a new literacies reader

Colin Lankshear and Michele Knobel
General Editors

Vol. 66

The New Literacies and Digital Epistemologies series
is part of the Peter Lang Education list.
Every volume is peer reviewed and meets
the highest quality standards for content and production.

PETER LANG
New York • Washington, D.C./Baltimore • Bern
Frankfurt • Berlin • Brussels • Vienna • Oxford

a new literacies reader

EDUCATIONAL PERSPECTIVES

Edited by Colin Lankshear & Michele Knobel

PETER LANG
New York • Washington, D.C./Baltimore • Bern
Frankfurt • Berlin • Brussels • Vienna • Oxford

Library of Congress Cataloging-in-Publication Data

A new literacies reader: Educational perspectives /
edited by Colin Lankshear, Michele Knobel.
pages cm. — (New literacies and digital epistemologies; vol. 66)
Includes bibliographical references and index.
1. Internet literacy. 2. Computer literacy. 3. Information literacy.
I. Lankshear, Colin. II. Knobel, Michele.
TK5105.875.I57N4876   004—dc23   2013003345
ISBN 978-1-4331-2280-4 (hardcover)
ISBN 978-1-4331-2279-8 (paperback)
ISBN 978-1-4539-1094-8 (e-book)
ISSN 1523-9543

Bibliographic information published by **Die Deutsche Nationalbibliothek**.
Die Deutsche Nationalbibliothek lists this publication in the "Deutsche
Nationalbibliografie"; detailed bibliographic data is available
on the Internet at http://dnb.d-nb.de/.

Contents

Acknowledgments

Our thanks go Chris Myers and colleagues at Peter Lang for the opportunity to put together a collection based on books published in our *New Literacies and Digital Epistemologies* series that samples the range of recent and current work within the loosely scribed field of "new literacies" research and scholarship. We would especially like to thank Bernie Shade for her unstinting good cheer and helpfulness in her role as production manager.

This collection represents the strong international mix that characterizes the books in the series and we wish to thank our authors for so willingly consenting to having their work republished in this collection.

We especially want to thank Jillian Walmach and Beverly Plein for their unstinting formatting and proof reading assistance. Both went above and beyond in helping us produce this Reader from a collection of files to a tight timeline.

Finally, we wish to convey our thanks to the many readers who have supported this series and helped us sustain it through a decade. We greatly appreciate your interest in the series and support for it. In this regard our thanks extend to the many librarians who order new books for their institutional stock and to colleagues who have found a place for various books in their course reading. Your support has been crucial to the series' sustainability and we thank you very much.

Social and Cultural Studies of New Literacies from an Educational Perspective

Colin Lankshear & Michele Knobel

This volume aims to provide a Reader—in the sense of a general introduction and overview—for a field of inquiry we think of as social and cultural studies of new literacies from the perspective of an interest in education. Its publication coincides with the 20th anniversary of a symposium published in *The English and Media Magazine* titled "Towards new literacies, information technology, English and media education" (1993) and the 10th anniversary of the New Literacies book series being launched by Peter Lang Publishing (USA).

New Literacies: Early Statements

Throughout the 1990s talk of new literacies remained quite marginal as a formal academic concept, at a time when terms like "digital literacy," "computer literacy," and "information literacy" were more prominent as names for reading and writing mediated by digital technologies—particularly in published work. In everyday conversation among education academics, "new literacies" seemed mainly to serve as a convenient shorthand for recognizing that new "species" of written language were emerging in daily life with the increasing uptake of myriad software applications and mobile and online communication services and practices.

A Starting Point

There were significant exceptions, however. In 1993, David Buckingham, in collaboration with Chris Abbott and Julian Sefton-Green, made the first formal recognition we can find within professional literature of "new literacies" as a potentially viable construct for organizing ongoing theoretical, conceptual, and pedagogical work across diverse cultural sites including formal education. In a series of articles addressing the theme "Towards New Literacies," Buckingham, Abbott, and Sefton-Green discussed aspects of video gaming, the role of information technology within English teaching (e.g., word processing, notebook computers and CD-ROMs), hypertext, and the implications of digital multimedia for media education, from the broad perspective of culture and communication.

Individually and collectively the authors approached new literacies more as a thematic frame for addressing issues arising in public debate at the time than as a concept to be closely defined, and explicitly rejected any sharp division between old and new technologies. They recognized that a key lesson to be taken from the history of print literacy is that "the ways new technologies are developed and used depend very much upon existing practices" (Buckingham, 1993, p. 20). At the same time, however, they were responding to the fact that public debates around the rapid uptake of digital technologies at the time largely framed technologies in terms of established and emerging technologies positioned in opposition to each other: computers were widely perceived as threats to print literacy, and video games were often seen as leisure pursuits that could lead to addiction, rather than contribute to human improvement in the manner of many established leisure pursuits. From the perspective of Buckingham and his colleagues, the familiar frame of the debate needed to be contested and revised.

Buckingham argues that it can never be proved one way or the other whether video games encourage violence. Moreover, focusing on this question is counterproductive: it actually undermines our capacity to understand violence as a phenomenon, by isolating it from other social forces involved in constituting violent behavior (Buckingham, 1993, p. 22). For parallel reasons, it can never be proved one way or the other whether computers have deleterious effects on print literacy.

By contrast, however, it *is* possible—indeed, it is *fruitful*—to focus on certain trends and tendencies that can be understood in terms of continuity, evolution, and incremental change. For example, as Buckingham argues (1993, p. 25), it is possible to detect "a blurring of boundaries between texts and between media" in cases like computer games that invoke "trans-media intertextuality." It is possible to discern a blurring of conventional distinctions between readers and writers, and producers and consumers, contingent upon the take up of new production technologies. In such cases, "new" is not understood in juxtaposition to "old" but, rather, in terms of continuities that result in evolution over time. "New" can serve as a provisional or heuristic reference point or vantage spot from which to conceive, explore, and understand phenomena in process.

The appropriate stance to adopt is one that enables us to improve our concepts about and theories of what is going on around us, such that we can make expansive and fruitful responses to the conditions we encounter. In the case of Buckingham, Abbott, and Sefton-Green, adopting the term "new literacies" offered a way to make creative and constructive responses to debates they were observing at the time—debates that have continued, and in some cases intensified, during the past 20 years. Ultimately, argues Buckingham (1993, p. 20), the debates around literacy and new technologies that impute causes and effects, that polarize opinion, and that limit our capacity to understand important aspects of our world, "point to the need for *a new definition of literacy*": a definition "that is not tied to particular technologies or practices" but, rather, "that allows us to look at the competencies that are developed across the whole range of culture and communication" (Buckingham, 1993, p. 20, our emphasis).

"New Literacies" and a New Technologies Emphasis

Nearer the end of the 1990s it was more common to find literacy researchers and writers using "new literacies" to formally mark an increasing awareness of the scope and role of post typographic texts in everyday life, and their significance for greater educational attention. For most, "new literacies" referred to reading and writing texts mediated by digital electronic technologies. Writing within the context of his professional interest in second language/foreign language/English as a second language acquisition, Mark Warschauer (1998) co-identified new literacies and electronic literacies, asking "what new literacies does multimedia technology demand?" He referred to learning to compose electronic mail and making effective use of the World Wide Web as typical examples of new literacies that have a role in language acquisition and beyond (p. 758). Anticipating issues of equity and critical perspective raised by other theorists to be surveyed below, Warschauer urged theorists and researchers to move beyond determinist and instrumental conceptions of new literacies and, instead, to take up a socially and culturally informed approach that can address in rich and deep ways questions about how development of new literacies intersect with race, class, gender, and equity issues; how learning and practicing electronic literacies are affected by the social and cultural contexts of institutions and communities, and what new literacies are demanded—within and beyond schools and classrooms—by multimedia computer technology (1998, p. 759).

In his inaugural "Technology" column for the *Journal of Adolescent and Adult Education*, titled "New Literacies," Bertram (Chip) Bruce (1998) describes the column's purpose as providing a venue for exploring new communications and information technologies and what they mean for literacy. He speaks of "rapidly evolving literacy practices"—new literacies—within the context of the "hypertextual, multimedia world we are entering" (p. 46), and identifies the challenge of understanding the "yet to be designed world" that unfolds as people engage in new practices made possible by new technologies (p. 47).

In a similar vein, Donald Leu Jr. (2000, pp. 423–424) identifies "the new literacies of the internet" in terms of the ways in which and the ends for which people read and write within networked information and communications technologies. These new literacies, says Leu, are constantly emerging and evolving as internet technologies themselves evolve, in accordance with the principle that literacies in any age change alongside changes in technologies for literacy. Leu (2001, p. 568) takes the example of literacy in contemporary work life to illustrate the stakes for education in coming to terms with the new technologies of the internet. He argues that members of modern organizations must know how to accomplish certain key tasks rapidly. They must be able to (1) identify key problems and issues for their work unit; (2) access relevant information and evaluate it critically; (3) use this information to address the issue or problem; and (4) communicate the solution throughout the organization as appropriate. On the assumption that at least part of what schools should be doing effectively is contributing to the development of future workers who can perform well, Leu poses the question of how educators can prepare students within networked classrooms for "the increasingly collaborative, problem-oriented, and critical nature of literacy" (pp. 568–69).

"New Literacies" through a Wider Lens: Beyond a Focus on New Technologies Alone

Other authors, particularly researchers and writers with interests in media education and cultural studies, associated new literacies with a range of post-typographic texts and technologies that included, but also went beyond, a focus on new digital-electronic media alone.

Carmen Luke (2000, p. 424), for example, talks of new literacies in relation to "a changing information, social, and cultural environment" that renders inadequate "book- and print-based literacies" and school learning approaches based solely on book culture. Within this context, new approaches to preparing teachers become necessary. Luke discusses an intervention in the teacher education program at her university intended to better prepare teachers for addressing the demands of new literacies. While far-reaching changes in everyday communication interactions and practices associated with electronic media provided the immediate catalyst for developing the program she discusses, the concepts and theory informing the program reflect phenomena and insights integral to issues, priorities, and practices within media studies and cultural studies dating from at least the 1960s. These include a concern with deconstructing media texts and representations via print and imagery within such media as "popular magazines, TV programs and advertising, and related forms of media representations," together with understanding "the social uptake" of such texts (2000, p. 425). Building a new literacies perspective into teacher education, for Luke, involves finding ways to "blend and synthesize" conventional and new technologies, and to inform computer education/literacy with insights and questions from media and cultural inquiry—such as by applying "tools of media analysis to Internet information" (2000, p. 426).

In "New technologies/new literacies: Reconstructing education for the new millennium," Douglas Kellner (2001) presents a similar and overlapping perspective to Luke's. Kellner observes that in modern societies the rapid introduction and uptake of new digital-electronic technologies has occurred alongside large-scale demographic and multicultural change resulting from intense migration. These forces in tandem present pressing challenges to the ideal of progress toward more democratic and egalitarian societies. In the interests of such progress, Kellner seeks ways that new technologies and new literacies can be developed and taken up such that they provide effective learning tools that can help realize democratic and egalitarian ends, rather than further benefiting already privileged groups and individuals in terms of social power and cultural capital (pp. 68–69).

By "new literacies," Kellner means new ways of using socially constructed forms of communication and representation. As with the position argued by Carmen Luke, Kellner's conception of the kinds of new literacies we need to develop builds strongly on ideas, techniques, and values integral to media literacy and critical practice forged since the 1960s. The explosion in new media increases the relevance of critical media practices and critical forms of reading and writing, along with analytic and interpretive techniques and procedures that have been developed within areas like semiotics, social semiotics, narrative analysis, and textual deconstruction, and projects their further development into spaces of intensifying engagement with electronic multimedia. Kellner argues that the current technological revolution "brings to the fore more than ever the role of media like television, popular music, films and advertising," since these are absorbed by the internet and become integral to "new cyberspaces and forms of culture and pedagogy" (2001, p. 70). The emphasis upon and approaches to interpretation and evaluation found in traditional media literacy becomes still more urgent under current conditions of technical and cultural change, since media culture is profoundly pedagogical. It socializes participants into taking up values, identities, and ways of experiencing and perceiving the world.

For Kellner as much as for Luke, just as the conditions of new media up the ante for media literacy and call for its further development in the interests of progressive social, political, and ethical ideals, so they also call for developing expansive conceptions of and approaches to computer literacy. Far beyond technical know-how and the ability to access, process, and generate content using typical computing applications, computer literacy calls for "heightened capacities for critically accessing, analyzing, interpreting, processing, and storing both print-based and multimedia material" and sophisticated visual literacy competence (Kellner, 2001, pp. 73–74).

The extent to which the link between new literacies and digital-electronic technologies is regarded as contingent—albeit strong—rather than necessary is argued in different but complementary ways by Ladislaus Semali (2001) and Brian Street (1998).

Semali defines new literacies as literacies that have emerged in the post-typographic era of intensified visual and electronic communication involving epistemological and cultural changes in the ways information is "designed, communicated and retrieved" (2001, no page). As interaction with "texts" has moved increasingly from engagement with print-dominated toward intensified multimodal content, traditional assumptions about what it means to read and write and how meanings are communicated have been disrupted and displaced. Semali refers to theorists who associate the rise of post-typographic modes of information and communication with a shift from modern to postmodern conceptions and practices of meaning and meaning-making. Where modernist meaning based on the model of the book as the default text type assumed linearity, logical progression, singularity and symmetry, postmodern meaning tends toward the non-linear, is multiple and hybrid, often communicated by means of disjuncture and asymmetrical means, may be fleeting, unstable, more impressionistic and intuitive.

Communicating and negotiating postmodern meaning mediated by post-typographic modes of inscription is intensified by digital-electronic technologies, but in no way depends upon them. For Semali, television literacy, visual literacy and media literacy—all predating the explosion in digital-electronic technologies—are new literacies alongside information literacy associated with electronic databases and the World Wide Web and computer literacy. Furthermore, echoing values and priorities expressed by the other authors we have referred to above, Semali emphasizes the importance of a critical and politicized dimension to new literacies, whereby examining how particular media texts generate meanings goes beyond "the aesthetics, modes and forms present" in visual and multimodal texts to also "locate them in their social and political contexts" (2001, no page). He asks how the "new languages of media" might enable us to generate and circulate meanings that enhance lives and reject oppression.

In "New literacies in theory and practice: What are the implications for education?," Brian Street (1998) presents three examples of texts typical of the kinds that mediate new literacies in the sense he intends. Two of these are hard copy hybrids of words, images and symbols (published on card or paper). The third example involves the creative appropriation within certain youth subcultures of sign and sound sequences on electronic pagers or beepers for passing idiosyncratic messages to one another, using the technologies in ways not intended by their designers and manufacturers. For Street, what makes the kinds of literacy practices that are mediated and constituted by such texts "new" is partly that they depart from the conventional identification of literacy with written speech governed by traditional views of grammar, lexicon and semantics. They mobilize a much "wider range of semiotic systems that cut across reading, writing and speech" (1998, p. 9). Traditional or conventional literacy comprises but one part of communicative competence. Street argues that within the "new communicative order" of the "new media age" (Kress, 2003) and an age of rapidly changing and "globalizing" population demographics, and across the multiple domains of everyday life, being literate involves much more than competence with conventional reading and writing and conventional print texts. We must increasingly negotiate meanings within contexts mediated by multimodal texts, and where making meaning successfully is not a matter of mastering abstract formal grammatical conventions but, rather, draws on "grammars" that provide a means for "representing patterns of experience…[and enable] human beings to build a mental picture of reality, to make sense of their experience of what goes on around them and inside them" (Halliday, 1985, p. 101, cited in Street, 1998, p. 10).

Being literate in this sense entails bringing lives and texts together within contexts in ways that "work": in the sense of successfully negotiating meanings, by managing a grammar/semiosis that brings together a text, one's experience, and features of the current context in a functional manner (i.e., serves an immediate purpose, helps realize a task, enables effective communication, etc.). Street's example of a chart designed to help people in South African communities to recognize when a water source is likely to be safe for drinking highlights the kinds of semiotic competence needed to read the text in ways that will enable sound judgments about water quality: distinguishing logos from symbols relating to relationships between animal life and pollution levels; relating text to degrees of shading, etc. Anyone who, like Street himself initially, reads the dark shading on the chart to mean impurity and light shading to mean purity, would get the chart "wrong." Similarly, someone not familiar with "pager" or "beeper"-using subcultures could not possibly read "07734" to mean "hello," since they would not know to turn the screen upside down and make the creative (leet-speak like) jump from numbers to letters. For Street, the new literacies of the new communicative order invoke myriad "grammars" and forms of insiderliness that bespeak patterns of experience and relationships between texts and experience that wreak havoc with conventional conceptions and norms of literacy grounded in print.

New Literacies without New Technologies at All

We end this brief survey of typical examples of conceptions of new literacies from the early life of the term within educational theory and research with an interesting outlier: the kind of case that has influenced our own approach to thinking about new literacies during the past decade. In "Culturally responsive instruction as a dimension of new literacies," Kathryn Au (2001, no page) associates new literacies with pedagogical interventions designed to help students from diverse backgrounds attain high literacy levels by "promoting engagement through activities that reflect the values, knowledge, and structures of interaction that students bring from the home." She claims that developing forms of culturally responsive instruction may create within classrooms *new* literacies that connect to home backgrounds.

Au argues that in the context of education policies that may narrow the literacy curriculum—such as by seeking to raise measured literacy performance levels in standardized tests—opportunities for students from diverse backgrounds to develop higher order skills through interaction with texts may be diminished. Resisting such a trend calls for creative attempts to bring student backgrounds to bear on literacy education by building bridges between cultural ways and strengths and engagement with texts in class. Au reports some of the ways teachers involved in culturally responsive instruction do this. For example, in a "talk story" approach, teachers participate in reading lessons in ways that resemble a familiar Hawaiian community speech event. In "talk story-like reading lessons" learners do not wait for the teacher to call on them but speak when they have something to say, and formulate answers to questions in a collaborative manner, "speaking in rhythmic alternation with a great deal of overlapping speech" (2001, no page). Such "hybrid events," says Au, incorporate features of community and school. They generate "literate activities" that are similar to those of school and community respectively, but are not identical to either (Au, 2001, no page). The talk story hybrid activity comprises "teacher-guided discussion of literature following talk story-like participation structures." Such discussions constitute "a new literacy that makes connections to students' home culture" (Au, 2001, no page).

The range of new literacies identified by Au emphasizes the normative association between "new" literacies and the pursuit of educational ideals, in a way that resonates with some of Kellner's arguments. Unlike the cases discussed by Kellner, however, Au's examples have no necessary link to post-typographic texts and technologies, far less to the use of digital-electronic technologies.

Adopting a Focus on New Literacies

The kinds of ideas surveyed above influenced our own thinking and activity. Until the late 1990s we had thought of "new literacies" as a convenient shorthand for changes in literacy practices associated with larger changes going on in the world. Influenced by our own experiences of researching diverse literacy practices within a variety of formal educational, community, and domestic settings from a broadly sociocultural perspective, and noting deep qualitative differences often apparent between young people's activities within formal educational settings and elsewhere, we became increasingly interested in rhetorical, theoretical, and practical-pragmatic means for naming these differences, pointing to patterns between and across different settings, and mounting critiques of formal educational literacy business as usual. The idea of new literacies, with some of the connotations attaching to "new," struck a chord with such purposes, and we adopted "new literacies" as a focus for our subsequent work as literacy researchers and writers. Since 2000 this has involved us in three related tasks:

(a) Thinking about "new literacies" conceptually and theoretically
(b) Mapping some dimensions of a new literacies research space
(c) Conceiving and editing a book series on new literacies

(a) Thinking about "New Literacies" Conceptually and Theoretically

For us, the challenge expressed by Bruce in his inaugural "Technology" column referred to earlier, needed to be taken seriously. Bruce says:

> We find ourselves engaging in new practices made possible by the new technologies. These new ways of communicating, or relating to one another, and of accomplishing our daily lives create possibilities that go beyond what even the designers of the new technologies envisage. It is this yet to be designed world that we seek to understand. (1998, p. 47)

Pursuing such understanding seemed to us a pre-eminent task for literacy researchers and literacy educators. An invitation to participate in an international working seminar convened by James Gee at the University of Wisconsin-Madison provided us with an opportunity to think in a more focused way about new literacies. The seminar sought to generate elements of a research agenda within the broad area of the New Literacy Studies under conditions of global change. At this seminar we presented a paper called "The New Literacy Studies and the study of new literacies" (Lankshear & Knobel, 2000). It focused on the extent to which work formally identified with the New Literacy Studies had to that time largely bypassed the theme of new literacies.

We adopted the idea that "new literacies" was best understood in terms of practices that were increasingly mediated by new technologies, but not *necessarily* mediated by new technologies. We also distinguished two ways we thought the idea of "new" might usefully apply to work in the area of literacy studies. One was a *paradigmatic* sense: the idea of the New Literacy Studies as a sociocultural paradigm for literacy theory and research that had been developing around the study of literacies as social practices from the time of Sylvia Scribner and Michael Cole's work in the late 1970s and onwards (Scribner & Cole, 1981; see also Street, 1984; Gee, 1990). The other was what we called an *ontological* sense, where one might plausibly talk about new forms of literacy practices emerging, that could in significant ways be distinguished from previously existing ones. Within this ontological sense of new literacies we included forms of literacy practice that were emerging in association with new technologies, along with others that might or might not involve the use of new technologies. It was the ontological sense of "new literacies" that became the focus of our work, largely undertaken from a New Literacies Studies perspective.

At the same time, we recognized two things that seemed important to us when thinking about new literacies in relation to education. The first concerned the continuity as well as disruption that occur within literacy practices within contexts of technological change. As Buckingham and others had noted much earlier, the ways new technologies are taken up and used in daily practice are strongly influenced by existing practices. Much of what we had seen in schools reflected the absorption of computers and other digital electronic devices into existing routines and "ways": established literacies changed only to the extent that they were now sometimes done with word processors rather than pencils.

By contrast, there were many instances of new technologies mediating influential emerging literacy practices that were significantly different in nature, scope and consequences from what had previously existed. For example, blogging was impacting journalism in quite profound ways; mobile devices were impacting cultural practices and communications in the streets, extending to political activism, as well as to gaming, group cultural practices and maintaining relationships. We recognized that if literacy practices in education are to stay in touch with the world beyond the classrooms, educators must become informed about creative disruptions and not merely adapt new technologies to familiar practices and routines. This calls for ongoing work that aims to map and understand such evolutions and project them to educational audiences.

The second thing that seemed important to us from an educational perspective when thinking about new literacies was the existence of influential *contemporary* literacy practices that did not necessarily involve new technologies but, nonetheless, should (in our view) be on educators' radars. At the time, such "chronologically"—though not "technologically"—new literacies included examples like producing paper-based zines and works of fan fiction, and scripting scenarios within the practice of scenario planning (among many others).

Beginning with "The New Literacy Studies and the study of new literacies (Lankshear & Knobel, 2000, 2003), and continuing through successive editions of our book *New Literacies* (Lankshear & Knobel, 2003, 2006, 2011), we have tried to understand new literacies in ways that honor the increased mediating presence of digital-electronic technologies within everyday literacy practices, while maintaining a place for popular and influential literacy practices that do not presuppose new media—always with a view to recommending that educators, education administrators and policy makers, and educational researchers attend to the importance such literacies assume within the everyday lives of students, their families, their networks and their communities.

(b) Mapping Some Dimensions of a New Literacies Research Space

While wrestling with conceptual and theoretical aspects of new literacies we were also thinking about the kinds of questions discussed at the Wisconsin seminar. We pondered what a sociocultural research agenda for new literacies might involve and look like, and how attempts to generate a critical mass of new literacies research endeavors might be fostered and nurtured. Two specific questions interested us:

- To what extent might investigating new literacies—notably, perhaps, those with substantial online components—call for developing innovative *methodological* and/or *theoretical* approaches and mixes?
- What might be some fruitful options for *research orientations* within the sociocultural study of new literacies?

At the level of theoretical innovation, it was evident that studies of new literacies were encouraging a push into domains of theory substantially new to literacy research. These included an interest in games studies (see, for example, http://gamestudies.org), Actor Network Theory, recent developments within theories of space and time hitherto most commonly associated with fields like geography and architecture (e.g., Appadurai, 1996), "flow theory" (e.g., Csikszentmihalyi, 1990, 1996), developments in socio-technical studies (e.g., Perkel, 2006), social network theory (e.g., Wellman, 2001), social informatics, and so on. Research in video gaming was generating new twists on concepts and theories of play, design, and learning.

With respect to methodology, researchers were responding to diverse challenges posed by practices emerging around developments in new media and communications. Some (e.g., Jones, 1999; Lemke, 2000; Leander, 2003) addressed issues raised by researching across online and offline environments: for example, how far it would be necessary to develop new methods and techniques to undertake participant observation. Others raised issues about how researchers might get at meanings generated within popular cultural practices involving multimedia text production, and the extent to which text-based analyses need supplementing with field-based inquiry to get at insider meanings (Burn, 2004).

The question about the need for theoretical and methodological innovation within new literacies research is empirical, not *a priori*. The only way it can ultimately be answered is by seeing what plays out in the course of making theoretical and methodological progress within a field. The point is to get on with the work and, as it were, see what shakes down. This relates to our question about fruitful options for research orientations within studies of new literacies.

As educationists interested in new literacies we were aware that researchers in this area often sense an expectation that their research should aim to make some active and more or less direct contribution toward enhancing teaching and learning within formal education settings. While this is a valuable research outcome, we thought it important to acknowledge that the very "newness" of the phenomena under investigation, plus the fact that to a considerable extent the field of literacy studies needs to reinvent itself in order to address the changes going on around us, should caution against adopting unduly goal-directed and functional/applied orientations at the outset. From this perspective, along with "Educationally applicable research," we considered the potential value of what we thought of as "Let's see" and "Try on" orientations toward new literacies research.

(i) "Let's see" Research

"Let's see" research is undertaken largely for its own sake, with the primary aim of understanding in depth a "new" social practice and the literacies associated with or mobilized within this practice. A "let's see" orientation encourages researchers to get as close as possible to viewing a new practice from the perspectives and sensibilities of "insiders." The existence of striking differences in mindsets with respect to social practices involving new technologies establishes the value of attending to how "insiders" engage with new literacies on their (i.e., insider) terms (cf. Jenkins, 2006).

(ii) "Try on" Research

"Try on" research encourages experimentation with concepts, theory and methodology, including innovative "mash ups" of theories and methods, together with the development of new techniques and modifications of existing techniques for data collection and analysis to explore and understand emerging and changing literacy practices. Such orientations parallel the quest for innovation and willingness to pursue "virtuous circles" (Castells, 1996, p. 67) that have enabled so much recent technological change and its creative appropriation, including those that issue in new literacy practices themselves. As with technological innovation, there are leading edges in research innovation to be encouraged and brought to wider attention and take up.

(iii) "Educationally applicable" Research

This focuses more directly and self-consciously on pursuing findings that can potentially be applied to better understanding or enabling learning in school and other formal learning spaces or, perhaps, to applying ideas and findings from extant studies to formal learning settings. Typical examples might include: studies addressing the nature, role and efficacy of reviewer feedback in honing young people's artistic craft or Standard English written narrative expression, which might be trawled for clues about how to mobilize effective features of reviewer feedback for school learning purposes (e.g., Chandler-Olcott & Maher, 2003; Black, 2005); case studies of participants who are working collaboratively with others on projects requiring them to learn through participation; or research on gaming where concepts and principles are identified that can be "interpreted and translated" into possible approaches to creating good learning environments.

(c) The "New Literacies" Book Series

Within the context we have described here, the idea of pursuing a book series made obvious sense as a practical-pragmatic strategy for encouraging and enabling the dissemination of work that could further the conceptual and theoretical development of new literacies and research into new literacies from a broad social and cultural perspective. We believed this should be a series that would be as open and diverse as possible and where there was scope to encourage work that might involve commercial risk but should nonetheless be published on the basis of its quality and significance.

Peter Lang Publishing (USA) agreed to publish a series on "New Literacies" that aimed "to explore some key dimensions of the changes occurring within social practices of literacy and the educational challenges they present, with a view to informing educational practice in helpful ways." The series would ask: "what are new literacies, how do they impact on life in schools, homes, communities, workplaces, sites of leisure, and other key settings of human cultural engagement, and what significance do new literacies have for how people learn and how they understand and construct knowledge?" It would aim to challenge "established and 'official' ways of framing literacy," and to ask "what it means for literacies to be powerful, effective, and enabling under current and foreseeable conditions." We hoped that, collectively, the works in the series would help "to reorient literacy debates and literacy education agendas" (Peter Lang USA, 2012).

To date the series has published 45 books and the following chapters have been drawn exclusively from recent contributions to the series' corpus.

Organization and Scope of the Book

This book aims to be of interest to a diverse audience comprising teachers and teacher educators, education administrators, curriculum developers, education policy makers, professional development specialists, post graduate research students and other literacy researchers. It is interested in the ways that participating in social practices of new literacies can be seen and understood in terms of people becoming insiders to ways of doing life that are considered desirable or worthwhile. It involves learning how to do things that are worth doing and being in ways that are worth being. The ideal of education in the sense intended here is concerned with processes by which human beings acquire the means and dispositions to live well, to live some version or versions of "good lives." Education involves learning how to take on identities, be members of groups and communities, take on civic responsibilities, develop an ethical stance toward other people and the world, and so on. Within societies like our own, schooling/formal education is invested with responsibility for much of this initiation and preparation. At the same time, education is much wider than formal education and, indeed, it is commonplace to hear complaints of formal education failing to do an acceptable job of preparation. Increasingly, we find educationists and others with interests in formal education looking to spaces beyond schools and other formal learning institutions for clues about how we might collectively do a better job of educating.

In terms of its organization and scope, the book is based on the idea of the school as a learning institution that occupies a particular location along a "learning spectrum" of institutional, quasi-institutional, and non-formal spaces. Five such spaces have been identified for the purposes of this collection, and the book is organized in five sections corresponding to these spaces.

(a) The Space of the School Classroom

The opening section focusing on classroom contexts addresses a rich and diverse array of settings, ranging from a formal class within an Alternative to Incarceration Program for young men, via a social class and race-ethnic mix of Norwegian secondary schools, an urban middle school journalism class, two senior English classes in a majority Black urban high school, to classes in a high-end private Grades 5–12 all-girls school. All four chapters engage in educationally applicable research, although none has set out to address particular school-based issues or problems. Rather, they all reflect a high commitment to what we have called "Let's see" research, with a focus on trying to understand processes and events from the perspective of the teacher and student participants.

In their opening chapter on multimodal pedagogies, Lalitha Vasudevan, Tiffany DeJaynes and Stephanie Schmier identify "the profound act of teachers and students *knowing* each other through multimodal play in order to teach and learn together" (p. 35) witnessed and related by the researchers and experienced by them as central to all three cases in their study. Kevin Leander's discussion of interview material (Chapter 3) provides rich insights into the play of dueling discourses in the consciousness of teachers in his study, and how this playing out of tensions contributes to producing classroom space-time in ways that constrain student opportunities for learning with laptops and internet access. Ola Erstad's discussion of trajectories of remix (Chapter 2) taps into student and teacher responses to pedagogical approaches built on recognizing that "learning takes place in many contexts, taking experiences from one context over to another" (p. 54). Bronwen Low's study of slam poetry in senior high school English classes (Chapter 4) pays particular attention to aspects of student and teacher identities through analysis of spoken data, performance, and poems.

With respect to conceptual, theoretical and methodological developments tailored to getting at *new* literacies, these chapters reflect a mix of careful innovation and exploration with appropriate combinations of existing approaches to researching literacy practices. Vasudevan, DeJaynes and Schmier innovate conceptually around their idea of "multimodal play," introducing this concept to the study of new literacies and tapping its potential for understanding and explaining the way multimodal play opened up opportunities for learning and personal development in the cases they present. Erstad extends existing discussions of "remix" and adopts a methodological approach designed to describe and understand the *trajectories* of remix practices that afford new student perspectives on what it means "to be at school" (p. 49). Kevin Leander brings a spatial perspective to bear on the theme of technology refusal in schools. He shows how Ridgeview school was caught "in a struggle of expansion and contraction" through which school space-time was constituted in ways that powerfully constrained the potential for integrating new technologies into classroom learning (p. 60). Bronwen Low makes a conceptual and theoretical case for "low tech" new literacies in her account of slam poetry, and draws on concepts from cultural studies and literacy theory to explore how a slam language arts unit *leveraged* out-of-school rap and freestyle literacies and *extended* them in ways that show how erstwhile literacy topics like audience and purpose in writing might be taught in characteristically contemporary ways.

(b) Bridging "The Classroom" and "The Wider World"

The second group of chapters considers contexts where schools might be seen as a kind of bridge between classrooms and the rest of the world. After-school clubs provide one kind of example of this space. Another kind of example represented here is where a school and a teacher make school resources available to students for pursuing their interests. Such spaces are often especially well-suited to promoting efficacious learning in the sense that the learning going on *now* has organic and motivated connections to what goes on in "mature" versions of a social practice during the course of life trajectories beyond the school (Gee, Hull, & Lankshear, 1996, p. 4).

In Chapter 5, Leif Gustavson presents the case of Gil, a 15-year-old African American turntablist enrolled in an elite private school where the jazz teacher had made a space backing off from the music room available for after school activity by students. This popular and heavily used space included a large set of music records and two turntables. Gustavson's account is a form of "Let's see" research that aims to understand Gil's turntabling interest as "creative practice." It is also, however, a highly applied case of educational research, whereby Gustavson uses his study to present a sequence of instructive ways for teachers to develop complex understanding of how youth like Gil work and learn "on their own terms" (p. 101). On the basis of such understanding teachers may transform classrooms into learning environments that actively appropriate the skills and sophistication inherent in creative practice that youth bring with them to school. Gustavson's account of "creative practice" brings Aristotle's concept of *tekhne* together with Paul Willis's idea of *grounded aesthetic*, focusing on the social practices of (youth) production rather than the products *per se*. Gustavson explores the "habits of mind and body"—performance, improvisation, self-reflection, interpretation and evaluation—integral to Gil's creative practice. These are habits he carries with him everywhere as part of his everyday life, in the same way gamers, skateboarders, rappers, digital remixers and other popular cultural aficionados do. Such habits of body and mind can, and should, be mobilized in formal educational activity, and Gustavson suggests practical and exploratory ways for doing so.

Althea Nixon's study of children engaging in digital storytelling (Chapter 6), and Kylie Peppler and Diane Glosson's account of youth undertaking projects using e-textiles in projects based on electrical circuits (Chapter 7) are both situated within organized programs occurring outside school hours. Nixon examines children aged 5–11 years creating digital stories in an after-school club serving low-income Hispanic, African American, Pacific Island and Asian children in a southern California city. The study focused on benefits and limitations of digital storytelling for youth-identity play, as well as on the extent to which digital storytelling as a new literacy practice might be used to engage children in critical dialogue about issues of race, ethnicity and gender. It has educational applicability, but might also be seen as a form of "Try on" research where components of sociocultural and narrative theory are brought together to understand identity from the standpoint of narration as *multimodal*. There are likewise elements of a "Let's see" approach as the researcher and undergraduate participants seek to understand the children's sense-making through interviews/conversations with a purpose and cognitive ethnographies in the process of the children creating their digital stories.

Peppler and Glosson's study is designed to have direct and functional educational application. They are interested in the extent to which using e-textiles might enable young people to understand electronic circuits in ways that often prove challenging when taught using conventional resources like batteries, insulated wire, and light bulbs. The study seeks to provide "a foundation for integrating e-textile materials with standards-based practices in formal education systems" (p. 140) and indicate how teaching and assessment in classroom settings might be approached. It proceeds from Seymour Papert's insight into "the impact of specific tools ("objects to think with") on the ways that we learn and perceive subject matter" (p. 139). The researchers recorded and analyzed conversations among participants in the course of their hands-on activity, collected pre- and post-activity artifacts to evince changes in conceptual understanding, and recorded conversations between participants and outsiders which tapped participant understandings.

(c) Teacher Learning and Professional Development

The third section of the book contains chapters that range over the diverse spaces of teacher learning as commonly referred to in terms of teacher education, teacher professional development, teacher growth, enhancing teacher expertise, and the like. Of course, in many ways it is confusing to think of this in terms of space at all, since learning travels all over. Like everything else it is connected to "everything else." Teachers carry the learning they do that is related to their professional work wherever they need to carry it, and find it wherever it arises. This section of the book is concerned with work that has sought consciously to focus on different kinds of initiatives where teachers are consciously involved in learning how to do and be in ways that enhance their understanding of and engagement with new kinds of literacy practices germane to their professional lives.

In Chapter 8, Andrew Burn presents an open, wide-ranging exploration of the work of an artist-teacher-animator/machinamator, Britta Pollmuller. The study focuses on Pollmuller's activities teaching animation in different forms (claymation, stop motion, machinima) to learners in a range of settings, culminating in her most recent involvement teaching machinima with 13–17-year-olds enrolled in the Open University's Schome (school + home) project in Second Life. Burn traces a rich trajectory in Pollmuller's recent experiences, as she transitioned from working as an artist-teacher in a school, to working as a freelance educator running projects in schools, discovering Second Life and exhibiting her art in its online galleries, teaching herself machinima and then teaching machinima to Shome-enrolled learners. Burn draws on interview data and observations conducted in Second Life, and frames his discussion around questions and issues arising at the interfaces "between media and art education, and between new technologies and adaptive uses of them by teachers and students" (p. 152). Throughout the elaboration of this case Burn draws on theory concerned respectively with art produced by mechanical means (Benjamin), aspects of performance (Goffman), collective intelligence (Levy), play (Sutton-Smith), and creativity (Vygotsky), among other threads, to elucidate his focal questions. The outcome is a classic "Let's see" study that speaks in interesting and fruitful ways to understanding online learning and its similarities and differences with respect to face-to-face learning.

Teresa Strong-Wilson and Dawn Rouse's chapter, "New wine in old bottles?" (Chapter 9), is grounded in a two-year professional development project—Learning with Laptops—undertaken by university-based researchers, school board personnel, and teachers within a school district in Quebec. Excerpted from a book-length study, this chapter revisits the two years of experience in the project from the standpoint of Bolter and Gusin's concept of remediation—the ways in which new media "refashion older media, and the ways in which older media refashion themselves to answer the challenges of new media" (Bolter & Grusin, 2002, p. 15). Data collected throughout the project period by means of interviews, in situ observations, photos, logs, and teacher literacy autobiographies are analyzed to understand the ways in which and extent to which the past hovered over the present in the life of the project: "How were teachers 'remediating' their classroom practices and stories through their use of new technologies?" At the heart of the chapter is an extended analysis of the ways teacher experimentation with new technologies during the second year of the project generated a parallel pedagogy, involving improvisation and bricolage: meshing print and digital media in the best mixes the teachers could manage for handling teaching and learning tasks at hand. This study exemplifies a retrospective "Let's see," aimed at understanding from the inside how the learning processes and their applications unfolded from the perspective of the participants.

Chapter 10 presents a study by April Luehmann, Joe Henderson, and Liz Tinelli of a cohort of 20 pre-service teachers in a graduate science teacher education program who maintained individual professional blogs as a course requirement. The chapter presents an in-depth account of one blogger (Maya) plus two contrasting snapshots (Niklas and Elisabeth). Blogging occurred over 15 months and across all courses in the program. The researchers report a thematic analysis of Maya's blogging corpus: 60 posts, 1880 lines, 129 comments received and 200 comments posted to peer blogs. The result is a rich explication from the perspective of the researchers of the nature, scope, and role blogging played in Maya's professional growth as a reform-minded science teacher in the course of preservice preparation. The brief summative contrasting snapshots of Niklas and Elisabeth's blogging, together with a report of analytic results of the entire cohort's responses to a self-assessment task augment the central case in the study. Key findings from the analysis of all data are presented by way of conclusion, with preference to opportunities, constraints, and productive purposes served by this instance of blogging in the context of professional preparation.

In Chapter 11, Margaret Hagood, Emily Skinner, Melissa Venters, and Benjamin Yelm report research focusing on two teachers involved in a two-year initiative designed to implement new literacies strategies within content-area instruction in classrooms. Informed by theory and research from studies of adolescent literacy and popular culture, multimodality, and new media, the chapter focuses on how the teachers (Melissa and Ben) designed instruction to address state standards for social studies in ways that employed digital multimedia within visual literacy formats—photostories and comic strips—as means for their students to learn curriculum content. Drawing on artifacts and transcriptions of in situ speech and interviews, the chapter offers a vivid account of classroom activity within a wider analytic frame that emphasizes connections between identities, content area instruction, assessment, and student outcomes in the course of teachers' professional learning "on the job." Of particular interest is the way the study reflects the teachers' drawing on their intersecting identities as knowledgeable social studies teachers and proficient new literacies exponents to keep multiple literacies—academic literacy, content literacy, new literacies, performance and formative assessment—*together* within schoolwork as they learned new instructional strategies; thereby resisting the kinds of literacy dichotomies that foster perceptions of students in "unsatisfactory" schools as being "unsuccessful" in academic literacies "when in fact they are competent" (p. 224).

(d) Spaces of Popular Cultural Affinities

Apart, perhaps, from classroom settings, the space addressed in the fourth section is the best-subscribed space within new literacies research. This is the non-formal domain of participation in popular cultural affinities like game playing and media remixing.

This section opens with Rebecca Black's chapter on language, culture and identity (Chapter 12). It focuses on how networked technologies and fan culture provide a teenaged migrant English language learning student (Nanako) with a context for developing her English language and writing skills while simultaneously developing an online identity as a popular multiliterate writer of fan fiction. For its theoretical base, the study draws on concepts of identity/identities, D/discourse and dialogic resources, from Second Language Acquisition theory and Literacy, Cultural and Media Studies. Methodologically, it employs a form of discourse analysis informed by Bakhtin's concept of dialogic resources and Gee's notion of language as part of Discourses, and applies this to transcribed excerpts from Nanako's fan fiction works, her author notes, reader feedback, and Nanako's responses to reader feedback. The analysis helps us understand phenomena like shifts in Nanako's writing and language use, narrative resources she draws upon to produce her fiction, the aspects of self she foregrounds as a fan fiction writer, and how these aspects of self change over time. These understandings inform an educationally applicable discussion of the play between ascribed and achieved identities. First and foremost, however, the study is an illuminating instance of "Let's see" research.

In a similar vein, in "Communication, coordination and camaraderie" (Chapter 13), Mark Chen draws on an online participant ethnography of a group of players in *World of Warcraft*. Part of a larger study, this chapter contrasts two nights of game playing—one successful, the other unsuccessful— to describe and understand communication and coordination practices within group endeavor. This account is informed by competing strands of emergent computer game (playing) theory, one of which emphasizes the *modeling* of game-playing behavior and mechanics-based motivations, while the other emphasizes *player practice* within social situations and foregrounds *social* norms and responsibilities defined by social contexts. During the several-months life of the group—before it imploded beyond possible revival—Chen amassed a rich data set of online interactions inside and outside of game play. Vivid instances and episodes are presented and analyzed throughout the chapter, providing a rich "as if I were there" experience for the reader. Chen takes a "look and see" approach to making sense of what he was involved in as a key participant. He concludes that for a team to succeed it needs "good communication and coordination," and this occurs when "team members trust each other in their specialized roles." In Chen's experience, strong trust was based on "strong goals and well-established relationships" rather than on "individual incentives" (p. 265).

Angela Thomas' chapter on youth participation (Chapter 14) explores ways of learning among a group of young people engaging in a range of online activities centered on strong interests in the Tolkien world of Middle Earth. Participants role play, discuss, perform poetry recitals and engage in story writing within a role-playing web forum created by four members of the group, and in an online graphical chat world (a Middle Earth palace). The study is strongly informed by Etienne Wenger's social model of learning within communities of practice. A key theme for Thomas is that the participants in her study (average age 13 years) learned from and with others like themselves—*novices* learning as they go—without reliance on the availability of recognized experts. The study trawls online interviews, stretches of chat and role play, and artifacts created by participants, to understand how they learned together and individually (as individuals in relationship with others sharing common purposes) to create, maintain, and grow their community; how they learned the language of role playing and, more generally, how to be literate online; how they combined "modes of being" (p. 275) in order to learn and expand repertoires of role playing; how to push the limits of their available technologies; and so on. This is an example of "Let's see" inquiry conducted from the standpoint of a peripheral observer seeking to understand learning within spaces of shared interests and, in doing so, providing insights relevant to learning within more formal settings.

This section concludes with Bronwyn Williams' investigation of how a population of students draw on popular cultural resources and "ways" to compose identities in online social media sites (Chapter 15). Williams draws on theory and research from the ethnography of literacy, and studies of discourse, culture and media to inform his analysis of web site content and interview material. He seeks to understand from the perspectives of the study participants how and why they have composed and performed online identities the ways they have, as well as to explore the range of readings such performances make available, and the social "work" these composed/performed identities do. Williams also considers how the kinds of identities in question might be understood in terms of larger constructions of identity like gender, race, sexual orientation and social class (p. 282). The study concludes that the students' uses of popular culture for composing identities online is not haphazard but, rather, "is a conscious process of self-inquiry and self-editing [which is] as considered and reflected on as what clothes to wear and which group to sit with at lunch" (p. 300).

(e) Researcher Perspectives on New Literacies

The concluding section of the book contains three chapters approached here from the "space" of researchers making sense of people engaging in new literacies in ways that are of educational interest. To some extent our interest and purpose with respect to these chapters lies in what they have to say about what happens and how within particular contexts and cases of engaging in new literacies. Primarily, however, we are interested in what they demonstrate about *how* to undertake research into new literacies, paying particular attention to conceptual, theoretical, and methodological considerations.

James Gee introduces the concluding section to this Reader with what might be described as an auto-ethnographic case study of learning to play a real time strategy video game (*Rise of Nations*) blended with an analysis of the experiences of learning the game in terms of the kinds of understanding such analysis may provide on the nature of "deep learning." To a large extent this analysis takes the form of looking for patterns in the data; patterns that can be categorized as instances and types of principles of good learning. Gee's study is informed by theory from cognitive science, social cognition, discourse processes, the New Literacy Studies, neural science/brain studies, social linguistics, and social semiotics. Methodologically, Gee proceeds by collecting data from the game as *artifact*, the game as *played*, and the game as a *system* of process potentialities, rules, feedback mechanisms and so on. The analytic approach is hybrid, reflecting techniques employed in discourse analysis, philosophical analysis, categorical analysis, and content analysis, mobilized in a version of grounded theory. There is a subtle interplay between grounded analysis through which patterns emerge from the data and are interpreted into, or distilled as, principles (of good learning), on one hand, and analysis that is guided to some extent by extant theory as identified above. The chapter concludes with a statement of 25 learning principles Gee identifies as being built into *Rise of Nations*. While this research has important educational implications, and Gee makes regular reference to the challenges good video game learning principles raise for formal education, it is also very much a form of research undertaken for the purpose of understanding the game in its own terms as a kind of learning system.

The penultimate chapter continues the theme of learning in the content of computer and video games. Aaron Hung's "Situated play: Instruction and learning in fighting games" (Chapter 17) investigates what and how players learn when they interact with a video game and, in this case, with other players at different levels of video game expertise in the process of learning a new game. This chapter demonstrates an exponent of Ethnomethodolgy/Conversation Analysis at work. Hung states his purpose in terms of an ethnomethodological maxim that "people's first experience with a phenomenon is an interaction that cannot be fully recaptured in a *post hoc* recollection" (p. 322). Since learning is messy and does not proceed in any kind of linear fashion it needs to be captured at the time, and captured as fully and accurately as possible. Hung further specifies his purpose by situating it in the company of work that aims to understand participants' orientation to a new activity through their social organization. To realize his purposes as optimally as possible Hung describes how he chose a mix of novice and expert game players, but asked them to choose a game they were not familiar with, and arranged for them to play the game in physical proximity. His data collection employs standard conversation analytic proce-dures, producing transcripts in accordance with routine conventions of conversation analysis, and pro-ceeding to explicate the analysis in the immediate context of the transcription and with very close reference to it. At all points the analysis aims to address the messy complexity *and* orderliness inherent in what "the players do and say as they try to instruct another player [in] how to play the game" (p. 350). At key points the analytic explication is referenced to ideas, arguments and positions within eth-nomethodological literature. In a brief discussion at the end, which might also be seen in terms of apply-ing some findings, Hung uses the results of his analysis to problematize and recontextualize some familiar ideas and positions associated with the concepts of situated learning and just-in-time learning.

The book concludes with Sean Duncan's report of research that investigates participants' discur-sive practices and design talk, and how this design talk was employed within one forum in an online gaming affinity space. Duncan's study is a form of what we call "Try on" research that pursues fruit-ful innovation in methodology. It "experiments" with bringing versions of D/discourse analysis and content analysis together in a mixed methodology with a view to exploring its potential for expand-ing the nature and scope of new literacies research based on the notion of affinity spaces. The chap-ter reports, rigorously and in depth, the rationale, purposes, design, theoretical informants, data collection, data analysis method, and analytic results of the study, before discussing the main find-ings, drawing conclusions, and considering the implications of the study for further development of research into affinity spaces. From a theoretical perspective the study draws especially on Gee's the-ory of D/discourse and Donald Schön's work on "design talk" and its types and rules. The method-ological innovation involves bringing D/discourse analysis together with a form of content analysis derived from Philipp Mayring. This is intended to address what Duncan sees as limitations in the scope of affinity spaces research to date that draws on Discourse analysis alone. Duncan argues that Discourse analytic studies can investigate detailed meaning-making exchanges within affinity spaces, focusing on "specifics," and reveal "fascinating and compelling moments of verbal exchange between participants within affinity spaces," but is not suited to identifying and understanding "the overall char-acter of an affinity space's textual content" and discerning discursive *commonalities* within single affin-ity spaces and across affinity spaces (p. 354). Duncan's account of "Kongregating online" centers on exploring and demonstrating the potential of his multi-method Discourse + Qualitative Content Analytic approach, within the context of a motivated focus on two facets of design integral to the Kongregate affinity space: design at the level of learning about successful game design and engag-ing in design talk to this end; and design at the level of how the affinity space has been constructed by its managers, and how its design constraints shape activity within the space.

This Volume and the "New Literacies" Series

This Reader *samples* the past five years of the New Literacies book series. It has aimed as far as pos-sible to represent the full scope of the types of work and interests addressed by the series as a whole, but with a view to where inquiry has currently reached more than where it has come from. This is a pragmatic choice that incurs costs, foremost among them the inability to include interesting and important work undertaken in the early stages of development of a field. For readers not familiar with the series, but whose interest in new literacies may be stimulated by the content of the present book, we strongly encourage them to consult the full contents list on the Peter Lang USA website at: http://bit.ly/11YZfIl.

A Note on Spelling Conventions

Throughout the book we have preserved the respective authors' spelling preferences from the original publications of their work. Most chapters employ Standard American English spelling, but several employ alternative English spelling conventions.

References

Appadurai, A. (1996). *Modernity at large: Cultural dimensions of globalization.* Minneapolis, MN: University of Minnesota Press.

Au, K. (2001, July/August). Culturally responsive instruction as a dimension of new literacies. *Reading Online, 5*(1). Retrieved 7 December, 2012, from: http://www.readingonline.org/newliteracies/au/index.html

Black, R.W. (2005). Access and affiliation: The literacy and composition practices of English language learners in an online fanfiction community. *Journal of Adolescent & Adult Literacy, 49*(2): 118–128.

Bolter, J. D., & Grusin, R. (2000). *Remediation: Understanding new media.* Cambridge, MA: MIT Press.

Bruce, B. (1998). New literacies. *Journal of Adolescent & Adult Literacy, 42*(1): 46–49.

Buckingham, D. (1993). Towards new literacies: Information technology, English and media education. *English and Media Magazine,* Summer: 20–25.

Castells, M. (1996). *The rise of the network society.* Oxford: Blackwell.

Chandler-Olcott, K., & Mahar, D. (2003). 'Tech-savviness' meets multiliteracies: Exploring adolescent girls' technology-mediated literacy practices. *Reading Research Quarterly, 38*(3): 356–385.

Csikszentmihalyi, M. (1990). *Flow: The psychology of optimal experience.* New York: Harper & Row.

Csikszentmihalyi, M. (1996). *Creativity: Flow and the psychology of discovery and invention.* New York: Harper Perennial.

Gee, J. (1990). *Social linguistics and literacies: Ideologies in discourses.* London: Routledge.

Gee, J., Hull, G., & Lankshear, C. (1996). *The new work order: Behind the language of the new capitalism.* Boulder, CO: Westview Press.

Halliday, M. (1985). *An introduction to functional grammar.* London: Edward Arnold.

Jenkins, H. (2006). *Fans, bloggers, and gamers: Exploring participatory culture.* New York: NYU Press.

Jones, S. (Ed.) (1999). *Doing internet research: Critical issues and methods for examining the net.* Thousand Oaks, CA: Sage.

Kellner, D. (2001). New technologies/new literacies: Reconstructing education for the new millennium. *International Journal of Technology and Design Education, 11*: 67–81.

Kress, G. (2003). *Literacy in the new media age.* London: Routledge.

Lankshear, C., & Knobel, M. (2000). The New Literacy Studies and the study of new literacies. Paper presented at an international seminar on "A Research Agenda for the New Literacy Studies," University of Wisconsin-Madison. September 19–20.

Lankshear, C., & Knobel, M. (2003). *New literacies: Changing knowledge and classroom learning.* Buckingham, UK: Open University Press.

Lankshear, C., & Knobel, M. (2006). *New literacies: Everyday practices and classroom learning* (2nd edn.). Maidenhead & New York: Open University Press.

Lankshear, C., & Knobel, M. (2011). *New literacies: Everyday practices and social learning* (3rd edn.). Maidenhead & New York: Open University Press.

Leander, K. (2003). Writing travelers' tales on new literacyscapes. *Reading Research Quarterly, 38*(3): 392–397.

Lemke, J. (2000). Across the scales of time: Artifacts, activities, and meanings in ecosocial systems. *Mind, Culture and Activity*, 7: 273–292.

Leu, D. (2001). Literacy on the Internet: Internet Project: Preparing students for new literacies in a global village. *Reading Teacher*, *54*(6): 568–572.

Luke, C. (2000). New literacies in teacher education. *Journal of Adolescent & Adult Literacy*, 43 (5): 424–435.

Perkel, D. (2006). Copy and paste literacy: Literacy practices in the production of a MySpace profile. Unpublished paper. http://www.ischool.berkeley.edu/~dperkel/media/dperkel_literacymyspace.pdf (accessed 12 September 2007).

Scribner, S., & Cole, M. (1981). *The psychology of literacy*. Cambridge, MA: Harvard University Press.

Semali, L. (2001, November). Defining new literacies in curricular practice. *Reading Online, 5*(4). Available: http://www.readingonline.org/newliteracies/lit_index.asp?HREF=semali1/index.html

Street, B. (1984). *Literacy in theory and practice*. Cambridge: Cambridge University Press.

Street, B. (1998). New literacies in theory and practice: What are the implications for language in education? *Linguistics and Education*, *10*(1): 1–24.

Warschauer, M. (1998). Researching technology in TESOL: Determinist, instrumental and critical approaches. *TESOL Quarterly*, *32*(4): 757–761.

Wellman, B. (2001). Physical place and cyber-place: Changing portals and the rise of networked individualism. *International Journal for Urban and Regional Research*, *25*(2): 227–252.

PART 1

New Literacies in Classroom Settings

CHAPTER ONE

Multimodal Pedagogies

Playing, Teaching and Learning with Adolescents' Digital Literacies

LALITHA VASUDEVAN, TIFFANY DEJAYNES & STEPHANIE SCHMIER

In a computer lab on the sixth floor of a federal building, four young men and one young woman spread themselves out across the machines. Three iMacs were brought in that day and set up adjacent to one another on a long folding table, and eight PCs lined the perimeter of the room. Frankie, the young woman, used one of the PCs connected to the internet to search YouTube (youtube.com) for a video she had previously uploaded to the video-sharing site. Bruce sat down in front of an iMac, opened up iMovie, and named his file "slickone," after the moniker he had earned in his neighborhood. All of the images he wanted to use for his afternoon movie project were on his MySpace page, so he borrowed a flash drive from the facilitator of the digital media drop-in hours and accessed his online profile on a PC. After selecting six images, and with Joey's help, he transferred the images onto the iMovie clip palette. Joey and Bruce worked together to drag and drop the images onto the iMovie timeline, where images and video can be organized into a desired sequence. When Mathu,[1] the facilitator, asked if Bruce could find the "effects" tab so that he could apply them to his images, Joey, who was still sitting with Bruce, pointed to the tab and responded with laughter, "It says 'effects'." Bruce spent the next hour applying and then removing effect after effect and made accompanying noises of exclamation and dissatisfaction at regular intervals. He left for work before he could finish his movie, but felt confident that he had mapped out the story he wanted to tell: one of himself as a former graffiti artist who was now seeking new canvases by painting clothing, hats, and signs for friends.

The youth who used the computer lab during the digital media drop-in hours moved seamlessly between "online" and "offline" spaces, and their digital literacies reveal hybridity in their multispatial navigations. While this vignette does not offer a definitive description of a completed project or product, the interactions across youth and adults reflect the pedagogical nature of a space in which multiple modalities for expression, communication, and representation are present. In this and other digitally rich contexts in which youth are engaged in the composition of multimodal texts (Hull & James, 2007; Ranker, 2008; Ware, 2008), experimentation and exploration are encouraged and literacies are not tethered to "in-school" and "out-of-school" binaries.

The well-documented literacies of adolescents reflect the shifting terrain of young people's communicative practices and the technologies that mediate them (Alvermann, Hinchman, Moore, Phelps, & Waff, 2006; Chandler-Olcott & Mahar, 2003; Skinner & Hagood, 2008). Virtual worlds, social networking sites, microblogging services, blogs, and wikis are among the several new kinds of spaces that Web 2.0 technologies make possible. Wesch (2007), a cultural anthropologist, in his highly popular video in which he analyzes the participatory culture of Web 2.0, suggests that among the concepts we need to rethink in light of the communicative, archival, and design affordances of evolving internet technologies are authorship, identity, aesthetics, and even love. Recent studies of adolescents' literacies resonate with Wesch's claims and illustrate a range of emerging practices across a diverse digital landscape encompassing spaces online and offline. These emerging literacies are evident in the sophisticated layering of texts, images, and sounds involved in the production of anime music videos (Ito, 2006). Digital literacy proficiency is also required to navigate and communicate within the unfamiliar semiotic contexts of video games (Gee, 2005), in which participants confront new situations, assume a range of roles and identities, and find themselves in a variety of communicative interactions. These are not merely new forms of "letteracy" (Lankshear & Knobel, 2007) and not solely concerned with the production of written texts. The challenge to educators is to be pedagogically nimble in order to most effectively support the literacy learning of adolescents who are engaged in these and many other literacies, which move across spaces of home, community, and school.

Multimodal Play

To this discussion of youths' online and digital literacies we bring the concept of multimodal play (Vasudevan, 2006), which illuminates otherwise dismissed or overlooked interactions with digital media and technologies for purposes of composing. Often, youth use humor and playfulness to navigate their daily discourses. This approach is also evident in the ways that youth approach new technologies and cultivate new literacy practices. In this chapter, we draw on research with adolescents in media-saturated contexts in order to advocate for a "pedagogy of play" while making connections with adolescents' digital literacies landscapes. We suggest that through multimodal play—including textual explorations, reconfigured teaching and learning relationships, and the performance of new roles and identities *with* and *through* new media technologies and media texts—educators are better able to make pedagogical connections with adolescents' evolving literacies.

The theoretical concept of multimodality provides a framework for understanding new forms of composing—not only the composing of multiple texts out of multiple modes but also the engagement of myriad digital "tools" to participate in equally varied digital geographies (Vasudevan, 2009). Multimodal composing, therefore, refers to more than bringing together separate modes of expression, such as sound or image, in the production of a text. Two ideas are important to consider when applying a multimodal approach to composing. First, it is important to recognize that reading and writing have always been multimodal. As Jewitt (2005) notes, even printed texts "require the interpretation and design of visual marks, space, colour, font or style, and, increasingly image, and other modes of representation and communication" (p. 315). A multimodal approach allows educators and researchers to attend to *all* of the resources involved in composing, which are especially visible in digital composing. Second, the ability to bring a variety of modes—for example, print, image, sound—together in the same text not only changes the way a text can be conveyed but also opens up new possibilities for what kinds of meaning can be conveyed (Hull & Nelson, 2005; Jewitt & Kress, 2003).

Adolescents are engaged in these types of composing across the hybrid spaces they travel on a daily basis (e.g., instant messaging with written language within a virtual world in which they must communicate using an avatar or incorporating photographs taken with a smartphone camera to their latest blog post). Portable technologies and increased wireless connectivity enable greater variation in what is composed, where and when composing happens, and reasons for composing.

We recognize that when youth are tethered to virtual spaces, such as microblogging sites like Twitter (twitter.com) and online video services like Hulu (hulu.com), their physical location also matters. Thus, we draw on this framework of multimodal play to extend the ongoing discourse about multi-modal text production by considering the makeup of the physical spaces in which teaching and learning with multiple modalities occur. Outside of schools, in many youth-focused media organizations, the availability of a wide variety of expressive modes, multiple audiences, and opportunities for collaborative as well as individual composition is mediated through a shared understanding of what we refer to here as multimodal play. While many examples of multimodal play are found to exist outside of school and in spaces that afford different social arrangements, there is growing evidence that suggests ways in which this ethos is possible within school spaces (Fisher, 2007; Hill, 2009; Wissman, 2005, 2008). As the examples in this chapter illustrate, the pedagogical stance of multimodal play can be helpful when reimagining classrooms and can be generative of meaningful literacy practices and teaching and learning relationships.

In places like Youth Radio, which is a broadcast training program for youth in the San Francisco Bay Area, as well as other projects that provide youth with largely unrestricted access to technologies, their explorations yielded unexpected and unplanned digital innovations (e.g., the music sharing service, Napster; the footage shot by children involved with the documentary, *Born into Brothels*; on-the-ground documentation by young soldiers of the war in Iraq) (Soep & Chavez, 2005). Soep and Chavez (2005) urge adults "to recognize that young people's media experiments are pushing the work of many adults and the institutions created 'for' youth" (p. 417) so that educators can build on these digital innovations in purposeful ways. In a youth media organization like Youth Radio, adults and youth engage in a "pedagogy of collegiality" to accomplish collective goals of youth development and media production. This "[c]ollegial pedagogy, then, characterizes situations in which young people and adults jointly frame and carry out projects in a relationship marked by interdependence, where both parties produce the work in a very hands-on sense" (2005, p. 419). This approach to pedagogy works in such a setting where a spirit of experimentation abounds, and where there is both physical and figurative room to play with roles, composing repertoires, literacies, and goals. Youth Radio and similar settings (Goodman, 2003; Hull & Katz, 2006) exist outside of the school walls. While calls for rethinking literacies pedagogies with adolescents abound (Alvermann, 2002; Burke & Hammett, 2009; Hull & Schultz, 2002; Pahl & Rowsell, 2006; Schultz, 2002), we have fewer examples of this call to action coming to fruition inside schools.

In this chapter, we present three instances of practice from our research with youth across three unique, urban educational settings and focus on the significance of play with technologies and media in literacy teaching and learning with adolescents. Each of us assumed different positionalities in our research, which afforded us varied entry into these multimodal educational spaces. We offer three different perspectives on creating and sustaining sites of multi-modal pedagogy that are informed by understandings of adolescents' emerging literacies. One case explores an eighth-grade journalism and media studies class and illustrates the ways in which the teacher utilized online tools and resources in the creation of a monthly school newspaper. A second case looks at the unexpected affordances of blogging in a high school English classroom. And a third case examines the engagement of social networking and video-sharing sites in the negotiation of identities and relationships between teachers and youth in an Alternative to Incarceration Program. We conclude our chapter with a discussion on the implications of the increasingly digitally mediated lives of youth for the educational institutions in which they participate.

Becoming New Media Journalists in an Urban Middle School

Room 208 at East Side Middle School looks very different from most of the other classrooms in this large urban public school. Thirty-five eMac computers circle the perimeter of the room surrounding a large "conference" table in the center where the 43 students enrolled in the journalism and digital media studies class meet at the beginning of sixth period each day to discuss their current projects and ask for support or feedback from the class. Though many of these students did not have an interest in journalism or expertise in digital media prior to being randomly assigned to the class by the administration, most readily took up the task put forth on the first day of school by their teacher, Mr. Cardenas: "You report. Journalists report the facts…[In] this class you will be journalists."

> Over the three years that Mr. Cardenas has taught the journalism and digital media studies elective,[2] he has transformed his classroom into an authentic workspace where he and his students explore both traditional and new media journalistic practices such as podcasting. During sixth period, students are journalists. They are provided with "press passes" that afford them freedom to move around the school to report on issues of interest and importance to the student body and access to a few digital still and video cameras which they use to perform their role as journalists. This freedom comes with responsibility. Students are required to make appointments to obtain interviews from their "sources" which include faculty and administration as well as fellow students and community members. Mr. Cardenas encourages the journalism students to work hard and be creative, and reminds them often of the importance of their jobs to "dig a little deeper to find something interesting that's happening, things that will matter to [our] students." He also takes his students on a field trip to the major newspaper in the city to learn about how and where journalists work.

As the above description of his classroom depicts, Mr. Cardenas employs a pedagogy of play in his classroom informed by a view of adolescents' literacies as meaningful and complex. His students play out their role as journalists, using props such as reporters' notebooks, cameras, and press passes to write about important issues in their school ranging from the academic curriculum to the nutritional quality of the cafeteria food. In contrast to some recent attempts we have heard about of teachers bringing out-of-school online literacy practices such as social networking on MySpace into their classrooms to engage students in academic content (e.g., create a MySpace profile for your favorite English poet), Mr. Cardenas acknowledged that many of his students had gained proficiency in a range of technologies through their participation in online communities and drew upon their expertise as he introduced them to new forms of composing with which most were not already familiar.

When I (Stephanie) interviewed one student, Casey, about her experiences in the class, she shared how she appreciated the way Mr. Cardenas respected the knowledge that students brought with them into the classroom and didn't "waste time" teaching the students skills they had already learned outside of school. Casey noted "Like he [Mr. Cardenas] knew that we use cameras outside of school. He knows that you [Casey and her fellow students] know how to use them." Furthermore, Casey valued how Mr. Cardenas pushed students to learn about new ways of using familiar equipment and tools to explore topics of interest, saying, "He let us do our own topics and let us play around with the camera." Another student, Sabina, described how Mr. Cardenas incorporated new online literacies into the classroom in ways that valued what the students knew and positioned them as responsible. Unlike other teachers and her parents who she felt did not trust the students at the school to use the internet appropriately without strict supervision and instruction, she felt that Mr. Cardenas created an environment where the students could learn to use the technology responsibly and in Sabina's words, "let us learn how to fly," something that she described as essential for the youth at her school to succeed in our increasingly digital world.

Mr. Cardenas and his students drew upon the affordances of a variety of online resources throughout the academic year as the school newspaper developed from a print-based PDF posted to the school website to a series of audio and video podcasts hosted through a free third-party online classroom resource. The podcast project required students to create a digital and downloadable audio file of one of their news stories using GarageBand software[3] (http://www.apple.com/ilife/garageband), which Mr. Cardenas had introduced through a directed whole-class lesson. Just as with all new projects that Mr. Cardenas introduced, many students played with the format of the project in order to tell their stories in creative ways.

Rosy was one such student whose podcast documented the exceptional artwork of a student at the school. Through experimentation with the software, Rosy realized that she could use both iMovie and GarageBand together to create a video podcast. In her podcast, she juxtaposed an interview she conducted with the student artist with her artwork. In so doing, Rosy created a meaningful multimodal text that showcased the artist's work in a way that would not have been possible in a solely audio format. Rosy, who aspired to be a journalist, shared that the use of technology in the journalism and digital media studies class "open[ed] the doors to what is going to be in the future…Getting us prepared for what's going to come." In an era when traditional print newspapers are quickly becoming extinct, the curriculum that Mr. Cardenas designed clearly helped Rosy consider how she can blend her proficiency with online media and passion for journalistic writing. She was able to position herself as a "shape-shifting portfolio person" (Gee, 2002), with the ability to design and redesign her work processes and texts, a skill which some have argued will be essential for success in our emerging global economy (e.g., Gee, 2002; New London Group, 1996).

Marie was another student who played with the podcast project format, leading to the creation of a digital text that uncovered and critiqued concerns over the quality of the educational experiences available to students at East Side Middle School. In her core academic classrooms where the curriculum is mandated and designed primarily to prepare students for the state standardized tests, Marie, who is an avid writer and blogger in online spaces, often takes up the position of "disengaged student," especially when the task is a traditional type of print-based school assignment with strictly mandated parameters put forth by the teacher. However, this was not the case in the journalism and media studies class, as is exemplified in the way that Marie approached the podcast project. For the podcast, she chose one of the topics offered by Mr. Cardenas, a new teacher profile, though she had the option of coming up with a topic of her own as well. Marie wanted to interview her new English teacher, the fourth teacher that the eighth graders on her track had that year. Marie developed a list of thoughtful interview questions which included: "What made you want to teach at our school?" and "Are you still in teacher school?" When I asked why she inquired about whether he was still in school, she replied, "He doesn't look like he has a lot of experience." She went on to articulate her frustration with some of the English teachers who had taught at her school previously but was impressed with the fact that this new teacher agreed to come in during lunch and be audiotaped. Marie spent her own time during lunch recording the interview, editing her podcast, writing and recording an introduction and conclusion, and adding her own touches to the piece, including music. Clearly, the social space of the journalism and digital media studies class allowed Marie to take up a different subject position than in her core classes, and the multimodal affordances of the podcast project allowed her to reposition herself as a "successful and engaged" student in ways not available in her core classes. The space also allowed her to critique the circumstances in her school, and design a multimodal text, which articulated what she saw as a grave injustice: that she and her fellow classmates in this under-resourced school are not provided with the experienced teachers who can give them the quality education they deserve.

The case of Mr. Cardenas' journalism and digital media studies class exemplifies how educators can make pedagogical connections with adolescents' evolving literacies through creating an authentic and meaningful workspace in which they can explore topics and issues of importance to them and share their thoughts through the creation of multimodal online texts. Mr. Cardenas' openness and flexibility to both ideas from other educators as well as the students in the class created a different type of space than the classrooms where students spent most of their day taking core academic classes. In these spaces, strict pacing plans and standardized curriculum provided by the school district were employed, and a majority of the students in the school were positioned as "underperforming." By contrasting these dominant school spaces and routines, Mr. Cardenas afforded diverse students at East Side Middle School opportunities to tell the stories that they wanted to tell in new and different ways, allowing them to reposition themselves as successful authors and designers, as they played with literacies and identities through their roles as new media journalists.

Blogging and Other Social Media in the Classroom

In my bright, sunny classroom at a new, arts-focused small high school in Brooklyn, New York, I (Tiffany) have a small but revealing window into students' technology interests. I consciously incorporate media and various technologies into my class projects, have more technology tools available than any other classroom in the school, and invite students to participate in social networking spaces (i.e., Facebook, AIM) with me if they choose. In practice, this means that students often work on laptops from the school's computer cart during class and that I let them "get away with" more time on their sidekicks [smartphones] than many other teachers would, often to the dismay of my administrators. Over the course of the year, I've found that interacting with students through social media has been one of the key factors in knowing them more deeply and also building trusting relationships.

Being the "techy" teacher means that I have a broader range of media resources in my room. Most visible is the stationary Mac tower with a large flat screen monitor in the back of my classroom. As a teacher of 12th graders with college applications due and a yearbook to design, I negotiated having this nice and more or less unclaimed computer moved into my room. Because of my willingness to let students on the computer for various reasons any time of day (before and after school, during free periods, and often even during a lesson), a student is working on that computer almost all of the time. No less significant is that I have two drawers of my desk full of technology: two "unlocked" laptops that are special because they aren't blocked by Department of Education Internet filtering software and can be used to access YouTube and social networking sites. We often call these the "good" laptops, simply because of their unrestrained access to tools we need and use. Additionally, my desk drawers hold my personal SLR camera, a digital video camera purchased with an educational technology grant, a tripod, a projector, and speakers for streaming music into the classroom. Thus, the technology in the cart and desk drawers are used in this English classroom in a range of ways—from class work to college work, personal communications, and a range of visual documentation, presentation, and entertainment purposes.

Media have a real presence in our school often in terms of the arts; however, media rarely enter into content area or literacy classes in ways beyond "typing up" papers or doing loosely guided internet research. Of the various media projects that I've brought into my classroom this year, student-created blogs (short for web logs, journal-like personal web pages) have become the long-standing form of classroom multimodal text production that I've introduced as an educator. Student blogs fit into the classroom structure primarily as a "homework" assignment, free-writing that I read and comment on digitally and assess solely on completion. A content analysis of my students' blogs found that they focused their writing on the following issues: academic or financial stress, high school graduation, college, friendships, dating, national politics, hobbies, special events, identity, other media (i.e., games, music, films), and a few students used their blogs exclusively for creative writing—poetry and short stories.

Other technologies are brought into the classroom with implicit invitation. I often observe students with personal communication devices out on their desks—SideKicks, iTouches, BlackBerries, or the like. Students use these devices in class for a range of activities—from cell phone text messaging to instant messaging (i.e., AIM) to blogging to even typing up papers or doing research for class. My students have learned that only answering their phones in class will garner much disciplinary action, as it is distracting to others and socially inappropriate. Otherwise, small communication devices and social networking are invited into the classroom space when they aid in learning or do not get in the way of it.

As an English teacher who is a bit unconventional in her curriculum (more a writing and media teacher than a literature one), it has taken some time for students not only to trust me as an individual but also to trust my methods as a teacher. When I first asked them to start blogging many students expressed extreme dismay. "Why do we have to write so much? Can't you just give us a quiz? What's the point of all of these writing projects? Can't we learn the material another way?" Some of my students were fairly resistant to an unconventional, writing-based curriculum and my department peers weren't quite sure what to do with it either. Often these students are the ones who have been successful in more traditional literature-based classrooms. Other students, ones who struggle with print, were visibly delighted in being able to type in whatever script they like on their blogs, post photos and videos, and so on.

One particular student, A'idah, often does not want to do the assigned work for class and asks if she can blog. I don't always allow it, but her class happens to be at the end of the day and many students cut class. One afternoon A'idah asked if she could take a short story written by Junot Diaz (1997) with her to read on the train and blog during class instead. I nodded my head, handed her an "unlocked" or "good" laptop and told her I would check three entries at the end of the period. I'd learned to give her a goal and check it, because sometimes she only pretends to blog as she sifts through Facebook pages and music videos instead.

About midway through class, I sat down next to her and watched her type. She barely looked up but began to narrate without prompting. She said, "I'm trying to describe myself from the outside in." I watched as collected adjectives poured onto the page and she checked how they lined up visually next to the photo of herself that she'd pasted into the entry. Next, I watched her edit the html code in the entry, watched her delete the ads from the song she'd posted in the entry (from imeem, a social media outlet that allows users to watch, post, and share digital content). She didn't like how the ads cluttered up her post, so she went into the html code and started editing out the ads. She moved quickly and effortlessly in editing the code; however, when she had finished the html was broken. She said, "I hate that." I muttered, "Yeah, me too, because I can never figure out where I broke the html when I was deleting stuff." Nonetheless, she persevered, quickly found the missing bit of code, repaired and published the entry. I was surprised when the next thing I saw on the screen was an entry that looked different than the one we'd seen in "preview"—the words didn't roll alongside the picture just as she'd planned. When I asked her about it, she shifted to the larger question of how limiting the blog layout was. However, she exclaimed she loved blogging despite these limitations. Of course, I asked why. She started talking rapidly, rambling on. I said, "This would help me with my dissertation. Can I take notes?" She nodded, watching me begin to type up her words as fast as I could. Here's what I wrote as she talked:

> I hate writing stuff on paper because I feel like my hands can't keep up with my thoughts when I write on paper. When I get to the end of the page with my pen, I feel like I lost my thoughts. I notice that I have more good thoughts when I'm on the Internet, clicking on stuff is more efficient than writing. I can get to everything I want on the Internet. If I click on Wikipedia I can get to what I want. I have more access to things like turtles…pet section. Plus online you can find a lot of other people who think the same thing you do. Google is my favorite thing.
> You can research forums and just anything. It expands my thinking more than books.

[She pauses; I redirect with "Why blogging?"]

> Blogging is more exciting than a journal because people can appreciate writing more than if it's in a book. I also feel like people are more apt to read my stuff if it's on the Internet than it's in a book.

She was talking about how great it was to write more quickly than on paper, and I was barely keeping up transcribing her thoughts. She asked as I plugged away transcribing in real time, "You writing all this?" I nodded and kept typing. "Cool" she said. As she talked, she unplugged her SideKick from the wall, packed up her belongings, and when she'd said about all she needed to say, she mumbled toward the door, "Yeah, I'll text you Miss DJ, we can talk more about this when I get home." As she left, I handed her the short story and told her to read it on the train.

Audience is no small thing to A'idah. Her best friend often gets a shout out on her blog, and she was pretty delighted the day a girl she had a crush on began to publicly "follow" her blog. One afternoon, after I'd commented on something I'd liked in an earlier blog entry, she asked, "So do you really read all our blogs, Ms. DJ?" I said, "Yeah." Her response: "You're a good teacher, Ms. DJ." I laughed, "So you like it that I read your stuff?" "Well a lot of teachers don't actually read stuff." Writers need readers and blogs are a good shot at making that happen, if an imperfect one. A'idah told me that her favorite entry of the day was the one titled "apathy," one that I suspect she wrote for the art teacher—a mentor of hers for four years who reads her blog and keeps telling her to move beyond her newfound apathy. Instead of simply moving beyond it, A'idah uses her blog to explain how her apathy is a matter of coping with stresses for her. Thus, the blog has provided a space for A'idah to connect through writing with a few trusted readers who give her feedback on dilemmas she has experienced.

A'idah's story is not unusual. Many of my students used the space of blogging to gain an audience of trusted readers—friends, teachers, and sometimes even parents and siblings. Throughout the year, student blogs have provided me as a teacher with a sense of students' emotional states and their practical progress through many of the stresses of 12th grade—high-stakes high school exit exams, difficult classes, the college application progress, and more personal, individual issues. Thus, blogs provided a way to not only get to know my students better as writers and media-savvy young people but also enabled me to be a better advisor—to follow up digitally and in person, sharing in their successes and struggles and supporting students as they developed into independent young people.

Making Our Space by Engaging MySpace and YouTube

In a classroom context where new geographies of teaching and learning were being crafted on an ongoing basis (Vasudevan, 2009), the online literacies of both youth and adults played an important role. This was evident during a brief exchange I (Lalitha) witnessed while talking with two teachers one afternoon. Joey, a young man who was 18-years-old at the time, walked into Christina's office as she, Norman, and I were discussing potential candidates for the digital media class I was planning. Joey, who we all agreed should certainly be one of the participants, was finished with classes for the day and had come to hang out with Christina for a few minutes before he headed off to his internship at a media design company.

The four of us squeezed into Christina's office and Joey, a born storyteller, regaled us with the latest tale of his adventures around town. He told us that while riding the subway on his way home the previous afternoon, he started talking with a young woman whose cell phone he admired aloud. It was the latest SideKick, a newer version of the phone he currently owned. Being a tech savvy teenager himself, Joey felt he had found a kindred spirit as he observed her navigate her multifunction communication device with ease. Not wanting to lose touch, Joey and the young woman "swapped URLs" so that they could access and be linked to each other's MySpace profiles. The three of us listening to the story laughed out of curiosity, and Joey clarified that "they"—presumably, youth of his generation—are more inclined to share online profile information than phone numbers. He identified a shifting communicative lexicon that is readily emerging in the social practices of youth.

Far from being dismissive, however, Norman and Christina were engaged in the story and probed Joey further. They asked him about his online profile, made note of his URL, and agreed to "friend" him so that his profile could be linked to each of their profiles as well. These teachers, like many of the other teachers, counselors, and other staff members at this Alternative to Incarceration Program (ATIP), also used the social networking site and actively communicated with others via their online profiles. Some of them were linked to participants via the "friending" function of the site. As Christina once noted, MySpace messaging was sometimes the quickest and most consistent way of contacting the participants when they couldn't be reached otherwise. I created an online profile for myself as a way to maintain contact with some of the youth, particularly after they graduated from the program, and found Christina's observation to ring true. Sometimes cell phones and home phones were shut off for periods of time, but the youth could always find a way to access their MySpace pages.

At the ATIP where Christina and Norman taught, and where Joey was a participant, educational classes were organized to support participants' preparation for the General Equivalency Diploma (GED) test. ATIP provided a range of services for youth who had been arrested and mandated to attend the program by a judge, in consultation with a court representative who worked with the program. Only a small percentage of the mostly young men who attended the program already had their high school diplomas or equivalency certificates. Many had dropped out of high school prior to their arrest and most had a history of interrupted school experiences. However, many displayed a range of digital competencies including, but not limited to, participation in online social networking spaces.

Amid a steady stream of photocopied math and grammar worksheets—that, on first glance, seem out of place in a context that places primacy on a holistic approach to education—are consistent pedagogical practices that draw on youths' digital literacies.

One afternoon, following the administration of a GED predictor that eligible participants take to assess their readiness for the GED exam a few weeks later, Norman was conducting a mini-lesson about basic economic principles. He asked the class of eight young men seated in the classroom what they knew about investing. There was a long pause, and then one young man asked for clarification: "You mean, like, how white people invest their money?" Norman, who was of South Asian descent and who had recently cut his long dreadlocks, looked at the young man wearing an over-sized plain white tee-shirt with curiosity. He probed for a longer response. The young man continued, "Cuz, people in the hood—they *wear* their investments." A smile began to creep across Norman's face and, seeing the computer lab unoccupied, Norman shifted the physical location of that afternoon's class across the hall. He asked Martin, the young man who made the observation about racial differences and investment strategies, to find evidence for his claim. A couple of the other participants sitting near Martin laughed when he initially logged into his profile. The humor was due in part to the cacophony between Martin's "tough guy" pose seen in his profile photo and the good-natured persona he often displayed at ATIP. In response to Norman's invitation, Martin clicked on several of his friends' profiles, repeating "See?" after each one. As he brought up several images of youth adorned with large pieces of jewelry or pointing to customized accessories, Norman wrote terms on the whiteboard on the wall adjacent to Martin in a manner reflective of free association. He wrote "consumption" next to "supply/demand" and then underlined both with a double line and underneath wrote, "personal economics." During the next 45 minutes of class, everyone in class opened up their own MySpace profile and began identifying images that reflected some of the economic terms that Norman had highlighted. The room was filled with a steady stream of laughter as the young men looked over each other's shoulders, and as they waved Norman over to share their visual artifacts.

The teachers at ATIP recognize the importance of the visual media for the youth who filter through their classrooms every day. They are equally aware that these youth are inhabiting and participating in a variety of digital spaces that are multimodal and online in some way. Similar to Martin's navigation of MySpace to support his economic argument, ATIP participants routinely brought up video clips they had either viewed or uploaded to YouTube, the video-sharing site. Like Frankie, the young woman who used her YouTube video to simultaneously communicate a narrative about her sexuality and her identity as a multimedia artist, other participants named and shared videos they found terrifying, funny, realistic, and unbelievable.

Along with Norman and Christina, Tony was another teacher at ATIP whose pedagogy was responsive to the cultural funds of knowledge that youth brought with them into the classroom (Moje et al., 2004; Moll, 1992). One of the classes Tony taught was Next Steps, a college preparation seminar designed to meet the needs of ATIP participants who either had obtained their high school diploma or who had taken the complete GED test. During one of the cycles of Next Steps that I documented, the writings of James Baldwin served as the main texts for the seminar. Tony, who had been teaching at ATIP for four years at the time, had begun to explore the visual realm in his teaching and was increasingly aware of the participants' familiarity with digital technologies and YouTube in particular. He began to incorporate this resource into his teaching as a way of illuminating the words and messages of a prolific author like Baldwin. By using a familiar resource like this video-sharing site, whose access is blocked in many public schools, Tony aimed to disrupt any dichotomizing that might have occurred between a revered author and current popular texts. In doing so, he was not

Table 1. YouTube Exploration of Representations of Blackness [4]

Topic of Video Clip	Description and Context [5]
James Baldwin	James Baldwin being interviewed by Kenneth Clark about race in American—his own personal experiences, and his thoughts on the nation. A long list of related clips includes several different people talking about Baldwin. http://www.youtube.com/watch?v=Rt-WgwFEUNQ
Reflection on Baldwin and *Little Black Sambo,* by Margaret	A woman reflects on having James Baldwin as a houseguest, and her embarrassment at having her young daughter share her copy of *Little Black Sambo*[6] with Baldwin. http://www.youtube.com/watch?v=47qAZWkwOaw
Little Black Sambo[6]	An animated illustration of the children's book of the same name, noted in the previous clip. http://youtube.com/watch?v=qSfGvptL_TY
Tom & Jerry	A popular children's cartoon featuring a wily mouse, an easily duped cat, and a Black housekeeper (Mammy Two Shoes) who is always depicted from the shoulders down.
Jeffersons	George, the patriarch of a middle class Black family, living on the Upper East Side of Manhattan with his wife, Louise, and son, Lionel. They were prosperous enough to hire a housekeeper, Florence.
Good Times	A sitcom from the 1970s that portrayed a Black family, headed by Florida and James Evans, living in a housing project in Chicago, Illinois.
All in the Family	The show about Archie & Edith Bunker, a seemingly mismatched couple, living in a working-class neighborhood in Queens, New York. Archie's prejudice towards anything outside of his world view was the driving source of the show, which was the genesis of both *The Jeffersons* (a direct spin-off) and *Good Times* (a spin-off of *Maude*, a direct spin-off of *All in the Family*).
Cosby Show	A show about an affluent Black family living in Brooklyn, New York, made up of two professional parents—Heathcliff (Cliff) and Clair Huxtable—and their five children.
Sanford & Son	Another 1970s sitcom about Fred Sanford, an antiques and junk dealer, and his son Lamont.

Table 1 (*continued*)

Topic of Video Clip	Description and Context [5]
Martin	A 1990s sitcom that focuses on the life of Martin Payne, a disc jockey and later television host, and his friends. Much of the comedy comes from Martin Lawrence's own stand-up comedy act.
Paul Mooney	An American comedian whose comedic material often addresses race in America, and which has been the object of critique and adulation.
Cedric the Entertainer roasting Secretary of State Condoleeza Rice	A clip of the White House Correspondents' Association annual dinner (2005) during which Cedric the Entertainer pokes fun at Secretary Rice by suggesting that she has two distinct personalities: her public persona and a second, which he demonstrates using racialized and gendered gesticulations. http://www.youtube.com/watch?v=T-bDO92S1jU

merely using "out-of-school" literacies and texts to bridge "in-school" objectives, but rather strived to construct a hybrid space constructed of shared understandings—among Next Steps participants and teachers—toward the realization of collective goals.

On one particular afternoon, this hybrid space lived in the context of Tony's office where he had access to his computer and loudspeakers. Rather than continue a discussion on the way Baldwin moved and held his cigarette during interviews, Tony shifted the location of class so that he could share a video of the author in different contexts. What ensued was a visual journey of representations of Blackness across various media clips found on YouTube. Table 1 offers an overview of this journey.

It was clear from Tony's enthusiasm and the ways he punctuated the video clips with commentary that this was a person and a subject for which he had great passion. Tony thought of himself as an artist and writer and used multimedia texts to elicit these and other identities from the young men who were enrolled in his classes. Tony's objective in this class session, and with his emphasis on Baldwin's work throughout Next Steps, was to illustrate the power of language for the youth seated around him. Not only did he share the writing of a beloved author with young men who had not been exposed to this work before, he also provided another way into *reading* Baldwin: by seeing and hearing the author, and interacting with other media texts, which Tony felt reflected the lasting impact of this pioneering African American author.

Afterwards, Tony reflected on his decision to move the class to his office with a characteristic smile and look of amusement on his face. He was surprised that "it worked," referring specifically to the conversational rhythm and observational insights about the representations of African Americans across various media that emerged in between the collective viewing of clips. The young men in the class took a cue from Tony's engagement with and spontaneous analysis of the texts and began to share their own intertextual connections: comparing reruns of the *Cosby Show* with current representations of Black families; recalling the cartoons they had watched as kids when the clip of *Black Sambo* appeared on the screen; musing about the ways in which President Obama had been characterized in the news as, alternatively, "not Black enough" or "too Black." Many of the video clips that the group watched were not familiar to most other than Tony, but each was evocative of multiple connections and engendered further inquiry that was nurtured during the next several weeks of the Next Steps seminar.

Although YouTube was a familiar resource for the young men in Next Steps, the setting and purpose of this class session suggested new uses for this popular video-sharing site. This pedagogical move, reminiscent of recommendations for educators to effectively leverage the funds of knowledge about popular culture that adolescents bring into the classroom (Alvermann, Moon, & Hagood, 1999; Morrell, 2004; Staples, 2008), was consistent with Tony's objective to connect with the youth with whom he interacted every day. Even in his role as a teacher, he sought to be a "student of students" (Staples, 2005). Like Norman and Christina, Tony embraced spontaneity and play in his pedagogy. Multimodal play is a pedagogical stance that holds real possibilities for the youth at ATIP to be reengaged in their educational trajectories. This is an approach that is culturally responsive, digitally intuitive, and grounded in a commitment to teaching and learning *with* youth.

Creating Classrooms of and for Multimodal Play

We conclude this chapter by widening the lens once more to consider the vast landscape of the increasingly digitally mediated lives and literacies of youth. In their three-year study of the online habits of teens, Ito and colleagues (2008) found that youth regularly navigate various new media and technologies including social networking sites, online games, video-sharing sites, mobile phones, MP3 players, and the like. While these artifacts of digital culture saturate the daily lives of youth, Ito and her colleagues assert that when youth engage in these practices and spaces, they are developing a range of social, intellectual, cultural, and technical knowledge that should not be dismissed. Thus, they argue, adults who impact the lives of youth—including educators, caregivers, and policymakers—must take seriously the ways in which "new media forms have altered how youth socialize and learn" (2008, p. 2). Their findings echo the arguments we have made in this chapter about the impact of youths' digital cultures and practices for literacy teaching and learning across contexts. As youth are engaged in the processes and practices of exploring, making, and remaking their identities across a wide array of representational modalities and spaces, both online and offline, the role of the educator becomes more complicated and, we would argue, ripe with possibilities.

In this chapter, we offered a brief look at three different classroom contexts in which we explored adolescents' online and digital literacies from a variety of perspectives. At the center of each example is the profound act of teachers and students *knowing* each other through multimodal play in order to teach and learn together. We invite readers of this chapter to consider the implications of these instances of practice for other settings, such as non-urban classrooms, school libraries, and afterschool programs. We wonder how institutional spaces such as these might more effectively engage the digital knowledge and practices in which young people are *already* proficient. When educators are more aware of adolescents' digital literacies and composing repertoires, they can more effectively marry instructional goals that children and youth need to meet in order to successfully navigate formalized education with pedagogical agility that affords adolescents multiple ways to construct and represent knowledge. Thus, as our work and that of others (e.g., boyd, 2008; Soep & Chavez, 2005) suggests, educational institutions must become spaces that can more readily accommodate and encourage literacy experimentation, exploration, and discovery.

Notes

* This chapter was originally published as: Vasudevan, L., DeJaynes, T., & Schmier, S. (2010). Multimodal pedagogies: Playing, teaching, and learning with adolescents' digital literacies. In D. Alvermann (Ed.), *Adolescents' Online literacies: Connecting classrooms, digital media, and popular culture* (pp. 5–26). New York: Peter Lang.

1. Mathangi (Mathu) Subramanian worked with Lalitha as a research assistant on the project Education In-Between: A Study of Youths' Lives, Learning, and Imagined Futures within and across the Justice System.

2. The class was referred to as an elective by school administrators though students were predominantly assigned to the class based on scheduling needs.

3. GarageBand is a software program available on Macintosh computers that allows users to author various types of audio recordings by composing, recording, and mixing music.

4. This table originally appeared in Vasudevan, L. (2009). Performing new geographies of literacy teaching and learning. *English Education*, 41(4), 356–374.

5. Some clips were only played for a few seconds and thus not all of the clips' URLs were documented accurately. Here, I briefly note the context for each clip that was viewed, drawing from field notes of the ongoing, intermittent discussion. I intentionally do not offer an extensive analysis of these clips but rather present this table to provide additional background for the Next Steps class.

6. A children's book that originally depicted a caricature of a South Indian child given the name "Sambo." In the 1930s, newer versions of the book gained popularity in the United States but were widely criticized for depicting racially insensitive stereotypes.

References

Alvermann, D. (2002). Effective literacy instruction for adolescents. *Journal of Literacy Research, 34*(2), 189–208.

Alvermann, D., Hinchman, K., Moore, D. W., Phelps, S., & Waff, D. (2006). *Reconceptualizing the literacies in adolescents' lives* (2nd ed.). Mahwah, NJ: Lawrence Erlbaum.

Alvermann, D., Moon, J. S., & Hagood, M. C. (1999). *Popular culture in the classroom: Teaching and researching critical media literacy.* Chicago, IL: International Reading Association.

boyd, d. (2008). Why youth (heart) social network sites: The role of networked publics in teenage social life. In D. Buckingham (Ed.), *Youth, identity, and digital media* (pp. 119–142). Cambridge, MA: MIT Press.

Burke, A., & Hammett, R. F. (2009). *Assessing new literacies: Perspectives from the classroom.* New York: Peter Lang.

Chandler-Olcott, K., & Mahar, D. (2003). Adolescents' anime-inspired "Fanfictions": An exploration of multiliteracies. *Journal of Adolescent and Adult Literacy, 46*(7), 556–566.

Diaz, J. (1997). *Drown.* New York: Riverhead Trade.

Fisher, M. T. (2007). Writing in rhythm: Spoken word poetry in urban classrooms. New York: Teachers College Press.

Gee, J. P. (2002). Millennials and Bobos, *Blue's Clues* and *Sesame Street*: A story for our times. In D. E. Alvermann (Ed.), *Adolescents and literacies in a digital world* (pp. 51–67). New York: Peter Lang.

Gee, J. P. (2005). Learning by design: Good video games as learning machines. *E-Learning, 2*(1), 5–16.

Goodman, S. (2003). *Teaching youth media: A critical guide to literacy, video production, & social change.* New York: Teachers College Press.

Hill, M. L. (2009). *Beats, rhymes and classroom life: Hip-hop, pedagogy, and the politics of identity.* New York: Teachers College Press.

Hull, G., & James, M. A. (2007). Geographies of hope: A study of urban landscapes and a university-community collaborative. In P. O'Neil (Ed.), *Blurring boundaries: Developing writers, researchers, and teachers: A tribute to William L. Smith* (pp. 250–289). Cresskill, NJ: Hampton Press.

Hull, G., & Katz, M. (2006). Crafting an agentive self: Case studies of digital storytelling. *Research in the Teaching of English, 41*(1), 43–81.

Hull, G., & Nelson, M. E. (2005). Locating the semiotic power of multimodality. *Written Communication, 22*(2), 224–261.

Hull, G., & Schultz, K. (2002). *School's out!: Bridging out-of-school literacies with classroom practice.* New York: Teachers College Press.

Ito, M. (2006). Japanese media mixes and amateur cultural exchange. In D. Buckingham & R. Willett (Eds.), *Digital generations: Children, young people, and new media* (pp. 49–66). London: Routledge.

Ito, M., Horst, H., Bittanti, M., et al. (2008). *Living and learning with new media: Summary of findings from the digital youth project.* The John D. and Catherine T. MacArthur Foundation Reports on Digital Media and Learning.

Jewitt, C. (2005). Multimodality, "reading," and "writing" for the 21st century. *Discourse: Studies in the cultural politics of education, 26*(3), 315–331.

Jewitt, C., & Kress, G. R. (2003). *Multimodal literacy.* New York: Peter Lang.

Lankshear, C., & Knobel, M. (2007). Researching new literacies: Web 2.0 practices and insider perspectives. *E-Learning, 4*(3), 224–240.

Moje, E. B., Ciechanowski, K. M., Kramer, K., et al. (2004). Working toward third space in content area literacy: An examination of everyday funds of knowledge and discourse. *Reading Research Quarterly, 39*(1), 38–70.

Moll, L. C. (1992). Funds of knowledge for teaching: Using a qualitative approach to connect homes and classrooms. *Theory into Practice, 31*(1), 132–141.

Morrell, E. (2004). *Linking literacy and popular culture: Finding connections for lifelong learning.* Norwood, MA: Christopher-Gordon Publishers.

New London Group. (1996). A pedagogy of multiliteracies: Designing social futures. *Harvard Educational Review, 66*(1), 60–92.

Pahl, K., & Rowsell, J. (2006). *Travel notes from the new literacy studies: Instances of practice.* Buffalo, NY: Multilingual Matters.

Ranker, J. (2008). Composing across multiple media: A case study of digital video production in a fifth grade classroom. *Written Communication, 25*(2), 196–234.

Schultz, K. (2002). Looking across space and time: Reconceptualizing literacy learning in and out of school. *Research in the Teaching of English, 36*(3), 356–390.

Skinner, E., & Hagood, M. C. (2008). Developing literate identities with English language learners through digital storytelling. *Reading Matrix, 8*(2), 12–38.

Soep, E., & Chavez, V. (2005). Youth Radio and the pedagogy of collegiality. *Harvard Educational Review, 75*(4), 409–434.

Staples, J. (2005). *Reading the world and the word after school: African American urban adolescents' reading experiences and literacy practices in relationship to media texts.* Unpublished doctoral dissertation, University of Pennsylvania.

Staples, J. M. (2008). "Hustle & Flow": A critical student and teacher-generated framework for re-authoring a representation of Black masculinity. *Educational Action Research, 16*(3), 377–390.

Vasudevan, L. (2009). Performing new geographies of literacy teaching and learning. *English Education, 41*(4), 356–374.

Vasudevan, L. (2006). Pedagogies and pleasures: How multimodal play helps us reimagine and represent adolescents' literacies. Paper presented at the American Educational Research Association, San Jose, CA.

Vasudevan, L. (2009). Performing new geographies of teaching and learning. *English Education. 41*(4), 356–374.

Ware, P. D. (2008). In and after school: Teaching language learners using multimedia literacy. *Pedagogies: An International Journal, 3*(1), 37–51.

Wesch, M. (2007). Web 2.0…The machine is us/ing us. Retrieved April 20, 2009, from http://www.youtube.com/watch?v=6gmP4nk0EOE

Wissman, K. (2008). "This is what I see": (Re)envisioning photography as a social practice. In M. L. Hill & L. Vasudevan (Eds.), *Media, learning, and sites of possibility* (pp. 13–45). New York: Peter Lang.

Wissman, K. (2005). "Can't let it all go unsaid": Sistahs reading, writing, and photographing their lives. *Penn GSE Perspectives on Urban Education, 2.* Retrieved July 11, 2008, from http://www.urbanedjournal.org/archive/Issue3/notes/notes0006.html

CHAPTER TWO

Trajectories of Remixing

Digital Literacies, Media Production and Schooling

OLA ERSTAD

Cultural transformations in recent years have been strongly linked to the developments of technology (Castells, 1996; Jenkins, 2006; Buckingham & Willett, 2006). Such transformations can be seen in the ways we as citizens change our everyday practices; as with the introduction of email systems early in the 1990s that changed fundamentally how we communicate, developments in virtual reality and later on simulations, the development of the World Wide Web as a source for information and in later years the developments of online games and Web 2.0.

One of the key challenges in these developments is the issue of digital literacy. This relates to the extent to which citizens have the necessary competence to take advantage of the possibilities given by new technologies in different settings. In a fundamental way it raises discussions about what it means to be able to "read" and "write" as part of our cultural developments today, understood as interpretation of and access to information and how we communicate and express ourselves. My focus in this chapter is on the implications these developments have for the way we think about education and the institutional practice of schooling.

From these more general considerations there is one aspect of digital literacy that I believe is of special importance; that is the issue of media and content production, especially what I term "trajectories of remixing." This is seen in the developments of Web 2.0 and the increasing number of postings on sites like YouTube, MySpace, Flickr or Facebook, during just a couple of years. We can also see similar trends in television concepts like Current.com, where it is the audience that produces the content, as well as in television shows like "So You Think You Can Dance" or "Idol." This represents a shift in the role of audience and the impact of production practices.

Remixing activities as an essential part of digital literacy represent processes of change in our schools today, from knowledge development being based on predefined content in school books and the reproduction of knowledge provided by the teacher, towards a situation where students take available content and create something new, something not predefined. Some schools have already implemented these new possibilities provided by digital media, and several theoretical developments are highlighting the educational implications of these developments (Scardamalia & Bereiter, 2006). However, our education system is still fixed in the traditional ideals of literacy.

I will use my own country, Norway, as an example of a country trying to address these challenges through its education system and policy changes. I will start with some contextual information about developments in Norway. The next step will be to outline some issues and frameworks about digital literacy in the research literature. From this I will orient myself more towards discussing the concept of remixing, and advancing my point that this has to be seen over longer processes of media production and not only as an expression of putting different content pieces together. I will use three cases as examples of such processes within school-based settings. These are taken from different projects in Norway where remixing activities are part of project work in schools using digital media. Towards the end I will look at some of the implications this has for our conceptions of schooling.

The Norwegian Context

Developments in Norway during the last 10 years can be divided into three main phases indicating the overall national agenda for scaling up activities using digital media in Norwegian schools. The three phases are also expressed in specific "action plans" from the Ministry of Education. The first phase, from 1996 until 1999, was mainly concerned with the implementation of computers into Norwegian schools. There was less interest in the educational context. In the next phase, from 2000 until 2003, the focus was more on whole school development with ICT and changing learning environments. The next phase, from 2004 until 2008 (the time of writing this chapter), put more emphasis on digital literacy and knowledge building among students and what learners do with technology.

One immediate challenge in these developments has been the balance between "top-down" and "bottom-up" strategies. At one level it has been important to commit the Ministry of Education to developing ICT in Norwegian schools. At another level it has been important to get schools to use ICT more actively. The latter has been more difficult. From 2003–2004 onwards, this changed somewhat in the sense that more schools started activities themselves, since access to computers and the internet was no longer a problem either in school or at home.

The national curriculum from 2006 defines digital literacy/competence[1] and the "skill to use digital tools" as being as important as reading, writing, numeracy and oral skills. The implication is that all students on all levels and in all subjects should use and relate to digital media in their learning processes in Norwegian schools. The emphasis is mainly on skills in using the technology although broader issues of competence such as evaluating sources critically when using the internet and using ICT to collaborate are also implied. At the same time research has shown that even though the access to digital media and the internet has been steadily improving, teachers hardly use these media in their activities with students. The students report that they use such media much more at home, and for a broader scope of different purposes (Erstad, Klovstad, Kristiansen, & Soby, 2005).

The conception of "digital competence" has been important on a policy level to create more awareness of the impact of digital technologies on our education system. In a Norwegian setting we are now in a situation where the main question is what students and teachers use these new technologies for, both inside and outside of schools. During the last few years many initiatives have been taken to stimulate productive use of new technologies in schools, as in numerous other countries. This has often been informed by how young people use new technologies outside of schools.

Norwegian youth, like youth in many other countries, are very active users of new digital media. Television is still the medium most youth use on an average day, but the time spent on the traditional mass media like television, radio and newspapers (paper versions) has been steadily declining since 2000. Most young people use a broad range of different digital media. Compared to young people in some other European countries, proportionately more Norwegian youth fall into the category of "advanced users" (Heim & Brandtzæg, 2007). This implies that Norwegian youth have good access to technology and use such technologies for "advanced" purposes. However, in a general sense several studies have shown how young people gain most of their competence in using digital technologies outside the formal institutions of knowledge building (Livingstone, 2002; Buckingham, 2003; Alvermann, 2002).

It should also be mentioned that young people in the Nordic countries have been involved in online networking sites and online content production for several years. In all Nordic countries there are examples of online communities for social networking and media production by youth since the end of the 1990s, which have been very popular. Most famous is the Swedish "Lunar Storm."

What is interesting is that these developments in policy initiatives towards digital literacy and media use in general have brought Norwegian educational initiatives to a point where new cultural practices start to appear, making us look at literacy in new ways. Remixing is such a turn in the way digital media allow the user to create new content based on other peoples' content production and sharing it with others. What is important is to frame remixing as such within broader discussions about digital literacy.

Digital Literacies: Conceptions, Frameworks and Issues

In recent years there has been an interest in how traditional conceptions of literacy change due to new digital technologies. An important point is that literacies change over time due to socio-cultural processes (Scribner & Cole,1981; Olson & Cole, 2006). Similar perspectives are reflected in socio-cultural theories of learning, where learning is related to the use of specific artifacts and tools (Säljö, 1999). James Wertsch (1998) uses concepts like "cultural tools" and "mediational means" to discuss these transitions in human development:

> One could focus on the emergence and influence of a new mediational means in sociocultural history where forces of industrialization and technological development come into play. An important instance of the latter sort is what has happened to social and psychological processes with the appearance of modern computers. Regardless of the particular case or the genetic domain involved, the general point is that the introduction of a new mediational means creates a kind of imbalance in the systemic organization of mediated action, an imbalance that sets off changes in other elements such as the agent and changes in mediated action in general. (Wertsch, 1998, p. 43)

Similar ideas are expressed by the German literary scholar and media theorist Friedrich Kittler who described this as the development of different "cultural techniques" over time (1990). Wertsch (1998) also makes a point of distinguishing between mastery and appropriation in relation to different cultural tools. Concerning digital literacy, this relates to being able to operate the technology itself, to master it, versus having the competence to reflect on the use of digital media in different contexts as part of your identity as a learner.

This implies that we constantly have to keep in mind the more general question of what it means to "read" and "write" in a culture and, thereby, how we learn (Pahl & Rowsell, 2005). In the *Handbook of Literacy and Technology*—subtitled, "Transformations in a Post-Typographic World"—David Reinking and colleagues (1998) present several perspectives on how the development of digital technologies changes conceptions of text, of readers and writers and ultimately of literacy itself. This implies that digital literacy relates to changes in traditional cultural techniques like reading and writing, and yet, at the same time, opening up new dimensions to what it means to be a competent reader and writer in our culture.

In her book, *Literacy for Sustainable Development in the Age of Information* (1999), Naz Rassool presents an overview of different debates on literacy during recent decades. Her point is that research perspectives on technology and literacy need to reconceptualize power structures within the information society, with an emphasis on "communicative competence" in relation to democratic citizenship. Digital technologies create new possibilities for how people relate to each other, how knowledge is defined in negotiation between actors and how it changes our conception of learning environments in which actors make meaning. Empowerment is related to the active use of different tools, which must be based upon the prerequisite that actors have the competence and critical perspective on how to use them for learning. Literacy, seen in this way, implies processes of inclusion and exclusion. Some have the skills and know-how to use them for personal development, others do not. Schooling is meant to counteract such cultural processes of exclusion.

What exactly should be included within the conceptual domain of literacy has become increasingly fuzzy, especially among those educators and researchers whose professional interests are tied to how literacy is understood. This is, of course, due to the fact that literacy is not a static term but relates to technological innovations, and cultural and political strategies and developments. It is necessary to distinguish between more of a skills orientation and a higher level of competency.

One report often referred to is *Digital transformations. A framework for ICT literacy* (ETS, 2002) written by a team of experts for the Educational Testing Service in the U.S. In this report they identified some key concepts of what they called ICT literacy. One interpretation of such key concepts is presented in Table 2.1 (which comprises my own elaboration of key concepts in this ETS report). This consists of more general competencies that are not connected to specific subjects in school or specific technologies. They can be taught and are related not only to what is learned in school settings but also to situations outside the school.

Other frameworks have used "digital competence" as an overall term. One example is the working group on "key competences" of the European Commission's "Education and Training 2010." This program identifies *digital competence* as one of the eight domains of key competences; that is, as

the confident and critical use of Information Society Technologies for work, leisure and communication. These competences are related to logical and critical thinking to high-level information management skills and to well-developed communication skills. At the most basic level, ICT skills comprise the use of multi-media technology to retrieve, assess, store, produce, present and exchange information, and to communicate and participate in networks via the internet. (European Commission, 2004, p. 14).

Table 2.1: Key Concepts of ITC Literacy (my elaboration based on key concepts in the ETS Digital Transformations report, 2002)

Basic skills	Be able to open software, sort out and save information on the computer, and other simple skills in using the computer and software.
Download	Be able to download different information types from the internet
Search	Know about and how to get access to information
Navigate	Be able to orient oneself in digital networks, learning strategies in using the internet
Classify	Being able to organize information according to a certain classification scheme or genre
Integrate	Be able to compare and put together different types of information related to multimodal texts
Evaluate	Be able to judge the quality, relevance, objectivity and usefulness of the information accessed. Critical evaluation of sources
Communicate	Be able to communicate information and express oneself through different meditational means
Cooperate	Be able to take part in net-based interactions and learning and take advantage of digital technology to cooperate and be part of different networks
Create	Be able to produce and create different forms of content: generate multimodal texts, make web pages, and so forth. Be able to develop something new by using available tools and software

Digital competence in this framework encompasses knowledge, skills and attitudes related to such technologies.

Another interesting conceptual background is the term "media literacy" (Buckingham, 2003), which has been part of the media education movement since the 1980s. Discussions of media literacy during the last ten years, especially in the UK (Buckingham, 2003), are relevant here; first, because the media themselves are the object of analysis; second, because the reflective and critical dimensions of analysis are central; and third, because media production among the students is a key component (see Case 3 below). Kathleen Tyner (1998), who uses "media education" and "media literacy" as reference points in her discussions, studies some of the elements of a modern interpretation of literacy both related to what she terms "tool literacies," to indicate the necessary skills to be able to use the technology, and "literacies of representation," to describe the knowledge needed to take advantage of the possibilities that different forms of representation give the users. This describes a division between a tool orientation of literacy and a more reflective social process.

An important cultural development in recent years has been the processes of convergence (Jenkins, 2006). This relates to how technologies merge, how production of content changes, how new text formats are developed, and how the users relate to information as part of communication networks in different ways. Parallel to such convergence processes some literacy theorists have sought to hold together the many new literacies under some umbrella concepts, emphasizing the plurality of literacies, such as "multiliteracies" (Cope & Kalantzis, 2000; Snyder, 2002) and "metamedia literacy" (Lemke, 1998). According to Kellner (2002, p. 163), "[t]he term 'multiple literacies' points to the many different kinds of literacies needed to access, interpret, criticize, and participate in the emergent new forms of culture and society." Kress (2003), however, argues against the multiplicity of literacies, suggesting that it leads to serious conceptual confusion. He believes that instead of taking this path, it is necessary to develop a new theoretical framework for literacy which can use a single set of concepts to address the various aspects of literacy.

In addition, it is important to stress that technology literacy is related to *situational embedding*; that is, the use of technology within life situations. To understand such processes we have to look at different contexts where literacy is practiced and given meaning. This is especially important when relating it to how children and young people use digital technologies across contexts. In line with this perspective, Lankshear and Knobel (2006) have defined literacy in this sense as:

> Socially recognized ways of generating, communicating and negotiating meaningful content through the medium of encoded texts within contexts of participation in Discourses (or, as members of Discourses). (Lankshear & Knobel, 2006, p. 64)

This definition is not bound by certain technologies. It proposes to study literacies in practice (what people do with technologies and digital texts) and not as something pre-described, indicating that we need to understand what people are already practicing concerning technological literacies and what the role of education should be in employing such literacies for new knowledge levels. The important message is that digital competence among young people today is of direct relevance to discussions about learning in schools, and it seriously confronts earlier conceptions of literacy and learning.

As shown in this section, there are different frameworks to relate to in our understanding of digital literacy/competence. However, the key challenge is to go deeper into the implications of increased use of new technologies in educational practices. I believe the concept of remixing points us in the right direction, because it raises some key issues concerning educational work with digital media.

Conceptual Developments of Remixing

As several authors have pointed out (Lankshear & Knobel, 2006; Manovich, 2007), the conceptual understanding of remixing is nothing new. Issues of reusing and reworking from other texts have been known since the early days of the Greeks. In more recent times we see such issues expressed in the developments of more visual media, in painting using inspiration from other art, or everyday objects put into paintings, creating new contexts for interpretation—for example, as seen in the Dada movement—or in photography as seen in collage and photomontage (Ades, 1986) or in film as seen in the theories and films of Eisenstein on montage, putting images and scenes together in specific ways, creating new ways of interpretation (Bordwell, 2005).

The concept of remixing is first and foremost connected to developments of producing music through available mixing equipment and in the way DJs work. As explained by Manovich (2007), "[r]emixing originally had a precise and a narrow meaning that gradually became diffused. Although precedents of remixing can be found earlier, it was the introduction of multi-track mixers that made remixing a standard practice" (no page). Since the mid-1970s we have seen many examples of how artists take existing music pieces or recordings and make something new from them; "[g]radually the term became more and more broad, today referring to any reworking of already existing cultural work(s)" (Manovich, 2007, no page).

For my purpose here it is especially the developments of new digital technologies and the way these technologies have become available both at home and in schools that are interesting. As a consequence, remixing as cultural practice has changed dramatically in recent years. Digital tools create new possibilities for getting access to information, for producing, sharing and reusing. The main point is that more and more people in our culture can take part in these remixing activities, not only elite or specific groups. Most evident, it is young people who take a lead in creative practices using digital media.

Some even talk about a remixing *culture* (Lessig, 2005; Manovich, 2007) as characteristic of the changes we see in our culture today. Remix is seen as evident in every domain of cultural practice (Lankshear & Knobel, 2006, p.177). Everyone engages in remix in this general sense of the idea, and remix is everywhere, and defined as a condition for cultural development. What is new is, of course, the impact of digital technologies. The possibilities of remixing all kinds of textual expressions and artifacts have thereby changed. And, as mentioned before, these kinds of practices have become central to the ways young people make meaning and express ideas. In his writings on copyright issues and intellectual property legislation in the digital age (as seen in the guidelines on Creative Commons), Lawrence Lessig (2005) highlights remix as a key rallying point. For Lessig, digital remix constitutes a contemporary form of writing.

Several writers have been looking at remixing as new ways of conceiving text production. Manovich (2007, no page) sees developments of remixing in "music, fashion, design, art, web applications, user created media, food"—cultural arenas that "are governed by remixes, fusions, collages, or mash-ups." Moreover, "if post-modernism defined the 1980s, remix definitely dominates the 2000s, and it will probably continue to rule the next decade as well."

One aspect of the development of remixing as a concept and practice is the theoretical development of multimodality, especially by scholars like Gunther Kress, Theo van Leeuven and Carey Jewitt. Multimodality expresses the combination of different media elements into a new textual expression. This combination of media elements is not just a sum of the different elements, but creates something new; a new quality as text. Some also talk about this as "remediation" (Bolter & Grusin, 1999), as partly building on what exists to develop something new, and partly that digital texts represent something new as hypertext (Landow, 2006). However, this literature has paid little attention to the dynamic process of media production made possible by digital tools.

The Bricoleur of Remixing

As stated in my introduction, my main argument in this chapter is that "digital literacies" *per se* does not tell us very much about these new cultural practices mentioned above. How digital technologies, for example, influence educational practices needs to be specified through the activities students and teachers are involved in, and this is where remixing becomes interesting and an important facet of digital literacy. This implies a conceptual understanding of remixing that involves the actor to a larger degree than stated in the section above.

Together with some colleagues I have defined re-mixing as "selecting, cutting, pasting and combining semiotic resources into new digital and multi-modal texts (bricolage), which is achieved by downloading and uploading files from different sources (internet, iPod, DV-camera, digital camera or sound recording devices)" (Erstad, Gilje, & de Lange, 2007, no page). This implies a focus on the process of remixing and text production.

Studying such processes can be traced back to the concept of "bricolage" from the cultural studies tradition, mainly associated with the Birmingham Centre for Contemporary Cultural Studies during the 1970s. Dick Hebdige, in his classic book, *Subculture: The meaning of style* (1979/1985), used the concept of "bricolage" to discuss cultural practices that different youth subcultures were involved in at the end of the 1970s, especially the expression of style. This constitutes processes of sign making done by people in specific sub-cultural settings, called bricoleurs. One of the groups Hebdige was studying was the Mods, characterized by their scooters, grubby parka anoraks, and so forth. According to Hebdige, "the mods could be said to be functioning as bricoleurs when they appropriated another range of commodities by placing them in a symbolic ensemble which served to erase or subvert their original straight meanings" (1979/1985, p. 104). Similar sign-using practices can be seen in how the punk movement used swastikas, rubbish, and safety pins in the face, excessive hairstyles, and so forth to create new interpretations of traditional meaning making from specific signs.

This also raises the question of authoring in remixing activities. In school-based activities the question of copy and paste has been raised as a concern since students have been said to just take elements from other texts and copy them into their own texts without much reflection. However, research that has been done on these activities shows that if we look at this in longer trajectories of activities we find both discussions and reflections on the selection, implementation and expression of different media elements into new textual expressions by students (Rasmussen, 2005). Multimodal practices could be said to give young people a voice to express their positions and interests as agents of remixing. This can be seen in several initiatives about digital storytelling and self-representation using digital tools, where these activities with young people often are defined outside of school-based settings in order to avoid the contextual constraints of schools and build directly on everyday experiences with technologies (Hull & Greeno, 2006).

Lessig (2005) refers to a particular practice of creative writing within the school curriculum in parts of the U.S., where students read texts by multiple authors, take bits from each of them, and put them together in a single text. This is described as "a way of creating something new" (Lessig, 2005, no page). Lankshear and Knobel (2006) relate this perspective from Lessig more specifically to issues of literacy in the sense that learning to write is done "by doing it." For most adults, the act of writing means writing with letters, while for young people writing today means something much more, such as using images, sound and video to express ideas (2006, p. 177–178). In their discussions of remixing, Lankshear and Knobel (2006, p. 178) include both "practices of producing, exchanging and negotiating digitally remixed texts, which may employ a single medium or may be multimedia remixes," and "various practices that do not necessarily involve digitally remixing sound, image and animations, such as fanfiction writing and producing manga comics."

How can we then understand these trajectories or acts of remixing, and how do they relate to literacy and learning? Nicholas Diakopoulos (2005) has developed an illustration of different acts of remixing combining media elements/pieces and the person involved (see Figure 2.1).

The "romantic authorship" is what we traditionally think about as the writer creating the text; that is, "the author as a lone creative genius." The person/author writes a text, the media piece, which is read by another person. Diakopoulos' point is that this is more of a romantic conception of the writer than what the real situation of authorship has been. This other conception he describes as "collaborative authorship," which has been central throughout history. Diakopoulos suggests we think of "the

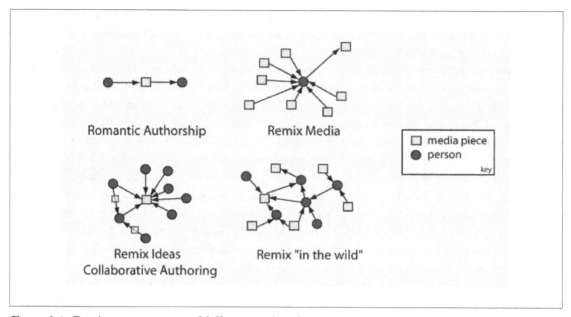

Figure 2.1: Graph representations of different modes of remix as they relate to people and media elements (Diakopoulos, 2005, no page).

myriad of different traditional productions which rely on the creative input of multiple people: orchestra, film production [and] architecture" (Diakopoulos, 2005, no page). He goes on to describe how "[t]his notion is reflected in Barthes' argument that a text does not release a single meaning, the 'message' of the author, but that a text is rather a 'tissue of citations' born of a multitude of sources in culture (Barthes, 1978). In this light, the author is simply a collaborator with other writers, citing them and reworking their ideas" (Diakopoulos, 2005, no page). In this sense, Diakopoulos distinguishes between remix ideas and remix media. "Remix media" implies that the remixer starts with concrete instantiations of media that are then segmented and recombined, as putting different elements together. Further, "remix ideas" may involve one or more people combining ideas gleaned from different sources (i.e., interpretations of media), which are then potentially instantiated in media, as by bringing ideas together for developing a specific text. "Remix in the wild" can then be related to Web 2.0 and the way media production is done through different people creating different media pieces, which are then reworked by other people through new steps of media production in a complex remixing trajectory.

Mimi Ito has written extensively about such complex cultural production practices, specifically on how Japanese youth are involved in "media mixes" in different ways. Her perspective is that "digital media broaden the base of participation in certain long-standing forms of media engagement. This includes the growing accessibility to tools of media production, as well as more diverse internet-enabled means for communicating about and tracking in cultural content" (Ito, 2006, p. 50). She uses Japanese animation media mixes as an example of combinations of various analog and digital media forms. She argues that "children's engagement with these media mixes provides evidence that they are capable not only of critical engagement and creative production, but also of entrepreneurial participation in the exchange systems and economies that they have developed around media mix content" (Ito, 2006, p. 50). She then goes on to show how these practices represent a media literacy that young people are involved in as part of their everyday culture.

Another interesting example of such creative media production among youth can be seen in the not-so-publicly known free online software called "Scratch" (http://scratch.mit.edu) (Peppler & Kafai, 2007). It has been made to stimulate kids' creative processes, to use a set of available modules, like Legos, to build a short animation, or create something new using available programming possibilities, download animations that others have done, and/or upload one's own to the website. When I logged on at the time of writing (October 12, 2007) there were available 34,991 projects with a total of 537,575 scripts and 192,959 sprites created by 7,506 contributors among 40,036 registered members. One of the uploaded animations I found on the front page was called "Stick Fight Remix" by Abudeok. This was a simple animation showing two characters fighting and flying between buildings, clearly referencing computer games and television cartoons (e.g., *The Powerpuff Girls*). Towards the end, text-boxes are included indicating communication between the two characters, and then ending the short film with the message: "The End. Want a part 2? Put it in my comments :)."

Remixing, in this sense, illustrates how young people today are involved in taking different media extracts and putting them together in new ways. My aim here is to show how these new possibilities of media production, expression and cultural practice of reading and writing change how we perceive literacy and learning within school-based settings and how digital literacy will be understood and worked on within these settings.

Remixing Activities in Schools

Media production has a long history in schools, through traditional writing activities, and later on (in the 1980s and 1990s) with audio-visual media in media studies and during more recent years with the massive introduction of computers and internet access (Buckingham, 2003, 2007). The question that arises is how media production practices in schools today indicate a change of what it means to read and write, building on the experiences of young people from outside of schools, and the importance of media production through all subjects and levels and not only as part of specific media-related subject domains.

Schooling in this sense refers to the process of relating to all aspects of being at schools as we usually know them today. Several studies have shown that there is a gap between how much and for which purposes digital media are used in- and outside of schools (Erstad et al., 2005). At school, children report that they use digital media to a much lesser degree than at home or with friends, and that when they use such media at school it is often to make traditional literacies of writing letters and numeracy more effective, while their use outside of schools is more made up of many different activities, especially gaming, downloading music and communication and creation. There are, however, some schools that have managed to create new spaces for literacy and learning, taking advantage of the possibilities represented by digital media, often connected to project work (Erstad, 2005).

Three Cases

Below I will briefly describe three cases where I see that trajectory of remixing, as part of digital literacy, being expressed. These are taken from different projects I have been involved in and are not unique. Many similar examples could have been mentioned. An interesting development in Norwegian schools is, for example, the introduction of digital storytelling as a method of telling personal stories remixing images, music, sound, visual effects and voice over (for more on this, see Erstad & Silseth, 2008). The first case is taken from one of the Norwegian cases in a large international project focusing on "innovative pedagogical practices using information and communication technologies" (Kozma, 2003, no page). The second is from a small project involving two classes of students at two different schools in Oslo, who collaborated on a project on prejudices and created online newspapers. The third is taken from ongoing research on media studies in Norwegian schools. None of these was initiated to study trajectories of remixing explicitly. Nonetheless, they raise issues about how this now becomes part of digital literacies in schools, showing both possibilities and constraints. I will not analyze the interaction among the students in these projects in an empirical sense. The intention here is to describe and reflect on the activities themselves related to the way they illustrate remixing using digital media in schools.

Case 1: Crossing Borders and Modalities

At one lower secondary school just outside Oslo a pair of teachers initiated a project called the "Antarctica project." It all started in October 1999 when the explorers Liv Arnesen (Norwegian) and Ann Bancroft (American) presented their ideas for an education program connected to their Antarctica 2000–2001 expedition. This was presented as a global activity where schools in different countries could participate. A special database was developed where anyone could follow the expedition. In addition the school had a special arrangement with one of the explorers, Liv Arnesen, whereby they would have direct interaction before, during and after the expedition. This was both to get factual and research-based information, and information of a more personal nature about the experiences of the two women in Antarctica. The student project was about the Antarctic. On using new technologies and related to remixing in the school the principal says that:

> It relates to being able to use many senses, and to do things and to see that it works. To learn about another country by reading about it in a book compared to having it presented through internet, images, sound and experiences, you might say, and communication with students in other countries directly through email and chatting and all that which now is possible. (Interview with school principal)

Two teachers and eight students took part in this project. The aim of the project was to create a web page that would contain different kinds of reports and information gathered by the students about the expedition and Antarctica.

The online version of one of Norway's major newspapers was a collaborator in the project. It had a special agreement with the expedition organizers to get up-to-date information from them. The newspaper also established a link to the students' web page. In addition, the students used the internet to get access to more general information about Antarctica, and they downloaded some video-presentation programs and also digital editing programs to edit the audio interviews with the explorers and put it on their web page.

The main technology used in this project was connected to the creation of a project web site. Additional activities consisted of collecting information from different sources and presenting it on the web site. The web site was created as part of the national school net and thereby became available to all schools in Norway. They had about 3,000 visitors per week. For working on their web page the students used Page Pro, Photoshop and FrontPage 2000. Mainly one PC was used for updating the web site. They used the internet to get access to information and email to stay in contact with the explorers and other students in and outside Norway. They used Word and learned the basics of html editing and coding. A couple of the students were reasonably familiar with programming, knowing more than their teacher.

Different kinds of technologies were used in different phases of the project. It started out with ordinary information retrieval from the internet about Antarctica followed by extensive use of email to exchange information with students in other countries. The next step was to create web pages about the expedition. On their web site, the students made a digital map on which they plotted the route that the explorers took from week to week. One of the teachers mentioned that he also used SMS messages on mobile phones to get in touch with the students after school hours. He sent out SMS messages to the students when the satellite connection with the explorers was established, and then all the students came to the school to participate. In addition, as a consequence of the project, they started to use video conferencing in their collaboration with other schools.

This project illustrates, in a simple way, processes of remixing in the way students searched for, brought together and combined different media elements made possible by digital technologies. It was also evident that for the students this project created some new perspectives on the school as a knowledge institution. By commenting on the use of technology in such a project some students mention that:

Boy: It becomes more fun to be at school. When you split it up a bit more. Instead of having six
              hours in one stretch, then it becomes easier to get through the day.

Girl: For some it might be a big shock when they get into the work market, because you do not
              sit and make mathematical assignments as such. When we work on projects you get a bet-
              ter grasp on what is happening in real companies and such.

Boy: We should get more experience of how it is in real working life.

In relation to this project the technology has given the students some opportunities and arenas for negotiation that creates exciting consequences for how they work on subject matter. As shown, remixing activities are a central part of the whole project integrating different modalities and knowledge domains in the making of the website and following the expedition.

Case 2: Challenging Prejudices of the Other

This case is taken from a project involving two lower secondary schools: one in the eastern part of Oslo and the other in the Western suburbs. Both schools had long experiences of project work as the main school activity all year round. At each school a group of students took part in the project during a two-week period (approximately 20 students in one school and 40 students in the other). The teachers at the two schools had for some time talked about collaborating on a project focusing on the differences between the two schools. The school in the Western suburbs had students from families with a high socio-economic background with only one non-white student, an adopted child born in Chile. At the school in the Eastern inner-city part of Oslo, the students came from many different cultural backgrounds, with about 65% of the students belonging to minority language-speaking families. After discussing this with the students the teachers decided that the students should collaborate on a project about prejudices concerning east and west in Oslo, and that they should use technology as a central part of the project work. When the project was starting up there were several headlines in the national newspapers about a study showing huge differences in the expected life course and death rate of people living respectively in the east and west of Oslo. This shocked the students and was an important stimulus for their discussions.

In the project the students used different digital tools to collaborate and create an online newspaper, one for each school, which consisted of reports about the students on the other side of town, their community and their school. In each student group they divided themselves into an editorial board with responsibilities for different sections of the paper; on culture, religion and ethics, sport, statistics about their communities and interviews with inhabitants. They created questions that they sent to each other using a collaborative online platform and MSN. Halfway through the project a group of students from each school traveled, without the teachers, to visit the students at the other school using public transportation. None of the students had ever been in the area of the other school. To document this visit each group made a video film and took still pictures to use in their own production.

My interest here is not to discuss everything that happened in the course of this project or the outcome concerning the prejudices about the Others, which turned out to be a very stimulating process in itself. I use this case as an example of a project where the dynamic use of digital media is integral to the ways students work and to what they create.

Throughout the project the students worked with different modalities and information sources in the making of the online newspapers. They worked individually on different computers looking for images, statistical data, graphs, illustrations, written texts, or editing audio interviews with players from the local soccer team, editing the video films to put on the web, and then got together to negotiate how to integrate and remix the different content sources into something new on their online newspaper. The two online papers turned out very differently. One had many different visual effects, with numerous images on the front page and links to other sections of the paper consisting of more text and images. The online paper of the other school had simpler aesthetics on the front page and more video material, such as video interviews with students at their own school and with students from the other school recorded during their visit.

What was interesting in this project were the ways the students combined different content they found on the internet with their own content, either written texts through collaborative writing or audio- and video-tapes. The editorial group at each school had the last word concerning how things should be presented on their online newspaper. Reviewing my video observations of the two groups revealed a very intense and creative process among the students working on different content materials and sending them between the two schools. Often there were rapid changes in the way they related to content materials, such as when one of the Muslim girls at the school in the eastern part of Oslo described why she was wearing a veil. This subsequently generated a lot of questions to her from the students at the other school on what this meant in everyday activities like what she did during gymnastics lessons, did she have ethnic Norwegian friends, what were her interests in music or films, and what did her parents think about her growing up in Norway. In documenting this story, the students remixed different content materials they found on the internet about the Muslim religion, about world incidents connected to religious conflicts and then connected to this girl's personal story, which was then presented on the online newspapers of both schools. In a simple way this project generated a lot of online and offline discussions about different themes triggered by their own prejudices towards each other and documented through collaborative efforts of remixing different content materials in an online newspaper for each school.

Case 3: Media Production in Media Education

The third case is taken from a subject domain in schools where digital media are at the core, both as embedded in learning activities and as an object of analysis. In the year 2000, a new subject was introduced at the upper secondary level in Norway, called "Media and Communication," as an optional three-year program in vocational training but also with academic components. Media education has been part of Norwegian education for many years but only as a marginal area comprising a non-compulsory part of school programs. However, this new program has become very popular among students, and more and more schools are establishing it and investing in infrastructure and teacher competencies for offering it. For my purpose here, the interesting part is the strong emphasis on media production in this subject made possible in new ways by digital tools. My interest is not in what they make (i.e., the end product) but, rather, in the process of media production, what I have termed "trajectory of remixing," using digital tools.

The first example of such remixing activities was collected by one of my Ph.D. students, Øystein Gilje, as part of his research on this subject in Norwegian schools (see also Erstad, Gilje, & de Lange, 2007). The students in this example were working on a short documentary film about a house occupied by young people in Oslo called "Blitz." They were using different digital resources to include in the film employing Photoshop. In the sequence below they are working on the opening title to find the right font, which is very important for them. They did not like the available fonts already in Photoshop, so they went on the internet and found a specific site with alternative fonts where they discovered what they were looking for and then tried to download it to their own computer without succeeding. This is when they asked the teacher to help them.

Teacher:	You are going to import a *new* font into Photoshop? (..).
Girl 1:	Yeah. We have downloaded a new font from the internet. That's the problem we want you to help us to solve....(approx. 4 seconds of silence)
Teacher:	Well, I don't know how to do that. Why can't you just use one...There're plenty of fonts in the program! (scrolling the font menu in Photoshop)
Teacher:	Waste no time doing this! Use time on. (...) What's important here is telling the story! You have to work with journalism!
Girl 2:	But maybe the font could tell something important about the Blitz.
Girl 1:	It gives the expression...(interrupting each other)
Girl 2:	No, use the ordinary one.

The creative element in choosing a particular font for the title is not accepted or is at least difficult to understand for the teacher. The confrontation develops further when the teacher tells them that the task is to work with journalism, not with design and "details" in the process. This leads to a discussion about the importance of the downloaded fonts. The students argue that these fonts are important because they express their understanding of the "blitz" concept.

The second example was collected by another doctoral student, Thomas de Lange, as part of his own research on "Media and Communication" (see also Erstad, Gilje, & de Lange, 2007). In this example a student (Boy 1) wishes to supplement his Flash production with a specific jingle from a Play Station game called *Final Fantasy*. He wants to include this jingle in his production as a personal attribute. Together with a fellow student (Boy 2) he first tries to search for this jingle on the internet. The following extract initiates the overall sequence:

Boy 2:   (…) who did the music for *Final Fantasy*?

Boy 1:   Nobuo Uematsu.

Boy 2:   How is it spelled?

Boy 1:   N (O U B) ((spelling the name))

Boy 2:   (No), say it again.

Boy 1:   Let's see. <N O B O U E:::>, <no::u:: bou:: Nubou::…>

The excerpt below takes place about one minute later, after the students have found the jingle on the internet and downloaded it to their computer. It starts with Boy 2 playing the jingle loudly on the computer, getting the attention of the teacher who is standing nearby.

Teacher: Quit playing.

Boy 2:   …was only looking for some music from this game here. I'm not going to play, just getting the music.

Boy 1:   I'm not just sitting here watching him play, right?

Boy 2:   No! ((Ironic))

Boy 2:   A film with Japanese subtitles.

Teacher: That you are going to put into ehh…use the music in flash?

Boy 2:   Yeah.

Teacher: Uhm. ((Teacher walks away))

Both these classroom situations show specific remixing practices among the students as part of larger media production projects. They go on the internet to find a specific font or a jingle that they have clear preferences for and download these to use in their own media productions. These extracts also show how the students operate by themselves and how the teacher has problems dealing with these remixing activities among the students.

Remixing as Literacy

Building on the different conceptions and frameworks of digital literacy discussed earlier in this chapter, especially conceptions of multiliteracies and multimodality, I defined remixing as a key issue in the way digital literacy is developed in contemporary cultural practices. As shown, remixing is nothing new in a cultural sense. What is new, however, is the way digital technologies make it possible to combine many different resources by an increasing number of people. Something new is created based on existing content and then shared with others for further reworking. In this way people take an active part in content production and sharing of multimodal texts. As such it makes a fundamental change in the way we conceive reading and writing as cultural practices of meaning making.

In the cases mentioned above an important aspect of remixing has been the process of creation; what I have termed trajectories of remixing. I have used the context of school to show how this can be played out in a specific setting traditionally framed by the use of books. The cases mentioned are not spectacular in their technology use, and they are representative of what is happening in many classrooms at the moment. What is important is partly that project work is a working method used in many Norwegian schools, which allows students and teachers to work in interdisciplinary ways with a particular theme over time, and partly that there is good access to technology in Norwegian schools, which makes it more interesting to ask questions about literacy practices involving new technologies. All the cases mentioned above show how available digital tools support the students' remixing activities of using different information sources, combining them in different ways, creating something new, and then sharing this with others for possible reuse. It is the trajectories of remixing that are important in these specific school contexts. At the same time they indicate some of the constraints of doing this in schools. This has not been so obvious in the case descriptions, but through interviewing several of the students involved in these projects they identify clear differences between doing such activities at home and doing them at school. This is mainly connected to the role of the teacher that restricts the students more than supporting or challenging them, partly due to lack of digital competence. This raises questions about what kinds of teacher and student roles such remixing activities open up.

The important challenge is to move away from a simplistic understanding of digital literacy as the skills in operating the technology, towards the more complex set of competencies involved in multiliteracies. Remixing encompasses many of these competencies, such as selecting, organizing, reflecting, evaluating, creating and communicating. And, as a literacy, it is closely related to the developments of new digital media (Olson & Cole, 2006).

The Idea of Schooling

In an increasing number of documented projects we now see how students use their experiences with creating media content in schools as part of remixing activities. Going from these micro levels of analysis we can move to more macro levels and see how these developments also challenge the traditional conception of schooling.

My point is that remixing as a cultural activity, especially present in the way young people today use digital media, opens up fundamental questions about "reading" and "writing" and about what schools are for. This creates new conceptions about texts that we read and write, about the student as a producer of content and knowledge, about the roles of teachers and students as part of knowledge-building processes, about identity and learning, and about reproduction versus creation. In the examples mentioned above, we see examples of how new literacy practices are developing in schools, as well as the constraints traditional schooling presents to the development of such practices. A basic requirement of schools today is, therefore, to deal with changes that have resulted in part from technological developments.

Many schools have problems in developing learning strategies supporting remixing practices because the structure of the school day, teacher competencies, examination systems, and so forth, do not take into consideration developments in the ways young people use new technologies. The institutional practice of schooling is thereby challenged by remixing as a literacy practice, entailing students in taking a more active role in developing knowledge. A key question in these developments involves interrogating what we have traditionally meant by the distinction between formal versus informal learning. From the perspective of young people, learning takes place in many different contexts, and in taking experiences from one context over to another. Remixing is an activity that cuts across such educational conceptions.

Conclusion

Norway is an example of a country that has taken the step from looking at digital media as an object that has to be implemented in school settings to asking questions about the real implications this has for how we conceive learning and literacy. Digital literacy has now been written into its national curriculum as one of five key competences. The consequent challenge is to discover how to make this work in educational practice and to let the experiences of young people outside schools inform the constant redefinition of the social practice of schooling. I believe remixing represents an area that we have to take seriously for future developments in schooling.

Notes

* This chapter was originally published as: Erstad, O. (2008). Ch. 8: Trajectories of remixing: Digital literacies, media production, and schooling. In C. Lankshear & M. Knobel (Eds.), *Digital literacies: Concepts, policies and practices* (pp. 177–202). New York: Peter Lang.
1. In Norwegian there is no word for the English term "literacy." Traditionally it has been translated with the term "alphabetization," but during the past 20 years the term "competence" has been used instead, with a broader conception of reading and writing implied.

References

Ades, D. (1976). *Photomontage*. London: Thames and Hudson.

Alvermann, D. (Ed.). (2002). *Adolescents and literacies in a digital world*. New York: Peter Lang.

Barthes, R. (1978). *Image, music, text*. London: Hill and Wang.

Bolter, J.D., & Grusin, R. (1999). *Remediation: Understanding new media*. Cambridge, MA: The MIT Press.

Bordwell, D. (2005). *The cinema of Eisenstein*. New York: Routledge.

Buckingham, D. (2003). *Media education: Literacy, learning and contemporary culture*. Cambridge, UK: Polity Press.

Buckingham, D. (2007). Defining digital literacy: What do young people need to know about digital media? *Nordic Journal of Digital Literacy, 4*, 263–276. Oslo: University Press.

Buckingham, D., & Willett, R. (Eds.). (2006). *Digital generations: Children, young people, and new media*. Mahwah, NJ: Lawrence Erlbaum.

Castells, M. (1996). *The rise of the network society, the information age: Economy, society and culture*. Vol. I. Oxford: Blackwell.

Cope, B., & Kalantzis, M. (Eds.). (2000). *Multiliteracies: Literacy learning and the design of social futures*. London: Routledge.

Diakopoulos, N. (2005). Remix culture: Mixing up authorship. Retrieved November 20, 2007, from http://www.nick diakopoulos.com/publications

Erstad, O. (2005). Expanding possibilities: Project work using ICT. *Human Technology: An Interdisciplinary Journal on Humans in ICT Environments, 1(2)*, 109–264.

Erstad, O., Klovstad, V., Kristiansen, T., & Soby, M. (2005): *ITU Monitor 2005: Digital kompetanse i skolen* [ITU Monitor 2005. Digital literacy in the school]. Oslo: The Norwegian University Press.

Erstad, O., Gilje, Ø., & de Lange, T. (2007). Re-mixing multimodal resources: Multiliteracies and digital production in Norwegian media education. *Journal of Learning, Media and Technology. Special Issue: Media education goes digital,* D. Buckingham & S. Bragg (Eds.). London: Taylor & Francis. 32 (2), pp. 183–199.

Erstad, O., & Silseth, K. (2008) Agency in digital storytelling: Challenging the educational context. In K. Lundby (Ed.), *Digital storytelling, mediatized stories: Self-representations in new media*. London: Peter Lang.

ETS. (2002). *Digital transformation: A framework for ICT literacy*. Princeton, NJ: Educational Testing Service.

European Commission. (2004). *Key competences for lifelong learning: A European reference framework*. Directorate-General for Education and Culture. Retrieved November 20, 2007, from http://ec.europa.eu/dgs/education_culture/publ/pdf/ll-learning/keycomp_en.pdf

Hebdige, D. (1979/1985). *Subculture: The meaning of style*. London: Methuen.

Heim, J., & Brandtzæg, P.B. (2007). Patterns of Media Usage and the Non-professional Users. Paper presented at the Computer/Human Interaction Conference, April 28—May 3, San Diego, US.

Hull, G., & Greeno, J. (2006). Identity and agency in nonschool and school worlds. In Z. Bekerman, N. Burbules, & D. Silberman-Keller (Eds.), *Learning in places: The informal education reader* (pp. 77–98). New York: Peter Lang.

Ito, M. (2006). Japanese media mixes and amateur cultural exchange. In D. Buckingham & R. Willett (Eds.). *Digital generations: Children, young people, and new media* (pp. 49–66). Mahwah, NJ: Lawrence Erlbaum.

Jenkins, H. (2006). *Convergence culture: Where old and new media collide*. New York: New York University Press.

Kellner, D. (2002). Technological revolution, multiple literacies, and the restructuring of education. In I. Snyder (Ed.), *Silicon literacies. Communication, innovation and education in the electronic age* (pp. 154–169). London: Routledge.

Kittler, F. (1990). *Discourse networks 1800/1900*. Stanford, CA: Stanford University Press.

Kozma, R. B. (Ed.). (2003). *Technology, innovation, and educational change: A global perspective*. Eugene, OR: International Society for the Evaluation of Educational Achievement.

Kress, G. (2003). *Literacy in the new media age*. London: Routledge.

Landow, G. (2006): *Hypertext 3.0: Critical theory and new media in an era of globalization*. Baltimore: The Johns Hopkins University Press.

Lankshear, C., & Knobel, M. (2006). *New literacies: Everyday practices and classroom learning*. Berkshire, UK: Open University Press.

Lemke, J. L. (1998). Metamedia literacy: Transforming meanings and media. In D. Reinking, M. McKenna, L. D. Labbo, & R. D. Kieffer (Ed.), *Handbook of literacy and technology: Transformations in a post-typographic world*. Mahwah, NJ: Lawrence Erlbaum Associates.

Lessig, L. (2005). *Free culture: The nature and future of creativity*. New York: Penguin.

Livingstone, S. (2002). *Young people and new media*. London: Sage Publications.

Manovich, L. (2007). What comes after remix? Retrieved November 20, 2007, from http://remixtheory.net/?p=169

Olson, D.R., & Cole, M. (2006). *Technology, literacy, and the evolution of society: Implications of the work of Jack Goody*. Mahwah, NJ: Lawrence Erlbaum.

Pahl, K., & Rowsell, J. (2005). *Literacy and education: Understanding the new literacy studies in the classroom*. Thousand Oaks, CA: Sage.

Peppler, K.A., & Kafai, Y.B. (2007). From SuperGoo to Scratch: Exploring creative digital media production in informal learning. *Journal Learning Media and Technology. Special Issue: Media Education Goes Digital,* guest editors: D. Buckingham & S. Bragg. London: Taylor & Francis. *32(2)*, pp. 149–166.

Rasmussen, I. (2005). *Project work and ICT. Studying learning as participation trajectories*. Dissertation, Faculty of Education, University of Oslo, Norway.

Rassool, N. (1999). *Literacy for sustainable development in the age of information.* Clevedon: Multilingual Matters Ltd.

Reinking, D., McKenna, M.C., Labbo, L.D., & Kieffer, R.D. (Eds.). (1998). *Handbook of literacy and technology. Transformations in a post-typographic world.* Mahwah, NJ: Lawrence Erlbaum.

Scardamalia, M., & Bereiter, C. (2006). Knowledge building: Theory, pedagogy, and technology. In R. Keith Sawyer (Ed.), *The Cambridge handbook of the learning sciences* (pp. 97–115). Cambridge: Cambridge University Press.

Scribner, S., & Cole, M. (1981). *The psychology of literacy.* Cambridge, MA: Harvard University Press.

Snyder, I. (Ed.). (2002). *Silicon literacies. Communication, innovation and education in the electronic age.* London: Routledge.

Säljö, R. (1999). Learning as the use of tools: A sociocultural perspective on the human-technology link. In K. Littleton & P. Light (Eds.), *Learning with computers: Analysing productive interaction* (pp. 144–161). London: Routledge.

Tyner, K. (1998). *Literacy in a digital world: Teaching and learning in the age of information.* Mahwah, NJ: Lawrence Erlbaum.

Wertsch, J. (1998). *Mind as action.* New York: Oxford University Press.

CHAPTER THREE

You Won't Be Needing Your Laptops Today

Wired Bodies in the Wireless Classroom

KEVIN LEANDER

E ver since it had implemented its wireless laptop program three years previously, Ridgeview Academy struggled with a number of contradictions between traditional schooling and ubiquitous internet access. As one teacher put it, "You're kind of opening Pandora's box [the internet] and trying to just kind of stick it in a different box [the school]." Even as Ridgeview had heavily invested in providing internet access to its single gender (female) student body, it has also structured, over three years' time, an array of implicit and explicit means of closing this access. In short, Ridgeview Academy was a contradiction of social spaces: on the one hand it presented itself and technically structured itself to be an "open" wired social space for 21st-century girls, while on the other hand, official school practices and discourses domesticated, or pedagogized (Street & Street, 1991) potential openings of space-time provided by the wireless network. In official school practice, the wireless network was "rewired" or closed off and anchored in ways that reproduced traditional school space-time.

This chapter, then, begins with a puzzle. Suppose we imagine a school where access to computing and the internet is not a problem? Say, for instance, a private school for girls in grades 5–12, where parents buy new laptops for their daughters, who then carry them from class to class and home at night? What if this school had a wireless network installed throughout all of the buildings on its 38-acre campus? What might happen to schooling as we know it?

Technology Refusal

In an important article on the failure of most technological innovations to change the culture of schooling, now dated by two decades, Hodas (1993) examines how technologies are value-laden, as is schooling itself, which is also a type of technology. Hodas argues that the mismatch between school values and technology values explains a great deal about why school practices are seemingly so intransigent. While critics of schools might conceive of them as failing or floundering in their relationship to technology, Hodas reminds us that schools, as institutions, are "doing exactly the jobs they were set up to do and have been refined over generations to perform" (no page). Even when new technological tools are introduced into this flow of practice and valuing, these tools fail to change what Hodas calls the "look-and-feel" of schooling, marked as it is by the "conservation and transmission of pre-existing, pre-defined categories of knowledge and being" (Hodas, 1993, no page).

Hodas' (1993) argument is primarily sociological, considering schooled practice as institutional practice and examining something of the working conditions, career paths, and culture of teaching. The argument is also partially historical. Drawing from Cohen (1987), for example, Hodas argues that school structure and teaching practice has remained substantially unchanged for seven hundred years. He also cites Cuban (1986) to argue that new developments in information and entertainment technologies, as they move into the popular realm (e.g., radio, film, television, computers), bring with them a popular hope that they will "bring the classroom out of the dark ages and into the modern world" (Hodas, 1993, no page).

In this chapter, I follow the impulse of Hodas' insight to consider how technologies are essentially social, and thus serve to constitute particular values, ideologies, preferred practices, power relations, social relations, and modes of learning. Likewise, schooling may be seen as a (heavily institutionalized) technology, and "refusal" or acceptance of technology in school must be understood as a relational construct—as some potentially frictional or smooth movement along the interstice of new tech/school-as-tech. However, I would also like to push beyond the sociological constructs that Hodas is drawing on, including institutional reproduction, school-as-factory, historical inertia, institutional self-preservation, and institutional irrationality. Sociologically and culturally, I argue that we need to consider a very basic dimension of school in order to understand its relation to technology: the production and organization of school space and time. While I posit this dimension as a general construct of interest for thinking about technological integration in schooling, I focus in particular on the relationship between school space-time and space-time as practiced by youth on the internet in their everyday lives. I argue that the challenge of "integrating" the internet into school is not chiefly technical, in the sense of providing tools and tool training, but rather spatial and temporal.

In this vein, Jones (2005) discusses features of the schooling of space-time in his analysis of school-related digital literacies in Hong Kong. Drawing on Hall (1959), Jones contrasts the school's perspective as essentially monochronic (treating time as linear and tangible, and divisible) in contrast to the students' perspectives as essentially polychronic (seeing time as more fluid, layered, and simultaneous). In the monochronic orientation, one action occupies time to the exclusion of all other actions, an approach to activity that would be quite foreign to many cultural contexts, including much of the modern workplace (Gee, Hull, & Lankshear, 1996), and interestingly, the historical cultural practices of Mayan mothers interacting with their children (Rogoff, Göncü, Mistry, Mosier, Chavajay, & Heath, 1993).

Technologies That Support School Space-time

Hodas (1993) briefly discusses several technologies that appear to be perfectly suited to traditional schooling, including the blackboard, the overhead projector, and the duplicating (photocopy) machine. The primary sources of cultural match that Hodas discusses in most of these cases are that such technologies reduce the physical labor of teachers to communicate written information, and they also enhance the teacher's authoritative position. Rather than imagining the shoring up of authority as an explicit goal of such technologies, however, we might conceive of them as more implicitly involved in the constitution of school space-time. The blackboard and the overhead projector, for instance, gather entire classrooms of students around a common textual surface. The overhead projector has the added affordance of being run in a dimly lit room, so that other possible interactions are muted. Moreover, both blackboards and overhead projectors are used to temporally organize lessons and classroom activities; lessons often move left to right, across a single or multiple blackboards, and some teachers scroll entire sequences of activity (e.g., problem sets) on overhead transparency rolls. The photocopy machine provides for the repetition of a common text across the space of the classroom (or school), and is an important technology for creating lessons and common texts that span years and even decades of pedagogical practice. It is critically important to recognize that each of these technologies is typically controlled by a teacher or teacher assistant, not in an explicit display of power, or even toward that end. Rather, teacher bodies/technologies as ensembles are disciplined and configured to spatio-temporally produce and organize schooling as a particular kind of activity.

Given this background, it may come as no surprise that the most prevalent literacy practices in using the laptops at Ridgeview included the following:

1. Writing process pedagogies
2. Student note-taking
3. An online newsletter for the school community, produced by the central office
4. Distributing assignments and submitting work
5. Keeping absent students up-to-date
6. Quick searches for online information

With the exception of the last two practices, the most common uses of the laptops either did not require a wireless network, or were simply online versions of former print technologies and distributions (e.g., the school newsletter). Julie, one of the teachers, summarized the dominant practices as follows:

Julie: I mean mostly in English it's still pretty staid, I still…I'm sure you know 90% of their work is…on a computer…is with a word program.

Kevin: Taking notes?

Julie: Taking notes, writing assignments, and writing papers. A lot of the stuff that I…I can do now though is rely on email to…email or our web to post assignments or if they were missing that day it's so much easier now to be able to say, "Boom, here's the worksheet; or here's the assignment sheet or whatever …"

At the same time, even though the laptops and network were used to support traditional school practices, these practices themselves were undergoing some internal change at Ridgeview; changes which can be conceived in terms of their spatial and temporal dimensions. For example, with respect to writing process pedagogies, students researched topics on the web in and out of school, and used email to gather information and conduct interviews. The laptops encouraged a constant writing process and the girls quickly moved into a project at whatever stage it was at: brainstorming, information gathering, drafting, revising or editing. The laptops also facilitated feedback as students exchanged drafts with peers and teachers via e-mail and loosened the boundaries of the school day and calendar. For instance, one teacher told students she would be giving them feedback on a project over spring break. Although the process of turning in a final draft of a paper could be chaotic and the laptops appeared to encourage last-minute completion, they also seemed to encourage the final moments to become a dynamic space of feedback that was reportedly less present when students arrived in class with print versions of their pieces. In the new temporal arrangement, students enquired of themselves, peers, or the teacher regarding citations, grammatical points, and if enough textual support was present in their text in the final moments prior to online submission.

Discursive Conceptions of (Online and Offline) Social Spaces at Ridgeview

As I examine the case of Ridgeview in detail and attempt to bring a spatial perspective to its technology refusal, I dialectically interpret social space (Leander & Sheehy, 2004; Leander, 2002; Lefebvre, 1991; Soja, 1989) across representations (e.g., classroom texts, discourse, official documents concerning the wireless network), material structures (the network itself, classroom spaces), classroom practices (pedagogy as discursive and material practice) and the lived experiences of space-time by the students and teachers. In what follows, I engage two broad approaches on the constitution of social space. I first examine discourses (Fairclough, 1995; Gee, 1999) of social space, considering discourses (or, Discourses; Gee, 1999) as not only ways of using language, but as the ways in which language use is related to thinking, valuing, acting, and identity work of all kinds (Gee, 1999, p.17). For Lefebvre (1991) and Soja (1989), discourses are a powerful constitution of second space, or conceived space; such conceptions have a hold on how spatiality is lived out, even more so than visible perceptions of space. I attempt to examine these discourses as multiple and conflicting; the first two sets are dramatized as "duels" to suggest how Ridgeview was caught up in a struggle of expansion and contraction. These discourses are primarily investigated by drawing on material from extended (1–2 hour) interviews with the high school principal and four faculty members: Barbara, Fran, and Julie (all of whom teach English) and Bill (who teaches Psychology). Following the discussion of these discourses, I examine specific vignettes of practice in order to consider how conceptions and perceptions of social space come together, and in particular, how the online space was domesticated and closed off at Ridgeview.

Strong Wired Women vs. Vulnerable Girls in Frightening Online Spaces

A first set of dueling discourses involves the school's construction of tech-savvy, strong young women on the one hand, and, on the other hand, the school's construction of them as girls who are vulnerable to all of the dangers on the internet and who need to be protected. The first discourse imagines the internet as a space for experiences that would help these young women compete and succeed in a (male-dominated) technology world, whereas the second discourse imagines the internet as a space of stalkers, of uncontrolled behavior, of unknown dangers. The first discourse is constructed on the school's website, which uses technology as an artifact (Hine, 2000) for identity construction and recruitment:

> [Ridgeview] is committed to preparing students to be effective users of information and ideas, because a well-rounded education requires preparing students for any type of career they might choose. [Ridgeview] strives to weave technology into everyday activities in the classroom and around the school.

The principal of the high school also constructed this discourse in relation to academic preparation for girls in areas previously dominated by boys:

> If you're going to have an all-girls' school, you need to afford them opportunities that they may not get in a co-ed environment, or may not get as concentrated in a co-ed environment. And so technology, math and science courses, areas that are not traditional to girls…that girls traditionally follow, I should say…are just, we feel are part of the mission. And they're part of the mission of the Coalition of Girls Schools, too, which is one of our associations, professional associations, is to push math and science. And along with that, technology in girls' curriculum.

In this instance, technology becomes described more as a curricular topic, akin to math and science, rather than as a set of social practices.

Barbara brought the two discourses together around the issues of teachers' and parents' goals. She related technology to the broader project of making the girls "stronger," and as part of developing the "whole student":

> I always have in the back of my mind what's going to help them be stronger. Now whether that's stronger than I was or stronger than they are right this second…and again, that's always a kind of intellectual, emotional and spiritual thing that I'm thinking about all the time. That whole student. So I'm always aware of that. And yet I also really want them to think of themselves and really enjoy being women. I don't want them…I'm not trying to…even though the men at the school sometimes accuse us of this because of some of the texts that we read, no I don't want them to be in that what used to be radical feminist sense of being angry with men. I want them to be able to really be great women and have great lives and get into the best college their parents can afford. Because finally that is our narrower mission. I mean, I think that's the reason most of their parents send them here, other than just to be safe. But we have broader goals for them.

Multiple tensions are apparent in Barbara's response, including the tension between being a "whole student," rather than an unbalanced student, with, for example, intellectual preparation but no emotional or spiritual preparation. Another evident tension involves the idea of being strong versus the idea of being angry with men, or a radical feminist. A final tension in the interview excerpt involves the narrower goal of "getting into the best college their parents can afford" and yet experiencing the broader goals of the faculty, which, presumably, include preparation as a "whole student." Safety is attributed to parent goals, and somewhat associated with the "narrower mission" of parents. Yet, safety was also more generally apparent as part of Barbara's discourse in responding to the internet and its potential threats to girls, many of which were relatively unknown. This discourse was apparent as Barbara described one of her teaching innovations with an internet-based chat room:

> And in fact this year started something that two or three other people picked up in the department and that I plan to pick up next year, which is this online forum where the kids are…they're in their own little chat…they have their own little chat room basically. You post questions for them. I mean, it's closed. That's the other thing that's so scary about teaching girls and having them out in cyberspace. But that's a whole other story. But you have to have the proper I.D. to get into this chat room.

While Barbara couldn't think of any direct danger to the girls from being online, she had heard a story of one of the girls who had "gone off to meet someone" once she was in college, and she also recounted a story of a private school in Kentucky, where a friend of hers worked, that had been infected with an internet virus that downloaded porn into its network. The discourse of internet danger appeared, for Barbara, to be a site or node where the parents' narrow goals (of safety, and preparation for the best colleges) came together with the teachers' goals of educating the "whole student," including the student who was savvy about internet safety. Moreover, the idea that the internet was potentially dangerous, even though nothing particularly dangerous had happened to girls they knew, was a common feature of the discourse around internet danger among the faculty.

Other teachers more directly described the actual and potential dangers of internet spaces. Fran, for instance, described certain areas of the internet as containing "frightening places," such as "diary.com." She seemed to have a vague sense of such sites, but considered them as "filled with positive [possibilities] and fraught with some negatives":

> Well, they're sexual; they're inappropriate for people 13 and 14 years old. The language, you would…I would not quote to you the language that is on some of the…like dear diary or diary.com. I mean, it's blatant misuse of the computer, and one girl was suspended for it. I don't know. They have access to sites. I mean, I don't know how the word spreads.

The internet danger discourse here seems particularly gendered around the idea of protecting girls from sexual knowledge, such as contained also in inappropriate language. Fran also draws generally on policy to support her stance: "It's blatant misuse of the computer." Extending her discussion of this kind of event, Fran framed danger around the issue of development:

> There's a long time between 7th grade and your senior year. And I later learned…yeah my source of information is the [high school] girls. They spend a lot of time in [my classroom]…that a 7th grader was involved in one of those sorts, one of those sites where you post all sorts of information about what you're doing. And a lot of it has to do with drugs, alcohol and sex.

Here, the issue for Fran was not merely that girls would find their way into such knowledge and interaction (of drugs, alcohol, and sex) but that young girls, who weren't developmentally ready for such information, would encounter it before their time. Fran's discourse, including the use of general problem descriptors such as "drugs, alcohol, and sex," and the way in which she was relying on informants (older girls) to learn of internet dangers, shares with Barbara's discourse the feature that the greatest fears are those that are the most unknown.

One of the events that crystallized the dangers of the internet for the school community at a relatively early period in its development of the laptops program (i.e., in the third year of the program) was one student's Xanga site which was censored by the school. The principal of the high school described this event:

> [The student] was talking to friends outside of school and in school about her teachers and about people in the school, and very vulgar, very…in one instance I thought very threatening. And so she was caught and we…and now if you'd ask me how she got caught, I can't remember. Anyway, it came to me. I can't remember who brought it to me, but anyway somebody got their hands on it and brought it to me, and she came before the discipline committee and received a five-day out of school suspension, which is pretty devastating. We don't do that much around here. Thank goodness we don't need to. And I think all in all the embarrassment of it and the realization of it made her want to leave the community. And she eventually left. And then…so that would be the most egregious thing we've had.

This event framed the discourse of internet danger around the idea that the internet could be used to do dangerous things. In this case, it is the girls themselves, under the influence of the internet, who are potentially dangerous and are putting others in the school community at risk. The idea that "teachers and other people in the school" were represented in the student's blog interactions in "vulgar" and even "threatening" ways was seen as a direct threat to the school as a certain type of community, with an investment in its own image and how this image was protected. The offender's response of "want[ing] to leave the community" is described as a natural outcome of her individual offense of harming the community and its agreed upon values. With respect to social space, this case is particularly noteworthy in that the student was posting to her blog both in and out of school. She was constituting and challenging representations of the school in space where the school had little control. Hence, her danger to the reputation of the school, through representations, was responded to, eventually, by helping to constitute her identity as (spatially) outside that of the school. In this case, relatively isolated, but nonetheless significant in the eyes of the students, faculty, and administration at Ridgeview, the discourse of internet danger became framed as a threat to the school community: students engaging in internet dangers threatened the integrity of the school community. Here, internet danger was supported by institutional discourses of school community, school policy, and school reputation.

Open and Closed Information Spaces

A second set of dueling discourses among the Ridgeview faculty and administration involved, on the one hand, opening up the classroom to a wide range of available information, and on the other hand, reconstructing the classroom as a closed information space. Key in this spatial dilemma are containment and closure as ways of measuring individual knowledge. With ubiquitous online access, the individual can become connected to an unprecedented world of texts. The vision of open information access—seeing the internet as an unlimited digital library—is supported by the discourse of the liberal arts tradition, which was dominant in the school. From this perspective, the internet is the new library at Alexandria, containing all classic and modern works, print and paintings alike. Fran expresses something of this tradition:

> Well [the internet] certainly has enlarged their world within the walls of this school because they can go anywhere or do anything as they're…and some of it is terrific. And for example, I had them do broadsides on poets and several of them pulled up art, pieces of art to put…that they thought…there's a "Starry Night" poem by Ann Sexton, and somebody had on her broadside "Starry Night" by Van Gogh. So that kind of access is fabulous. It breaks down the world, the walls.

In making their broadsides or posters, the students could "go anywhere," with "anywhere" defined as a voyage through the liberal arts where new texts would be found to support canonical texts and authors authorized by the school.

The discourse of bounding the school as a closed information space is constituted and supported in different ways. One relatively simple way is through online/offline distinctions as formed by the faculty, where offline texts are privileged, as in Barbara's following remark:

> You know, at first we had to make them do certain things with technology. For example, in our research that we do…used to be the kids automatically went to books and you had to build into the assignment, and you must use at least one online source. Well now it's the opposite. They immediately go to the online sources and you have to say, "You have to look at so many books or printed articles or things like that."

The online/offline distinction functions as the definitive quality of a "source," a binary of two different types of media. Since the students wanted to give online sources primacy, Barbara and other faculty suggested that they now needed to be taught to focus attention on offline print. Another discourse on closing the information space indexed in Barbara's response involves distraction from schooling through too many texts, or too many unauthorized texts. This discourse is connected to how adolescent identity is more generally constructed as easily distracted:

> And you know…and teenagers have always been distracted, but it's a difference, I feel, between being distracted by a magazine and being distracted by every magazine ever written. You know…and on top of having at their fingertips every magazine ever written, they have every book ever written, every comment on every book ever written, every piece of art, their boyfriend's e-mailing them from [another school]. And it's difficult. And we've got some ways that we're going to try to be able to control that in classroom settings in later years.

The idea of distraction, discussed in the following section, is even more strongly related to the notion of the problem of the internet being a mode for communication (rather than information), which severely disrupts schooled assumptions about containment and surveillance of individual activity in identifiable locales.

The most powerful conflicts with the discourse of an open information space involve, unsurprisingly, testing and writing events imagined as individual performances. Test cheating and writing plagiarism are seen as supported by the internet as an open text space. While these issues can be described as school practices that enter into conflict with new technology practices, a spatial perspective here is instructive in examining the conflicting assumptions and ideologies of school and widespread internet activity spaces. The school test is typically based on the idea of the individual who is isolated from her or his environment, with the "open book" test being an exception to this idea. (Even open book tests are often temporally structured in school such that, while books are available, they are not practically of much use in the given time slot of the test.) The school test is also often structured around the idea that much of what is taught and tested is known information, available in the world in the format in which it was given. With an open information space, the idea of the skill set necessary to succeed changes entirely. In this case, rather than remembering information, locating, and, if necessary, combining and synthesizing information are at stake. The laptops program at Ridgeview brought these two discourses into direct conflict, and with respect to testing, began to close the newer space of open information through the containment of testing, as captured in Fran's remark:

> The downside is that there are things like Sparknotes. We had two girls last year that were doing in-class essays and apparently had Sparknotes up and then minimized and were cutting and pasting to their own essay. Now when I have an in-class essay…and I have them sit on the inside of the circle so I can see all the screens. Next year we have, as a department, agreed that in-class essays will be hand written.

Fran also described how she had begun to rethink how she assigned compositions for the students, given that students could just go online and either order papers from essay mills for "$9.95," or would simply cut and paste from other papers and put a patchwork together of their own. Fran primarily framed this issue as one of moral failure on the part of the students: their lives were simply too busy, and the temptation was too great to cut corners and plagiarize. Thus, the machinery she described putting into place for her own teaching involved more steps on the part of the student to document how information had been accessed and combined:

> I have had to redo how I assign papers to avoid, to help them avoid, the temptations of plagiarism. I now, they always do a topic outline in class. They always do their full outline in class. I require that they use citations from the Tennessee Electronic Library. They have to print their article and highlight what they're using. In other words…and I develop topics that don't lend themselves to being pumped into the computer.

Again, as in the case of testing, the idea of what it meant to be knowledgeable or to do knowledge work was not challenged. The space of where knowledge was located (in authorized texts and individual memories) and how it was measured (in individual performances) and what it was characterized by (unique voices) was held stable. Indeed, in some ways, the school's response to the open information space became hyper-schooled and closed, where processes that were relatively less visible in early eras of school research (e.g., uses of source material) were now being brought under scrutiny. Barbara explains:

> And in fact with our freshmen we've decided we're going to go back to paper note cards that they have to use first. And then we do have an electronic note card program that we teach the kids that is pretty fun. But if they don't have a sort of visual sense of what a note card is and what you're supposed to put on it to start with, it's hard to understand what you're supposed to do with an electronic card except just download information into it.

The Damaged Classroom Interaction Space

In addition to the duels of discourses that positioned the girls online, and with respect to access to texts, a powerful discourse among the faculty regarded the damage to classroom interaction from online activity. This discourse is most strongly associated with how the communication dimension of ICT's (the "C") is down-played or denied with respect to the information dimension, but as the previous section discussed, the information dimension is not unproblematic for school space either. In this discourse, with respect to communication, the laptops were seen as damaging to classroom interaction in that they distracted girls into forms of communication and activity other than the core communicative activity at hand. Second, beyond their promotion of multi-spatial activity, the laptops were seen as damaging by putting up physical barriers between interlocutors in the classroom.

Prior to considering these activity and physical aspects of the discourse in turn, it seems useful to consider some assumptions common to English and social studies courses, where texts and talk play a central role. At a semi-abstract level, we might describe the flow of texts and talk in many such classes as moving through the following stages:

1. Some common print text is given as "input" (e.g., a poem, an image, an historical description).
2. Oral interpretation by the teacher and students follows, in the form of recitation or discussion.
3. The teacher has full access to this oral interpretation and all participants in it, and a key role in guiding it. The oral interpretation has one common context or "footing" (Goffman, 1981).
4. Later, some common print output (e.g., test or composition) is assigned that draws on the input text and the oral interpretation.

The sequence may seem painfully obvious, but these basic assumptions about the constitution of space through texts and talk are important to recognize in considering that it is not only through the common (monospatial) text that wireless practices might challenge these assumptions, but also through the types of literacy practiced, often against the common flows of the classroom.

Following is a re-description of classroom interaction as shaped by wireless online access:

1. A common print text is given as "input" and accompanied by many other uncommon textual inputs that are read simultaneously to it, and against it.

2. Oral interpretation by the teacher and students follow, which is highly mixed with (digital) print interpretations developed by individuals.

3. The teacher has only partial access to the interpretations, many of which extend beyond the classroom space to distal online spaces and persons, taking on multiple footings and emotional "keys" (Goffman, 1981). The teacher is one participant in the interaction, but much less central and sometimes at the periphery.

4. Oral (schooled) interaction is seen as something to record in print for further study rather than something to engage in for its own right.

5. Later, a print output, once assigned, can draw on input text, on the print record of schooled interaction, and from a pastiche of online and offline texts.

These contrasting lists begin to suggest how monospatiality is contested through ubiquitous online access, and also through the "hyperliteracy" of online interaction in the classroom. Teachers lament that everyone seems to be writing, but no one talking. The classroom space of common talk around common texts is damaged. For the text-talk-text pedagogue, the classroom becomes asocial, nonsensical. The discussion below suggests more of how this discourse is constituted and sustained.

Distraction. One of the most common complaints about the laptops in the classroom space involved how online interaction distracted the girls into a range of individual activity, most of which involved communication of some type. This type of activity was seen as off-task by teachers, and often framed through the lens of management and discipline, as evident in the high school principal's consideration:

> I'm sure kids order their summer wardrobe off of AOL in their spare time. One of the keys to making a laptop program work is classroom management. And teachers really have to watch what their kids are doing. I think it's a lot of kids who appear to be taking classroom notes, are actually just e-mailing their friends. And it's…we call it electronic note passing. It's just a little harder to police…But you know, if a teacher can watch a kid, then that really keeps it from getting to the disciplinary level, before it comes before a discipline committee.

Teachers often lamented that just before they could correct a student's behavior, the student would minimize the computer window of the off-task, and thus the procedural display (Bloome, Theodorou, & Puro, 1989) of "good student" would be maintained.

Julie noted coming to a kind of compromise for herself: if the students appeared to be taking notes and participating at the same time in the common talk of the classroom, then she would back off policing their activity:

> And sometimes if they're taking notes and if I can tell they're on task and they can also look up and you know sort of participate at the same time that's fine. If they don't need it and if they're not taking notes and if I have a suspicion that, you know, what they're looking at instead is, I don't know, some kind of email or you know it's hard to tell sometimes and you don't want to stop in the middle of class and be the laptop police but I'll just tell them, "Put your laptops down we don't need them, let's just talk." So that's what we'll do instead.

This movement to limiting the use of the laptops to only times when they were specifically needed, as deemed by the teachers, was a common response across the classrooms we observed and teachers we interviewed. In interview, Fran frames this response as a return to the "old fashioned class," which seems most appropriate for indexing the reconstitution of classroom space:

Fran:	But I don't want to spend my time wandering around the backside of this classroom trying to catch people who are e-mailing. I want to spend my time thinking about what we're talking about and getting them to engage in a conversation. And one of the things I think I have to try…now maybe…you'll have to ask me next year. I think I've got to limit the use of the computer.
Kevin:	To get that attention focused.
Fran:	Yeah, and to make it more like the old, an old fashioned class. I've noted to you that I think that first period class is very quiet and not interactive, that I find myself having to survey that class. And a lot of it is they all use their computers. They're all behind those screens.

Fran further described how she felt that the laptop use was responsible for the classroom losing its "unity," "personality," and "spark": "…if they're not instant messaging or e-mailing, if they're just staring at the pictures that they've put on their screen, they're not really with you." This experience of being "with" the teacher is central to the discourse of the laptops interfering with the classroom interaction space, as is the idea of "unity." The teachers often described nostalgia for the pre-laptop days, in which interaction was more focused, common conversations richer, and teacher roles within these common conversations were clearer.

Atypically, Barbara departed somewhat from the discourse on distraction and considered how different practices might reframe the use of the laptops in the classroom. In particular, Barbara was impressed with the use of an online forum by one of the young, new science teachers in the school, who would structure online conversations among students prior to their arrival in class. Barbara saw Kristen's ability to create this activity as linked to her generational mindset being closer to that of the students: "I mean…for Kristin it's not a problem. For me it's a problem. But she's…she's in her 20s, I'm in my 40s. That's the difference." Barbara, however, also asserted the importance of verbally arguing one's ideas in public as central to English education, to the school's broader purposes of educating strong young women, and to their future prospects in college. At the same time, she questioned and challenged how such values might be changing:

> You know you have all this clicking sound all over the place in ways that you didn't when people were just taking notes on a piece of notebook paper. I don't know. It changes the dynamic of your classroom. I mean that seems really trivial, but for an English class that's a big deal because so much of what…even when we used to talk about part of what we want our students to learn. It's to articulate verbally certain ideas and to be able to have that kind of debate and intellectual debate. And again I think that's important for young women. You've got to be able to have an idea and defend it.
>
> And that's important for all young people, but you know, it becomes particularly important, I think, as we send these girls off into other academic institutions where they're just going to have to hold their own. And maybe they don't need to anymore. I don't know. Maybe I just need to get into a few college classrooms for a while and see what they're asked to do. Maybe it doesn't matter if they articulate it in [an online] forum or if they articulate it verbally.

Physical barriers. Faculty at Ridgeview conceived that the classroom interaction space was damaged not only by the lack of common activity, but also by the physical barriers created by the laptops. In this manner, first space (materially observable) and second space (discursively constituted) (Lefebvre, 1991; Soja, 1989) appeared to be coordinated, not in opening up thirdspace, but rather in affirming the loss (and nostalgia) experienced in the classroom space under the reign of the laptops program. Many of the teachers described how their own physical positions were affected, and how they could no longer see students' faces and eyes with the laptops. The essential primacy of physical interaction was very strong in these responses, as reflected by Bill, the psychology teacher:

Bill: But in terms of…I could sit at a student desk with all the other ones and psychologically that's where I like to be. And I think it works better in terms of drawing out discussion. What also is bad, just from a purely physical standpoint, many of the girls can't be seen. Their faces are shielded from peers because they're behind the screen. And I personally have to tell them to lower the screen, or they'll look and they're talking between their screen and their neighbor's screen. I can't always…I have to read lips a lot of times and I have to say, lower your laptop, I can't see you. I have to…and it just . . .

Kevin: You don't see their mouth and you don't see their eyes.

Bill: Right. It walls them off and I can't…if their head is down I don't know if they're working at the…I don't know always what is going on. So in that sense I don't like what it's done to that part of the atmosphere in here. It's made it a little less open. Does that make sense?

First, Bill reflects in this segment on his own position vis-à-vis the students: he likes to take a position on the same physical level as the student, but feels this is affected by a physical laptop barrier. This physical barrier also creates a fragmented classroom space where the girls can carry out verbal, offline conversations with peers. Bill also suggests that this physical shield prevents him from monitoring activity-in-common, as we saw with the distraction of online interaction, previously considered. Finally, Bill notes that the physical (and presumably, digital) barriers have made the face-to-face interaction in his class "a little less open." His discourse asserts how closure had been affected by the physical erection of new boundaries.

Likewise, Julie expressed a notion of physical separation similar to that of Bill:

Julie: Right off the bat as soon as we got [the laptops out] I was amazed that day at how much it changed [everything] because immediately those black cases went up, their faces were in the computer and it looked to…from my perspective like a classroom full of tombstones…it literally deadened the class because everybody was involved, you know, in their individual little program, their individual little projects, you know. There was no interaction.

Kevin: This was supposed to be discussion?

Julie: No, no, no. I was just trying like, oh, they had just gotten their laptops. Let me create, you know whatever we were going to do, let's do this online or whatever and ah and I lost them I just felt like I had no connection with them whatsoever.

Particularly striking in Julie's response is the embedded assumption that even when the teacher and students are not involved in some activity of common interaction, such as classroom discussion, a kind of habitus (Bourdieu, 1977) or embodied assumption of being able to see, monitor, and immediately recognize some type of activity in common was at the base of her experience of the class as a space of life. Individual activity online, within the classroom space, with its privileging of face-to-face, verbal interaction, was experienced by Julie as death, and as a loss of her own personal sense of connection and purpose. Finally, not only did virtually all of the teachers interviewed conceive of the laptops as interfering with the physical space of the classroom by erecting barriers, many of them also commented on how difficult it was for them to attempt to move about the classroom and monitor laptop activity. In classrooms that already felt small, the addition of laptops, cords, power strips, new desk arrangements (to allow for monitoring), computer cases, and books on the floor contributed to teachers' constructions of loss of the classroom space and loss of their mobility within it.

The Schooling of Digital Space at Ridgeview: Vignettes of Practice

The most obvious examples of the bracketing of school space and time that might come to mind for secondary schooling would be the walled divisions of classrooms (and respective student groups) and the separation of learning into 50- or 55-minute periods. Beyond these obvious features of the pedagogization (Street and Street, 1991) of space-time, a number of other prominent features of pedagogization were recognizable within the digital literacy practices at Ridgeview:

- Defined plans precede resources and activity; actors know what they need or are seeking in advance.
- Sequential activity is dominant, and everyone follows the same sequential path.
- Asynchronous communication is primary to synchronous communication (e.g., e-mail or web searching is more "schooled" than instant messaging).
- A single space is dominant (and under surveillance) for each task; "task" is mono-spatial and "off-task" is partially defined as departure into another social space.
- Public social spaces, including the internet, must be bracketed for student use; school needs to produce kindergartens of public spaces for students to understand them, learn within them, and be safe within them.
- Material print texts and print spaces (the built environment) are primary and are authorized, while virtual texts are unauthorized and supplemental.
- The internet is primarily a tool for information rather than a tool for communication. Information and Communication Technologies (ICTs) are primarily "ITs" in school.

These features of schooling or pedagogizing digital space at Ridgeview, where the thinking, valuing, and identity work of space-time practices becomes evident not only in discourse but also in activity, are briefly captured below in four vignettes of practice. This discussion is not intended as a critique of particular pedagogical practices (in fact, some of the experiments with new online forms of pedagogy were admirable), but more broadly aims to understand how schooling involves the production of space-time that remains invisible until challenged by other spatialities and temporalities, such as those produced by ICTs.

Vignette one: Library research. All of the 9th-grade English classes were sent to the library during different class periods to conduct research on a poetry project. The project, assigned over a few weeks, included gathering several poems around a common theme, formal explications of two poems, a foreword, and other work. On the library visit, the teachers and the librarian put a great deal of emphasis on the idea that the girls should privilege the material space of the library over access to texts in virtual space. Directions given by the librarian about resources targeted specific shelves and carts:

> This side of the cart has books for freshmen on it. Check the books here first. Then do a power search of the card catalogue. Check the websites at home on your own time.

The directions to first make use of the material library space may be considered part of a practical consideration of what was being made available only at official times (the school library). However, several well-schooled assumptions about space-time are built into this activity that are made more evident by the eventual responses of the girls. Among them, everyone was directed to follow the same sequential path in searching for information, print texts were primary to digital texts, "checking websites" was associated with home space-time, and the built environment was primary over the virtual. (In this latter regard, it is noteworthy that, while the school is entirely wireless, the girls went to the library to do a search in its online card catalogue.)

The practice of separating and bounding space-time was not limited to making distinctions between the material and virtual worlds, however, but was also evident in boundaries within online space. The school had bracketed its own card catalogue as a primary source on the web and the librarian had also provided a list of key poetry websites, including "Poet's Corner," "Favorite Poem Project," and "Poetry 180." A common assumption in this case was that the school had taken a piece of the web that was prepared and authorized for student engagement—a type of web *kindergarten*. To search the card catalogue and other resources culled by the librarians, the library staff had attempted to teach the girls what they termed a "power search," using particular Boolean operators to find information:

> Barbara: Today you are trying to get the poems you love. What words would you use to do a power search of what's here in the library?

An operating assumption across the teachers and librarian was that the students needed a large degree of guidance directing them toward specific online texts, and that online space needed to be greatly simplified and selected for these explorations. On the other hand, browsing was an encouraged practice among the books. Barbara remarked that she was worried that students would go online and simply end up with "poetry written by some kid in Kansas." (On more than one occasion, Kansas or other Midwestern locations were represented as sources of low-quality online texts composed by students.)

Several of the girls' individual practices during this library visit are indicative of the difficulty of structuring and enforcing a single space-time with the wireless network and the developed histories of information searching that the girls brought to the event. As the first girl we observed entered "American Poets" into the search engine Google, a second pulled a book from a library shelf and used the directory Yahoo to verify whether the author was American (a project requirement). A third girl attempted a power search of the online card catalogue on fairy poems, with no results, while a fourth, her partner, searched for fairy poems in Google. A fifth girl had brought a book of poems with her from her friend's locker and browsed through it. Another student spent some of her time looking through books on the cart shelves, while also talking with Barbara about her possible theme. Yet another student used most of the searching time in the library to work on a report for her psychology class, including conducting research online. None of the students that we observed followed the sequential, ordered path across resources and space-time as ordered by the librarian and teachers, and only a minority used "power searching" or the online card catalogue.

Vignette two: Online information and text hunt. A second example makes evident some of the same ways in which online space-time was schooled or pedagogized (Street & Street, 1991) within school. Figure 3.1 is a copy of a web-based assignment that the students received from Fran in relation to the text *The Joy Luck Club*. As with the work in the library, the assignment involves a bracketed selection of websites made available from the school's "Webliographer" (moreover, a pre-selection of a few sites is made in this case), and the assignment is structured uniformly and sequentially (note the teacher's recommendation to "check off" steps). Moreover, in this case it is very clear that using the web is of secondary importance to following directions. For instance, step 5 simply involves printing off a compass image, which resulted in the same image being printed by every girl in the class. Concerning this assignment, Fran remarked that she thought that following directions was particularly important for girls to learn, who did not "get as many experiences following directions as boys do," and in particular, directions for technical processes. Boys, for instance, would be more apt to build models from a kit and have such direction reading and following experiences.

Besides Fran's particular discursive construction of what girls are lacking, and what might be necessary to help construct strong girl identities with respect to technology, a striking characteristic of this assignment is the way in which it presents the internet as a strange territory, and positions the girls as tourists in this foreign land. Indeed, like many online assignments at Ridgeview, the assignment reveals more about the teacher's relationship to online spaces than the girls' histories in such spaces.

Vignette three: Discussion board. On another occasion, also associated with the study of *The Joy Luck Club*, Fran had set up a discussion board for students to post responses to her specific questions about the text. The online discussion was relatively short-lived and appeared in some ways even more formal than did oral classroom discussions. The space-time bracketing of the discussion board had much in common with how web spaces were bracketed in other forays into cyberspace. In this case, the dis-

---

Joy Luck Club: An investigation of Chinese culture

This assignment is designed to give you a sense of the cultural heritage of the Chinese American. In addition, it will familiarize you with another form of writing. Hopefully you will become a little bit Chinese. This assignment is specifically designed to improve your ability **to read and follow directions**; thus, this will be an **important** part of your grade.

Since the directions are so integral to the assignment, I suggest you begin by printing the directions. They are complicated and involve several steps. Printing them will allow you to reread **when** you need to do so. You might even want to **check off** what you have done.

1. Go to the Webliographer. Put in the following address: www.ocrat.com. Go to "Animated Chinese Characters" in the list of selections to the left. Write the word "east" using the Chinese character on unlined paper of your own. Enrichment: write the name of someone you admire or have a crush on.
2. Go to the Zodiac. First write the date of this year's Chinese New Year. Next, find which animal represents you. You do this by pulling down the menu until you find the year you were born. The year you were born determines the animal that represents you. Record this information. Also record the years and animals which represent the rest of your family and the boy you have a crush on. Write the character which represents your animal.
3. Go to the category "Numbers." Write your age in Chinese characters.
4. Go to "Countries." Write in Chinese the name of a country you would like to visit.
5. Go to "Compass." Print the illustration of the compass.
6. Go to a new site: www.new-year.co.uk/chinese. Send a card to a friend or teacher here at school. Check out the Fortune Cooking sayings. Record three that you like. You will need these for a class activity so choose well.

Figure 3.1: Web-based assignment from Fran's class.

cussion board was set up as part of the school's intranet, separate and not available to others outside of the school. Despite her detailed instructions (steps written on the black board) on how to access the discussion board, the class activity and computers broke down when it was introduced. Only three students in the class appeared to have permission to reply to the postings that Fran had made. The teacher circulated around the room to solve problems, and asked for students who seemed to be having computer problems to take their computers down to the "Lion's Den" (a computer repair center staffed by the school). Three students responded and left the room with their laptops immediately, returning ten minutes later, when a fourth student left.

Fran instructed the students to write down the web link for the discussion board in their notebooks, and moved on to a different plan of discussing the novel. This planned activity and its breakdown could be analyzed from different angles; my primary interest is in how the breakdown is at least partially created by the attempt to create a separate, well-schooled space for interaction. The discussion board isn't very accessible because it is made to be difficult for those outside of the school to access. But, like a pill bottle, no one can seem to get easily past the child- and adult-proofing placed upon the discussion board. This closure is even more evident by how, ironically, during this event of failed access to a well-schooled web, several students in the class were simultaneously involved in online activity that reached far beyond school space-time: one read others' Xanga entries and composed a new entry on her own blog, another student was playing a computer game, and other girls used instant messaging, all officially unsanctioned school activities that depended upon its wireless network and upon publicly available media spaces.

Vignette four: Testing. Over time, while there were some experiments with new forms of pedagogy that involved new forms of digital literacy practice at Ridgeview, attempts with these new practices, or even passively allowing the laptops to be present, were beginning to be closed off during the period of our study. For example, near the end of the third year of its laptops program, the English department agreed to have students write in-class essay exams by hand rather than with their laptops for the following academic year. This policy was to prevent students from cheating on literature tests by culling information from the internet, a practice that had been only partially contained through the teachers' efforts to survey the offline/online social spaces of student work through panoptic practices (e.g., rearranging the desks in a circle for easy walk-arounds). Rather than challenging the tests themselves, the use of texts that are canonized for school on the internet, or the social-spatial assumptions of knowledge existing "inside" the individual and needing to be assessed, the teachers reproduced classic school space-time and had the students close their laptops.

Reform, Technology, and Social Space

This chapter began with a dilemma: Why might it be that a school that has solved the computer and internet access problem, a school in which online access is nearly ubiquitous, would ultimately find itself refusing technology? Why does school seem so intransigent? By examining discourses and pedagogical practices at this school, I have argued that in order to understand the mismatch of schooling on wireless practices, we need to think more fundamentally, beyond the evidence of apparent social practices, values, institutional reproduction, and historical inertia. We need to think, I have posited, about the schooled organization of space-time. History does not provide its own explanation for refusal, or stasis, or reproduction. Rather, as argued by Soja (1996), the social, the historical, and the spatial are tied up in complex dialectical, (or trialectical) relations. Social life is both productive of space and produced within the spatialities that precede it; schooled life is never far from schooled space as it has been historically produced and socially reproduced in everyday practice.

However, both schooling and new technologies are often seen as located within social space rather than productive of it. At Ridgeview, this perspective on technology was most apparent in discussions of how reform might occur. A prominent conception was that curriculum must remain at the center of anything "new," and that new technologies must support goals already in place from the curriculum. The dominance of this conception of technology, curriculum, and reform is apparent across the following interview excerpts:

Fran: I start with the belief that the technology must be an outgrowth of the curriculum and that the curriculum can't be formed to appease the technology. And that has been a difficult thing at this school. We have a very strong technology force that even though…that expects you to develop curriculum so you can use the technology, even though they don't see that they're doing that.

Julie: Yeah and all we've gotten, which is great, from the administration is just reassurance, keep doing what you're doing, include them if it works with the curriculum, include it if it enhances the curriculum but not just as busy work or just because they're there.

Barbara: And my own colleagues, I think, would be the place that I'd like to start and really hear what they have to say and what they're doing. You know, I mean…I guess what I've tried to do, my two rules of thumb: number one, make sure that whatever I'm doing really does enhance the curriculum rather than just being the tidal wave that washes over it. It's very difficult, though.

Bill: And I felt pressure with kids coming out of our middle school doing a lot of laptop stuff. And then they get to my class and I'm sitting there saying, I don't care if you bring it or not.

The idea that teachers might "keep doing what [they're] doing," and that technology might "enhance" or be an "outgrowth" of the curriculum, is essentially a guarantee that the social space of schooling will be saturated by the relations set forth in current curricular practice, including the dominance of mono-spatial activity, sequential activity, text-talk-text cycles, the school as a safe harbor, and other dimensions of schooled spatiality examined across the course of this chapter. Neither the curriculum nor technology is fully spatialized in this view; technology, in particular, is seen as an add-on, a "tool" to support forms of practice that are well-rehearsed circuits that travel along deep grooves.

A key difficulty, of course, is that "keep doing what you're doing" discourse is not merely about refusal, but about giving reassurances to teachers that change can happen gradually and incrementally. While almost everything (the curriculum and pedagogy) can stay the same, technology can be brought in to "work with" teaching and learning, adjusting here, supporting there. However, when the package of technology brought into school involves ubiquitous wireless computing, this kind of promissory note to teachers is fundamentally unsound and even unethical. Because, even as teachers keep doing what they're doing in well schooled space-time, wired kids like many of the girls at Ridgeview bring the following productions of space-time with them to the classroom, through practices and orientations that we have observed in online activity across school and home contexts (see Table 3.1).

Table 3.1: Space-time productions

Schooled Productions of Space-time	Productions of Space-time Common to Everyday Online Practices
• Defined plans precede resources and activity; actors know what they need or are seeking in advance.	• Plans develop within activity; actors seek out materials that they need in the course of acting.
• Sequential activity is dominant, and everyone follows the same sequential path.	• Simultaneous activity is normative. Simultaneity is an orientation toward social practice and not a psychological deficit, overload, or resistance, or something else.
• Asynchronous communication is primary to synchronous communication (e.g., e-mail or web searching is more "schooled" than instant messaging).	• Synchronous communication and simultaneity involves monitoring and responding to fluctuating demands of diverse activities as they emerge over time; attention economy.
• A single space is dominant (and under surveillance) for each task; "task" is mono-spatial and "off-task" is partially defined as departure into another social space.	• Multiple spaces are the norm of practice; action happens *relationally*, *across* spaces.
• Public social spaces, including the internet, must be bracketed for student use; school needs to produce kindergartens of public spaces for students to understand them, learn within them, and be safe within them.	• Decision-making regarding trustworthy and safe social spaces is embedded in routine practice. Public-private-institutional boundaries are not fixed.
• Material print texts and print spaces (the built environment) are primary and are authorized, while virtual texts are unauthorized and supplemental.	• Online/offline distinctions concerning textual authority are not strongly held; no material bias and online preference likely.
• The internet is a primarily a tool for information rather than a tool for communication. Information and Communication Technologies (ICTs) are primarily "ITs" in school.	• Communication and information are highly integrated; information and communication flows are co-constituted in practice.

This chart only begins to suggest some key differences among traditionally schooled productions of space-time and those practiced by wired kids. It is not intended as a list or recipe of what school ought to become, but rather as one means of understanding the dilemma of introducing laptops and wireless internet into well-schooled space. If the goal of such an introduction is to move beyond the domestication of online space-time—to not experience the meeting of schooling and online technologies as containment and closure—then educators must re-imagine and re-enact the social life of schooling as spatial practice.

Note

* This chapter was originally published as: Leander, K. (2007). "You won't be needing your laptops today": Wired bodies in the wireless classroom. In M. Knobel and C. Lankshear (Eds.), *New literacies sampler* (pp. 25–48). New York: Peter Lang.

References

Bloome, D., Theodorou, E., & Puro, P. (1989). Procedural display. *Curriculum Inquiry, 19*(3): 265–91.

Bourdieu, P. (1977). *Outline of a theory of practice.* Cambridge: Cambridge University Press.

Cohen, D. (1987). Educational technology, policy, and practice. *Educational Evaluation and Policy Analysis, 9* (Summer): 153–70.

Cuban, L. (1986). *Teachers and machines: The classroom use of technology since 1920.* New York: Teachers College Press.

Fairclough, N. (1995). *Critical discourse analysis: The critical study of language.* London: Polity.

Gee, J. (1999). *An introduction to discourse analysis: Theory and method.* London: Routledge.

Gee, J., Hull, G., & Lankshear, C. (1996). *The new work order: Behind the language of the new capitalism.* Boulder, CO: Westview.

Goffman, E. (1981). *Forms of talk.* Philadelphia, PA: University of Pennsylvania Press.

Hall, E. (1959). *The silent language.* Garden City, NY: Doubleday.

Hine, C. (2000). *Virtual ethnography.* Thousand Oaks, CA: Sage.

Hodas, S. (1993). Technology refusal and the organizational culture of schools. *Educational Policy Analysis Archives* 1(10). Retrieved June 5, 2006, from http://epaa.asu.edu/epaa/v1n10.html

Jones, R. (2005). Sites of engagement as sites of attention: Time, space, and culture in electronic discourse. In S. Norris & R. Jones (Eds.), *Discourse in action: Introducing mediated discourse analysis* (pp. 141–154). London: Routledge.

Leander, K. (2002). Silencing in classroom interaction: Producing and relating social spaces. *Discourse Processes, 34*(2): 193–235.

Leander, K., & Sheehy, M. (Eds). (2004). *Spatializing literacy research and practice.* New York: Peter Lang.

Lefebvre, H. (1991). *The production of space* (D. Nicholson-Smith, Trans.). Cambridge, MA: Blackwell.

Rogoff, B., Göncü, A., Mistry, J., Mosier, C., Chavajay, P., & Heath, S. (1993). Guided participation in cultural activity by toddlers and caregivers. *Monographs of the Society for Research in Child Development, 58*(8): i, ii, v–vi, 1–179.

Soja, E. (1989). *Postmodern geographies: The reassertion of space in critical social theory.* London: Verso.

Soja, E. (1996). *Thirdspace: Journeys to Los Angeles and other real-and-imagined places.* Malden, MA: Blackwell.

Street, J., & Street, B. (1991). The schooling of literacy. In D. Barton & R. Ivanic (Eds.), *Writing in the community* (pp. 106–131). Newbury Park, CA: Sage.

CHAPTER FOUR

Slammin' School

Performance Poetry and the Urban School

BRONWEN E. LOW

Thirty high school poets compete in a poetic "mock Olympics" in which they perform original pieces, ranked on a scale of 1 to 10 by judges picked randomly from the audience. In keeping with the principles of slam poetry, the poets use neither props nor musical instruments in this war of words, relying instead on the expressiveness of their bodies and voices. No performance can exceed the 3-minute time limit. The teen poets parade on and off the stage, dreadlocked and ponytailed, braided and buzzed, some squeezed into stretch pants and baby T-shirts, while others, in the words of poet Patricia Smith (2007), are "drooped as drapery" (p. 49). Iolet, headwrapped and regal, tells of police brutality. A boy from New Jersey dedicates his poem about being "surrounded by a raging sea called heterosexuality" to "anyone who's ever felt left out of society's categories, or been to a really boring sweet-16 party in Westchester county." There is a poem about Puerto Rican nationalism, an ode to a mother, another to a brother locked up, and many tales of sex and heart break. The crowd hollers its approval and disagreement with the judges' scoring. Asheena McNeil, who writes her poetry on the 125th street bus to and from school in Harlem, won the slam with a perfect score for her "125th Street Blues." She cites as inspiration Maya Angelou and her grandmother who "lives poetry rather than writes it." And like most of the other student poets, she credits rap music, and hip hop culture in general, as having made poetry "cool." From these examples alone, it is clear that rap music opens up an important space of communication and expression for many youth, including and even especially for young men.

This auditorium packed with youth going wild for poetry at New York's inaugural Teen Slam was the tip of the iceberg of a popular resurgence of interest in poetry which has important implications for youth writing in the here and now. Slam poetry is one manifestation of "spoken word culture," a category used to describe forms of poetry and performance in which an artist recites poetry, often to musical accompaniment which might range from a jazz ensemble to a bongo drummer. The 1960s coffee house reading is back, and most cities feature "spoken word" poetry nights and series in bars, cafés, and community centers. But this is poetry reading with a difference. In the early 1990s, poetry went mass market and mass media as MTV and Much Music began to televise clips of poets performing their work in between music videos. Performance poetry also hit the road, touring with the music festival Lollapalooza. In 2001, HBO began airing Def Poetry Jam, a half hour of spoken word poetry hosted by well-known rapper Mos Def and orchestrated by famous rap producer Russell Simmons. Performance poetry is gathering media interest, much of which is focused on the dynamic and competitive slam poetry movement. Started in the mid-80s at the Get Me High bar in Chicago by poet and construction worker Marc Smith, poetry slams now take place across North America, and culminate each year in the National Slam. Each is held in a city in the U.S. before audiences of thousands. In August 2006, 73 teams from cities across the United States (and teams from Canada and from France) met in Austin, Texas, to vie for the title of Grand Slam champions. While performance poetry and its implications for education are just beginning to garner academic attention (Fisher, 2005; Jocson, 2005, 2006; Low, 2006), community-based organizations which offer spoken word programs for youth have been going strong since at least the mid-1990s. The largest of these, Youth Speaks, was founded in 1996 in San Francisco, works with 45,000 youth a year in the Bay area, has partner organizations in 36 cities, offers a wide range of programs including after-school and in-class writing and performance workshops, and hosts the yearly International Youth Poetry Slam festival (see their teaching guide, *Brave New Voices*, by Weiss & Hearndon, 2001, and their website at http://www.youthspeaks.org).

Spoken word has a passion for language. At odds with the rhetoric of literacy crisis which pervades popular representations of education, youth—and in particular the urban youth usually deemed most at risk in the rhetoric—are embracing cultural forms in which language matters a great deal. This fact has largely escaped mainstream education's attention. This oversight is beautifully represented by the opening of the movie *Dangerous Minds* (Smith, 1995). White teacher, Louanne Johnson, played by Michelle Pfeiffer, peers into her new classroom and sees a group of African American students "freestyle" rapping, improvising rhyming verse to a beat, while other youth listen and dance to rap music. "Noisy bunch," she comments nervously. After realizing that she's going to have to "rewrite" the curriculum in order to engage her class of disenfranchised black and Hispanic adolescents, she develops a poetry assignment in which the students compare the songs of Bob Dylan to the poetry of Dylan Thomas. The students rise to the challenge of interpreting poetry through their engagement with Ms. Johnson's 1960s "popular culture," a plot point that insists they were without poetry (and popular culture) to begin with, in contrast to the poetic force of the freestyle scene.

That certain forms of poetry are now alive and well, even cool, among youth may come as a surprise to many language arts teachers; in this chapter, I examine this popular resurgence of interest in poetry and argue for slam poetry as a powerful conduit for youth expression. In order to think through some of slam's implications for youth writing, I describe and reflect upon a high school performance poetry course which I developed in conjunction with a creative writing teacher and a spoken word poet. This chapter therefore engages closely questions of pedagogy. This investigation of slam pedagogy places a priority on three of Johnson's (1996) four moments in the cycle of a cultural form: the processes of production or authorship, including the conditions which were set up to facilitate a culture of student writing and performance in these classrooms; the texts the students produced; and lived culture, for the data we draw upon hundreds of hours of audio and video tapes of classroom life as well as interviews with teachers and students.

Slam as New Literacy

Even more so than rap music, slam complicates discussion of adolescent literacies as chronologically "new" because it is a "low tech" genre, requiring only a stage, performers, and an audience. Slam draws on some of the most ancient forms of entertainment: competition, pleasure in language, storytelling, and self-expression. Central to the appeal of slam poetry to youth is performance, a return to the oral traditions of the bard or African griot. Here slam draws upon African-American musical traditions in which performance is central; as Frith (1983) describes, "Black music is immediate and democratic—a performance is unique and the listeners of that performance become part of it" (p. 17). The emphasis on performance in slam also revives 1960s and 1970s interactive avant-garde arts scenes and phenomenon such as dada soirées and "happenings"; in these, notes oral poet Jerome Rothenberg (1981), performativity broke down the boundaries between art and life, the arts and non-arts, music and noise, and poetry and prose.

At the same time, slam is a creation of its technologized context. The live, intimate communion between poet and listener in slam is awash in contemporary communication technologies including websites and chat rooms that publicize slam events and share slam's history, such as Poetry Slam, Inc. (http://www.poetryslam.com), About.com Poetry (http://www.poetry.about.com), An Incomplete History of Slam (http://www.e-poets.net/library/slam), and slampapi (http://www.slampapi.com); websites for the yearly National Slams such as for Austin Slam (http://www.austinslam.com); and international sites such as Poetry Slam Sverige [Sweden] (http://www.estradpoesi.com). Spoken word record labels, including Kill Rock Stars and Mouth Almighty/Mercury, produce recordings. Feature films *Slam* (1998) and *Love Jones* (1997) and the documentaries *SlamNation* (1998), *Slam America* (2001), *Slam Planet* (2006), and *Poetic License* (2001) translate the intimacy and immediacy of slam's storytelling onto screen and into larger dramas. Television journalism reports expand slam's audiences and communities of participation and interest. Algarín (1994) gives a sense of slam's imbrication in contemporary culture when he writes that the extensive media coverage of slam means "that it is now possible to cull from the endless articles a sense of the poetics that is being created in midair from one article to the other as these poets are made to think about content, quality, and craft" (p. 22). This is a poetics of the moment, forged in cafés and bars as well as in the pages of *Newsweek*, and within which poets learn from journalists. Granted, despite the media attention, slam is still largely the stuff of grass roots and community forms of distribution and promotion (an instance of the internet fulfilling some of its democratic promise), and of independent film production companies, recording labels, publishers, and documentaries. Many teachers are not yet familiar with slam, nor are their students. However, as noted above, slam is but one manifestation of a growing spoken word scene that includes the Def Jam poetry series on cable channel HBO and is intimately related to massively influential hip hop culture. Slam might be considered the "B side" of increasingly corporate rap music, and given some of the limitations of the genre conventions and formulas structuring contemporary hip hop culture, slam poetry is opening up some important possibilities for youth expression.

Why Poetry?

I've always enjoyed poetry as a way of reading and thinking…the language and methods of poetry have always seemed right to me; they push at the boundaries of thinking; they play in the noise and excess of language; they upset and they surprise. To write critically I've always written poetry. (Fred Wah, 2000, p. 1)

Poetry is a powerful form of youth expression that bridges the past and the present in new literacies. The term "poetics" stems from the Greek *poesis* or "making." Through-lines in theories about the work and importance of poetry are its ability to make language both new and strange. For instance, Shelley's 1840 "Defense of Poetry" argues that poetry revitalizes language by disrupting conventions of expression and by building fresh associations between the word and world, especially through metaphor. The Romantic poet warns that "if no new poets should arise to create afresh the associations which have been thus disorganized, language will be dead for all the nobler purposes of human intercourse" (cited in Richter, 1989, p. 325). The idea of making language strange, what the Russian formalists called *ostranenie* or "defamiliarization," argues that art "exists to recover the sensation of life…to make the stone stony" (Shklovsky, 1917, cited in Richter, 1989, p. 741); for the Formalists, poetry estranged reality in order to disrupt literary and aesthetic conventions but also to open up a space of social critique. Poet Fred Wah's sense that poetry is a place to push at the boundaries of thinking and language provides a contemporary articulation of *ostranenie*. Given the close ties between thinking, language and identity, the defamiliarisation and renewal of thought and language works also to make the subject new and strange. Poetry can open up a space of creative possibility for the self, disrupting fixed models in favor of a theory of identity as evolving, experimental, and dynamic. Committed to renovation and making strange, poetry celebrates the limits of what we know about language and identities and so can be the grounds of curiosity and surprise about the world, the self, and others.

Why Slam?

Slam poetry and contemporary spoken word more generally are not the work of the poet-hermit, isolated from society in contemplation. Instead, slam poets tend to see themselves as embedded within and responsible to particular communities and the poem comes to life in its performance. At the same time, writing is also a space of introspection, and so slam lies at the intersection of the personal and public. The importance of the national Grand Slam poetry competition to the scene means that poets associate with venues and cities, and poets end up representing specific places (for instance, New York City is usually represented by a team from the Nuyorican Poets Café). And slam is populist and accessible; as slam poet Miguel Algarín (1994) describes there "is no discerning of 'high' or 'low,' all in the service of bringing a new audience to poetry via a form of entertainment meant to tune up fresh ears to a use of language as art" (p. 16). Given the importance of audience appeal in the judging process, slam poets work to make an impact, to get noticed. This means that slam poetry is often funny, irreverent, and sexy; it is also frequently personal, sometimes hard hitting and even raw, a vehicle for exploring painful life stories. The confessional quality of much of the poetry performed at slams has been a source of criticism, as in the question posed by *Sixty Minutes* reporter Morley Safer to teacher Gayle Danley: "Isn't slam poetry, then, really therapy?" Her ready reply, "Yes," and the question she writes on the board of the middle-school classroom in which she is teaching slam poetry, "Have you dug deep?," suggest that poetry as healing self-expression is not a designation shied away from by slam poets (cited in Hewitt, 28/11/1999). However, slam poets are just as likely to speak out against social injustices as they are to explore their own feelings, and the confessional and critical modes are often connected, the ties between the personal and political writ large. For all these reasons slam poetry appeals to adolescents who see it as a space for explorations of self and society, within which to express anger and sorrow, and to entertain and educate.

Slam in the Classroom

New Literacy Studies examinations of youth literacy practices in out-of-school contexts have convincingly demonstrated their complexity and the ideologically driven disconnect between these practices and schooled forms of literacy (Gee, 1996; Heath, 1983). Also made clear are ways the split between academic and home/community literacies furthers the social marginalization of racial, ethnic, and language minority youth (Luke & Freebody, 1997). Hull and Shultz (2001) ask, in response to such findings, "How might out-of-school identities, social practices, and the literacies that they recruit be leveraged in the classroom?" and, "How might teachers incorporate students' out-of-school interests and predilections but also extend the range of the literacies with which they are conversant?" (p. 603). One significant barrier to the incorporation of non-academic literacies into school is the deficit model that characterizes many teachers' attitudes towards such literacy practices, particularly those that stem from black popular culture. The performance poetry course which I helped to develop and teach took up Hull and Shultz's challenge to both leverage and build upon the interests and skills students brought with them from their literate engagements in out-of-school contexts. It also worked to challenge deficit models about hip hop culture by placing rap music within the larger genres of spoken word and performance poetry, and situating it within multiple artistic traditions.

In the spring of 2002, I began collaborating with a high-school English teacher and a performance poet involved in arts education at an urban arts school in a mid-sized, northeastern U.S. city, helping to develop and lead a performance poetry or "spoken word" unit for two senior English classes. The school's district has the highest poverty rate among the state's largest districts, and 88% of its students are eligible for free/reduced priced lunch, with 50% of the schools at a 90% or higher poverty rate. The teacher, "Tim," is a middle-aged European male, and the performance poet and arts educator, "Rashidah," is a black woman in her early 30s. Tim, Rashidah, and I drew and built upon student interests in rap music and freestyle oral poetry and the class culminated in a competitive poetry slam. The students were all 17 or 18 years of age. I was actively involved co-teaching and researching the course in 2002 and in 2004; in what follows, I draw here on poems performed in the slams in those years as well as audio and video recordings of full-class discussions and performances, students' in-class writing, and one-on-one interviews with the students and teacher. I also examine the pieces performed in the slams in 2003 and 2006 in order to discuss some recurring themes in the students' writing over the years: 46 poems in total. The student poems included here are copied with as much fidelity as possible to the hand-written and typed versions students submitted. I will examine some of the recurring themes in the students' poems, as well. This chapter also discusses whole and parts of student poems, an important part of taking youth writing seriously.

The spoken word curriculum was first offered as a six-week unit in Tim's two senior English classes. One of these classes, the "boys' class," was designed as an alternative to the academic college-level English class and was composed only of male students who chose to be in a same-sex class. Their teacher called them "the survivors"—students who have not traditionally done well in English, but who have managed to persist into their senior year. More than two thirds of the boys were black, the rest Hispanic and white. The other class was an Advanced Poetry class (which I'll call the "AP class"), which attracted some of the top academic students in the grade including most of the creative writing majors. It was co-ed and most of the students were white. In 2004, the term-length course was again offered as "English IV," the alternative to the college-stream class, composed that year of young men and young women who Tim felt were the weakest group academically of the three years the course had been offered. All the students in this class had had to take the state wide English

Language Arts exam the previous year and more than half had just passed it with 55% overall grade. The class shared the racial demographics of the boys' class mentioned earlier, but was co-ed.

Due to the popularity of the courses and to the repeatedly high quality of students' poetry and performances, spoken word poetry has now been institutionalized in this school as part of the middle school creative writing program and as a senior English option. The school's graduating class regularly votes the poetry slam as the "best school event," no mean feat in an arts magnet school with a continual roster of drama, dance, creative writing, and visual arts productions. Students clamor to get into the spoken word classes and attendance is consistently high. Fisher (2005) argues that spoken word poetry series in the black community act as "African Diaspora Participatory Literacy Communities": these communities are shaped by respect, audience engagement and participation, explorations of identity, and learning. Tim, Rashidah, and I tried to develop within the classroom a community of poets similar to those found outside of school. During the course we immersed students in spoken word forms through videos, CDs, visits by local poets, and a series of workshops in which students developed and rehearsed their own poems. Students also brought in examples of rap music, jazz poetry, and other spoken word forms that moved, interested, or challenged them to share with the class. In the first year of the project we examined various contexts in the history of poetics for thinking about rap's experiments with word and sound, including dada sound poetry, Stein's modernist decompositions of language, jazz poetry, and blues poetry. In 2004, led by a literature professor from the local research university and Rashidah, we explored some of the history of black poetics: spirituals, the blues, and poetry from the Black Arts Movement. However, more time was dedicated in class to writing and performance workshops, in part because this particular group was much less interested in the more academic investigations into poetry than the two classes in 2002. Always integral to the course are journals within which students freewrite to various creative writing prompts, write drafts of poetry to be workshopped in class, and respond to texts and audio and visual recordings of poetry as well as to their classmates' performances. The course culminates in a poetry slam at the end of the school year in an auditorium filled with all of the senior students, selected classes of juniors, and some invited members of the community. Judges are picked based on a formula in which 2 or 3 are selected from inside the school, such as teachers, librarians or current students, and 2 or 3 are from the larger community, including local artists, parents, and school alumni. This formula strays from the original slam rules in which judges are picked randomly from the audience, but this move was designed to increase the possibility of balanced and disinterested scoring in a high school context.

Reinventing Language: "We are the Public Enemies Number One!"

Near the beginning of the project in both years, the film *Slam* (1998) was screened; it became central to the students' interest in and understanding of the genre. *Slam* (1998) tells the story of Ray Joshua, spoken word poet and subsistence-level marijuana dealer, and his experiences with both the criminal justice system and the redemptive force of poetry. Largely improvised and shot on location in the Washington, DC, city jail, the Anascostia "Dodge City" housing project, and a genuine poetry slam at the Nuyorican Poet's Café, the film, a "drama *vérité*" in the words of its makers, uses inmates and project residents as cast members and extras, and stars actual spoken word poets Saul Williams (Grand Slam national champ in 1996) and Sonja Sohn (now of HBO series *The Wire* fame). The filmmakers' commitment to working with extras and actors playing close versions of themselves as well as to shooting in real settings is not only a product of their limited budget, "guerilla" shooting-style and *cinéma vérité* aesthetic, but is also a marker of the relationship rap and slam poetry—and by extension the film—have with the "real" conditions of the lives of the disadvantaged. The film shares its emphasis on authenticity with the genre of spoken word, and with hip hop culture's insistence on "representin'" and "keepin' it real" in relation to the lived conditions of the urban blacks and other minorities who have traditionally been rap music's thematic centre.

In an early scene, Ray (Saul Williams) hears a fellow inmate, Bay, drumming and rap freestyling in the adjoining jail cell. Ray joins in the rap, and the two voices rise in conversation, weaving a freestyle tandem to the rhythm which Bay drums and Ray strengthens as he whispers under Bay's lyrics—"Ba bam, ba bam bam. I had to be strong, I had to be real." The rappers finally stumble, laugh, and stretch their hands through the bars, holding a handshake from cell to cell. "That shit was tight, mo," says Bay (in the film and out, a seventeen-year-old convict about to find out if he is jailed for life) to Ray. Of their rap, the screenplay notes: "the symmetry and rhythm are the culmination of two centuries of slave chants, prison work songs, and blues; a modern, hip hop slave song for the 90s. And as long as they can hold it, they're free" (Stratton & Wozencraft, 1998, p. 200). Locating this rap within a tradition of black aesthetic resistance, the writers suggest that the scene encapsulates *Slam*'s larger theme of the power of poetry to help the socially marginalized temporarily transcend the prisons that constrain them: the prison of a political and economic system that discriminates against minorities and the poor, the prison of an individual's life circumstances, and, in the moment of synchronicity with a fellow prisoner, the cell of the self.

The power of spoken word to reconcile and transcend is taken to its extreme in a later scene in the jail in which Ray defuses a confrontation mounting between himself and two rival gangs in the yard by blazing forth with his poem "Amethyst Rocks," a diatribe against the system which ends with the lines, "i am the sun / and we are the public enemies number one! / one one one! / one one one!" Here spoken word announces itself as the poetry of the disenfranchised. The poem literally stops the jailyard gangs in their tracks in the film and is one of Williams' best-known works (he gave it as title to his first spoken word album). Evident in the poem is the poet's freedom of reference, as he builds a collection of classical allusions that coexist with references to rap group Public Enemy and singer Prince. This creative freedom might also be considered a characteristic of slam poetry, for as Algarín (1994) insists, there is no discerning between high and low art in slam. Viewing the film was a powerful experience for the students for a number of reasons. The jail freestyle scene opened up a discussion in the boys' class about freestyle poetry, a genre Tim had not yet heard of. In response, two black young men, the school's most gifted freestylers, performed for him individually and in a "cipher" in which they stand in a circle and each improvise poetry in turn. One of these freestyle poets, Gerard, has gone on to some celebrity: he reigned as freestyle champion for seven weeks on BET's nationally televised freestyle battle show, *106 and Park*, opens for rappers at local shows, has toured campuses, and produced his own rap album, which is available for download on the net (see also Hoechsmann & Low, 2008, Ch. 1). Tim was very impressed by the freestyles and that moment seemed to confirm for the students that this was a class in which their skills and interests were greatly valued. Carlos, one of the most enthusiastic supporters of the project, had hinted at some of the students' talents when Tim mentioned the course the previous term. Carlos had requested a tape recorder to start chronicling some of the poetry action in the hallways, saying "there's a lot going on in this school that teachers don't know about." After watching the freestyle scene in *Slam*, the students were asked to compare and contrast the two different styles as a way of having students pay close attention to questions of form and content. Saul Williams' style is particularly metaphoric, abstract, and philosophical, while Bay's is more direct and colloquial, ridden with "fucks." The students reflected upon these differences, often associating the first with education and the second with the "streets." Saul Williams and his more literary style and intense, often frenetic flow (or style of delivery), became a poetic role model for a number of the Black male students, evident in some of the performances in the slam.

The film was also used to introduce students to the role played by various communicative modes in the production of meaning: students first read, then listened to, and finally viewed different versions of "Amethyst Rocks": the written text, Williams performing the poem on his spoken word CD by the same name, and finally the scene from the film. After each version, they were asked to journal about and then share what they were getting from the text. Their journal entries make clear how the students' interest in and understanding of the poem grew as the audio and then visual elements were added; in reflecting on the slam many of the students observed that the performances of their poetry were less likely to be misinterpreted than written versions of them. This seemed to be very reassuring to them.

Opening the Floodgate

The spoken word course continually opens floodgates of student writing and creativity. This was especially striking with the weaker English IV group who were generally less engaged in the class discussions than the previous groups, but who Tim felt produced as a whole the highest quality of performance poems. For instance, on the second day of class Clayton, a student who was very shy and had not once spoken in class the prior term, came to see Tim in the morning to show him a poem he had written and wanted to read for the group. By the third morning of class, Tim was surrounded by students with open notebooks and had started a performance signup list with six names. Pablo, an English IV student who was on the brink of failing English and who rarely showed up for the first half of term, began actively participating when the focus turned to producing and workshopping poems for the slam. He performed a powerful poem at the slam called "Just Another Baby Dad"; when Rashidah ran into him in the hallways of the local community college two years later, he told her that since the slam he had been doing "nothing but writing." The first year of the project, Jaz, one of the few black students in the AP class, was the slam's Master of Ceremonies and also won the slam. He was a creative writing major, unlike the majority of the students in all three classes, and felt that the course "rekindled a fire in me to write more, it just got me excited and I just started writing crazy and, like, I wake up in the middle of the night writing poems and stuff. It's got me excited again about writing." He added that he felt that this passion for poetry was improving his writing more generally, even his essays which "really needed some work," but within which he now finds he can "still put a sense of poetry in it, the way you use the words and the way to be figurative." He added that he wished that the slam had been at the beginning of the year for it let people know that he writes poetry and just "opened so many doors" because now he knows about "other people writing poetry" and can have conversations with them about their work. Jaz's thoughtful slam poem and impassioned performance had some of the intensity of Saul Williams' work:

> Continually I shadow box
> silhouette soldiers
> defeated
> I'm beaten, but naked
> until I bleed infinite
> beads of blood

the world shows not its own love
the streets give not hugs but through
drugs delivers amphetamine slugs
slow like forest I try to outrun the streets
escape its heat but these braces that bind
my feet won't bust
fallin unconscious I get caught in my sleep
my lion roar subdued to a
simple hush
Hush somebody callin my name
a once confident brother downsized to feel in
pain
Broken down hollowed out like an
abandoned window pane
this my major pain my daily
growing pain
My new white suit with a baby's kool-aid stain
my five heartbeats like Big Daddy Kane
and nights like this I wish raindrops would
fall, and christen my dome
I click my heels close my eyes
there is no place like home
There is no place like home
there is no place like home
But once awakened there's no Kansas for me
No scarecrow no tinman or cowardly lion as far as the eye
can see
Just darkness
and pissed off family
cause I interrupted their
sleep

Jaz creates an evocative scene of a man at night in his bedroom fighting his demons—the drugs and unemployment, the streets and despair which drag him down. He dreams of being transported away into the world of Oz but is (screamingly?) jolted back into the realities of his life. The poem is powerfully imagistic, filled with sound and color and stark contrasts between the lion roar and the subdued hush, the kool-aid stain on the white suit, the fire of the heat, and the rain on the roof. Like the narrator in "Amethyst Rocks," the one in Jaz's poem figures himself as at war, and this war also involves drugs, bullets as "amphetamine slugs." Jaz's performance greatly complemented the poem: he accentuated its use of repetition, imagery, and alliteration by varying his speed and volume. It was a symbiosis of poem and performance that brought to life the struggles of the poem's persona.

Getting Students to Write: "I'm Reading off the Top of the Head"

The performance poetry students' enthusiasm for writing poetry stands in sharp contrast with the feelings of many about writing more generally. One of the reasons Tim makes journaling a central piece of the course, including its assessment (50% of the class grade is usually based on their journals) is that he wants the students to be constantly writing. Classes often begin with "writing practice" about which Tim says, "Don't edit yourself. Be adventurous with your language. No talking." The students write to specific prompts, such as William Carlos Williams' "Men die everyday for what they miss in poetry," "Poetry heals the wounds inflicted by reason," and "Write down the words for a song or poem you wish you'd written. Then explain why." One year, the morning after the Oscars, the prompts included phrases from the broadcast including "And the winners are_____" and "Outcast no longer." The students are also given the following series of sentence openers to help them to start formulating in writing their "first thoughts" about something: "I don't understand / I noticed / I wonder / I was reminded of / I think / I'm surprised that / I'd like to know / I realize / If I were / The central issue here is / One consequence of could be? If then / I'm not sure / Although it seems." While Tim's prompts are engaging enough that the students usually do some writing to them, they are also often very reluctant to read what they have written. This is particularly the case for the black men in the classes.

In the second year of my involvement in the course, one male student started to paraphrase what he had written during the writing practice, saying "I'm reading off the top of the head." Tim responded, "you need to read what's on the page," to which the student replied, "then I don't want to do this." In conversation with Tim and me after the class period, Rashidah explained that regularly in her writing workshops with black children and youth the students would share what they "wished they had written" instead of what they actually had. Tim explained that he had them read "what's on the page" in order "to put the attention on their writing" for they'd eventually be writing poems. He also did this to keep the class focused, for students can "ramble on" in discussions. Tim tried to grapple with students' anxieties about writing up front, and on day two of the English IV class held out a cup in front of one of the students and told him to "spit in it." He then asked him to drink it, which the student laughingly refused to do. Tim surmised aloud that this refusal stems from our sense that what was once now private is public, that it has been exposed to others but also to ourselves, and then drew an analogy to writing in which we are usually our own worst critics, censoring ourselves for fear of being exposed. Rashidah next emphasized to the students that they should think of their writing as a performance, not to be scared of it as some kind of permanent record but to allow it to remain imperfect and in process.

Students' fears of exposure shone through in year three as soon as they began performing their work in class. One young woman prefaced her performance by saying, "I don't want people to talk too much about it," to which Tim responded that the authors should specify in advance the kind of feedback they are looking for. At another point in that class Jamir worried that he didn't "get" one of his classmate's poems. During a discussion about the group with Rashidah and me, Tim suggested that these generally low academic achievers would be particularly plagued by worries about the validity of what they have to say. For many of them, English classes had been deadly places where they had learned to get by through playing the rules of the game; these don't generally involve taking creative risks. He pointed out that Jamir's "I don't get it" epitomizes how students have been taught to respond to poetry: to mistrust their own instincts in favor of the teacher's "true" interpretation. In order to help change this dynamic, I regularly read through the students' class journals and validated their responses by putting selections on an overhead for discussion. And Tim offers the students concrete strategies for responding to each other's work. One is the concept of "pointing," where the students write down words and phrases that jump out at them from a poem. He also recommends that they initially structure their responses around the following prompts:

I believe your poem because _____

I doubt your poem because _____

When I hear your poem what goes through my head is _____

These prompts ask the students to be specific in their feedback and so help them avoid simplistic judgments about something being either good or bad. They also make clear the personal and subjective nature of all responses.

Poetry as Cool

This context of anxiety and low achievement makes the poetry the English IV students performed at the slam and all term all the more remarkable. In order to explain this, we need in part to revisit Asheena McNeil's comment about hip hop having made poetry cool. One valuable aspect of rap music for literacy educators is its commitment to linguistic skill, with rappers proudly proclaiming themselves as word warriors. The links between rap and the other spoken word forms we explored in the course redefined what counts as poetry in school; in the words of one male from the boys' class, "I think people really like poetry, they're just afraid to admit it." In all of the classes, many students wrote poetry and/or shared it publicly for the first time. This was consistently a source of surprise to the students. For instance, one student in the boys' class, Darren, spontaneously wrote a poem in class and then performed it, inspired by Rashidah's first visit to the class. His poem began: "My notebook is my horse and saddle / With this / I ride / I ride into the creativity of my emotions and embrace them as one would their child.…My thoughts laid out on piece of paper / for all to see / for all to see that through me / you can see / that I myself / Am poetry." A classmate expressed shock that Darren and others wrote poetry, "because I didn't see that part of him and I was like oh—well they deserve my attention because this is something that I didn't know about." In the Advanced Poetry class, one male announced, "I've seen things come out of people that I didn't know they had in them, and like we've been together since the ninth grade." In this same class, Jaz, commenting on his powerful invective that won the slam, said, "I didn't know I had that in me" and later in conversation added that "a lot of people found a lot of things within themselves."

Seven of the forty-six slam poems reviewed took poetry and/or writing as an explicit topic. These explorations of the significance and importance of writing and poetry in the students' poems work in the tradition of rap music, which is often self-referentially about the importance of writing and rhyming. Clayton, the shy young man discussed above whose poetic voice erupted in the course, performed a piece at the slam about the power of poetry which included these lines:

A poet opened my ears to poetry.
A diva like no other
she reminded me of hip hop.
Like her I'm often told me that I sound white
cause I can't flow to the beat of my block.
It's cause I'm misunderstood.
Don't get it twisted though,
me and you parked in the same hood.
A poet spits knowledge.

Knowledge—she's not from college
but damn she's the truth.

. . . .

At a time when my life was ticking away,
I was bound to be a statistic too.
Who knew rhymes could enter the solitary crevice
of an unanswered question?
Thank you bringing culture into me
at a time when I had drowned
in the sea of preconceived notions of a life
once known as the black man's struggle.....

Clayton's ode to poetry and to one poet in particular contains themes which reoccurred in many of the students' poems: the problem of social misperception and stereotyping and the challenges of being a black man. For instance, his classmate Aisha's poem "I write" also addressed some of these themes and in its final lines drew on pieces of the language from Clayton's poem, putting these works into conversation:

. . . .

I write about naked minds
and twisted allusions
of the so called American dream.
Naked minds
filled with empty aspirations
and preconceived notions of the life and times of a Black
man.
In a time when people in America are just a technicality
on a piece of paper
I write.

Aisha's powerful refrain, "I write," punctuated the poem throughout and offered a strong argument for the urgency of written self-expression in the face of a culture of deception and alienation.

Making Selves Strange and New

Contributing to the widespread sense of surprise about the poetry slam and course more generally, students in both classes took significant risks with their poems. Many seemed to experiment with different identities, making themselves strange and new to their peers and themselves. Given that the writers are all adolescents, it won't surprise that adolescent identity was the top theme (found in 15 of the 46 poems). Many of the poets tried on different personae. This experimentation was encouraged by a couple of experiences in the course. The first year, the boys' class had participated in a "many selves, many voices" unit in which they explored the different ways of speaking and communicating that they adopted in different situations in their lives. They wrote a monologue adopting one of their particular voices. In both years, we explored the concept of the persona poem and "mask," and studied a poem by Patricia Smith (1992) written from the perspective of a skinhead. A number of students performed these at the slams, adopting personae such as Pablo's "just another baby dad who leaves his child without a man," an Iraqi civilian, and an American soldier in Iraq. The latter was adopted by Don who dressed in fatigues to add authenticity; when he forgot his lines he was greeted by a chorus of support from the audience whose comments included "alright," "no pressing," and "you tell it," an example of the Participatory Literacy Community in practice. Another persona poem was written from the perspective of a much aggrieved planet Earth, and opened with the following lines:

> Since you were here, I couldn't breathe cause you polluted
> my air.
> Since you were here, I've bled thousands of times from
> endless warfares
> Giving me third degree burns from your careless acts
> ripping each single strand of hair right off my back.
> . . . .

This poet, Jeff, identified strongly as a rapper and mostly dressed in hip hop outfits: baggy clothes, a baseball hat, and a heavy chain necklace. His angry tone and hip hop stance and style made the poem initially seem like a rap "beef" (or complaint); when it became clear that he was speaking as the Earth rather than as a human, the message surprised and then demanded one's attention.

While some students used the slam to publicly explore different personae, others used it as an opportunity to share some aspects of themselves that they previously had not. For instance, one of the biggest surprises for many students the first year, as well as for their teacher, was a poem entitled "Who Can Defeat Me," delivered with force by Clifton, a student in the boys' class known for his soft-spoken, easy-going manner:

> WHO CAN DEFEAT ME
> Inside me
> is an inner me
> that inner me
> wants to be free
> but should I let it free
> therefore releasing
> my enemy
> . . . .
> is it reality
> to see
> Rodney King join hands w/ his enemies
> after his tragic police brutality
> or to see Afghanistan Refugee
> eat w/ the ones dat made them flee
> . . . .
> our ancestors wanted to be free
> their spirits live deep in me
> telling me
> "FREE ME" "free me"
> my mind is the key to my individuality
> telling me
> no one can defeat me
> but me.

The poem's ambiguity gets at some of the complexity of this "inner me," at once Clifton's "enemy," the voices of his slave ancestors whose spirits "live deep in me," and his "mind." I read this "inner me" as in part a personification of this student's anger at the injustices of the world, from the treatment of Rodney King to the bombing of Afghanistan. While he fears his anger, he recognizes its source in historical and contemporary racial violence and also its potential for resistance, for working in particular towards the liberation of black people. He suggests that paths towards freedom lie both with the individual, particularly the individual mind, and the community. Clifton delivered the poem with such vehemence and intensity that he was almost shouting, which suggested that this normally reserved student was using the poem as one vehicle for exploring different aspects of himself: part of the journey, perhaps, towards freedom.

Other students also experimented with different perspectives and ways of being. For instance, after controversy about Gerard's performance of "Streetlife" at one Talent Night at school (stopped as it was getting started by the school principal who was worried about possible profanity or sexual references; for more, see Hoeschmann & Low, 2008, Ch. 1), Tim suggested Gerard write a poem about being labeled and misinterpreted, which Gerard (and other students in this and subsequent groups) seemed to take to heart. Gerard performed a poem entitled "Cry" that critiqued gang violence, and implicitly, models of masculinity that suggest that men have no feelings. "Cry" starts with, "Misunderstood is the definition when a man cry," and ends with the lines, "And you ask why? Why you think I'm crying you bastard? / It's cause I'm at your funeral putting flowers on your casket." The first line takes up the popular theme of misinterpretation, but in relation to a man's tears rather than to generational and cultural stereotyping. "Cry" is a plea for peace in a world of violence. While the poem could still be titled "Streetlife" for it discusses its battles and its victims, Gerard is here the critic and teacher, not the "player." In another line in the poem he writes: "No degree in philosophy but when I talk, I teach." The difference between the two versions of "Streetlife" also suggests that Gerard has in part switched genres, moving from gangsta rap with its playful, hyberbolic conventions to the slam poetry genre, which is often politically provocative, critical, and self-reflexive. However, the poem also draws on some common themes in rap music, especially in its "conscious" renditions: poetry as pedagogy, as tool for healing, and as vehicle for street wisdom.

While the Advanced Poetry students, many of whom were creative writing majors, were already comfortable writing and sharing poetry publicly in school literary events, they also made themselves vulnerable through honest explorations of identity. In year two of the project one young white woman, an accomplished poet who had won several national poetry prizes, performed a love poem to another woman.

Around the corner from the billboards that the sun rises
over
Is a little take-out place. The manager there has eyes that
burn
Like unattended egg rolls.
She makes me get mooney-eyed. She makes me go gaga.
She makes me go and get moo goo gai pan
At three a.m. I take the bus.
. . . .
I love her spicy wings. I love her breasts
Served over rice, her legs, her thighs
The shine of the grease on her arms when she cleans the

rotisserie light
Her simple grin as she brings me my Buddhist's Delight
I asked her out for coffee one day. Outside it rained
Dark tea-leaf patterns on the smokestacks and drains
She leaned close and told me
that's not what "take-out" means.

Given the widespread expression of homophobia in high schools, unfortunately reinforced by some of the lyrics of a good deal of rap music, this was a very risky poem to choose. The response from most of the audience members was muted and many seemed taken aback by the student's honesty. Only one other poem performed in the slam over the four years directly addressed homosexuality, and it was in a list of people a student wished she could speak for, including "If I spoke for everyone the fearful silence of lesbians bi's and gays would be slain and it would end the pain of their disdain."

Only one of the 46 poetry students took up the theme of body image—a white male named Kurt. My speculation is that disinterest in this topic with these youth speaks to the fact that "body image" is still mostly the concern of middle class white young women, a very small number of whom participated in the poetry slams in this urban school. Kurt's poem, however, also speaks to more general issues around adolescent identity, the most common theme in the slam poems, and of love relationships, another recurring theme (though not necessarily one of the most important). Kurt was the class clown in the Advanced Poetry class and wrote a poem about being fat:

A dose of truth
no a large portion.
Some own their blackness
their whiteness
I own my fatness.
But I do wish to sell it
at some lonely garage sale
with its bad memories
but till then that day comes
it is mine
all mine
until I shed its burden
I will never stop striving
to fit in—
to the damn pants.
I can't fit into the pants
that I bought for fifty
bucks cause I said to
my mom they would fit
shit.
A sidewards glance
is all I ask
from one of those
slim girls
those beautiful, elusive girls
with smooth plains for stomach
and golden locks for hair

> Is a dance so hard
> so difficult to try
> maybe they are afraid to see
> that I am not a novelty or a means to a better
> rep.

Kurt uses humor very effectively here to both talk about something difficult and to make his classmates laugh. It shows insight into dating relations (the notion that one might dance with or date the "fat" boy in order to try something new or to get yourself a good reputation—as a caring person perhaps?) and also some limits of vision, given that Kurt is also seeking the attention of the "slim"—the girls with smooth stomach plains (from his performance it did not seem that this reference was knowing or ironic).

In an interview at the end of the course, Kurt spoke about the way he normally "bottled things up" that bothered him, erecting a "force field" of humor, and that,

> to finally get that out in my senior year, a lot of the things that I just wanted to yell at some people, but to get it out in a way that they won't be offended or they won't be taken aback…if you say it like that and you can get it all to everyone at one time…it was just this huge weight off.

We see here Kurt working, like Gerard, to say something he feels needs to be said without offending his audience; while Gerard's comment suggests some of the difficulties involved with speaking across cultural and generational differences, Kurt reminds that these shape communication more generally, especially in the fishbowls that high schools can be. This repeat theme of misconception is a reminder of how often adolescents feel that everyone is watching and making judgments about them. Another white student in the Advanced Poetry class, Nathan, also spoke to this dynamic when he said that "there are a lot of people that you just don't know, you don't even form a relationship" with and that one can go through school with "tremendous misconceptions about people." Nathan saw the slam as working against this, and argued that the slam demonstrated

> the importance of the individual as not answering to a stereotype, as not being necessarily what people expected, and saying, well, this is me, this is no one else talking. I've been inspired yes, but those inspirations are a part of who I am because my experiences make me. So this is about me the individual…we're all just people and we don't need to be divided by anything unless we decide that we are.

The slam is a space where students can express themselves as individuals, which helps them to move beyond stereotypical notions of each other, and so facilitates the coming together across differences.

While Kurt felt liberated by his performance, he was disappointed by the reaction of one of the judges whom he described as overweight and whom he feels "either doesn't address it or has given up on it." The judge approached him afterwards and

> you know she kind of defended me…to me…she kind of defended me and it was just kind of disheartening to see…she couldn't get over the fact in the poem I was saying that I was fat…she couldn't get past that to get to the poem and if she didn't get to the poem, she couldn't understand what I was saying…so. You know, but she's a teacher, so I just…I took her words and went into class. But it's interesting to see how some people have a shield, have like a force field up when they don't want to hear someone talk the way they do or listen to somebody.

According to this student, his teacher couldn't hear him because of her own issues with weight; whether or not this is the case, it is interesting that Kurt felt that she couldn't even "get to the poem" and that her defense missed the point. This scenario adds another dimension to the dilemma of adults reading or listening to youth: the relationship between adults and young people is burdened by adults' baggage, including unresolved feelings about their own adolescences (Gilbert, 2007). In both classes that first year we discussed possible reasons for the collective risk taking in the poetry slam. Several students suggested that they were more willing to explore difficult subjects because performance allowed them greater control over the audience's interpretation of their message. A few students suggested that their risk taking was in part due to the fact that they were graduating seniors, leaving this particular community behind in a few weeks. One student responded that "freedom" was at stake in their choice of topics, not "vulnerability," and that the slam presented the "perfect opportunity" if "you just want to express yourself."

Spoken Word and Hip Hop Performativity

The students' experimentation with different styles and identities in school is also very much in the spirit of hip hop performativity, which celebrates the power of what Toni Morrison (1995) calls "word-work" to continually forge new selves, worlds, and meanings. And as noted above, not only has hip hop culture helped legitimize spoken word poetry among youth, but the course also drew upon students' interests in rap music. One important dimension of hip hop's ethos of reinvention is its language, "Hip Hop Nation Language" (HHNL) (Alim, 2004), which is a hotbed of linguistic innovation whose distinct and ever-evolving lexicon, syntax, and phonology draw upon African American Vernacular English (AAVE) word play traditions and then accelerate them through hip hop culture's mass-mediated high-speed networks of distribution and influence. As Alim (2004) has noted, while AAVE is the "cutting edge" of sociolinguistic innovation in the U.S., HHNL is the "cutting edge of the cutting edge" (p. 296). Three mass market examples of this spirit of word-work and self-invention and expression in hip hop culture are the changing identities of prominent rappers: Sean "Puffy" Combs' multiple reincarnations, first as Puff Daddy and now as P Diddy; Shawn Carter/Jay-Z/Jigga/and Jay-HOVA, the new God of rap; and, perhaps most infamously, the three personae of the character known alternately as Slim Shady, Marshall Mathers, and Eminem. Hip Hop Nation Language embodies a dynamic poetics of the moment.

Making Society Strange

Not only was the self interrogated and reworked through the composition of poems, but so was the social. In every class, students grappled with important issues at the individual, local, and international levels. While adolescent identity was the top theme, it was quickly followed by general critiques of the state of the world, with most poems implicating current politicians and the older generation (13), drugs (13), race and racism (13), and then violence, crime, and gangs (10), and poverty (10). A number of the poems critiqued the American "War on Terror" and the Iraq War (7). Here are some excerpts from two of these:

"Blinded" (Only to shed a little light on the eyes of the "blind")
The sky is filled with society's pollution that infects our
world as a whole

It was our goal to unite our nations as one but I guess that
idea was too far fetched
Instead Osama Bin Laden gathered some planes together
and told the world to catch

. . . .

How are we the young people of tomorrow when
tomorrow's opportunities are no longer?

And

. . . .

Yet things are still the same.
More bombs over Baghdad.
More innocent victims left sad.
To everyone who lost someone,
I'm sorry they had to go out that way.
But maybe next time
someone will make the right decision on election day.

One of the most powerful poems on race was by three young women in the 2002 Advanced Poetry class—one black, one white, and one who self-identified as mixed race. They performed a group poem, "Me," in which they interrogated race and racial stereotyping, including being "Too black," "Too white," and "two things combined, intertwined / Through society's eyes blinded by color / Do I have to be one or the other?" Each poet had a solo section and some group choruses, and they explored the limits of the racialized identities imposed upon them by others, including, "They only see my mistakes as defeat / If I stand up for myself / I am considered defensive / And when I make it to the top / It is considered rare" and "You see my pale skin and think I'm innocent / My blond hair, you think I'm naïve / My blue eyes and you think I'm blind."

Several black women wrote poems in which they spoke directly to black men, as in for instance the winning poem in 2003, Danielle's "Stay High":

Every time I look at you I just want to cry
You are wasted opportunity
You are time gone by
You are unspent knowledge
You are unfulfilled worth.
Nigga you are far from a nigga
Ignorance is not what you are
Or were
But now, Shit nigga
Stay high
Stay posted on street corners
Provide me with that high
That fucks me up

. . . .

This poem speaks to some of the tricky politics of representation. It is an undeniably powerful poem, as was Danielle's performance, and was recognized as such by the very high scores it was given by a mixed panel of judges. But it is filled with expletives (five "shits" and two "fucks," which Tim refers to as the "F-bomb"). "Stay High" was the final product of a creative negotiation between the student and Tim, who advises his students to use all "precious pieces of language" with thought and care and not to "cast pearls among swine" by overusing expletives to create sensation rather than meaning. Tim did not want to censor the poem but recommended editing what started out as 14 "F-bombs." And what "Stay High" conveys is both the language of the streets, the speaker's anger, and the urgency of the message. In the four years of slam poems, most of the expletives were used thoughtfully and with impact, as in the line "I wish I was rich, cause living in poverty in America's a bitch," as well as in Kurt's "cause I said to / my mom they would fit / shit."

Race shaped the entire project in very interesting ways, given that predominantly black groups of students (the Advanced Poetry class was the exception) were exploring hip hop and "spoken word" with a white teacher, a white university professor, and a black poet. The contrast between the two classes the first year—one mostly black and all male, the other mostly white and co-ed—brought to the fore some of the usual racial dynamics of the school, and then overturned the usual order of things. The very top academic students in the grade that year were mostly white, and many of them were creative writing majors in the Advanced Poetry class who tended to receive all of the school's literary awards. The boys' class was a less academically successful group with only two creative writing majors—many of the others were majoring in theatre tech. The first year of the project was a particularly surprising one on a number of levels. While one of the creative writing majors from the Advanced Poetry class won the slam, he was black with a strong hip hop style. And many of the students from the boys' class wowed the audience with their work. Two of the strongest students in the school in the Advanced Poetry class spoke of how much they learned from and about the poets in the boys' class who performed. One young white woman, Laura, explained to me that while she had not "made an effort to get to know the students in the boys' class" (for she hadn't been in their classes and had few friends who were boys) she was very impressed by the way they "expressed emotions and social ideas." I asked Laura if she noted any patterns of difference between the poems performed by both classes, and she responded that the black students "tend to have a better cultural awareness from being on the other side of the whole dominant culture," giving Gerard's poem as an example:

> his poem, the one about the tears, crying, and he addressed a whole slough of issues on racism on different counts, racism against Arabs, and racism against black people, and gender issues and all sorts of things. That just the way he talked about this, what he knew and his experience of those things. To some degree all of us have known some of that because we're all in this school together, but I think that the black students understand better.

Laura also speculated that an experience of marginalization meant that many of the black students spoke "straight from the heart," and she pointed to the ways their poetry became powerful through "the type of language, the slang, the kind of the grittiness of the language or the bam bam bam." One of the white students remarked on these differences during the slam performance when he introduced his love poem by saying: "I'm sorry if I'm not angry." This comment can be read as an attempt at minimizing the impact of the black poets' words, or as a recognition, like Laura's, of the very different experiences faced by students who grow up marginalized by white privilege. But these comments also make clear that slam poetry is an inclusive genre that can accommodate different poetic styles; while it is ideally suited for hard-hitting expressions of social critique, it also makes room for more introspective self-analysis.

In contrast with the number of poems which engaged current social problems, only 4 of the 46 slam poems spoke primarily about love, while 2 spoke about friendship. This challenges the common portrait of youth as mostly preoccupied with their romantic relationships and friendships. Why did so many of the students choose to tackle social problems? The spoken word poems such as Saul Williams' which were explored in class might have in part inspired and provoked students to be so socially aware in their pieces. However, Rashidah conducts performance poetry workshops with children and youth around the city and regardless of what they read or watch together finds that her students want to address weighty social issues in their poems. While people tend to think she asks this of them, instead Rashidah feels that her students "just go there, unprompted." That the students frequently choose to tackle important topics in the poetry slam suggests that they crave a venue and permission to take a stand on social issues, in their own language. Or in the words of a male in the Advanced Poetry class, "I think everyone was saying things that needed to be said, but didn't know how to put them, but once everyone said them they were said so eloquently it was amazing." Another pointed out: "racism, terrorism, image, society, love—you can tell exactly what runs through our minds every day." In the boys' class, Carlos put out a call towards the beginning of the project for the group to be as thoughtful as possible:

> cause we think about a lot of things they don't know we think about, you know what I'm saying. We write a lot of things they don't know we write about. So we care about issues they don't know we care about. If we show them that we care about these issues and we learn about these things and we can do it in this creative way of language…with our poetry what I want us to do—me personally—is to have them leave the theatre thinking like damn those are some talented young men and women you know what I'm saying like damn—they got things to say—know something else…that's the future of all of us—we're the future and they got to know that…the things we have to say even though we might say it in a different way, that shit is important.

Carlos' appeal was heard; given the space to share what they think and write and care about, in their own creative language, the students treated their classmates and slam audience with their intelligence, wit, insight, honesty, and emotion. Carlos' comments also speak to my argument that youth are particularly interested in tackling serious issues when "they" are listening, a reference in this context to adults in general and teachers and administrators in particular. This makes a case for the importance of youth writing in schools, for despite many of the students' frustrations with high school (expressed in class conversations and in some of their poems), the committed nature and seriousness of the performances at the slam suggest that these youth still see schools as places where one works to be as smart as possible in the presence of peers but also of adults. Their awareness of an adult audience was made particularly clear in one piece in year three of the project, which began, "All administrators you might want to have a seat with this one" and then proceeded to critique many aspects of the school's bureaucracy and regulations, including what was seen as "learning in city schools." Another powerful local critique was of the city school district's budget crisis and the decisions being made to cut arts and sports program, all within the context of the testing and standardization of No Child Left Behind. Sample lines are:

> . . . .
> We, and by we I mean we who are coming of age, need to
> tell the world
> What's what. That we don't give a fuck about color, gay,
> straight or bi, all
> You need to do is give us the material for wings and we can
> make ourselves
> fly.
> So don't cut the arts, cause we need to learn to express,

don't cut sport
because without sport we're a mess, the answer here is to
spend more
money on learning, and less money on tests

Learning from Slam

There are a number of elements which contribute to the course's ongoing success. First of all, Tim is a very experienced and talented creative writing teacher who has been working as an English teacher in the city school district for over 20 years, and for the last ten as a creative writing teacher in an arts magnet school. He is passionate about teaching and writing, and is a published haiku poet. He draws upon many of his creative writing teaching skills such as the freewrite and response prompts discussed above. In interviews, his students shared their awareness that Tim is genuinely curious about them, and willing to learn from them about their lives and culture. He asks them lots of questions and is a careful listener. In illustration of this, Tim proposed co-developing the performance poetry course to me, feeling that his lack of knowledge about hip hop presented a missed opportunity to engage his students. Tim's students also say that they feel that he is himself with them and shares easily of that self through his storytelling. He is willing to relinquish the role of authority and reject traditional school power dynamics. The students feel that, unlike many of their teachers, Tim isn't on a "power trip" and that he doesn't judge. All of these things help Tim cultivate a lower risk classroom environment for writing and creativity more generally.

The partnership with Rashidah has also been a key factor in the course's success. She was invited into the course the first year through a local artists-in-residence program so that the students could work with an experienced performance poet; she connected and worked so well with them, injecting a real professionalism and dynamism into the course, that she is now an integral piece of the school's performance poetry program. Rashidah is especially good at helping the students think about the elements of performance and at workshopping their poems. Tim described her as "tremendously talented, a wonderful teacher" who had the "respect and admiration of the kids." She shares the trials and rewards of her own creative writing processes, performing polished works as well as works in progress in class. As some of the students explained in reflections about the course, Rashidah is "poetry." Aside from Rashidah's particular talents, her role in the course speaks to the importance of bringing professional poets into the classroom as resources for teachers who are not usually spoken word poets so that the students have a strong sense that performance poetry lives in the community as well as the school.

Finally, I argue that the slam genre itself is key to the course. Rogoff (2003) explains how our thinking is shaped by the cultural tools we work with. As discussed earlier, slam poetry—vernacular, urban, often politicized, playful, sexy—opens up certain possibilities for thinking, and for trying on new modes of expression and being. Students described some reasons slam poetry seemed like the right vehicle for self-expression and exploration: for one student it is "written and read in the author's own voice" and for another it has "more emotions in it, more of the writer inside the piece." Laura explained that while poetry can seem elitist or pretentious to people, slam doesn't. And central to slam is the fact that it is a competitive performance which brings together the poets and audience into a community of shared engagement in the works. As Laura put it, central to slam's power is "the way the audience reacts to the poetry slam. It's amazing, gave me chills almost as much as the poetry slam itself, but I think it's just that everybody's going to give them a shot, and you get all different types of people who are going to give it a try, and people are funny, and people talk about things that affect everybody." The audience invests in the poems and the poets in vocal and visceral ways, yelling, clapping, stomping feet, laughing, even dancing in order to express disagreement or support for the judges' scores. That said, the competition is one of the contradictions that slam impresario Bob Holman (1994) argues are central to slam's dynamism: just as the audiences tend to be both heckling and attentive, playful as well as very serious, the competition is both important enough to fight about and so insignificant that in his "Slam Invocation," Holman proclaims that "the best poet always loses" (p. 1).

A cultural studies approach to literacy takes youth culture seriously as a resource of creative, provocative literate practices. Given that adolescents might be saying what they have to say in a "different way," the challenge for educators becomes learning how to listen differently. The language arts unit "leveraged" (Hull & Shultz, 2001) the youths' out-of-school rap and freestyle literacies and "extended" such literacies: the students who were accomplished rappers and freestylers experimented with performance poetry, written in advance and performed without musical accompaniment. Experienced creative writers placed greater emphasis on the performance of their works. Some familiar practices were made strange, worthy of analysis; others were situated within the historical and contemporary context of spoken word culture. And given the students' expressions of surprise, not only were the teachers and administrators shown that "we think about a lot of things they don't know we think about" but so were the "talented men and women" in question. The surprise factor speaks to the way "business as usual" in the school was interrupted by the spoken word course. The students were often in the position of knowing more than the teacher. The teacher was collaborating extensively with a local spoken word teaching artist and a university professor, and a range of poets visited the classroom over the course of the project. The school's usual hierarchies of academic achievement were destabilized for none of the winning slam poets were the top students or thought of as the "best" creative writers in the grade. Part of this interruption of the order of things was racial, for in this majority black school, a disproportionate number of the highest achieving students are white; in the poetry slam, the poetic and performance talents of many of the black and Latino students came to the fore and were respected by teachers and peers. In particular, the slams value a poetry of the margins: as Laura described, the cultural insights and hard-hitting social critique of many of the black and Latino students' poems, as well as the powerful, gritty, language and "bam bam" delivery, were what moved and impressed audiences most.

Students in all of the classes practiced important literacy skills as they wrote and performed poems in order to grab the attention of and engage audiences. Many of the poems built and sustained arguments using appeals to logic, humor, and emotion. Some spoke to multiple audiences, hoping to speak to their peers while trying not to alienate the older generations in the crowd. Students had to draw upon all of their expressive instruments—their minds, words, voices, eyes, hands, bodies—and practice the elements of oral performance, including tone, pacing, modulation, and volume. As a result, the course asks us to rethink how even longstanding literacy topics like audience and purpose in writing might be taught. It also asks us to open up what gets valued in school by emphasizing that popular cultural forms like rap music are central to the evolution of culture and communication. At another level, the spoken word curriculum encourages the development of a community of learners who are genuinely invested in each other's work because it makes clear that writing is something to care deeply about. It is a place for exploring what matters most: figuring ourselves out, sharing our worries about the world, getting angry, telling stories, making each other think, laugh, and feel. In this place of exploration, notions of therapy or of healing aren't to be dismissed but instead are integral to the growth of individuals, classrooms, and larger communities. Ultimately, these concerns need to be seen as integral to learning rather than as separate from or counter to it.

Note

* This chapter was originally published as: Low, B. (2008). Slammin' School: Performance Poetry and the Urban School. In M. Hoechsmann & B. E. Low, *Reading Youth Writing: "New" Literacies, Cultural Studies & Education* (pp. 99–126). New York: Peter Lang.

References

Algarín, M. (1994). Introduction: The sidewalk of high art. In M. Algarín & B. Holman (Eds.), *ALOUD: Voices from the Nuyorican Poets Café* (pp. 3–28). New York: Henry Holt.

Alim, S. (2004). Hip hop nation language. In E. Finegan & J. R. Rickford (Eds.), *Language in the USA: Themes for the 21st century*. Cambridge: Cambridge University Press.

Fisher, M. (2005). From the coffee house to the school house: The promise and potential of spoken word poetry in school contexts. *English Education, 37*(2): 115–131.

Frith, S. (1983). *Sound effects: Youth, leisure, and the politics of rock*. London: Constable.

Gee, J. (1996). *Social linguistics and literacies*. London: Taylor and Francis.

Gilbert, J. (2007). Risking a relation: Sex education and adolescent development. *Sex education: Sexuality, society and learning, 7*(1): 47–62.

Heath, S. B. (1983). *Ways with words: Language, life, and work in communities and classrooms*. Cambridge: Cambridge University Press.

Hewitt, D. (Producer). (1999, November 28). Slam [Television series episode]. *Sixty Minutes*. New York: CBS.

Hoechsmann, M. & Low, B.E. (2008). *Reading youth writing: "New" literacies, cultural studies & education*. New York: Peter Lang.

Holman, B. (1994). Congratulations: You have found the hidden book. In M. Algarín & B. Holman (Eds.), *ALOUD: Voices from the Nuyorican Poets Café* (pp. 1). New York: Henry Holt.

Hull, G., & Schultz, K. (2001). Literacy and learning out of school: A review of theory and research. *Review of Educational Research, 7*(4): 575–611.

Jocson, K. (2005). "Taking it to the mic": Pedagogy of June Jordan's Poetry for the People and partnership with an urban high school. *English Education 37*(2), 132–149.

Jocson, K. (2006). Bob Dylan and Hip Hop: Intersecting literacy practices in youth poetry communities. *Written Communication, 23*(3): 231–259.

Johnson, R. (1996). What is cultural studies anyway? In J. Storey (Ed.), *What is cultural studies? A reader* (pp. 75–114). London: Arnold.

Low, B. (2006). Poetry on MTV? Slam and the poetics of popular culture. *Journal of Curriculum Theorizing, 22*(4): 97–112.

Luke, A., & Freebody, P. (1997). The social practices of reading. In S. Muspratt, A. Luke & P. Freebody (Eds.), *Constructing critical literacies: Teaching and learning textual practice*. St. Leonards, N.S.W: Allen & Unwin.

Morrison, T. (1995). Nobel lecture. *The Georgia Review, 49*(1): 318–323.

Richter, D. (1989). *The critical tradition: Classic texts and contemporary trends*. New York: St. Martin's Press.

Rogoff, B. (2003). *The cultural nature of human development*. Oxford: Oxford University Press.

Rothenberg, J. (1981). *Pre-faces & other writings*. New York: New Directions.

Smith, J. (Director/Writer) (1995). *Dangerous minds* [Motion Picture]. In D. Simpson & J. Bruckheimer (Producer). USA: Hollywood Pictures.

Smith, P. (1992). Skinhead. *Big towns, big talk*. Cambridge, MA: Zoland Books.

Smith, P. (2007). Building Nicole's mamma. *Rattle e.2, Spring*, 49.

Stratton, R., & Wozencraft, K. (Eds.). (1998). *Slam*. New York: Grove Press.

Wah, F. (2000). *Faking it: Poetics of hybridity: Critical writing 1985–1999*. Edmonton: NeWest Publishers.

Weiss, J., & Hearndon, S. (2001). *Brave new voices: The YOUTH SPEAKS guide to teaching spoken word poetry*. New York: Heinemann.

PART 2

New Literacies and Semi-Formal Learning beyond the Classroom

CHAPTER FIVE

Influencing Pedagogy through the Creative Practices of Youth

LEIF GUSTAVSON

My motivation to conduct the study on which this chapter is based came from teaching middle school students and witnessing the creative work they were doing outside of school. Before returning to university to pursue a Ph.D., I taught English/language arts for seven years. In that time I established numerous work relationships with students who were engaged in what I thought was interesting learning outside of school. On the basis of this recognition, I eventually organized my seventh-grade class so that many of the students would bring their projects into class to develop and share with others. These projects included writing computer code for online adventure games, writing and illustrating comic books, composing music for various instruments, publishing zines, sculpting, drafting scripts for one-act plays, painting, and building stereo speakers. Many would call what these youth did "hobbies" or "passing fancies," but in conversation with these youth and through watching them work, I could hear and see that they were incredibly passionate about what they did and eager to discuss it. In addition, the craft involved in this kind of work was technically sophisticated and disciplined.

As I came to know their "out-of-school" work better, I could see how their ways of working within my class were often prescriptive and unimaginative. They would go through the routine of writing an essay, for example, and the result would be adequate. However, it would lack that personal touch or distinctive voice that sets powerful writing apart from merely adequate writing. At the same time, the same students were constructing sophisticated processes to do their out-of-school work. They were fashioning discourses in which to communicate with others. They were continuously representing themselves in refreshing ways as readers, writers, and thinkers. They were also evaluating their work and performing it. These sophisticated processes were not foreign to the ways of working that I valued in my class. In fact, I could see how the ways in which they worked outside of school often complemented skills and work habits that I wanted them to develop in my class. They were simply idiosyncratic and personally relevant to the students when they worked "on their own terms." I saw these youths' ways of working as an untapped resource for my teaching and as having the potential to transform the look and feel of the way we worked and learned in my classroom. With this in mind, I set out through my Ph.D. research to investigate particular creative practices to see the ways in which youth engaged in them and made them a part of their lives.

I understand the term *creative practice* to be a hybrid of Aristotle's notion of *tekhne* and Paul Willis's "grounded aesthetic." Aristotle defines *tekhne* as "the art in mundane skill and, more significantly, in day-to-day life…an intrinsic aesthetic or crafting that underlies the practices of everyday life…'a reasoned habit of mind in making something'" (Cintron, 1997, p. xii). According to Willis (1998), grounded aesthetic is "the everyday application of symbolic creativity to symbolic materials and resources in context, whereby new meanings are attributed to or associated with, or seen in them, thereby re-organizing them and appropriating them to common concerns and issues" (p. 173). Willis argues that to understand the way youth understand and live in the world, we need to shift our focus away from products that they consume or make (e.g., CDs, websites, jewelry) to the "social practice" of making these products. The creative practices of youth, whether skateboarding, gaming, redesigning cars, or Parkour, are part of their everyday lives. They literally carry the practice with them wherever they go. Youth spend hours and days practicing their craft, swapping techniques, and scrutinizing their own practice. These creative practices take youth to all different kinds of spaces: friends' houses, conventions, skate parks, studios, concerts, clubs, and stores where they know they will find people and texts that are interesting and will inform their work. This characteristic of youth engaged in creative practices, to me, is the "intrinsic aesthetic or crafting that underlies the practice of everyday life" that Aristotle speaks of. And through this conscious and unconscious "mapping" and constructing of their everyday lives, youth employ a "grounded aesthetic." Their creative practices are part of who they are and how they understand the world around them. The way they live their lives informs their practice, and their practice influences the ways in which they live day to day.

In this chapter, I show how the creative practice of Gil, a fifteen-year-old turntablist, can serve as an analytic frame for thinking about how teachers can use the ways in which youth work in the everyday to inform pedagogy. I first show how performance, improvisation, self-reflection, interpretation, and evaluation are a part of the everyday practice of Gil as a turntablist. I then translate these aspects of practice—what I call habits of mind and body—into pedagogy. Through this approach, I wish to build on the critical work in "everyday" learning of scholars such as Schultz and Hull (2002), Heath (1998, 2000; Heath & McLaughlin, 1994), Lave (1997), Csikszentmihalyi (1991), and Wenger (1998) by turning my newly constructed knowledge of how youth work "on their own terms" back on to the classroom; in essence, having youth inform us what a productive learning environment would look like if it were more finely tuned to the ways they work.

The Participant

At the time of the research, Gil, fifteen years old and African American, lived with his mother just within the western border of Philadelphia, a stone's throw from the elite private school that he attended. Gil's mother sold medical insurance to senior citizens—an incredibly demanding and stressful job because of the weekly quota that she had to fill. Gil worked hard during the summer before the research to help pay for an exchange trip to Spain offered through the school that coming year and for equipment he wanted to buy for his turntablism. He also worked during the school year, picking up a few hours bagging groceries at a nearby store as well as DJing for parties. In terms of academics, Gil was doing very well. He registered for an advanced class in math, to his mother's surprise and pleasure. At the beginning of the research, Gil took his studies seriously and appreciated the positive feedback he received from teachers and peers regarding his schoolwork.

During my Ph.D. program, I worked with Gil on a research project investigating student identity formation in school. He proved reliable, working with me on multiple drafts of the report. What I found most invigorating about this work with Gil was his ability to challenge me on observations that I was making about him and his willingness to question the research and its purpose. Not so coincidentally, this study provided insight into the creative practices of youth and exposed ethical difficulties inherent in collaborative research (Gustavson & Cytrynbaum, 2003). Perhaps the most challenging aspect of researching with teens is designing a study that indeed supports and utilizes their wisdom, not only in the collecting of data but in the writing of the manuscript as well. After the project, Gil spoke with me, critiquing the products and processes of the work and outlining what he felt could be done to improve it in the future. The study from which this chapter comes implements many of Gil's suggestions.

Turntablism

Turntablism, the art of manipulating vinyl records on turntables, is one of the four elements of hip-hop. Hip hop began in the Bronx at a time when the area was undergoing dramatic and traumatic social change. The early 1960s were a time of racial unrest and economic inequality. The established African American and Hispanic communities in the Bronx of the early 1960s began to disappear with the introduction of an expressway that cut a swathe of asphalt through the Bronx—or, more specifically, directly through Hispanic and African American homes and neighborhoods. With this intrusion into their lives, people started to leave the Bronx for other boroughs such as Queens. With the exodus of people the businesses followed, and by 1965 the Southside of the Bronx was a picture of urban decay. Not surprisingly, without the vibrant and supportive neighborhoods of the past, both crime and unemployment rose. Soon, street gangs followed. Within this bleak context, hip hop was born.

Turntablism, like all the elements of hip hop, is a distinctly youth-oriented art form. It was created by mainly African American and Puerto Rican American youth in the 1960s and is sustained by youth of diverse cultural and class backgrounds today. Turntablism is a form of music: by remixing and reassembling sampled sounds, beats, and melodies on records, the turntablist creates a new piece of music. Turntablism perhaps most thoroughly embodies Kress and Van Leeuwen's (1996) and Street's (2000) theorizing on the multimodality of literacy. Kress and Van Leeuwen define multimodality as "a range of representational modes…a range of means of meaning-making, each affecting the formation of their subjectivity" (p. 39). When Gil composes, for example, he takes a form of representation—the vinyl record—and manipulates it with turntables to produce a new sound, a new form of representation. The "interactive elements," the found sounds on records, are "made to relate" to each other in new ways, thus creating new texts and new meanings (Kress & Van Leeuwen, 1996, p. 176).

For further explanation of how a turntablist works and what kind of work is produced, I defer to Sam, another young turntablist who taught me a great deal about the art form. Gil thought of Sam as a mentor. They would often get together to talk shop about their practice. Sam was a senior in the same high school as Gil. I knew him because he used to spend time in my classroom before school started. We shared similar musical tastes. We would spend the fifteen minutes or so before the bell rang swapping names of bands that we were listening to at the time. Part of Sam's way of educating me on turntablism was through giving me writing he had done on his creative practice. His essay entitled "Turntable Philosophy" clearly draws the connection between turntablism, multimodality, and the act of writing:

> The DJ represents this idea of reassembly in its purest form. Pieces from the past are put together to arrive at a present purpose, thus creating the aural collage that is called the mix. In this way the turntable/mixer combination is a tool, no different in its elemental sense than the pen and paper, for they provide a means to pull "words" and "quotes" from records and place them in a consistently new and different context. The idea of turntable language may seem farfetched, but when the roots of the language are examined, it is seen that it was not only an essential, but inevitable part of the guerilla-art social reaction (i.e. that of Black America), similar to the origins of many arts and humanities.

There is a certain kind of reading and writing involved in turntablism. Sam suggests that manipulating records is a form of language. There is the interpretation of words. There is the fashioning of a message out of words, phrases, and sentences that have been captured from other sources. The turntablist's "referencing" of words and phrases and the manipulation of preexisting words and notes on a record resemble the way in which teachers expect students to quote from the work of scholars within their essays, for example. In addition, the sampling of phrases from various albums to construct a new text reminds me of the way Shakespeare "borrowed" themes from Ovid to write his plays. Like writers of more traditional texts, turntablists make meaning out of language and ideas they did not create or conceive. Sam also mentions that turntablism is a means of social action. Turntablists create music in part to subvert the status quo. We will see this in Gil's work later in this chapter.

While rap still garners all the media attention within hip hop culture, the turntablist is back in style now and in high demand. One needs only to watch television for an hour or so to see the influence of turntablism on our broader society. Zima ads feature turntablists. Lee Jeans and Gap ads use turntablists. IKEA catalogues represent posh adolescent bedrooms with two turntables and a mixer. MTV has a turntablist how-to show. The internet contains hundreds if not thousands of turntable websites.

The creative practice is global as well. There is an international federation for turntablists—the International Turntable Federation (ITF). This organization and others host international turntable competitions, including Disco Music Competitions (DMCs) and the ITF World Championships. Even jazz artists such as Steve Coleman and Medeski Martin and Wood are now recording with turntablists as part of their bands—not to mention all of the popular bands that have a "turntablist," if only the sampled sound of someone scratching. Turntablists such as QBert, DJ Shadow, and The Invisibl Skratch Piklz have attained rock star status among many youth. Gil is a product of this renewed interest in the art form, and it is informing what he reads, the messages he chooses to "write" on his turntables, and how he works and learns in his everyday life.

I would like to illustrate through two vignettes the ways in which Gil works in his chosen creative practice. These glimpses into the ways he works on his turntables highlight specific habits of mind and body that have the potential for influencing how work and learning are conducted in classrooms. The first vignette focuses on Gil at work on his turntables in a school space. The second vignette shows Gil at home practicing. In both spaces we can see how performance, improvisation, self-reflection, interpretation, and evaluation are essential habits of mind and body within Gil's craft as a turntablist.

Playing at School: Turntablism as Performative, Self-Reflective, and Interpretive

Through the jazz teacher's generosity, Gil and other students interested in turntablism had a room off of the main music room where they could set up their equipment, practice, and record together. It was through this space, and the community of practice formed therein, that Gil and others were able to transport their out-of-school creative practices into school. The room was a popular place at the end of the school day. The sound of needles scratching vinyl always drew a crowd. Within this space, Gil had the opportunity to observe other turntablists at work, to share his playing with others, to talk about turntablism as art and craft, and to use his skills to think about and comment on his own life experiences.

This small room off of the jazz room had several tables of equipment. One held two turntables with a mixer between them. A sampler and drum machine faced the turntables. There was also a four-track machine and tape recorder. Facing all of this equipment was an electronic keyboard. All of this material rested on top of an old Persian rug. A mic stand stood at the ready to the right of the four-track machine. The rest of the room was filled with a worn Victorian-style couch, a baby grand piano, and a fairly new computer with laser printer. Bookshelves, haphazardly stocked with all kinds of records and sheet music, lined the walls. Posters hung on these walls. Two advertised the movie *Goodfellas*; one *The Godfather*. Others included a *Superfly* movie poster, a poster of Bob Marley smoking a large joint, a poster of Tupac Shakur, and one black-light print of two people standing on a mountain with their arms upraised.

Del, a senior and mentor for Gil, sat behind the table that held his turntables. He was rapping to a beat, half to himself. When Del saw us, he took the headphones off his ears, rested them around his neck, and asked, "What's up?" Gil walked over to him, shook his hand, and introduced me. Del nodded at me. He then asked, "You want to listen to the intro to the album?" Gil nodded, "Definitely."

Del turned around to the DAT player and put in the tape. The intro blasted an aural collage of phrases from recent rap albums out of the speaker to the side of the turntables: *My sound surrounds you like racism. You feel it all around you.* The three of us stood and nodded to the beat, made sounds of agreement when we recognized particular phrases or rappers: *I'm trying to catch my people in all different stages, all different phases.* No phrase was repeated: *If knowledge is the key then show me the lock.* Each blended seamlessly into the next. At the end of the intro, which was about two minutes in length, both Gil and I said, "Damn." Del smiled. I asked, "How long did it take to put that together." Del sighed, "Over eight hours."

Del checked the clock and realized that he had to go. Gil pointed to his turntables, "Can I spin for a while?" Del said, "Sure, just take care of my babies and put away any albums you use." On the way out the door, he added, "And yo, don't let anyone else mess with them, OK?" Gil put the headphones on, "Promise." With that, Del left. Gil told me that this was usually what he did: went up to this room and played for hours before catching up with his friends at around six.

As Gil warmed up, by scratching various phrases on two albums that he found in the stack of vinyl on the floor, we talked about the ubiquity of turntablism in the media. I sat on the couch and asked, "You ever see that Zima ad where that dude is spinning at a party so intensely that the records on the decks melt?" At this point in the ad, the turntablist picks up a Zima that miraculously cools everything off, and he is able to get back to spinning records. Gil winced, "That ad's corny: corny because Zima is corny and because Zima has nothing to do with hip hop." He added, "Zima's not advertising with turntablism because they care about hip hop. They're just out to make money." Gil, like Sam, felt strongly that playing on his turntables was in part a political act. Honing his craft helped sustain hip hop as a cultural form that avoided commodification. The commercial, on the other hand, was only capitalizing on the rising popularity of the art form, with no recognition of its roots and cultural significance. Through ads such as this, turntablism ran the risk of being merely a product.

About a half-hour into spinning, he looked up from the turntables and said, "Guess I'm not going to practice." I asked him what he meant. Gil said, "I was supposed to go to track practice." The conference championships were this weekend, and the team was traveling to the track to check it out. Gil did not seem too concerned about missing what sounded like a fairly important practice. I asked, "You want to run and catch the bus?" He shrugged, "Nah," and went back to the turntables.

A few minutes later, three long-haired eighth-grade boys came in and lounged on the couch to listen to Gil play. One of them leaned against the table, "Can I spin? Gil? Gil? Gil?" Gil smirked and shook his head no. With this audience, Gil accentuated the physicality of a turntablist. He put the headphones on and rested them on his temples when he was not using them. When checking for a phrase on a record, he would hold one earphone to his ear with his shoulder. At one point, the eighth-grader who wanted to use the turntables said half-sarcastically, "Gil! I love you!" as Gil played. He smiled.

Students would drift in and out of the space, sometimes staying for only a few minutes, other times hanging out for an hour or so. When the eighth-graders eventually left, two seniors entered the room and flopped down onto the couch. Gil was experimenting with several albums that he had recently acquired. The first one was entitled Mr. Noisy, a children's novelty record that contained mini morality plays. He sampled phrases such as "must try harder" and "the police." He played a break beat behind what he scratched, meaning that he manipulated one of the records on the turntables to maintain a consistent beat as he scratched phrases on the other album. Gil looked over at me while experimenting with the beat he found: "Sounds like a car chase." It was subversive. He smiled, "Runnin,'" like evading the law. The seniors nodded in agreement. Other students drifted in while he played. They sat down on the sofa and nodded to this beat. Sometimes they would laugh at phrases Gil selected to scratch. Other times they would walk over to the table and watch Gil spin.

In the midst of this activity, Gil and I, and the two seniors who had come in earlier, talked about the ability of the turntablist to, in the words of one of the seniors, "tell a new story out of one that already exists." For example, Gil experimented with the soundtrack to The Rescuers, a children's movie from the 1970s about two mice that rescue an orphaned girl from an abusive woman, and scratched certain phrases that created a completely different story from the original, particularly with the break beat behind it.

Later, I asked the two seniors and Gil, "Why are the samples that you pick so interesting when you take them out of context?" This came up while Gil spun the soundtrack to Raiders of the Lost Ark. While experimenting with various voices and sounds on the album, Gil found the sound of a gunshot. Through scratching this sound, he transformed the gunshot into something different—a drum beat. Through the improvisational freedom of reappropriating this sound, Gil took a dominant discourse (gunshot as violent act) and invested it with his own particular inflection (gunshot as rhythm). One senior suggested, "It's the timing of the phrases." The art of phrasing to him was the element of surprise, catching the listener off-guard with a quirky or familiar pop culture reference or found sound. The other senior added, "You got to be able to kinda recognize where the sample's coming from or from what kind of music." The comfort of the familiar perhaps makes it possible for the listener to suspend his or her disbelief and create an alternative reality of sorts. The pleasure is in recognizing the familiar sound, voice, passage, or beat juxtaposed with another sound, voice, passage, or beat from a disparate source. For example, at one point, Gil scratched the phrase "Sunday school," playing it over and over again. By taking this easily recognized idea in the form of a phrase out of context and placing it within the context of that music room at that moment in time, Gil essentially made the familiar strange. He suggested, "Sampling's a lot like wearing a *Sesame Street* T-shirt to high school. You're fucking around with what's expected of you."

In considering the applicability to pedagogy of Gil's craft as illustrated within this vignette, there are several points I wish to make. First, the kind of work that Gil enjoys doing on his own time is highly experimental, and it involves working to create something original. Second, there is also a subversive quality to it: the recognition that the composition challenges normative behavior or language use contributes to the desire to practice and play for others. Third, notice too that the practice of being a turntablist at times involves playing in a semipublic space, where people can see you practicing/performing. This semi-public space makes possible the occasional conversation that arises out of the work, a pause either to think about what has been playing or to consider what the most recent composition means. Fourth, work within this realm involves others coming up and looking closely at what Gil is doing, not necessarily to judge him, but instead to watch him work: to see the way he uses his hands, to understand the effect that he is making, and to check to see the album he decided to play. Finally, the everyday practice of a turntablist involves working in spaces where many things are happening at once. People are listening, watching, talking to each other and the turntablist, and flowing in and out of the space. It is this multiplicity that contributes to the vitality of the creative practice.

Toward the end, once the seniors left, just Gil and I remained, with the hum of the amps in the background. Gil said he wanted to play a song for me. "Have you heard 'E Pluribus Unum' by The Last Poets?" He pulled the vinyl out from the record jacket. I told him that I had. Gil smiled and placed it gently on the platter of the left turntable. He placed the needle on the outer edge of the record. The popping and hissing of a well-worn record filled the room.

At the time, as we sat and listened to this song together, the anger and frustration of the lyrics did not register with me nearly as powerfully as they do now, looking at this song on the page. In the midst of listening to the song, I was swept away by the raw and minimal beat. I "heard" the lyrics, but not as deeply as I think Gil wanted me to. When the song ended, Gil said only that he "agreed" with a lot of what they said and proceeded to put away the albums, much like someone would reshelve books in a library. I was struck by the image of Gil putting the records away and did not ask him to explain what he meant by agreeing with the song.

Reading the lyrics now, and hearing the beat only faintly in my head, I think I understand more clearly why Gil wanted to play me that song, at that particular time, in that particular place. I hear the way the song resonated with Gil, how it had a context beyond being just an interesting piece of music. Finally, I see how the turntable can be a place for Gil to be self-reflective and construct an interpretation of his current life situation through an important piece of hip hop history.

The Last Poets brutally deconstruct the dollar bill, showing how money has corrupted those in power and how those in power—white men—have oppressed African Americans. Not a particularly new idea now, but the message of the song—originally recorded in 1972—is fresh to me because of the way they deconstruct the text and images on the dollar bill. The Last Poets take each image, each word, and explain its significance and culpability in the history of oppression in America: *so the people don't get any in the land of the plenty / because E PLURIBUS UNUM means One Out of Many* (all lyrics taken from Lyrics2, 2006). What is perhaps the most powerful and lasting image of this song for me is the way in which The Last Poets show how racism is ingrained, even printed, in our society. The way money is used can be oppressive, they argue, but what is even more sinister is how images and text can be used to weave racism into the infrastructure of society: *Then there's the pyramid that stands by itself / created by Black people's knowledge and wealth / and over the pyramid hangs the devil's eye / that stole from the truth and created the lie.*

Back to that day, in the music room, listening to the song. *Racism and greed keep the people in need / from getting what's rightfully theirs.* The lyrics of this diatribe against racial and economic injustice poured out of the speakers and slid underneath the door into the second-story hallway of the auditorium, which is part of the campus of an upper-middle-class, predominately white private institution. *Seclorum is a word that means to take from another / knowledge, wisdom and understanding stolen from the brother.* By the time the lyrics made their way down to the end of the hall, they were probably faint, the message indecipherable to a group of students who may have been sitting on the faded Oriental rug. *And so the power is in the hand of the ruling classes.* However, through Gil's act of playing the song in this room, the lyrics were now a part of this institution. I interpret Gil's playing of this song as an acknowledgment of the subtle and not so subtle racism that he experienced at this school.

Gil came across this song *through* his work as a turntablist. He heard about The Last Poets through other hip hop that he listened to as well as through other turntablists talking about the music that influenced them or that they used. He read about them in liner notes on albums in his collection. Gil learned through his practice that they are an important part of the lineage of hip hop. By playing them, Gil signified his knowledge of their significance and in a way authenticated that he *was* a turntablist. He also connected his current life situation with the life experience of his hip hop "ancestry."

About a year before we sat in that space off from the music room, listening to "E Pluribus Unum," Gil and I had worked on a different research project. In this project, Gil and I explored the concept of inscribed and chosen identities in his high school. In the process of working on this project, Gil shared with me that there were times when he felt he needed to prove himself academically as a young black man in a predominately white school. As a way of explaining this feeling, he sent me this e-mail:

> I always feel the need to prove myself…I was in the bathroom…Chris walks in, and says hi. He ok so far. Then out of the clear blue sky he says "All of the black teachers in this school were hired because they are black." Now I know that Chris is something of a mathematical genius, but his social skills are horrible…I don't want to prove to him that they are qualified, because its not so much what he said, but what it revealed about what he is thinking…One time I said to Dan [a friend of Gil's] "I think I might have gotten a 100 on the lit test." Right away two guys come over and ask me if I want to bet. They both bet $5, and even though I stay away from gambling, I took their money. Now if that's not having to prove myself I don't know what is.

Gil jumps to a conclusion in this story that the two guys who questioned whether he aced the test were in fact implying that because Gil was black, he could not possibly have scored that high. They could have just been teasing him like they would any other student or friend, regardless of his/her race. However, Gil's response to their taunt is indicative of the social climate in which we live. It is powerful and quite frustrating to think that regardless of the two students' motives, in the back of Gil's mind was the possibility that they were being discriminatory, and because of that, he had to respond defensively to prove his worth or intelligence.

Imagine for a moment the two incidents that Gil mentions in the e-mail above somehow being in that room on the day when Gil played "E Pluribus Unum" for me on that turntable. Perhaps they were in his head when he put down the needle. The song speaks to the discrimination and oppression present in those two stories. It makes me think of the money that changed hands in the story that Gil told in the e-mail. As in the song, money in Gil's story was used as a vehicle for forcing Gil to prove that what he said was true. The money was a mechanism for placing the two white students in a position of power over Gil. Through laying down five dollars each, they were in the position of being able to judge whether Gil was right. I would argue that Gil played "E Pluribus Unum" in part to tell the story of incidents such as this where issues of race, class, and power put Gil in the position of constantly negotiating his identity. It was an act of witness in a way. Playing the song provided Gil a way of articulating feelings, thoughts, and ideas that were swirling around in his head at the time. The turntable concretized those feelings, thoughts, and ideas.

Gil worked on the turntables for a good three hours on that day after school. In that time, he performed his skills on the turntables to those who came in. Instead of a formal performance, it was a series of mini/in-process performances where Gil tried out new moves to see the reaction he would get. He also reflected with other turntablists in the room about his practice, exploring with them why he does what he does, what hip hop means to him, and why turntablism intrigues people. Finally, Gil used his turntables to make connections between certain pieces of music and his own life. On the way out I asked him whether spending that much time in the room was normal, and he said, "Definitely. One time my mom got so pissed at me because I was here until, like, 7:30."

Gil on the Decks at Home: Turntablist as Historian

Gil did not practice only at school. His primary place to practice was in his room at home, where he kept his equipment and records. When I would show up at Gil's house to watch him spin, he would greet me at the front door and ask whether I wanted to see what he had been working on on his turntables. We would then jog up the flight of stairs to his bedroom.

The first thing that inevitably grabbed my attention upon entering Gil's room was his enormous queen-size bed. It took up most of the room, the wooden headboard occupying the space between the two windows that looked out on to the street. Listening to Gil play, I often started off sitting on the edge of the wooden footboard of this bed until it became far too uncomfortable and I would end up sitting on the plush tan carpet.

Across from the footboard of his bed were Gil's turntables and mixer. They sat in his black *coffin*—the term used for the long, rectangular carrying case needed to lug around a turntablist's equipment—on top of his white chest of drawers. Gil said it was the perfect height for him. To the right of his turntables were his cardboard boxes of records: four in all. The records that he most often used when he spun stood stacked on their edges either directly to the left of his feet as he played or behind the mixer. To the left of his turntables was a wardrobe, on top of which sat his TV. Often, the TV was on when he played. Around the room were objects that represented his other interests. I got the sense that his room was a collage of many years of life and that some objects may have clashed with the way Gil thought of himself in the present. For example, there was the computer drawing of a human figure holding a guitar, resembling the symbol used to delineate the men's restroom from the women's. A pair of stilts leaned against a slim floor-to-ceiling bookshelf. Next to these stilts was his hockey stick. "I used to play when I was in sixth grade," Gil told me. His paintball gun hung over his bed, and an army helmet sat on one of the shelves of the bookshelf.

Next to his bed hung a corkboard with one small article from *Jive* magazine thumb-tacked to the bottom:

DJs: Perhaps the easiest parallel one can draw between the South Bronx mixing OGs and their effect on future generations is the legacy of the 1940s and '50s blues legends on the rock guitar gods of the 1960s and '70s. Just as the instrumental and compositional creativity of modern rock predecessors like Chuck Berry, Bo Diddley, and Muddy Waters inspired the amplified fretwork frenetics of Jimi Hendrix, Eric Clapton, and Jimmy Page (subsequently causing kids worldwide to pick up guitars), so too did DJ Kool Herc, Afrika Bambaataa, Grand Wizard Theodore, and Grandmaster Flash inspire the first wave of post-old school pyro-techno-theatrical phenoms: DJs Scratch, Cash Money, Jazzy Jeff, and Aladdin.

On one particular day, Gil wanted to show me some work he had been doing with two albums of Martin Luther King Jr. and Malcolm X speeches. A friend from school had loaned him the albums a few days before. He placed one album on each of the turntables, turned on the mixer, placed the headphones over his ears, and dropped the right turntable needle on the revolving record. Malcolm X's voice boomed out of the speaker:

Malcolm X:...are waking up and they are gaining a new political consciousness, becoming politically mature, and as they develop this political maturity, they are able to see the recent trends in these political elections. They see that whites are so evenly divided that every time they vote, the racist polls have to go back and count the votes all over again...In fact I think we would be fooling ourselves if we had an audience this large and didn't realize that there were some enemies in it.

Gil started scratching the phrase "in it" from the Malcolm X speech and then allowed it to continue playing: *This afternoon we want to talk about the ballot or the bullet.* Gil then sampled and scratched "bullet" over and over again. At this point in his playing, I asked Gil what interested him about these two albums: "Well, like, it relates to today. I'll show you specifically with me and [my school] how it relates."

The turntable with Malcolm X continued to spin; however, with the cross-fader of the mixer moved over to the left, no sound came out of the speaker. Gil then placed the Martin Luther King album on the left turntable. He placed the needle on the album and flicked the cross-fader to the right again; Malcolm X's voice bellowed, *Well, this country is a hypocrite. They try to make you think they set you free by calling you a second-class citizen. No, you nothing but a twentieth century slave.* Gil flicked the cross-fader to the left, and Martin Luther King spoke: *This nation is wrong because it is nothing but a new form of slavery.*

Gil started juggling the phrases "You nothing but a twentieth century slave" from Malcolm X and "This nation is wrong" from Martin Luther King Jr. By juggling, I mean that he went back and forth between these two phrases, sometimes allowing the whole phrase to play before he spliced the other in, sometimes playing only bits and pieces of each. Sometimes, he played both at the same time, so that the voices overlapped or lay on top of one another. I asked him why he made the choice to juggle these two phrases:

The contrast between what they are saying and the similarities...They are talking about two different things. He is talking about colonization with the second-class citizenship [referring to Malcolm X]. And he is talking about segregation [referring to Martin Luther King Jr.] and they are sort of the same thing but they are kind of different names for it. They kind of look at it from a different point of view...segregation is sort of a name that is sort of geared toward the Sixties and the Civil Rights Movement. And second-class citizenship and colonization sort of like general and sort of like looking at history in general...so they are both saying that it is basically slavery. He's saying the new form of slavery or twentieth-century slavery [referring to Malcolm X] and he is saying new form of slavery [referring to King]. That is pretty good contrast and similarity.

The act of sampling from these speeches for Gil was not simply one of indiscriminately dropping the needle. Part of his personal work was hours of listening to the albums until he knew them inside and out. Thus, on the day he showed me this work, he constructed a spontaneous message out of bits of text he knew by heart, much like the improvisational playing of a jazz guitarist. Gil never "performed" this piece. In other words, he did not play it for a larger audience than me. However, this space served as more than a time to hone his technical skills as a turntablist. Through this space and time, Gil drew from other sources and manipulated messages to construct his own meaning. In this case, he also used his turntables to analyze a historic event—the civil rights movement—as well as the different connotations of the term "slavery" from the perspective of two of its leaders. Through playing these voices on his turntables, remixing them the way that he did, he was able to hear the rhetorical differences in the way Malcolm X and Martin Luther King Jr. understood the climate of racial injustice in the 1960s.

It is useful to compare Gil's work with the kind of writing work that many teachers expect of their students. In this case, the two ways of making meaning are surprisingly similar. Gil worked and learned the way we wish all of our students would when they write. For one, Gil conducted research. He first went *grave robbing*: the DJ's expression for finding albums to use in compositions. This search involved hours at various new and used record stores and yard sales, as well as trading albums with friends and fellow turntablists. Then Gil spent several more hours, over a period of days, listening to these albums, first all of the way through to get "the message," and then in bits and pieces, experimenting with particular scratches and phrases; Gil deconstructed the vinyl texts. A part of understanding the messages of the albums also entailed conversations with Sam. He would document these conversations in a notebook he carried in his pocket. This notebook also contained ideas for turntable pieces, lists of records he wanted to obtain, and names and contact information of people associated with turntablism. After finding the phrases he liked, he would begin putting the new text together. To construct this new text, or new argument, Gil cited from other people's work—citing, in this case, the phrases that he sampled from the records. This whole practice created a way for Gil to make what he "read" personally meaningful to him.

After Gil played his piece, he told me that he had read the Malcolm X speech that he was manipulating in his English class that semester. But the act of reading the speech did not interest him nearly as much as playing it on his turntables:

> I think the idea of having a voice played of someone who's dead is really cool...Because it kind of brings them back to life, and not many things have that power. I actually feel that he is talking. I feel that he is alive when I hear the voice. We read the script of the speech in Lit class, the one where he's like, "I would be mistaken if we had a turnout this big and there weren't some enemies in here." And it was really cool to read that, but I felt like I was reading the speech of a dead guy...but when I play it on a record, it's almost like he's not here but he's over there (pointing to the corner of his room).

Through his turntables, the words of Malcolm X and Martin Luther King Jr. were no longer disembodied or "embalmed speech," to use Denzin's (1997) term. Rather, Gil had the power to resurrect their voices *and* embody their messages in the life he lived. In the quotation above, and through his process of work, Gil speaks to a critical characteristic of an effective teacher: the ability to work with youth to find ways to make the texts with which they interact feel like they are "not here, but…[right] over there" within arm's reach, malleable, and connected to their lives in relevant ways.

The amount of time and effort that Gil devotes to his creative practice is considerable, the envy of any teacher I would think. The interesting thing to me is that it is not only the subject that stimulates Gil to work long hours on his creative practice. It is also the way in which he gets to work, the *craft* of his creative practice, that makes him stay up all hours on the turntables. In fact, the physicality of the work, and the freedom he has in determining when he wants to do it, influence the meanings that Gil makes in and through it.

To return to my comparison between traditional methods of teaching English and Gil's ways of working, my experience in schools has shown me that often writing is taught as a linear skill. The writing process is presented as brainstorming, prewriting, first draft, sharing, editing, final draft, and publishing. Writing assignments are presented axiomatically as well. In other words, students are to work on one piece of writing at a time, finish that piece of writing, and then move on to the next piece, often with little to no connection between the two other than the fact that both pieces of writing involve commenting on something that they have read. This process seems artificial and manufactured in light of the ways in which Gil works. In the remainder of the chapter, I offer ways for teachers to develop complex understandings of how youth like Gil work and learn on their own terms as a means to move beyond these artificially constructed learning environments and into classrooms that take advantage of the skill and sophistication that students like Gil bring to school.

How Can Gil's Way of Working Inform and Influence Pedagogy?

Because of my background as a teacher and my current work as a teacher educator, I am committed to forging linkages between my research and the ways in which teachers work and learn with students in classrooms. I make this commitment recognizing the real constraints that standardized tests, core curricula, class size, uneven distribution of funding, and other state and district mandates place on curriculum and pedagogy. However, I choose to believe that these constraints need not get in the way of allowing students to work and learn on their own terms. I say this because core curricula and other mandates more often than not merely emphasize which skills and concepts need to be developed within a certain time frame. While it may be difficult to cover those skills and concepts within the time allotted, this does not prohibit a teacher from teaching those skills and concepts through the ways in which youth work in their everyday lives. In other words, the curriculum is not the issue here; it is the way in which students and teachers interact with the curriculum that needs reexamination.

This idea of having the way youth work inform the practice of teaching is not new. In fact, John Dewey argued for this approach to teaching and learning early in the twentieth century. More recently, scholars such as Shirley Brice Heath, Donna Alvermann, Greg Dimitriadis, and Elizabeth Moje have explored this idea from various perspectives.

Heath (1997, 1999) shows how teenagers organize their personal time: they "take up mixed patterns of learning, working, and [take] seriously their leisure time" (p. 2). Often adults construe this work and learning as play. Heath argues that this "work" of teens is filled with risk and challenges and in many ways mirrors the work of adulthood. She describes how youth are involved in creating "developmental assets" to better themselves and their community (1999, p. 3). Heath argues, like Street and

Barton and Hamilton, that "youth draw upon multiple symbol systems, engage several versions of themselves depending on circumstances, and call on multiple discourses according to need, motivation, and domains" (1997, p. 120).

Educational research that seeks to understand youth perspectives on work and learning also provides us with useful perspectives on how youth go about interpreting pop cultural forms. Alvermann (2003), for example, researches the way youth interpret the culture of rap and rap songs through observing them "in the action" of interpreting this art form. For instance, through his interest in the Goodie Mob, Ned, a fourteen-year-old African American eighth-grader, develops strategies for "acquiring facts" about the group. Alvermann also shows how he gains "independence" in pursuing information about the group. She writes of "Ned's command of several multiple and overlapping literacies gleaned through personal, familial, and social interactions both in and out of school that afforded him the opportunity to act like—and, just as important, to be recognized as—a competent and literate person."

Dimitriadis (2001) has done interesting work on how African American youth "mobilize" forms of popular culture to construct understandings of where they live, of generational identity, and of iconic rappers. Moje (2002) argues that the way to acknowledge "unsanctioned" forms of literacy such as graffiti in the classroom is to recognize their complexity and power. In addition, she recommends that teachers work with youth who are engaged in these practices to develop a critical understanding of why the practices are marginalized. She writes, "As educators, we need to work with youth to learn how the language and literacy practices they value might be used productively in other contexts to challenge dominant assumptions about literacy and social practice" (p. 48). Moje's suggestion recognizes the importance of the practice involved in these creative forms. In addition, she speaks to making connections between the seemingly disconnected phenomena of youth cultural forms and school learning.

This kind of research is extremely helpful in terms of understanding how youth make meaning with popular culture products that often have been produced by people other than the youth themselves or how youth-produced popular culture products could be used in classrooms. In this research, the cultural products of youth provide ways of expanding or exploding the literary canon in schools, for example. Novice and veteran teachers with whom I work are intrigued by the idea that they should be integrating songs by the Goodie Mob and Tupac Shakur into their units on poetry. It is not a difficult leap for them to see how their students could be reading the rap of the Goodie Mob or Tupac Shakur alongside *The Scarlet Letter*, for example. This orientation still positions books and other forms of literature as objects to be studied by students, not written by them, so it fits nicely with the way learning looks in traditional classrooms. What these teachers have a difficult time understanding is how the way a young rapper works, for example, could influence how youth do learning in their classrooms. Teachers with whom I work struggle with conceptualizing how the ways youth "draw upon multiple symbol systems, engage several versions of themselves depending on circumstances, and call on multiple discourses according to need, motivation, and domains" could alter the way they teach in a classroom setting.

Lave and Wenger (1991) argue that "there is a difference between talking *about* a practice from outside and talking *within* it" (p. 107). Teachers often make youth culture "work" in their classrooms by designing units of study around the products of the practice: graffiti, rap, zines, and so on. This pedagogical approach talks *about* the practice because it positions the teacher and students as outside observers of the cultural form, gleaning meaning from studying it rather than constructing meaning about the cultural form through *doing* it. Teachers who design these kinds of units are interested in and influenced by popular culture. They value popular culture as high art and potentially part of the "canon." For example, they believe that Tupac Shakur and Bob Dylan have a place in poetry. These teachers help their students to see that they can view anything as a source of learning. Placing popular culture at the center of the curriculum legitimates it and allows students to speak about their own experiences within the classroom.

Nevertheless, youth do not necessarily want their cultural practices to be legitimated or co-opted by schools. In fact, adult sanctioning of youth culture may ironically delegitimate it as an interesting world of experience. Youth might see through this practice as trying to trick them into learning: an attempt to motivate them to participate. If the teacher's interest in the practice is merely as a tool of motivation, students will read this as a dismissal of their interests, rather than as a "cool" way to learn. Also, not everyone is "into" turntablism, and not everybody needs to be into turntablism. If teachers head down this road, they could be setting up all sorts of obstacles for certain students to get involved with whatever it is that they are exploring in the classroom. Finally, making something a subject of study can "fix it" in such a way that it loses its vitality. In the same way that a Shakespearean play can be boring to read as opposed to *acted*, turntablism could be boring if it is something to study rather than something *lived*.

We need to think of other ways of informing pedagogy through youth creative practices. We need to look at the ways in which youth engage *in* the practices—how they do what they do—and have those habits of mind and body influence the way we design learning environments in classrooms.

Wenger (1998) writes that "what we think about learning influences where we recognize learning, as well as what we do when we decide that we must do something about it—as individuals, as communities, and as organizations" (p. 9). How can teachers teach in ways that capitalize on the need youth feel to develop communities of practice, to perform their work, to improvise, to self-reflect, and to assess work that they are committed to? Teachers can open their practice to these forms of youth work in two interconnected ways: as an ethnographer in her/his classroom and then as a conscious designer of the learning experience.

Teacher as Ethnographer

One way to get at answers to the questions above is through developing an ethnographic understanding of how youth make meaning in their own lives (Ben-Yosef, 2003; Dimitriadis, 2001; Goswami & Stillman, 1987; Schultz, 2003; Sitton, 1980). Ethnographers approach their phenomena realizing that they know little and that the people who are part of the phenomena, the "natives," know a lot (Gallas, 1994). With this realization, ethnographers position themselves as the learners and the people who are part of the phenomena as the teachers. When we make this role recognition analogous to teaching, it is our job as teachers to figure out how our students are mathematicians, historians, writers, and scientists *in their lives*, instead of assuming that they are not or that they need to be taught how to be. Therefore, a teacher who is influenced by ethnographic practices would no longer look at Gil's interest in turntablism as simply a product. Instead, the teacher would recognize that he is involved in a practice—a craft, a habit of mind and body—that enables him to do the work. From a curriculum standpoint we would call this "experience" (Dewey, 1997). The teacher would realize that it is part of her or his job to understand the how and why of the practice because it is one of the ways in which Gil makes meaning in the world. A teacher who takes an ethnographic stance would find ways to understand the depth and complexity of Gil's turntablism. She would work to see how Gil is self-reflective, experimental, and analytic in the way that he works on his own terms. She would come to know the community of practice Gil keeps to be able to do his work. She would honor that sophistication through the way she teaches.

Understanding youth cultural practices as an ethnographer requires that we look at youth as inherently creative problem solvers, problem posers, solution finders, and so on. The teacher enters her room assuming that her students are already some form of mathematician, scientist, poet, architect. Karen Gallas (1994) writes that she "suspend[s] [her] disbelief as a teacher and [leaves her] judgment in abeyance in service of a child's development" (p. 96). She continues, "Rather than my 'teaching'…what science [is], we [struggle] together to understand [our] changing picture of science" (p. 96).

Edward Said (1996) would describe Karen Gallas as a "professional amateur," someone who does not limit herself through special knowledge of a discipline. Experts, Said contrasts, only feel comfortable approaching problems, issues, ideas, through their rarefied knowledge. He warns that specialization, as opposed to competence, can result in the "sacrifice of one's general culture to a set of authorities and canonical ideas" (p. 76). He adds:

> Specialization means losing sight of the raw effort of constructing either art or knowledge; as a result you cannot view knowledge and art as choices and decisions, commitments and alignments, but only in terms of impersonal theories or methodologies.…In the end…you become tame and accepting of whatever the so-called leaders in the field will allow. Specialization also kills your sense of excitement and discovery…giving up to specialization is, I have always felt, laziness, so you end up doing what others tell you, because that is your specialty after all. (p. 77)

When people present an expert with a problem that grows out of their creative practice, the expert often feels that she or he cannot even discuss it because it is beyond the purview of her or his expertise. What the expert knows has nothing to do with the problem. Teachers often think of themselves or approach their subject as experts or specialists. For example, a math teacher may see her job as teaching students how to factor polynomials and therefore may not afford the time to link mathematics with presidential elections or even be able to entertain a provocative tangent related to everyday life. Said suggests that teachers who view themselves as specialists are not able to see the "raw effort" of work and learning. They are blind to the practice—the daily habits of mind and body—that lead to the construction of knowledge. Instead, they focus on the end result—the knowledge itself. This blindness may also lead to a lack of genuine interest or "excitement," to use Said's term, regarding understanding the world around us. Specialization makes it difficult for teachers to believe that youth are creatively intelligent human beings. It narrows a teacher's sense of what or who a mathematician, scientist, writer, historian can be and makes it difficult to connect turntablism, for example, to any of these disciplines.

On the other hand, teachers who view themselves as professional amateurs pounce on these opportunities to think about things differently and learn from others. Said defines amateurism as "an activity that is fueled by care and affection rather than by profit and selfish, narrow specialization" (p. 82). Teachers as professional amateurs relish the chance to get involved in conversations where they can take what they know and grow new understandings. They see their students as allies in a common project. They expect to learn from their students not just how to be a better teacher or how to understand fractions in a new way but also about the world in general. Said writes that teachers as professional amateurs "can enter and transform the merely professional routine most of us go through into something much more lively and radical; instead of doing what one is supposed to do one can ask why one does it, who benefits from it, how can it reconnect with a personal project and original thoughts" (p. 83). Teachers who see themselves as professional amateurs value a student's experiences in creative practices as resources for their own understandings of academic subject knowledge in particular and the world more broadly.

Gil, like so many youth, is a professional amateur as well. What makes him a professional amateur is the range and variety of things that he does that somehow influence how he embodies a turntablist. For example, Gil reads widely and disparately. He plays guitar in his church band. He raps, break dances, and views films. He writes music and listens to music. Gil redesigns his car. He does not pursue these experiences solely because of his interest in turntablism. Nevertheless, they inform and influence what and how he decides to work on his turntables. Like Gallas, teachers who understand youth work as a craft provide a space where students can see for themselves that the skills and concepts they are developing within their creative practices are assets in the classroom. All of Gil's varied experiences can be used in the classroom to do the work of the class. Students as professional amateurs see their craft as informing and influencing the way they engage in the work of the class. They see academic disciplines and their creative practices as equal resources for their work. Youth already do this kind of work. For example, Gil used his skill as a turntablist to explore more deeply and thus make more relevant the class discussions on Malcolm X through manipulating one of Malcolm X's speeches on his turntables.

As teachers, it is difficult for us to see the classroom as a space to encourage these ways of working. Heath writes:

> Schools face imposing constraints of structure, disposition, resources and externally imposed guidelines for curricula and outcomes...teachers have to neutralize their methods and materials to satisfy a constituency of wide-ranging interests....The constraints with which schools must wrestle and within which they must define practice make deep inroads into educators' autonomy, especially in areas most central to authentic curricula. (p. 485)

This "constituency of wide-ranging interests" often gets appeased by viewing teaching as always trying to find something to do with students instead of designing learning experiences that encourage enduring understandings of essential conceptual ideas. Wiggins and McTighe (2005) describe this way of teaching as "engaging experiences that lead only accidentally, if at all, to insight or achievement" (p. 16). Another problem with this practice is that the search for the best activities is never over, and teachers are always hunting for more ideas to fill time. Jean Lave (1997) captures this perpetual crisis of teaching by comparing a curriculum that supports the creative practices of youth with a curriculum that delineates what that practice must be:

> The problem is that any curriculum intended to be a specification of practice, rather than an arrangement of opportunities for practice (for fashioning and resolving ownable dilemmas) is bound to result in the teaching of a misanalysis of practice...and the learning of still another. At best it can only induce a new and exotic kind of practice....In the settings for which it is intended (in everyday transactions), it will appear out of order and will not in fact reproduce "good" practice. (p. 32)

Lave cautions us that the focus in classrooms should not be *about* practice, meaning an emphasis on learning how to do something out of the context of doing it. Instead, teachers should spend their pedagogical energy on designing experiences where students can learn through doing. Lave calls these experiences "ownable dilemmas." These are challenges, problems, obstacles that students want to take on, see the purpose in solving, and feel the need to overcome. A curriculum where youth utilize skills and conceptual knowledge developed through creative practices is designed around ownable dilemmas, for that is exactly the way in which Gil engages in his creative practice on his own terms. His daily practice places him in perplexing, confusing, or challenging moments where he must do more work to move forward in his art form. This orientation to work and learning is more sustainable than the kind of curriculum that focuses on covering material or is built from a collection of one-off activities. Instead, teachers design learning environments that encourage a way of being in the classroom, as opposed to a collection of methods of teaching.

Implementing this sort of curriculum gives teachers a "solution" to the problem of constantly trying to find one day, one month, or one hour of something to do in the classroom. Lemke (1997) reminds us that "practices are not just performances, not just behaviors, not just material processes or operations, but meaningful actions, actions that have relations of meaning to one another in terms of some cultural system" (p. 43). There is value in building a "common culture" of "professional amateurs" in our classrooms to enable our students to "learn not just what and how to perform, but also what the performance means" (p. 43). It is in this spirit that we can build with our students a "community of classroom practice" through the conception of creative practice—youth work—as craft.

Classroom as Youth Space

While it is important to develop a sense of the culture of work of one's students, it is just as important to translate that understanding into how one designs the learning experience. In fact, these two perspectives go hand in hand, with the ethnographic stance informing how one goes about designing a learning experience. In the case of classroom as youth space, I mean that informed by an ethnographic understanding of her students, the teacher now needs to open up space in the classroom for youth such as Gil to utilize the technical skills and conceptual knowledge acquired through their creative practices. She can do this in several ways: by allowing for multiple forms of performance, by embracing idiosyncratic ways of working, and by working alongside her students.

Multiple Forms of Performance

Performance often has a narrow definition in classrooms. In a classroom context, performance often means displaying some kind of product at the end of a unit. Performance is used as a sign of the end of learning a concept or set of skills: the culmination of several weeks of work. It could be a "public" reading involving students sharing their writing in front of the rest of the class. A performance could be a museum of artifacts produced through research students have done in a history class. The performance is polished and practiced. It is meant to be one's best effort. The performance is also a way for teachers to assess the work of their students. When the performance concludes, the class moves on to something else, and this something else is tied to curricular objectives that are often not connected at all to the learning that led up to that performance.

Gil's multidimensional use of performance in his turntablism pushes us to expand the ways in which we design performances in our classrooms. Many times, Gil developed a particular product out of snippets of ideas amassed over a period of time. In fact, Gil would purposefully perform works in progress designed in this way to bring his creative practice forward. Recall Gil's layering of the Malcolm X and Martin Luther King Jr. speeches. He wanted to perform for me what he had been working on, not as a final product but as a work in progress that, by performing, he could think about more critically. He performed this work in progress to open a space where we could talk about the issues introduced by the material.

In addition to the end-of-unit culminating performances, we need to offer more informal forms of performance where our students can try their work out, in mid-production, as Gil so often does. These informal performances serve a crucial purpose: they provide essential feedback from peers to determine where to go next or even whether it is worth proceeding with the project at all. They also open up avenues for critical conversation about the craft itself and the meaning of the products being constructed. These performances provide opportunities for discussing the ideas within the work. Freedom must be given to allow students to decide, after such performances, to abandon works and move on to other ideas that they are pursuing.

How would this look in the classroom? Imagine a teacher teaching a unit on short stories. The teacher decides to have her students write their own short stories. This teacher, informed and influenced by the creative practices of youth, would not only have a culminating performance at the end of the unit where students would pick their "best" short story to read aloud or display. She would implement weekly performances, informal readings for example, where her students could try out stories as works in progress to see where to take them next or whether to drop them entirely for another idea. After all, isn't this self-reflection and assessment what many writers do? They work on getting ideas down on paper and then share those rough ideas with others whom they trust. In fact, this is different from sharing a rough draft of a piece that needs polishing. Youth and adults involved in a creative practice see feedback throughout the process of developing an idea. We need to enact this kind of practice in our classes.

Gil also performs widely. During the research, Gil performed in the music room, in his own room, in a studio, in a record store, in his friend's house, and at parties. If we want to design learning environments where the learning has the potential to be personally meaningful and resonate with how youth learn in the world, we must provide our students the chance to perform in small and large ways outside of the confines of our classrooms or schools. This pedagogical move creates the possibility of our students identifying multiple audiences for their work. These different audiences can push our students' work in new directions. For example, if students are investigating how to improve the safety of a local intersection in a math class, they should not perform their findings only to a high-level official in city government. They must also meet with urban planners, transportation advocates, and pedestrian advocates while they are doing the project. At this time, students perform what they are learning not just to show what they know but also as a way of figuring out what needs to happen next.

Embracing Idiosyncratic Ways of Working

Gil has an idiosyncratic work process. He has a peculiar and individual way of making work meaningful to him. When you spend time with any youth you will find that they have their own personal ways of understanding the world around them and they have personalized ways of working to construct that understanding. These processes are certainly not axiomatic or linear. They do not follow the regimented work patterns of classrooms: one day to brainstorm ideas, another day to read and take notes, another day to write a rough draft, and so on, or study a topic for a prescribed amount of time and then take a test on it. Instead, Gil, like other youth involved in these kinds of practices, works in starts and spurts, sometimes dabbling, at other times working for many hours at a stretch. While at work, they experiment. They test out ideas by themselves and with members of their community of practice. They hone particular technical skills.

Gil told me that there were days when he came home from school and immediately got on his turntables. The next thing he knew he would look up at the clock and realize that he had been on them for six straight hours. By the end of the session, records would be strewn about the floor, evidence of intense work. Gil even rigged a cross-fader so that he could take it to bed with him and practice crabbing, a technique for moving the toggle switch of the cross-fader to create various effects as the record plays.

Another important characteristic of the work that Gil did was that when he came up against an insurmountable obstacle or was not satisfied with what he had done, he moved on. He may or may not have put the work away and come back to it at another time. This meant that Gil's work involved experimentation and partially completed projects. He had the freedom to determine when a project did not merit completion. For example, Gil used his notebook to scribble ideas for turntable pieces. Some of these ideas became compositions. Others did not. He also gave me several audiotapes of partially completed pieces. These starts and stops on their own may not seem to amount to much, but when put together they actually enabled Gil to bring other projects within his practice to completion.

This particular aspect of how youth work on their own terms can have direct implications in terms of the way we teach, for it turns upside down the idea that the goal in learning is the product. Gil shows us that the accumulation of attempts that lead up to an eventual turntable composition is where we should be focusing our pedagogical energy if we want youth to produce powerful and meaningful work in our classes.

The way we design learning spaces in schools needs to honor the idiosyncratic nature of real work. Instead of making everyone follow the same steps for a research paper, for example, teachers need to recognize everyone's personal way of exploring something by establishing a set of criteria that enable students to construct their own way of finding what it is they want to explore and how they want to explore it. These criteria should be shaped by listening to youth describe their ways of attacking a problem, exploring an issue, or developing an argument balanced by our understanding of the ways mathematicians, historians, writers, and scientists pursue their craft. In addition, teachers need to design ongoing conversations where teachers and students articulate to each other and themselves how they go about working. This form of work dialogue honors the ways youth are making meaning in their worlds and acknowledges that the classroom can be a place to put that understanding of practice to work as well.

Teachers Doing Work with Their Students

Teachers need to be working *with* their students. One thing that struck me about Gil's practice is that he surrounded himself with others who were engaged in the same or a similar practice. This meant that when they got together, they were all speaking from experience. Gil played with and watched Del and others work on the turntables. He hung out with seniors who were part of the hip hop scene in his school. He taped up articles about other turntablists in his room. These real and imagined communities of practice introduced new skills to be developed, books to read, movies to see, words to learn, places to go, and concepts to understand.

Too often in classrooms, work is assigned and the last thing that the teacher would ever consider doing is the work that her or his students are doing. School districts, schools, and teachers *package* learning in such a way that teachers would never want to do the work. It is boring, childish, contrived, and meaningless. This division-of-labor approach to learning contradicts the way youth, and I would argue adults outside of schools, do real work. Part of what makes Gil productive in his practices is the fact that his friends are actively engaged in the work as well. This egalitarian approach to the work provides a shared language in which the youth can communicate with one another and establishes a set of rituals and behaviors that are common to everyone. What keeps this community of practice together is a belief that the work they are doing is purposeful and meaningful as well as a sense that the work connects them to possibilities of meeting new people, exploring new places, and progressively getting better at what they do. Imagine if these qualities of work were the driving force behind curriculum.

Surprisingly, there is little writing to be found on this idea. Certainly, Dewey (1997) advocates for this kind of engaged pedagogy when he writes that "the very nature of the work done [is] a social enterprise in which all individuals have an opportunity to contribute and to which all feel a responsibility" (p. 56). This way of working resonates with people such as Kirby, Kirby, and Liner (2003), who suggest writing teachers are readers and writers "modeling the life of a literate person" (p. 10). Foxfire's Core Practices include "The work teachers and learners do together is infused from the beginning with learner choice, design, and revision….The role of the teacher is that of facilitator and collaborator" (Starnes, 1999, section 2, para. 1). Even with this work we have somehow lost this idea in middle and secondary schools for the most part. It is a rare classroom space where the teacher collaborates with the students. Put simply, teachers need to write with their students, do scientific experiments with their students, and research alongside their students. This way of being a teacher in the classroom goes beyond modeling how we would like students to be working and learning. Often times modeling in classrooms is used simply to show students what to do or how to do something. It does not stem from real work in which the teacher is engaged. Del and Sam modeled technical skills through their work on the turntables. Their modeling was a natural outgrowth of their practice. Doing work *with* students meant that teachers are personally interested in the work. The modeling, then, is done not just to show students what to do but actually to help the teacher continue the work as well. Teachers need to be engaged in the act of *learning* within their classroom. With that, teachers need to engage in conversations with their students around what it means to work, how they do it, and so on. This discourse is a fundamental part of how youth work in the everyday.

The classroom should be a space of mutual work. Instead of the traditional "detached spectatorship" where teachers observe and evaluate the learning of their students, we need to shift to a classroom space of actors—both students and teachers engaged in the challenges, frustrations, and benefits of real work (Rorty, 1998).

Conclusion

> To engage with our students as persons is to affirm our own incompleteness, our consciousness of spaces still to be explored, desires still to be tapped, possibilities still to be opened and pursued…We have to find out how to open such spheres, such spaces, where a better state of things can be imagined…I would like to think that this can happen in classrooms, in corridors, in schoolyards, in the streets around. (Greene, 1986, p. 29)

Throughout this chapter, I have been arguing that when educators investigate and acknowledge the creative practices of youth within their pedagogy, opportunities for authentic learning emerge: teachers tune their teaching practices more closely to the ways in which youth learn and make meaning in their everyday lives; they heed the clarion call of writers such as Maxine Greene who encourage educators to make the ways in which students work and learn in their everyday lives explicit in their teaching.

An ethnographic understanding of the ways in which youth perform, improvise, self-reflect, form communities of practice, and assess their work allows us to treat students as people with "desires still to be tapped, possibilities still to be opened and pursued"(Greene, 2003, p. 111). In classroom environments driven by prepackaged curricula or standardized testing, students are figured as finite, closed systems. These classrooms lack the open-ended fluidity of authentic, meaningful learning. They make it difficult or almost impossible for students and teachers to develop a shared sense of *how they can learn together*. In this chapter, I have argued that one of the most underutilized ways of weaving into the fabric of the class habits of mind and body that are at the heart of the work that Gil and so many youth choose to do is gaining a deep ethnographic understanding of how youth make meaning in their everyday lives. Indeed, by honoring the *personhood* of each of our students, we can reframe traditional questions such as "How can I (teacher) teach them (students) these skill and concept objectives?" as "How can we as a community of practice develop these skills and concepts, utilizing my (teacher) understanding of the creative intelligence at work in my students' daily lives?" While this reframing may seem insignificant, in fact it opens up the possibility of adopting curricular standards as a guide rather than a set of constraints to be slavishly followed. In this light, curricular standards are not the source of the problem as many teachers feel. Rather, they become useful tools for learning. We can then work with our students to meet the current high-stakes testing curriculum in the same ways these students meet challenges in the work of their daily lives—by implementing what I have discussed above as authentic forms of performance, improvisation, self-reflection, interpretation, and evaluation. Through this recasting of teacher and student roles as well as how learning looks, sounds, and feels, we transform the classroom into a space where the multisited nature of the ways in which everyone makes meaning is embraced and put to work.

Note

* This chapter was originally published as: Gustavson, Leif. (2008). Influencing pedagogy through the creative practices of youth. In M. Hill & L. Vasudevan (Eds). *Media, Learning and Sites of Possibility* (pp. 81–114). New York: Peter Lang.

References

Alvermann, D. (2003). Image, language, and sound: Making meaning with popular culture texts. Retrieved July 1, 2007, from http://www.readingonline.org/newliteracies/action/alvermann.

Ben-Yosef, E. (2003). Respecting students' cultural literacies. *Educational Leadership, 61*(2), pp. 80–82.

Cintron, R. (1997). *Angel's town: Chero ways, gang life, and rhetorics of the everyday*. Boston: Beacon Press.

Csikszentmihalyi, M. (1991). *Flow: The psychology of optimal experience*. New York: Perennial.

Denzin, N. K. (1997). *Interpretive ethnography: Ethnographic practices for the 21st century*. Thousand Oaks, CA: Sage.

Dewey, J. (1997). *Experience and education*. New York: Macmillan.

Dimitriadis, G. (2001). *Performing identity/performing culture: Hip hop as text, pedagogy, and lived practice*. New York: Peter Lang.

Gallas, K. (1994). *The languages of learning: How children talk, write, dance, draw, and sing their understanding of the world*. New York: Teachers College Press.

Goswami, D., & Stillman, P. (1987). *Reclaiming the classroom: Teacher research as an agency for change*. Upper Montclair, NJ: Boynton/Cook.

Greene, Maxine. (1986). In search of a critical pedagogy. *Harvard Educational Review, 56*(4), 427–441.

Greene, M. (2003). In search of a critical pedagogy. In R. D. Torres, A. Darder, & M. Baltodano (Eds.), *The critical pedagogy reader* (pp. 97–112). London: Routledge.

Gustavson, L., & Cytrynbaum, J. (2003). Illuminating spaces: Relational spaces, complicity, and multisited ethnography. *Field Methods, 15*, 252–270.

Heath, S. B. (1997). Culture: Contested realm in research on children and youth. *Applied Developmental Science, 1*(3), 113–123.

Heath, S. B. (1998). Working through language. In S. Hoyle & C. T. Adger (Eds.), *Kids talk: Strategic language use in later childhood* (pp. 217–240). New York: Oxford University Press.

Heath, S. B. (1999). Rethinking youth transitions [Review of the book *Everyday courage: The lives and stories of urban teenagers*]. *Human Development, 42*(6), 376–382.

Heath, S. B. (2000). Seeing our way into learning. *Cambridge Journal of Education, 30*(1), 121–132.

Heath, S. B., & McLaughlin, M. W. (1994). Learning for anything everyday. *Journal of Curriculum Studies, 26*(5), 471–489.

Kirby, D., Kirby, D. L., & Liner, T. (2003). *Inside out: Strategies for teaching writing.* Portsmouth, NH: Heinemann.

Kress, G., & Van Leeuwen, T. (1996). *Reading images: The grammar of visual design.* London: Routledge.

Lave, J. (1997). The culture of acquisition and the practice of understanding. In D. Kirshner & J. Whitson (Eds.), *Situated cognition: Social, semiotic and psychological perspectives* (pp. 17–36). Mahwah, NJ: Lawrence Erlbaum.

Lave, J., & Wenger, E. (1991). *Situated learning: Legitimate peripheral participation.* Cambridge, UK: Cambridge University Press.

Lemke, Jay. (1997). Cognition, context, and learning: A social semiotic perspective. In D. Kirshner & J. Whitson (Eds.), *Situated cognition: Social, semiotic and psychological perspectives* (pp. 37–55). Mahwah, NJ: Lawrence Erlbaum.

Lyrics2. (2006). Retrieved March 14, 2006, from http://www.lyrics2.co.uk/The-Last-Poets-E-Pluribus-Unum-lyrics2-59608.php [Now defunct, see instead: http://lyrics.wikia.com/The_Last_Poets:E_Pluribus_Unum]

Moje, E. (2002). But where are the youth? On the value of integrating youth culture into literacy theory. *Educational Theory, 52*(1), 97–120.

Rorty, R. (1998). *Achieving our country: Leftist thought in twentieth century America.* Cambridge, MA: Harvard University Press.

Said, E. (1996). *Representations of the intellectual: The Reith Lectures.* New York: Knopf.

Schultz, K. (2003). *Listening: A framework for teaching across differences.* New York: Teachers College Press.

Schultz, K., & Hull, G. (Eds.). (2002). *School's out! A review of theory and research on literacy and learning outside of school.* New York: Teachers College Press.

Sitton, T. (1980). The child as informant. The teacher as ethnographer. *Language Arts, 57*(5), 540–545.

Starnes, B. (1999). The Foxfire approach to teaching and learning: John Dewey, experiential learning, and the core practices. *ERIC Digest.* Retrieved March 14, 2006, from http://www.ericdigests.org/1999-3/foxfire.htm

Street, B. (2000). Literacy "events" and literacy "practices": Theory and practice in the "new literacy studies." In K. Jones & M. Martin-Jones (Eds.), *Multilingual literacies: Comparative perspectives on research and practice* (pp. 17–30). Amsterdam: John Benjamins.

Wenger, E. (1998). *Communities of practice: Learning, meaning, and identity.* Cambridge, UK: Cambridge University Press.

Wiggins, G., & McTighe, J. (2005). *Understanding by design.* 2nd ed. Alexandria, VA: Association for Supervision and Curriculum Development.

Willis, P. (1998). Notes on common culture: Towards a grounded aesthetics. *European Journal of Cultural Studies, 1*(2), 163–176.

CHAPTER SIX

Engaging Urban Youth in Meaningful Dialogue through Digital Storytelling

ALTHEA NIXON

This chapter focuses on the digital storytelling practices of Latino, African American, and Pacific Islander children in an urban, after-school club in Southern California. Specifically, this research shows how digital storytelling, as organized through collaborative, joint activity between children and undergraduate students, can be a critical digital literacies practice that supports meaningful dialogue around sensitive issues of identity, race, ethnicity, and gender. Digital storytelling blends image, sound, print, and other communication media in a dynamic, real-time environment (Center for Digital Storytelling, 2011; Lambert, 2010; Lundby, 2009). Children use different media to help them tell a story about an important aspect of their lives. This multimodal practice provides children, who are at a developmental age when issues of identity are salient, the opportunity to be expressive using not just written or oral modalities but also by incorporating multiple media to reflect on questions of who they are and what is important to them.

Researchers have studied identity from several different theoretical perspectives, including consciousness (Dennett, 1991), modernist and postmodern (see Kellner, 1995, for a discussion), psychological (Erikson, 1970; Marcia, 1980) and sociocultural theories (Holland, Lachicotte, Skinner, & Cain, 1998). From a sociocultural perspective on identity, there are different versions of the self-performed (Goffman, 1959), enacted, and lived in moment-to-moment interactions: "Identities are lived in and through activity and so must be conceptualized as they develop in social practice" (Holland et al., 1998, p. 5). Digital storytelling is one such practice in/through which youth can construct identities as they tell their personal stories (Davis, 2004). Children in this study created digital stories about their lives and interests and provided narrative descriptions of themselves as they participated in figured worlds; the socially and culturally constructed worlds in which particular identities are lived: "Figured worlds could also be called figurative, narrativized, or dramatized worlds...[where] many of the elements of a world relate to one another in the form of a story or drama, a 'standard plot' against which narratives of unusual events are told" (Holland et al., 1998, p. 53). The figured worlds of these youth included, for example, their lives in school, in their neighborhoods, in society, and within online communities. Identities are formed as youth participate in these figured worlds, and their digital stories narrated this process.

There is a long-established research tradition of studying identity through narratives (e.g., Ochs & Capps, 1996, 2001; see also Holstein & Gubrium, 1999; Mischler, 2006; Rymes, 2001; Sfard & Prusak, 2005). Recently, researchers have argued that identity is not only understood through the expression of storytelling, but that identity is the personal narrative: "Lengthy deliberations led us to the decision to *equate identities with stories about persons*. No, no mistake here: We did not say that identities were *finding their expression* in stories—we said they *were* stories" (Sfard & Prusak, 2005, p.14, emphasis in the original). Yet words cannot communicate everything about identity because words do not represent the repertoire of lived experiences in practice (Wenger, 1998).

Studying identity through narratives has limitations if the stories or words are the only focus; however, it is important to understand that narratives include much more than words since "[n]arratives are not usually monomodal, but rather they integrate two or more communicative modes. Visual representation, gesture, facial expression, and physical activity, for example, can be combined with talk, song, or writing to convey a tale" (Ochs & Capps, 1996, p. 20). There are not only speakers and hearers of stories, but also bystanders and addressed and unaddressed recipients of narratives (Goffman, 1981) who use gestures, body position, gaze, and intonation to co-construct stories collaboratively (Goodwin, 1986). In digital storytelling, children use these multiple modalities as they tell stories to each other, but they also incorporate additional modalities with the use of different technologies. These technologies offer a variety of "mediational means or cultural tools that people employ to construct their identities in the course of different activities and how they are put to use in particular actions" (Penuel & Wertsch, 1995, p. 91). Digital storytelling has the potential to provide youth with opportunities for new sense-making of who they are, using digital stories that incorporate images, text, and sound. This sense-making is not additive; instead, it is qualitatively different: "Multimodality can afford not just a new way to make meaning, but a different kind of meaning" (Hull & Nelson, 2005, p. 225). Through the multimodal sense-making of digital storytelling, youth create new meaning as they are pushed to talk, think, and engage in identity play.

In addition to studying children's identities through the digital stories they tell, identity can be understood through social categories of race and gender. Recent research on identity in the context of new technologies has focused on how these institutional categories of identity are expressed within the domains of technological innovations, such as chat rooms and video games (Tynes, Reynolds, & Greenfield, 2004) or through digital artistic production (Sandoval & Latorre, 2008). The utopian rhetoric of a colorblind internet challenges the salience of race, class, and gender in this domain; however, although many of the physical cues (i.e., skin color, clothing) children regularly use in the real world are not present in digital worlds, social categories of identity are indeed relevant (Smith & Kollock, 1999). Gender, for example, continues to be important in digital worlds through the use of language that is indexing particular social meanings (Ochs, 1992) and gendered activities (i.e., boys' use of violent video games and girls' use of computer games with friendship themes) (Kafai, 1998). This study shows how the literacy practices of digital storytelling are gendered and raced, as children take up these new technologies.

Only recently have researchers (e.g., Davis, 2004; Hathorn, 2005; Hull & Nelson, 2005; Myers & Beach, 2004) begun to study literacy and identity through storytelling that includes these additional media. In the age of new technologies used by growing numbers of children and adolescents (Lenhart, Madden, & Hitlin, 2005; Rideout, Foehr, & Roberts, 2010), it is important to understand the richness and depth of expression the many tools afford youth and how the literacy practices of digital storytelling encourage or constrain identity expression. I refer to this process as "mediation." Indeed, a major tenet of Vygotskian sociocultural theories (Vygotsky, 1978) and cultural-historical activity theories (Cole & Engeström, 1993; Cole & Levitin, 2000) of learning and development is the concept of cultural mediation. There are multiple components to this definition, but the basic premise is that individuals interact with the world through the use of cultural artifacts, ranging from basic material constructions like tools to elaborate symbolic constructions like language and online media the children find during digital storytelling.

This interaction with artifacts affects how individuals think about the world and act on the world. Moll (1998) argues that cultural artifacts are used so frequently in our everyday activities and thought processes that it is easy to forget their influence on us. Yet all human activity in the cultural world is mediated by artifacts, and artifacts change how we view the world and develop cognitively (Cole & Derry, 2005). I studied how the tools and media of digital storytelling helped mediate discussions around identity. Moreover, while the focus of this study is on digital storytelling, it is important not to lose sight of the whole ecology, the contexts in which digital storytelling is embedded, that makes possible the potentials of digital storytelling. This study focuses on both the benefits and limitations of digital storytelling on youth identity play within the settings of a media-rich learning environment, and how digital storytelling, as a digital literacy practice, can be a tool for helping children engage in critical dialogue around issues of race, ethnicity, and gender.

Methods

Setting and Participants

This study takes place at Las Redes After-School Club, located in Southern California. Las Redes, originally directed by Dr. Kris D. Gutiérrez, is part of a growing network of Fifth Dimension sites in California, across the United States, and internationally (Gutiérrez, Baquedano-López, Álvarez, & Chiu, 1999; Nixon & Gutiérrez, 2007). Researchers at the Laboratory for Comparative Human Cognition started the first Fifth Dimension site in San Diego, California (Cole, 1996), as a design experiment (Brown, 1992; Collins, 1992) based on Vygotskian (1978) perspectives on learning and development and cultural-historical activity theory (Cole & Engeström, 1993; Cole & Levitin, 2000). Guided by these theoretical orientations, elementary school children at Las Redes learn through participation with undergraduate students enrolled in colleges and universities, using goal-directed activity in game playing with different technologies. Digital storytelling is one such technology practice begun at Las Redes with the goal of encouraging meaningful and empowering multimodal literacies praxis for the students.

Las Redes is an imaginary world, called a tertiary artifact (Wartofsky, 1979), where play is one of several leading activities (Griffin & Cole, 1984) for learning and development. At Las Redes, children imagine a world in which they suspend their disbelief in the existence of a wizard "El Maga," who is said to have created the after-school program. The wizard communicates with the children via online letter writing and encourages them to reflect on their learning during game-playing activities. As children play games in the imaginary world of Las Redes, they also suspend their understanding of what experts and novices look like and act like. Children teach undergraduate students, and each other, the rules of the game, how to use new technologies (such as those employed in digital storytelling), and how to use new strategies in their game playing. In this way, Las Redes is an envisioned space of unconventional learning and untraditional roles.

The demographic background of participants at Las Redes is important, considering that "digital storytelling involves access to a medium which was very recently unavailable to low-income individuals [and] youth" (Davis, 2004, p. 1). The participants at Las Redes included children, ages five to eleven, from a predominantly low-income and working-class community. Approximately 50 children out of slightly more than 1,400 students in the elementary school attended Las Redes afterschool club. They were either chosen by the principal or joined the program through word of mouth from family members and friends who had been past participants. Of these 50 children, approximately 20 participated in digital storytelling. A core group of 10 to 12 children participated daily, and the others moved between digital storytelling and other game playing at the after-school program. More girls (almost 60 percent) than boys participated. At the elementary school, 95 percent of the students were Latino/a, 2.5 percent African American, 1 percent Pacific Islander, and 1.5 percent "Other." However, to create greater ethnic and racial diversity at Las Redes, there was a greater representation of African American and Pacific Islander children. At Las Redes, slightly less than 90 percent of the children were Latino/a, approximately 10 percent were African American, and a few of the children were Pacific Islander or Chinese. This study focuses on the core set of children who most regularly participated in digital storytelling, and the digital storytelling work of five children: Maya (a 6-year-old Latina girl), Eva (a 9-year-old Latina girl), Corey (a 10-year-old African American boy), Ryan (a 9-year-old Latino boy), and Teresa (a 10-year-old Pacific Islander girl).

Undergraduate students attended Las Redes as part of their Education Studies Minor class assignments. Each academic quarter, approximately 30 undergraduate students worked with the children in helping them create their digital stories. The majority of the undergraduate students were women and each quarter roughly equal numbers of Latino/a, European American, and Asian teacher education students participated, with a few African American students. There was a Latina coordinator at Las Redes, who oversaw the general club activities and El Maga's role, and I (an African American woman) was the digital storytelling coordinator at the after-school club. I designed the digital storytelling learning environment and oversaw the collaborations between the undergraduate students and children. As a researcher, I was also a participant-observer who interviewed the children and collected the following data.

Data Sources and Analysis

To study digital storytelling at Las Redes, there were a variety of data sources. The data analyzed in this chapter include digital stories (a set of two- to three-minute digital stories); video data recorded of the children creating their digital stories and being interviewed; cognitive ethnographies (Hutchins, 1995) the undergraduates wrote about their collaborative, joint activity with the children; and letters the children wrote to and received from the wizard, El Maga. Across the school year, 55 videotapes were collected (each tape holds 60 minutes), 20 digital stories were created, and hundreds of cognitive ethnographies and letters were written; however, this chapter focuses on five children's digital storytelling work and their corresponding videotaped interviews and activities, letters, and cognitive ethnographies specific to these children.

The data sources included activities that were already a part of the after-school club. For instance, undergraduate students wrote cognitive ethnographies for their class requirements. The cognitive ethnographies showed the undergraduate students' perspectives on digital storytelling. Considering distributed cognition, it is important that studies are "collaborative in that they depend on the knowledge and co-work of practitioners" (Shavelson, Phillips, Towne, & Feuer, 2003, p. 26).This is important because in order to understand practice, researchers need to include practitioners in their studies (Erikson & Gutierrez, 2002; Feuer, Towne, & Shavelson, 2002; Pellegrino & Goldman, 2002). I addressed this need by including observations made by the undergraduate students who helped implement digital storytelling at Las Redes. Undergraduate students wrote their cognitive ethnographies after each visit to Las Redes (once or twice a week, depending on the number of units in which they were in enrolled).

In addition, it is a long-established practice that children write letters to El Maga every day. Most often, their letters include what they did that day at Las Redes. El Maga usually responds with questions about what they learned, and why they liked certain things. These letters are written within an online discussion board as well as on paper. This study highlights a salient exchange of letters with El Maga about the children's digital story composing, providing a perspective on how children themselves think about the process.

The digital stories children and adolescents created show how the participants expressed their identities through the literacy practices of digital storytelling. Moreover, because identity is expressed in the stories we tell about ourselves as well as through the activities we engage in, video data captured moment-to-moment interactions throughout the digital storytelling process. For instance, video showed how they collaborated and helped each other or even had conflict or competition in their activities (M. H. Goodwin, 1990, 1998).

To understand participants' decision making, motivations, and rationales for creating the digital stories using particular themes and tools, recordings included a developmental dialogue—a conversation about their meaning-making and new understandings—with them throughout the process. As they were working on their digital stories, I moved around the room with a video camera to sit next to them and talk through their ideas, focusing on the artifacts (such as pictures and music) that they incorporated into their digital stories. I asked them questions about these artifacts (e.g., why they selected the artifacts, what the artifacts meant to them, and how the artifacts tied into their digital stories). The data were collected to answer the following research questions:

1. What are the benefits and limitations of digital storytelling on youth identity play within the settings of a collaborative, media-rich learning environment?
2. How can digital storytelling, as a digital literacy practice, be a tool for helping children to engage in critical dialogue around issues of race , ethnicity, and gender?

To answer these questions, the data were analyzed in an iterative, non-linear process. First, macro-level analyses of identity themes and multimodal literacy practices/tools used across digital stories were conducted. Second, the ways in which conversations around identity, race, ethnicity, and gender unfolded throughout the digital storytelling activity were analyzed, with a focus on multimodality as a method and text within the social organization of and learning within digital storytelling activities. Third, digital storytelling artifacts, such as writing and images, undergraduate students' cognitive ethnographies, and children's letters to El Maga that documented their perspectives on the digital storytelling activities, were coded to show children's identities, interests, voice, and interactions with their co-participants. Last, activity logs of the observational videos were created to document students' sense-making processes as they researched—via online websites, multimodal media, and among themselves—their self-selected topics for their digital stories.

The Multimodality of Race, Ethnicity, and Gender

Examining Gender Identity through New Media Practices of Digital Storytelling

The children in the after-school club examined intertextual, complex understandings of identity through their own and others' practices around media representations. Gender was evident in the types of digital stories girls and boys created. Of the total digital stories selected to analyze, which were representative of the body of digital storytelling work done at Las Redes, 80 percent of the girls wrote about their family and personal life aspirations, and 80 percent of the boys created fictional tales of adventure. This gender difference in digital storytelling themes is consistent with studies of gendered literary socialization and genre of reading preferences of young children (Mohr, 2006). However, it is much too simple to understand gendered practices through digital storytelling themes alone, or in isolation from the ways in which race, ethnicity, and gender were also at work in these narratives. The following is a prototypical example of how images of gender, race, and ethnicity in popular media were appropriated, as well as challenged, by youth and adults at Las Redes, and how this created a site for a cross-age exchange of ideas. This exchange led to a more critical analysis of the social construction of gender in popular media.

While participating at Las Redes, the children introduced me to the popular culture group RBD/Rebelde, whom a few girls wanted to write about in their digital stories. Rebelde is both a musical group and a telenovela or Spanish soap opera. The group originates from México but is televised in the U.S. Many of the girls at Las Redes watched Rebelde at home and at times with their mothers. As one undergraduate co-participant noted,

> A lot of the girls in the class like Rebelde….At home [Susana's] mother is into it too. In a way Rebelde is a way for Susana to connect what is seen at home with what girls talk about at school. (Amy, field notes)

I documented that the children at Las Redes brought Rebelde stickers, pictures, DVDs, CDs and other collectibles from home. These media became shared artifacts among not just the Latino community at Las Redes, but also among several African Americans. For instance, an undergraduate co-participant documented the popularity of Rebelde among African American girls at Las Redes. He noted,

> I remember once in the beginning of the quarter, Noreen told me that she watched RBD by satellite with subtitles in English. Ever since, I have been very interested to discover why the African American community at Las Redes, specifically the girls Noreen, Charlotte, and Tracey would take interest in an otherwise Mexican pop-culture phenomenon. They all collect stickers. Write letters to El Maga requesting pictures. They know all of the characters' names. They even like to listen to their music despite the language barrier. (David, field notes)

Although the Rebelde media indexed particular ethnic codes about being Latina, these digital-storytelling media and codes were taken up in hybrid ways across ethnic groups. Undergraduates documented non-Latina children incorporating images from the Rebelde website into their digital stories, even though they spoke no Spanish. The children learned with each other and shared their knowledge about Rebelde. These conversations occurred spontaneously in the everyday activities of the children. For instance, an undergraduate described the scene at the school when he arrived at the beginning of site:

When we walked into the school, I noticed all the parents standing, waiting for their kids by the gate, and as I turned around, there I saw a lot of little kids running, jumping on each other, play fighting, talking about Rebelde (OC: which I still do not know what it's about), and just walking home. (Renato, field notes)

The repeated mention of Rebelde in undergraduate field notes about children's digital stories and discussions in the undergraduate course illustrate the popularity of Rebelde among children, although many adults at the after-school club (myself included) were not initially aware of this fandom. Thus, a valued practice of the children, and the adults' curiosity to learn more about what excited the young girls, provoked interaction and conversation in which children shared with each other their interests and adults learned more about the cultural worlds of the children. By drawing on children's interests and out-of-school literacy practices, strong relationships between adults and children formed.

Although there were clear affordances in encouraging children to incorporate valued media practices in digital storytelling, such as Rebelde, such media often may promote static or problematic notions of gender identity. Here we begin to see the constraining sides of technology as well.

Gender and sexuality were salient in the media images and songs from Rebelde. The soap opera had a large storyline about high school girls and boys singing in a group, being close friends, and dating each other. The girls were hyper-sexualized in short skirts and shirts, similar to the "naughty schoolgirl" outfits made popular by what Britney Spears wore in her music-video debut. Several children at Las Redes, mostly girls, wanted to find online images of Rebelde and create digital stories about why they loved the group and why Rebelde was important to them.

The children's interests in Rebelde media merged into their digital storytelling work. One example comes from Maya, a 6-year-old girl at Las Redes, who wrote a simple explanation in a digital story of why she likes Rebelde. She wrote, "Rebelde is pretty because she always paints herself around her eyes. She is also pretty because she is nice to her friends, Mia and Lupita. They are always together so they won't get lost." This narrative shows Maya's understanding of a dual nature of beauty: physical appearance and interpersonal, social behavior. Yet the physical appearance important to young Maya was not what many adult participants at Las Redes valued in the images. Maya didn't write about Rebelde's clothing or dress but focused on her eyeshadow. Similarly, the social behavior of Rebelde, which Maya appreciated, is reflective of Maya's experiences as a young child. Being nice to friends and sticking together so no one will get lost is something that Maya did each day at this site. She stuck by her older brother, who was 9 years old, and at the end of the day waited close by him so that they could walk home from school together. Maya's own experiences served as the interpretive lens for making sense of Rebelde.

Interestingly, Maya's interests in Rebelde conflicted with the undergraduate students' concerns about Rebelde's attire and the hypersexual images conveyed by the group. Even though the children and undergraduates were usually more aligned in their joint activity, their relationship allowed the undergraduates to point out problematic notions the children held and to write about these concerns in their field notes. As one undergraduate reported,

I moved on to observe a group of three girls who were working on their project very intently. As I came closer I noticed that they were making their digital story on a Mexican pop music group called Rebelde. When I asked them who those people were, all three girls seemed kind of surprised that I had no idea about this group. Then one of the girls proceeded to explain that they are really popular in Mexico and that all of them are really pretty. She told me that their show comes on Univision and that I should watch them next time. (OC: By observing the scantily clad pictures of the singers I wasn't too sure if they were good examples of role models and someone these kids should be looking up to. But it seemed that their clothing did not bother the kids at all). I thought so because when I asked her what she liked about them so much she told me that she thought they were all really pretty and cool looking. (OC: So I think without even real- izing these kids are attracted to the physical appearance of these celebrities. So I don't think it's a good idea to promote such celebrities who instill superficiality in these kids). (Sam, field notes)

We see in this field note a generational gap but also different conceptions of gender at work. For exam- ple, the children were surprised at the undergraduate's lack of cultural knowledge about the popular group Rebelde. In addition, although the children saw Rebelde as "cool" and "pretty," the undergrad- uate thought the members of Rebelde were bad role models because of their mode of dress, which encouraged superficiality.

The example of Rebelde made visible that there was not an uncontested object shared by all par- ticipants. The staff and undergraduates were in a double bind. On one hand, children were encour- aged for drawing on their valued practices and agentive behaviors of choosing their own topics for digital storytelling; but at the same time, adults felt that there were also opportunities for develop- ing critical thought around one's meaning-making practices. Undergraduates, like Sam above, as well as the wizard, wrote about Rebelde. Through letter-writing to the children, El Maga tried to reme- diate digital storytelling activity around Rebelde to include social thought on Rebelde's mode of dress and effects of the television media. As El Maga wrote in response to Maya's letter about her digital- storytelling activities,

How are you? I am doing good. I didn't know that you liked RBD. They are really cool. I don't like all the things about them though. I like their songs and the way they sing. I don't like the way they dress because they don't wear a lot of clothes. I think it's ok not to like something100%. What do you think? Do you like everything about them? What do you think TV does to us? I think that it hypnotizes us. It makes us for- get about a lot of things and it shows us a picture of something that is fake. Then we believe that it is the truth. I like RBD even though I know that some of it is fake. What do you think? Do you think that the girls and boys in RBD are always that happy? I think they are like everyone else and that they get mad, sad, and happy too. Well, I have to go now but please write back soon. Adios. El Maga.

In this letter, El Maga is critical of the way Rebelde members dress while also acknowledging that Rebelde has appealing songs. However, while reflecting on both the strengths and limitations of Rebelde, El Maga neglected to write about both mediating aspects of television media. The response that television "hypnotizes us" and is "fake" shows a one-sided analysis of television media, in general, and the popular television show Rebelde in particular. In doing so, El Maga was able to encourage social critique by asking the children to think about the media they use, but also could at times shut down conversations about the children's digital storytelling interests by conveying strong opinions that did not encourage critical analysis of the media, multiple perspectives, and joint prob- lem solving.

Encouraging social critique through joint problem solving required a critical analysis of both the enabling and constraining aspects of mediation through Rebelde. There needed to be a balance between discussing with children the limitations of Rebelde, why Rebelde reproduced gendered and sexualized stereotypes, and discussing the strengths of these media in children's lives by listening to the children's voices about why they liked Rebelde.

I had conversations with some of the girls at Las Redes about Rebelde, and through digital sto- rytelling, I learned more about the importance of Rebelde from the children's words. Digital story- telling required children to talk about images, and rich conversations around these images occurred during production time. For instance, a developmental dialogue with Eva, a fourth-grade girl, documents her sense-making around her digital story on Rebelde and why Rebelde is important to her. As illustrated below, unlike the undergraduates—who focused on the outward image of the characters in Rebelde, including their mode of dress—Eva never mentioned how the characters dress or their outward, physical appearance in our entire conversation. Instead, she reflected on Rebelde's interpersonal relationships and their singing, music, and dance.

Althea:	So tell me a little bit about your digital story.
Eva:	Um, I'm doing the digital story about Rebelde. It's my favorite telenovela
Althea:	Why?
Eva:	I don't know. It has a lot of cute music. I like some of the characters, how they act and everything
Althea:	Which are your favorite characters?
Eva:	My favorite characters are Mia, Roberta, um Diego, and Miguel.
Althea:	Why?
Eva:	They act good.
Althea:	What's good? What do they do?
Eva:	A little bit about the novela is some, Mia and Miguel like each other and, but there's a new girl that entered to school, so then she wants to take away Miguel from Mia, and that's a little bit sad.
Althea:	Yeah.
Eva:	So Roberta used to not like Diego but now they got used to each other and they like each other.

As documented in this interview transcript, Eva shared with me the love interests among the main characters of Rebelde and how two characters in particular are best friends. As a pre-teen, issues of dating and friendships are salient to Eva. Peer affiliation is a leading activity for youth Eva's age (Griffin & Cole, 1984). The social aspect of peer relationships in Rebelde was motivation for Eva to engage in the multimodal literacy practices of digital storytelling. In Eva's words, she "tried to make it like a film" (transcript continued below), and her engagement in story development centered on the social networks of friends in Rebelde. As part of this social network, the friends of Rebelde sing together, and in Eva's words, the show "has a lot of cute music" (line 45). Eva values the musical attributes of Rebelde, as further illustrated in the next part of her conversation with me. The interview highlights Eva's appreciation of Rebelde's singing, dancing, and music. She repeated many times that she likes Rebelde because "they just express their music," and she wanted to "put them singing" in her digital story:

Eva:	And so they sing, sing, dance. They just express their music. They express their things. (Starts scrolling through pictures.)

Althea:	Awesome. Are they on these pictures?
Eva:	Lemme show you. (Scrolls through iMovie project.)
Althea:	(Points to an image.) What's that?
Eva:	That's Mia. These are all (Points to members of Rebelde individually) This is Miguel, that's Mia, this is Roberta, and this is Diego.
Althea:	How did you get the pictures?
Eva:	Well, I just went to www.Rebelde.com. You see something like that. (Motions with her hands at the screen.) And then you get the pictures of them. You just search them, you make your folder, and you put them and drag them all in there. (Makes gathering motion with hands.) And that's how I got all of this.
Althea:	So what's happening down here? (Points to project timeline.)
Eva:	Well, here. Lemme show you from the beginning. (Drags timeline to the beginning.)
Althea:	What's happening here?
Eva:	(Points to screen.) What I, what I tried to do something here is that I tried, I tried to make it like a film. Like I tried it with Rebelde. And then I put, tried to put all the characters like Mia, Roberta, Diego. And here I put all of them. Here I put the two best friends. (Points to screen).
Althea:	Um hmm.
Eva:	I put them right here, all of them.
Althea:	Um hmm.
Eva:	I put them singing.
Althea:	Um hmm.
Eva:	I tried to put all types of pictures from them singing.

Eva also likes to sing herself, and as she told me her favorite Rebelde songs, she sang a few lines of music (transcript continued below). When asked if she would like to sing for her digital story, she smiled and said yes. In the days that followed, Eva sat with her best friend at Las Redes (who was making a digital story about *High School Musical*), and together they sang quite loudly and confidently in front of the computer to an audience of anyone who walked past them.

Alethea:	Do you like to sing, too?
Eva:	Yeah. (Nods head.) Some of my favorite songs were "Es Así, Así Es," "Un Momento," "Y Soy Rebelde" (sings the song titles) and those, those are my three favorite songs from the whole thing.
Althea:	Would you like to sing on your digital story?
Eva:	Um. (Nods.)
Alethea:	Awesome! You have a good voice. That would sound nice!

The incorporation of cultural media in the digital storytelling activity gave children like Eva the opportunity to engage in meaningful literacy practices that mixed popular culture with her interests in relationships, music, and dance. These cultural practices might have been censored in formal educational environments (Lewis, 2001; Revilla, Wells, & Holme, 2004), but at Las Redes, while El Maga and some undergraduate students initially wanted to censure Rebelde media, these controversial media were introduced, challenged, and expanded on by the participants. The media and practices of digital storytelling, like all practices, were therefore both enabling and constraining. The media of Rebelde enabled Eva to express her love of music and to consider story structure and character development, as Eva explained, "to make her story into a film." It enabled children to bring their home experiences to the after-school club, and groups of Latina and African American girls came together and created hybrid media practices.

Examining Race and Ethnicity through New Media Practices of Digital Storytelling

The centrality of child-driven interests and teaching and learning opportunities in the digital storytelling activity created the space where undergraduate students positioned the child as someone with knowledge on important subject matter to be discussed. To further elaborate this pattern of analysis, Corey, an African American fifth-grade boy at Las Redes, had open conversations about race with a Latino undergraduate student, Jesús, who documented this interaction in his field notes. Jesús explained that while Corey was working on the computers creating his digital story, Corey showed him a personal website he designed. On this website, Corey wrote, "I'm African American and proud of it." The technologies and learning contexts of digital storytelling provided the opportunity for Corey to talk with Jesús about why being African American was important to him. Corey shared with Jesús the cultural practices of African ancestors and the relevance of the African American leader Rosa Parks to issues of prejudice. Jesús noted,

> Corey showed me and read to me what he had written on his info link. The very first sentence read "I am African American and proud of it"…I [asked] him if he [would] tell me more about his culture.…After this I asked him if he knew who from the African American community had recently died. He answered and said that Rosa Parks had died recently adding that she was an inspiration to everyone. I then asked Corey to tell me about why Rosa Parks should be an inspiration and he told me that she had sat where only white people were allowed to sit and refused to get up. I [asked] him if he knew the history that had led up to this and [he] told me that all white people weren't bad but some of them were prejudiced. Having heard Corey use the word prejudice, I asked him if he knew what the word meant and he blew my mind by saying that prejudice was prejudging someone based on the way they look. (By this point I wondered if I was talking to the next Martin Luther King Jr.) (Jesús, field notes)

Digital storytelling technologies, as in the case of Corey and Jesús' collaboration, provided the tools to promote rich conversations on racial pride, identity, and prejudice. Corey paused from working on his digital story to show Jesús his website. This pause was a rupture in the digital storytelling activity—a valuable rupture made possible by the flexibility of rules and the centrality of child-directed goals of digital storytelling—and Corey was able to share with Jesús his understanding of these complex issues. Corey took a nuanced stance on prejudice by acknowledging its relationship to the challenges Rosa Parks and other African Americans faced and also by explaining that "all white people weren't bad but some of them were prejudiced." Jesús was impressed by the discussion and promoted this dialogue. In this space, the dialogue with Corey and Jesús was mediated by the technologies and learning contexts of digital storytelling that gave Corey the opportunity to showcase his website and knowledge of African American cultural history and racial prejudice, a conversation that spoke of race and its importance to Corey's identity and sense of pride. Digital storytelling technologies and the social relations the activity promoted enabled meaningful dialogue around such critical issues.

Digital storytelling resulted in digital literacy practices that supported meaningful discussions of race and ethnicity but also engendered critical dialogue around topics of prejudice and racism. Teresa, a fifth-grade student from the Pacific Islands, sat at a computer to find images to go along with her digital story about her interest in wrestling. She came to the after-school club wearing a t-shirt with images of WWE (World Wrestling Entertainment, Inc.) and her favorite wrestler, John Cena. She wanted to create a digital story about how she and her brother are wrestling fans. While searching for online images for her digital story, Teresa found pictures of WWE professional wrestlers JBL (John "Bradshaw" Layfield) and Rey Mysterio. Teresa worked alongside an undergraduate co-participant, Celia, who came to the after-school club as part of her education minor class to work with children creating digital stories, among other activities. Teresa explained to Celia that she did not like JBL because he was a "racist." In this moment of digital storytelling activity, Teresa had a conversation with Celia about what racism meant to her and how it related to the popular media of the WWE she valued. As Celia noted,

> Then [Teresa] came across a picture of JBL and Rey Mysterio and she told me that she does not like JBL. I asked her why and she said "He's racist against Mexicans. He does not like Rey Mysterio because he won the championship and he said that Mexicans win everything and that Americans don't win." [JBL reportedly called a Smack Down wrestling crowd a bunch of "fruit pickers" in 2005, and when they responded by calling him names, he answered that he doesn't "speak Mexican" (Wrestle Zone, 2005)]. (OC: I was in shock that she used the word "racist" and I wanted to hear what she thought that word meant. I wanted her to elaborate more on this word.) She said that it means that "Someone is against [a] certain culture and I don't like people that are racist." I asked her what was her reaction when she heard what JBL said, and she said that she was shocked and that he should not have said that, she said that "A match is a match, he shouldn't have thrown in something about race." (Celia, field notes)

As evidenced by Teresa and Celia's interactions, the technology and media practices of digital storytelling supported discussions about race and racism, as did the social relations encouraged by this kind of joint activity of undergraduates working alongside children with a shared goal. Through the technologies made available to the children and the social relations formed between the co-participants at Las Redes, digital storytelling promoted this meaningful discourse to help extend children's understandings of race and racism. Children have experiential knowledge of forms of racism at young ages and recognize this behavior in others (Quintana & McKown, 2008). Digital storytelling drew upon this knowledge, and the conversation between Teresa and Celia documents the importance of participation in meaningful conversations where children can openly discuss their understandings of racism.

Using the technologies of digital storytelling as tools for meaningful discussions, the children at Las Redes shared their experiential knowledge and perspectives on race and racism with the undergraduates, as shown in the examples with Corey and Teresa. Although the children initiated these conversations, it is important not to minimize the roles undergraduate students had in mediating these types of discussions. For instance, one undergraduate, Isabel, shared with a fourth-grade student, Ryan, the cultural origins of the anime drawings he was using for his digital story. She wrote,

> I told him, "Oh, you chose an anime character!" He then said: "What is anime?" (OC: I figured that since he had chosen an anime character that he would have known what anime was. To be honest, I was kind of

shocked that he liked the character so much to put in his story, but did not know the type of animation that he was looking at. But, I stepped back and realized that I should not assume that he knows something just because I know it and have been exposed to information about it.) Given this, I then explained that anime was a form of drawing that came from Japan, and gave him examples such as Pokemon and Yu Gi Oh! (OC: I know this because I have a 9-year-old brother who is into those shows.) In order to not confuse him, I told him that anime was made up in Japan, but that anyone could draw it whether they were Japanese or not. And then he said, "Oh, so, like you learn from the Japan or the Chinese, I mean Japanese, to do this and then you can do it too?" (OC: Here I realized that Ryan learned that just because something comes from one place and is used by certain groups of people, that it does not mean that someone else somewhere else cannot use it also.) (Isabel, field notes)

In sharing with Ryan that anime originated in Japan, Isabel also explained that anyone could draw it. Ryan immediately drew from this explanation that cultural practices can be shared by different groups of people, regardless of their ethnicity or nationality. This is an understanding that Gutiérrez and Rogoff (2003) argue is oftentimes misunderstood by researchers who equate culture with race or ethnicity. Yet through discussions around his digital storytelling activity, Ryan gained new knowledge about the meaning of the cultural practices of which he had become part.

Conclusion

The tools of digital storytelling, as well as the social relations that this type of activity promoted, provided the space and opportunity for youth to engage in meaningful practices to represent and extend their understandings of complex issues with which they grappled personally and intellectually. There were both affordances and limitations of these media practices for non-dominant youth. Developing a more expansive technological toolkit has both enabling and constraining dimensions that re-inscribe as well as challenge static notions of identity. Through the remediation of their newly acquired media tools, youth engaged in meaningful examinations of gender, race, and ethnicity, topics too often ignored or sidestepped in learning environments (Lewis, 2001; Revilla, Wells, & Holme, 2004).

In the organization of learning in the digital storytelling activity, the children were the central decision makers in choosing a story around their interests and ideas. This agentive role is important for the process of self-representation. The children constructed texts that represented themselves, their life interests. As with most efforts to introduce student-directed elements into education, there is a tension between the interests of the student and the constraints of the educational environment. Digital storytelling can be a powerful tool for engaging urban youth in discourse about identity, but only if the environment allows them to bring in elements that may initially not be seen as fitting well (e.g., the telenovelas). Many service-learning efforts contain the implicit assumption that university students are going to be teaching K–12 tutees (as do many of the Fifth Dimensions sites around the world), but there is also an assumption that there will be mutual learning by university students; each is a tutor to the other on different aspects of what is to be learned. The traditional hierarchy of adults as teachers and children as students also did not exist in the digital storytelling learning environment because today's youth are "digital natives" (Prensky, 2001a, 2001b) who bring their own areas of expertise with new-media practices to the activity. Digital youth are resources in this technology-based learning environment, and children worked together through joint activity and collaboration.

The social relations the digital storytelling activity promoted enabled meaningful dialogue around critical issues such as race, ethnicity, gender, and power. Using the media of digital storytelling as tools for meaningful discussions, the children shared their experiential knowledge and perspectives on these issues. Children deepened their understandings through this firsthand interaction and discussion around their interests, with adults mediating these types of discussions. Undergraduate students, researchers, and program directors listened to, challenged, and encouraged the children to expand and question their understandings of messages in media.

Images of gender, race, and ethnicity in popular media were appropriated, as well as challenged, by youth and adults at the after-school programs, creating a site for a cross-age exchange of ideas. This exchange led to a more critical analysis of the social construction of gender in popular media. Youth participated in intertextual, complex discussions of race, ethnicity, gender, and power through a critical examination of their own and others' practices around media representations. The tools of digital storytelling, as well as the social relations that this type of activity promoted, provided the space and opportunity for youth to engage in meaningful practices to represent and extend their understandings of complex issues with which they grappled personally and intellectually. A critical examination of gender, race, and ethnicity is oftentimes ignored in public discourse and traditional educational settings (Lewis, 2001; Revilla, Wells, & Holme, 2004), but this practice was promoted and valued at Las Redes and in the digital storytelling activity.

By making race and the intersections of race, ethnicity, and gender central to the study of digital storytelling, children's practices may challenge the utopian rhetoric of a colorblind internet, a rhetoric that wrongly states these social categories of identity are no longer relevant in digital worlds (Smith & Kollock, 1999). In doing so, these practices also introduced a conversation that critical race theorists argue is often missing in education research (Ladson-Billings & Tate, 2006). It is important to focus on the consequences of new media and digital literacies on youth identity play within a framework that addresses these critical issues, in order to understand the diversity of participation and representation in digital worlds.

Note

* This chapter was originally published as: Nixon, A. (2013). Engaging Urban Youth in Meaningful Dialogue on Identity through Digital Storytelling. In J. Avila and J. Pandya (Eds.) (2013). *Critical Digital Literacies as Social Praxis: Intersections and Challenges* (pp. 41–62). New York: Peter Lang.

References

Brown, A. L. (1992). Design experiments: Theoretical and methodological challenges in creating complex interventions in classroom settings. *Journal of the Learning Sciences, 2*, 141–178.

Center for Digital Storytelling. (2011). http://www.storycenter.org

Cole, M. (1996). *Cultural psychology*. Cambridge, MA: Belknap Press.

Cole, M., & Derry, J. (2005). We have met technology and it is us. In R. J. Sternberg & D. D. Preiss (Eds.), *Intelligence and technology: The impact of tools on the nature and development of human abilities* (pp. 209–228). Mahwah, NJ: Lawrence Erlbaum.

Cole, M., & Engeström, Y. (1993). A cultural-historical approach to distributed cognition. In G. Salomon (Ed.), *Distributed cognitions: Psychological and educational considerations* (pp. 47–87). New York: Cambridge University Press.

Cole, M., & Levitin, K. (2000). A cultural-historical view of human nature. In N. Roughley (Ed.), *Being human: Anthropological universality and particularity in transdisciplinary perspectives* (pp. 64–80). Berlin: Walter de Gruyter.

Collins, A. (1992). Toward a design science of education. In E. Scanlon & T. O'Shea (Eds.), *New directions in educational technology* (pp. 15–20). New York: Springer-Verlag.

Davis, A. (2004). Co-authoring identity: Digital storytelling in an urban middle school. *Then, 1*(1). Retrieved 4 Dec., 2012, from http://thenjournal.org/feature/61/

Dennett, D.C. (1991). *Consciousness explained*. Boston, MA: Little, Brown.

Erikson, E. H. (1970). Reflections on the dissent of contemporary youth, *International Journal of Psychoanalysis, 51*: 11–22.

Feuer, M. J., Towne, L., & Shavelson, R. J. (2002). Reply. *Educational Researcher, 31*(8): 28–29.

Erikson, F., & Gutierrez, K. (2002). Culture, rigor, and science in educational research. *Educational Researcher, 31*(8), 21–24.

Goffman, E. (1959). *The presentation of self in everyday life*. New York: Doubleday.

Goffman, E. (1981). *Forms of talk*. Philadelphia: University of Pennsylvania Press.

Goodwin, C. (1986). Audience diversity, participation and interpretation. *Text, 6*(3): 283–316.

Goodwin, M. H. (1990). *He-said-she-said: Talk as social organization among black children*. Bloomington: Indiana University Press.

Goodwin, M. H. (1998). Games of stance: Conflict and footing in hopscotch. In S. Hoyte & C.T. Adger (Eds.), *Kids' talk: Strategic language use in later childhood* (pp. 23–46). New York: Oxford University Press.

Griffin, P., & Cole, M. (1984). Current activity for the future: The zo-ped. *New Directions for Child Development, 23:* 45–64.

Gutiérrez, K., Baquedano-López, P., Álvarez, H., & Chiu, M. (1999). A cultural-historical approach to collaboration: Building a culture of collaboration through hybrid language practices. *Theory Into Practice, 38*(2): 87–93.

Gutiérrez, K. D., & Rogoff, B. (2003). Cultural ways of learning: Individual traits or repertoires of practice. *Educational Researcher, 32*: 19–25.

Hathorn, P. (2005). Using digital storytelling as a literacy tool for the inner-city school youth. *Charter Schools Resource Journal, 1*(1). Retrieved 4 December, 2012, from: http://www.cmich.edu/academics/educ_humanservices/units/EHSTCSRJ/Documents/phathorn.pdf

Holland, D., Lachicotte, W., Skinner, D., & Cain, C. (1998). *Identity and agency in cultural worlds*. Cambridge, MA: Harvard University Press.

Holstein, J. A., & Gubrium, J. F. (1999). *The self we live by: Narrative identity in a postmodern world*. New York: Oxford University Press.

Hull, G. A., & Nelson, M. E. (2005). Locating the semiotic power of multimodality. *Written Communication, 22*: 224–261.

Hutchins, E. (1995). *Cognition in the wild*. Cambridge, MA: MIT Press.

Kafai, Y. (1998). Video game designs by girls and boys: Variability and consistency of gender differences. In J. Cassell & H. Jenkins (Eds.), *From Barbie to* Mortal Combat*: Girls and computer games* (pp. 90–117). Cambridge, MA: MIT Press.

Kellner, D. (1995). *Media culture: Cultural studies, identity and politics between the modern and the postmodern*. New York: Routledge.

Ladson-Billings, G. J., & Tate, W. (2006). *Education research in the public interest: Social justice, action, and policy*. New York: Teachers College Press.

Lambert, J. (2010). *Digital storytelling cookbook and traveling companion*. Berkeley, CA: Digital Diner Press.

Lenhart, A., Madden, M., & Hitlin, P. (2005). *Teens and technology: Youth are leading the transition to a fully wired and mobile nation*. Washington, DC: Pew Internet & American Life Project.

Lewis, A. E. (2001). There is no "race" in the schoolyard: Color-blind ideology in an (almost) all-white school. *American Educational Research Journal, 38*: 781–811.

Lundby, K. (Ed.). (2009). *Digital storytelling, mediatized stories: Self-representations in new media*. New York: Peter Lang.

Marcia, J. E. (1980) Identity in adolescence. In J. Adelson (Ed.), *Handbook of adolescent psychology*. New York: Wiley.

Mischler, E. (2006). Narrative and identity: The double arrow of time. *Studies in Interactional Sociolinguistics, 23*: 30–47.

Mohr, K. A. J. (2006). Children's choices for recreational reading: A three-part investigation of selection preferences, rationales, and processes. *Journal of Literacy Research, 38*: 81–104.

Moll, L. C. (1998). Turning to the world: Bilingualism, literacy, and the cultural mediation of thinking. *National Reading Conference Yearbook, 47*: 59–75.

Myers, J., & Beach, R. (2004). Constructing critical literacy practices through technology tools and inquiry. *Contemporary Issues in Technology and Teacher Education, 4*(3). Retrieved 4 December, 2012, from: http://www.cite-journal.org/vol4/iss3/languagearts/article1.cfm

Nixon, A. S., & Gutiérrez, K. D. (2007). Digital literacies for young English learners: Productive pathways toward equity and robust learning. In C. Genishi & A. L. Goodwin (Eds.), *Diversities in early childhood education: Rethinking and doing* (pp. 121–135). New York: Routledge Falmer.

Ochs, E. (1992). Indexing gender. In A. Duranti & C. Goodwin (Eds.), *Rethinking context: language as an interactive phenomenon* (pp. 335–358). Cambridge, UK: Cambridge University Press.

Ochs, E., & Capps, L. (1996). Narrating the self. *Annual Review of Anthropology, 25*: 9–43.

Ochs, E., & Capps, L. (2001). *Living narrative: Creating lives in everyday storytelling.* Cambridge, MA: Harvard University Press.

Pellegrino, J. W., & Goldman, S. R. (2002). Be careful what you wish for—you may get it: Educational research in the spotlight. *Educational Researcher, 31*(8): 15–17.

Penuel, W. R., & Wertsch, J. V. (1995). Vygotsky and identity formation: A sociocultural approach. *Educational Psychologist, 30*(2): 83–92.

Prensky, M. (2001a, September/October). Digital natives, digital immigrants. *On the Horizon, 9*(5), 1–6. Retrieved 4 December, 2012, from http://www.marcprensky.com/writing/Prensky%20-%20Digital%20Natives,%20Digital%20Immigrants%20-%20Part1.pdf

Prensky, M. (2001b, November/December). Digital natives, digital immigrants, part II: Do they really think differently? *On the Horizon, 9*(6), 1–6. Retrieved 4 December, 2012, from http://www.marcprensky.com/writing/Prensky%20-%20Digital%20Natives,%20Digital%20Immigrants%20-%20Part2.pdf

Quintana, S. M., & McKown, C. (Eds.). (2008). *Handbook of race, racism, and the developing child.* Hoboken, NJ: John Wiley and Sons.

Revilla, A. T., Wells, A. S., & Holme, J. J. (2004). "We didn't see color": The salience of color blindness in desegregating schools. In M. Fine, L. Weis, L. P. Pruitt, & A. Burns (Eds.), *Off white: Readings on power, privilege, and resistance* (pp. 284–301). New York: Routledge.

Rideout, V. J., Foehr, U. G., & Roberts, D. F. (2010, January). *Generation M^2: Media in the lives of 8- to 18-year-olds.* Kaiser Family Foundation. Retrieved 4 December, 2012, from http://www.kff.org/entmedia/mh012010pkg.cfm

Rymes, B. (2001). *Conversational borderlands: Language and identity in an alternative urban high school.* New York: Teachers College Press.

Sandoval, C., & Latorre, G. (2008). Chicana/o artivism: Judy Baca's digital work with youth of color. In A. Everett (Ed.), *Learning race and ethnicity* (pp. 81–108). Cambridge, MA: MIT Press.

Sfard, A., & Prusak, A. (2005). Telling identities: In search of an analytic tool for investigating learning as a culturally shaped activity. *Educational Researcher, 34*: 14–22.

Shavelson, R. J., Phillips, D. C., Towne, L., & Feuer, M. J. (2003). On the science of education design studies. *Educational Researcher, 32*(1): 25–28.

Smith, M., & Kollock, P. (Eds.). (1999). *Communities in cyberspace.* London: Routledge.

Tynes, B., Reynolds, L., & Greenfield, P. M. (2004). Adolescence, race, and ethnicity on the Internet: A comparison of discourse in monitored vs. unmonitored chat rooms. *Journal of Applied Developmental Psychology, 25*: 667–684.

Vygotsky, L. (1978). *Mind in society: The development of higher psychological processes* (M. Cole, V. John-Steiner, S. Scribner, & E. Souberman, Eds.). Cambridge, MA: Harvard University Press.

Wartofsky, M. (1979). *Models: Representations and the scientific understanding.* Dordrecht, the Netherlands: Reidel.

Wenger, E. (1998). *Communities of practice: Learning, meaning, and identity.* Cambridge, UK: Cambridge University Press.

Wrestle Zone. (2005, October 30). *JBL's latest racist rant, & backstage news on Warrior DVD.* Retrieved 4 December, 2012, from http://www.wrestlezone.com/news/229295-jbls-latest-racist-rant—backstage-news-on-warrior-dvd

CHAPTER SEVEN

Learning about Circuitry with E-Textiles

KYLIE PEPPLER & DIANE GLOSSON

The relationship between various tools and the structuring of subject matter is central to many examinations of disciplinary learning. Papert (1980, p. 23), for one, called attention to the impact of specific tools ("objects to think with") on the ways that we learn and perceive subject matter. Of potential interest to anyone working with e-textiles in educational settings is the impact that working with these tools has on our ontological understanding of robotics, computing and engineering, particularly in the ways that it contrasts with learning outcomes that derive from the use of more traditional tools (e.g., batteries, insulated wire, nails, thumbtacks, paper clips, bulbs, and so on). The historical prevalence of youths' conceptual misunderstandings of simple circuitry from learning with these traditional materials (Evans, 1978; Tiberghien & Delacote, 1976) provides additional justification for this exploration. For instance, traditional circuitry toolkits possess numerous design elements that make invisible what makes them work (e.g., the connecting wires in an incandescent bulb disappear behind an electrical contact foot and metallic screw cap; insulated wires prevent crossed lines from shorting out). By contrast, e-textile toolkits reveal underlying electrical structures and processes in tangible and observable ways, allowing designers to investigate aspects of circuits and computational technologies that are otherwise invisible to the user (Buechley, 2010; Kafai & Peppler, in press). Furthermore, dramatically changing the nature of the tools used to explore circuitry concepts (e.g., fabrics, threads, and other soft materials) inspires youth to ask questions they otherwise wouldn't have. Is cotton conductive? What makes energy pass through *this* material but not *that* one? Re-evaluating garments and textiles beyond their immediately practical or aesthetic functions encourages youth to think more deeply about the circuitry concepts at play and the qualities of the physical materials, themselves.

Seeking to explore whether the visibility inherent to these materials could prove significant for youths' conceptual understanding of circuitry, we invited youth at a local Boys and Girls Club to design a host of e-textile projects and reflect upon their production practices in a 20-hour workshop. All the while, we observed and analyzed the youths' projects and interactions in the process of creation for evidence of improved understanding of core circuitry concepts. Results indicate that youth participants significantly gained in their understanding of multiple core circuitry concepts as well as their ability to diagram and create working circuits in parallel and series formations (Peppler & Glosson, 2012). This work seeks to provide a foundation for integrating e-textile materials into standards-based practices in formal education systems and to illustrate how this might be taught and assessed in the classroom.

Workshop Description

Our e-textile workshop was designed as part of the local Boys and Girls Club summer program. Seventeen youth, ages 7–12 years, participated in the entire twenty-hour, ten-session e-textile curriculum lasting for two hours per day over a two-week period. The e-textile workshop targeted five central concepts important to the study of circuitry but are more commonly taught using traditional materials: current *flow* (Osborne, 1981; Osborne, 1983; Shipstone, 1984), battery *polarity* (Osborne, 1983; Osborne et al., 1991; Shepardson & Moje, 1994; Asoko, 1996), circuit *connectivity* (Osborne, 1983; Asoko, 1996), and the diagramming of circuits in *series* (Osborne, 1983; Osborne et al., 1991) and *parallel* (Shepardson & Moje, 1994) formations which are further defined below:

1. Current *flow* is defined as the circular path electrons take around a circuit (Osborne, 1981). For e-textile projects, we assessed participants' ability to stitch loops with no redundant lines or instances of shorts (i.e., loose threads touch the opposite terminal line).

2. Battery *polarity* involves connecting battery terminals to the corresponding output terminals in a circuit (i.e., + to + and - to -). In the context of e-textiles, we assessed whether youth could orient the positive and negative terminals of circuit components correctly in relationship to the power source.

3. Circuit *connectivity* pertains to the joining of the battery, bulb and wires to form a working circuit (Osborne, 1983; Osborne, et al., 1991; Shepardson & Moje, 1994). In the absence of these materials, we adapted the term in our assessment of youths' e-textiles projects to define connectivity as the craft of the circuit. That is, the lines (i.e., conductive thread) had to securely connect one component to another with attention being paid to the particular points of conductivity (e.g., looping the conductive thread through the terminal hole for a strong connection).

4. A *series* circuit is one where electrical current flows sequentially through every component in the circuit. In a series circuit, any electron progresses through all components to form a single path, meaning that energy diminishes as it progresses through each component in the circuit (such as a string of light-emitting diodes [LEDs]).

5. In a *parallel* circuit, the electrical current divides into two or more paths before recombining to complete the circuit. Working with e-textiles, electrons in a parallel circuit go through two (or more) LEDs at the same time, meaning that the electron's energy given to each LED is identical.

These circuitry concepts were explored in a series of three projects selected by the youth participants over the course of the 10 sessions, of which two are presented here: an introductory simple circuit quilt square and a programmable wristband with persistence-of-vision (POV) tracking. Taking place in an informal environment, participants' creative production with these tools was largely defined by free exploration and experimentation; direct instruction was limited to three brief presentations, and youth often turned to peer or mentor support for advice and inspiration on their individual projects.

Below, we address the science concepts manifested in two of the youths' e-textile projects—the quilt square and the POV bracelet—as well as what the youths' projects revealed about their understandings of current flow, circuit connectivity, battery polarity, and series vs. parallel circuits. Throughout, we augment these findings with vignettes of how these understandings were cultivated through moment-to-moment interactions with the tools, peers and workshop mentors.

Learning about Simple Circuits: Simple Circuit Quilt Square

The quilt square project provided an introduction to designing simple circuit forms, as well as an opportunity for youth to play with the new materials—threading a self-threading needle, sewing with conductive thread, practicing making secure knots—and reflect on the basic requirements of creating a complete simple circuit with an illuminated LED.

Each square consisted of a 12 x 12 inch swatch of fabric upon which each youth stitched a closed circuit using one LED, a battery, a switch (button or slide), and conductive thread. Before the youth began their projects, we asked them to draw circuit diagrams in order for us to assess their preexisting understanding of current flow, connections and polarity. In this first drawing, the youth attempted to diagram a simple working circuit using pencil and custom LilyPad component stickers [Editors' note: "Lilypad" here refers to the Lilypad Arduino kit, "the first construction kit to make e-textile construction accessible to non-engineers" (Buechley, et al., 2013, p. 12)]. Once their diagrams were complete, the youth then adapted their drawing to their quilting square. However, once engaged with the physical materials, initial misunderstandings of circuitry in the abstract came to the fore. The evidence that these misunderstandings had been amended through the experience of

Start of Workshop	End of Workshop

Initially, Courtney lacked the understanding of:

- Current flow: there is no circular path from the battery to each component.
- Polarity: the LED's negative terminal is incorrectly oriented toward the battery's positive one.
- Connections: the lines drawn don't connect to any of the small terminal holes in any of the components.

By the end, Courtney showed an improved understanding of:

- Current flow: there's a clear circular path in the diagram connecting all of the components in the circuit.
- Polarity: the LED is positioned correctly toward the battery terminals (- to -).
- Connections: there is a mindful consideration that the drawn lines extend over the edge of the sticker, directly into the terminal ports.

Figure 7.1: Courtney's circuit drawings at the start and end of the workshop.

working with the e-textile materials was abundantly clear when compared with the hand-drawn circuit diagrams the youth made later in the workshop. Through projects like these, the youth revealed significant gains not only in their ability to diagram a working circuit, but also in their demonstrated understandings of current flow, connectivity and polarity (Peppler & Glosson, 2012). Figure 7.1 provides an illustrative example of how one youth's circuitry understandings developed over the course of working with the e-textile materials.

As illustrated here, 10-year-old Courtney in her first drawing appeared to understand the need for three parts to a circuit—switch, battery holder and LED—in the (unprompted) labeling of the parts and that a connection needed to be made from the battery holder to the LED. However, she lacked the understanding of current flow (circuit path), polarity and the importance of solid connections of conductive thread to the conductive holes. This would have been immediately evident when she first attempted to realize this drawing using the physical materials. By contrast, Courtney in her later diagram showed an understanding of a working circuit including the current flow, connections and polarity.

To see this understanding developing in the moment-to-moment interactions over the course of the workshop, we recorded and analyzed conversations taking place between the youth, their peers and the research team that touched upon the key circuitry concepts at play in these projects. The following excerpt is from a conversation between a researcher and an 8-year-old boy working on his quilt square about the importance of tracking polarity in the context of e-textiles:

Researcher: So you want to do the same thing to the LED that you did...

Ryan: No, I mean...where is this one *(pointing to the switch part sticker)*?

Researcher: I'll get that one for you in a second *(gestures towards parts table)* but first go through the LED.

Ryan: *(positions LED to sew)*

Researcher: You are about to make a fatal mistake. *(Points towards Ryan)* What is it?

Ryan: The plus is going to the minus.

Researcher: Yes! So you want to switch this (LED) around *(gestures in a circle)*. Now plus is going to plus.

In this early example with sewing the quilt squares, the youth had already learned that the plus terminal of the battery needed to be connected to the plus terminal in the LED with conductive thread or an electrical short would occur. So when the researcher warned Ryan of a "fatal mistake" as he was about to sew the negative terminal connecting it to the positive battery terminal, polarity was one of the first things Ryan checked for. His response could have been due to a phrase that was used extensively by the staff and the youth: "plus to plus and minus to minus" (i.e., the positive terminal in the battery should connect to the positive terminal in the LED, just as the negative terminal in the battery should connect to the negative terminal of the LED). We believe this mantra may have contributed to the significant gains in the youths' understanding of polarity as reflected in the pre- and post-test diagram assessments.

After the workshop, the completed "e-Quilt," comprising 16 working circuits designed and created by participating youth, was highlighted and displayed at the Boys and Girls Club annual art exhibition at the local City Hall, which was attended by the mayor, community members, Boys and Girls Club staff, the youth artists and their family and friends. At the exhibition, workshop participants anxiously searched for their circuits to light, shared stories with their parents about the making of their quilt square and were excited to locate their friends' circuits, as well. The e-Quilt project provided not only a valuable showcase for the Boys and Girls Club to highlight what learning opportunities the Club can offer youth in the community, but the exhibition provided youth with an occasion to introduce their artistic and scientific skills to their broader community.

Learning about Series and Parallel Circuits: Persistence of Vision (POV) Wristband

The LilyPad POV wristband is a wearable version of a persistence of vision (POV) display; POV is the illusion that an image continues to persist even though part of the image has changed. The LilyPad POV wristband or bracelet can be thought of as a digital version of the old-fashioned zoetrope used for simple animation. The zoetrope is a cylinder with static images pasted on the inside. Each image is a slight modification of the previous image. By cutting slits in the cylinder and spinning it, the viewer effectively sees motion. The POV bracelet creates words by rapidly alternating patterns of LEDs stitched in a row. When youth sweep their arms horizontally, the flashing LEDs appear to spell a visible word in the air.

Workshop youth stitched LEDs into their bracelets in a parallel circuit configuration to enable each LED to be lit separately through LilyPad Arduino programming. In order for each LED to be programmed separately, the positive LED terminal holes were connected to individual LilyPad petals (i.e., terminal holes) and the negative LED terminals were stitched as one line into the negative petal of the LilyPad Arduino (which they also stitched into their bracelets) (see Figure 7.2). Youth worked with a computer programmer to convert text into Arduino code that could be uploaded to the LilyPad board. Constraints of time and a primary emphasis on the basics of circuitry in this workshop prohibited us from dedicating more time to the youths' learning of programming concepts. However, we hope that some initial transparency into the process of computer programming will provide youth with a foundation for future explorations with creative computation, which we have explored more fully in our later workshops (for more, see Buechley et al., 2013).

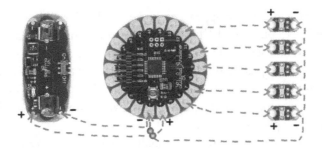

Figure 7.2: Diagram of the POV wristband design.

During the electricity lesson, parallel circuits were explained in terms of not only the LED's being in parallel form (placed next to one another) but also how this placement allowed for the LEDs to produce a brighter light. It was explained as "in a parallel circuit, an electron goes through EITHER one LED or the other" while the series circuit electrons had to progress through both LEDs, losing energy along the way and thus producing a dimmer light as the series progressed. Similar to the circuit diagrams that youth drew before and after their quilt square projects, we asked youth to draw a parallel circuit diagram before and after the POV bracelet activity. The following (Figure 7.3) is an illustrative example of Jovita's understanding of a parallel circuit as drawn in her circuit diagrams at the start and end of the workshop.

<table>
<tr><td align="center">Start of Workshop</td><td align="center">End of Workshop</td></tr>
<tr><td align="center"></td><td align="center"></td></tr>
<tr><td>Jovita's drawing shows an understanding of polarity and current flow (circuit path for a series circuit) however, lacks understanding of the importance of connections of conductive thread and incorrectly places the LEDs in a series as opposed to the requested parallel circuit form.</td><td>Jovita's diagram shows an understanding of polarity, connections, and current flow as well as correct placement of the LEDs in a parallel formation.</td></tr>
</table>

Figure 7.3: Jovita's circuit diagrams, drawn at the start and end of the workshop.

In the pre-test, 10-year-old Jovita appears to understand polarity and current flow for a series circuit, yet lacks the ability to place the LEDs in a parallel configuration in her diagram (e.g., all the LEDs are, instead, aligned in a series). The post-test, by contrast, correctly places the LEDs parallel with one another. However, the placement of the switch (opposite to both of the battery holder's terminals) allows the LEDs to stay lit continuously until the switch is pushed. This is in effect the opposite of the solution to the prompt where the push button switch would turn on the circuit. While not incorrect, *per se*, it is a rather peculiar design.

In the following, two researchers engage a small group in a conversation about 10-year-old Dalmar's POV wristband, calling specific attention to the workings of parallel versus series circuits:

Researcher 1: The one on the left is called series, why do you think it's called "series"?

Dalmar: Because they [the LEDs] are by each other.

Researcher 1:   And why do you think the other one is called "parallel"?

Dalmar: Because they are parallel to each other.

Researcher 2:   Yes, exactly. So it's easy to tell the difference, right? Series and parallel. OK, so this is how all electronics works…when you put an electron in the battery, it wants to go to the other side of the battery, right?

Dylan (age 8):   Yeah.

Researcher 2:   It's attracted to the other side. So it will go through these LEDs to get to the other side *(points to series circuit diagram on the laptop screen)*. Now with a series circuit the electron loses some energy in going from this side of the battery to the other side of the battery. And in a series circuit it loses half of its energy on one LED and half of it on the other one…But in a parallel circuit *(points to the parallel circuit diagram on the laptop screen)* the electron either goes through one LED or it goes through the other LED. So the electron gives all of its energy to one LED or the other LED. So how do you think this is going to affect the brightness of the LED? You guys found this out yesterday, you did this parallel versus series.

Shawnte (age 9):   Hook it up to some wires.

Researcher 2:   Which one was brighter? Parallel or series?

Many Youth: Parallel.

Researcher 2:   Right, right. Because of this *(points to the parallel diagram)*. The electron goes across the LED and it gives all of its energy to the LED, while in the series it divides energy between the two LEDs. That's why it's dimmer in series. So which one do you guys want to use?

Many Youth: Parallel.

This exchange between the youth and the researchers took place the day after the youth had played in small groups while building series and parallel circuits. During that playtime, the youth were left to explore the connections while using multiple LEDs in making both series and parallel forms. The exchange captured above calls attention to two things: (1) the youth could apply the definitions of series and parallel circuits correctly, and (2) the youth had learned the implications of these designs for the circuits (i.e., that parallel circuits produced brighter LEDs while series circuits produced dimmer ones with the battery power available).

Moving beyond the Club

Beyond learning about circuitry, the real promise of e-textile artifacts is their capacity to follow youth into their peer and family settings, potentially transforming their identities in these social circles and sparking relevant conversations. Demonstrating the power that physical artifacts can have to cultivate these conversations, we present a sample exchange between two workshop participants, 8-year-old Ryan, 10-year-old Noah, and Ryan's mother at the end of the workshop:

Mother: What is "L.D."?

Ryan: L.E.D.—it's a special type of light. And, guess what? In Chicago there is a museum with 4,000 LED lights on one dress.

Mother:	What is the idea behind this? *(gesturing towards the square)*…that this works, how?
Ryan:	It's the plus…I mean. That here's the plus *(points)* it goes to plus *(points)* and through the minus. *(To Noah)* How does that work *(pointing to switch)*?
Noah:	It doesn't matter which way that goes.
Ryan:	Oh, it doesn't?
Noah:	No.
Ryan:	Then it goes through that *(points to switch)* and then minus goes to minus.
Mother:	So, this is minus?
Ryan:	And it doesn't really matter what side this is on *(points to switch)*.
Mother:	How does this [project] work? *(Passes Noah the 3V battery)*.
Noah :	Yeah *(takes the battery)*.
Ryan:	You have to put this [battery] on the conductive tape *(points)*.
Noah :	Yeah.
Mother:	Where is the tape? Is it conductive tape? *(Looking closer at the project)*.
Ryan:	Yeah, that means it has electricity through it and we have electricity through us.
Mother:	We have electricity…through us?
Ryan:	Electricity is basically electrons and protons.
Mother:	Ohhh.
Noah :	Actually we have a small amount of [it]…Your brain takes 100 watts to work.
Mother:	Ohhh.

The conversation highlights the opportunities for Ryan and Noah to display what they learned, facilitated and illustrated by the presence of tangible, mobile artifacts. As shown here, several of these circuitry concepts were new to the Ryan's mother (at least in this physical incarnation), and the youths' ability to take these projects home with them increased the likelihood that these STEM-related [i.e., Science, Technology, Engineering and Mathematics] conversations could continue with other family members and peers, and in the other spaces in their lives.

As it turns out, new conversations were sparked back at home through the youths' experiences with e-textiles, though they weren't limited to science content. Another youth's mother reported back the following day that her 7-year-old son had taken notice "as if for the first time" the cross-stitching work she had on display at home, having a newfound respect for her crafting techniques. She reported that Caleb had exclaimed, "Ooh, Mom, your stitching is so good here! It's nice and even." Caleb's mother later explained to us that, having all boys, she never anticipated that she could have these types of conversations with her kids. Conversations such as these underscore the ability for artifacts that sit at the intersection of high and low tech to spur meaningful conversations among family members.

Discussion

From the marked shifts in the workshop participants' circuit diagrams, as well as their ability to create a variety of functioning circuits using the e-textile toolkits, we gather that the youth learned at least five traditional circuitry concepts—current flow, battery polarity, circuit connectivity, and diagramming circuits in a series—within the context of e-textiles throughout the workshop. The diagramming-plus-"hands-on" components of each workshop activity mirror several of the pedagogical methods that employ more traditional toolkits, and some of the intermediate results—the youths' exuberance at having the bulb in their circuit illuminate, or the need for youth to reassess their diagram if their physical circuit failed to work, for example—were shared across both approaches. However, the learning outcomes of the e-textile workshop, where participants significantly gained in their understanding of all five targeted circuitry concepts (Peppler & Glosson, 2012), stand in contrast to the difficult learning curve and frequent lingering misconceptions promoted by the instruction of circuitry through more traditional kits as described in numerous studies (Osborne, 1983; Shipstone, 1984; Osborne et al., 1991; Shepardson & Moje, 1994; Asoko, 1996). We believe that the e-textile materials, themselves, may be largely responsible for this difference in outcomes.

What makes these materials so different with regard to youths' learning trajectories? Until further research is conducted, we can only speculate, though we have a number of hypotheses based on our observations:

1. E-textile tools are "unforgiving." Coated wires, magnets and snaps to easily affix lines and components together are design elements of traditional toolkits intended to prevent mistakes, and consequently have some inevitable trade-offs for how electricity operates. The materials explored here, by comparison, did not put in place such safeguards, so youth were put in positions to make mistakes through which they could learn about polarity, shorted circuits and other concepts in the process of troubleshooting. By enabling such opportunities to happen, these tools may afford greater visibility into what makes one circuit work and not another.

2. E-textile projects provide opportunities for embodied learning of circuitry. Working with e-textiles or traditional circuitry toolkits provided tangible, hands-on experiences with building a circuit in both cases. However, youth must invest substantially more time in an e-textile project to create a functioning circuit (whereas this could be done in about two minutes using a kit consisting of magnets and snaps seen in many youth science exhibits). From our observations, we found that deeper, continuous engagement with the e-textiles materials over a longer period of time led the youth into deeper and more sustained reflection than what could have been achieved in only a few minutes. In this regard, the speed in which one arrives at an answer may not necessarily be the one that produces the richest learning outcomes.

3. E-textile projects encourage youth to see familiar phenomena in unfamiliar ways. Youth have close relationships with their clothing, as the various types of materials that adorn their persons are seen, touched and manipulated daily. However, youth don't associate fabric materials or threads as something conductive. Seeing the qualities of these soft materials in unexpected ways enables youth to forge new connections; both because they have previous familiarity with clothing, but also because they haven't thought about the qualities of conductive materials, more broadly, as a way of sorting the world.

Our investigation into e-textile creation as a potential vehicle for learning circuits acknowledges that the tools we use and make available play a formidable role in shaping our conceptual understandings, and, moreover, that new tools can bring clarity to concepts that are often challenging. As shown here, e-textile projects can successfully engage youth in core science content, subject matter that has been difficult in prior approaches to make conceptual sense to youth. The workshop youths' aforementioned gains as well as their ability to explain their understandings to peers and parents demonstrate that e-textiles can offer an alternative and efficacious introduction to electronics.

Workshops such as the one described here demonstrate that classroom teachers can leverage e-textiles for efficacious science content learning. Further research into how to best translate these types of informal workshop environments into classroom pedagogy is still required. Workshop models that occur within the school day are one potential answer (see Buechley, et al., 2013 for more on this). Furthermore, while this study focused on simple working circuits and five core circuitry concepts, future research studies could include adding directional flow to the current model, as well as more advanced constructions to complex circuitry.

Acknowledgments

This material is based upon work supported by the National Science Foundation under Grant No. 0855886 awarded to Kylie A. Peppler. Any opinions, findings, and conclusions or recommendations expressed in this material are those of the author(s) and do not necessarily reflect the views of the National Science Foundation.

Note

* This chapter was originally published as: Peppler, K., & Glosson, D. (2013). Learning about Circuitry with E-textiles in After-School Settings. In Buechley, L., Peppler, K., Eisenberg, M., & Kafai, Y. (Eds.), *Textile Messages: Dispatches from the World of E-Textiles and Education*. New York: Peter Lang.

References

Asoko, H. (1996). Developing scientific concepts in the primary classroom: Teaching about electric circuits. G. Welford, J. Osborne, & P. Scott (Eds.), *Research in science education in Europe* (pp. 36–49). London, Falmer Press.

Buechley, L. (2010). Questioning invisibility. *Computer, (43)*4: 84–86.

Buechley, L., Peppler, K., Eisenberg, M., & Kafai, Y. (Eds.), *Textile messages: Dispatches from the world of e-textiles and education*. New York: Peter Lang.

Evans, J. (1978). Teaching electricity with batteries and bulbs. *Physics Teacher, 16*(1): 15–22.

Kafai, Y., & Peppler, K. (in press). Rethinking transparency in critical making with e-textiles. In M. Boler & M. Ratto (Eds.), *DIY Citizenship*. Boston, MA: MIT Press.

Osborne, R. (1981). Children's ideas about electric current. *New Zealand Science Teacher, 29*: 12–19.

Osborne, R. (1983). Modifying children's ideas about electric current. *Research in Science and Technological Education, 1*(1): 73–82.

Osborne, J., Black, P., Smith, M., & Meadows, J. (1991). *Primary SPACE Project research report: Electricity*. Liverpool University Press, Liverpool, England.

Papert, S. (1980). *Mindstorms: Children, computers, and powerful ideas*. New York: Basic Books.

Peppler, K., & Glosson, D. (2012). Stitching Circuits: Learning about circuitry through e-textile materials. *Journal of Science and Educational Technology*. November 17. Retrieved 8 December 2012, from: http://link.springer.com/article/10.1007%2Fs10956-012-9428-2

Shepardson, D.P., & Moje, E.B. (1994). The nature of fourth graders' understandings of electric circuits, *Science Education, 78*(5): 489–514.

Shipstone, D. (1984). A study of children's understanding of electricity in simple DC circuits. *European Journal of Science Education, 6*: 59–87.

Tiberghien, A., & Delacote, G. (1976). Manipulations representations de circuits electrique sample chex les enfants de 7 a 12 ans, *Review Francaise de Pedagogie, 34*: 32–44.

PART 3

New Literacies and Teachers' Personal and Professional Learning

CHAPTER EIGHT

Machinima, Second Life and the Pedagogy of Animation

ANDREW BURN

A nimation has a long history in media education, though it belongs equally in art education. The two domains bring different emphases: the one exploring animation as popular culture and as a filmic production medium; the other looking at it as an art form and emphasising its component elements of drawing, painting and model-making as well as its aesthetic properties. However, in recent years this traditional distinction has diminished to some degree with a disciplinary shift in art education towards a curriculum for "visual culture," involving a move away from the institutions of fine art towards a more inclusive engagement with practices of visual representation (e.g., Duncum, 2001). This effort represents a move from a conception of art education as elite, cut off, and situated firmly within the project of modernity to a postmodern diversity of practices (Addison & Burgess, 2003). In this new dispensation, traditional oppositions between word and image, artistic medium and technology, the sense of sight and the other senses addressed by contemporary multimodal texts are challenged. Importantly for this chapter, this new diversity also implies a breaking of disciplinary boundaries, a new collaboration with other education practices occupied with visual culture.

At the same time, it is possible to see media education shifting away from its traditional character and curriculum location. Where once its central emphasis, inherited from its origins in English teaching, was on literacies and the critical analysis of texts, moves in recent years have involved a more pluralistic engagement with the Arts. Media specialist schools in the UK, for example, are formally designated as "Media Arts Colleges" by the government's specialist schools programme, and while this term is arguably intended to locate such schools within a rationale of training for the "creative industries," it has also given impetus to productive collaboration between media educators and educators in drama, music, art and dance (see Burn & Durran, 2007: Ch. 8, for an account of this kind of work).

At the same time, the digital era has brought new possibilities to both subject domains, and this is true of the cultural practice of animation as it is of other media forms. Where a few schools used to make animations using traditional stop-frame techniques and a rostrum film camera, the arrival of digital video allowed the easy capture of individual images as frames, editing with a non-linear editing program, and a wide range of formats for exhibition and publication.

The most recent cultural form in the world of animation—both shaped by and shaping new technologies, in this case those of 3D computer games and virtual worlds—is the art of machinima. Machinima, as has often been noted, is a portmanteau word combining machine and cinema, with a substitution of the "e" by an "i," implying animation and anime. It is defined by Kelland and colleagues as "the art of making animated films within a realtime 3-D environment" (2005: 10). It can be thought of as animation made from the 3D environments and animated characters of computer games or virtual immersive worlds. The first machinima films were produced by players of the game *Quake* in the mid-1990s.

Machinima-making in schools requires a rethink of animation as an artistic practice and as a form of media production. How is it different from, or similar to, earlier kinds of animation, in terms of its cultural context, its technical resources, the skills it requires, the pedagogies it implies, the creative possibilities it affords?

This chapter will focus on the work of artist, animator, machinimator and teacher Britta Pollmuller, who has taught animation to teenagers in many ways, ranging from stop-frame and claymation techniques to machinima made in the immersive virtual world Second Life. It will explore the interface between media and art education, and between new technologies and adaptive uses of them by teachers and students.[1]

Animation and Digital Video

This story begins with a project recorded as a case study for the BECTa DV (Digital Video) evaluation[2] (Reid et al., 2002). Britta was working with a Year 8 group in her school in Norfolk on animations of African folktales. BECTa had provided one iMac and a DV camera, and like many teachers in other schools, Britta had found creative ways around this restricted provision. One group of children was animating plasticine models against painted backdrops with clip-on lights, filming and recording frames onto the iMac with a freeware capture tool. Other groups were scripting, storyboarding, painting backdrops, designing characters, and writing haiku-form credits.

This work can be seen as a hybrid of media and art education (see also Burn, 2009). In respect to media education, the children were learning through production about the language and grammar of animation and of the moving image more generally. They learned through design and practise about the speed and duration created by the quantity of frames, about the meaning of lighting and set design, about the grammar of shot composition and camera angle, about the function of sound, dialogue and music. They also learned collaboratively, through group work, a process typical of media education production projects, where responsibility for authorship is shared, students may adopt different roles in the production process, and practices of the industry may be simulated (Buckingham, et al., 1995). Group work is much less typical of art education, where individual endeavour is still a common model for creative production.

At the same time, a number of emphases were in evidence which were more characteristic of the art classroom. The "word wall" at the back of the classroom displayed words like "harmony," "composition," "rhythm." In fact, the wall combined media and art-related terminology, as Britta explained in an interview:

> Well, I have got, to start with here, animate, abstract films, storyboard, digital, focus, rhythm, composition...tone, 2D, find a sense of space, harmony, and so on.

The process paid a good deal of attention to the component craft skills involved, especially drawing, painting and model-making, and to the aesthetic effects of these elements. Britta insisted on quality, overseeing the careful production of the artwork, demanding reworking or reconstruction or refilming where necessary, and conducting frequent discussions to reflect on the quality of work so far.

Something which emerged from the case study was a sense of the varied cultural contexts which animation work invokes and the different kinds of cultural value attached to them. While the chosen subject of the work, the African folktales, and the craft skills of the art classroom invite fine art references such as the tradition of European animation, the children's own experience imports references to popular animation which appeared in aspects of the visual style, especially those constructing ironic or parodic humorous effects. This oscillation between a fine art and popular aesthetic can be seen as a consequence of the cross-disciplinarity of the project.

Finally, this project was infused by the status and experience of the teacher-as-artist. This kind of role varies through the arts: found most strongly in teachers of Art and Music, and perhaps least strongly in teachers of Literature, with Drama somewhere in between. Britta had worked as a painter, was familiar with a range of digital media, had completed an MA at the Norwich School of Art, and worked part-time for a regional arts education project. The teacher-as-artist can be seen as complementary to a pedagogic role though it brings other practices, such as co-creator, quasi-professional mentor, and studio director. It can be seen as a pedagogic stance, which backgrounds the statutory frameworks of schooling—curriculum design, assessment requirements, compulsory attendance—and foregrounds the creative endeavour and the social context in which it takes place.

A number of issues arise from this kind of animation work. Three are raised in the BECTa report, which, though general, are applicable here. One is the importance of the "language" of the moving image: the projects perceived as the most successful in the evaluation, including Britta's, were those which made the "grammar" of moving image composition explicit.

A second was the nature of creativity: teachers in the project all strongly emphasised the creative nature of students' work though all had difficulty in defining exactly what was meant. Recent research studies and literature reviews of creativity in education have shown that creative work in schools is beset by competing definitions and interests of different stakeholders (Banaji, Burn, & Buckingham 2010; Loveless, 2002).

A third issue was the affordances of digital media. Clearly, many instances of classroom work in the BECTa pilot could have achieved their results using analogue equipment. To distinguish the specific benefits of the digital filming and editing tools, the report focused on three affordances, derived from Moseley and collagues (1999): *feedback*, *dynamic representation* and *iterative opportunities for editing*. An important reservation made in the report, however, is that these affordances could not be guaranteed by the technology alone, but depended on pedagogic intervention and the quality of reflection the teacher could encourage during the production process.

In addition, there are specific issues raised by Britta's work. These include, as suggested above: the nature of animation and the specific cultural and semiotic resources it offers for creative work with students; the constraints of formal educational settings; the meeting of art education and media education and their respective practices and pedagogies; and the identity of the teacher-as-artist.

The next section will follow Britta's move into contexts of informal education, new contexts of artistic production and exhibition, and her current work with machinima. The questions raised above can be followed through; though it will be necessary to ask new questions too.

The Artist in Second Life

Britta left her job as a classroom teacher to work as a freelance educator in animation, running projects in schools in Norfolk. These projects continued to develop a range of animation techniques and hybrid practices of art and media education. Students were encouraged to learn specific filmic conventions, and to consider the artistic quality of their work, while incorporating resources from their experience of popular animation. Britta helped them to use the work as an expressive tool for their own interests and preoccupations and the exploration of their social roles and identities.

At around this time, she came across Second Life, the immersive virtual world created by the American internet company Linden Lab. It shares some characteristics of a Massively Multiplayer Online Roleplaying Game: it offers avatar-based interaction in a persistent online world; it provides resources for roleplay, fantasy and the building of communities; its aesthetic is derived in many ways from gaming cultures. Nevertheless, in other ways it is not a game in the same sense as an MMORPG: it provides no ludic resources, goals or other structures.

Britta had no background in gaming culture but was intrigued by the possibilities of Second Life for an artist. She exhibited her own paintings in Second Life galleries and sold her first painting for a couple of hundred Linden dollars (the currency of Second Life). In an interview with Diane Carr, project leader of our own research in Second Life,[3] Britta described her feelings about exhibiting her paintings in Second Life:

> I had to present my paintings in this world of modern technology; wondering how relevant painting is in our digital age? This grows out of a certain anxiety I sense about the influence of technology on art and our culture as a whole. How can art reposition itself in relation to image production in our technological age? Second life certainly transforms the ways art is produced, exhibited, and valued, and how new art forms, new tools for representation and new conditions for communication are now generated. There are private views where avs [avatars] can drink virtual champagne and talk to the artist, poetry readings in an Irish pub, museum exhibition tours and talks, photography exhibition, avant-garde video art, scripted kinetic sculpture exhibitions, music live performances and even ballet. The SL art learning experience is endless, resourceful and stimulating.

Britta's remarks, though inspired here by a new medium, recall older debates about what happens when works of art are produced by mechanical means. Perhaps the best-known discussion of this question is Walter Benjamin's influential essay on "The Work of Art in the Age of Mechanical Reproduction" (1938), which is still relevant to Britta's comments in three ways. Firstly, Benjamin's original question about the effect of mechanically reproducing a work of art with a unique original applies here. What is still at stake is the ontological and aesthetic status of different technologies of inscription (Kress & van Leeuwen, 1996). Equally at stake are the social practices which deploy these resources. What is already clear is that the art of the machine in Second Life does not imply the inevitability of the forms of corporate exploitation that the Marxist thinkers of the Frankfurt School anticipated. Corporate motives continue to co-exist with independent artistic motives; popular art styles with fine art. Furthermore, Britta's *perception* of the images of her own paintings as they are exhibited in Second Life is not of reductive, mechanical copies, their aesthetic quality flattened and depleted. Rather, she is surprised by their "strength":

> My first day in SL was to see a photography exhibition, and I was offered a show so I learned to set up my first virtual exhibition. I was amazed how strong my paintings looked, digital.

It seems likely that, while the technical production of high resolution images plays a part here—what Sinker calls the "digital aesthetic" (Sinker, 2000)—at least as important is the participant's view of the authenticity of the images and their context of exhibition and interpretation. In social semiotic terms, this would be seen as a modality judgment (Kress & van Leeuwen, 1996). The credibility, truth to genre, authenticity—all qualities relating to Benjamin's "aura"—can be seen as a meeting of claims made by the representation, and judgments made by the participant.

What Benjamin could hardly have imagined, however, is the immersive, persistent virtual world which in this case provides the social context, where the avatars of artists, spectators, critics and poets can conduct replications of the social genres which surround the exhibition, consumption and interpretation of art in the "real" world. The artistic community of this world, as Britta describes it, reinstates the social practices of the art world, from the meetings and exhibitions of independent fine art, to the commercial practices of professional studios making corporate videos using the resources of the virtual world.

As well as producing the work of art, artists and spectators are producing themselves, with an emphasis on fluid performance, whose semiotic resources range from the customisation of the avatar to the typing of chat dialogue, the deployment of emote repertoires, and the use of expressive and functional animation resources in Second Life to sit, fly, play musical instruments, laugh, drive cars, and so on.

This kind of performance replicates aspects of performance in "real" life (RL), of course. In Goffman's sense of the presentation of self through dramaturgic structures (1959), artists, students, critics and spectators have always performed their social roles in studios, galleries, museums, streets and cafes. The simple but difficult question begged by Second Life is, how to specify the differences?

These can be considered in terms of semiotic resources. For instance, Britta is able, as avatar, to adopt and change appearance much more fluidly, and with considerably more freedom, than she would be able to in RL. Her avatar, Pigment Pye, is a colourful figure with flying braids, patterned translucent garments, tattoos and cyberpunk decorations. Figure 8.1 shows her in conversation with me on her own island on Second Life.

Figure 8.1: Pigment Pye and Jupiter Mapp in conversation.

At the same time, there are constraints. The communicative repertoires of gesture, facial expression, intonation etc. are much more limited than in RL ["real life"], for instance. However, the consideration of affordance in semiotic terms doesn't entirely explain the performance of self here. Britta's accounts, like those of other occupants of virtual worlds, insist on a strong feeling of presence in this world, a sense of embodiment which invites a phenomenological consideration. The identity of the participant is projected onto the avatar, as you become the actor in your own movie—except that it is played out in real time. At the same time, there is a concern for a cognitive centring on as well as an affective commitment to the virtual body of the avatar; a dissolution of the barrier between the objective viewing of the image on the screen and the subjective experience of embodied selfhood.

In relation to Benjamin, we can recall, of course, that his interest was not limited to the artistic object and its mechanical proliferation but extended later to contexts of consumption and the social figure who occupied them—to the Arcades of his unfinished final work and the flâneur who strolled through them (1999). These metaphors are still resonant and applicable to the avatars and islands of Second Life. Indeed, while the technology of Second Life might have been beyond Benjamin's imagination, he would surely have recognised the fantastic figures who loiter in its art galleries and shopping malls. The difference is in the application of the word "mechanical" in Benjamin's earlier essay. In Second Life, the world itself and its social agents are mechanically reproduced, struggling between the attempt to capture the aura of the original and the dawning recognition that it can produce its own aura, a mechanical aesthetic, sensibility, habitus.

Having exhibited her paintings in Second Life, then, Britta encountered the art of machinima. For professional animators as well as educators, machinima offered many attractions. Because it is made in real time, it avoids the laborious process of frame-by-frame animation. It makes possible forms of character behaviour which are hard to achieve in amateur animation: a "walk cycle," for instance, is hard to achieve with frame-based animation, whereas machinima in SL merely needs to capture footage of the avatar walking. In many respects, it is closer to live film, with avatars acting parts, events filmed in real time, and virtual camera work which in conventional animation would be simulated by the animation process.

In relation to Benjamin's argument, machinima is a recent example of his category of the technological *generation* of an art which has no original, and therefore no aura to be dispelled. For Benjamin, the exemplary instances were of course photography and cinema. In the case of machinima in Second Life, it is the common sharing of resources made in Second Life itself, using scripting tools and other authoring devices. No discernible "original" seems to be generated by the artist here, so that no possibility of the aura remains. Rather, existing representations: characters, landscapes, sounds, objects, are adapted and incorporated into new productions. In fact, however, many entities in Second Life are conspicuously authored, retaining the signatures of their makers, sometimes freely available, sometimes for sale and paid for in Linden dollars. In this respect, some sense of an originating text remains, with claims either in the aesthetic domain, to be an original creation, or in the legal-economic domain, to intellectual property rights or to payment.

Britta taught herself the art of machinima, becoming acquainted with the Second Life machinima community, learning from them, and meeting them at specialist events. She attended seminars, festivals and exhibitions in Second Life, such as one addressed by Spector Hawks (real name: Paul Jannicola), a member of the ILL Clan which made the first machinima films. Britta made a number of films of her own and exhibited them on YouTube and elsewhere. One film was made as an entry for a film competition and festival in Second Life: the Ed Wood festival. Films had to address a given title and had to be made in 48 hours. Britta's entry won first prize in the festival, which was sponsored by the machinima company Shortfuze, based in Cambridge, UK. The film is notable in two ways for the purposes of this chapter.

Firstly, it exemplifies Britta's parallel life as an artist, involved in the professional production practices which inform her work in education. She describes in an interview how she found a suitable online location, used a horror-film avatar as a character, and worked with other machinimators to produce the film:

> I went to the site Sleepy Hollow, excellent location of an orphanage…but this is why machinima is so amazing in SL as you have all this fantastic sets…so the title the origin where bad things come from…I worked with two or three people so we all had an input of what that might be? Pure evil…so we had to have pin head. Oh, Dalinian helped. .he is a crazy artist…he makes weird avatars all the time…but has not been online in ages.

Secondly, the aesthetic of the film represents something of the range of cultural contexts in which Britta is working. The film is redolent in many ways of the surreal folktale animations of Eastern Europe, such as those of the Czech animator Jan Svankmajer. At the same time, it retains something of the game aesthetic, a residue of its inscriptional source. It also makes intentional reference to popular horror, in deference to the theme and title of the festival, employing the iconic villain of the horror film *Hellraiser*, available as an avatar in Second Life. This range of contexts, as observed above, might be expected also in the classroom of an educator whose pedagogies and cultural rationales are derived both from art and media education.

More broadly, we might note the nature of the social contexts of fine art, avant-garde art, and independent film-making here. They are replicated in Second Life, not only through forms of mechanical representation, but through systems of belief, commitment and social networking. While "communities of practice" may be rather more open to anti-social practices than their proponents sometimes recognise (Oliver, 2008), in this case they do exhibit the forms of solidarity and organisation which are often claimed for them. Perhaps a better term is the one borrowed by Henry Jenkins from Pierre Levy: "collective intelligence." The processes of self-education, knowledge-sharing, and communal viewing and critique undertaken by the machinima groups in Second Life closely resemble Levy and Jenkins' new knowledge communities, which are "voluntary, temporary, and tactical affiliations, defined through common intellectual enterprises and emotional investments" (Jenkins, 2002).

Teaching Machinima in Second Life

Having taught herself the rudiments of machinima, Britta became involved with the Open University's Schome project (a portmanteau of school and home). Schome has built an island in the Second Life Teen grid (Schome Park), in which young people are separated from the adult Second Life in a protected environment, to which only accredited adults have access.[4]

Britta has developed within the Schome project's general remit a specific project growing out of her long-term interest in animation. She teaches an after-school class in machinima, working with students aged between 13 and 17 to create animation using the virtual world, avatars, and creative tools provided in Second Life to make short films.

Britta described in an interview[5] how her work here began:

> I started 3 weeks ago [July, 2007]. First, I set up a film-makers forum where Schomers (under 18s) and Sparkers (their supporters) can learn all about machinima. We meet from Monday to Friday, from 17.00–19.00 on an airship that I transferred over from the main grid [the teen grid is for under 18s, the main grid is age open].
>
> Schome Park has a media centre that is entirely made, organised and set up by Schomers. Between meetings we "talk film" and get organised via the discussion forum, which is regularly visited by all.

In many ways, this project displays continuities with Britta's earlier work: a strong commitment to animation as a cultural medium for her own work and for students' expressive needs, a fusion of art and media educational aims and pedagogies; a productive interplay between her own professional identity as an artist and the pedagogic practices of the classroom.

However, while there are also differences, these are surprisingly difficult to pin down. Britta comments in interview on what feels different in this project:

> I taught media studies for 12 months in a secondary school in East London a few years ago, and as part of my work and research I'm teaching new media technology to all ages [see http://www.mediaprojecteast. co.uk/projects/index_animation_schooltoons.html].
>
> Teaching in a virtual environment is a very new experience. There is no classroom I have to walk into. No bell, no stress, no staff room (hurrah). Pupils are not sitting and waiting for their lesson.
>
> In Schome Park the students are independent learners, they are in this world because they want to be. By the time I arrive at the machinima session the core group is already IMing [instant messaging] me to get started. We teleport each other to the ship and discuss what scene we can do and who is in world for acting. Sometimes we have to wait for a particular team member to log in. But we ALWAYS talk, type, which is amazing. There is never silence. The team is always very keen to demonstrate props they made for the movie. I had one student build a grand piano in 10–15 minutes!

Some of the differences here can, of course, be accounted for in terms of the shift from formal to informal educational contexts. The latter can change the emphasis from the preparation of students for a future world of work to an emphasis on their immediate expressive and cultural interests and their engagement with the world of leisure. More practically, it can escape the constraints of compulsory attendance, mandatory curriculum and assessment frameworks, and disciplinary regimes.

However, there are differences. The physical context of informal education, often based in school buildings, carries its own cultural overtones; and, most significantly, the students are present as themselves, in the flesh. All their performances of self through speech, clothing, gesture, could never eliminate certain fixed points of identity in the body, and, indeed, in such fixed social conventions as naming. Britta's students, by comparison, are not present in her class except as avatar presences: the names they choose are recently adopted and mutable; their physical appearance is freely editable; their gender might have been changed.

These identities accomplish social purposes and desires arguably distinct from those they might adopt in school, though the comparison cannot be directly made. Britta makes the point that one of their purposes may be to escape the identities required by traditional schooling:

> Well, it is such a new field to investigate how these kids already take on a virtual identity with 12 years of age, but they feel safe in this new "skin" and e.g., voice somehow was neglected as it is too close to RL.
>
> They enjoy to be what they cannot in RL…as of peer pressure, schooling and so on. School is limiting most of them, so they like to express themselves differently and not like the norm. We have one teen who is a blue fox or raccoon; one is a giant marshmallow who changes colour; one always wears a top hat….

While these performances of identity may be frequently re-designed, the markers of difference from the conventional performances of pupil identities can be generally described as playful. Exactly what kind of play this might be is difficult to pin down. In some respects, in that it fits well with a clearly structured educational project, it resembles the form of play Sutton-Smith (2001) describes as "progressive," in the educational sense: pro-social, collaborative, developmental. However, the avatar forms chosen by the students and the names they adopt also display elements of Sutton-Smith's notion of play as phantasmagoria: anarchic fantasy operating quite outside the regulatory structures conventionally imposed by education and parenting. The "ambiguity of play" proposed by Sutton-Smith challenges older oppositions between work and play which have bedeviled play theory. In the case of these young machinimators, a productive confusion between these categories is helpful in the manner proposed by T.L. Taylor in her discussion of the playful work, or the work-like play, of power gamers (2006).

For Carroll and Cameron (2005), educational drama specialists who have explored the pedagogy and practice of process drama in relation to roleplay in computer games and virtual worlds, both educational drama and roleplay in games and machinima offer "role protection"—the "psychosocial moratorium" which protects the roleplayer from real-life consequences. Here, the performance of teacher and student roles themselves are subject in various ways to the role protection Carroll and Cameron describe. Students—and teachers—can wear clothing or hair styles which might occasion comment or even prohibition in a school environment but which are in Second Life subject to a modality of identity play and fantasy. Students may adopt social roles quite different to those they would feel obliged to play in RL classrooms. However, the Teen Grid has more limited resources, so Britta has to create a different avatar for her Schome work, and says:

> It took me two weeks to finally have a moment to change my avatar because I was always busy when logged on. It is relatively limited in Schome Park as you have no access to other shops. Yes, I do miss my outfits from the main grid! In fact, I miss a lot from the main grid. It is frustrating to move between the Teen Grid and the main grid because you're always aware of what you have to leave behind—like my Dragon avatar!

So, while there are considerable freedoms available for teacher and students in terms of dramatic expression and the representation of self, the resources are by no means unlimited, and the limitations are subject to a range of social motivations. Main grid avatars have access to outrageous tattoos, highly realistic skins, even graphic representations of full nudity, while the Teen Grid, for obvious reasons, is debarred from some of these resources.

Similarly, SL has a dramatic topography—selfhood can be realised not only by what you wear but where you visit. Again, there are many freedoms here. When Britta visited a seminar we held in SL as a visiting avatar-lecturer,[6] she took us to an SL machinima studio, where our Master of Arts students were able to question professional animators about how they made their films. By comparison with RL, this was remarkably easy: no lengthy negotiations, complicated and time-consuming travel, difficulty of access: we teleported to the studio in a matter of seconds, and the educational "visit" was in full flow.

However, Britta comments on the constraints which apply to her students:

> We can't take the teens out of the Teen Grid for obvious reasons…but I still imagine taking "day trips" with the students to visit machinima facilities and neighbourhoods on the main grid. Similarly, there are so many amazing educational sites in the main grid, but we can't take the teens there. For instance, I recently met a Geologist in the main SL. She built an entire island on the History of Geology. Amazing! I'd love to take them there and meanwhile the Geology island has no visitors!

In some respects, then, the barriers existing in RL between the worlds of adults and teenagers, permeable because they are mostly legal, social and conventional rather than physical, are rendered impermeable by the technological divide between the Teen Grid and the Main Grid. Similarly, "no-go" areas in the Main Grid are defended by technological barriers which will not allow an avatar to pass through them. While such physical barriers—to property and so on—exist in the real world, they seem to be strengthened here.

Nevertheless, it may be that the context of Second Life does make a shift away from the constraints of formal education that conventional informal teaching and learning never quite manage. While the aims, curricula and evaluation practices of informal education may escape the constraints of formal schooling, the pedagogic practices may remain very similar. Indeed, it can often be the case that "informal" classes are curiously formal and instructional, while "formal" practices can be fluid, innovative, student-centred and collaborative. In the case of Britta's Schome class, the agency of the student-as-avatar perhaps determines an informality in the teaching and learning process which is complemented by the fantasy setting—a huge airship on which Britta and the Schomers meet.

Britta's comments about how she has adapted her teaching for Second Life are worth considering in detail.

> As a classroom teacher you are always taught and reminded about classroom management. After ten years of teaching in real life I think I established a good routine of what works and what doesn't. I have worked in a variety of schools, with a variety of learners of all abilities. But teaching in a virtual world is totally different. First of all, most obvious, there is no physical presence of the teacher and students, so there's no eye contact, no voice to raise if you need them to be quiet, a very new personal space.

This seems a startling juxtaposition of affordance and constraint. While the sense of presence and social agency is strong, the sensory experience of this is quite different. The noise which all teachers experience as stressful, something necessary but also necessary to constantly manage, is gone, and though Britta sees this space as "never silent" in the sense that the students are always typing chat and instant messages, it is clearly "silent" in sensory terms. The lack of eye contact might be read as communicative constraint though there is also a sense that to make eye contact with 30 students in a "real" classroom might be a heavy responsibility from which the teacher is relieved in the virtual environment.

If we look at the chat dialogue between teacher and students, the sense of constraints becoming affordances becomes stronger still. The nature of chat dialogue, with its variety of affective devices, abbreviations which also serve as neo-tribe argot, and adaptation to specialist purposes (in this case, the teaching and learning of animation), deploys a range of features strikingly different from the genres of traditional classroom discourse. The effect is to foreground humour, speed up turn-taking, and flatten social hierarchies. In other ways, however, Britta acknowledges some similarities with the conventional teaching context:

> However managing a group is still similar—you need to be fast! The first two sessions were totally mad as I organised everyone and gave everyone jobs to do. Here I found myself in a situation not very different from being in an ordinary classroom. You speak and ask the students what they like to do and about how they think they can do it—and what they think they are best at, and so on.

One specific difference between teaching in Second Life and Real Life depends on a technical resource—the private instant messaging function available in SL:

> The thing is that I found that I had more "quality" time with the students because I could chat with them in IMs too…I never had time to talk to real life students in schools.

The ability to switch instantly into private communication with a student is impossible to achieve in a conventional classroom, where a "private chat" inevitably requires a highly visible movement of the student to another space, even another room. However, the question arises about whether the "quality time" Britta refers to is replicated in other ways in conventional school environments, whether in informal after-school activities, school trips, or "corridor" talk, all opportunities which teachers use to build relationships with students that escape the limitations of classroom-bound subject teaching. The difference, perhaps, is that such communication is here integrated into the teaching session rather than found with difficulty in the interstices of the school day.

Student Machinima

The students' main production to date has been a 12-minute film about the destruction of the airship *Hindenburg* in 1937. It was inspired by the airship Britta transported from the Second Life main grid to the teen grid:

> ...so I had the chance to take a few things from the mg to SP so I took the ship: my first pirate home I had in SL. So I gave that to the teens. Very tricky to move objects from mg to teens...so that inspired their idea to make the *Hindenburg* film.

The process of devising the film is an important aspect of the pedagogy. Media, Art, Drama and creative writing classrooms always have a choice here: to specify the topic (perhaps under constraints from exam syllabuses) or to leave it to the students. In this case, Britta strongly feels the students should choose what to film:

Pigment Pye: I am just a technician you see, and let them imagine. But sometimes I do interfere...like with the plan to refilm the TITANIC. I challenge them to tell me WHY? AGAIN? I encourage them to think again...to explain why they want to do this movie in that style—it has been done so what do they want to make different?

Juniper Mapp: creativity?

Pigment Pye: yes...as I think teens refer first to what they know, but then once encouraged refer to their imagination. I think so. But once their imagination is going there is no stopping.

This raises a number of questions about the creative process which are not specific to machinima or teaching in virtual worlds. The relation between freedom and constraint (Sharples, 1999) was a theme of the BECTa DV pilot project evaluation, in which many teachers considered that freedom was the key to creativity, yet the evaluation repeatedly found that the most effective projects were those which constrained what the students did in some way. In Britta's *Hindenburg* project, there is both freedom and constraint. Importantly, this includes the freedom to choose the content: though, as Britta's account makes clear, this choice is challenged and refined. Creativity may involve the deployment of cultural resources students retrieve from their prior experience of the media, but it also involves the transformation of these resources in two ways. As Britta says, one aspect of the transformation is imaginative: the ability to rework remembered or found cultural resources into something new. But as her account implies, another aspect is reasoned discussion. In Vygotsky's account of creativity (1931/1998), this element is criterial to creativity, seen as the alliance of imagination with conceptual understanding, rational thought. While it is commonplace for models of media literacy to specify a critical and a creative dimension (Buckingham, 2003; Burn & Durran, 2007), this instance shows how closely connected these apparently discrete dimensions can be. The ability to critically evaluate and assess the function, meaning or aesthetic effect of a media text is closely associated with the ability to imagine how it might be different. Conversely, the ability to produce something which has never existed before depends not only on re-imagining images, sounds, spaces and events, but on a rational assessment of what these resources might be made to mean.

A perennial debate in media education concerns the collaborative nature of creative work. Successive models of media education have resisted traditional essentialist post-Romantic notions of individual genius and inspiration, preferring accounts of group production which rationalise the creative process, democratise the function of authorship, and promote social ideals of co-operation and solidarity (see Buckingham et al., 1995, for an extended account of rationales and practices of group production work in media education). It is possible, even desirable, to challenge these ideals to some degree. A case can—perhaps should—be made for individual creativity, and this remains, as noted above, the dominant model of creative work in Art education. Similarly, the virtues of collaborative work can be overplayed, even sentimentalised. Group work can easily conceal emergent hierarchies, covert or overt competition, forms of exclusion and power-brokering, and disunited intentions.

Nevertheless, the evidence in this case is that group production lives up to its ideals. Students choose production roles in negotiation with the teacher:

Decimus—editing/SFX
Prof—story
Faz—explosives/props
Achilles—recording
Martin—casting/storyboards
Hapno—Directing/animation
???—Music/sound effects, costumes
(the "???" indicates that we still need someone to do those)

In the case of Britta's class, the Schome students make some of their own assets. Her evaluation of the project's outcomes referred to these processes: "Skills included character design and realisation of objects and sets using second life interface building and scripting tools."

The content of the film shows clearly the kinds of transformation of genre, semiotic resource and given information to which Vygotsky's notion of creativity can apply. It is a hybrid of documentary elements—the historical narrative of the *Hindenburg's* destruction—and fantasy elements suggesting murder and thriller genres, which produce a mysterious saboteur who kills a guard and plants the explosive which destroys the ship. The process of negotiation which accepts the various ideas here, as well as the joyful exploitation of big disaster scenes which machinima allows amateur film-makers to do (Kelland, et al., 2005), and fuses all this into a coherent narrative, is a distinctive feature of this project.

On the other hand, where constraints and structures are clearly apparent is in the pedagogy Britta describes here, which recalls, as in her earlier work in schools, the synthesis of art education and media education. There is a strong emphasis on the "language" of the moving image, as well as the metalanguage of the digital medium:

We have a specific media discussion forum where we set up topics, such as the machinima workshops. We post ideas, scripts, and I also manage to include terminology about film language. We discuss a lot of technology too, how things work such as streaming media, what codec to use.

The teaching combines old and new—the grammar of shot types developed in the early days of cinema and still fundamental to the art of machinima, and the social processes of film-making, along with the specific filming tools provided in SL:

> We are very "hands-on" and the students learn a variety of skills. It's not just about technology. I help the team to be a complete film crew, from script writing, prop making, clothes design, filming, to editing. This means that the participants learn how to use the alt-zoom camera, the SL interface camera, how to set up shots, including wide, medium, close as well as over shoulder shots, etc.

The pedagogy recalls the emphasis of media education and art education on the craft of creative production work. On the one hand, this is rooted in what Metz (1974) called the cinematic language: filming and editing. In some respects, this seems to resemble closely the production processes typical of media education:

> We get organised via the forum, and in-world everybody makes what is needed, or I train and teach camera skills and recording techniques. That can be very demanding once we get to film. The *Hindenburg* took 3 months to make…I was filming alongside Achilles (16 years old), so we had two sets of files….Editing was tricky as the teens haven't got very good editing software. Most use movie maker and that really is not very good, so that is what I like to develop with them further.

However, there are specific differences. A screenshot used by Britta to teach different roles shows the student camera operator floating in mid-air to film the ship from the outside. Machinima makes possible, then, shots which would normally be quite beyond the technical possibilities of a school production: shots which are only possible in professional production with cranes, planes, or, indeed, CGI.

If the teaching focusses on Metz's cinematic language on the one hand, however, it also recognises what he saw as the wider filmic language: the multimodal nature of film, and the other signifying systems it incorporates, such as costume, words, dramatic movement:

> Acting—he he, that was hard as I had to probe the teens and the camera man, all by typing. But we had a script, and the teens followed their basic idea…e.g., the guard shooting and the bomb. They negotiate via chat of how to film and what to do…I only took over when it got too complicated or I wanted to focus them back to their ideas.

The dramatic element is, because of the nature of machinima, a much stronger component than in traditional animation work, where it is really limited to speech characterisation. Here, the process is much more like live action moving image production work in education, in which students act roles as well as filming, editing and directing. Performance is perhaps the feature of machinima which most obviously distinguishes it from conventional animation. Avatars perform roles in real time, filmed by themselves or others, replacing the atomised production process of cel or stop-frame animation with the performative continuity of virtual bodies and running cameras.

The dramatic element in the multimodal ensemble of moving image production is under-recognised in media education: at its worst, the acting roles can be given to students perceived to be less competent with filming and editing. More generally, however, it is simply a failure of dialogue between the pedagogic traditions of media and drama education: the one has equipped itself with a language of representation, mediation, screens and distributed exhibition; the other with a language of dramatic presence, phenomenological embodiment, and local, immediate display. The truth is that the two need each other.

Figure 8.2: Britta's teaching guide for filming Second Life.

In the case of the *Hindenburg* project, it is not immediately clear what the nature of the dramatic work might be. It is clearly a form of roleplay, as Carroll and Cameron argue:

> Both process drama and machinima possess the kind of agency that Murray wants to build into the form she calls Cyberdrama [20]. Both of these forms lead to a type of dramatic creative work that is intermediate between dramatically 'linear narrative' and functional 'game' play. Role distance allows the required 'psychologically present entity,' which is somewhere between 'me' and 'other' to operate within the framed context. (2005: 8)

Role distance offers here the possibility of critical distance, in effect a descendant of Brechtian alienation, which process drama in education has at its core. The point is not so much to be emotionally immersed in a role as to be able to move in and out of role to reflect on the development of the drama and its meaning for the various participants and spectators. A different metaphor is offered by Henry Lowood:

> This was a first step towards what Paul Marino, one of the founding members of the Ill Clan, would call the virtual puppetry of machinima, that is, the careful synchronization of avatar actions (moving, speaking) to voice actors/game players via keyboard bindings. (2005: 20)

The avatar as puppet resembles in some ways Augusto Boal's notion of the *spect-actor*—the member of the theatre audience who crosses the threshold and becomes part of the drama (Boal, 1992). Most importantly, both offer critical distance. But there are differences of emphasis. The spect-actor implies a serious political project. The puppet, by contrast, suggests play, carnival, street theatre, childhood. Of course, the future of machinima, whether as art form or as educational process, can embrace both.

In general terms, the question here is about the pragmatic diversity of creative work in education. This kind of work moves beyond the traditional practices of the media classroom or the art classroom. We can no longer be certain of whether the work of art belongs to the world of popular culture or the avant-garde, or both; whether students are fledgling filmmakers, visual designers or actors; whether their work belongs to literacy, visual culture, popular cinema, digital drama, or all of these. Whatever the case, it is clear that the teaching intelligence at work here is quietly refusing to throw out pedagogic babies with the bathwater. The old order may be giving way to something more pluralistic, more fluid, more easily characterised by postmodernist modes of thought than modernist, but the process of creative making still needs to retrieve the detailed procedures of older media, their grammars and their cultural echoes. This is as true for the Schome students as it is for the adult machinima community.

Conclusion

One possible conclusion of this study is that new media raise old questions, albeit in new forms. Britta's work with the Schome students suggests that students need a stake in the content of their work, that approaches to creative production which somehow balance play and work are successful, that a detailed attention to the semiotic specificity of the moving image pays dividends. It raises the question of the differences between the aesthetic practices of art education and media education but also suggests that this kind of project can be situated within changing practices in both disciplines, the one moving towards a more pluralistic, critical approach, the other towards a closer engagement with the arts in education. It raises the issue of the advantages enjoyed by informal education and its freedom from the constraints of statutory mechanisms of curriculum and assessment. It demonstrates the advantages in both art and media education of a teaching approach rooted in and informed by professional artistic practice. It shows the complexity and the benefits of collaborative production work. This much is a reinforcement of older lessons about media education, though ones which need repeating and refreshing, especially in the context of new media.

But what can be said that is distinctive and different about machinima—its culture and its technology?

Machinima is both enabled and constrained, defined and confined, let loose and tied down by its dependence on game worlds and the resources they offer. It can never start from scratch, but must always adapt, transform, re-purpose. This is its strength and its weakness. Maybe not too much of a weakness—the art of collage, synthesis, and the transformation of found materials has an honourable history in the modernist period (Braque's newspaper collages, Picasso's bike saddle bull's head), while practices of bricolage are well-established markers of postmodernist culture, in the sampling practices of contemporary popular music; or in the material and semiotic transformation of codes in fashion and design, in which military uniforms become garments of dissent, or the severe lines of Shaker domestic style become markers of bourgeois wealth.

More specifically, an aesthetic practice based in the adaptation of existing resources is conducive to the cultural work of schools and education. The forms of cultural raiding represented by mash-ups, fan art, fan fiction, modding, reverse engineering: these are all grist to the mill of the educational project. In this sense, school students and their teachers resemble always the textual poachers of Jenkins and de Certeau's metaphor (1992): they create in rented space, with borrowed tools, in genres and forms invented by other people.

Furthermore, these practices enact the central processes of creativity envisaged in Vygotsky's (1931/1998) essay on the subject, as noted above. His emphasis on the transformation of semiotic and cultural resources serves as a vindication of the use of machinima in education. To provide resources which are already heavily culturally shaped, and shaped within contemporary gaming cultures, is to offer a starting point full of possibilities for young animators to play with. While social semiotics has always regarded language and other systems of signification as being systems of meaning potential, to regard games and gamelike environments in the same way is a productive way forward. Lowood cites Manovich's notion of the "cultural economy" of games in this respect, seeing them as toolkits for creative work, rather than fixed textual entities (Lowood, 2005).

It must be acknowledged, though, that metaphors of border raiding and trespass run the risk of romanticising educational creative production work. There are counter-arguments: schools *are* in many ways authentic and distinctive cultural spaces owned by teachers and students, with no need to trespass; their creative work is more like professional apprenticeship than amateur production: it is their day job, not a transgressive leisure activity. In particular, if the teacher's identity derives as much from professional artistic practice as from a pedagogic role, as Britta's does, then apprenticeship becomes an even more appropriate idea. In addition, there is an important question about the ontology of the artistic work, which is in many ways made from scratch by the Schome students, who script and shape their own assets for their animated films rather than adapting them from found objects within Second Life. This looks much more like a digital equivalent of the plasticine modelling of stop-frame animation than like the bricolage of culturalist rhetoric.

Nevertheless, if they are a professionalised production team, as Britta's machinimators in many ways are, they work with restricted tools, budgets, time. They beg, borrow and steal, as well as design, invent and transform; and, while its future may hold something quite different, this is the dominant aesthetic practice of machinima in its early years and what makes it so suitable for educational animation work. What is clear already is that it is a mistake to over-generalise. As Kelland and colleagues emphasise (2005), there are already many different genres of machinima, some of which depend on gaming culture, some of which derive from established film genres, others which occupy a new kind of indie space. Plenty of room and time, then, for art and media educators to find the creative spaces and resources for their young machinimators to play, work and learn with.

Notes

* This chapter was originally published as: Burn, A. (2009). Machinima, Second Life and the pedagogy of animation. *Making New Media: Creative Production and Digital Literacies* (pp. 133–154). New York: Peter Lang.
1. The chapter draws on two funded research projects: Learning from Online Worlds; Teaching in Second Life, funded by the Eduserv Foundation; and the Digital Video Pilot project, funded by BECTa. It also draws on the work of the Schome project at the Open University.
2. BECTa (the British Education and Communication Technology Agency) is the UK agency supporting the development of ICT use in schools. THE DV pilot project involved giving an i-mac and a digital video camera to 50 schools and monitoring and evaluating their use of this equipment. The uses ranged across different subject areas and different ages from early primary to post-16.
3. Learning from Online Worlds; Teaching in Second Life, Eduserv Foundation, 2007–8.
4. There are distinctions to be made between Schome, the Schome Initiative and the Schome Park Programme:
   • Schome will be the education system for the information age.
   • The Schome Initiative is developing Schome.
   • The Schome Park Programme (which Britta was involved with) is a subset of the Schome Initiative which was set up specifically to help us to give people 'lived experiences' of radically different models of education. More details can be found on the project website at www.schome.ac.uk.

5. With Diane Carr, Principal Investigator of Teaching and Learning in Virtual Worlds. The interviews cited in this chapter were all conducted in Second Life via in-world chat.

6. The Learning from Online Worlds; Teaching In Second Life project held a series of Masters seminars in Second Life, which included two sessions addressed by visiting lecturers. The report of the study, Learning to Teach in Second Life, can be found at http://learningfromsocialworlds.wordpress.com/learning-to-teach-in-second-life/

References

Addison, A., & Burgess, L. (Eds). (2003). *Issues in art and design teaching*, London: Routledge Falmer.

Banaji, S., Burn, A., & Buckingham, D. (2010). *The rhetorics of creativity: A literature review.* 2nd edn. London: Creativity, Culture and Education.

Benjamin, W. (1938/1968). The Work of Art in the Age of Mechanical Reproduction. In H. Arendt (Ed.), *Illuminations: Essays and reflections.* Trans. Harry Zohn. New York: Schocken.

Benjamin, W. (1999). *The arcades project*, edited by Roy Tiedemann. Boston: Harvard University Press.

Boal, A. (1992). *Games for actors and non actors.* London: Routledge.

Buckingham, D. (2003). *Media education: Literacy, learning and contemporary culture.* Cambridge: Polity.

Buckingham, D., Grahame, J., & Sefton-Green, J. (1995). *Making media: Practical production in media education.* London: English & Media Centre.

Burn, A. (2009). *Making new media: Creative production and digital literacies.* New York: Peter Lang.

Burn, A., & Durran, J. (2007). *Media literacy in schools: Practice, production and progression.* London: Paul Chapman.

Carroll, J., & Cameron, D. (2005). Machinima: Digital Performance and Emergent Authorship. *Proceedings of DiGRA 2005 Conference: Changing Views—Worlds in Play.* University of Vancouver, June 2005.

Duncum, P. (2001). Visual Culture: Developments, Definitions and Directions for Art Education. *Studies in Art Education, 42*(2): 101–112.

Goffman, E. (1959). *The presentation of self in everyday life.* New York: Anchor.

Jenkins, H. (1992). *Textual poachers: Television fans and participatory culture.* New York: Routledge.

Jenkins, H. (2002). Interactive Audiences? The "Collective Intelligence" of Media Fans. In D. Harries (Ed.), *The new media book* (pp. 157–170). London: British Film Institute.

Kelland, M., Morris, M., & Lloyd, D. (2005). *Machinima.* London: Course Technology PTR.

Kress, G., & van Leeuwen, T. (1996). *Reading images: The grammar of visual design.* London: Routledge.

Loveless, A. (2002). *Literature review in creativity, New technologies and learning.* Bristol: Futurelab.

Lowood, H. (2005). High-Performance Play: The Making of Machinima. In A. Clarke & G. Mitchell (Eds.), *Videogames and art: Intersections and interactions.* London: Intellect.

Metz, C. (1974). *Film language.* Chicago: Chicago University Press.

Moseley, D., Higgins, S., Bramald, R., Hardman, F., Miller, J., Mroz, M., Tse, H., Newton, D., Thompson, I., Williamson, J., Halligan, J., Bramald, S., Newton, L., Tymms, P., Henderson, B., & Stout, J. (1999). *Ways forward with ICT: Effective pedagogy using information and communications technology for literacy and numeracy in primary schools.* Newcastle: University of Newcastle.

Oliver, M. (2008). Exclusion and Community in Second Life. Retrieved November 18, 2012 from: http://learningfromsocialworlds.wordpress.com/exclusion-community-in-second-life

Reid, M., Burn, A., & Parker, D. (2002). Evaluation Report of the BECTa Digital Video Pilot Project, BECTa.

Sharples, M. (1999). *How we write: Writing as creative design.* London: Routledge.

Sinker, R. (2000). Making Multimedia. In J. Sefton-Green & R. Sinker (Eds.), *Evaluating creativity.* London: Routledge.

Sutton-Smith, B. (2001). *The ambiguity of play.* Cambridge: Harvard University Press.

Taylor, T.L. (2006). *Play between worlds: Exploring online game culture.* Cambridge, MA: MIT Press.

Vygotsky, L.S. (1931/1998). Imagination and Creativity in the Adolescent. *The collected works of L.S. Vygotsky* (pp. 151–166). Vol. 5. New York: Springer.

CHAPTER NINE

New Wine in Old Bottles?

Remediation, Teacher as Bricoleur, and the Story of Antaerus

TERESA STRONG-WILSON & DAWN ROUSE

> ...one assumes oneself to be in the present when one is not.
> —WILLIAM PINAR,
> *THE METHOD OF CURRERE*

> There is no new thing under the sun.
> —ECCLESIASTES, 1: 9

In the field of education, as in life, it can feel as if there is a continual pursuit of the "New." One can't help but want to echo Ecclesiastes: Is there really anything new under the sun? Some propose that Technology with a capital "T" is education's latest salvation, with an accompanying rush to equip public and private school classrooms accordingly (Buckingham, 2006). For many teachers, this prospect feels intimidating. New technologies do not fit the typecast of curricular reforms that come and go (and then come back again). With the evolution of computers and related technologies (cell phones, digital cameras, iPads, Kindle readers, to name but a few), a massive cultural shift has been occurring in one life span. Technology's presence does not simply call for new training and professional development. It implies changes to teachers' lives, within school as well as outside of it. But how "new" are new media? While each new device is heralded as a novelty, how new are our encounters with "new" technologies?

Bolter and Grusin (2000) suggest that "[w]hat is new about new media comes from the particular ways in which they refashion older media and the ways in which older media re-fashion themselves to answer the challenges of new media" (p. 15). With technologies such as the iPad or Kindle, the main appeal lies in "on-demand" access to written text, which is then being read. Cell phones refashion traditional telephones. Even digital cameras trace their roots back to cave paintings and the desire to capture images. As Bolter and Grusin state: "Media can best be understood through the ways in which they honour, rival and revise linear perspective painting, photography, film, television and print" (p. 15). One of the ways in which new media do this is through "immediacy" (p. 30). Immediacy seeks to erase the distinction between the "Real" and the "Realistic" (p. 53). It is no accident that a computer interface is referred to as "The Desktop," that our MP3 music players have "Play Lists" or that the newest Blackberry device is called a "PlayBook." These terms are intended to assist the user in reorganizing perception but in familiar directions. In this way, we all implicitly participate in remediating the "new."

In this chapter, we explore the phenomenon of "remediation" (Bolter & Grusin, 2000, p. 5) and the broader question of how the past hovers over the present. How are teachers "remediating" their classroom practices and stories through their use of new technologies? We begin with a time before the laptops made available to teachers as part of a three-year university-school board research partnership project called Learning with Laptops (LWL) became firmly embedded in a cohort of six teachers' practice. This was a professional development initiative located at a "rurban" school board (including a mix of students from rural and suburban areas), south of Montreal, Quebec. Where did the teachers situate themselves with respect to new technologies upon starting the project? We then look at how they moved from print to electronic media, concentrating on the first year. By the second year, immersion in the new media was virtually complete, but with a twist. We found that rather than being wholly steeped in new media, teachers had become bricoleurs engaging in "parallel pedagogy": deciding when and how to most productively use print and/or electronic media. Leander (2009) situates parallel pedagogy within a "remediation stance," whereby familiar texts and practices are mediated through less familiar ones (p. 148). Specifically, "[p]arallel pedagogy is a way of describing how old and new literacy practices, including print texts and visual texts, may be fruitfully taught side by side, rather than the 'old' being a precursor to the new or being replaced by it" (Leander, 2009, p. 149). We look at how teachers' classroom projects exemplified this principle as well as how they talked about crossing thresholds. We conclude by considering deeper, more inward evidence of remediation, including how change is embraced even as it may be unconsciously resisted through the persistence of a teacher self-formed through previous literacy encounters. We ask: Do remediated practices simply constitute "old wine in new bottles" or is a different metaphor necessary to account for the complexities of change and how new learning is incarnated?

Starting Out

Fall 2006. Teacher excitement was high. The initial LWL [Learning with Laptops] teacher meetings focused on fears and doubts: How can I use the technology effectively? Will student learning improve, especially their writing? Spelling was a preoccupation but so too was coherence of the text. Compounding these fears for Genevieve was that she felt as if she was already falling behind; she wasn't familiar with the portal and was missing important messages sent to the group by Bob. The secondary school teachers shared the troubles they were having finding spaces for the laptops in classrooms and arranging student access. They were also being run off their feet with questions. Students didn't know how to turn on the computer, let alone gain access to the portal. The students were losing some of their texts and having to start over again. (Field Text)

We began the research by inviting the teachers to align themselves with names of movies playing at the time: *Crash, Fearless, Step Up,* and *March of the Penguins.* Our intention was to find out where teachers stood *vis à vis* the laptops, as well as, consistent with the action research, to raise teachers' awareness about their beginning vantage points. Chart paper with the different movie titles was hung around the room. The first question was: How do you feel about new technologies? The second reiterated the first, but in the context of classroom practice: How do you feel about incorporating new technologies in your classroom? Some frequented the same "movie" for both questions, whereas others chose a different one. Of the teachers, four were new to the Learning with Laptops project, while two were teacher coaches who had already been through one two-year iteration of the project. One participant was a principal at the Learning with Laptops school where the teacher coaches taught. Another was the Learning with Laptops coordinator (Bob Thomas). The university research team also participated in the activity. Comments reflected a group consensus while also bringing out individual perspectives.

Affiliation with a movie title indicated a provisional identification; the comments then nuanced the affiliation. For instance, in gravitating towards *Step Up* for the first question, participants conveyed their willingness to learn about new technologies. However, comments ranged from optimism to perceived gaps in their own or others' knowledge. The comments were:

- Willing to learn
- Staff has to "step up"
- Some things are "scary"
- How to "apply" it?

Those participants choosing *March of the Penguins* specified needing a community in which to grow, but also one from which they could pull ahead:

- It makes me feel good when I see my students using "Les ordis" [les ordinateurs; the computers]. However, I still need as much support as "Bébés pingouins" [comment from new Learning with Laptops teacher]
- This is how I started. I needed to follow. Now, I still need to follow but I want to cut ahead of the line. [comment from one of the teacher coaches]

Those who chose *Fearless*, not surprisingly, displayed an unalloyed confidence about new technologies:

- Love new technology and working on the computer
- Catch on easy, ready to go, minimum instruction
- Keeners
- Fun—worry-free—mistakes

No one chose *Crash* to reflect their personal feelings on new technologies.

This was not the case with the second question on how the educators felt about "integrating new technologies into one's classroom." Two participants (one of whom was the principal) brought forward a litany of concerns and worst-case scenarios,[1] wherein "mistakes" (unlike for the *Fearless* group) were seen as disruptive of learning:

- It fails us when we need it
- Creates holes because students lose work
- Printers are unreliable
- Costly (Principal wants to buy, but not enough $$)
- Head Crashing—Pulled from one student to another
- Technology holding us back from using technology

- Slows down or interrupts
- By the time the school gets the technology, it is already outdated.

The two teachers (both new to the Learning with Laptops project) who chose *March of the Penguins* re-emphasized the need for support:

- Slow Process
- Sometimes the Technology is slow or not available
- Working as a group works well

For the second question, which comprised the focus of the research study (integration into practice), despite concerns in one case (*Crash*) and some cautious optimism in the other (*March of the Penguins*), *Fearless* remained a popular choice. After all, teachers had voluntarily chosen to participate in Learning with Laptops. We might also consider that teachers may have wanted to present a certain positive "face" in the presence of an administrator, the Learning with Laptops coordinator, and the university team. Nevertheless, the comments indicate that confidence may not have resided so much in the technology or in themselves as teachers, but in a certain faith and optimism in the students:

- Student attitude and enthusiasm
- Potential for teacher learning from students
- Teacher confidence in our developing knowledge
- Access to information/world
- Technology as a facilitator
- Reveals potential for other skill sets
- Teachers relinquish control and let kids run with it—we are developing their competencies via ICT not ours
- Kids need to have an active role (not be presented to)

The movie exercise revealed that teachers began the project from different places, but that most felt more confident personally than they did professionally. A different way of understanding this outcome is to emphasise not what teachers lacked, but what they anticipated and hoped for from the project.

A similar pattern emerged in the individual teacher surveys, which were also administered in the fall of 2006, and likewise tried to gauge teachers' personal and professional levels of confidence and knowledge of new technologies. At home, teachers mostly used computers for social communication with others (e.g., email) as well as for research, either for planning for teaching or for personal purposes (e.g., shopping for clothes). While some used computers to engage with family (e.g., travel planning), others sought in it a measure of privacy. At the time, only one (Colleen) actively engaged in online social communication with family members, saying that electronic communication had largely replaced the phone; Colleen was among those in the *Fearless* group. Genevieve avoided email or making online purchases (although she searched the internet for information on what she might buy), mainly because of security fears but also because of her lack of familiarity with computers.

Whereas most teachers were actively using the laptop personally, especially since they were now bringing their project-provided laptops home, they identified themselves as novice-level or average in their professional knowledge of using new technologies. The first professional use of the laptop that increased was planning: creating lessons, finding websites, conducting online research. The first classroom change was that more writing assignments were done using the laptops. Teachers were modest in indicating what they wanted to learn how to do, which suggests that their knowledge of classroom applications of new technologies was quite limited in these first months of the project. For instance, they expressed a desire to learn website design, video conferencing, and how to create PowerPoints, with only one teacher identifying blogging as an area of interest.

From both the movie activity and the surveys, we gain a picture of motivated teachers whose classroom knowledge of new technologies was just beginning. Even the teacher coaches were experiencing extended use of the laptops for the first time; their previous classroom encounters had been confined to two rounds of 90 days over a two-year period (for more on this, see Strong-Wilson, 2012, Ch. 2). However interested and confident any of the teachers may have felt around new technologies, the fact was that their practices were immersed in print. Sustained access to the laptops began to change that situation.

Moving from Print to Electronic: Which Texts? Which Practices?

When we consider how steeped the teachers' classrooms were in print, teachers moved from print-based practices to largely electronic ones in a remarkably short space of time. And yet, this movement also happened gradually and selectively. One of the best sources of evidence for this change is the photographs that the university team took in the classrooms. Some classroom elements quickly withered away, receding from lack of use as the laptops took centre stage, for instance, a recycled paper towel tube mailbox in Arden's classroom or loose-leaf binders, which were relegated (archived) to bins under the students' chairs, in both Arden's and Enza's classrooms as the laptops took centre stage. Other elements simply remained, like the prized reclining chair that luxuriously sat in a reading corner in Colleen's classroom; it was there in 2006 in her Grade 5/6 classroom and was transferred in 2010 to her Grade 1 classroom, although the original side table and book display disappeared.

New objects could displace old ones. As soon as she learned how to use the SMART Board, Genevieve created uses for the electronic timer, which she regularly draws on to this day (the time of writing, April, 2011).[2] She used it as an incentive to help students manage their time on task. When students finished their work, they would come up to the SMART Board and use a marker to record their finishing time around the timer's perimeter. She also used the timer in the more traditional way as a countdown, for students as well as for her, to signal when a class was ending and another period (e.g., recess or lunch) about to begin.

We found that teachers organized their changing pedagogical responses around two main areas: texts and practices. By "texts," we mean the actual materials students were asked to read and view as well as those they were asked to produce for others' reading and viewing. "Practices" is a complex, multifaceted notion. We understand it to mean how teachers choose, consciously or unconsciously, to approach texts and concepts within a given duration of time and organization of space. What constituted their typical "habitus" for teaching and learning (Bourdieu, 1990)? Which pedagogical approaches did they usually use? What tools did they rely on? How did these change over the first and second years? Choice of texts and the enactment of practices come under the provenance of curriculum at the classroom level: "this process of selection, this determination that something matters, is the very heart of curriculum. The choosing and naming of what matters and the presentation of those values for the perception and engaged participation of others are the deliberations that constitute curriculum development" (Grumet, 1991, p. 76).

Another area related to practices, which received considerable teacher attention in the first year, was classroom management: instituting routines for student use of the laptops (e.g., managing transitions, cooperative learning strategies), including ease of student access to the machines through the ways in which the laptops were stored and, especially, charged (see: Figures 9.1 and 9.2). The laptops were first stored in cramped quarters in Arden's classroom, adjoining the teacher's desk, with tangled cords going every which way. The laptops were then moved to a secure hallway cupboard, so that the adjoining Grade 5/6 Learning with Laptops classes could access them more readily and without dis-

Figure 9.1: Laptop storage "Before" (2006–07).

Figure 9.2: Laptop storage "After" (2007–08).

rupting either group. The sharing of classroom routines was especially important for the beginning teachers. However, all teachers made use of this shared knowledge, which laid the groundwork for deeper exchanges around issues of curriculum development and pedagogy.

Texts Read

With respect to fiction, over the two years, teachers continued to rely on class sets of print texts. Moreover, the novels and plays reflected titles familiar to Canadian classrooms: *Underground to Canada, Hatchet, The Island of the Blue Dolphins, Macbeth, Romeo and Juliet.* Teachers also read novels aloud and frequently reported on how students clamoured for the next installment (e.g., when Arden read *Hatchet* and Colleen read *Romeo and Juliet*). Only short fictional texts were likely to be accessed online. In the first year, teachers scanned texts, mostly picture books, which were then read aloud. Most dropped this practice as scanning took considerable time. Innovation occurred in the area of literary response, as students produced slideshows in year one and digital stories in year two.

With respect to information text, teachers travelled back and forth between print and electronic formats in the first year; a common practice during this period, for example, was searching for information online and recording it on paper templates. Indeed, the internet became the primary source for research, although students were often expected to seek out multiple sources, including from books and magazines. Class sets of informational texts produced by educational publishers also continued to be used. Teachers often vetted websites for content or language level (e.g., especially for second-language learners). Depending on teacher preferences and the topic at hand, student searching could be a closed activity (using teacher-chosen links to websites), while other searches were more open ended. If the latter, students were enlisted, or volunteered, to google key words. Information was then shared with the class, as when Colleen asked students to help find tongue twisters online; a flurry of sharing ensued (Interview, Colleen, 2007). Teachers relinquished more control at the same time as involving students in conversations on how to appropriately search for information.

Over the course of the first year, the viewing material expanded to include more visual content: photographs, PowerPoints, slide shows, iMovies. Initially, the digital productions were often created by the teacher who was learning by experimenting with the new technologies; these artifacts were posted in the teacher blog. The presence of laptops precipitated an overall shift, setting the stage for guided inquiry, self-regulated learning, and other student-centred practices.

Texts Produced

At the very start of the project, at least one teacher was having students copy handwritten text onto the computer. Such print-dependent practices were quickly phased out as teachers shared alternative ways to use the media. One teacher reported that she rarely used photocopied worksheets, replacing them with digital graphic organizers. In the first year, text composing was done using Microsoft Word. Through informal teacher-conducted surveys, its spell check feature emerged as one of the aspects of having laptops that students most valued. Second-language students also regularly relied on online programs to verify the accuracy of their texts.

Over time, written texts were transposed to electronic formats. Although still in recognizable (print) form, they also subtly altered the landscape, supplanting traditional practices previously organized primarily around a teacher. For instance, individual journal writing expanded into entries in a class (public) blog. Brainstorming, with one teacher writing students' ideas on a blackboard or whiteboard, was often decentralized through student-generated Cmaps.[3] Increasingly, too, the focus turned away from the printed word and towards predominantly visual representations: slide shows, Power-Points, comic strips, and iMovies, which the teachers called digital stories. Enza set things off in this direction when, midway through the first year, she and her students began working on a Grade 6 graduation book using the program Comic Life. Students brought in photographs to scan and added dialogue bubbles, thus generating their own personal graduation pages in a comic-book genre. By the second year, the emphasis had markedly shifted towards production, in which students were creating digital texts, with Arden introducing the term "digital story."

Teachers also began to depend more on the portal, which increased the sustained use of ePEARL.[4] Using ePEARL, students could post their artifacts as well as respond to others' work. Refinements to ePEARL combined with the school board's growing expectation that schools and teachers make use of the portal resulted in an overall increase of student-shared electronic texts. The portal and e-portfolio were also used with parents for student-led conferencing.

Practices

At the beginning of the second year, it was as if one switch turned off and another turned on. New technologies drove practice in the beginning stages of the project. Practice then started to drive the use of new technologies. In the first year, teachers had paid greater attention to acquiring technical competencies. Their first-year achievements were quite modest, technologically speaking (e.g, PowerPoints, slide-shows)—"baby steps," as Arden called them (Interview, Feb. 2007). While large projects were planned in the first year, they often paled in comparison with what teachers later achieved. Some first-year projects failed for being too grand or pedagogically flawed, and teachers resolved to try again. Establishing classroom-management routines was also a major hurdle in the first part of the project, paving the way to practice driving new technologies.

Because questions could be posed to the "collective LWL mind" and a solution quickly found in the Learning with Laptops professional learning community, any difficulties that cropped up in the Fall of 2006 were short lived. Teachers profited from one another's experience, avoiding the same "mistakes." For instance, the problem of storing and charging of laptops (initially a perennial problem, especially in the secondary school where students change classes frequently) was discussed and principals "hit up" for the purchase and installation of storage shelves as part of schools' "buy-in" to the project. One of the most useful classroom-management practices that Enza and Arden (the teacher coaches) shared was for students to be designated as "experts" and help other students; the strategy of "Ask 3 Then Me" spread like wildfire and bolstered student confidence.

> We had "captains" that would guide their teammates through certain activities. If a problem arose, I would ask the students, "Is anyone an expert in this area?" There always seemed to be someone that was! That student would help their classmate and then return to their own assignment. The students were very respectful and always offered a word of thanks to the expert that helped them out. I particularly encouraged my students to share their discoveries with the class. We were all in this together, and everyone was invited to share his or her expertise. (Colleen; Professional Journey, 2006–07)

Certain tools provided a "good fit" for existing teacher practices. Because it resembles a blackboard or whiteboard, the SMART Board tends to blend invisibly into the classroom environment. Two of the teachers had SMART Boards in their classrooms, while a third regularly accessed a mobile one. In the first year, the SMART Board was used to display texts. With time, teachers found more innovative uses. One example comes from Genevieve, the most technologically reluctant teacher in the Learning with Laptops group. In the first year, her uses of the SMART Board were largely text based; she transposed printed text to the screen and read from it. She would often scan books and project them to the board. With time, her use of the tool became much more versatile and interactive. We witnessed how she deftly used the erasure feature of the board to slowly reveal, as in a puzzle, a portion of an image, slowly, slowly—the students were riveted, trying to guess who the image portrayed—until finally the full picture was displayed: Maurice Richard, famous hockey player and local legend. The image was then linked to a video on the player.

Blogging provided a "good fit" with existing practices while also pushing teachers in new directions. One of the challenges of print journals is timely feedback. With the blog, teachers could post a question in the Learning with Laptops online portal and the response was almost immediate. Teachers could also adjust criteria so that students altered their prose accordingly. Students, for their part, could edit their entries (as well as share them with other students for feedback) and decide when to hit the "Send" button. When the audience was wider and their voices heard, there was also a greater incentive for students to participate. The importance of an authentic audience is one of the key findings that emerged from the teacher research (for more, see Strong-Wilson, 2012, Ch. 6). Another use of the blog was for polling students. The poll was usually tied to an important classroom decision that needed to be made.

Struggles existed between the media and teacher practice; they were few, but telling. Mild tensions were evident in the first year from the tendency of new technologies to dominate practice and as teachers felt pressure to incorporate the new technologies into their lessons; these issues disappeared by the second year. Deeper tensions arose when the teacher could not reconcile print and classroom practices. One teacher, for instance, developed deep reservations about iMovie. She was concerned with what she saw as the banality of content being produced by her students (Interview, Pauline, Feb. 15, 2007). More profoundly, she resented how the program infringed on her pedagogy. It affected her teacher autonomy, her "story to live by" (Connelly & Clandinin, 1985). Shared laptop time among the secondary teacher team was such that, when the students entered class in the morning, they proceeded immediately to their laptops. Missed was the crucial "reading aloud" time with which Pauline, on principle, had always started the day, a practice tied to a love of literature deeply rooted in her schooling history (Interview, Nov. 2007). Pauline nevertheless perceived enough value in the software to return to iMovie, but with significant modifications.

As time passed, teachers became more judicious about laptop use, with some using the laptops more, but others using them less, strategically linking them to specific aspects of projects and thereby exploiting their pedagogical possibilities. In videotaping the teachers' inclusion of digital story production in Year 2, the usual phases of projectwork were observed: brainstorming, choosing/settling on a topic, discussing (in small groups and whole group), reflecting (e.g., through journaling or blogging), and using storyboarding (print and/or electronic) to plan the project. What was different was the emphasis on the visual, which translated into innovative practices that moved student response to new planes of engagement.

In summary, teachers strayed least from the fictional stories they liked to use in their practice. The greatest leap from print to electronic text, not surprisingly, occurred with informational text, as the internet was resourced as a research tool. Teachers adapted print graphic organizers to electronic form and, in the second year, began to experiment with blending research with story through students' production of digital stories. The teachers initially expected a sharp change in their practice, and behaved as such in Year 1, going out of their way to enfold the laptops in as many lessons as possible. However, in Year 2, there was a relaxation as well as deeper exploration, with a seeming reversion to familiar practices but with transformations that came more from the teachers' interests and students' stories. In the second year, teachers behaved more like bricoleurs, practicing a new artistry through parallel forms of pedagogy.

Teacher Bricoleurs

What we have learned through Learning with Laptops is that teachers become more committed to meaningfully incorporating new technologies when they are given room to approach the challenge in their own ways rather than following a predetermined script or prescribed approach. When they are allowed to explore on their own and through talking with others, they will look for ways to use the tools to support the best pedagogical practices that they know—even as they search for new ideas or expressions of ideas.

Levi-Strauss first proposed the term "bricoleur" in his 1966 book, *The Savage Mind*. He wanted to distinguish between the theorists—or "Engineers," as he called them—and the more practical class who made do with the materials of the here and now, crafting solutions out of what was at hand. Strauss' bricoleur was the ultimate realist artisan dealing with the "art of the concrete" (Harper, 1987, p. 74). There is potential for the term to be applied to teachers' improvisational talents (e.g., although he doesn't use the term, Max van Manen [2002], among others, has emphasized the artful aspect of teaching). However, the term has also been used disparagingly to reinforce teaching as conservative: teachers unimaginatively drawing on a finite "bag of tricks" to solve pressing classroom problems. For instance, Hatton's (1989) teacher bricoleur exhibits "limited creativity brought about by limited repertoires of means and limited approaches to repertoire enlargement on both intellectual and practical levels" (p. 84). Hatton's bricoleur solves practical problems, but never in an innovative way, perpetually building and rebuilding castles on theoretical sand. If teachers would use theory more, she argues, they would experience the benefit of "being able to rationalize their pedagogic problem, to deflect criticism, and to protect their status as competent professionals" (p. 81).

Perhaps, Scribner (2005) counters, teacher bricolage is instead to be found in the in-between spaces. As Huberman (1995) points out, "there is always a general frame/script/set of conventions, but within them, anything goes. Improvisation is the art of moving about freely in that space and exploiting as many possibilities as the situation allows" (p. 133). Pushing the argument further, teaching (improvisational, practical) is the eclectic art that leads to knowledge that is both theoretical and practical: an art of the concrete. While the Learning with Laptops teachers experimented with new technologies in both years of the project, the evidence suggests that experimentation was greater when they were engaging in a parallel pedagogy; in other words, when they were using their prior knowledge of effective pedagogy to construct something new and innovative. This is an interesting outcome for what it suggests about the relationship of past and future to teacher identity. A memory-studies perspective (see Strong-Wilson, 2012, Ch. 1), for example, can contribute to understanding how teachers can productively address change even as we remain aware of the well-founded concern that new technologies are simply being co-opted by print-based, traditional school practices (Lankshear & Snyder, 2000; Knobel & Lankshear, 2010) and that, as former practicing teachers, we are implicated in that culture.

For the Learning with Laptops teachers, clearly, knowledge of effective pedagogy was grounded in print. This was so even for the newly graduated teachers. In the first year, teachers subsisted primarily in "technician" mode. They focused on how to apply something external to teaching (namely, new technologies) to their pedagogy. Their moves were rudimentary: "baby steps" (Interview, Arden, June, 2008), not just technologically but more fundamentally, pedagogically. In the second year, teachers' artfulness emerged as they took back control of the print and electronic "tools" at their disposal, appropriating them in their own fashion. This was accomplished when their attention shifted to the curriculum, with new technologies seen as a means of achieving curricular goals in an innovative fashion.

By way of illustration, Table 9.1 contrasts the two main projects of Years 1 and 2 for Learning with Laptops teachers at two different schools. Year 1 was characterized by using digital tools to construct bar graphs or plan for writing. Projects in Year 2 were not only more complex, they also drew on more than one medium as well as engaged with new media that were more of the students' social world. The projects in Year 2 also did a better job of integrating new media, such that a digital story was not the icing on the cake (as in Arden's *Macbeth* project in Year 1), but the cake itself. Although a book was created by Blue Metropolis, Arden's community partner, VoiceThread was Arden's contribution.[5]

Table 9.1: Two LWL Teachers' Classroom Projects (Year 1; Year 2)

Year 1	Year 2
ARDEN	
Macbeth	*Heroes in our Community*
Book read aloud	Oral brainstorming (recorded on a blackboard and chart paper)
Scriptwriting	
Students taking digital photos of themselves in costume	Classroom blogging
	Writing (on laptop)
Creating individual iMovies (using the Apple editing software)	Students taking digital photos
	Creation of a book
	Digital stories using VoiceThread (online software)
	Community presentation of digital stories
COLLEEN	
Careers	*Community: Romeo and Juliet*
Oral interviews	Oral brainstorming (recorded on SMART Board)
Blogging (unsuccessful)	
	Student research (online)
	Classroom blogging
	Interview with mayor (questions composed on laptop and tracked online during class interview)
	Reading print story aloud
	Storyboarding (print/digital)
	Group digital stories using GarageBand

Another way to gain insight into how teachers were approaching new technologies is through examining their discourse. How did they talk about their use of new technologies? Specifically, how did they envision new technologies as continuing in their practice after their formal participation in Learning with Laptops came to an end?

The teachers agreed that things would change when the laptops would not be "at hand." For one novice teacher, it meant "going back" and "doing without," while for her colleague, it entailed finding different tools:

> Pauline: Well, it will change because we won't have the laptops. The laptops were a great resource and tool to have in the classroom. And we're not going to have that as handy as it was, where for example in English class we'll stumble across a word and need to look it up, and of course we could use a dictionary.
>
> Murray: So it's up to us now to find different tools.
>
> Pauline: For sure we can do without. We'll just have to adapt. (Interview, June 2008)

For the more experienced teachers, there was no question of going back; there could only be a moving forward. "I think now it's become part of the way I teach and I don't want to go back to not having laptops," Arden explained. She continued: "I thought about that on the weekend again, I thought: how are we going to go back? All paper? Really, this is ridiculous. After four years we need to keep going, not go backwards now" (Interview, June 2008). Likewise for Colleen, who was optimistic: "We'll end up being really resourceful" (Interview, June 2009).

Teachers connected having the laptop "on hand" to greater spontaneity within their practice. It led to greater experimentation as well as fine-tuning, bringing out the artistic and playful aspect of the teacher bricoleur, as Enza testifies:

> I just love the fact that the kids are always motivated too, so if we have a discussion, a topic comes up and the kids say, can we research that more? And that wouldn't happen if we didn't have the laptops. They wouldn't say, can I go get an encyclopedia and look that up for you? They wouldn't do that! The spontaneity of always wanting to work and being motivated. (Interview, June 2008)

Enza was the most philosophical about the relationship between the teacher and her/his tools. After participating in the Learning with Laptops initiative, Arden and Enza assumed a greater mentoring role in their schools as half-time resource teachers and half-time teacher ICT Pedagogy coaches (for more on this see Strong-Wilson, 2012, Ch. 8). Teachers need to appropriate the tools, Enza emphasized: "[T]he teachers are going to have to go through the same learning that we have in the sense that it's not just magic that it does it for you. You have to do it" (Interview, June 2008).

Enza was also the most articulate in elaborating the relation between "old" and "new," theorizing remediation:

> Because there is value in everything else as well, there has to be a good mixture. If you only have one, it becomes only having what we had before, which was also good, but…I think a teacher's role is always finding new resources and putting it together and making a good blend, a good mesh between new and old. I couldn't forget the value of acquired things. (Interview, March 2007)

> Whatever we acquire tends to be reused. (Interview, June 2008)

Enza's perspective represents the teacher as improvisational artisan/pedagogue: as someone who not only does not want to forget, but whose artistry depends on remembering; specifically, on "productive" remembering (Mitchell, Strong-Wilson, Pithouse, & Allnutt, 2011). Productive remembering is the opposite of nostalgia; it is remembering for the future. Such a notion is consistent with parallel pedagogy, which implies consciousness and deliberation on the part of the teacher bricoleur who selects the best means (or "affordances," Kress, 2003) for arriving at a future learning place; who, given her/his knowledge of different media, meshes old with new so as to produce something new or creates a context that allows students to reach this goal.

Did all Learning with Laptops teachers achieve this artistry within the two years of the project? The most experienced teachers certainly did, with the two novice teachers making considerable headway in that direction. Learning with Laptops also provided a context that supported the development of teacher as bricoleur through the sharing of practices. In large part, the task would seem to involve having the right tools at hand. For instance, iMovie remained somewhat problematic for Pauline, even with creative modifications in the second year. It is also possible that Pauline was caught unawares between what Leander (2009) has identified as two "foils" (p. 148): the technophobe's resistance stance and the replacement stance of the technophile. This was mirrored in her love-hate relationship with new technologies. It was not just that online journaling, blogging, and "book talk" PowerPoints provided a closer fit with her reader-response, literature-based pedagogy. It was that the match was perfected; with the online tools, she could more readily do what she had already been doing with print, thoughts she shared in a McGill Research Exchange Forum presentation (in December 2007).

In the final analysis, for the teacher bricoleur, "[p]edagogy has to be first all the time. No matter what tool and what materials you're using, you really have to go by the same process, thinking, well, this is what needs to be done. How are we going to get there?" (Interview, Enza, June 2008). Students ought to also be invited into this process, by learning to ask themselves: "[W]hat are all the tools that are available? Why would it be—why should we use it?" Enza suggests that when these conversations take place, learning is enriched (Interview, Enza, June 2008).

New Wine in Old Bottles?

Giambattista Bodini cannot remember his name. He wakens into a "milky gray" that is like sleep (Eco, 2005). The grayness is filled with sounds that are like remnants from a past time ("A-tisket, a-tasket, a green and yellow basket," p. 21) but they don't make sense because he cannot remember who he is, where he comes from or how he came to be here. The only other sounds are of people (doctors, his family) telling him what he "should have been seeing" (p. 3).

This is how Umberto Eco's (2005) novel *The Mysterious Flame of Queen Loana* begins; the story comprises the frontispiece for an article on Learning with Laptops teachers "gathering in the dusk" (Strong-Wilson, 2008, p. 211). The image of the dusk comes from Innis (1951/2003), who used the metaphor to describe the liminal space that occurs when one technology is receding and another is coming to the fore. Applied to the present context, the grayness refers to the uncertainty—as well as to the excitement—of operating without a map.

Teachers come to initiatives like Learning with Laptops because of the "demands for literacy" (Kelly, 2007, p. 11), in this case, technoliteracy. They don't want to be left behind. They want to remain connected to their students, which means tapping into contemporary culture. Prevailing assumptions would seem to be that: (a) practicing teachers resist forgetting their past formations in print culture;

it is like a millstone around their neck, hampering new learning; and therefore, (b) practicing teachers need to successfully cross over to the other side. "There is first of all the problem of the opening, namely, how to get us from where we are…to the far bank" (Coetzee, 2003, p. 1). As pointed out elsewhere (Strong-Wilson, 2008), it is as if teachers are being asked to forget who and what they are; to begin life anew untainted by outmoding ways of being or thinking. However, even Giamabattista Bodini, who does have this opportunity (in fiction), cannot help but start to remember, such as that he likes apricot marmalade best. He is driven to know who he is because, until he remembers, he cannot stitch together and make sense of the fragments of his "new" experiences. "I couldn't forget the value of acquired things," Enza said (Interview, Oct. 2007). With Kress (2003), we ask: "[w]hat shapes" are being carried forward, "unbeknown to ourselves" in times of "deep change" (p. 83)? Do the Learning with Laptops teachers' practices with new technologies amount to new wine in old bottles? Are they unconsciously reenacting "touchstone" practices with print (Strong-Wilson, 2006)? In what ways do their practices mark a departure, an opening?

The Learning with Laptops professional development initiative was distinctive in creating an informal context for learning within a formal structure.[6] The formal structure consisted of the teacher action research model. The training was informal in that teachers were essentially free to teach what they wished, flexibility being one of the main characteristics of informal learning (Ernaut, 2004). The only constraint was that their planning conformed to curriculum reform guidelines. Informal learning can take place on several levels of consciousness: implicit, reactive, and deliberative (Ernaut, 2004, cited in Hoekstra, Beijaard, Brekelmans, & Korthagen, 2007, pp. 191–192). Implicit learning happens independently of a conscious intention to learn. Reactive learning occurs primarily at the level of action—in the middle of a situation—when there is little time to think. Deliberate learning is done in accordance with a learning goal and in a dedicated space or time. Of greatest interest in this section is the role played by memory in implicit as well as reactive learning. Memory selectively constructs links between past and present episodes, but often does so unconsciously. How does the past carry forward into the present? Three examples follow.

Genevieve

Astride her father's knee, Genevieve continually asked for the story of her father's lost dog. "When I think about someone who read to me, the image of my father immediately springs to mind. I was sitting on his knee and asked him, 'Papa, tell me a story.' I often asked for the same story, the one in which he lost his dog. Without realizing it, this experience stimulated my imagination and helped me understand the world around me" (Literacy Autobiography I, Fall 2006). This beloved story entered unconsciously into Genevieve's pedagogy in the first year of the research, months after she had first written her literacy autobiography.

Robert Graham (1989) suggests that autobiography bears a deeper resemblance to Antaeus (giant son of Poseidon and Gaia, the Earth) than to the self-enamoured Narcissus. As long as Antaeus was in touch with the ground, he found his strength. When removed from it (as Hercules discovered in holding him aloft), Antaeus lost his power. The myth is interpreted thus: keep to your own ground. Genevieve would seem to have done just that when she posted a story on the SMART Board to read aloud and analyze, serving as an example of the good writing she hoped would follow from her students. The story was about a dog lost amid the storm: "…the electricity cut out and the house plunged into darkness. It was as dark as a motionless night in the forest. As I became very scared, I called my dog. Mika would protect me. But where was she? I called several times. No answer" (Classroom videotaping of lesson, May 18, 2007). Shivers travelled up and down Teresa's spine as the videotaping proceeded because the story was the same as the one narrated in the literacy autobiography.

In the fall of 2007, we conducted another literacy autobiography. Genevieve reiterated her positive memories of being on her father's knee hearing about the lost dog. When asked if she had this story in mind during her spring writing lesson, she was visibly startled. She nevertheless immediately recognized the resemblance. We had presumed it was a story she had composed for the class. To compound the uncanniness further, she explained that she had instead found it in a writing resource (for a fuller discussion of this episode, see: Strong-Wilson et al., 2008). We presume that she was unconsciously drawn towards this story; indeed, on some level, reenacting it with her students.

Enza

Riggins (1994) has suggested that we can tell a lot about a person from analyzing the objects positioned in rooms belonging to them. Things are social; they are part of a social-semiotic web or "cosmology" of meaning (Riggins, 1994). Riggins meticulously examined the objects in his mother's living room. Classrooms are like living rooms; for teachers, these spaces are often continuous with domestic spaces and are configured in the mould of "home" (Grumet, 1988, 1991). The choices we make about which things to include matter: "Choices are affective decisions that construct and respond to the significances and consequences of things and the human relations with which they are associated" (Edwards & Hart, 2004, p. 6).

We spent the fall of 2006 taking photographs of the teachers' classrooms. In Enza's classroom was a narrow shelf that resembled a living room mantel. Above it was a map of Canada. On the mantel was the replica of a galleon. Beside it was propped a hardcover book, one in the *Tintin* series. As we learned from Enza, she developed a love of *Tintin* early in her life, reading all of the books in the series. She later acquired all of the books and associated paraphernalia. Following the writing of our first literacy autobiography, Enza brought in her collection, spreading the titles out on the table. "I couldn't forget the value of acquired things," Enza later explained in an interview (Oct. 2007).

Enza's love of *Tintin* was part of her love of comic books. This love had not been left behind in childhood. She often used comic books in her pedagogy. Her classroom was littered with piles of comic books. While *Tintin* was her preferred one, she had since found others that were more in keeping with the competency level of her students, who were learning French as a second language.

One of the first print projects that we observed in Enza's classroom involved inserting dialogue, in French, into existing comics. It is therefore not surprising that a program to which Enza was drawn in the first year of the project was Comic Life (see: http://plasq.com/products/comiclife2/win). Enza has also had an abiding interest in photography, an interest that goes back to high school. She also married a photographer. They installed a dark room for photography in their house. Enza's interest in oral language pulled her towards podcasts in the second year of the project, but in the first year, it was her interest in the visual that provided a bridge between what she knew and loved and what she was experimenting with.

Colleen

The teachers were asked why they chose to use the texts they did, and later, why they chose the digital story projects they did. Dawn tells the story of Colleen's use of *Romeo and Juliet*. What follows is a brief summary of key elements of that story, from the point of view of memory and remediation.

Colleen was determined to include *Romeo and Juliet* within her long-range planning for 2007–08. In the fall of 2007, teachers had a workshop on the Ministry's new requirement of a Learning Evaluation Situation. Colleen had wanted to do a project on the Middle Ages, culminating in the story of Romeo and Juliet. An educational consultant pointed out that, because the Quebec Education Program mandates that each Learning Evaluation Situation conform to a competency-based approach that aligns with its Broad Areas of Learning, this was not an option. The Broad Areas of Learning are intended to link classroom pedagogy with students' contemporary lives. The Middle Ages could therefore not be a focal point for a Learning Evaluation Situation.

Colleen was deeply disappointed, as she had planned this thematic unit over the course of the summer. She found a way around it by making *Romeo and Juliet* the culminating digital story project of an Learning Evaluation Situation on "Community." The mayor was invited to speak about what it was like to be in charge of a town; the analogy was made to Shakespeare's story: the challenges in navigating among competing, often conflicting, visions. What was it about Shakespeare's story that drew Colleen to it so strongly?

Colleen did not have a vivid recollection of stories read when she was young, although she had imbibed many "proprioceptive understandings" (Mackey, 2011). She remembered the "wooden book-case" with its Golden Book series. She remembered the small record player that her father had bought for her from the Legion; he had painted it pink for his daughter. "The record player was in my room and my mother used to put my favorite record on it for me at naptime. It was Wilma Flintstone telling Pebbles the story of Bambi. I still have that record today. It was beautifully told. I listened to this story over and over again" (Literacy Autobiography, Fall 2006).

Over the course of the research, Colleen also alluded to, in passing, her fairy-tale second marriage, which was an event fresh in her mind. A favourite story she liked to tell was that, when her teaching partner called her to ask if she wanted to be part of the school's project submission, she was on her honeymoon. In her first life-history interview, she mentioned that before this life event, she had been a less happy Colleen. The digital stories that the students created around *Romeo and Juliet* (for they came to love the story as much as Colleen did) marked a high point in Colleen's experience in the Learning with Laptops project. *Romeo and Juliet* thus seemed a less than random choice, given the tenacity with which Colleen held onto her intention to enfold the story within her pedagogy. We are left to surmise that a deeper lived connection was likely implicit.

What can we make of the teachers' accounts? The story of Antaeus, although "just" a story, is instructive. It reminds us that teachers may feel most committed to new technologies when they can experience the excitement and ambiguities of disequilibrium on their own lived ground. The presence of new technologies in the classroom is most often experienced, on some level, as an "intensification" of teachers' practice (Apple, 1986; Hargreaves, 1998). While Hargreaves saw intensification as undermining teachers' autonomy, Ballet, Kelchtermans, and Loughran (2006) have suggested that teachers can actively seek out as well as choose change. Especially within a context of teacher action research, in which teacher knowledge is valued, intensification "differs from imposed change because it involves teachers in 'enhancing' their practice (Ballet et al., 2006, p. 226) through deepening their knowledge of practice" (Strong-Wilson et al., 2008, p. 457). And yet, even as teachers choose intensification, they may resist its effects, here through "the implicit and largely unconscious continuation of favourite narratives in new forms and transformative contexts" (Strong-Wilson et al., 2008, p. 457). This kind of resistance is different from the reactive kind that Leander (2009) identified. It may be a reminder of the presence of the teacher as person within the situation called "incorporation of new technologies within practice."

With the teacher, willy-nilly, comes memory and life history. We say "willy-nilly," but as the three narratives above suggest, a certain coherence is present that arises from the teachers' subjective interpretations of life events. As Day and Leitch (2001) rightly caution, we need to be careful about making fragments of lives speak for lives in their entirety. Our own account is its own "narrative story produced by the researcher[s], not an image-like replica" (Heikkinen, Huttunen, & Syrjälä, 2007, p. 11, cited in Strong-Wilson et al., 2008, p. 456). The teachers have read these accounts, though, and have agreed with them. A life-history perspective alerts us to the fact that teachers appropriate change in their own fashion. Such selves are not necessarily closed entities, but open to, and often highly receptive to, change. However, when speaking about lived lives, we are clearly operating in the realm of remediation.

Conclusion

To reiterate Bolter and Grusin (2000): "What is new about new media comes from the particular ways in which they refashion older media and the ways in which older media re-fashion themselves to answer the challenges of new media" (p. 15). Over the course of the two years of the research project, a reciprocal process of remediation occurred within the teachers, who became bricoleurs *vis à vis* the print and digital affordances at hand. This artistry, which reached its highest point in the digital stories, developed through sustained use and continuous experimentation as well as sharing of practices within the school teams and in Learning with Laptops.

This chapter has focused on how the past hovers over, as well as informs, the present: first through the teachers' initial fears, which were dispelled; then through their chosen texts and practices, which were kept as is, left behind, or translated into a new form; followed by a more deliberate artistry and use of the past in the service of the future; and finally, the persistence of certain implicit threads to remind teachers of where they came from and what mattered to them. Based on the evidence provided through the Learning with Laptops research, attention to the role of the past in teacher subjectivities needs to be an integral part of understanding a change process with "new" media.

Notes

* This chapter was originally published as: Strong-Wilson, T., and Rouse, D. (2012). New wine in old bottles? Remediation, teacher as bricoleur and the story of Antaeus. In T. Strong-Wilson (Ed.), *Envisioning New Technologies in Teacher Practice* (pp. 67–96). New York: Peter Lang.

1. This principal was one of the staunchest defenders of integrating new technologies into schools, so in this exercise, rather than expressing her own anxieties, she may have been articulating teachers' worst fears, anticipating the challenges she would be facing as a new principal.

2. The SMART Board was developed by Smart Technologies (http://www.smarttech.com/us) and is an interactive electronic white board.

3. The Cmap software, created by the Florida Institute for Human and Machine Cognition (IHMC), according to its website, "empowers users to construct, navigate, share, and criticize knowledge models represented as Concept Maps" (http://cmap.ihmc.us).

4. ePEARL stands for Electronic Portfolio Encouraging Active Reflective Learning (http://grover.concordia.ca/epearl/en) and is a bilingual electronic portfolio system developed by CSLP (Centre for the Study of Learning and Performance), a multi-institutional provincial research centre of excellence based at Concordia University, with collaborators from various colleges and universities throughout Quebec (see http://grover.concordia.ca/epearl/promo/en/information.php).

5. Arden's use of Voice Thread is explained in more detail in Strong-Wilson (2012), Ch. 7.
6. This paragraph and Genevieve's story include summarized material from Strong-Wilson, Harju, & Mongrain, 2008.

References

Apple, M. W. (1986). *Teachers and texts: A political economy of class and gender relations in education*. London: Routledge.

Ballet, K., Kelchtermans, G., & Loughran, J. (2006). Beyond intensification towards a scholarship of practice: Analysing changes in teachers' work lives. *Teachers and Teaching: Theory and Practice, 12*(2): 209–229.

Bolter, J. D., & Grusin, R. (2000). *Remediation: Understanding new media*. Cambridge, MA: MIT Press.

Bourdieu, P. (1990). *The logic of practice*. R. Nice (Trans.) Cambridge, UK: Polity Press.

Buckingham, D. (2006). Is there a digital generation? In D. Buckingham & R. Willett (Eds.), *Digital generations: Children, young people, and new media* (pp. 1–18). Mahwah, NJ: Lawrence Erlbaum.

Coetzee, J. M. (2003). *Elizabeth Costello*. London: Secker & Warburg. (Originally published 1999).

Connelly, M., & Clandinin, D. J. (1985). Personal practical knowledge and the modes of knowing: Relevance for teaching and learning. In E. Eisner (Ed.), *Learning and teaching the ways of knowing* (84th Yearbook of the National Society for the Study of Education, part 2, pp. 174–198). Chicago, IL: University of Chicago Press.

Day, C., & Leitch, R. (2001). Teachers' and teacher educators' lives: The role of emotions. *Teaching and Teacher Education, 17*: 403–415.

Eco, U. (2005). *The mysterious flame of Queen Loana*. G. Brock (Trans.). Orlando, FL: Harcourt.

Edwards, E., & Hart, J. (Eds.). (2004). *Photographs, objects, histories on the materiality of images*. New York: Routledge.

Ernaut, M. (2004). Informal learning in the workplace. *Studies in Continuing Education, 26*: 247–273.

Graham, R. (1989). Autobiography and education. *Journal of Educational Thought, 23*(2): 92–105.

Grumet, M. (1988). *Bitter milk: Women and teaching*. Amherst, MA: University of Massachusetts Press.

Grumet, M. (1991). Curriculum and the art of daily life. In G. Willis & W. H. Schubert (Eds.), *Reflections from the heart of educational inquiry: Understanding curriculum and teaching through the arts* (pp. 74–89). New York: State University of New York Press.

Hargreaves, A. (1998). The emotions of teaching and educational change. In A. Hargreaves, A. Lieberman, M. Fullan, & D. Hopkins (Eds.). *International handbook of educational change* (pp. 558–575). Dordrecht, Netherlands: Kluwer Academic Publishers.

Harper, D. (1987). *Working knowledge: Skill and community in a small shop*. Chicago, IL: University of Chicago Press.

Hatton, E. (1989). Levi-Strauss's "bricolage" and theorizing teachers' work. *Anthropology & Education Quarterly, 20*(2): 74–96.

Heikkinen, H. L. T., Huttunen, R., & Syrjälä, L. (2007). Action research as narrative: Five principles for validation. *Educational Action Research, 15*(1): 5–19.

Hoekstra, A., Beijaard, D., Brekelmans, M., & Korthagen, F. (2007). Experienced teachers' informal learning from classroom teaching. *Teachers and Teaching: Theory and Practice, 13*(2): 189–206.

Huberman, M. (1995). Networks that alter teaching: Conceptualizations, exchanges and experiments. *Teachers and Teaching, 1*(2): 193–211.

Innis, H. A. (1951/2003). *The bias of communication*. Toronto: University of Toronto Press.

Kelly, U. (2009). *Migration and education in a multicultural world: Culture, loss, and identity*. New York: Palgrave.

Knobel, M., & Lankshear, C. (Eds.). (2010). *DIY media: Creating, sharing and learning with new technologies*. New York: Peter Lang.

Kress, G. (2003). *Literacy in the new media age*. London: Routledge.

Lankshear, C., & Snyder, I. (2000). *Teachers and technoliteracy: Managing literacy, technology and learning in schools*. Crows Nest, Australia: Allen & Unwin.

Leander, K. (2009). Composing with old and new media: Toward a parallel pedagogy. In V. Carrington & M. Robinson (Eds.), *Digital literacies: Social learning and classroom practices* (pp. 147–164). Los Angeles, CA: Sage.

Mackey, M. (2011). Readers remember: Text, residue, and periphery. In C. Mitchell, T. Strong-Wilson, K. Pithouse, & S. Allnutt (Eds.). *Memory and pedagogy* (pp. 81–97). New York: Routledge.

Mitchell, C., Strong-Wilson, T., Pithouse, K., & Allnutt, S. (Eds.). (2011). *Memory and pedagogy*. New York: Routledge.

Riggins, S. H. (1994). Fieldwork in the living room: An autoethnographic essay. In S. H. Riggins (Ed.), *The socialness of things: Essays on the sociosemiotics of objects*. Berlin: Mouton de Gruyer.

Scribner, J. (2005). The problems of practice: Bricolage as a metaphor for teachers' work and learning. *Alberta Journal of Educational Research, 51*(4): 295–310.

Strong-Wilson, T. (2006). Touchstones as *sprezzatura*: The significance of attachment to teacher literary formation. *Changing English, 13*(1): 69–81.

Strong-Wilson, T. (2008). Gathering in the dusk: Circling back to literacy formations as teachers "learn with laptops." *Changing English, 15*(2): 211–222.

Strong-Wilson, Harju, M., & Mongrain, N. (2008). Changing literacies, changing formations: The role of elicitation in a teacher action research project involving new technologies. *Teachers and Teaching, 1*(6): 447–464.

van Manen, M. (2002). *The tone of teaching*. London, ON: Althouse Press.

CHAPTER TEN

Supporting Pre-Service Teachers' Development

The Place of Blogging in the Get Real! Science Teacher Preparation Program

April Luehmann, Joe Henderson & Liz Tinelli

In this chapter, we report on how teachers engaged in blogging as part of an education experience that included maintaining a personal professional blog as a requirement. These teacher bloggers were a group of 20 *pre-service* teachers who participated together in a cohort-based graduate science teacher preparation program during the U.S. 2009–10 academic year. Their blogging experience took place throughout the 15 months they were in their program in connection with and across a series of four consecutive courses with four different instructors. A few blogging assignments and overall requirements were carefully constructed to make these blogging experiences as productive as possible, building on what was learned from a number of earlier case studies (and reported in Luehmann & Borasi, 2011).

Findings from our studies of this practice showed us that all 20 pre-service teachers took up blogging to support their own personal professional work, although to varying degrees and in varying ways. Each of them inserted images, hyperlinks and video (some more than others), most constructed "rants" about some injustice or inappropriateness they were passionate about, and all wrestled with issues related to teaching and learning—including those unique to a reform-minded agent of change. Many brokered knowledge and resources they felt would be useful to their peers and some developed a perceived sense of community with their readers. Though there were commonalities across the teacher blogging experiences, each pre-service teacher made personal decisions about what, when and how they engaged in blogging that ultimately crafted her and his own blogging experience, engagement and effects.

To give readers an in-depth appreciation of the power of blogging in this context, in this chapter we feature the in-depth exploration of the unique ways one pre-service teacher, Maya (pseudonym), took up blogging for her own personal, professional development as a reform-minded science teacher. After offering this in-depth look into Maya's blogging, we offer snapshots of two contrasting cases—Niklas's and Elisabeth's blogging—to give a sense of the very different ways individual pre-service teachers within this group engaged in blogging literacies. These analyses will be complemented by a report of how all 20 participants *perceived* their blogging experience, based on data collected from a reflective assignment given toward the end of the program. This metacognitive task asked them to explicitly identify benefits and drawbacks of blogging for their own development and meaning-making as teachers-to-be, as well as for developing community and support within the cohort. Main take-aways from these analyses will conclude the chapter.

We begin by giving you a sense of the learning context for these teacher bloggers—namely, that of their teacher education program known as the Get Real! Science (GRS) program. We share with you both key experiences and key players (i.e., various types of mentors) to enable you to better understand and interpret the content, relevance and importance of the blogging content.

The Context

The Pre-service Teacher Program

The Get Real! Science program is a 15-month graduate teacher preparation program specifically focused on preparing reform-minded science teachers with a commitment to supporting meaningful science learning and investigations for *all* students—especially for students who have traditionally been underserved in schools and marginalized in science. The program is grounded on the premise that teachers learn reform-based pedagogy best through "real" and supported inquiry-based teaching experiences. Throughout the Get Real! Science program, prospective teachers experience a carefully sequenced series of four reform-based learning-to-teach experiences concurrent with four science methods courses—as summarized in Table 10.1 and described in more detail in what follows:

(1) *Conducting an authentic science investigation as learners.* During the first methods course, pre-service teachers experience the richness (e.g., excitement, challenge, frustration) of conducting personally meaningful, extended scientific investigations as learners—often for the first time!

(2) *Facilitating a week-long summer science inquiry camp for middle-school students: collaborative science teaching in a low-stakes out-of-school setting.* After experiencing scientific investigations as learners, participants in the Get Real! Science program have a first opportunity to "try-on" their identity as reform-minded teachers as they work together in small groups to design and implement a week-long science inquiry camp for middle school students. The overarching driving question for the camp investigation is the same as the one the prospective teachers engaged with as science learners in the previous course. The instructor of the concurrent methods course serves as the mentor-teacher for these out-of-school teaching experiences, thus affording participants guidance and feedback on their teaching that is informed by and grounded in reform-based theories.

(3) *Facilitating a weekly after-school science inquiry club for urban middle school girls called Science STARS: collaborative science teaching in a second low-stakes non-traditional setting.* During the fall, prospective teachers work collaboratively to implement inquiry-based lessons in an after-school program that is similar to, but intentionally different from, the camp. Designed to transition beginning teachers from the open-ended experience of teaching in a camp, situated in a highly motivating setting (i.e., the beach), STARS situates learning and teaching within the more structured context of a traditional school. Prospective teachers support the urban teens in developing and conducting a 10-week investigation around a topic that is interesting and relevant to the girls (e.g., energy drinks, blood spatter, dancing, video games, rockets). The methods course instructor and other mentors support beginning teachers in the development of reform-based pedagogy, language and identity as well as classroom management strategies.

(4) *Formal, school-based teaching experiences.* Throughout both the third and fourth methods courses, candidates have multiple opportunities to work in traditional classroom settings. Toward the end of the third methods course in the fall, candidates are required to teach a series of three "innovative lessons." Toward the end of the program, during the fourth methods course in the spring, candidates engage first in a four-week middle school formal student teaching placement, followed by an eight-week high school formal student teaching placement. They are now expected to consider and implement aspects of reform-based practices in classroom settings that resemble contexts of likely future employment and learn strategies to be successful in existing culture while maintaining a reform-minded vision.

Table 10.1: Get Real! Science teacher preparation program at a glance

Semester:	Summer A (May–June)	Summer B (July–Aug.)	Fall (Sept.–Dec.)	Spring (Jan.–April)
Methods course:	EDU487. Integrating science & literacy	EDU486. Technology in service of science teaching	EDU434. Theory and practice in the teaching & learning of science	EDU448. Implementing innovation in science education
Learning-to-teach-experience:	*Conducting an authentic science investigation as learners*	*Facilitating a week-long summer science inquiry camp for middle-school students*	*Facilitating a weekly after-school science club for middle school urban girls*	*Formal, school-based teaching experiences*

Throughout the program, participants also engage in ongoing narrating, reflection, critique and recognition of their professional practice and growth. Besides professional blogging (the focus of this chapter), these opportunities include engaging in collaborative post-teaching debriefing sessions (where pre-service teachers and mentors identify "pluses"—i.e., positive aspects of the day's teaching—and "arrows"—i.e., ways they plan to change future approaches and strategies), constructing a comprehensive portfolio as a way to demonstrate one's learning and growth, and presenting at professional conferences.

This science teacher preparation program is especially demanding and challenging, as participants are asked to constantly juggle concurrent graduate-level coursework and the work associated with teaching in these varied contexts. These teacher learners are not only preparing for a demanding profession (teaching) but are also asked to do things that are outside the norm (i.e., being a reform-minded teacher and a change agent working toward social justice).

Blogging as an Assignment and Expectation

April Luehmann, as the program director, made some overarching decisions about the blogging requirements connected with the program. Those included the decision to have the participants blog throughout the 15 months of the program, to publish their blogging work on the internet so that they would be publicly accessible, and to connect specific blogging assignments to the concurrent methods courses.

That said, specific blogging assignments were somewhat tailored to each science methods course, as course goals and instructors varied. The first methods course offered to participants, *Integrating Science & Literacy*, required only two blog posts for the entire 12-week course. The syllabus asked that students post a blog at the start of the course reflecting on themselves as science learners and at the end of the course, to blog reflections about how they have grown as science learners. The instructor (Dawn) gave verbal instructions to students that blog posts were intended to be an extension of classroom discussions.

In the second methods course, *Integrating Technology in the Service of Science Learning*, the requirements for blogging became more specific and a greater number of posts were required. The syllabus encouraged pre-service teachers to "post your reflections, struggles, and successes of integrating technology in science instruction on your blog so that you can track your developing understanding and so that you can invite others to contribute to your learning." The instructor of this course (Michael) required that students adhere to weekly posting (a programmatic requirement) as well as contribute a reflection after each day of teaching camp (6 days, for a total of 6 posts). The instructor also read and commented on all student blogs.

Blogging requirements became more explicit in the fall when students took *Theory and Practice in the Teaching and Learning of Science*, taught by the program director (April). Class participation—40% of the total course grade—included weekly blog posts and comments. As documented in this excerpt from the course syllabus, the guidelines became considerably more structured than the previous two courses, and identified specific requirements:

> By the end of the semester, you need to have A) posted 14 significant posts; B) engaged in 4 different professional practices (labeled by categories or tags such as rant, share resources, reflect, build community, engage in a conversation); C) used blogging technological affordances in at least 4 creative ways (such as post a series of images, include a video, construct an intensely hyperlinked post that connects to peer's work as well as outside resources, author a poem, scan one of your creative drawings); and D) engaged in your peer's professional work by commenting on their blogs at least 14 times.

It is worth noting that the decision to explicitly require that participants explore different blogging practices and technological features came from the instructor's appreciation of the value of those practices and features as a result of previous, related studies (see Luehmann & Borasi, 2011). In addition, this specific set of blogging expectations came from the desire to have participants experience professional blogging as a way to build productive long-term meaning-making and community-building routines that could sustain their continuing development as teachers beyond their teacher preparation program. These intentions were shared and discussed often with participants to ensure that both the spirit of the expectations and the goals were clearly understood.

The fourth methods course, *Implementing Innovation in Science Education*, occurs concomitantly with pre-service teachers' student teaching placements and was taught by yet another instructor (Lisa). The blogging requirements for this course were identical to the expectations for blogging in the previous course, asking students to engage in four different professional practices, four different technological skills, and to complete a minimum of 14 blog posts and 14 blog comments (one of each per week). The instructor for this course was purposeful in verbally reinforcing blogging expectations during each class meeting and also referenced specific blog posts during class for the purpose of highlighting shared experiences. The instructor read and posted comments on blogs every other week. In addition, she arranged for another instructor within the program to read and comment on blogs during the alternate weeks.

The Blogging Community

Each of the 20 participants maintained her/his own personal professional blog. While this group comprised only pre-service teachers, there were some interesting, varied member characteristics within this group: five males and 15 females; four "career changers" as well as students who had recently completed an undergraduate degree in one of the sciences, and individuals seeking primary certifications in one of the following sciences: biology (9), chemistry (6), physics (4) and earth science (1). Most were seeking certification in at least two of these science disciplines.

Not only did these 20 pre-service teachers read and comment on each other's blogs, but so did a diverse group of science teachers and teacher educators serving in various mentoring roles. These significant others included:

- The program director and program advisor for most students (April).
- Course instructors (Dawn, Michael, April and Lisa), who each chose the level at which they wanted to comment on their students' blogs.
- Student teaching supervisors (including retired science teachers Jo Ann—lead supervisor, Mort, Sue, and Jim, as well as former teacher, former GRS student and current doctoral student Joe).
- Programmatic mentors—these were practicing science teachers or administrators who each supported a small group of 4–5 pre-service teachers in assignments such as innovative lesson and unit plans and their final portfolio (Jay, Michael, Lisa and Joe).
- A few former Get Real! graduates who helped facilitate some of the out-of-school experiences (Ashley and Tonio) and a few former graduates who were interested by the blogging and wanted to support the new cohort (e.g., Chris).

An In-depth Look at Maya's Blogging

The power of blogging as a tool for professional identity learning and development in a semi-structured setting (as a part of a graduate-level course and program) is made clear through the in-depth, unique and personally-meaningful ways one preservice teacher, Maya, was able to wrestle with the nuance of becoming a professional. In her own unique ways, Maya blogged to engage in each of five core teacher learning practices shown to be effective in supporting teachers' development: reflecting on practice separate from practice, engaging in learning within a community, integrating one's autobiography in the lessons being learned, engaging in critical inquiry, and participating in sustained inquiry over time. In what follows, we will examine in depth how each of these practices played out, after a few considerations about Maya's background and style.

Maya and Her Blog

Maya was a career-changer who enrolled in the University of Rochester's Warner Graduate School of Education after leaving a previous job as a molecular neuroscience lab technician at a nearby medical research hospital. Maya's husband was also a teacher, and she spoke often about how different this program was from the one her husband experienced. She also has three young boys and her experiences with them shape how she understands science and science teaching. Indeed, the primary lens Maya brings to her learning and development is that of a mother, as her children are extremely important to her, and she writes about them often, especially as the demands of the program and student teaching responsibilities build over time.

The tagline on Maya's blog reads: "Aspiring Science Teacher." The visual theme she chose for her blog has a heading image of reeds being reflected in water, which fits with her perceived value of blogging as a reflective practice. (You can explore Maya's blog in full at http://www.getrealscience.com/PreserviceBlogging1.)

Maya published a total of 60 posts between May 2009 and June 2010 with a total of 1880 lines (an average of 31 lines per post) that received 129 comments. Her blogroll lists 21 other blogs, consisting of the other 19 students in her cohort, the main cohort blog and a blog from a member of the previous GRS cohort. The left toolbar of her blog displays a number of other resources that appear to be important to Maya's professional development and practice, including "Cool Science Links" (5), "Journals" (4), "Photos" (1) and "Teaching Tools" (2) as well as her personal identity "I Lean Left" (6).

The categories she defined to organize her blog posts, and the number of posts she wrote within each category, were: community building (4), learning (9), my Life (outside Warner) (2), reflecting (13), resources (3), teaching (12), teaching & learning (27), uncategorized (7), venting (6), wondering (2). Beyond the categories that Maya developed for labeling her own posts, our codes revealed an even wider range of topics related to her own identity development as a teacher including: self as learner (6), self as teacher (8), planning (4), management (6), professional learning and development (5) and pedagogical practices and dilemmas (12). At the time of this writing (July 10, 2010), her last post (published June 1, 2010) is titled "Making a commitment" in which she publishes a commitment to continue her blogging as a way to remain a reflective practitioner.

Although every once in a while Maya made what might be seen as sarcastic or frustrated digs about her course requirements in her posts, she took up blogging participation in rich and diverse ways that far exceeded any programmatic or course expectation. Maya's blogging was unique in a number of interesting and complementary ways: (1) the relatively consistent way she approached and processed her lived experiences, (2) her exceptional use of creativity and wit in communicating lessons learned, (3) her attention to and success with building a community and (4) the many and varied ways she employed her lens as a mom to make sense of her learning-to-teach experiences as well as to advocate for what she felt were priorities in effective teaching. Her blogging also represented unique forms and powerful interpretations of the types of practices research has shown to be supportive to teacher learning. Though each of the categories was certainly integrated and dialogic in Maya's practice, in what follows we will highlight her unique forms of participation by organizing them around five research-based teacher-learning practices (for more, see Luehmann & Borasi, 2011, Ch. 9). These include: studying practice separately from practice, learning through engagement with her community, autobiography and teaching practices, engagement over time, and integration of expert voice.

Studying Practice Separate from Practice

Within this project, pre-service teachers were encouraged to "wrestle" with "dilemmas that are specific to particular content (e.g., science) and specific topics within that content (e.g., chemical change)" but within a "space removed from the immediacies of the classroom" (Luehmann & Borasi, 2011, p. 170). This was referred to as "studying practice separate from practice." The "distance" afforded by blogging about "wrestles" with practice was also aimed at promoting critical inquiry among the participating pre-service teachers.

Throughout Maya's blog, there is much evidence of her *wrestling* with many significant issues that she explores in complicated grey—revealing her awareness of the nuanced complexity of everyday situations and her role as teacher within them. These issues include when and how to engage students with homework, how to *really* (and accurately) measure student understanding (and the shortcomings of school-based on-demand requirements), how to process, survive and react to what she feels are injustices of the world that hurt her students, to what extent and in what form inquiry can actually make its way into the classroom, as well as many others. These wrestlings appear to be deep explorations that complement and are sometimes inspired by other significant forms of meaning-making Maya engaged in through blogging, namely self-evaluative lists of effective and ineffective practices. These "pluses" and "arrows" are reflections on and connections to a specific instance of teaching practice that both celebrate competence as well as direct future efforts. Out of these wrestlings and reflections, Maya takes regular pause to define general take-aways about teaching, herself and the world that she defines as "lessons learned."

Lessons learned: Inspired by practice, informed by program.

> One thing that I've learned already—planning a science lesson is time-consuming and difficult. Planning inquiry is even harder. Planning inquiry that is student-led and meaningful is much harder. That said, it's also a lot of fun (July 13).

As well illustrated by the above quote, Maya's statements about what she has learned are articulated in general, take-away terms and, though most often inspired by a particular situation, were phrased such that they were no longer tied to that instance or specific goals for future practices. When Maya's blog transcript is searched for the word "learned," it appears 33 times—27 times having to do with her own personal learning about course outcomes (7), teaching (17) or about herself (3). She titles two different posts "Lessons Learned." Certainly the most interesting and elaborate claims of lessons learned were those that were inspired by her teaching practice. As can be seen in the following example, these lessons learned were deeply rooted in her on-the-ground experience and thus impacted Maya because of the investment she had made in understanding the nuance of the professional work of being and becoming a teacher.

> Those who can't teach, do (insert job title here).
> On Monday I had my first experience really "leading" class. And I learned a lot:
> 1. Always calling on the first hand up in the air: Cost = 10 students. Enough said. I know better than to do this, but it's like an unstoppable instinct.
> 2. Kneeling down to help one student with my back to the rest of the class: Cost = 30 students (doing whatever). For goodness sake, I have kids so I know you're not supposed to let them out of your sight!
> 3. Handing back four assignments at the same time: Cost = 35 (confused) students. This is the problem with blocks—there is a lot of work to hand back all the time.
> 4. Handing out homework at the beginning of class: Cost = 5 students (doing it during class). My thoughts were that they would have it if they finished group work early, but I noticed students doing it during the discussion.
> 5. Knowing names: priceless. I am so grateful that I spent so much time really learning names. I used them constantly, especially to get the room quieted down. And once I started realizing how often I call on that same hand-raiser, I started randomly calling on students (which may or may not be a good idea???)....(September 29)

The following reflection represents a thoughtful interplay between practice and theory—Maya aptly uses the lens "reform-based pedagogy" to make meaning of her own *trajectory* of practice-based experiences—having truly experienced success and competence at a new and powerful level (for her) than she had (or at least was aware of) before.

> ### STARS (love active learning)! Week 4!
>
> I put that in my title because I learned a giant lesson (for me) on Thursday: not all activities are hands-on even if the students are doing something. What I mean by this is that hands-on does not equal engaged in active learning. This week my group nailed active science learning. Finally!.... Above when I said hands-on doesn't mean active learning, I was referring to some of my group's previous activities (e.g., girls drawing their dream homes for our river of pollution activity) where the girls were busy but not actively learning. It's not a shot at myself but rather a reminder that hands-on activities are great but they should also involve learning as much as possible! (October 10)

This connectedness to real practice comes through so clearly in Maya's blogging, not only in the explanations and justifications of "lessons learned" (as illustrated by the previous examples) but also in the evolution of them. Using phrases such as "It would not have occurred to me that . . ." (July 18) or "I realized," she made transparent the *how* of coming to know these lessons. These realizations may or may not have been things she was aware of before she authored the posts. Maya also made clear that these lessons often came at a cost.

Maya and her peers engaged in two distinctly different types of reflection on practice separate from practice—what we refer to as "day-to-day" reflections and "benchmark" reflections. "Day-to-day" reflections occurred at the end of any given day—sometimes after watching a mentor teacher teach, but most often as a self-critique of personal pedagogical practice. The 13 different posts Maya authored that were coded as "day-to-day" lessons learned were inspired by the following events:

- Course/professional development work (4)
- Grant writing assignment
- Micro-teaching for mentors
- Analyzing expert teaching through video
- Final write-up of innovative unit
- Out-of-school teaching (6): prior knowledge concept interviews with campers-to-be, camp teaching days—3, after-school club teaching—2
- Profound experience at placement (3)
- Student arriving at school having been beaten (Maya was not teaching yet)
- Feeling "thrown into teaching" by mentor unexpectedly
- Confession of a mistake of great personal significance

Specific examples of lessons learned through day-to-day practice included the following:

- Activity directions are best when they are "**explicitly clear** AND **short** AND **visible**" (emphasis hers).
- Scripting (being prepared with what you will say to students) is necessary and important to the flow of the lesson.
- "Dry runs are not only necessary, but they are also very informative."

- Learning student names is "intensely important." Knowing students personally—including the things they know about science—is also very important.
- Having a deep understanding of content is necessary to address the range of student questions that emerge.
- Students need support in establishing a sense of safe community amongst themselves—especially newcomers.
- "Big ballers" (students with power among peers) can be used to a teacher's advantage.

In addition to these lessons learned in the midst of everyday teaching interactions, Maya took five pauses throughout the year to stop and reflect on lessons learned at the end of key benchmark periods of her program (as required of all students in the program): after each of the two summer methods courses (June 23 and August 8), after teaching camp (August 4), after fall semester's field placement (December 1) and after first student teaching placement (January 28). An excerpt from the August 4th reflection on lessons she learned from teaching at the camp reveals nuanced and well-articulated take-aways inspired from a very specific and uncommon experience (running an inquiry camp at a lake) that are phrased in language that could easily inform future classroom practice:

> …I learned quite a few lessons from camp week that I'll carry with me to the next phase of learning to teach. First, the importance of scripting cannot be understated for a beginning teacher. Lesson plans don't just flow from within like magic. They must be planned with the goal and the objectives in mind—backward design. Second, regardless of how prepared you feel regarding a specific lesson, there is always more that might have been done. Third, the students are very forgiving if you take the time to get to know them and to demonstrate that you honestly care about them. This is important as it relates to the previous lesson learned in that if you're not prepared fully, the students will forgive you provided they know you care about them and thus they care about you, too. Finally, teaching is a complex and demanding endeavor that requires one hundred percent of your focus to be done at it's best. (August 4)

Even though writing a reflective post at this stage was assigned, how each pre-service teacher engaged in this reflection and to what degree was up to them. Maya's 70-line post, which concluded with the above quote, represents an important piece of recognition work in a teacher's development. The 61 lines that preceded this conclusion afforded Maya the opportunity to reflect on, evaluate and recognize specific instances of competent reform-based science teaching in a public place and way that makes it available for others to similarly recognize. In this conclusion, Maya engaged in the important translation work of understanding the concrete ways the specifics of the camp critique served to mold, shape, direct and inform the professional identity she had developed that would serve her future work and be further developed in the next teaching experiences.

How she rolls…Maya being Maya

Maya has a unique way in which she processes and makes meaning from practice and thus engages in critical inquiry. She often begins with what many might call "ranting" or "venting" and then, later in her post, she takes a distinct turn toward a positive and constructive perspective. The venting sometimes focuses on context (e.g., organizational structures of a teaching situation or programmatic expectations for her as a graduate student) and sometimes focuses on her own performance and competence. In the post that follows, Maya starts with a list of wrestlings and ventings that followed the leading sentence: "STARS this week was tough for the following reasons …" The very next section of the *same* post was, "So what can I do about all these things" followed by an item-by-item exploration of positive things she could try to address each problem.

STARS (week 3)

STARS this week was tough for the following reasons:
1. **What!? Photo Club? Seriously?** We only had 5 of our 9 girls show up. One girl dropped for another club, one girl hasn't shown up for two weeks in a row (despite a very cheerful and encouraging call home from me), and our two new additions last week failed to show this week. Overall, it was just depressing. We keep hearing that it's too early to lose our girls, but I'm not sure what else we (team purple) can do to keep them coming. And no matter how you look at it, it seems like a reflection of something we didn't do right last time. Are we not awesome enough? One of my biggest worries is that the two new additions last week were a bit intimidated and we failed to introduce them into the established group well enough…lesson learned, maybe, but clearly not soon enough.
2. **The RUSH.** Please, let's figure out some way to change (rather than embrace) the rush. I am talking about the rush to get the room set up (since we have literally zero minutes to do it ahead of time), to find plates, to get supplies, to set up demos, to organize whatever it is you want organized, AND TO GREET THE GIRLS AS THEY COME INTO THE ROOM. It's nearly impossible to do all of that well. As a result of this week's chaos, I spent a lot of time running around behind the scenes trying to keep our group together and on time. I was setting up demos during the team building activity or looking for our misplaced rope during pizza time. In addition, due to our location and our planned activities, we ended up with a lot of little transitions that stole time away from our end goal.
3. **Oh, team unity…where art thou?** So we failed to unite our team well. This was partly due to the big rush, partly due to time constraints, and partly due to the discrepancy in ages between our two groups. Mainly we just had a hard time getting the girls to talk with each other and the awkwardness of the situation was difficult for us teachers as well as the girls. Our team building event was fun, but it failed to really get the girls to connect. We just did not expect the age difference to matter as much as it did. . . .

So what can I do about all of these things?
1. For starters, I can call home again, though I'm not sure that two new additions last week left contact information. We can also drop off an encouraging card at the girls' homerooms.
2. In regards to the big rush.…I don't have any ideas other than to stop doing so many activities. Which is a bad idea. In my previous job, I was quite used to the general mayhem and rush that is benchwork science under the pressure of "need to publish to get funding." I was great at running around running six or seven different experiments while cloning on the side. But this is a different kind of pressure (these girls look up to us; they're coming to hang out with us after school!) and I'm cracking underneath it…Perhaps having a list of immediate needs followed by less urgent needs might help. Or enlisting one of the girls to help get notebooks or fill water bottles?
3. As far as team building, we're going to work really hard to get the power in the hands of our 7th graders for the videoconferencing. We also know now that it's going to be a bit tough when we go to the other location…so we can plan more productive team building activities. (October 2)

Maya's mentors as well as her peers understood that this was the unique way she processed the world, and were supportive of and encouraging towards her in ways that both respected this tendency and tried to nurture her into a slightly more balanced initial perspective. For example, in the exchange that follows, Maya targets the venting toward herself with a critique of a specific aspect of her teacher performance that day, and her blogging readership responds:

> **I failed.** Specifically I crashed-and-burned during the concept map part of my interview with my ladies. I didn't want to lead them. So after some dead air, I moved on to the next activity. And that kinda fizzled too. I need to work on this, but I'm not sure how—any ideas? (September 17) (6 comments)

Jo Ann, the lead supervisor, responds quickly to emphasize that this outcome should not be considered failure, and Maya replies with gratitude and evidences her awareness of this personal pattern of interaction:

> Thanks for the new (upbeat) perspective. I think I tend to lean towards a hard-on-myself approach (which works for me) but it's always nice to hear what other people think, too. Thanks! (September 20)

The next comment posted was written by Ashley, a programmatic mentor and alum of the program who had been mentoring Maya in person and through blogging for the past three weeks:

> Maya—you crack me up! Somehow even through your negativity, I find you extremely positive. I know your type…such a hard worker who expects nothing but the best and is disappointed that they cannot please everyone all of the time. You are a great person:) Look at what a great support system you have from your Warner buds. They will be the ones to get you through this, because they are really the only ones who know exactly what you are experiencing. That was how it was when I went through the program. As you settle into a routine, before you know it, you will be done with Warner and starting a new job. It flies, so try to keep that in mind. I know it seems grueling at times, but I assure you 1000% that you will be better prepared than ANY other new teacher by going through April's program. It's just a given:) (September 23)

Not only did her mentors support and encourage Maya through this form of meaning-making, but her peers were a consistent source of support. Maya recognized and publicly appreciated this specific form of peer-support. For example, on March 5, she wrote and published (and has since removed) the following post to her peers:

> Dear GRS Cohort 2010 (That's YOU!): Thank you for putting up with me over this past year. I know that often times I bring a bit (or a lot) of negativity and pessimism to the table. Personalities are complex, and I appreciate that you upbeat, sunshiny, happy-go-lucky teachers-to-be listen to me complain all the time. I wouldn't have survived this far along without the whole lot of you around supporting me! So, very sincerely, thank you! (March 5).

Learning through Engagement with Her Community

Maya was known by her peers and mentors for her community work through blogging. She clearly read and commented on more peers' blogs than anyone else in the cohort. On July 13 in one of her posts Maya wrote, "I am working on creating a google reader so that all of my wonderful cohort's blogs are within my instantaneous reach." In addition to commenting on others' blogging, she reached out to her community through her own blog posts and comments in a number of complementary ways:

fleshing out her critical inquiries in her post and explicitly asking for input; connecting her posts to those of her peers through "shout-outs" and other hyperlinks, sharing resources and accompanying critique, and authoring entertaining posts for the enjoyment of all.

Creativity and wit

Maya was unique in her integration of wit throughout her blogging. What follows is just one of many examples:

> **Got A.L.E.?**
>
> I've got a name for a phenomenon I've observed every single day thus far in my middle school placement. I now refer to the (subtle) chaos I observe in whichever class I have immediately after lunch as ALE (After Lunch Effect)....Students suffering from ALE generally demonstrate 2 or more of the following characteristics:
> 1. Incessant chatting
> 2. Uncontrollable giggling
> 3. Continuous fist bumping, handshaking, or any other form of human contact
> 4. Unstoppable note-passing ("the look" has no affect whatsoever on this activity)
> 5. Melodious outbursts
> 6. AAA (Alarming Amounts of Activity)—These include (but are not limited to): pencil sharpening, paper tossing, nose-blowing, hand-sanitizing, stapler/hole-punch overusing, finger-tapping, etc.
>
> WARNINGS: ALE is highly contagious. If one or two students are already affected prior to entering your classroom, it will spread at a rapid rate to all students in the room. No amount of hand sanitizer will stop the spread…(September 22)
>
> Comment from peer: This made me laugh, thank you! You're so clever!

Another blog post Maya constructed that was recognized and spotlighted as being creative and witty during class one night as well as through six responding comments expressing enjoyment and appreciation was Maya's use of famous lines from movies to characterize lessons learned from her first field placement (December 1). A sample is provided below.

> Lessons Learned (in movie quotes)
> 1. "Toto, I've got a feeling we're not in Kansas anymore" (?) ⊠The world of education has changed (a lot) since I've been a student at one of the little desks.
> 2. "They're here" (?) ⊠First day jitters…that lasted for a few weeks.
> 3. "Good morning, Vietnam!" (?) ⊠For me, this represents my first "uh-oh" moment: when my CT tossed me the dry erase marker and left the room, at the beginning of a class, without telling me anything. Every single day after that, I entered the room prepared for whatever else might come my way.
> 4. "I love the smell of napalm in the morning!" (?) ⊠Loving your job. . . .
> 5. "Snakes! Why did it have to be snakes?" (?) ⊠..even when you are forced to face your worst fears.
> 6. "Go ahead, make my day" (?) ⊠This one goes out to that first student whom I had to ask to leave the classroom (the one who refused to change seats) but I stood my ground a la Dirty Harry (not really).
> 7. "I'll be back" (?) ⊠Every day, no matter what happened the previous day. (September 22)

Still another example of Maya's witty blogging presence followed a very serious and deep wrestling with respect to the design, role and usefulness of homework (September 8). Maya concluded this thoughtful exploration with the block-quote disclaimer:

> Disclaimer: The interpretation and the ideas presented here are those of the author and are based solely on three days of observation plus zero discussion of the homework policy with her CT.

This special way in which Maya processed her learning and meaning-making was attractive to and valued by peers and mentors and thus helped her experience success with one of the most difficult aspects of blogging—nurturing an involved readership and community. She consistently made little quips in the midst of passionate arguments such as, "3. Make science fun. Are metric conversions really necessary? Seriously? Does anyone really go from deci to dekameters in life?" (From "Untitled," October 1). It is difficult to imagine other venues or participation structures teacher learners have to creatively author their development in such personally relevant, deeply thoughtful *and* entertaining ways.

Reaching out

Another common occurrence in Maya's blogging was an explicit bidding for support and advice:

> So, my fellow cohort members and surrounding support network that diligently read my blog posts, please offer me advice on the following: 1. How do I motivate this student? 2. How much is too much when it comes to helping during class? How much hand-holding is acceptable? (February 4, 2008, five comments—two from peers, three from mentors).

Interestingly, this sense of cohort as audience did not happen right away, and it appears to begin as an interesting tension for Maya. During the summer (first 3–4 months of her program), Maya's posts seemed to be written for the professor or for no group in particular, yet within the posts are mini-experiments to reach out to her peers. For example, on June 23, though she *titled* a post "Send me your ideas (please)" requesting ideas for a field trip to a local provider of an alternative energy source, she *starts* this post with this commentary:

> Given the discussion in class on Friday (July 10, 2009) about blogging (specifically that we are required to blog on an "at least once per week" basis and the format of this blogging is flexible), I've decided that I should post often so as to create a habit. Maybe I'll even end up liking the entire blogging experience. As for right now, I am still uncomfortable with the idea that others are reading what I've written. (July 13)

As Maya and her cohort developed a sense of community in face-to-face experiences, those to whom she addressed most of her blogging shifted from a more general audience to her peers *very* specifically. Factors that may have positively impacted this perceived sense of online community early in her program could likely be (a) the intense in-person collaborative learning experiences of the program (i.e., conducing an authentic scientific investigation and presenting findings to the county health department or running a week-long summer science inquiry camp when you have never taught a day in your life), (b) the developing relationships with peers face-to face, and/or (c) the increased peer participation on her blog. It is unclear given our data, how and to what extent each of these impacted her sense of readership and audience.

You can see from Figure 10.1 the large number of people who engaged with Maya through her blogging across this academic year: 28 people total, 18 of whom were current cohort members (out of a possible 20, shown in ovals), 2 of which were near peers who were recent graduates of the program (rounded rectangles), and 8 of whom were different types of programmatic mentors such as professors or supervisors (rectangles). This figure also makes it clear that Maya was a strong presence in her own blogging comments as she posted more comments on her own blog than anyone else—thus engaging her readership in conversation by explicitly and publicly reacting to their contributions.

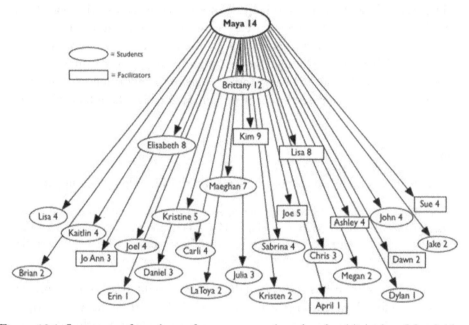

Figure 10.1: Summary of numbers of comments authored and published on Maya's blog.

Maya's professional blogging practices clearly involved reading and interacting with peers through their blogging. At the time of this writing, Maya had written 200 comments to her peers, an average of 10.5 comments/peer and had written no less than 3 comments (199 words) to any one of the 19 peers. These comments totaled 17,595 words—much longer than the length of this chapter! The depth of her comments is well illustrated by the following quote:

> One quick thing. I disagree that it's a cultural issue (towards the end of your post). I think it's more of a socioeconomic effect...and I think the differentiation between the two is really important. I was thinking about this a bit on my ride home tonight. I think when I was responding to your post I was thinking about the word culture having only a limited definition, which isn't the case...just look at how we all talk about classroom culture. So anyways, I hope that my comment didn't come across as rude (it was 5:45am)...and you are right, both are important! Thanks for the post! It reminded me of how far we've come collectively. (Maya's comment on Carol's blog)

A primary purpose that was served by Maya's comments was the acknowledgment of innovative teaching ideas from her peers. As evidenced in the following comments, Maya showed that she valued her cohort's ideas by thanking them, acknowledging their ideas in practice, and eliciting further ideas and contributions from her cohort:

Finally, your demos sounded great. I think we might use at least one next week, so thanks for the good ideas!

I loved your idea about using the GPS systems as a treasure hunt! That's not simply because it sounds like fun (and there was candy involved). It put the students in touch with usable technology, thus teaching them while they weren't aware. That's great!

It's funny that you wrote about wanting your lesson to be a bit less like school next time. We had the opposite with our lesson this week…we need to work on bringing a bit more structure/teaching into the mix. We should get together to trade ideas …

The following quote best illustrates Maya's recognition of the value of her peers' ideas:

I second the need for an investigatable question bank. I set up a post on the GRS [cf., http://getrealscience.com/getreal] blog so we can all contribute ideas. I was thinking of trying to make them a bit open-ended so that the girls would have access to idea but be able to modify it to make it "their own"…I love your idea about sharing pictures from camp (of real scientists)! It's a good one that I think team purple will use in the coming weeks. Finally, I agree that next week, when we have more control, it's going to be SO much more fun (and so much less like school)!

In this comment, Maya not only recognizes a fellow pre-service teacher's idea of a question bank for STARS ("I second the need for an investigatable question bank"), but she also followed through by setting up a virtual space for this work. This level of engagement in her comments demonstrates her acknowledgement of the value in collaborative and participatory teaching ideas.

Maya also engaged in other "work" in her comments, including commiserating with her peers about the difficulties inherent in adopting reform-minded practices and offering encouragement:

Hey! This sounds awesome—modifying "cookbook" labs isn't easy and neither is introducing them to students that are used to (and like the "not thinking" aspect of) cookbook labs! I also agree with Lisa, that they will learn to expect it. I also wanted to add that I also struggle with the implementation of my lesson plan procedure and getting the outcome I visualized. For me, a lot has to do with modifications I make "on the fly." I often reflect on my lesson and realize something that I wished I'd done I already wrote about BUT forgot. I'm not sure if that's exactly what you meant by mind the gap, but it's how I took it. My thought is that, with time, good things will happen…So….GOOOOOOOOD LUCK:-)

Maya also revealed her avid readership by commenting on peers' comments, providing links to other blogs, and publically admitting in one comment, "I'm taking a break from my lesson planning to surf my newest addition (blogging) and your post just cracked me up! Thanks for the laugh!" Finally, Maya acknowledged that, "I'm proud that I made the effort to post responses on everyone's comments as much as possible." (blogging reflection, December).

Emotions in community

Like many bloggers, Maya engaged in blogging to express and work through emotions. Developing a new professional identity is a personal and often risky process for many, and the charge of becoming "reform-minded" *and* an "agent of change" working toward "social justice" makes it even more challenging. We have found that our pre-service teachers understand and embrace this (somewhat crazy yet) important charge, but continue to wrestle (for years) with what that means for their everyday life as a professional. Maya's blogging was replete with demonstrations of emotion as evidenced by the use of capital letters, multi-colored texts and many, many exclamation points (268 in 60 posts)! We decided to explore Maya's emotional work under the category of "learning with community," because so many of her intensely emotional posts were explicitly directed to her audience, often with explicit invitations to respond.

Using blogging "categories" she created, Maya labeled five of her posts "venting"—which correspond to what the blogosphere refers to as "rants," i.e., passionate arguments about an issue or injustice. Maya aptly described the work in all five of these posts in her opening sentence to this "vent:"

> This purpose of this post is to officially vent about a topic in education that gets under my skin, drives me bonkers, eats at my insides…however you want to say it. Here it is: **teaching science with a large group of students in a non-science classroom because of "budget cuts"** (December 1).

In each of these passionate "venting" posts, Maya reached out to connect with her readership in explicit and intentional ways. For example, in "My Official Vent" (December 1) after expressing anger and frustration with respect to the unfair access to resources she has in her current urban placement compared to suburban science students and teachers, Maya wrote

> "…and that brings me to the real purpose of my vent" which she addressed to other teachers who are find themselves in the same situation and are not as motivated to make the best of the situation: **Get off your teacher's chair, sit in a student seat, and realize how crappy your science class currently is…really, it's no wonder you have discipline issues! I, receiver of no detentions my entire educational career, WOULD ACT UP IN YOUR CLASS—IT'S THAT BORING. For goodness sake!…**Perhaps, just maybe, I will be an "agent of change." She further pleaded with these teachers to advocate for their students: In summary, please do science in your classroom, even if you have to walk two miles to the prep room, up hill both ways and through knee-deep (no NECK-deep) snow in a blizzard to do it. I am begging you, all of you, to take on this challenge— do real cool science in your classrooms! Similarly, in "What is the NYS [New York State] Dept of Education thinking?" (February 24, emphasis hers).

In a post inspired by her own cross-case comparison of implementing a state-mandated lab in two dramatically different contexts, Maya articulated four nuances of implementation that made this experience ineffective and untenable in her current urban placement. She concluded this "vent" with the following plea:

> So please, NYS, please rethink these state-mandated, featured-on-the-regents-exam [a high-stakes test] laboratories before you insist we, the teachers, integrate them into our classroom curriculum.

In each of these venting posts, Maya published passionate arguments about specific changes needed to realize education that is more fair and just—especially for urban students. Maya invited the engagement of her online community through the intense emotions she shared in these venting posts as well as the posts in which she "wrestled" with unclear or unknown solutions to tough, nuanced problems or situations. She also invited her readership to share in her joy as she shared success, her frustrations with the demands of graduate student life, and even her pain as she shared failures. For example, she titled one post "Please read this one." In which she wrote, "I was so wrong it hurts to write about it." Clearly this wrestling work is an emotional process, as well illustrated by this quote:

> Tonight as I was reading for class, I began to notice an increase in heart rate, a decrease in appetite, and an overall sense of unease settle over me. In particular, the Chinn & Malhotra (2002) reading was making me feel as if each lesson I would be creating in the not-too-distant-future would need to take place in a research laboratory in order to be authentic inquiry….Then I came across this quote: **"Of course, there is no need for every inquiry task to incorporate every feature of authentic science"** (p. 205). And I breathed an audible sigh of relief. So many thanks go out to you, Chinn & Malhotra, because you've now given me permission to sleep a little bit more each night during my future years as an awesome authentic-inquiry-providing super cool science teacher. (January 22)

Few practices and spaces in traditional teacher education allow for the expression and working through of these and the many other emotions that are integral to becoming involved in developing a new professional identity. And even fewer occur in spaces that afford peer and mentor encouragement, commiseration, resource and advice sharing, and just plain listening.

Integration of Autobiography

Understanding and explicitly considering "self" as having a cultural, social and historical background and make-up in developing as a teacher is valuable and essential to developing a professional identity as a teacher. Authoring a *personal* professional blog—even when it is a requirement—is uniquely personal. Maya's wrestling and meaning-making through blogging naturally integrated these historical, cultural and social aspects of herself—her self as a former student, as a former lab technician, as a mom, and even as a person small in stature who likes to plan and does not love chaos.

For example, within a thoughtful reflection on effective design, and appropriate role and use of homework (that, by the way, did not result in a published resolution), Maya uses her perspectives as former-student to explore and consider her decisions and roles as future teacher:

> …Then I started reminiscing about how much I disliked homework (and still do). Mostly this was due to the nature of the homework (e.g., defining vocabulary words or filling out maps). Which led me to thinking about the difficulties of making homework assignments meaningful (for both student learning and assessment). Meaningful assignments would not only help the students to learn but also make potential copying difficult…(September 8)

In addition to using her autobiography as a former student as a lens to interpret the options around a professional issue, she also used the lens of a science lab technician to relate to the chaos that can exist in a classroom, and her understanding of herself to wrestle with confidence around management issues:

> My CT handles the students' (poor) behavior pretty well. He's tall and has a strong presence (I don't). These students say things to each other that are offensive which leads to lots of almost-fights (I'm not great at reading these tentative, important moments yet). A lot of "on the fly" judgment calls are made (I'm a thinker/planner). A minimum of once/week some students get "bounced" out of class for some problem or another (I'm not a fan of sending students down to some higher authority (but what do I know?)) (October 6).

Most distinctive was Maya's consistent use of her lens as a mom for interpreting her development and experiences, as well as framing her advice as a teacher and teacher learner. For example, when Maya wrestled with the costs of teaching and learning-to-teach, the majority of her posts articulated deeply felt loss with respect to time and connectedness with her sons (e.g., August 1). The following post highlights Maya's use of personal experiences with her children to construct advice for her peers that simultaneously solidifies her own position regarding this practice as a teacher:

> While it might be easier to send home a letter, it is undeniable that a telephone conversation is much more personal. It makes a connection with the p/g that might be useful for the entire school year (and beyond). How do I know this? Well…what really drove home the importance of connecting with p/gs is a personal experience. My own children have started to attend daycare and every single day I call to touch base with their day. (On a side note, just imagine the patience this woman must have to deal with me—this reminds me to remind all of you to have patience with parents). Every day she tells me something good that each of my children did in her presence. And every day that makes me smile. Now, I know what a lot of you are probably thinking…in high school chemistry, what parent is really going to care what I think of their kid? My answer is every single one of them. Seriously, it makes such a difference to hear good things about your children even if it's not related to learning or the content area whatsoever. ("Calling Home With…(wait for it)…GOOD NEWS!" September 15). (6 comments—4 from mentors and peers; half of which articulated gratitude for sharing a parent's perspective; 2 comments were responses from Maya).

In the following final example of Maya's use of her Mom-lens to frame and support her understanding and development, Maya's experiences as a parent help her problematize what real assessment of student understanding involves. This thoughtful and in-depth thinking about the nuance of an issue is evidence that Maya used her blogging to engage in the core teacher-learning practices of critical inquiry.

> Why? Well, in analyzing my student work, I realize just how difficult it is to really ascertain whether or not students LEARNED and UNDERSTAND something from a written or illustrative or oral assessment. *Did they "learn it" long enough to write it down? Did they really "get it" or were they able to just make sense of it for a short period of time? How do I really measure student learning/understanding?*
>
> **My personal experiences today:** This morning I took my boys to visit my mother at work. All my kids were early talkers (as defined by current medical parameters), which they no doubt get from me because I rarely stop talking. So while at my mom's office (Brady mountain!), a bunch of her coworkers came out to see the boys, too. And my mom, typically, gushed about how awesome (smart) they all are and then started to prompt my kids to talk. **My kids talk all the time.** They never stop. And they refused to say a word. In short, they refused to put on a show for all these ladies going ga-ga over them. No words whatsoever. No songs, no counting, no ABC's.
>
> **What's my point?** Well, my kids know how to talk, sing, and count. They can even count in French, Spanish, and German (sometimes they get confused). But in refusing to do so it made me think…most assessments of student learning/understanding are on OUR (teacher) schedule. This is obviously a necessity of life…but at the same time, *students have to know/understand what we demand when we demand it.* They have to know what we are asking of them, in other words be able to interpret our questions and respond in ways we are looking for specifically. As a side note, this is kinda like interviewing for teaching jobs, right? We know certain places are looking for us to say certain buzz words (which bothers me enormously).
>
> *Does this matter?* I think it does. *Do I think we should ask students when/how we should assess them?* No (at least not most of the time). But I do think it's important to ensure that students know why we are assessing them and how we are going to assess them. I also think it's impor-

tant to provide them with the chance to show what they know in multiple ways. Finally, why not allow them the chance to correct/make changes to their work (see Megan's Blog). Each of these ideas (and there are more out there) will help make assessments LESS of a "performance on demand":-)

It was clear that Maya's identity as Mom was central to who she was, how she saw her worlds, how she wanted to engage with her worlds, and how she went about making decisions—professional and otherwise. Integrating autobiography was natural for Maya and was appreciated and encouraged by her online (and offline) community. This realization begs the question about what might happen if one's core identities were not as well understood or appreciated by the blogger's community.

Sustained Work over Time

As Maya authored a total of 1880 lines in 60 posts across 14 months of reflective and metacognitive reified statements of her development, several themes re-emerged over time. Among these themes were the importance of building relationships with kids, the need to script questions to be well-prepared for lessons, the need to teach *all* students science through meaningful, authentic, hands-on work, and her on-going efforts to improve her time management skills—just to mention a few. In most cases, none of these fundamental issues was ever fully "resolved," although Maya kept adding new insights as she progressed in the program.

Most importantly, throughout her teacher preparation program and its concurrent blogging, Maya was working to develop her professional identity as a reform-minded science teacher and an agent of change. Blogging offered Maya ongoing opportunities to recognize herself and simultaneously bid for recognition by others as a teacher, as a certain kind of teacher (e.g., reform-minded, student-centered, accessible), and as a certain kind of teacher with a certain amount of competence. The following sequence of quotes is indicative of this work over time:

- August 1. "I am beginning to feel as if I may not be a good teacher because I am too focused on my home life and missing my children."
- August 5. "You now know that I may turn out to be a decent teacher after all, what with all this learning and reflecting going on in my life."
- September 29. "So many thanks go out to you, Chinn & Malhotra, because you've now given me permission to sleep a little bit more each night during my future years as an awesome authentic-inquiry-providing super cool science teacher."
- March 18. "This discussion was especially helpful for me given the readings we had in our class this past Monday, as they left me feeling doubtful about my ability to be a great teacher (especially right now)…This video watching experience gave me hope that I will be able to *truly* apply what I believe in (in terms of teaching to learn)." ("Finally! Uncovering in Action").
- April 16. "The part of your post that stuck out for me was the last few lines. While interviewing this week I realized that I have a lot to say that I truly mean.…I kept trying to get my energy across, sometimes to the point of raising my voice to get the interviewer's attention (it was a crowded event). I agree…we want to share our stories, because we are well-equipped and READY TO TEACH!" (Maya to Hayley on Hayley's blog).

Integration of Expert Voice

While Maya did integrate the expert perspectives in her blogging, this did not occur often. It was rare for her to mention professors by name. However, on two occasions, in the midst of her wrestling, she described hearing their voices. The following quote references both the well-known urban teacher educator and scholar, Martin Haberman, as well as one of her graduate school professors, Lynn Gatto:

> So I'm a totally nervous/scared/anxious that these students are just going to keep right on talking while I'm up there "teaching"...or do any other of the myriad little misbehaviors that are common practice in these classes right now. This relates to my bigger issue of how to assume responsibility for these classes in a few months. *And I hear Haberman (and Lynn Gatto) in my head telling me to "hook them in" with a cool demo and to make class interesting, meaningful, etc.* But right now I'm dealing with my CT's lesson plans (which is great) because that is all that I can handle given the time constraints and my need for sleep. ("I can't sleep (AGAIN)!" (October 6)

Though she made mention of course readings and professor's advice on occasion, Maya's blogging was much more focused on her own meaning-making in the context of her own life experiences.

Maya clearly took up blogging in ways that were personally meaningful and rewarding to her. It was clear from the language she chose and the way she addressed her posts that she felt an increasingly supportive presence from her community over time. Over the course of her program, Maya moved from someone who is "not that into blogging" to a final post in which she committed to continue to blog after coursework. In between these posts, she authored 200 comments and 60 posts, shared heart-wrenching failures and many proud moments of success, wrestled with many nuanced professional issues, and passionately advocated for change she felt was necessary. Blogging for Maya focused primarily on the teacher-learning practices of studying practice away from practice, engaging in learning with her community, and integrating her varied histories and identities into current development. She used her blog to integrate voices of experts (science, pedagogy or other) less frequently.

As we take a brief look next at two of Maya's peers, you will see how each took up blogging in interesting and very different ways.

Comparison with Two Other Pre-Service Teachers' Blogging

Niklas's Blogging

Niklas comes to the program directly after finishing an undergraduate program in the geosciences from a local state university, where he studied geology and archaeology, and worked as a teaching assistant. These experiences were formative in shaping Niklas's identity as a scientist and educator. In his first blog post he wrote, "I already know for a fact that I love geology and know that I am pretty good at it too. I also know that I want to teach the earth sciences to young students, but know I don't have all the tools that I need" (Lines 42–43). Niklas enrolled in the Get Real! Science program based on the advice of a close friend who was a graduate of the science education program.

Niklas absolutely loves the earth sciences, and this passion flows into and through everything he engages in as a teacher and learner. He leverages his prior undergraduate experiences to share resources and information with the rest of the cohort. Many of his blog posts include links to interesting geoscience activities and images from some of his scientific sampling adventures, which he then relates to future lessons and his own vision of himself as an educator. When talking with Niklas in person, you notice immediately that he is a passionate and interested individual, often exuding so much energy that he cannot stand still as he moves arms in grand gestures to accentuate whatever point he is attempting to make.

As you skim through Niklas's blog (available at http://www.getrealscience.com/Preservice Blogging2), you will immediately notice two things: (1) an extensive integration of images, YouTube videos and hyperlinks to other resources and (2) Niklas's love for geology—so much so that you can't help but love it if you spend a little time with him through his blogging. More than the other two bloggers featured in this chapter, Niklas used the multimodality available in blogging to teach his readership geology content and concepts alongside sharing valuable instructional resources and lesson ideas.

Niklas frequently posted blog entries where he takes something that he is excited about, sometimes from the past and sometimes current events, and carries it forward into his new role as an educator. Niklas is also passionate about music and followed around his favorite band, often posting YouTube videos of the band that represented some aspect of his current life situation. This music was important to Niklas and shaped how he presented himself.

While Maya searched for her own expert voice as it pertained to her pedagogy, Niklas engaged in a different sort of *integrating expert voice*. Maya's blogging often situated teaching experience and pedagogical process at the locus and focus of her expertise. Niklas situated the content of the Earth Sciences and located his own expertise in relation to other scientists and researchers. As a result, *integrating expert voice* is a very prominent blogging practice for Niklas.

In contrast to Maya's focus on teaching, Niklas engaged in reflections on his teaching practice only when required by the specific blogging assignment after each key learning-to-teach experience. That said, each of these required posts was very thoughtful and demonstrated his ability to *reflect on practice separate from practice* and identity work. One might wonder if he would have missed out on these valuable blogging affordances if these reflections weren't assigned.

Elisabeth's Blogging

Elisabeth is a quiet and deeply thoughtful scientist turned teacher. Elisabeth had worked for a few years in a dermatology lab conducting scientific investigations that she both loved and of which she was very proud. She had recently married and shared a love of teardrop trailer camping with her husband. They constructed and towed their small caravan behind their vehicle and travelled to different parts of the state. Elisabeth took many pictures on these trips and often posted them to her blog with relevant descriptive information.

While Elisabeth was often quiet in large-group settings, her blog (available at http://www.getrealscience.com/PreserviceBlogging3) is full of rich reflection and detailed ideas. On one occasion she even addressed her more reserved nature:

> I know that throughout this year I will be struggling to develop who I am as a teacher and how I will interact with my students. While I love laughter and fun in the classroom, I have learned this week that I am not a comedian. This is just not my nature while in the classroom. That doesn't mean I never say anything funny or don't like to have fun, but I am not a natural at inserting funny or outrageous comments into discussions with students. (September 9)

A post titled "Musings from today's garage sale" (see below) is typical of Elisabeth's blogging—deeply thoughtful and reflective consideration of students' schooling experiences and her responsibility and role in shaping those experiences.

Musings from today's garage sale

April 24th, 2010 . Posted in <u>Teaching Science</u> | <u>1 Comment</u> »

Yesterday and today I participated in one of our friend's multi-family garage sales in Rush, NY. And naturally while sitting around doing next to nothing I began thinking about teaching and how it was kind of like a garage sale.

Each family/person that brought stuff to sell all brought different things and what they brought said a little something about their personality. Of course, I thought that what I had brought would be desirable and would sell (nice stuff, in good shape…etc.) But here's the catch, each person who came to the sale had their eye out for something totally different. Every customer was interested in something different. I was amazed at how much of my stuff didn't sell and was clearly therefore not appealing to anybody. I may have sold 30% of what I brought and what did sell were the items that I thought would be last to go!

So this is where I began thinking about teaching. I am going to bring things to my classroom that I think students are going to want to learn about and experience. But they are all going to come with very different interests. They will likely not be looking for what I think they are looking for. What happens if my students only respond to 30% of what I bring to them? It is easy to see at a garage sale what people like and don't like…if it doesn't sell, it was not a hit. But what about in the classroom? Will it be so easy to tell what isn't working for my students? At best, we will only capture our students' interests 30% of the time unless we commit ourselves to constantly consider what they are looking for and reflect on what we brought to the classroom.

Long story short, I will bring more jeans next year!

Participants' Reflections on Their Blogging Experience

To complement the information and perspectives provided by examining the content of a three individual blogs, we would like now to report on this group of pre-service teachers' reflections on their blogging experience. For this we will draw from the 20 pre-service teachers' responses to a blogging self-assessment task given in December, in about the middle of their Masters program, and which was prompted by the following questions (using the shared Get Real! language of "pluses"—i.e., strengths—and "arrows"—i.e., elements calling for some improvement):

- In what ways did your blogging support your meaning-making? (pluses & arrows).

- In what ways and to what degree were you able to nurture your own personal professional community through your blog? (pluses & arrows).

Some significant categories emerged from this data analysis regarding what the teachers gained, as well as their struggles with the practice of blogging, as summarized below (see also Luehmann & Borasi, 2011, Appendix B). It is also worth noting that this exercise was very valuable for the pre-service teachers themselves, as it stimulated metacognition regarding the process and utility of blogging as a professional practice. Students reported that this explicit attention and thinking, in turn, led them to come to a better appreciation for the value of blogging and, thus, a renewed commitment to continue to engage in these practices.

Drawbacks and Challenges

The most frequently mentioned "arrow" regarding blogging related to feelings of not having enough time to blog during the day given the demands of other aspects of life (as mentioned by about a third of the participants). This frustration was complicated by the fact that some of the blog posts were required at different points in the program. Some teachers reported being frustrated with this requirement and ended up just completing the blog for the sake of satisfying the course requirement:

> The required posts were actually less helpful. I found it more helpful when the idea to post came from myself and not from a requirement. I did it as soon as possible so that I wouldn't forget to do the assignment thus making my reflections rushed and not as reflective as they could have been.—Bethany

The public nature of the blog space was perceived by about one-fourth of the participants as another limiting factor and frustration:

> The blogs were a bit constraining because I felt like I had to censor the types of things I put up there. There were a lot of things that went on in my field placement that I would have liked to blog about and get my colleagues inputs on.—Mary

Privacy concerns and professional sensitivity meant that some things could not be written about, posted or wrestled within the blog space.

Participants also mentioned some technical issues they experienced as a challenge—especially referring to one point in the semester when all the blogs stopped working and the pre-service teachers were not able to post for approximately four weeks until the technology could be fixed. Another technological challenge mentioned by two bloggers was the difficulty to follow comment threads to their end (due to limitations of the technology used).

It is also important to note that one pre-service teacher reported frustration with the process and technology of blogging and resisted engaging in these practices:

> I have a lot of arrows for blogging. I think that blogging can certainly support meaning making, but I have not taken advantage of that. I find myself putting blogs at the bottom of my priority list, and then having to catch up, which does not necessarily make it so meaningful anymore.—Evelyn

Another pre-service teacher expressed a similar frustration with time constraints and required posts:

> I did not gain much from the (lesson) reflections other than a summarization of the events I already knew and have worked on fixing.—Ben

Benefits of Blogging for Meaning-Making and Community Development

The criticisms expressed by the participating pre-service teachers, as summarized above, need to be interpreted in the context of an overwhelming appreciation for what blogging allowed them to do in the course of a very demanding teacher preparation program.

A majority of the pre-service teachers (15 out of 20) reported that blogging allowed them greater connection with other cohort members (both peers and mentors) outside the formal confines of the teacher education program, as reflected in the following comment:

> I learned a great deal through blogging conversations and reading fellow cohort members' blogs. It was a beneficial forum outside of the classroom that extended my learning.—Katie.

The teachers were able to leverage the blog space and participation and interaction opportunities outside the normal course structure to share and make sense of teaching practices and ideas in ways that might not have occurred otherwise. Blogging served as a means of capturing and sharing teaching resources and lesson ideas. Many of the teachers commented that they used these practices to share and learn about teaching resources and also to collaboratively problem-shoot future lessons. It was through this process that the teachers were able to witness that they were part of a larger community of like-minded educators, and some expressed catharsis in knowing that they were not alone in their struggles:

> It allowed me to post questions to other and others responded with ideas or empathy regarding my question. Whether they had an answer or not, it was nice to know I wasn't alone.—Bethany

Blogging also served another intrapersonal function, as many of the teachers reported that they appreciated seeing their ideas and thinking change over time, and this would not have happened so explicitly were it not for blogging:

> Blogging allowed me to go back and revisit my thoughts. This was powerful because I could go back and clearly see my conceptual framework, making it easier for me to modify it when I was presented with new knowledge.—Jim

Blogging also allowed them to develop an appreciation for reflection as a professional practice, with many reporting that blogging space (forum and time…and maybe excuse) to reflect on a myriad of educational issues, from lessons and content dilemmas to student needs and the larger politics of education.

Concluding Thoughts and Main Take-Aways

The findings reported in this chapter show the many benefits that blogging could add to a teacher preparation program. As explicitly recognized by the pre-service teachers' own reflections and objectively demonstrated by the in-depth analysis of Maya's blogging, both writing posts in one's blog and interacting with other classmates' blogs provided multiple opportunities for engaging in valuable "teacher learning practices"—such as *reflecting on practice separate from practice*, engaging in *learning within a community, integrating one's autobiography* in the lessons being learned, *engaging in critical inquiry*, and *participating in sustained inquiry* over time—at a very critical time in these teachers' development. Indeed, while we would argue that learning to teach is a life-long enterprise, the teacher preparation stage is a time specifically focused on learning and is a period when a teacher is likely to be most open and disposed to consider new ideas.

At the same time, the 20 pre-service teachers participating in the program took advantage of those opportunities to varying extents and in different ways, as they used the flexibility of blogging to create their own space to work on what mattered most to them. Indeed, as well illustrated by the three examples we chose to feature in this chapter—Maya, Niklas and Elisabeth—the personal nature of blogging provided each pre-service teacher blogger unique angles and paths as they processed and participated in different aspects of their teacher preparation program, allowing each of them to start where they were, respecting the varied inputs into their professional growth (words from husbands, experiences with their own children at home, etc.) while making sense of new experiences and identities formation. *Autobiography* was a core theme for each of these blogs, as Maya, Niklas and Elisabeth each integrated past experiences, self-perceptions of dispositions and competing demands on their time into the meaning-making going on in the program. Each of the 20 blogs, in turn, provides an invaluable window into the experience of each individual pre-service teacher as she went through her teacher preparation program—a lens that we demonstrated to be very valuable for teacher educators, learning scientists and the science teacher education community more broadly.

In the particular case described in this chapter, blogging occurred within a closely knit community. These 20 pre-services teachers worked alongside one another for 15 months learning to become reform-minded science teachers, taking courses and engaging in key formative experiences, together, sharing many of the same fears, joys, challenges and successes. The various "mentors" that supported them throughout this process, and often read and commented on their blog posts, were also part of this community and shared many of the same goals, experiences, and even "specialized language" such as "pluses and arrows" as the teacher learners. As such, this existing community provided a very natural and rich ground to develop a highly interactive and vibrant blogging community.

Even within these very favorable conditions, the instructors struggled with many decisions about how to best structure the participants' blogging experience—trying to balance the importance of giving each blogger sufficient freedom and agency with offering each blogger sufficient opportunities and motivation to explore the many different facets and affordances of blogging. It must be said that blogging represents *new* literacy practices (emphasis on "new") for many, and thus it naturally follows that this learning may need to be explicitly supported and scaffolded. For example, teacher learners will likely tend toward some types of professional meaning-making and identity work than others (i.e., Maya had a natural inclination toward engaging in learning with community, and Niklas demonstrated a natural blogging tendency to explore and share multimedia collections of disciplinary content). In order to support their learning of other professional blogging literacies, teacher learners may need support and feedback from instructors and programmatic mentors—as well as the gentle nudge to try.

With these considerations in mind, we would like to highlight the following key "take-aways" from this study:

- **Blogging within a teacher preparation program presents unique opportunities and advantages.** A teacher preparation program is a very special and formative time in a teacher's development—not only because this is when key beliefs, expectations and practices are formed, but also because teachers are by definition in a "learning mode." Teacher preparation programs in which students move through as a cohort can additionally provide a natural "blogging community" whose members have common knowledge and experiences. For example, evidence of this shared culture within the context studied in this chapter includes references to "our" definition of inquiry that differed from that of other teachers (Elisabeth, March 16), reporting and peer feedback on a profound by-experience event that made *real* a lesson learned in the program (Elisabeth, "What was that all about?" November 6), framing personal critique of teaching in terms "pluses" and "arrows," language of the program that emphasizes moving beyond minuses by looking forward to what will be different next time (arrows). Sharing common goals, language and experiences can act as a powerful motivator for wanting to engage with each other's blogging.
- **Programmatic expectations for blogging, when sufficiently flexible, do not stifle blogging learning affordances.** All of the these pre-service teachers were able to use blogging to work through the issues that mattered most to them, as the blogging requirements focused more on frequency (as they were

asked to blog at least once a week through most of their program and after each of their out-of-school learning to teach experiences), more so than subject-area content *per se*.

- **Blogging assignments requiring the use of specific blogging features and genres can be helpful to extend one's blogging practice—as long as it is not overdone!** We are convinced that several of the participants would not have tried out certain blogging practices and features—which they eventually found valuable—on their own without the additional "push" of meeting a course requirement. That said, some participants complained that given the time constraints, these additional requirements sometimes got in the way of writing what they really wanted to blog about.

- **Blogging can serve as a place for pre-service teachers to publish (and narrate) "lessons learned" as well as "work in progress" (issues not yet resolved).** These stated and narrated claims occurred in two different circumstances on the blogs: first, at benchmark transition periods in the program when the blogger chose to pause and take a reflective consideration of perceived growth and future goals (e.g., "Looking back, thinking ahead…," Elisabeth, August 3) and second, as outcomes of studying *practice separate from practice* as the blogger wrestled with the complex circumstances of a given situation, and whether responding effectively or not, defined the lessons learned that she/he is taking away from the experience. (Note that by "narrated" claims, we mean that claims rarely are stated without explanation and justification.)

- **Sharing resources is especially valuable for and appreciated by novice teachers.** Whenever knowledge brokering took place, it was greatly appreciated by other pre-service teachers who were eager to learn about new tools and ideas for their practice.

- **Blogging offered pre-service teachers uncommon opportunities to support one another.** As participants are engaged in teaching experiences that vary across cooperating teachers, scientific disciplines, student populations, schools and districts, they used the blog to commiserate, encourage and share common wrestlings (e.g., how to get a class's attention in ways that align with one's philosophy of education). Peers, at least if not more often than mentors, helped get each other "unstuck" in difficult, nuanced wrestling issues.

- **Pre-service teachers' blogging provides a unique window into how individuals develop during their teacher preparation program.** Teacher educators can learn a lot about the personal processes of becoming a teacher, and how such processes can be supported, by reading about the specific struggles and meaning-making recorded in pre-service teachers' blogging—both those of the pre-service teachers they personally supervise, and those in other programs.

Note

* This chapter was originally published as: Luehmann, A., Henderson, J., and Tinelli, L. (2011) Ch. 12: Supporting pre service teachers' development: The case of blogging in the Get Real! Science teacher preparation program. In A. Luehmann and R. Borasi (Eds.), *Blogging as Change: Transforming Science and Math Education through New Media Literacies* (pp. 236–270). New York: Peter Lang.

References

Chinn, C.A., & Malhotra, B.A. (2002). Epistemologically authentic inquiry in schools: A theoretical framework for evaluating inquiry tasks. *Science Education, 86*: 175–218.

Luehmann, A., & Borasi, R. (Eds.) (2011). *Blogging as change: Transforming science and math education through new media literacies*. New York: Peter Lang.

CHAPTER ELEVEN

New Literacies and Assessments in Middle School Social Studies Content Area Instruction

Issues for Classroom Practices

Margaret C. Hagood, Emily N. Skinner,
Melissa Venters & Benjamin Yelm

Adolescents' engagement in literacy practices that extend beyond the page to incorporate multimodal texts in out-of-school contexts is not new terrain. Research on adolescents' new literacies practices outside of school has shown that they read and utilize texts that demonstrate their competencies as engaged, literate citizens (Alvermann, Hagood, Heron, Hughes, Williams, & Yoon, 2007; Black, 2005; Guzzetti & Gamboa, 2004; Knobel, 2001; Lewis & Fabos, 2005; Mackey, 2003; Mahiri, 2004; O'Brien, 2003; Skinner, 2007a; Vasudevan, 2006). Many of these literacies involve accessing popular culture; using visual and digital technologies such as zines, instant messaging, and fanfiction; creating documentaries; and analyzing television. Most of this research is predicated on the assumption that literacy is no longer singular and print bound; instead the iconic and digital demands of the 21st century have opened up literacies that require transversals across print and non-print-based formats.

Although literacy practices outside of school demand engagement of an array of multimodalities, school-based literacy competencies in the United States continue to be determined by end-of-year statewide assessments of content that examine students' proficiencies of functional and autonomous literacies (Hull & Schultz, 2002; Street, 1995), which include solely the decoding and encoding of reading and writing print-based texts usually from the standpoint of receiving an author's message. All the while, research continues to reveal that adolescents, especially those who struggle with academic literacies in schools, are more apt to engage with and to realize the relevancy of traditional academic content when teachers make connections between out-of-school and in-school literacies and adolescents' lives (Hobbs & Frost, 2003; Mahar, 2001; Morrell, 2002).

Even as adolescents engage in new literacies and show competencies with multi-modal texts, other indicators such as Annual Yearly Progress (AYP) scores determined by end-of-year assessments and federal initiatives to assist underserved students with literacy improvements in schools suggest that many adolescents continue to struggle with engagement and success on school-based content area literacies. This inconsistency between out-of-school and in-school achievement with respect to literacies practices is felt throughout the United States, and little research has examined the transfer of adolescents' new literacies skills to traditional academic content learning. Perhaps the dearth of research in this area results from the false dichotomy that separates out-of-school and in-school contexts, and from various groups' interests in keeping these literacies separate. It is this very transversal between engaging new literacies and learning across contexts that we take up in this chapter.

Drawing upon studies of using popular culture and new literacies to engage students in learning (Alvermann, Moon, & Hagood, 1999; Hagood, 2007; Skinner, 2007b), we examine the connections between instruction and assessment of two middle school teachers' pedagogical implementation of new literacies using students' out-of-school interests and texts to further their understanding of social studies content. The work presented here stems from a larger research study of implementing new literacies strategies in content areas (e.g., social studies, science) in underperforming middle schools (Hagood, Provost, Skinner, & Egelson, 2008). In this chapter, we look at how these teachers—who were part of a two-year implementation of new literacies strategies in their respective schools—designed instruction that addressed state standards for social studies using new literacies strategies. Using observation data concerning teaching, individual interviews on the teachers' instructional practices and views of literacies, and student artifacts, we examine how the teachers worked to engage students in social studies content and literacy objectives by incorporating new literacies. We also show how students demonstrated competencies on these standards by means of a variety of assessments. Finally, we scrutinize the connections between identities, instruction, assessment, and student outcomes on performance and formative assessments of social studies content when using new literacies.

Meet the Teachers

Ben and Melissa are European Americans in their mid-twenties, and are energetic middle school teachers, working in two underperforming Title One middle schools (Grades 6 to 8) populated by a majority of African American students and a minority of Latino, Asian and White American students. Both schools have been rated "unsatisfactory" on the South Carolina Report Card, which reflects students' statewide assessment scores. Both schools were selected by the school district to participate in a two-year implementation of new literacies teaching strategies, and all English language arts and social studies teachers in the schools were mandated to participate. Over the two years, these two teachers, along with other teachers from their schools, attended four two-day Institutes on using new literacies strategies and participated in bimonthly grade level meetings to reflect upon their implementation of new literacies strategies, learning how to connect their students' out-of-school and in-school literacies for improved engagement and performance. As part of this research, they implemented these strategies in their social studies classrooms and studied their students' content engagement and academic performance.

Ben has an undergraduate degree in secondary education/social studies (Grades 7 to 12). Because he taught three years of middle school prior to South Carolina teaching level certification policy changes, he was grandfathered under previous policy that allows him to teach any grade level in middle school. Ben recently completed a Masters degree in Technology Education. In addition, for the past two years, Ben has participated in a group of 13 educators to prepare for a Fulbright funded five-week trip to Sierra Leone and Guinea to learn about West African culture and to make connections between West African culture and local Gullah and Geechee cultures, to which many of his students relate.

Ben has taught sixth and seventh grade classes for over four years, all at Northside Middle School (a pseudonym). The Northside administration puts a significant emphasis on preparing for the statewide assessment, the Palmetto Achievement Challenge Test (PACT), illustrated recently during a faculty meeting when the principal announced that the school planned to have a community pep rally for teachers to ride around in a bus on a Saturday afternoon hyping up the community about the upcoming test. In the past, students at Northside had scored the lowest on the social studies portion of the PACT. However, for the past couple of years, students at Northside have scored highest on the social studies portion of the PACT, an achievement of which Ben and his social studies teaching colleagues are proud. Like all teachers at Northside, Ben spends a substantial amount of time during the "PACT Push" (50-day countdown prior to the beginning of PACT), preparing his students for the test with activities such as reviewing big ideas, making PowerPoint presentations about historical figures and events, playing Jeopardy review games, answering daily review questions, and reviewing *unitedstreaming* (Discovery Communications, 2008) video clips. *Unitedstreaming* is an on-demand digital online service provided by Discovery Education that provides teachers with a multitude of video clips related to content area curriculum (e.g. social studies, science, math, health, language arts, etc.).

During the time of this research, Ben taught three sections of 6th grade and one section of 7th grade social studies for general education students. The previous three years he exclusively taught 7th grade social studies, but received a new placement for the current year based on a shift in grade level student enrollment numbers. Sixth grade social studies standards in South Carolina include world history content from early humans to the 1600s and the Age of Exploration.

Melissa has an undergraduate degree in history and secondary education, and is currently working during the summer on a graduate degree in social studies. She has taught for three years, all at Westside Middle School (a pseudonym). Because of Westside's "unsatisfactory" rating, teachers feel pressure from the administration to raise end-of-year test scores. Therefore, much of Melissa's classroom instruction includes coupling new literacies with course content so that students understand content and are prepared for state testing.

As an 8th grade social studies teacher, Melissa teaches all social studies courses (honors, general, resource, and self-contained). Middle school students in the district that Melissa and Ben work in are tracked into all academic classes (math, science, social studies and English language arts) dependent on their math proficiency. Math is the only course that has different standards for the different tracks, whereas in the other content areas, teachers address the same standards at all levels, but generally modify their instruction and expectations based on their students' track placement.

At the beginning of the academic year, Melissa knew she had her work cut out for her when she learned that approximately half her current students scored "Below Basic" on the social studies portion of the PACT state testing as 7th graders. She resolved to assist students in making connections from out-of-school to in-school literacies to engage them in learning and to prepare them for the year-end assessment. In an interview about new literacies and history, she said, "History is boring to kids; I am always looking for ways to connect their lives to what I am teaching. Using new literacies helps to make things relevant to students because it's connecting what they are already comfortable with, with new information. I also think that using new literacies strategies will help my students be more engaged with content. As an 8th grade teacher, I teach only South Carolina history. To make connections for students using their literacies brings the content to life and improves their engagement with it, and hopefully their retention of the information."

The New Literacies Classroom Implementations

Drawing upon research that makes connections between adolescents' out-of-school literacies and in-school academic content (Morrell, 2002; O'Brien, 2003; Skinner, 2007b) and between new literacies and academic literacies (Hagood, 2007), our approach to new literacies professional development within the context of this project has been to provide a repertoire of new literacies teaching strategies for teachers, such as comic strip writing (Bitz, 2007), digital storytelling, and blended narratives (Harris, 2007), that they could then draw from to address specific academic content area standards. In selecting new literacies strategies, we asked teachers to consider the academic literacy areas (e.g., vocabulary, writing process, fluency, applying comprehension strategies, grammar, decoding, reading/writing connections, understanding text genre and structure, etc.) that their students struggle with as identified by the teachers' own classroom observations as well as by their review of district assessment scores.

It is our view that new literacies strategies can be implemented during any or all stages of content area reading instruction (before, during, and after) (Hagood, 2007) and writing process instruction (Skinner, 2007b). New literacies strategies also can be used to address any stage (e.g., pre-unit, in-unit, post-unit) of content area unit plan implementation. In the following two sections, we show how Ben engaged students in a new literacies project using visual literacies and digital technologies at the beginning of a unit, and Melissa utilized visual literacies within new literacies strategies through students' comic strip creation at the end of a unit in order to build upon students' facilities with new literacies formats and to improve their competencies with academic content.

Using Digital Storytelling to Build Prior Knowledge about Classical Roman Civilization: New Literacies as an Introduction to Content

Ben frequently drew upon new literacies strategies, projects, and references in his teaching. He often stated that in comparison to the English language arts teachers participating in our new literacies professional development and research, social studies teachers had much more freedom to assess new literacies. During a grade level meeting where teachers discussed their implementation of new literacies strategies and assessments, Ben commented, "All we have to do to assess is [evaluate] are they addressing content? Can they spell? We don't care. We have so much stuff—we cover 30,000 years of history. For us to take time out to work on that stuff is unrealistic. It's unrealistic to teach them to be fluent [readers and writers]."

And yet, during our observations of Ben's teaching, we found that he explicitly incorporated literacy teaching into social studies content area teaching.

In this section, we describe how Ben developed, implemented and assessed a digital storytelling project at the beginning of a unit of study that addressed the sixth grade world history standard, "Summarize the significant political and cultural features of classical Roman civilization, including its concept of citizenship, law, and government: its contribution to literature and the arts; and its innovations in architecture and engineering such as roads, arches, keystones, and aqueducts" (Charleston County School District, 2007a). At the same time, he fluidly integrated literacy instruction into the digital storytelling project through addressing multiple sixth grade language arts state standards regarding writing process, reading comprehension, reading response, communication and research skills, and assessed the organization component of a *6 + 1 Traits* (Culham, 2003) district-wide writing initiative that Ben noted was "just common sense."

In preparation for this project, Ben used the online resource, *Filamentality* (Knowledge Network Explorer, 2008) to develop a home page where his students could gather images of Roman architecture, historical icons, art, maps, and government. This step of project development proved crucial in providing students with access to online images, a task that had been challenging for one of Ben's English language arts colleagues who had previously implemented digital storytelling with his students and run into challenges regarding the district's internet filter, which teachers characterized as blocking out all websites recognized as used for social networking (and thus excluded Flickr.com, among others).

Using Ben's *Filamentality* home page, his students worked online to immerse themselves in print-based and visual texts related to Rome, selected images they planned to present in their digital stories on Roman architecture, and then imported these images to their personal district network folders. Concurrently, Ben taught students how to use the free software, *Photostory* (Microsoft, 2008), a program that allows users to design digital stories using still images, narration, music, subtitles, motion, and transitions.

Ben modeled how to use *Photostory* in whole class minilessons that included: importing images, adding motion to images, writing and recording narration, and adding music. He also individualized instruction regarding many of these digital literacy skills as students worked their way through developing their photostories noting that, because this was the students' first experience with this particular software, he had to re-teach each skill to about half of the students, who then retaught the skills to the other half. In addition, Ben developed a photostory model that students used as a mentor text when developing their own photostories. In addition, Ben developed a rubric for evaluating students' photostories (see Table 11.1).

Table 11.1. Photostory Project Grading Rubric

Score Criteria	Below Average: 70% or lower	Average: 70%–85%	Excellent: 86%–100%
Photos	Less than 75% of photos used do not have to do with Roman history or culture.	75%–95% of all photos have to do with Roman history or culture.	All photos have to do with Roman history or culture.
Captions	Over 50% of captions are difficult to understand or have nothing to do with the photos.	Less than 50% of captions are difficult to understand or have nothing to do with the photos.	All captions are easy to understand and deal with the photos they were placed on.
Narration	Narration is confusing/off topic.	Narration is not confusing, but not completely on topic.	Narration is easy to understand and completely on topic.

In reviewing students' photostories, we found that their projects all integrated multiple images of ancient Roman architecture and engineering (e.g., roads, arches, keystones, and aqueducts). In addition, students' projects included a diversity of other Roman images such as current architecture, ancient and modern day geographical and political maps, and historical Roman leaders and gods. Students designated captions for each image included (e.g., Roman aqueducts, theatre of Marcellus, Roman arch, etc.). At the beginning of their photostories, students orally introduced their photostories using the narration tool.

In order to modify instruction for the variety of learners in his classes related to English language oral fluency and reading and writing competencies, Ben offered his students a variety of options for narrating their photostories, including composing their own narration, reading their narration from their social studies text book, and providing background music in lieu of narration (following the introduction that all students were required to record). Students' chosen background music included popular hip hop (e.g., Beyonce, Soldier Boy, Alicia Keyes) and Latina (e.g., Shakira, Esperanza) music that provided viewers with clues as to the cultural identities of the *Photostory* designers in relation to age, race, ethnicity and gender.

At the culmination of the week-long project, students presented their photostories to their classmates. Then, having facilitated building prior knowledge about classical Roman civilization through digital literacy practices, during the following weeks Ben facilitated direct whole group teaching of classical Roman civilization content, presenting activities such as having students draw diagrams of Rome's bridges and roads, reading a variety of short shared texts including comics and short stories, viewing parts of the Hollywood-produced movie, *Julius Caesar* (2004), and completing worksheets on content. Ben framed these activities with interactive PowerPoint lectures and notes that purposefully included many of the images students had used in their photostories so that they would recognize the images as part of their prior knowledge and be interested in learning more about the content.

Ben observed that during the Roman architecture digital storytelling unit students took ownership over their projects, learned a lot about Rome, and were extremely engaged. He noted that for months after the project's completion they viewed it as one of their most memorable experiences from 6th grade. At the end of the academic year, Ben said his students still recalled the pictures they had included and the songs they had selected. Ben recognized that working on this project for a week's time was so engaging and inviting that, "for some of them, it got them to school that day, and that got them to math and science . . ." (Yelm, 2008). He further elaborated on a particular student who had been retained twice and regularly missed school, and yet during the week of this project's implementation was present every day and additionally showed up at his classroom door during lunch to work on her Roman architecture photostory.

Ben also concluded that the project worked well for English language learners, a conclusion that he had likewise drawn when implementing a new literacies comic strip project that drew upon visual literacies earlier in the year. Ben delineated the teaching challenges inherent in the project, including the necessity that teachers both develop a depth of knowledge of *Photostory* and then are able to offer their students substantial individual assistance in order to complete their individual photostories.

Using Comic Strips to Study South Carolina's History: New Literacies as Culmination of Content

Most of the South Carolina 8th grade social studies standards address issues of slavery and race relations. Working in a predominantly African American school, Melissa wanted to make the content real to the students and to connect their contemporary lives with the academic standards relevant to life in the state 300 years ago. Melissa drew upon the predominant standard that students must "draw conclusions about how sectionalism arose from events or circumstances of racial tension, internal population shifts, and political conflicts, including the Denmark Vesey Plot, slave codes, and the African American population majority" (Charleston County School District, 2007b, p. 20) in order to weave together the main ideas of race relations and tensions that led to stricter state laws. She used several school and out-of-school sources to cover this standard. These texts included primary source documents such as those provided by the curriculum guide (Charleston County School District, 2007b), the section on Denmark Vesey provided in the district-wide 8th grade social studies text, *The History of South Carolina in the Building of the Nation* (Huff, 2006), and other websites and information she found online that she included in her classroom discussions.

Melissa decided to use the case of Denmark Vesey as a central point of discussion and to connect his story through new literacies strategies as a culminating activity so as to improve students' engagement with the content and retention of information of the larger theme of slavery, race relations, and repercussions in the law as a result of whites' concerns for slave uprisings. A brief history of Denmark Vesey (1767–1822) shows how students would be drawn to his story. Melissa explained to the students, through their readings and discussions, how Denmark Vesey was a unique and interesting man. A West Indian slave, he won the lottery in Charleston, and then used the $1,500 prize money to buy his freedom and to help found the African Methodist Episcopal Church (AME). According to *The History of South Carolina in the Building of the Nation* (Huff, 2006), Vesey believed God spoke to him and told him to be the Moses of his people, and with approximately 9,000 supporters he plotted a slave revolt in 1822. Peter Prioleau, another slave, told his master what Denmark planned. The revolt was squelched, and Vesey and others were hanged. Outcomes of the attempted revolt resulted in stricter slave codes in South Carolina, tightening slaves' few privileges, taxing free blacks, and strengthening the Whites' pro-slavery stance.

Melissa worked with her students on this topic for a week, covering content, vocabulary, main ideas, and making inferences. Students first read the textbook selection on Denmark Vesey as a class and picked out the main points. Then, they summarized these points on the whiteboard in a whole group discussion, and students copied this information down in their notebooks. To conclude the unit of study, Melissa wanted students to demonstrate their knowledge of content and vocabulary. She planned to have students critique the Wikipedia entry of Vesey and to add their own information to the site during a review of the unit of study, but due to the school's cyber-patrol system, the students were blocked from making any additions to the entry on Denmark Vesey on the Wikipedia site. Instead, Melissa chose to use a comic strip, one of the new literacies strategies she learned about during one of the New Literacies Institutes she had attended. First she reviewed the key information with the students. The following transcript shows how Melissa engaged in the method of Initiate, Respond, and Evaluate (IRE) (Mehan, 1979) to quickly review content with the students and to set the stage for comic creation:

Melissa: Where did Vesey live?

Student 1:   Charleston

Melissa: He was a slave and brought here from the West Indies. How did he get his freedom?

Student 2:   He won the lottery.

Melissa: How much did he win?

Student 3: $1,500

Melissa: How much did he pay for his freedom?

Student 1: $600

Melissa: Who did he pay?

Student 4:   The slave owner.

Melissa: Then he founds a church. Which one?

Student 5:   AME

Melissa: What was his job?

Student 3:   He was a carpenter.

Melissa: His house was near the College of Charleston. He thought he was the Moses of his people. What does he plan? Recall, we got mad at your social studies text because it calls it the "Vesey Insurrection." Why shouldn't we call it that?

Student 5:   Because it never happened.

Melissa: Why?

Student 4:   Because they were caught before it.

Melissa: Right. Vesey and other leaders were hanged. Some others were enslaved and because of what Vesey does they are re-enslaved. How is that?

Student 1:   The slave code was put into effect after the other rebellion.

Melissa: Yes, what was the name of that one?

Student 6:   The Stono Rebellion.

Melissa: Okay so two plots had occurred before this one. The Stono Rebellion is where slaves were trying to get free in 1739 in south Florida. Was the rebellion successful?

Students (most of class): No!

Melissa: So that resulted in stricter slave codes and blacks had to wear negro cloth—certain kinds of clothing.

[The other plot occurred in Santo Domingo in 1791 and was successful.]

Melissa: So you need to create a 6 slide comic that would teach 3rd graders about Denmark Vesey. You have to summarize what happens to him. You need to include words and pictures. If you can't draw people, that's okay, but try to make it colorful and use the background to show the setting. You have markers, colored pencils, rulers. You have until the end of class [40 minutes] to create your comic.

Then, students eagerly engaged and completed this assignment in the allotted time frame. Examples of their work are presented in Figures 11.1 and 11.2.

Figure 11.1: Student 1's comic of the Denmark Vesey Revolt.

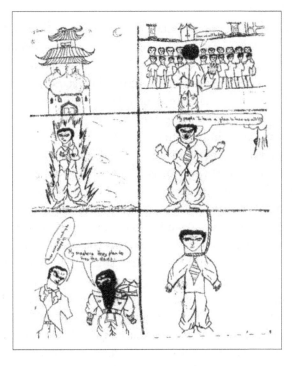

Figure 11.2: Student 2's comic of the Denmark Vesey Revolt.

After completing this assignment, students shared their work with each other, summarizing the result of the Vesey-led attempted revolt and critiquing each others' comics related to content and presentation. In this exercise, Melissa attempted to have students transfer their uses of visual literacies and their new literacies creations of comic strips into a more formalized academic literacy. Using the comic strips as a form of prewriting, Melissa had students write essays summarizing the outcome of the Vesey plot, explaining the tightened slave laws that ensued, and discussing the historical significance of these events on South Carolina history.

Finally, in an end-of-unit test, Melissa had students discuss in an essay question the story of Denmark Vesey, including the result (i.e., stricter slave codes). She explained, "What I really wanted students to gain from the comic was the result of the plot, and I even showed them actual examples of South Carolina slave codes from the 1840s. As a PACT review question, I asked students the multiple choice question, 'What was the result of the Denmark Vesey plot?' This was five months later, and most students got the answer to the question correct."

Discussion

Finally, we scrutinize the connections between identities, content area instruction, assessment, and student outcomes on performance and formative assessments of social studies content. In implementing the *Photostory* project, Ben did not regard himself as a literacy teacher; instead he viewed his primary purpose as being to teach his students social studies content. He recognized the difficulty for social studies teachers to hang back and to involve their students in inquiry-based learning, as he had done with the *Photostory* project, stating, "Social studies teachers know everything, and we want to teach you everything we know."

And yet, Ben's *Photostory* project implementation allowed students to build prior knowledge about ancient Roman civilization *before* he indulged in telling his students, whom he assessed as knowing very little about ancient Roman civilization, everything *he* knew about Roman ancient civilization. Furthermore, Ben explicitly addressed social studies curriculum standards while at the same time integrating numerous English language arts state standards including: reading comprehension, writing process, reading response, communication (speaking, viewing and listening), and research skills (i.e., gathering, preparing and presenting information). In addition, the rubric Ben developed to evaluate students' projects addressed writing organization, one of three *6 + 1 Traits* (Culham, 2003) areas his administrators had selected for school wide focus across the content areas.

Melissa, unlike Ben, did not initially see the connections between social studies and the teaching of literacy. Like many other middle school teachers, Melissa's undergraduate program did not prepare her to be a literacy teacher in a social studies classroom. Speaking to this issue of identity and teaching, she said, "I don't know about all of those terms you use with literacy. No one ever explicitly taught me in my undergrad program how to teach students how to read the text. We were just taught how to teach the content." Seeing herself as an outsider to literacy instruction and her role in the classroom solely as one of history content transmission, she used new literacies to break down the content so as to assist students in comprehending the difficult aspects. Drawing upon what she taught them with key vocabulary, main ideas, summarizing, and inferencing, she completed the unit of study with students' creation of a six-panel comic. Students were able to visually display their understanding of the ideas and connected this visual aid to their construction of an essay that demonstrated their understanding of content in more academic representation.

Ben and Melissa's teaching illustrates that sometimes new literacies strategies build upon foundational, academic literacies. Ben's work with augmenting students' schema at the beginning of a unit of study and Melissa's use of new literacies as a culmination to solidify main ideas and inferences illustrate the intricate coupling of foundational/academic and new literacies practices in the classroom. Through incorporating new literacies, Ben and Melissa validated their students' engagement as crucial to content area learning and their students' development and display of multimodal competencies (Siegel, 2006) as legitimate sources for performance-based assessments of social studies content area learning. Furthermore, both Ben and Melissa integrated English language arts standards and important foundational literacy components into their teaching and assessment. Melissa, in particular, worked to assist students' transfer of content from the creation of visual, new literacies texts to more traditional essay format assessments.

Because students were able to work first from their areas of interest and expertise with comic creation, Melissa felt that they understood better the content and were more willing to do the work to translate and to transfer their understanding to a more traditional form of assessment: writing a brief summative essay. The essays made it apparent to Melissa that the students understood both the main ideas and the details of the Vesey case, as well as the nuances of the race relations that were exacerbated by the outcome of the slave revolt that never occurred.

Conclusion

Through incorporating new literacies instruction and content assessment into their pedagogy, teachers like Ben and Melissa can assert their intersecting identities as knowledgeable content area teachers and sophisticated new literacies practitioners, an assertion that maximizes students' engagement and furthers students' acquisition of competencies. Melissa often critiqued the structure within her school that subtracted her contact time with students and replaced it with *Read 180* (Scholastic, 2008), a reading intervention software program targeted for below-grade-level readers that focuses on decoding drills to improve students' print-based reading skill.

Relatedly, Ben highlighted that students at Northside (where they also were pulled out of their regular classes in 7th and 8th grade for *Read 180*) were doing better on the social studies PACT than any other area. Perhaps, if schools and districts recognized and supported teachers such as Ben and Melissa's competencies in integrating social studies content with literacy teaching objectives through new literacies projects, students in "unsatisfactory" schools might have more opportunities to display their own competencies while at the same time extending their content area knowledge and raising their literacy achievement. Moreover, as literacy practices change to reflect multimodalities and new literacies, appropriate assessments must follow suit. Assessments must allow for students to demonstrate their competencies within new literacies, but students must also be able to show those competencies in more traditional formats and high-stakes statewide assessments such as the PACT.

Instead of dichotomizing literacies—separating new literacies from academic literacies, content literacies from each other, and performance assessment from formative assessments—we need to find spaces to meld these forms of literacies to aid in both instruction and assessments in classrooms. To keep literacies separated marginalizes new literacies to continue to be the "hook" that gets students involved and fails to recognize the necessity to teach and assess students' new literacies in order to prepare students to be competent literacy users in the 21st century (Johnson & Kress, 2003; Kalantzis, Cope, &

Harvey, 2003). Such division between these literacies also precipitates perceptions that students in "unsatisfactory" schools are unsuccessful in academic literacies, when in fact, they are competent.

As illustrated in the model in Figure 11.3, teaching literacies in the 21st century must incorporate academic and new literacies simultaneously. Efforts must be made to assist students in using new literacies to connect to content and then to loop around so that competencies can be translated into assessments that are current markers of success in school.

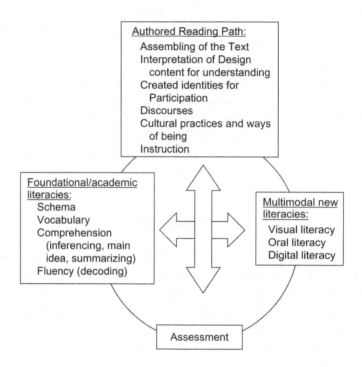

Figure 11.3: Transfer of content across foundation/academic and new literacies in school.

Developing and recognizing students' foundational literacies and new literacies concomitantly is especially important for students and teachers in schools that have been rated as "unsatisfactory," a label that unfortunately is internalized by teachers in these schools (Venters, 2008) and yet neither describes nor defines the depth or breadth of Ben and Melissa's teaching and their students' learning.

Note

* This chapter was originally published as: Hagood, M., Skinner, E., Venters, M., & Yelm, B. (2009). New Literacies and assessments in middle school social studies content area instruction: Issues for classroom practices. In A. Burke & R. Hammett (Eds.), *Assessing new literacies: Perspectives from the classroom* (pp. 77–93). New York: Peter Lang.

References

Alvermann, D.E., Hagood, M.C., Heron, A., Hughes, P., Williams, K.B., & Yoon, J. (2007). Telling themselves who they are: What one out-of-school time study revealed about underachieving readers. *Reading Psychology, 28*(1), 31–50.

Alvermann, D.E., Moon, J., & Hagood, M.C. (1999). *Popular culture in the classroom: Teaching and researching critical media literacy.* Newark, DE: International Reading Association and National Reading Conference.

Bitz, M. (2007). The comic book project: Literacy outside and inside the box. In J. Flood, S. Brice-Heath, & D. Lapp (Eds.), *Handbook of research on teaching literacy through the communicative and visual arts* (Vol. II, pp. 229–237). New York: Routledge.

Black, R.W. (2005). Access and affiliation: The literacy and composition practices of English-language learners in an online fanfiction community. *Journal of Adolescent and Adult Literacy, 49*(2), 118–128.

Charleston County School District. (2007a). *Social Studies: Grade 6 coherent curriculum.* Charleston, SC.

Charleston County School District. (2007b). *Social Studies: Grade 8 coherent curriculum.* Charleston, SC.

Culham, R. (2003). *6 + 1 traits of writing the complete guide (Grades 3 and up).* New York: Scholastic.

Discovery Communications, LLC (2008). *Unitedstreaming.* Retrieved on May 16, 2008 from http://streaming.dis coveryeducation.com/index.cfm

Guzzetti, B.J., & Gamboa, M. (2004). Zines for social justice: Adolescent girls writing on their own. *Reading Research Quarterly, 39*(4), 408–436.

Hagood, M.C. (2007). Linking popular culture to literacy learning and teaching in the 21st century. In B.J. Guzzetti (Ed.), *Literacy for the new millennium: Adolescent literacy* (Vol. 3, pp. 223–238). Westport, CT: Praeger.

Hagood, M.C., Provost, M., Skinner, E., & Egelson, P. (2008). Teachers' and students' literacy performance in and engagement with new literacies strategies in underperforming middle schools. *Middle Grades Research Journal, 3*(3), 57–95.

Harris, R. (2007). Blending narratives: A storytelling strategy for social studies. *Social Studies, 98*(3), 111–116.

Hobbs, R., & Frost, R. (2003). Measuring the acquisition of media-literacy skills. *Reading Research Quarterly, 38*, 330–355.

Huff, A.V. (2006). *The history of South Carolina in the building of the nation.* Columbia, SC: Capital City Publishing Enterprises.

Hull, G., & Schultz, K. (Eds.) (2002). *School's out: Bridging out-of-school literacies with classroom practice.* New York: Teachers College Press.

Johnson, D., & Kress, G. (2003). Globalisation, literacy and society: Redesigning pedagogy and assessment. *Assessment in Education, 10,* 5–14.

Julius Caesar [Television mini-series] (2004). New York: Good Times Video.

Kalantzis, M., Cope, B., & Harvey, A. (2003). Assessing multiliteracies and the new basics. *Assessment in Education, 10,* 15–26.

Knobel, M. (2001). "I'm not a pencil man": How one student challenges our notions of literacy "failure" in school. *Journal of Adolescent and Adult Literacy, 44*(5), 404–414.

Knowledge Network Explorer. (2008). *Filamentality.* Retrieved on May 16, 2008 from http://www.kn.att.com/wired/fil

Lewis, C., & Fabos, B. (2005). Instant messaging, literacies, and social identities. *Reading Research Quarterly, 40*(4), 470–501.

Mackey, M. (2003). Television and the teenage literate: Discourses of *Felicity. College English, 65*(4), 389–410.

Mahar, D. (2001). Bringing the outside in: One teacher's ride on the anime highway. *Language Arts, 81*(2), 110–117.

Mahiri, J. (2004). Street scripts: African American youth writing about crime and violence. In J. Mahiri (Ed.), *What they don't learn in school: Literacy in the lives of urban youth,* (pp. 19–42). New York: Peter Lang.

Mehan, H. (1979). *Learning lessons: Social organization in the classroom.* Cambridge, MA: Harvard University Press.

Microsoft. (2008). *Photostory.* Retrieved on May 16, 2008 from http://www.microsoft.com/windowsxp/using/digital photography/Photostory/default.mspx [now defunct; see instead: http://www.microsoft.com/en-us/download/ details.aspx?id=11132].

Morrell, E. (2002). Promoting academic literacy with urban youth through engaging hip-hop culture. *English Journal, 91*(6), 88–92.

O'Brien, D. (2003, March). Juxtaposing traditional and intermedial literacies to redefine the competence of struggling adolescents. *Reading Online, 6*(7). Retrieved on May 15, 2008 from http://www.readingonline.org/newliteracies/lit_index.asp?HREF=obrien2

Scholastic. (2008). *Read 180.* Retrieved on May 16, 2008 from http://teacher.scholastic.com/products/read180

Siegel, M. (2006). Rereading the signs: Multimodal transformations in the field of literacy education. *Language Arts, 84,* 65–77.

Skinner, E.N. (2007a). "Teenage addiction": Adolescent girls drawing upon popular culture texts as mentors for writing in an after-school writing club. In E. Rowe, R. Jimenez, D. Compton, D. Dickinson, Y. Kim, K. Leander, & V. Risco (Eds.), *National Reading Conference Yearbook, 55,* 275–291. Chicago, IL: National Reading Conference.

Skinner, E.N. (2007b). "Teenage addiction": Writing workshop meets critical media literacy. *Voices from the Middle, 15,* 30–39.

Street, B.V. (1995). *Social literacies: Critical approaches to literacy in development, ethnography and education.* London: Longman.

Vasudevan, L. (2006). Looking for angels: Knowing adolescents by engaging with their multimodal literacy practices. *Journal of Adolescent and Adult Literacy, 50*(4), 252–256.

Venters, M. (2008, May 4). *Day of tears: Day of desperation; Using blogging to make literacies engaging and comprehensible.* Session presented at the International Reading Association Conference, Atlanta, GA.

Yelm, B. (2008, May 4). *Using Photostory to teach world history.* Session presented at the International Reading Association Conference, Atlanta, GA.

PART 4

New Literacies and Popular Culture Affinities

CHAPTER TWELVE

Language, Culture and Identity in Fan Fiction

Rebecca Black

Observers of the twentieth and the onset of the twenty-first century will note how these times are distinguished by a peculiar passion for identity: identities made around nation, community, ethnicity, race, religion, gender, sexuality, and age; identities premised on popular culture and its shifting sets of representational practices; identities attached to fashion and new imagined lifestyles, to leisure and work, and to the mundane and the exotic; identities made in relation to place and displacement, to community and to a sense of dispersal, to "roots" as well as "routes."
—Yon (2000, p. 1)

Language, Identity, and Discourse

Much current research on second language (L2) and literacy acquisition has centered on the contextual nature of language development and has highlighted the role of identity in English language learners' literacy practices. In addition, as new information and communication technologies (ICTs) facilitate the formation of "virtual spaces" that cross traditional cultural, linguistic, and geographic borders, scholarship in Teaching English to Speakers of Other Languages (TESOL) has turned its attention to such online spaces as new transnational contexts for identity development and language socialization (Cope & Kalantzis, 2000; Warschauer & Kern, 2000). Save for a few studies (Lam, 2000, 2004, 2006; Yi, 2005), there has been little inquiry into the roles of popular and fan culture in the online literacy and social practices of English language learning youth. Moreover, with the fast-paced propagation of new media and technologies, novel fan practices and "virtual" communities based on popular culture seem to spring up on a daily basis. The popularity of such communities generates many questions related to how youth from across the globe are affiliating around popular culture in online spaces. How do adolescents with limited English proficiency construct identities in online English and text-dominated spaces? How do these identities change and develop over time? What resources do these adolescents draw on for their interactions and presentations of self in online spaces? What role does popular culture play in their identity development and literate and social practices?

In this chapter, I draw from constructs in Second Language Acquisition, literacy, cultural, and media studies as theoretical bases for examining how networked ICTs and fan culture provide an English language learning youth with a site for developing her English language and writing skills. During this process, she also develops an online identity as a popular multiliterate writer. To understand how this happens, I explore the notion of *identity* as a fluid construct that shifts over time with this English language learner's long-term participation in a fan community. I also explore popular culture as a point of affiliation and as a *dialogic resource* that she appropriates both in her writing and in her interactions with other fans. In so doing, I show how popular culture and technology converge to provide a context in which this adolescent English language learner is able to develop a powerful transcultural identity that is discursively constructed through the different cultural perspectives and literacies that she and other fans from across the globe bring to this space.

Research on second language acquisition has often focused on individual learners' psycholinguistic processes as they learn to read, write, and speak in the target language. Some of this work conceives of identity, if at all, as a stable construct that exists outside of and/or that can be set in opposition to social context (see Harklau, 2007, for a review of research on second language writing and identity). For example, many theories of acculturation posit standard stages that learners go through as they come into contact with, assimilate to, and/or resist the host culture (Atkinson, Morten, & Sue, 1983; Gay, 1985). The research perspective has expanded to consider the development of *ethnic identity* as a fluid, dynamic, and often recursive process (Jeffres, 1983; Phinney, 1990) that is closely tied to learners' interactions in various social contexts. This focus on the social is mirrored by the aforementioned work being done within sociocultural or New Literacy Studies (New London Group, 1996) that conceives of literacy and language development as socially situated practices (Street, 1984) that are intimately tied to cultural, historical, and institutional contexts as well as to identity (Gee, 1996; Lankshear & Knobel, 2003).

Gee's (1999) notion of little-d/big-D Discourse bridges literacy, identity, and context in that it conceives of little-d discourse as everyday language use and big-D Discourse as various resources that act as an "identity kit" of sorts. Thus, big-D Discourse encompasses the wide range of representational resources such as clothing, text, language, and gestures that individuals use to be recognized as certain kinds of people within a given context. Such a construct is useful in looking at interaction in online spaces for several reasons. This construct recognizes the different semiotic and material resources, not only including but also exceeding traditional print-based language, such as images, avatars, icons, shape, sound, and space, that individuals use to convey meaning via computers. In addition, big-D Discourse highlights the ways in which individuals use language and text to index certain facets of their identities in online spaces where many traditional markers of identity are unavailable (Merchant, 2006). Thus, from this perspective, English language learners may have multiple fluid identities that are connected, not to some fixed stage of acculturation or some internal state of being, but rather to more flexible patterns of participation and self-representation in social events that change over time and according to the context and activity (Gee, 2001).

In our modern, information-oriented society, computer-mediated communication and the internet provide new opportunities for using discourse and text to discursively construct and enact achieved identities in online environments (Gee, 2004b; Thomas, 2004). In this spirit, researchers have started to explore how immigrants across the globe are using online spaces to aid in the formulation and/or continuation of their various ethnic identities and affiliations across geographic borders. As an example, Mitra (1997) explores how Indian expatriates use text to construct their identities and signal certain allegiances by selectively inserting themselves into the discourse of an online newsgroup community. Members of the newsgroup live in different parts of the Western Hemisphere and would typically be isolated by spatial constraints; however, computer-mediated communication and the newsgroup provide a common space for this population to gather and discuss "the identity crisis that the Indians negotiate every day in their everyday life in the new land" (p. 67). Thus, this online space provides a forum not only for the sharing of individual experiences but also for collective debate, commiseration, and reaffirmation of an immigrant Indian identity that takes on many different forms and carries across national borders.

Fan Culture, Second Language Literacy, and Identity

Although the role of popular culture in English language learning youths' practices of linguistic and cultural identification remains largely unexplored, recent scholarship has started to address the function of such technology-mediated fan practices in English language learners' literacy and/or identity development. As an example, Lam's (2000) innovative work includes an in-depth case study of a Chinese immigrant who created and maintained a web site devoted to a popular Japanese singer. Through authoring the web site and interacting with fans who visited his site, this youth was able to develop a "textual identity" that bolstered his confidence as he learned and practiced English with a transnational group of peers. More recently, Lam (2006) explored how an English language learning high school senior's webpage enabled him to gain status as a respected anime fan and webmaster. Moreover, the connections he established via the site also allowed him to develop fluency in multiple social languages, including online and anime-related discourses, as well as in the global forms of English spoken by the many English language learning anime fans he interacted with. Through such studies, Lam's work illustrates how these online, pop cultural spaces provide opportunities for youth to fashion linguistic and cultural identities for themselves—in essence, multiliterate and transcultural identities—that extend beyond traditional geographic borders such as the nation-state.

In a similar vein, Yi's (2007, 2008) work explores the multiliterate practices of generation 1.5 Korean-American youth participating in an online community called Welcome to Buckeye City. Drawing from ethnographic and case study data, Yi describes how youth in Welcome to Buckeye City use their first language (L1) of Korean and their second (or more) language of English to relax, socialize, write, and confer about problems from their everyday lives. Thus, Yi explains how this community was a "safe house" (Canagarajah, 1997, as cited in Yi, 2007) of sorts, where these bilingual youth felt comfortable conveying different aspects of their identities in multiple languages. In addition, Yi's case study analysis explores how Joan, a generation 1.5 Korean-American high school student living in the United States, drew from a wide range of multiliterate composing practices to develop a multifaceted "writerly" identity in the Welcome to Buckeye City community (Yi, 2007, personal communication). Joan composed distinct poems, short stories, cards, notes, relay novels, e-mails, and instant messages, and each of these texts provided her with the opportunity to take on subtly different identity roles according to the social context. Moreover, much like authors on fan fiction sites, Joan also received feedback on her publicly posted texts. This feedback provided Joan with opportunities to discuss her "adolescent thoughts and feelings" with other immigrant youth. Constructive feedback also helped her to improve her composing skills and positive comments helped to affirm her identity as an accomplished writer and poet (Yi, 2007).

Anime-based fan fiction is also an example of the highly participatory, agentive, and global nature of online popular and fan culture. In the anime section of FanFiction.net, the majority of fictions are written in English; however, analyses will demonstrate how many members of the site seem to display a global disposition in that they value and express interest in learning about the different cultural and linguistic backgrounds of other youth in the space. Hence, the emphasis of anime fan fiction writing does not center on English-only or print-based forms and conventions of writing and North American cultural values. Instead, interactions between writers and readers illustrate a cosmopolitan, shared appreciation for multiple languages, different cultural perspectives, and alternative forms of text. Texts from the web site also illustrate fans' strong allegiance to popular culture and emphasize the value of communication, social interaction, and pluralism in this online space.

In *Textual Poachers: Television Fans and Participatory Culture,* Jenkins (1992) challenges prevalent stereotypes of fans as "passive dupes" who uncritically ingest the messages of mainstream media. He instead argues that fan culture is based on the introduction, discussion, and dissemination of a multiplicity of perspectives.

> [Fans'] activities pose important questions about the ability of media producers to constrain the creation and circulation of meanings. Fans construct their cultural and social identity through borrowing and inflecting mass culture images, articulating concerns which often go unvoiced within the dominant media. (1992, p. 23)

The fan fiction texts presented in this chapter are a clear illustration of Jenkins' point, as through writing, reading, and peer-reviewing fan fiction, these youth are engaging in a *dialogic* process (Bakhtin, 1981; Dyson, 1997; Nystrand, 1997) of appropriating Japanese media characters and narratives and making them their own. As such, these youth refashion the preexisting media tales by infusing them with social and cultural themes, multiple literacies, various forms of expertise, and concerns from their lives. Moreover, these mass-produced media become resources for and are integrated into fans' day-to-day interactions and activities, and the cultures of online fandoms. In addition, through such appropriation, many youth in this space are able to take on identities, not as immigrants, or as struggling writers or readers of English, or as native or nonnative speakers of one language or another, but rather as learners and users of multiple social languages and discourses.

Building an Online Identity

Nanako

Nanako and her family moved from Shanghai, China, to a large Canadian city in the summer of 2000. When they moved, Nanako, a native Mandarin Chinese speaker, was eleven years old and did not speak any English. According to Nanako, at school in Canada, she struggled with all of her courses except for math and found it difficult to make friends since she is "a rather quiet person" and "couldn't even speak a sentence in English without thinking about [her] grammar and all" (interview, 2006). The winter after she moved, however, she was surfing the web for anime and happened upon some personal web sites that featured anime-based fan fictions. She became an avid fan fiction reader, and because many of the texts were posted in English, her interest in this form of Japanese popular culture also became a conduit for her language learning.

Two years later, Nanako joined FanFiction.net and created a personal page that offered her many different means of forging social connections and for presenting certain aspects of herself to the online community (Black, 2005). Two months after joining FanFiction.net, and only two and a half years after moving to Canada and beginning to learn a new language, Nanako began writing and publicly posting her own fan fictions on the site in English. Over the years, Nanako has been able to achieve the identity of a successful and wildly popular author in this space. Moreover, as this chapter demonstrates, the relationships she has built with readers and the dialogic nature of writing and participation have played a large part in her success and popularity on the site.

Research Questions

In the analysis for this chapter, I focus primarily on thematic topics that were related to identity, language, and culture (for additional analyses, see Black, 2008). To this end, I present texts that are representative of how Nanako actively constructed and enacted her identity in this space (and how this identity changed over time). I also chose salient types of reader reviews or feedback in which the reader responds or in some way contributes to Nanako's online presentation of self. I also conducted a closer discourse analytic examination of such texts with the following questions in mind:

- What sort of linguistic "work" are these texts doing?
- How and in what ways are the texts indexing Nanako's identity as a successful writer?
- How and in what ways are the texts indexing the readers' identities as knowledgeable participants in this space?
- How and in what ways do the texts reference and/or draw from language, culture, and popular culture?

In answering these questions, I coded data on multiple levels. First, I looked at separate lines to identify the main topic or thematic structure of each clause (Gee, 1999; Halliday & Matthiessen, 2004). Next, I returned and looked at each line in terms of the sort of *socially situated* identities that were being enacted, referenced, and/or were relevant to meaningful participation in the site (Gee, 1999). For example, in certain contexts, Nanako would present herself in the broader category of Asian, whereas in others she would self-identify as Chinese. She would also represent herself as a bad writer, a lazy writer, or an English learner depending on her particular goals at the time. I then compared across reviews, Nanako's interactions with readers, and interviews to identify potential thematic and/or structural patterns in these various texts and forms of self-representation.

Dialogic Resources

In Bakhtin's (1981) dialogic conception of language, to become literate in a certain social language entails more than solely learning the discrete, linguistic aspects of reading, writing, and speaking. Similar to Gee's (1999) notion of language as part of Discourses or "identity kits" that enable individuals to be recognized as certain kinds of people, Bakhtin conceives of language learning as coming to know, either consciously or implicitly, how to participate successfully in certain social situations and to enact the social values and ideological dispositions of certain cultural, linguistic, and/or social groups. This heteroglossic or multivocal (Bakhtin, 1981) vision of language also encompasses the ways in which individuals appropriate an array of available dialogic resources, such as media, texts, other utterances, and social voices, to assist them in constructing meaning and in projecting certain identities and social affiliations that may depart from and/or challenge what is standard or established.

In the following analyses, I discuss how Nanako's facility with different forms of literacy and popular culture, and the online fan fiction community provided her with many diverse resources that helped her to construct and enact the identity of a successful fan fiction writer in English. However, this identity was negotiated not only through English but also through Nanako's pan-Asian linguistic and cultural knowledge and affiliations. In addition, for Nanako's writing on FanFiction.net, she draws on a range of pop cultural resources from different countries, such as Japanese animation, music from the United Kingdom, and novels and motion pictures from the United States, to assist her in composing in English. I also discuss how these dialogic resources shifted over time as Nanako's facility with English and her comfort level in the online community increased. To conclude, I posit that Nanako's participation in this online space not only helped her to develop confidence and motivation for continued writing and language learning in English but it also provided her with a sense of pride and a renewed emphasis on her linguistic background and ethnic identity as an Asian.

From Beyblade to Card Captor Sakura

Nanako's initial fan fictions were based on two anime series, *Beyblade* and *Yu-Gi-Oh!*, that, like many media "mixes" (Ito, 2001) or "franchises" (Lemke, 2005), have corresponding toys, television shows, movies, and manga (comic books) and were wildly popular at the time. The plots of both series revolve around competitors battling or dueling either using Beyblades, which are spinning tops, or in the case of *Yu-Gi-Oh!*, using Duel Monster playing cards. While both shows have female characters and competitors, the action centers mainly on male protagonists and their skirmishes. In drawing from these media for her writing, Nanako appropriates only certain aspects of these texts and then uses them to create her own plotlines. For instance, in her first *Beyblade* fiction, Nanako develops her story around the characters from the White Tigers, a Chinese *Beyblade* team. In particular, the narrative events focus primarily on a romantic relationship between the characters Ray and Mariah. Thus, her choice of plot provides means for fusing elements of popular culture with the emerging interest in sexuality and/or romance that she and many adolescents on the site share.

The narrative of the story text itself is written entirely in English, aside from one spot where, interestingly enough, Nanako portrays one of the Chinese characters using a Japanese term as she is thinking to herself. The use of Japanese rather than her first language of Chinese here could be attributed to several factors. First, as discussed in subsequent analyses, Japanese language is often viewed as a badge of membership in anime fan communities. Also, while Nanako knows a great deal about the *Beyblade* show, she freely admits that she does not know details about some of the characters; hence, she may not have realized that this particular character was in fact Chinese.

Nanako's *Beyblade* fiction is what is known within the fan community as a "songfiction" or songfic, which is a "story based entirely around the lyrics of a song" (Fanfiction Glossary, 2006). This hybrid story structure can be seen in the following excerpt from Chapter 1 of *Complete*.

Chapter 1 The Pain

It was a cozy night, I was lying awake on my bed, I just couldn't help but thinking about Ray. His bedroom was just a few blocks away from mine. I wanted to go and see how he was doing, but I would probably get kicked off the team if Lee or Kevin see me wondering around Ray and his teammates' rooms. *Oh Ray, I wish you could come back to me, then we can be together just like the old times.*

~ Flash back of yesterday ~

If you see me walking down the street Staring at the sky and dragging my two feet

I was walking down the street with my teammates, and then we saw you and your team, the bladebreakers. I was so glad to see you again, you were as handsome as per usual, I wanted ran up to you and gave you a warm hug, but I know Lee won't allow me to so. I really missed you Ray.

Thus, the text is dialogic in the sense that she mixes both the Asian elements of the Japanese Animation with more Western pop cultural elements by using a song from an all-female pop band from the United Kingdom. Moreover, for a writer who was just learning English, the mixture of generic resources from both the song and the narrative story format provides an intertextual framework to scaffold Nanako's writing. Specifically, she was able to separate and use each stanza of the popular song, as well as readers' knowledge of the tone of the song, to augment and support the romantic nature of the narrative story she was crafting. Moreover, she did not have to construct the entire narrative from scratch.

Author's Notes and Self-Identifying as an English Language Learner

Nanako introduces the first chapter of *Complete* with an Author's Note (A/N). On FanFiction.net, Author's Notes are used by writers to address readers before, during, or after their stories. However, there is a fair amount of controversy surrounding Author's Notes in the broader fan fiction community. The debate hinges on the fact that many "serious" fan writers do not approve of such notes, arguing that they are jarring and/or detract from the readers' enjoyment of a text. Nonetheless, as evidenced by the copious amount of Author's Notes, readers' positive responses to such notes and general support for their continued presence in the community (e.g., online petitions), Author's Notes are an integral and, I would argue, valuable part of writing and participation in this space. On the Fanfic Symposium, a site devoted to meta-discussion of fan fiction, Gilliam (2002) writes about this very topic and argues that "fanfiction.net is less an archive in which finished stories are housed than a community in which the participatory process of constructing the story is as important if not more so than the finished product" (no page). Nanako's extensive use of Author's Notes supports this vision of FanFiction.net as a social and interactive writing space rather than a depository for text. She uses Author's Notes for a variety of notable purposes: to establish certain aspects of her identity, to introduce and help orient readers to her texts, and also to thank reviews for their feedback and support of her writing, to name just a few. Moreover, as discussed in the next section, Nanako uses her Author's Notes to elicit both social- and writing-related responses from readers in such a way that the readers and their feedback also become resources that support and inspire her participation on the site.

For instance, the following Author's Note serves several different functions. First, the note is a way for Nanako to begin establishing her identity as an anime fan. Second, it provides a guide to her text for readers to follow. And finally, it serves as a means for Nanako to negotiate her writing space with readers. In Segment A, Nanako begins not in her native language of Mandarin, but in Japanese. She greets readers (*Konnichiwa*) and tells them that "[She's] back" (*Tadaima*) from a few weeks of not writing or updating her stories. These Japanese terms are a means of indexing her identity and insider status in the realm of anime fan fiction, as many fans try to learn and/or integrate Japanese into their anime-based texts.

Segment A
L1 A/N: Konnichiwa!
L2 Tadaima!

L3   This is my first Beyblade song fic,
L4   so please go easy on it.

Segment B
L5   I just love Ray/Mariah fics,
L6   they are so kawaii together! ^_^

Segment C
L7   Read and Review!
L8   And no flames!
L9   Thank you!

Segment D
L10 By the way, this is in Mariah's POV
L11 on the night when Ray lost his bit beast. (2002)

In Segment B, Nanako is indexing another aspect of her identity, while at the same time eliciting a different sort of interaction from readers. Specifically, in Line 5 she identifies the couple that will be paired romantically in the story, and then in Line 6, in Japanese, says what a *kawaii* or cute couple she thinks they are. In this way, Nanako is establishing herself as a supporter of the romantic pairing of a certain anime couple. Interestingly enough, this is often a huge point of contention, as many fans are deeply invested in *shipper* or relationship-based texts and prefer to read stories that feature pairings that they are interested in and/or approve of. In this sense, Nanako is establishing a point of contact with her readers and is identifying herself as a Ray + Mariah fan. She is also eliciting responses that are not based on her writing per se, but are more related to other fans' interpretations of the anime itself and is in a sense engaging in the debate surrounding which characters make the best romantic fit.

Nanako also uses this Author's Note to negotiate her writing space with readers in a way that indexes the sort of online writer that she is, specifically, one that appreciates and encourages the participatory and social nature of FanFiction.net. For example, in Lines 3 and 4, she asks readers to be gentle with their comments as this is her first attempt at writing a *Beyblade* songfic. Then, Segment C is a clear example of Nanako's attempts to negotiate with readers as she elicits feedback by asking for "reviews" in Line 7; moreover, she specifies the type of feedback she wants in Line 8. In online register, "flames" are antagonistic, derisive comments. Thus, by writing "no flames," Nanako is parleying for gentle, constructive forms of feedback and making it known that harsh criticism is unacceptable. Nanako concludes, in Segment D, Line 10, by providing further orientation for readers by specifying the character point of view the story is told from, and in Line 11 establishes a specific timeline for the text.

One month later when Nanako posted the second chapter of this fiction, she introduced a new element of self-disclosure into the Author's Note. Specifically, she chose to foreground the fact that she is learning English, and, thereafter, this disclosure played a formative role in many readers' responses to her texts. She writes:

L1   Important note: English is my second language,
L2   so please ignore my grammar mistakes and spelling errors.
L3   I might have some typo
L4   since I wrote this story in a hurry. (2002)

In self-identifying as an English language learner, Nanako is again engaging in a sort of dialogic negotiation with readers. First, she explicitly requests that readers overlook conventions in her writing, which implicitly directs their focus to other aspects of composition such as content and meaning value. Also, at this point in time (one month after the initial chapter was posted), many readers were pleading with her to update the story. So in Line 4, she is also able to use haste as a disclaimer of sorts to mitigate any potentially negative responses to errors and typos in the text. In addition, as shown in the following examples of reader reviews, this new introduction to her Author's Notes generates interest in and questions about Nanako's linguistic and cultural background. As such, she is able to use the Author's Note in such a way that continues helping her to construct her identity as an accomplished fan writer. Moreover, this addition sets the stage for establishing her expert knowledge and insider status as an Asian writing anime-based fan fictions.

Card Captor Sakura *and Linguistic and Cultural Identity*

Three months after posting the *Beyblade* fiction, Nanako moved on to another anime canon, specifically, to *Card Captor Sakura*. *Card Captor Sakura* is what is known as a *magical girl* series, a popular subgenre of *shōjo* or anime for young women. In this series, the protagonist is a young Japanese girl named Sakura Kinomoto, who uses her magical powers to capture an enchanted deck of cards. Though the plot does feature many of Sakura's battles with the magical cards, it differs from the *Beyblade* and *Yu-Gi-Oh!* series in that it also places a great deal of emphasis on friendship, family, and implied romantic relationships between characters. Thus, when Nanako began writing *Card Captor Sakura* fictions that featured relationships between certain popular couples, her stories generated a great deal of interest in the community. One such fiction, her fourteen-chapter story *Crazy Love Letters*, became very popular in the *Card Captor Sakura* section of FanFiction.net and received more than 1,700 reviews from readers (as of May 21, 2005).

As a dialogic resource, *Card Captor Sakura* provided Nanako with new opportunities for creating texts that were linguistically and culturally hybrid. For example, although the series takes place in Japan, two of the main characters are exchange students from Hong Kong, and one of them, Syaoran Li, becomes Sakura's primary love interest. Unlike the *Beyblade* fiction that was written primarily in English with some Japanese interspersed, Nanako used these Chinese characters as an entrée for bringing her first language of Mandarin into her writing. At the same time, she continued to improve her English and also attempted to integrate more Japanese, which she is learning in school, into her texts. When I asked about her use of multiple languages in fan texts, Nanako explained that she used the languages to add to the realism of the story.

> I find add words of another language into a piece can be very effective in a way. For example, on FF.N [FanFiction.net], Sakura and Syaoran speak Japanese and Syaoran speaks Chinese as well. To give the story more realism, Japanese and Chinese should be added into the dialogues to give the reader the impression that the story is actually happening in some place in Japan or China. Using different languages is sometimes like attracting the readers into the writer's own made up world and make things seem more realistic than it actually appears. (2006)

In addition, as she begins revealing more about her cultural and linguistic background in her biographical statements, self-identifying as an English language learner in all her Author's Notes, and using different languages in her fan fiction texts, the multilingual nature of her texts becomes another crux of interaction and dialogic negotiation for her and a transnational group of fans. In the next section, I focus only peripherally on Nanako's text (for a more extended analysis, see Ch. 6, Black, 2008), and highlight instead how Nanako's selective appropriation of resources and reader reviews of this text enabled both Nanako and her readers to discursively position themselves within a diverse, pop cultural milieu made up of youth from across the globe.

Reader Reviews

According to Bakhtin, dialogism is a mode of meaning-making characterized by the meeting and interaction of diverse and often dissenting social voices and perspectives (1981). FanFiction.net provides a space for such dialogism in the provisions it makes for reader feedback. Specifically, each chapter of a posted story has an easily accessible link for submitting reviews. This allows readers to respond to each section of a text as they finish reading it. This is significant for Nanako as an English language learner writer because she received immediate, contextualized feedback on the effects that her rhetorical choices and uses of language have on different readers (Black, 2005). Then, this dialogism continues, as, through Author Notes, e-mail, and subsequent texts, Nanako is in turn able to respond to readers' responses. However, as Nystrand (1997) points out, "discourse is dialogic not because the speakers take turns, but because it is continually structured by tension, even conflict, between the conversants, between self and other, as one voice 'refracts' the other" (p. 8). Thus, Nanako is not simply composing her stories for some silent, anonymous audience. Instead, she is learning to write and to make language choices as part of authentic participation in what Nystrand calls a "dynamic, sociocognitive process" (p. 8) or event as writers and readers co-construct the "temporarily shared social reality" surrounding her text (Rommetveit, 1974). Readers in this space, as avid anime fans, feel a sense of ownership over the characters and media that Nanako is representing in her texts. Moreover, as members of this fan fiction site, they also have a proprietary attitude toward the writing environment and feel justified in putting forth their own ideas and perspectives in terms of how it should be shaped. Thus, in terms of content, reader reviews are not only resources for and responses to Nanako's writing but are also conduits for readers' distinct identities and cultural perspectives, which at times may differ or conflict with each other. Jenkins (1992) points out that "for most fans, meaning-production is not a solitary and private process but rather a social and public one" (p. 75). As such, FanFiction.net provides a meeting place for what Newkirk (2000) calls "the dialogic relations of multiple worlds" (p. 124) stemming from popular culture, school and academic practices, fans' home and friendship groups, online communities, as well as fans' varied ethnic and cultural affiliations, to name just a few. Moreover, these multiple worlds play significant roles in how youth construct, enact, and portray their identities.

In the following reviews, both reviewers respond to Nanako's fan fiction text as well as to her use of her first language of Mandarin. In addition to providing simple feedback on Nanako's writing, which supports her identity as a fan fiction author, these reviews also enable readers to demonstrate allegiance with Nanako and to index their own identities as Mandarin Chinese speakers. For example, the first reviewer begins by making this association in the first segment and holds off commenting on the text itself until Segment B.

Segment A
L1   so u speak manderin?
L2   cool!!
L3   metoo^^

Segment B
L4   i luv this story!
L5   keep up the good work!! (2003)

Similarly, in the next example, the reviewer begins by complimenting Nanako on her facility with Romanized Mandarin, indexing their shared knowledge in this area, and also relegates story commentary to the final segment.

Segment A
L1   Congratulations! I deem you another Han Yu Ping Ying champion! :D
L2   It's rare to find many people who understand how to use this phonetic spelling of the Chinese language correctly,
L3   but you have proven that you can through the Mei-Lin/Syaoran conversation!
L4   Great job on that aspect your fic!

Segment B
L5   Overall, of course, your fanfic is wonderful!
L6   I've been meaning to review but kept forgetting ^^;;
L7   Please update soon!: D (2003)

In deeming Nanako "another" Hanyu Pinyin champion in Line 1, the second reviewer is implicitly positioning herself as accomplished in this area as well. Moreover, the reviewer's feedback on this aspect of Nanako's writing sends a clear message that knowledge of and skill with multiple languages, not solely English, is valued in this space. Both the structure and the content of these reviews illustrate the social and participatory nature of writing in this space. Structurally, both readers foreground their shared linguistic background and appreciation for Mandarin, which immediately creates, albeit at the surface level, a social connection with Nanako. Both readers also end with segments of strong support and enthusiasm for Nanako's general abilities as a writer. In addition, the emoticons (smiling and crying faces), truncated spelling (u, luv, fanfic), and repeated exclamation points index the readers' knowledge of online social registers and display their affiliation with the participatory and interactive nature of writing and reading on FanFiction.net as they show strong support for the author.

Hanyu Pinyin itself is a hybrid form in that it represents Chinese phonetics with characters from the Roman alphabet. This system of translation is particularly useful in computer-mediated communication because keyboards are not set up to display the many thousands of traditional Chinese logographic characters (Wikipedia, Hanyu Pinyin, 2005). Moreover, Romanized forms of language are increasingly more prevalent as a medium for online communication between youth who are bilingual in English and Chinese. For example, Lam's (2006) work explores how a "mixed code" variety of Romanized Chinese and English was used by bilingual Cantonese/English speakers in a chatroom.

> This language variety served to create a collective ethnic identity for these young people and specifically allowed the two girls in this study to assume a new identity through language. This new identity follows neither the social categories of English-speaking Americans nor those of Cantonese-speaking Chinese. (p. 45)

Thus, online spaces are fertile grounds for observing the fluid nature of identity and language in use. Lam's study presents one of the many shifts taking place as English language learners adopt and adapt language varieties to communicate in global forms of English in online spaces. Moreover, it highlights how language and new ICTs are playing a new role in the ethnic and social affiliations of immigrant youth across many different parts of the world.

In addition, Nanako's extensive use of Romanized Chinese and even her minimal use of Japanese were means for positioning herself both as an insider in the Asian realm of anime and as an effective user of several different languages. Many of her readers contributed to this discursive construction of self with reviews that expressed enthusiasm and admiration for Nanako's knowledge of different languages, including but not limited to English. For example, in Segment B, the following reviewer claims to be learning Chinese and Japanese from reading Nanako's fan fictions.

Segment B
L4   This is really interesting,
L5   the plot is thickening every minute!
L6   I'm learning so much chinese and japanese every time I read! (2003)

Moreover, in terms of integrating her first language in her fictions, Nanako writes in a manner that positions her as an expert and makes the Mandarin accessible to speakers of other languages. For instance, she provides clear translations of all Mandarin Chinese text, essentially juxtaposing the English and Mandarin languages, as in the following example of a conversation between Meiling and Syaoran.

Meiling turned to face Syaoran and grumbled in Chinese. "Dan shi, Xiaolang, wo xiang he ta shuo ji ju hua. (But, Xiaolang, I just wanna talk to her.)"

"Ni bu yao fan ta, ren jia you shi gan. (You shouldn't bother her, people have things to do you know.)" Syaoran frowned and responded in Chinese as well. Sakura just looked at the two of them with a big question mark on her head. (A/N: Aww so kawaii!! Lol!) (2003)

Nanako, at times, inserts A/Ns into the fiction to explain different aspects of language, such as explaining that there are many different ways of saying "I'm sorry" in Mandarin. In a similar example, the next reviewer, a native English speaker, expresses her admiration for Nanako's skill with English, Chinese, and Japanese.

Segment B
L3   By the way, you are on my fave authors list!
L4   And your english is great!
L5   You should hear my japanese…;^^
L6   I don't know any chinese either,
L7   so you are very smart to know so much about these languages! ^_^ (2003–07–08)

In Line 4, the reviewer explicitly comments on Nanako's status as an English language learner. The reviewer then goes on to affiliate with Nanako as a fellow language learner by implying in Line 5 that her own Japanese is terrible. Then in Line 6, by conveying her ignorance of Chinese, the reader acknowledges not only the breadth of Nanako's linguistic abilities but also how "very smart" Nanako must be to use these different languages effectively in her texts. Moreover, the reader's point in Line 7 can be contrasted with how language learners are often positioned in the majority of English-speaking contexts, such as schools. In particular, bilingual speakers are often viewed from a deficit perspective in which their first languages are seen as something detrimental that interferes with acquisition of English. However, this reviewer positions Nanako as a smart, accomplished user of multiple languages.

In a different example, the review presents a somewhat dissenting voice as the reader asserts both her knowledge of the *Card Captor Sakura* series and her identity as a Cantonese speaker. However, it is important to note that even in presenting a critique of Nanako's writing, this reader still mitigates this dissent by finding other points of affiliation around Chinese popular culture and with Nanako's story itself. For instance, in Segment A, the reader begins with a humorous threat that implicitly expresses her appreciation for Nanako's story as she threatens to strangle her if she does not continue updating with new chapters. Then in Segment B the reviewer makes a further point of affiliating with Nanako over a popular Chinese film that they both like.

Segment A
L1 Meiling is so evil! Ha!
L2 Don't stop,
L3 if you do I'll strangle you! Haha!

Segment B
L4 I love Huan Gu Gak Gak as well.
L5 It's a great story huh?
L6 bu i watch it in Cantonese.
L7 My favourite character is Siw Yin Ge,
L8 The one Vicki Zhoa Wei plays.
L9 it's awesome.

Segment C
L10 Let me point out that Li and Leing are from hong Kong, not China
L11 and since they're from hong Kong they should be speaking cantonese
L12 but nevertheless i love it! (2003)

It is not until Segment C that the reader points out that, according to regional language differences, the Chinese characters from the *Card Captor Sakura* anime should be speaking Cantonese rather than Mandarin. However, it seems significant that the reader then mitigates this critique in Line 12 by using the coordinating conjunction "but" and then the conjunctive adverb "nevertheless" successively in a way that essentially renders the critique doubly unimportant. This is one example of how the site serves as a space where members can negotiate linguistic and cultural difference, but do so in a way that emphasizes connection and affiliation across potential barriers. Readers also, for the most part, express social and ideological differences in ways that still provide support and respect for the authors' creativity and artistic license.

Flames

It is important, however, not to reify FanFiction.net and other online communities as unproblematic socially and culturally harmonious spaces. To this end, I would like to discuss reviews that run somewhat counter to the previous samples. In the eighth chapter of *Crazy Love Letters*, Nanako introduced a plot twist that involved an arranged marriage between Sakura's love interest Syaoran and his cousin Meiling from China. Out of 137 reviews for that chapter, the reviews of only two readers questioned the propriety of marriage between cousins. One reviewer simply expressed confusion that a cousin could also be a fiancé; however, the other reader posted a flame that does not merit reprinting. Interestingly enough, neither Nanako nor any other members of the community directly responded to these reviews. However, within the story text itself, Nanako indirectly explains that Syaoran must marry his cousin to fulfill his obligation to his family. Also, about a year after the *Crazy Love Letters* series was completed, Nanako began a new fan fiction that focused explicitly on the role of arranged marriage in Asian society. Thus, rather than directly addressing the question and/or confronting the hostile flamer, Nanako addressed the topic through her writing.

Also in the same batch of feedback, another reader posted a flame complaining about a long list in which Nanako thanks many of her regular reviewers. Though it is unclear to which flame Nanako is referring, in her Chapter 9 Author Note she revealed that she had been considering retiring from FanFiction.net because of flames that she received, but that a good friend convinced her to reconsider. Following this mention of her possible retirement, Nanako received an outpouring of support from her readers. The ensuing anti-flame sentiments ranged from thoughtful, nearly page-long discussions of how best to deal with flamers, to threats and name-calling, all the way to general expressions of appreciation from readers coupled with recommendations to simply ignore hostile reviewers because "hey if they dont like the story then they shouldnt read it right? ^-^" (SakiGurl, July 11, 2003).

Shifts in Identity over Time

Daily Life Resources

McCarthey and Moje (2002) posit that one of the many ways identity is implicated in literacy and language learning is in how "readers and writers can come to understand themselves in particular ways as a result of a literate engagement" (p. 229). The shifts in Nanako's writing and participation in the fan fiction site over time reveal how her literate engagement in this space allowed her to draw on an array of dialogic resources to scaffold her writing and also provided her with a supportive social context for foregrounding and backgrounding different aspects of her identity according to her comfort level and the situation. During the years when Nanako was writing her first stories, she was just beginning to adjust to life and school in a new country. Her texts represented many different themes and issues from her life as an adolescent. Her early fictions have settings such as concerts, sleepovers, parties at houses where the parents are out of town, and school classrooms. In addition, the texts deal with concerns that would be familiar for many youth, such as popularity, friendship, first love, and the pressure to succeed academically. These early narratives also are filled with what are most likely references to and resources from Nanako's daily life in North America (e.g., she mentions certain products such as Tylenol; she inserts the book jacket text from a Nicholas Sparks novel written in English; she draws from many television shows set in the United States). However, as more time passed and as Nanako grew more comfortable in this space, there were some notable shifts, not only in her writing and language use, but also in the narrative resources she draws from and in the themes she works through in her texts. These changes can be related to Nanako's changing patterns of participation and self-representation over time.

According to Nanako, in her early attempts at writing on the site, she not only wanted to participate in the anime and fan fiction culture, but also was hoping to improve her writing ability. Her first fictions were written almost entirely in English, and the Author Notes at the beginning of each text clearly indexed her identity as a new learner of the language and asked that reviewers overlook her grammar and spelling errors. These Author Notes in turn shaped readers' responses to her texts in many ways. For instance, many readers gave her pointed but gentle feedback on how to improve certain aspects of her writing (Black, 2005). Readers also focused a great deal on the content rather than the conventions of her stories. In this way, FanFiction.net provided a safe space where Nanako as a learner could experiment and practice with different genres and forms of writing in English. At the same time, she was able to use her developing language skills to participate in a social environment that was meaningful for her and her fellow anime fans as they affiliated around different elements of adolescent pop culture. She was also able to develop both skill and confidence in her identity as a writer and to make lasting social connections with youth from many different countries.

Over time, the aspects of self that Nanako foregrounded through both her texts and Author Notes began to shift. For instance, it was not until she had been writing on the site for about seven months and had received hundreds of encouraging reviews from readers that she began incorporating her first language of Mandarin and a small amount of Japanese into her narrative texts. Then, as readers, such as those who affiliated with Nanako as fellow Chinese speakers and/or the many readers from other countries who expressed interest in learning about Asian languages and cultures, began responding positively to this integration of multiple languages, she began to present more of this aspect of her self to readers. For instance, her use of both Japanese and Chinese became more or less standard in her texts. Also, her Author Notes and her biographical statements on the site began to foreground a continued affiliation with her Asian heritage, as she devoted space to lists of new Chinese movies that she was watching or to discussions of popular Chinese actors, in addition to listing her favorite anime and manga series. Moreover, Nanako's fan fiction texts themselves began to turn toward themes and topics that she viewed as more closely related to aspects of her identity as an Asian female.

For instance, in an interview, Nanako explained that after attending school in Canada for several years, she began to realize that her schoolmates were largely unaware of either Chinese or Japanese history. Thus, she assumed that many fan fiction readers might also be unaware in this regard and decided to write stories that were grounded in the rich histories of these two countries. Specifically, she is referring to two recent fictions. In one, the popular novel/motion picture *Memoirs of a Geisha* serves as a dialogic resource for another crossover fiction in which she presents the anime character Sakura as a Geisha. The other, set in 1910 Kyoto, Japan, centers on Sakura's struggles with an arranged marriage. In addition, she has plans to compose a historical fiction based on the second Sino-Japanese war, or the war fought between China and Japan from 1937 to 1945. In reference to these shifts, Nanako points out that her writing has changed "dramatically" as she has matured, moving from the "utterly unrealistic high school happy, fluffy fanfics to something with more meanings" (2006). She goes on to explain that her desire to share her cultural heritage with others is in part the impetus for writing more stories about China and Japan.

> I guess you can say it's my Asian pride that urged me into writing more stories about China and Japan. At school, I realized that very few people knew the history of the far east. So I kinda thought, maybe not a lot of people on fanfic.net knew about it too. So I have decided to lead my readers into the world they didn't know existed and fascinate them with its rich history and culture, but at the same time, for myself to learn more about my own culture and history, since I often must go research for my fanfics. Lolz my knowledge is very limited too. (2006)

Thus, by writing these historical texts, Nanako has an opportunity to learn more about her own culture and history because she often conducts research to effectively represent the social and historical details in her fictions.

Achieved and Ascribed Identities

Gee (2001) posits that in many institutions (e.g., schools) those in power often draw from rules, laws, and traditions to authorize certain social roles in ways that also "author" a certain kind of identity for the occupants of these roles. Such authorized or ascribed social positions are clearly present in classrooms where teachers are placed in the role of expert, and students are often assigned roles as certain kinds of learners. Moreover, many students, including English language learners, are often ascribed roles based on deficit models of cultural and linguistic difference. These roles, in turn, connote certain types of identities and set up certain expectations for student ability and behavior, without sufficient attention to the part that school, classroom, curricular, and societal contexts play in our assessments of and ways of categorizing students. Ascribed social positions can be contrasted with the notion of *achieved* identities, which are identities that individuals actively construct and negotiate in their moment to moment interactions with others. From this perspective, individuals may be positioned in certain ways by categories that have been authored for them; however, they also may engage in dialogic negotiation with these ascribed roles, as they choose to discursively represent and situate themselves in ways that may challenge or subvert standard expectations.

Unfortunately, in many North American educational settings, English language learners are viewed from a deficit perspective, and abilities in their first language are viewed as a hindrance to learning English and/or are not taken into serious consideration as an additive element for participation and meaning-making in classroom activities. In addition, in many schools, youth are cordoned off into spaces delineated by official and unofficial lines drawn along race, ethnicity, social class, gender, and ability. These lines can be quite pronounced for English language learning youth who are isolated by linguistic and cultural barriers and/or who are completely relegated to classrooms that are separate from the mainstream school population. On the contrary, the online environment of FanFiction.net provides multiple routes that offer potential for traversing some of these real and imagined barriers.

On FanFiction.net, Nanako's writing was not constrained by an ascribed English language learner role and/or specific expectations and requirements for her texts. Neither was she expected to adhere to the identity of an immigrant, a Canadian, or a native Mandarin Chinese speaker nor was she forced to choose between the languages in her linguistic repertoire. Instead, Nanako's process of fan fiction writing enabled her to portray different aspects of her identity in different ways over the years. Moreover, who, what, and how she chose to represent was in many ways contingent on the feedback and positive interactions she had with readers. Through her self-identification as an English language learner, she was able to garner language-related support as well as social support from readers, which in turn provided her with the impetus to continue learning and writing in English. In addition, by drawing from a range of dialogic resources that were pertinent to her life at the time, she was able to establish her membership in a realm of adolescent popular culture. Then gradually as she grew more comfortable and received more supportive feedback from readers, Nanako was able to use her writing to demonstrate and also to explore aspects of her Asian heritage, as she moved into developing texts that center on the role of women in Chinese and Japanese society, and this sets her thinking about creating texts based on the tumultuous history between China and Japan. Rather than being constrained by the expectations of a monolingual, uniform group of readers, Nanako's process of self-representation and meaning-making was instead supported by a linguistically and culturally diverse group of youth from across the globe. Moreover, at the same time that she was learning English, she was also developing new skills related to Romanized writing in her heritage language of Mandarin.

As broad shifts along the lines of globalization, computer-mediated communication, and "virtual" spaces compel us to reconsider the notions of culture and community (Jones, 1997; Yon, 2000), it also becomes necessary to consider differences between how English language learners, and adolescents more broadly, are positioned in schools versus how they choose to position themselves in out-of-school spaces. Perhaps there are lessons to be learned from sites such as FanFiction.net, where the absence of imposed or ascribed social roles enables adolescents from a range of different backgrounds to act both as teachers and as learners. Through their online interactions, both native and nonnative English speakers alike are learning to use multiple languages, social discourses, school-based forms of writing, as well as knowledge of popular culture, in socially and linguistically appropriate ways. Also, they are able to discursively position and represent themselves as articulate members in a pluralistic space that fosters a positive sense of self. Moreover, the site also provides a safe, supportive, and meaningful venue not only for language learning and literacy development but also for affiliating and commiserating with other youth around social and cultural issues that are central to their lives. Finally, in this site, language learning and identity development are not characterized as movement toward some fixed, monocultural standard. Instead, literate and social engagement in this space involves a great deal of communication, and a fluid and ongoing process of meaning-making and identity negotiation that traverses national, linguistic, and cultural borders.

Note

* This chapter was originally published as: Black, R. (2008). Language, culture and identity in fan fiction. *Adolescents and Online Fan Fiction* (pp. 75–96). New York: Peter Lang.

References

Atkinson, D. R., Morten, G., & Sue, D. W. (1983). *Counseling American minorities: A cross-cultural perspective*. Dubuque, IA: Wm. C. Brown.

Bakhtin, M. M. (1981). *The dialogic imagination: Four essays by M.M. Bakhtin*. M. Holquist (Ed.), M. Holquist & C. Emerson (Trans.). Austin, TX: University of Texas Press.

Black, R. W. (2005). Access and affiliation: The literacy and composition practices of English language learners in an online fanfiction community. *Journal of Adolescent & Adult Literacy, 49*(2): 118–128.

Black, R. (2008). *Adolescents and online fan fiction*. New York: Peter Lang.

Cope, B., & Kalantzis, M. (2000). *Multiliteracies: Literacy learning and the design of social futures*. London: Routledge.

Dyson, A. H. (1997). *Writing superheroes: Contemporary childhood, popular culture, and classroom literacy*. New York: Teachers College Press.

Fanfiction Glossary. (2006). *Songfiction*. Retrieved January 15, 2006, from http://www.subreality.com/glossary/terms.htm#S [now defunct].

Gay, G. (1985). Implications of the selected models of ethnic identity development for educators. *Journal of Negro Education, 54*: 43–55.

Gee, J. P. (1996). *Social linguistics and literacies: Ideology in discourses*. London: Taylor and Francis.

Gee, J. P. (1999). *An introduction to discourse analysis*. London: Routledge.

Gee, J. P. (2001). Identity as an analytic lens for research in education. In W. G. Secada (Ed.), *Review of Research in Education* (Vol. 25, pp. 99–126). Washington, D.C.: American Educational Research Association.

Gee, J. P. (2004b). *Situated language and learning: A critique of traditional schooling*. New York: Routledge.

Gilliam, L. (2002). Gather 'round the campfire: Fanfiction.net and participatory writing. *Fanfiction Symposium*. Retrieved January 16, 2006, from http://www.trickster.org/symposium/symp95.html.

Halliday, M. A. K., & Matthiessen, C. M. (2004). *An introduction to functional grammar (3rd revised edition of Halliday's Introduction to functional grammar)*. London: Hodder Arnold.

Harklau, L. (2007). The adolescent English language learner: Identities lost and found. In J. Cummings & C. Davison (Eds.), *Handbook of English language teaching* (pp. 574–588). New York: Springer.

Ito, K. (2001). Images of women in weekly male comic magazines in Japan. *Journal of Popular Culture, 27*(4): 81–95.

Jeffres, L. W. (1983). Communication, social class, and culture. *Communication Research, 10*(2): 220–246.

Jenkins, H. (1992). *Textual poachers: Television fans and participatory culture*. New York: Routledge.

Jones, Q. (1997). Virtual-communities, virtual settlements & cyber-archaeology: A theoretical outline. *Journal of Computer-Mediated Communication, 3*(3), Retrieved Janauary 12, 2008 from, http://jcmc.indiana.edu/vol3/issue3/jones.html.

Lam, W. S. E. (2000). Literacy and the design of the self: A case study of a teenager writing on the Internet. *TESOL Quarterly, 34*: 457–482.

Lam, W. S. E. (2004). Second language socialization in a bilingual chat room: Global and local considerations. *Language Learning and Technology, 8*(3): 44–65. Retrieved January 15, 2005, from http://llt.msu.edu/vol8num3/lam/default.html.

Lam, W. S. E. (2006). Re-envisioning language, literacy, and the immigrant subject in new mediascapes. *Pedagogies: An International Journal, 1*(3): 171–195. Retrieved January 3, 2008, from http://www.sesp.northwestern.edu/docs/publications/42746077444b48507d46af.pdf.

Lankshear, C., & Knobel, M. (2003). *New literacies: Changing knowledge and classroom learning.* Philadelphia, PA: Open University Press.

Lemke, J. (2005). Critical analysis across media: Games, franchises, and the new cultural order. In M. Labarto Postigo (Ed.), *Approaches to critical discourse analysis.* Valencia: University of Valencia (CD ROM edition).

McCarthey, S. J., & Moje, E. B. (2002). Identity matters. *Reading Research Quarterly, 37* (2): 228–238.

Merchant, G. (2006). Identity, social networks and online communication. *E-Learning, 3* (2): 235–244.

Mitra, A. (1997). Virtual commonality: Looking for India on the Internet. In S. G. Jones (Ed.), *Virtual culture: Identity and communication in cybersociety* (pp. 55–79). Thousand Oaks, CA: Sage.

New London Group. (1996). A pedagogy of multiliteracies: Designing social futures. *Harvard Educational Review, 66:* 60–92.

Newkirk, T. (2000). Misreading masculinity: Speculations on the great gender gap in writing. *Language Arts, 77*(4): 294–300.

Nystrand, M. (1997). Dialogic instruction: When recitation becomes conversation. In M. Nystrand, A. Gamoran, R. Kachur, & C. Prendergast (Eds.), *Opening dialogue: Understanding the dynamics of language and learning in the English classroom* (pp. 1–29). New York: Teachers College Press.

Phinney, J. S. (1990). Ethnic identity in adolescents and adults: Review of research. *Psychological Bulletin, 108*(3): 499–514.

Rommetveit, R. (1974). *On message structure.* New York: John Wiley & Sons.

Street, B. (1984). *Literacy in theory and practice.* Cambridge, MA: Harvard University Press.

Thomas, A. (2004). Digital literacies of the cybergirl. *E-Learning, 1:* 358–382. Retrieved May 1, 2005, from http://www.wwwords.co.uk/rss/abstract.asp?j=elea&aid=2010.

Warschauer, M., & Kern, R. (2000). *Networked-based language teaching: Concepts and practice.* Cambridge: Cambridge University Press.

Wikipedia. (2006). *Hanyu Pinyin.* Retrieved May 1, 2005, from http://en.wikipedia.org/wiki/Hanyu_pinyin.

Yi, Y. (2005). Asian adolescents' out-of-school encounters with English and Korean literacy. *Journal of Asian Pacific Communication, 15*(1): 57–77.

Yi, Y. (2007). Engaging literacy: A biliterate student's composing practices beyond school. *Journal of Second Language Writing, 16*(1): 23–39.

Yi, Y. (2008). "Relay writing" in an adolescent online community: Welcome to Buckeye City. *Journal of Adolescent & Adult Literacy, 51*(8): 670–680.

Yon, D. (2000). *Elusive culture: Schooling, race, and identity in global times.* New York: State University of New York Press.

CHAPTER THIRTEEN

Communication, Coordination and Camaraderie

A Player Group in *World of Warcraft*

MARK CHEN

Context

*T*his chapter is taken from Mark Chen's book-length analysis of one expert player group in World of Warcraft *(WoW), the massively multiplayer online game (MMOG). The group comprised roughly 60 people—most of whom have never met in their lives outside WoW. Players belonged to a range of different WoW guilds (e.g., Booty Bay Anglers, The 7/10 Split), but came together for the purposes of high-stakes "raiding" within the game (game mechanics forces this kind of collaboration; monsters and bosses are too strong for a single player to defeat successfully). Chen studied the origins, rise, and decline of this raiding group over a 10-month period as a participant-observer/ethnographer. He focused especially on shared activity, the role of communication in group trust and cohesiveness, the negotiation and renegotiation of roles within the group, and game-play practices. He also documented how "expert" players become like "noobs" (or newbies; newcomers to the game) as they learn new game-play strategies, or incorporate game add-ons (e.g., small programs that can help document game play, facilitate communication across chat channels, generate statistics about an in-game battle, etc.) to help facilitate group play. A central part of the study includes reporting how group values and relationships changed over time: starting with describing an informal group that saw itself as more of a "family" than anything else, and ending with a vivid and moving account of its ultimate demise in a fiery online meltdown that left everyone involved scorched in some way.*

Introduction

This chapter describes the communication and coordination practices of my group of players in *World of Warcraft* by contrasting two nights of game playing—one successful, one unsuccessful. The first night was chosen as it depicts representative practice for the group; the second lets us examine a poor-performing night and the repair work the raid group engaged in to recover from the resulting drop in morale. This chapter also contrasts the practices of this group against the generally conceived notion of how a group like this operates. My raid group went through a process of trial and error with many failures—a norm in gaming practice (Squire, 2005)—before we finally succeeded in defeating all the monsters in Molten Core (a location within WoW). Success depended on the ability of our group members to coordinate our efforts and maximize group efficiency by having each member take on a specialized role as determined by game mechanics, specific contextual details of the battles, and group norms. To achieve the desired level of group coordination, my group used a variety of communication channels, including specialized text chat channels for specific teams within the group. The general notion was that most players who participated with others to go into Molten Core needed to have characters that were specced in a certain way to maximize the efficiency of the group. It was also assumed that most players did this because they wanted valuable in-game equipment, which they could loot from the monsters after defeating them. The 7/10 Split-led group, however, was able to adapt and refine strategies and adjust to relatively nonstandard group compositions and nonstandard character specifications. The success of this group was because of its members' trust in each other and their shared goal of having fun rather than a collection of individual goals emphasizing loot. This approach—of giving preference to friendships—might be a way to think about how people can be encouraged to cooperate and participate in other types of groups.

(Computer) Game Theory

One prominent line of research about player behavior includes those focused on games from a perspective emphasizing incentives and decision making (Smith, 2005; Zagal, Rick, & Hsi, 2006)—a line of research from economics known as game theory—where an examination of game rules leads to ideas about how people will behave and, therefore, how designing games in certain ways can construct certain types of communities.

My interest in game theory literature stemmed from an experience I had while playing through *Star Wars: Knights of the Old Republic* (KotOR) twice a few years ago (in a galaxy far, far away). (In fact, it was after playing KotOR and reading James Gee's *What Video Games Have to Teach Us about Learning and Literacy* that I decided I needed to wade into gaming culture and player learning research, moving away from instructional game design.) KotOR is a computer role-playing game that lets players make moral choices as a Jedi Knight. I wanted to play it through once making all the Light Side choices and once making all the Dark Side choices, so I could see the whole set of outcomes for the progression of the story that the developers designed into the game. While I was playing a Dark Jedi, I noticed that sometimes the choices I made were the same ones I made as a Light Jedi. For example, in the game, I was presented with the classic game theory model, the prisoner's dilemma, which I had learned about in Psych 100 over a decade ago in my undergrad studies—only in KotOR it had Star Wars trappings. I had to choose whether to betray a friend (a Wookiee warrior) for selfish reasons, and he had to make the same decision about whether to betray me. In both cases, I chose to stand by my hirsute friend. I would never betray a friend as a Light Jedi, of course, because I was being selfless. As a Dark Jedi, I reasoned that if I betrayed my friend for immediate benefit, we would not be able to use each other for mutual personal gain in the future, so I actually ended up standing by him in my second play-through, too.

Making a selfless choice and making a selfish choice actually led to the same decision! Game theory simulates considering future interactions between participants by modeling iterated versions of the prisoner's dilemma. In this model, it has been demonstrated that mutual cooperation can be both stable and attractive, even for selfish players. Yet KotOR did not present this scenario as a recurring one. It could be argued that I brought my knowledge about the game's world and imaginings of future interactions with my evil henchman to the decision-making point in the game. In other words, my choices were motivated by how I saw myself playing a particular character situated in a specific setting rather than by "rational" thought as presented in the game developers' traditional game-theory model.

The prisoner's dilemma is part of a larger set of situations that economists and game theorists call social dilemmas (Axelrod, 1985; Hardin, 1968), wherein many people, rather than just two, are making choices about whether to cooperate or defect. Basically, a situation is considered a social dilemma when an individual's immediate self-serving choice is not the same as the choice he or she would make to benefit the community as a whole. A common feature of many models of social dilemmas is that the whole community benefits when a certain *critical* number of people cooperate. The most humorous explanation I could find that defines social dilemmas is embedded in *The Onion's* (2000) headline, "Report: 98 Percent of U.S. Commuters Favor Public Transportation for Others."

The Onion pokes fun at our human tendency to be selfish and stabs right at the heart of the issue: Individuals can defect—make the self-serving choice by free riding—so long as enough other people are cooperating, but if too many people free ride, the whole community loses any benefits. It is relatively easy to show how two people can rationalize cooperating with each other (by not betraying each other and maximizing their benefit over time). It is much harder to convince someone who belongs to a larger community that cooperating makes sense.

The body of literature from people looking at social dilemmas in games has mostly focused on how different games support cooperation through various game mechanics and rules. If a team of players is trying to figure out how to most efficiently beat another team of players or a set scenario in the game, they will choose to do such and such because of certain game rules and how the game works. I found, however, that my experiences with games, in general, and with KotOR and WoW, in particular, showed that the choices being made in certain situations were not so tied to game rules. Instead, they were more complex and tied to how I saw myself playing a particular person in a socially situated world.

This mirrors Gee's (2003, p. 55) notion of *projective identities* where players role-play what they want their characters *to be*. His idea here comes from a multiliteracies perspective where a player's multiple identities are grounded in the social discourses he or she participates in. The greatest power for role-playing games in education is the way in which players can think or take on a certain perspective by being someone who has that perspective. This perspective shifting allows understanding through situational experience.

In WoW, many norms and rules have emerged from the player community. Taylor documents this very well with her experiences in *EverQuest* (2006a) and WoW (2006b), recognizing how game culture that emerges in and around a game is co-constructed between all the various authors, including developers of the game and its players. Players start with the base game but need to develop myriad social norms, etiquette, and practices that ultimately help define what it means to be a player of a particular game. The same thing has happened with WoW, and some of these norms or rules could be looked on as socially constructed social dilemmas. These emergent situations are ignored when looked at through a game-mechanics lens. Additionally, even in situations that could clearly map onto social dilemma models, the choices I saw being made by both myself and other players were not so cut-and-dried and rational. They were contextually contingent.

One could argue about game mechanics all one wanted, but in doing so, a sense of actual game-playing behavior in a real game context rather than some sort of construct will never be realized. Smith

(2005, p. 7) made this same comment, and I would take that argument further by saying real social situations—like the ones I experienced in WoW—are messy and complex and problematize the very notion of constructs as convenient ways of modeling player behavior. Instead of starting with game mechanics, Taylor has been taking a different approach to looking at game behavior by looking closely at player practice. When one looks closely at practice, common assumptions are dispelled. All ethnography is about exceptions, about teasing out differences, about attending to the local pragmatics of situations. Taylor paints a rich world and is joined by other scholars doing ethnographic research in massively multiplayer online games (MMOGs)—relating it, for example, to literacy and learning discourse (Steinkuehler, 2004), social learning theory and emergent social networks (Galarneau, 2005), and general portrayals of player experience and meaning-making (Nardi, 2010). One thing to note from Taylor is that some players of *EverQuest* have the distinction between work and play blurred. I also see this happening in WoW, but, as Nardi (2010, pp. 95–96) also argues, there are definite differences in how some players take on responsibility in-game and out-of-game. These responsibilities—to the group, to friends, to the self—are intricately tied to game mechanics, the emergent game culture, and personal beliefs taken up by the players about what it means to play and have fun. I follow in this ethnographic tradition and discover that social norms and responsibilities defined by social contexts can play a large role in providing incentives and consequences for player behavior in a way that game-mechanics-based motivations fail to do.

A Typical Night in Molten Core

Gathering and Chatting

At about 5:15 p.m. server time on Friday, April 14, 2006, my raid group started forming up, as it had been doing every Wednesday and Friday for the past 6 months. Our raid leader, Maxwell, from The 7/10 Split guild, was inviting the rest of us into the group, and I was invited early this night. Meanwhile, the rest of us were all over the game world—working on other quests or PvPing (engaging in person-to-person combat) or whatever—or just logging into the game after getting home from work or school. Once invited, we knew we were supposed to make our way to the entrance of the dungeon in Molten Core, but getting everyone there so we could start took a while, *as usual*. Our official forming-up time was 5:30 p.m., and our official start time was 6:00 p.m., but we usually ended up starting at around 6:15 p.m. because some people tended to show up late. That night we started fighting monsters at around 6:10 p.m. In other words, I was in this raid group for almost an hour before the group actually started fighting monsters. The original task of forming a new raid group started by finding enough people who wanted to go raiding at a certain time, and, for my group, it was done through a combination of in-game chat and announcements and out-of-game web forum postings on guild-specific sites. Once that was done (which took several weeks because friends wanted to be invited with each other and it was difficult to find a time that fit the schedules of at least 40 different people), the raid leader still had to deal with the task of getting everyone in the group together at the agreed time every week, twice a week. That the composition of the raid group was made up of members from different guilds could not have helped the situation any.

Some of us resented the fact that we sat around for upward of an hour before actually fighting, and this is evidence of the tension some players had between their expectations of what it meant to play a game—that video and computer games are thought of as immediate gratifications—and the reality of playing—where participating in a shared activity required administrative overhead (i.e., work). Others of us, however, did not mind the initial wait time and used it to greet each other and catch up with old friends.

We discussed new things about the game, new discoveries about the game, and new strategies to try out, or otherwise engaged in small talk, and most of this talk was laid-back with a lot of joking around. For example, below is a snippet of what the rogues were talking about that night while we were gathering. (We were using the [Party] channel since we were all temporarily in the same 5-person party while Maxwell was organizing the 40-person raid and finalizing invites and the 8 in-raid party compositions.)

> 18:00:46.484: [Party] Rita: You guys have become familiar faces—I'm glad I'm with you all:).
> 18:01:04.734: [Party] Thoguht: Thanks! you too!
> 18:01:05.921: [Party] Rebecca: Hi Rita!
> 18:01:34.468: [Party] Thoguht: We've been having some crazy rogues nights recently.
> 18:01:37.578: [Party] Rebecca: What's everyone's best unbuffed FR?
> 18:01:43.234: [Party] Rita: 137.
> 18:01:52.468: [Party] Thoguht: I feel lame.
> 18:02:03.734: [Party] Roger: 92.
> 18:02:13.375: [Party] Thoguht: I feel cool!
> 18:02:18.937: [Party] Rita: I feel sexy!

Here one rogue, Rita, was just invited to the group that night. Then, as a way of greeting the other rogues who were in her party, at about 6:00 p.m., she made an explicit comment about how much joy has come out of being part of our group. Rebecca and I responded and greeted back. I echoed that the last few sessions in the group have been really good to us rogues. What I meant was both that rogue loot had dropped and that we had had good success as a subgroup in the raid in terms of performing our roles well by dealing out good damage during fights and minimizing our deaths. Implied in my utterance was that the rogues, and the raid in general, had a healthy attitude, and morale was high. Then, changing topics, Rebecca asked what each rogue's fire resistance was.

When characters took or dealt damage, the damage was of a certain type, one of which was fire damage. Along with building up resistances to the other types of damage, characters could acquire items that protected them from fire damage. These resistances were quantified in-game, like almost every in-game attribute, on a number scale with no theoretical maximum. In practice, because resistances are gained through equipment worn and temporary spells, for rogues the maximum tended to be around 250 to 300.

By talking to other players in other raid groups and reading strategies online, we knew that most people suggest that rogues have at least 180 fire resistance during the fight with the last boss in Molten Core, Ragnaros. When Rita said 137, I wrote that I felt lame because my fire resistance was low by comparison, but then Roger replied with a 92. I felt not so lame anymore (I had a fire resistance of 120). Playing off of my phrases, Rita said she felt sexy. This is a good example of the light atmosphere in our chat even when on-task strategies and assessments were talked about. It is also easy to see that we felt beholden to our fellow adventurers in a way that falls outside of normal game theory incentives and consequences.

Pulling, Coordinated Fighting, and Division of Labor

After we all sufficiently gathered, we buffed up and started pulling. "Buffing" is the term used to describe the act of casting beneficial spells on other characters. "Debuffing"—placing curses on enemies—is the opposite of buffing. "Pulling" is used to describe grabbing the initial attention of monsters that are found standing around at preset locations in the world. Once their attention was caught, they charged toward whoever did the pulling. The first encounter in Molten Core is with two Molten Giants who guard a bridge into the rest of the dungeon. Like most encounters in WoW, we initially had to learn how to approach the fight and what roles each different character class should play. For example, the warrior class was designed to play the role of the "tank," holding the monster's attention (a.k.a. "aggro") effectively. They can activate abilities that are specifically for angering enemies and keeping their aggro (e.g., Taunt and Intimidating Shout)—abilities that other character classes lack. We usually had about five warriors in our raid group. Because most encounters in Molten Core involve just one or two monsters, we learned to designate two of our warriors, Warren and Wendy, to be *main* tanks, so that all the warriors were not competing for aggro. The healers could then concentrate even more on these two warriors instead of all the warriors equally. Because we had multiple healers, too, we usually divided healing duty among them so that only a set of them were healing the main tanks while the rest were either spot-healing the rest of the raid group when necessary or were assigned to heal specific parties in the raid. Furthermore, monsters in WoW also have special abilities that they can activate against the players, and part of what we had to learn was the kinds of abilities to expect from each type of monster.

To aid us in this coordination, each role in the raid had a specialized chat channel. For example, the healers had a channel in which they managed the assignment of healing and buff duties:

18:21:48.843: [3. healsting] Paula: how about Pod 1, 2,…Paula 3, 4, 5…and Peter 6, 7, 8? For DS buff

Here, the priests and other healers used the [healsting] channel. Paula was suggesting that each priest be assigned certain parties in the raid (there were eight parties in the raid group, remember) on which to cast the Divine Spirit (DS) buff, which increases the party members' Spirit attribute, which in turn determines how fast spell casters regain spell points (a.k.a. Mana) that were needed to cast spells. This assignment of roles was common among all channels. Here is an example from the warlock channel:

18:11:20.421: [4. soulburn] Lori: Remember, ss target will change at Domo, but until then, your rezzer is to be ssed at all times.

Lori was reminding the other warlocks that one of their unique warlock abilities—to create a soulstone (ss) and apply it on other characters—should be active at all times. A soulstone allows whomever it is applied on to resurrect himself or herself after dying. This was important to keep active on characters who could resurrect others ("rezzers"). In this way, if the whole raid group died (wiped), our rezzers could come back to life and revive everyone else in the raid.

Note that in the above examples, Paula and Lori were in charge of their respective classes or channels. These leadership roles were consistent from week to week and were sometimes established on demonstrated leadership ability in previous raiding activities. (I'm told that in many raid groups, class/role leads were supposed to read up on the fights and brief everyone they were in charge of. This was not the norm for my group until we'd "banged our heads" on the fight a few times first.) What mattered more often, however, were previous relationships before the raid began, including rank in the main guild organizing the raid and out-of-game friendships. These existing social obligations (i.e., our built-up social capital) were important to the group because we had established a norm of valuing players for their social skills rather than just game-content knowledge.

Roles were also assigned by character class. These roles were generally determined by what each class was designed to do (e.g., priests tended to heal others). Most "serious" raid groups take these game-defined roles at face value and require that players design their characters to most efficiently take advantage of their class' roles. In other words, these roles were based on specialized functions within the group, akin to distributing responsibilities according to specialized expertise. This raid group, however, valued diversity and accepted variation in how people defined their character's abilities. In WoW, players can differentiate their characters by choosing special talents every time their characters gain an experience level. Priests could specialize (spec) even further into healing, for example, but they could also choose talents that let them be very capable damage dealers as "shadow priests." In general, though, even shadow priests could heal, and instead of mandating that a priest's abilities were maximized for healing, this raid group accepted any sort of priest, so long as there was *enough* total healing ability across the whole raid.

At other times, a player was assigned a role because he or she had participated in an encounter that no one else in the raid had taken part in before. If no clear candidates were suited for encounter-specific roles, these roles were taken up by players who had established themselves as capable of managing their cognitive load either through some competency or, more likely, through the use of add-ons. Cognitive load theory (Cooper, 1998; Sweller, 1988) posits that people's working memory has a finite capacity. In terms of instructional design, and all information design in general, elements of design and interface take up some of this working memory, thereby increasing cognitive load. Confusing elements put on more load than otherwise necessary, taking away people's ability to work with the content to be learned or the actual information being conveyed. Many players supplement WoW's built-in interface with user-created add-ons which replace or augment certain design elements to help them keep track of all the information in this world. A player having an add-on that notified him or her of specific events during an in-game encounter (e.g., the add-on called CEnemyCastBar) was sometimes the deciding factor when roles were being assigned or taken up.

All these different roles that people assumed—leadership, class, and fight-specific—were divided through a combination of game mechanics and emerged social practice. In other words, as Moses Wolfenstein (2010) describes in his research comparing leadership in WoW to leadership in schools, leadership tasks often were completed by various individuals who were not necessarily assigned "leaders." This division of labor process mirrors that found in work and school settings by Strauss (1985) and Stevens (2000), where the different tasks associated with a particular project are assumed by different people depending on social factors and emergent practice, which included the enrollment of various technomaterial resources that were distributed among the activity system. In WoW raiding, at the very least, those factors included game mechanics, players' understanding of the mechanics, players' ability and skill, and relationships of trust.

While chat was happening in these specialized channels, concurrent chat might have been happening in the [Raid] channel, the [Party] channel, the [Guild] channel, and any other channel to which a particular player was subscribed. Managing all the information coming from these various sources was challenging, especially when one had to concentrate on and navigate through the physicality of the virtual world at the same time. In fact, reading through some of my transcripts shows pretty clearly that I missed some utterances that were directed at me. In addition, sometimes the chat in one channel referenced chat in another channel, as well. In this way, chat could be—and often was—interwoven and layered. Furthermore, on top of the text chat, there was voice chat that was also sometimes running parallel to and sometimes interwoven with the text chat. Those who were not using voice chat were often exposed to non sequiturs in text chat. On the flip side, some people responded to the chat threads in a specialized text channel through voice, which was confusing to those not participating in that particular specialized channel.

So, and recapping a little here, to start off our night in Molten Core, we pulled a couple of Molten Giants (after sitting and talking and gathering together for an hour). Our fight with the Giants was routine and only lasted a little more than a minute. The text chat was relatively sparse because we all were familiar with the encounter and knew what to do. Even so, it was steeped in meaning:

18:11:34.671: [Raid] Willy: INCOMING Molten Giant!
18:11:34.687: Willy yells: INCOMING Molten Giant!
18:11:36.187: Larry thanks Mary.
18:11:40.640: [Raid] Lester: Pat is Soul Stoned.
18:11:45.203: Marcie hugs Lev.
18:11:45.562: [Raid] Roger: rebroadcast ct please?
18:11:49.343: Willy yells: ATTACK!
18:11:49.453: [Raid] Willy: ATTACK!
18:12:57.359: [Raid] Sherrie: This whole only shaman group is amazing!

First, Willy, who was the second in command for this evening (spontaneously asked to lead by Maxwell while Maxwell was still organizing and getting ready for the rest of the session), alerted the raid group that we were pulling the Molten Giants. To help him alert everyone, he employed a button macro that let him announce things in multiple chat channels in rapid succession. That way, all he had to do was target a monster and hit a key to tell us when something was "incoming!" In some cases, if he had spent some time upfront to set it up, an add-on that we all used called CT_RaidAssist (a.k.a. CT Raid or CTRA), would also make these announcements appear as pop-up text overlays, smack dab in the middle of our screens, while a loud alert sound further let us know that something eventful was happening. In other words, although the chat log shows that Willy used two channels to tell the rest of us that the Giants were incoming, it was in fact mostly automated text accompanied by an automated sound. In this way, Willy offloaded responsibility to a material resource that then carried out its ascribed duty.

"Incoming!" was actually the cue for one of our hunters in the group to take a potshot at one of the Molten Giants, which initiated the fight. After the potshot, the Giants charged our group and Warren and Wendy grabbed their attention. The two warriors then ran in opposite directions and positioned the Giants so that the Giants' Area of Effect damage from their Stomp ability was not overlapping. This way we could kill one Giant without taking damage from the other Giant. While this was happening, Larry thanked Mary for something. What we cannot see in the text chat is that Mary, who was a mage, gave some water to Larry. Spell casters, like Larry (a warlock), used up a certain amount of Mana with each spell cast. Casters had a finite reserve of Mana (depending on their class, level, and equipment), so after casting enough spells, they ran out and were no longer effective participants in a fight until their Mana pool replenished at a slow and steady rate. In between fights, however, they could consume water or other liquids to regain their Mana at a quicker rate. These drinks could be purchased in towns or cities from certain vendors. Mages, like Mary, however, could conjure up water and share it with other characters, thus, saving them from having to buy water. (Even in-game, some people didn't like paying for water.)

Next we see that Pat had a soulstone applied to her by Lester, so we had a safe rezzer in case something went horribly wrong. Then Marcie hugged Lev. In addition to soulstones, warlocks like Lev could create healthstones and pass them out to other characters. Consuming a healthstone would heal some damage, giving players a way to regain Health in an emergency during a fight if, for example, the healers had run out of Mana or if they were occupied in healing the main tanks. Lev had just given Marcie one of these healthstones, and she returned the favor with a hug.

Roger, an undead rogue, then asked if "ct" could be rebroadcast. This was in reference to the afore-mentioned CT Raid, which among other things, also allowed raid leaders to designate main tanks. Once designated, little windows showing who the main tanks were and what the main tanks had targeted appeared on every CT Raid user's screen. The CT Raid add-on worked by using its own specialized, hidden chat channel usually given a comical name by the raid leader. Anyone who used CT Raid would automatically be subscribed to that channel so long as the raid leaders synched everyone up by broad-casting in [Raid] chat a certain key phrase that CT Raid recognized. Players who joined the raid group late or who somehow temporarily lost connection to the game often had to be resynchronized by hav-ing the raid leaders rebroadcast. CT Raid was the most popular add-on for raiding groups in 2005/2006, and using it was often required or highly suggested by raid groups. Thus, game experience and prac-tice within the game was not defined just by the developers of the game. The practice around raiding and the coordinated work required for raiding allowed a common tool to be developed and propagated such that it was hard to imagine playing the end game without the CT Raid add-on.

About 4 seconds after Roger asked for the CT Raid channel to be rebroadcast, and about 15 sec-onds after pulling and separating the Molten Giants and then letting the main tanks build up aggro, Willy called the rest of the raid group to attack. It took us about a minute after that to kill the Giants, at which point Sherrie announced that she liked being in a shaman-only party. Shamans can place ("drop") totems on the ground, which gives some sort of benefit to party members standing near them, but each shaman could only drop two unique totems, so they often had to weigh the pros and cons of which totems to drop. By having five shamans in one party, they were able to drop a very effec-tive combination of totems because the party was no longer limited to only two totems.

Making Encounters Routine by Finding Balance

After this fight, we prepared for the next pull by making sure our casters had regained Mana and that people were healed. The next fight was with another kind of monster, which had different abil-ities, but it was just as easy with little danger of failure or of having lots of people die. In fact, our Molten Core experience had become a series of routine fights where we got ready, pulled, and killed in a systematic way until we reached a boss. These monsters were made so routine that the gam-ing community had come to know them as "trash mobs." They were "trash" in that they did not pose a threat, and the loot they dropped was often worthless in terms of making our characters more pow-erful but could sometimes be sold for in-game currency (gold). This loot was also known as "ven-dor trash." The term "mob" stands for monster object, which is how developers of MMOGs refer to game-controlled monsters or enemies.

Making these trash fights a routine activity took us several weeks. For me, a rogue, it took time finding the right balance between doing a lot of damage and not taking aggro away from the tanks. The problem was that if I did too much damage, the Molten Giant or Lava Annihilator or whichever mob we were fighting would consider me its greatest threat and start attacking me instead of pay-ing attention to the warrior who was tanking it. As soon as this happened, in most cases, I died. Early on, this happened to me often. Embarrassingly often. But at least I wasn't the only one who strug-gled with aggro. After 6 months, one or two of us still had a difficult time finding that balance, and drawing aggro happened to just about everyone in the raid at least a few times.

Once we matured as a raid group, grabbing aggro from the main tanks and dying in such routine pulls was met with laughter and people who did it were only jokingly chastised. Some even felt a bit of pride when it happened because it meant they were "out-DPSing" others in the raid.

Even non-damage classes had to find the right balance of abilities versus aggro. Healers, for example, drew aggro by healing the warriors. The monster would suddenly consider a healer more of a threat than the warrior in front of it. If enough of us attracted the attention of the mob we were fighting during a single encounter, the monster would "bounce" from person to person, moving to and killing whoever was the next highest threat. When this happened, usually we wiped—enough of us died that there was no hope of defeating the mob before it killed the whole raid group.

Learning each encounter could involve many wipes, and when it happened, it took time for our healers to resurrect themselves and then resurrect everyone else. If we did not have any safe rezzers, we all had to release our "ghosts" in the game at the nearest graveyard and then run back to the entrance of the dungeon to reclaim our bodies and reappear in the world. Although it could be frustrating to wipe over and over again, many of us in the raid, including the raid leader, took this opportunity (the time it took to either rez everyone or run back to the entrance from the nearest graveyard) to reflect on what had happened and suggest things to change about our approach or suggest completely new strategies to try. This mirrors the practice of another successful raid group that Sarah Walter (2009) wrote about in a different MMOG, suggesting that it is perhaps a necessary practice for successful raiding, no matter the game. Indeed, reflective thought is needed for metacognition (Bransford, Brown, & Cocking, 2000)—the ability to step back a bit from one's activity and assess where one is and where one needs to go—in any setting.

This practice of failing multiple times on new encounters might be unique to raid groups whose members are all relatively new to the raid encounters. Many players, after they hit level 60, attempt to find memberships in mature raid groups, often joining guilds that concentrate on endgame raiding. It is possible for these players to never experience multiple wipes. Unfortunately, I cannot speak to this experience much. It should be clear by now that raiding takes an enormous time commitment, so even if I had access to a mature raid group, I would not have been able to join both groups. My choice of participating with a new raid group, however, allowed me to see group learning and talk around shared understanding of encounters and the game world itself. As Walter demonstrated in her research about newcomers to established groups (2009), learning happened in a mature raid, but it was of a more individual nature where a newcomer learned the predefined role the raid group had established for him or her. In contrast, the raid group I participated with did not start out as a mature one, so the local instantiation of broader raiding practice was still being defined and shaped heavily by the collective endeavors of the group members.

A raid that had progressed enough to treat trash mobs as routine was one venue in which a social dilemma was present. Individual players may have been tempted to free ride off the efforts of the other raid members. In a mature raid, to defeat a monster, only a critical mass of raid members had to know what they were doing; it was often not necessary for all players to play their best. In fact, when I spoke to a member of a raiding guild that had put Molten Core on farm status (meaning that the task had become so routine that it had become repetitive and easy and a good, revisitable source of loot), he confided in me that he and other raid members tended to play *Tetris* or *Breakout* or other casual mini-games during the raid sessions. (Too bad *Farmville* didn't yet exist!) To combat this free riding, some raid leaders used certain add-ons that kept track of the individual performances of raid members and then reviewed the logs after each gaming session. The raid group I was in only used this common damage and healing meter to help troubleshoot times when we were failing and trusted that raid members were paying attention. Instead of relying on a technological actor to conduct surveillance on each other (cf. Taylor, 2006b, p. 329), at this point of our raiding group's life, we had established a social norm of trust in each other that served as a powerful disincentive to free riding. Our reliance on material actors was slowly manifesting, however, and, as will be discussed later, this shift from trust through humans' internal sense of right and wrong to trust that is enforced by technology would fragment the group, leading to its eventual downfall.

Welcoming Failure in Golemagg and Other Boss Fights

Because this night was several months into our raid instead of when we first started, we did not wipe on trash mobs. Also, we were not wiping on the early bosses. Our goal this night was to make an attempt on the last boss in the instance, Ragnaros. The way the dungeon is set up, our raid group had to kill all the other bosses before Ragnaros's lieutenant, Majordomo Executus (Domo), would appear. Then after we defeated Domo's guards, he would teleport away to Ragnaros's chamber and summon his lord. This was a Friday night, so we had already been in the instance once this week and had already cleared out some of the dungeon, including many of the early bosses, but we still had to defeat a unique Giant named Golemagg and his two Core Hound guards before reaching Domo. Boss monsters were special ones with more Health and more abilities. To fight one was to engage in an extended fight requiring more careful strategy. Boss monsters often had minions or guards near them, and challenging a boss in these cases was a matter of tanking each guard along with the boss then figuring out which ones to kill first.

We reached Golemagg a little after 7:00 p.m., about an hour after our first pull and about 1 hour and 45 minutes after we first started forming up for the evening. That is, we spent a good chunk of time just getting to a significant fight.

Our strategy for Golemagg was to kill him before his Hounds because, once he was down, his Hounds would automatically die, as well. To defeat Golemagg meant we had three warriors assigned to tank him and his two Hounds. While some healers were keeping the tanks alive, everyone else focused their attention on Golemagg. Golemagg had an ability that gave players debuffs that did steady damage spread out over a set amount of time ("damage over time" debuffs or "dots"), and he could apply this effect over and over again on anyone within melee range. A rogue's role was to run in, hit Golemagg a few times, run out of melee range when he or she had received enough dots, wait for the dots to wear off (because applying bandages could only be done when not receiving damage), bandage or otherwise heal (e.g., with a healthstone) himself or herself, then run back in to do more damage, backing off as needed. Again, learning the encounter was a balancing issue for rogues, maximizing damage-per-second (DPS) without getting too many dots. If I stayed within melee range to raise my DPS a little, I might have received more dots than I could wait out after retreating. The dots would kill me before wearing out, preventing me from applying bandages.

Learning how to engage in the encounter for the raid meant we had to know the overall strategy of concentrating on Golemagg. We knew this because some of us had been in a fight with him before with different raid groups, and some of us had read strategies online for the bosses in Molten Core. The majority of us, however, were disinterested in reading about boss strategies before encountering them for the first time. A handful of us even considered it outright spoilerish; bordering on cheating. Contrast this with raiding in WoW several years later when the norm is to blast through content as quickly as possible, which comes with an implicit assumption that everyone is intimately familiar with all the boss fights and studies strategy guides or watches YouTube videos of successful fights beforehand.

Golemagg had a plentiful amount of Health, and this night, killing him took us almost 8 minutes (in contrast, the two normal Molten Giants earlier took us a little more than 1 minute to obliterate). In long "endurance" fights such as this, it was common for healers and other casters to run out of Mana. If enough of our healers ran out of Mana at the same time, the warriors would no longer be healed. They would die, causing the rest of the raid to wipe thereafter because all the other classes could not take more than one or two hits from Golemagg. The first few times we did this fight, like the first few times we did any of our boss fights, we wiped. This was not seen as a bad event but rather as a necessary component of learning the strategy and finding the balance or "groove" needed to succeed. A raid member, Rebecca, an undead rogue from The 7/10 Split, had this to say:

Rebecca ‹The 7/10 Split›
Ultimately each of us can only control our own character; so the most important job we each have to do is make sure we are doing our part both effectively and efficiently.…[S]moothly executing a kill on a boss that used to kick our tail is very gratifying, I think.;)

For Rebecca, the sense of accomplishment from finally defeating a difficult boss was very satisfying, and most members of the raid shared her sentiment. It was not just loot we were after. We enjoyed the challenge and success that came with the hard work of failing multiple times. To succeed, each of us had to learn to play our role effectively. We also had to trust each other to take on this responsibility. It is very clear that, just as Taylor saw in *EverQuest* (2006), some players took on responsibilities very seriously and that fun and pleasure were not so easily defined. Generally, each player decided when to play and when to quit based on personal goals and ways of seeing fun. For most players, this fun came from a (sometimes obsessive) desire to improve their characters through what WoW players have come to call "itemization"—the act of acquiring better and better equipment. Time and again, however, the various members of the raid I participated in reiterated their desire to do raids as a way of doing an activity *together* to sustain and strengthen relationships. In the words of Penny, a Bay Booty Angler, on June 27, 2006:

Penny ‹Booty Bay Anglers› (5:09 PM)
You guys, how are we "falling behind"? We're not a raiding guild. There's no competition to keep up with other guilds here. I want to go to Gruul's Lair again, too (and this time be successful), but pushing people too fast, and wearing ourselves out to get there isn't the way to go about. It takes time and patience.
. . . .
And you know what? We, as a guild, are raiding successfully. Part of being in this guild is working with everyone else, and the majotiry of the people in this guild have insurmountable patience and want to take their time plowing through everything. So that meant I needed to stop rushing ahead, wait up, and enjoy the fact that our guild is filled with enough talented individuals who are willing to work with each other each week to make it happen. No one is getting left behind and everyone is getting a chance, if they take the opportunity.

For players like Penny, deep bonds were forming around shared experiences, and they recognized engaging in these participatory acts as a way to deepen trust and friendships. Sure, they wanted to be successful, but progression was not worth leaving each other behind.

Socially Constructed Social Dilemmas AKA the Problem of Rare Loot

This night, we killed Golemagg relatively easily, and therefore, we could loot his body for valuable equipment. This was standard action according to in-game mechanics, which rewarded player participation through valuable loot when a group of players defeated high-end monsters. Each monster that a group killed only dropped a handful of items, though, so only some of the group's members were to receive this in-game reward. Setting up high-end rewards as scarce commodities caused player groups to come up with rules on how to fairly distribute the loot.

This practice was so prevalent that almost all groups clearly defined loot rules before they set foot in a high-end dungeon, and many players had come to see endgame practice as only participating in these high-end encounters and winning loot. The most common way of dividing loot was through the DKP loot distribution system where participating in certain monster kills netted a player a certain number of points (Malone, 2009; Wikipedia, 2011). When loot was distributed, a player then bid his or her "dragon kill points" or DKP in an auction against other players to win a particular item that would benefit his or her character. Winning an auction subtracted however many points were bid, thereby limiting how many points the player could bid on a future item, thereby giving someone else in the group a chance to win it. This can be likened to a social dilemma, in that many players' bidding practices were motivated by selfish, individual benefits. Yet a particular player could win an item that would actually benefit the whole group more if *someone else* won the item. This is because not everyone had the same equipment, and someone else's character might have been more effective in combat than the winning player's character with the same loot item. From a more general perspective, no matter what kind of loot rules a group used (see Wikipedia, 2011, for many examples of other loot systems), the social dilemma of "who gets the loot?" existed. The addition of using a DKP system on top of the basic game structure reinforced the dilemma by more explicitly making the situation competitive.

Actions within this socially constructed social dilemma are not so easy to explain through social dilemma modeling, however. Other factors came into play, such as a player's relationship with others in the group. For example, two of the group members, Hizouse and Hatfield were brothers in off-screen life, and they tended to play games together, joining and leaving player groups together. Tight bonds like these were sometimes the cause for one player deferring to another when it came down to loot distribution. Additional factors also played a role: the attachment and commitment a player had with his or her character, how long the player planned on continuing to play the character, the fiction and role or identity he or she saw the character taking on, and personal values about what was an important goal and what constituted fun. This last point is important because if the group, as a whole, valued other things besides loot, the whole looting system itself had to be reanalyzed. The group that I played with, for example, took a completely different approach to loot rules—one which reinforced their approach to high-end content as an opportunity for shared experience. The loot was an added bonus to the more valued experience itself.

The system this raid group used included a random element, and it was not always clear who would receive a particular item. The group used a weighted loot-roll system in which players initially "rolled" a random number from 1–100. For each session that a character was present but did not win anything, he or she subtracted 10 from his or her roll range (e.g., after two sessions without winning anything, a character would roll from 1–80). The lowest number won the item and the winning character's range would reset to 1–100. Probabilistically speaking, those who had a history with the raid group and hadn't gotten any loot in the last few weeks had a better chance at winning something they wanted, but there was always the chance that someone who was relatively new could win an item. The raid's leaders, informed by a long, open discussion in the group's online message board (three different threads spanning dozens of pages), decided that they wanted this informal, slightly chaotic, loot system to reinforce the raid's de-emphasis on loot (i.e., the raid's desire to forge friendships and hang out with each other).

This night was a good night. After dividing loot from Golemagg, our raid succeeded in killing some trash mobs and then successfully defeated Domo and his eight guards. Frustratingly, we then moved onto three failed attempts at killing Ragnaros. He proved frustrating because his encounter became "buggy," where he was activating abilities at odd times. We eventually gave up, and by the time we were done for the evening, it was almost 10:00 p.m. Our gaming session was almost 5 hours and, other than Ragnaros, was relatively successful.

An Atypical Night in Molten Core

In contrast to our good night that Friday, the following week on April 19, 2006, we had an atypical night in Molten Core. It was atypical in that a series of events unfolded that caused us many wipes and generally gave us poor morale, which almost culminated in a "meltdown," where enough raid members fervently opposed each other on an issue that irreparable damage occurred to their friendships, effectively disbanding the raid. I believe it started with having enough people in the raid feeling stressed about other things happening in their offscreen lives. For example, about 30 minutes before the raid session started, a member of my guild made it known that she was depressed and contemplating committing suicide! As an officer and friend, of course, I was compelled to attend to her as best I could without knowing who she was offscreen. This meant I was engaged in a private conversation with her in-game, forcing me to miss some of the other chat that was happening. (I was also privately messaging other members of my guild and consulting an out-of-game friend about what to do. Thankfully, as I'd learn several weeks later, my guildie turned out okay.)

We also decided that night to try using two different warriors as our main tanks for the first time, so that in the future we'd have backup main tanks available, and it was clear that the warriors who were not used to tanking were not sure where to position their monsters. Furthermore, the warriors who were normally our main tanks did not know which abilities they should be using and which weapons they should be using while playing maximum damage-per-second roles. To add to this, we had an abnormal group composition that night, with more shamans and hunters and fewer warlocks and rogues than we were used to. Though our raid did not strictly proscribe the exact composition of our group, this night still presented us with a combination of character classes that we were not familiar with. Additionally, some of the players expressed concern about people bringing characters who were not their primary characters. Instead, a few players were trying their alts (i.e., alternative characters) in this night's raid session that they might not have been as proficient in playing. This uncertainty manifested itself in our chat. At various times in certain specialized channels, raid members were bickering with each other:

> 18:46:17.640: [2. healsting] Pod: Poll: Best Knockback
> 18:48:13.906: [2. healsting] Pod: a) The Beast
> 18:48:23.453: [2. healsting] Pod: b) The Fish Boss in ZG
> 18:48:31.296: [2. healsting] Sven: Hmmm?
> 18:48:45.625: [2. healsting] Pod: c) Garr's Lt.'s
> 18:49:01.062: [2. healsting] Pod: d) other
> 18:49:06.296: [2. healsting] Sven: Shaun's breath.
> 18:49:40.093: [2. healsting] Shaun: you know, if you want to be the next shaun, it might serve you well not to always insult me
> 18:49:51.593: [2. healsting] Shaun: i mean, why would you want to be just like somebody with bad breath?

18:49:54.515: [2. healsting] Sven: I don't want to be "the next Shaun!"
18:50:08.218: [2. healsting] Sven: You are simply going down. I shall overcome your shortcomings.

When Pod, an undead priest, was playfully polling the healers about which WoW encounter featured the "best" knockback—when a monster pushed or threw player-characters away from them—Sven suggested that Shaun's breath was the most memorable knockback in the game. Shaun was generally seen as the de facto leader of the shaman class (and, generally, all the other healers, too) within the raid group, and it is possible that Sven resented him for it, as evidenced by their talk of "the next shaun" and "going down." This tension between Shaun and Sven continued later into a disagreement about where Sven was standing during the fight with the first boss monster, a snake-man named Lucifron:

19:00:02.468: [2. healsting] Sven: I'm ranged for Will healing
19:00:10.515: [2. healsting] Shaun:....
19:00:17.578: [2. healsting] Shaun: Sven, you are fired.
19:00:21.484: [2. healsting] Sven: Hey, most people avoid you, Shaunny!
19:00:24.312: [2. healsting] Sven: It's the breath
19:00:32.218: [2. healsting] Sven: I'm giving an alternative!
19:00:46.406: [2. healsting] Shaun: an option that is closer to the caves.
19:00:49.015: [2. healsting] Shaun: you ...
19:00:55.625: [2. healsting] Shaun: you are trying to kill us all....
19:01:00.625: [2. healsting] Sven: Well?
19:01:05.109: [2. healsting] Sven: It hasn't happened, now has it??
19:01:17.703: [2. healsting] Sven: Stop being so paranoid!

Sven was positioning himself away from the main group of players, dangerously close to an adjoining cave with monsters the raid was not yet ready to battle. Shaun thought that Sven should have moved to the rest of the group, just in case those other monsters noticed Sven and attacked the whole group. This interchange gave more evidence that there was a distinct lack of trust this night, which did not help motivate raid members to concentrate.

We ended up wiping three times on trash mobs because too many of us were either distracted or consciously free riding. After our third wipe, no one said anything in text chat for 8 minutes. That is, no chat was happening in the [Raid] channel, none in the [Party] channel, none in the [say] channel, and none happening in the various specialized channels for 8 whole minutes. The longest idle time from our typical good night was 2 minutes. Those who were not already feeling less than 100% became frustrated from our three wipes and the bickering that they were seeing in their specialized channels. At one point, the raid leader asked the raid if we should continue:

19:10:10.046: [Raid] Maxwell: as fun as it is to goof around, we can't wipe to trivial stuff at the same time
19:10:43.937: [Raid] Heather: What? We can't?
19:10:55.093: [Raid] Pod: Yeah. I kind of need to make a profit tonight. Just spent most of my cash.
19:10:57.375: [Raid] Roger: well, maybe hunters can.
19:11:12.937: [Raid] Maxwell: time to be mean. If you are not all willing to focus and have a polished run
   I -know- we are capable of, let me know now and I'll find something better to do with my time.
19:11:25.578: [Raid] Maxwell: do you want to raid MC tonight?

We decided to continue, which in hindsight was probably a mistake because a few minutes later we had an argument break out over loot rules. One of the regular druids, Dierdre, had to take an emergency phone call during a boss fight and could not participate. When we killed the monster and looted it, an argument broke out whether she should be allowed to roll for a druid item that dropped. This argument proved to be a shock to many of our raid members. What's more, Dierdre was not even one of the vocal participants in the argument. She did not care either way, but other raid members (who were also druids and potential winners of the loot item) argued that she should not be eligible to win the item. This caused other raid members to jump to her defense, citing the core values of the group. Some heated exchanges took place over voice chat, followed by some heated text chat exchanges. It ended with some people, including our raid leader, retiring for the night. A partial excerpt (prior to this, Shaun, the target of Sven's insults and Dierdre's offscreen partner, had already logged off in disgust) reads as follows:

21:06:29.656 : [Raid] Maxwell: all right, Dierdre is passing and I am giving the hammer to Sam, but I have something to say about all this

21:07:37.953: [Raid] Maxwell: this is a somewhat unconventional raid in many ways

21:08:04.500: [Raid] Maxwell: I don't do dkp, I don't dock people for only showing up for part of the evening

21:08:11.156: [Raid] Maxwell: loot has never been the main focus of this

21:08:49.562: [Raid] Maxwell: I find it disturbing that this much drama was raised over something like this *["Drama" occurred when players had to deal with stress and arguments with other players.]*

21:09:31.343: [Raid] Wei: wasnt like it wasnt fueled

21:09:43.156: [Raid] Maxwell: I am sorry that some of you feel this strongly about loot, but Dierdre has contributed as much to tonight as any of it *[meaning Dierdre had helped all along the way up until that point, and that effort should have been considered reward worthy]*

21:10:22.734: [Raid] Maxwell: I am not having the best evening, I'm recovering from food poisoning and I feel like shit, so I am sorry if I seem a little out of sorts

21:10:46.265: [Raid] Maxwell: but I am quite disappointed and will be taking a break from leading raids for awhile

21:11:23.343: [Raid] Maxwell: this has been too much pressure on me, and I'm having a hard time with this right now

21:13:03.328: [Raid] Maxwell: I just ask that you think about why you are all on these raids. I do this for all of you, not for any pieces of loot and I hope you all realize it's the people that make this worth it

21:13:06.156: [Raid] Maxwell: good night

21:17:20.468: [Raid] Sven: On this depressing note, I'm tired and depressed. I'm going to call it a night.

21:17:33.250: [Raid] Iskaral: Ok guys I think I'm off for the night

21:17:45.953: [Raid] Dierdre: i have to log guys…i am really upset right now, and am not thinking clearly. i am sorry i caused an issue while not even at my own keyboard. i shall see you all again tomorrow perhaps when the day is new

Maxwell was already feeling "a little out of sorts" when the dispute over Dierdre's eligibility came up. In the moment, he attempted to remind the raid members of the values that went into the formation of the raid, but he had to retire for the evening and possibly take a break from future raid events, too. This precipitated a chain of players quitting for the evening. The group decided to continue but eventually ended the session for good when the remaining players realized they couldn't defeat the next boss with so few raiders.

For many of the raid members, the drama came as a shock because they did not see the entirety of the chat that was happening in the various channels. It also came as a shock to me because I was not paying as much attention as I should have to the chat while it was happening. I was dealing with some particularly stressful situations in my own guild (including suicide threats). This was similar to

Barron's observation that groups working on specific projects are often more successful if the group's members are able to maintain their attention on their discourse of problem-solving strategies (Barron, 2003, p. 332). The following day, many of us discussed what happened on the raid's web discussion board.

The raid members' values of friendship and ability to reflect and realign were clearly evident on the forums because the events that happened the previous night were seen as a fluke. One raid member said, "I personal find what happened tonight to be just plane old rotten luck. We had a bad run tonight and people where getting tired and a situation accrued." In light of this view, players were emphasizing the family nature of our raid group and how it is natural for people to sometimes disagree with each other. A tauren druid from The 7/10 Split, Drusella, said:

Drusella <The 7/10 Split>
I love our raid. I know we are all going to get burned out at times and frustrated and upset and disagree with one another. It is part of being human. We are like brothers and sisters really. Stuff like this is going to happen. However I think we have all been playing long enough to know that we have a pretty great group of people going here and truly we care about and try to do what is best for one another.

Drusella framed the events as normal disputes a family would have and then emphasized the uniqueness of the group's collegial nature. We also talked about how we should treat each other in the future. One raid member said, "Stress, it happens. We have a wonderful group of people here and we should always keep in mind that every last one of these people has feelings." What mattered most was that we learned from this experience that conflict is normal, and people should be careful not to hurt each other while trying to resolve the conflict. In other words, the raid group was treating this as cause for reflection by trying to identify the problem (or at least symptoms of it) and resolve it. I then suggested that we needed to consciously make the effort to lighten the mood:

Thoguht <Booty Bay Anglers>
I noticed that not many people were actually joking around with each other like we normally do. I think a lot of us were sick or tired or having a crappy day, and when we got together, we had enough people who weren't feeling 100% that it showed itself in chat, in our performance, and in our stress levels. It might seem artificial but if I notice that happening again in the future…I'm going to start making jokes.

Another raid member echoed my sentiments:

Hala <The 7/10 Split>
I also noticed the lack of joking around in raid chat, and vent was totally silent for the time [I] was on it. I agree hun…I will be right there with you making a nerd of myself to try and lighten the mood.

To sum up, our lack of camaraderie was an indication that many people in the raid were feeling stressed more than usual and that some of them did not trust themselves or others to play their roles in the raid effectively. Somehow the underlying goals of the raid as a whole became diluted or lost during our bad night. The fact that the ultimate dispute was over loot suggests that the goals of building relationships became eclipsed by individual motivations for progressing and winning loot—incentives that are built into the underlying mechanics of the game. In this instance, the effectiveness of the group was compromised when the motivations for cooperating with each other came from selfish sources. In other words, whereas one argument about how to address social dilemmas is to appeal to people's selfish, "rational" nature, the experiences of this night for my raid introduces doubt into this approach's power. Perhaps more important than how individuals in a group are motivated to do their work is that everyone in the group is in alignment with where their motivation comes from.

One alternative way to address this issue was through explicitly reiterating the group members' goals and how they emphasized our experience together much like the reification/participation work that had been done before. Reiteration of assumed goals and expectations could only have served to strengthen bonds. Free riding that may have been occurring because players saw their efforts as work or obligation might have been lessened if players had seen their efforts as play or as participating in simply hanging out. Additionally, players were not at their most attentive during this night, and it is possible that a look at how labor could have been divided differently would have helped. Finally, even though camaraderie in the MC raid group was just an indicator for effectiveness rather than the cause of effectiveness, one way to fix poor performance and wavering trust may have been for members of the raid to attempt to lighten the mood and be supportive of each other when trying new things.

Communication and Trust

Learning for this group of players occurred through iterative attempts to perform in-game tasks together. Failure was seen as progress so long as the raid group was given time to reflect on strategies and form new strategies. Failure inherently pushed at our initial concepts about how a particular fight worked. This poses two problems. First, failure is not often thought about in games where more attention has been paid to how games allow imaginary actions to become realized and/or how games allow players to reach a state of *flow* (Csikszentmihalyi, 1991), where players never fail in such an absolute sense. When failure is considered, it is usually associated with skill-based failure at a specific task rather than instances of non-coordination, which may stem from a lack of trust. This could be examined using a distributed cognition or actor-network theory view of failure as moments when the system of distributed roles and responsibilities fails to be in alignment (see also Chen, 2012, Ch. 3). I make the claim, like Iacono and Weisband (1997) when they wrote about developing *swift trust* in virtual teams, that trust is closely tied to communication practices, and, specifically, the frequency of communication turns along with the kinds of communication happening might be a good indicator of the level of trust in a group.

Second, time to reflect on failure and, more generally, time to talk, think, coordinate, and prepare for the actual in-game activity can represent much of players' actual experience. This also is not often the picture one conjures up while thinking about games as immediate gratification. As Walter (2009) demonstrates in her research on a different raiding group, the time to reflect was needed for any meaningful learning to occur, and time to talk through this reflection was necessary for group learning.

Frustrations for my group emerged not from actual failure but through an emergent social understanding of a particular night's gaming. We had failed many times before, over and over again, but in those cases we were "in it together." On our poor performing night, the raid collectively momentarily lost track of its goals, but it was able to reaffirm them on the web forums the day after in a bottom-up approach to management. These goals included maintaining friendships and having fun (i.e., socially constructed goals) over the more traditional purpose of obtaining loot to improve or progress (i.e., game-mechanics goals). The raid's realignment with these shared-experience goals after a bad night was done through reflection and the ability to see that it had strayed and the ability to make suggestions for finding the path again. In a sense, the raid was metacognitive. The raid was made up of 40 different players on any given night, however, and it was those people who thought and acted.

It is difficult to say whether everyone in the raid valued the same goals, and it is clear that they did not always agree; otherwise, there would have been no strife. Yet the majority of members felt very strongly about the familial nature of our group. In contrast to this, I have heard and read about other raiding groups in WoW permanently breaking up after a meltdown. It is possible that those groups did not establish alignment in the same kinds of goals, and the individuals in those groups valued raiding as a means to an end rather than the end itself.

Looking at game mechanics and systems to guess how players will behave can lead one to suppose that changing the rules of a game can encourage cooperation within situations that resemble social dilemmas. Actual player behaviors, however, are complex. The concept of social dilemmas cannot model all the different social aspects that go into the choices players make in their situated experiences. If one were to look at these decision-making points not as a series of rational choices but rather as points where players act out of emotion and role-playing—identity-taking and action in a social discourse—it becomes clear that the issue of trust is more complicated than merely thinking that one's peers will also think rationally. The raid group I was in was able to foster a different kind of trust in its members by ensuring that they were in it for the sake of the group and having fun rather than for individual, self-serving loot collection, and this trust was enforced through our social norm of camaraderie and coordinated communication. Our social norms and communication practices allowed us to exist without other game-induced incentives such as guild affiliation or technical surveillance tools. This could be a new way of looking at the problem of trust in social dilemmas. My raid group ensured this trust first by only recruiting players with whom other members had already established a friendly relationship (i.e., we had built up enough social capital among us to trust each other). Second, the raid group explicitly stated its goals in in-game chat and in the web forums and then reflected on its behavior in relation to these goals. Finally, the raid loot rules—socially established criteria for regulating group actions around collective goals relative to individual interests—were collaboratively agreed upon through its web forums—one of the key components Kollock and Smith (1996) claim is needed for creating a sustainable online community.

The approach this group took may suggest a way that teams in other settings (like work or school) can also take when working on a new task. Rather than focusing on the goal of doing the task right and reaping the rewards, teams can concentrate on building friendships and learning how to complete the task together. An analogy to schools, for example, could liken getting good grades to winning loot and that grades represent an individualistic notion of how students should approach school. If learning is the goal of school, however, and one thinks of learning as socially constructed meaning from practice, more emphasis should be placed on fostering self-sustaining cooperation in the context of individual and collective goals. To aid in this, dividing the labor up into specialized roles allows each individual to contribute to the shared experience, and developing efficient communication channels is necessary for coordinated work. This could only happen, however, in environments that allow the right kind of trust to be established among group members. The trust must be based on valuing the shared experience and forging relationships rather than individual grades. Fostering trust among group members in this way may actually lead to a more coordinated group, which is better prepared to handle future tasks and changing situations. Additionally, a group formed on friendship is able to rebound from instances of poor performance and realign or rally itself for future tasks.

By examining player practice, I conclude with this: Good communication and coordination is necessary for a team to succeed. Good communication and coordination happens when team members trust each other in their specialized roles. For the raid group I participated in, trust based on shared goals and well-established relationships was stronger than trust based on individual incentives.

Note

* This chapter was originally published as: Chen, M. (2012). Communication, coordination and camaraderie. *Leet Noobs: The Life and Death of an Expert Player Group in* World of Warcraft (pp. 55–82). New York: Peter Lang.

References

Axelrod, R. (1985). *The evolution of cooperation*. New York: Basic Books.

Barron, B. (2003). When smart groups fail. *Journal of the Learning Sciences*, 12(3), 307–359.

Bransford, J. D., Brown, A. L., & Cocking, R. R. (2000). *How people learn: Brain, mind, experience, and school. Expanded edition*. Washington, DC: Commission on Behavioral and Social Sciences and Education, National Research Council. National Academy Press.

Chen, M. (2012). *Leet Noobs: The life and death of an expert player group in* World of Warcraft. New York: Peter Lang.

Cooper, G. (1998). Research into cognitive load theory and instructional design at UNSW. Retrieved November 19, 2012, from: http://dwb4.unl.edu/Diss/Cooper/UNSW.htm

Csikszentmihalyi, M. (1991). *Flow: The psychology of optimal experience*. New York: Harper Perennial.

Galarneau, L. (2005). Spontaneous communities of learning: Learning ecosystems in massively multiplayer online gaming environments. *Proceedings of DiGRA 2005 conference: Changing views—worlds in play*. Vancouver, British Columbia, Canada. Retrieved November 19, 2012, from: http://ir.lib.sfu.ca/handle/1892/1629

Gee, J. P. (2003). *What video games have to teach us about learning and literacy*. New York: Palgrave Macmillan.

Hardin, G. (1968). The tragedy of the commons. *Science*, *162*: 1243–1248.

Iacono, C. S., & Weisband, S. (1997). Developing trust in virtual teams. *Proceedings of the 30th Annual Hawaii International Conference on System Sciences (HICSS)*, 2: 412–420.

Kollock, P., & Smith, M. (1996). Managing the virtual commons: Cooperation and conflict in computer communities. In S. Herring (Ed.), *Computer-mediated communication: Linguistic, social, and cross-cultural perspectives* (pp. 109–128). Amsterdam: John Benjamins.

Malone, K. M. (2009). Dragon kill points: The economics of power gamers. *Games and Culture*, 4(3): 296–316.

Nardi, B. A. (2010). *My life as a night elf priest: An anthropological account of* World of Warcraft. Ann Arbor, MI: University of Michigan Press.

Smith, J. H. (2005). The problem of other players: In-game cooperation as collective action. *Proceedings of DiGRA 2005 conference: Changing views—worlds in play*, Vancouver, British Columbia, Canada.

Squire, K. D. (2005). Changing the game: What happens when video games enter the classroom? *Innovate*, 1(6): 25–49.

Steinkuehler, C. A. (2004). A discourse analysis of MMOG talk. In M. Sicart & J. H. Smith (Eds.), *Proceedings from the other players conference* (pp. 1–12). Copenhagen, Denmark.

Stevens, R. (2000). Divisions of labor in school and in the workplace: Comparing computer and paper-supported activities across settings. *Journal of the Learning Sciences*, 9(4): 373–401.

Strauss, A. (1985). Work and the division of labor. *Sociological Quarterly*, 26(1): 1–19.

Sweller, J. (1988). Cognitive load during problem solving: Effects on learning. *Cognitive Science*, 12(2): 257–285.

Taylor, T. L. (2006a). *Play between worlds: Exploring online game culture*. Cambridge, MA: The MIT Press.

Taylor, T. L. (2006b). Does WoW change everything? *Games and Culture*, 1(4): 318–337.

The Onion. (2000, Nov 29). Report: 98 percent of U.S. commuters favor public transportation for others. Retrieved 19 November, 2012, from http://www.theonion.com/articles/report-98-percent-of-uscommuters-favor-public-tra,1434/

Walter, S. E. (2009). *Raiding virtual middle earth: Collaborative practices in a community of gamers* (Doctoral dissertation, Stanford University, 2009).

Wikipedia. (2011). Loot system. Retrieved November 19, 2012, from: http://en.wikipedia.org/wiki/Loot_System

Zagal, J., Rick, J., & Hsi, I. (2006). Collaborative games: Lessons learned from board games. *Simulation & Gaming*, 37(1): 24–40.

CHAPTER FOURTEEN

Youth Participation

Learning and Growth in the Forum

ANGELA THOMAS

In this chapter I examine the discursive and social practices of a group of approximately 60 children who are actively involved in a number of online activities related to the Tolkien world of Middle Earth [Editors' note: This builds on the argument that one of the most important aspects in shaping online identity is related to the sense of community and belonging to that community; see Thomas, 2007, Ch. 3]. These children, average age 13 years, engage in online role-playing games where they create collaborative and ongoing stories based on their created fictional Middle Earth characters. They participate in role-playing and discussions on a role-playing web forum that was created by a key group of four children who had met when they first started role-playing online at ages 10 and 11 years. In addition to role-playing on the forum, an asynchronous text-based world, they also participate in synchronous discussions and role-playing on a Middle Earth palace, an online graphical chat world, using avatars they have selected as visual representations of their characters. As well as role-playing, they do poetry recitals and storytelling, sometimes combining the words and visuals with midi files they share to create musical atmosphere. Some of the poetry is in character; some is out of character. Poetry and individual fan fiction writing are also posted on the web forums for sharing and critique by others. Both boys and girls regularly swap gender roles to enhance particular storylines. Some children deliberately adopt ugly or evil characters to enhance storylines. In "out of character" discussions both boys and girls willingly share the emotional effect of some of the more powerful storylines where lead characters are hurt or sad. They also discuss and critique the finer points of Tolkien's writing, Peter Jackson's directing, and the actors who portrayed their favourite Middle Earth characters. Out of character they discuss their offline lives, celebrate birthdays together with online parties, engage in quiz nights, and learn Elvish together. The four developers of the forum have spoken to each other by phone, but none of the 60 children have met each other offline. They have joined together because of their love of the Tolkien mythology, and they have developed a community where they learn together and work together for the common social goals valued by that community.

I will argue that the type of learning engaged in by the children in the *Gathering of the Elves* community is reflective of Wenger's social model of learning, a type of learning as yet rarely attributed to children. The field of Education often relies upon a Vygotskian (1981) theorisation of learning through interaction with expert others. In this study, children did learn from more experienced others, but more often than not they learned without an expert, using strategies such as brainstorming, trial and error, practice, and discussion. They learned through the process of becoming a community and engaging in its social and discursive practices. They learned through adopting identities mediated through text, image, and sound, and both within and out of their fantasy storylines. They learned through the repeated routines and activities that they constructed together, and they learned through ongoing interactions with each other. These ways and means for learning resonate closely with Wenger's notion of "Communities of Practice."

Communities of Practice

"Communities of Practice," according to Wenger and Snyder (2000), are informal groups of people bound together through a shared passion for a joint enterprise. Wenger (1998) explains that the conceptual framework, in which "community of practice" is a constitutive component, is that of a social theory of learning. A social theory of learning is based on a number of premises, including: the fact that as social beings, we learn through social interaction; the idea that knowledge can be equated to competence in a valued enterprise, and is realised through active engagement in that enterprise; and the understanding that learning occurs through our social experiences, which ultimately leads to meaning (Wenger 1998). A social theory of learning, then, is connected with learning and knowing within social participatory experiences. Wenger (1998) goes further to propose a model to represent a social theory of learning, which comprises four constituents: community, meaning, practice and identity. In explaining the constituents of this model, Wenger (1998), summarises the significant terms as:

- *Meaning:* a way of talking about our (changing) ability—individually and collectively—to experience our life and the world as meaningful.
- *Practice:* a way of talking about the shared historical and social resources, frameworks, and perspectives that can sustain mutual engagement in action.
- *Community:* a way of talking about the social configurations in which our enterprises are defined as worth pursuing and our participation is recognizable as competence.
- *Identity:* a way of talking about how learning changes who we are and creates personal histories of becoming in the context of our communities. (Wenger, 1998, p. 5)

Although the notion of "Communities of Practice" has traditionally been associated with adult and workplace learning (Falk, 2006; Wenger & Snyder, 2000), and also with business and employees (Wenger & Snyder, 2000; Mitchell, 2000; Young, 2000), there has been a cross-over of interest into virtual communities, albeit with a focus on e-commerce (Lipnack & Stamps, 1997; Tapscott, 1999; Turban, King, & Chung, 2000). Also the four aspects of the model of a social theory of learning and Wenger's definitions seem to lend themselves to a wider consideration of community and the types of learning that occur within communities which have no business or commercial enterprise at stake. Wenger and Snyder (2000) for example, remark: "people in Communities of Practice share their experiences and knowledge in free-flowing, creative ways that foster new approaches to problems" (Wenger & Snyder, 2000, p. 7).

In fact, Wenger (1998) proposes a rather different view of learning to that of other social views of learning such as constructivism (Phillips & Jørgensen, 2002) and Vygotskian notions (1981). Wenger claims that in communities of practice, certain practices and processes characterise learning, namely:

> *Evolving forms of mutual engagement:* discovering how to engage, what helps and what hinders; developing mutual relationships; defining identities, establishing who is who, who is good at what, who knows what...
>
> *Understanding and tuning their enterprise:* aligning their engagement with it, and learning to become and hold each other accountable to it...
>
> *Developing their repertoire, styles, and discourses:* renegotiating the meaning of various elements; producing or adopting tools, artifacts, representations; recording and recalling events; inventing new terms and redefining or abandoning old ones; telling and retelling stories; creating and breaking routines. (Wenger, 1998, p. 95)

Unlike Vygotsky's theory of learning (Vygotsky, 1981), Wenger's model does not require the combination of expert and novice. In this theory, members of the community work things out together, to achieve certain purposes for their mutual benefit. This closely relates to the notion of social capital. Social capital refers to the way in which people establish networks, participate and make contributions to the common good of a community, because of the high value members place upon the community. Cox (1995) further defines social capital as "the processes by which people establish networks...and social trust...[to] facilitate co-ordination and co-operation for mutual benefits" (Cox, 1995, p. 15).

Stewart-Weeks (1997) examined voluntary organizations and concluded that they produced social capital because they had the "capacity to achieve" (Stewart-Weeks, 1997, p. 97), and he attributed this to factors such as: communities creating allegiances, communities being learning organizations capable of transforming and developing, communities working together for a collective purpose and communities which can put new knowledge to work. Coleman (1990) further explains the notion of social capital as being those productive behaviors that are invested by people into a community to produce a social profit or resource that will be desired and consumed by others.

Falk (2006) argues that learning occurs when social capital is built. He states that, "learning occurs when the set of interactions utilizes existing knowledge and identity resources and simultaneously adds to them...Learning occurs *in* the interactions" (Falk, 2006, p. 5, italics in original). In discussing identity as a component of social capital in communities of practice, Lesser and Storck (2001) claim, "a sense of identity is important because it determines how an individual directs his or her attention...[t]herefore identity shapes the learning process" (p. 832). In these views then, it is clear that identity, learning and community are intimately linked.

Wenger (1998) also asserts that issues of identity are inseparable from learning, knowing and community, and in that, in fact, "the concept of identity serves as a pivot between the social and the individual" (Wenger, 1998, p. 145). Linking with the previously argued concepts of identity as both social constructs and constitutive of "lived experience," Wenger claims that his perspective on identity "does justice to the lived experience of identity while recognizing its social character—it is the social, the cultural, the historical with a human face" (Wenger, 1998, p. 145).

Much has been written about aspects of online community as far as adults are concerned (e.g., Turkle, 1995; Holeton, 1998; Jones, 1998; Smith & Kollock, 1999). Communities are developing in many forms and for many purposes. People are coming together through email lists, bulletin boards, text-based chat sites and graphical-based chat sites to name just a few. In these communities a sense of belonging is established and social capital is built through the motivated engagement of the community members to develop mutual relationships with others who share the same passions, hobbies and values. I now want to turn to the children of the *Gathering of the Elves* community, and highlight how these children are producing social capital and learning through the discursive and social practices of that community, in those ways as defined by Wenger above, for the purposes of mutual engagement, tuning their enterprises and developing their repertoires, styles and discourses. In particular I will use data drawn from extensive interviews with four children: Elianna (13, female, US), Lily (13, female, US), Percirion (14, male, Australian) and Leggy (13, male, US).

The Gathering of the Elves: Creating the Community

Elianna, the young girl who created the community, spoke extensively with me about the purposes, motivations and processes involved in its creation. When I expressed admiration for her achievement, she humbly deflected my praise to the team of friends who assisted her in administering the site. She identified each friend, telling me their particular area of expertise, and what they had contributed to the site. She claimed she just thought of the idea to create the community and it was easy because her friends helped her to develop it. She didn't see anything remarkable at all in what she was doing, labelling it as "just a game," "a bit of fun." When I pointed out all of the processes she had worked through to set up the community, she dismissed it, saying "…nah, it's easy…you just mess around for a bit and you get it.…You just have to figure out which 'button' works which part lol.…and yeah, just about.…most of it you have to change back and forth, and its like, ok, so this one changes this and that one changes that, and you just kept messing with it til you work it out."

There are two aspects to what Elianna told me that are important in beginning my discussion about the learning which occurs in the *Gathering of the Elves* community. The first aspect is that of collaboration. The process of creating the site for the community was a joint construction, involving Elianna's reliance on and valuing of the varying abilities of her friends to work together, contributing what they each had strengths in. The duality between making the world and participating in the world together with her friends constructed, as Wenger (1998) terms, a negotiated world of experience and meaning. The second aspect Elianna mentioned was the method for learning what to do—trial and error, or puzzling it out. Social theories of learning which emphasise the importance of social interaction focus on the ways in which children learn by observing expert others. In pedagogical terms, this usually means the teacher is the expert other, who models the behaviour to be learned to the class of children. What Elianna is doing here as she constructs the community is not a result of observation of another, it is the result of her testing, trialling, checking, confirming, changing, and playing with the tools available to her until she is satisfied. Additionally, it involves continually reflecting on what she has built, and modifying and changing it over time to adapt to her growing knowledge and the emerging needs and desires of the community.

Similarly, in asking Elianna about how she learned to role-play, there was an expert other in one sense: Tolkien! But what she learned from reading Tolkien was not the result of her direct interaction with and observation of his behaviour; it was a result of her intellectual and imaginative engagement with his writing and with Peter Jackson's movie adaptations. Elianna informed me that to role-play, she just read Tolkien, imagined a character for herself, and then created a storyline based on a Middle Earth fantasy as the subject of the role-playing and then "I hopped right in." This is not to say that modelling and social models of learning are irrelevant; quite the contrary, in fact. Children read each other's posts and learn from their observations of how they each use language to construct the role-play. The point I am making here is that learning is multilayered, involving exploration, experimentation, engagement and participation, practice, storytelling, rituals, discussion, overcoming difficulties, negotiating and valuing identities and motivation. The combination of many elements together produce sophisticated learning and it is my contention that these elements all seem to come together in an online community such as *Gathering of the Elves*. For this reason, I see such a community as the locus for the creation and development of knowledge, and one that teachers could well learn from!

When I asked Percirion to tell me what he had learned through his involvement in role-playing games, the following discussion ensued:

Percirion:	What we do teaches us...skills
Anya:	like what?
Percirion:	I have already become more mathematically minded because management of tasks
Percirion:	Patience as well...I was kinda impatient for a while
Percirion:	And it can take around days for a reply to your posts
Anya:	ahhhh I see....but I don't see about task management
Anya:	what are the tasks you are managing?
Percirion:	I help my regional lord manage the movement of supplies for war and such
Percirion:	And not only that, but I have already become quite articulate through using Zhou Wei's intelligent speech (tm)
Anya:	grin
Anya:	i am still not sure how you just learned how to use his intelligent specch
Percirion:	I studied it
Percirion:	I was given a reason to study better English
Percirion:	An incentive
Anya:	where? in books?
Percirion:	Books, society
Percirion:	Other people
Anya:	you went to the library or searched the internet?
Percirion:	Both
Anya:	and what do you mean by society?
Anya:	do you mean you listened to intelligent people you know?
Percirion:	I listened to articulate people
Pericirion:	People who knew how to use the words to make them sound good
Percirion:	Friends, teachers, sister
Anya:	ahhhhhh *smile*

| Percirion: | It was just piecing the words together |
| Percirion: | and slipping into the role |

Percirion's message to educators cannot be more explicit! In the pursuit of fun and the desire to create a character that would engage well in the community enterprise of role-playing, he voluntarily spent hours studying ways of sounding intelligent! At no time did Elianna or her friends ever conceive of this community being a "Learning Community," yet the literacy demands and challenges of the role-playing culture are so complex that children are learning simply by engaging in the situated practices of the community.

Learning the Language of Role-playing

The language of role-playing is highly sophisticated. From a linguistic perspective, the children's written role-playing language reflects a high lexical density and complexity, detailed descriptive nominal groups, and a high degree of symbolism and figurative expressions. It is poetic, beautiful and quite overwhelming for me to read—I feel a sense of great awe and wonderment at the inventive and creative ways these children are manipulating language for the sole purpose of "playing." Their characters come to life, as they inject the language of powerful description and emotion into them.

In my interviews with children, a common theme arose in response to my questions about learning how to role-play. This theme was the fact that children didn't really think of their participation in the community as a learning process at all. To them it is a game, and to become better at the game, you just do certain things to improve. One girl laughed at me when I asked about learning, and quipped, "you learn how to role-play? I thought you just did it." Lily, who is "almost 14, 13 and ¾" years old, also found it difficult to explain how she learned to participate in the role-playing, preferring to demonstrate to me how she role-played, and the following is an excerpt from the ensuing discussion:

Lily:	:-) But my favorite part . . .
Lily:	is bringing your character to life
Anya:	can you tell me how you do that?
Lily:	Well, my character Lalaith Elerinna is my favorite character. You just talk for them and it kinda lets you relate to the character you made up.
Anya:	can you pretend to be her now and show me how she talks?
Lily:	Sure :-) I'd be delighted...Want her warrior side or her Romance side?
Anya:	oohhhh can I please have an example of each?
Lily:	of course
Anya:	thanks . . .
Lily:	Lalaith: NO!!!! You touch him, you'll die before you ever see your life. You can trust your mind to it! Back up now or I shall throw my sword into your neck!
Lily:	that's her warrior side. :-) hehe

Lily:	now heres her romance
Anya:	excellent!
Anya:	ok :>
Lily:	Lalaith: My heart weeps at the site of your tears, tell me Tregallien, what makes you cry so?
Anya:	awwww how sweet
Lily:	I forgot what the rest of her words were
Anya:	so can we just go back to her warrior side for a minute
Lily:	Yes of course
Anya:	what special words or phrases do you use to act like a warrior?
Lily:	Lalaith sometimes cries out in anger and she mostly has this growling in her voice. At times if I look up a few of the words I make her yell in elvish
Anya:	what makes her angry?
Lily:	When someone hurts her friends, her, or threatens to destroy her kingdom. What you just experienced was a Nazgul holding her father hostage.
Anya:	Have you worked out some sort of background for the character
Lily:	hehe, I have her profile on CoE, its often changing though so it might not be totally accurate
Anya:	and did you think of the background before you started role-playing or did it just grow
Lily:	It just grew. It says in her profile what her name means . . .
Anya:	oh, what does it mean?
Lily:	Lalaith means laughter....Elerinna, I forgot
Anya:	where did you get that meaning from?
Lily:	looked it up
Anya:	is it an Elvish word?
Anya:	where did you look it up? online?
Lily:	Yes. It is from Sindarin....I looked it up on Council of Elrond, and found it in a thing that says Lasto Lalaith nin...which means Listen to my laughter
Anya:	wow that is beautiful
Lily:	lol it's beautiful but lasto lalaith nin is a threat
Anya:	really?
Anya:	how so?
Lily:	Well you're saying listen to my laughter, which is a threat to people who were being serious and you're pretty much saying 'I'm laughing at your seriousness' and it could be a serious matter. causing...trouble is what you're doing

Through her involvement in the community, Lily has learned to develop a complex history for her character, create varying subtleties of emotions to bring her character to life, and deploy a range of linguistic resources to convey her character's actions, moods and involvement with others. One of the interesting things Lily mentioned was how her character profile was evolving over time. As new aspects of the role-playing emerged and new ideas occurred to her, Lily adapted her character, Laileth, to include emerging knowledge she had gained. Lily's character, Laileth, had a narrative arc that adapted with Lily's newly acquired knowledge through her participation in the community. The community is clearly a site for learning and intellectual stimulation. To enhance her character's authenticity, Lily also studied the languages of Elvish (Sindarin and Quenya) and knew the time and place that was appropriate for the use of each. She and her friend Elianna read *The Silmarillion* (Tolkien, 1977) and discussed it with each other in a mutual discovery of the mythology and folklore of Tolkien, in an attempt to bring their characters to life.

The ability to tell stories about the exploits of one's characters is also valued and is a source of entertainment and pleasure. On the Middle Earth palace, a visual virtual world, the *Gathering of the Elves* community often meets to talk together in real time, and enjoy recounting their experiences to each other. One evening I visited to find Elianna telling stories in a room which had the image of a campfire as a background, with an animated fire sparkling, creating a sense of intimacy and warmth in the room. Soft Celtic music was playing to create atmosphere, and here is Elianna's story, edited of the oohs and ahhhs of the other listeners for my purposes here:

Elianna:	it started out in the Elf Hideaway Bar and Grill
Elianna:	and I met up with Rain, Lil, Linwelos, Galuwen, Inwe, and a few others
Elianna:	on my way back to Mirkwood
Elianna:	and in this RP, my chair is also the Lady of Mirkwood
Elianna:	(being married to the blondie we all love ^o^)
Elianna:	hehe but anyways we had been writing
Elianna:	and I had found out that our borders were under attack
Elianna:	and so I went off to go back because I was staying in Rivendell with my aunt uncle and cousins at the time
Elianna:	and then I met everyone at the Bar and Grill and they insisted on coming with me
Elianna:	that's when it turned into its own RP, Saving Mirkwood
Elianna:	in SM we did not get very far because Eli had an accident lol....
Elianna:	basically my horse was shot in the leg, threw me off down a hill and then rolled on me...lol
Elianna:	that hurt
Elianna:	and that's when Elrond joined
Elianna:	he was in the Inn RP
Elianna:	but he joined SM to come and rescue and heal me
Elianna:	now 90% of the Inn is beat up lol
Elianna:	(they also hopped over to the other RP so SM has not been written in for a while)
Elianna:	I woke up right as we were at the Inn and they took me inside
Elianna:	and then Elrond put forward some very cool power lol and healed me

Elianna: (you will def. have to read that part ;))

Elianna: but it drained him of strength and so he slept and I slept and everyone was tired

Elianna: so no one was paying much attention

Elianna: we had several guests come in that were injured

Elianna: and by the time we realized it was because of the orcs

Elianna: (that had shot Nenya (my horse))

Elianna: we were all under attack

Elianna: almost everyone was wounded

Elianna: (we just described it in our own words how they (the orcs) acted etc.)

Elianna: but 3 of us in the Inn were pregnant so that didn't help anything…LOL

Elianna: so the three of us and Glorfindel and Percirion played healers

Through the storytelling, we learn about the practices of role-playing—how there are several con-current role-plays being enacted at any one time based on different realms of Middle Earth, and how the characters will move in and out of the role-plays as they enter and exit the spaces of these dif-ferent realms. But it is the act of the storytelling ritual that is revealing. Elianna is creating and shap-ing a history of the community by retelling the events of the role-playing. She is also encouraging and directing other community members to read certain parts of it, as she celebrates the achievements of the role-players, showing pride in their collaborative narrative, and forging her identity in the com-munity as a leader. She is developing a sense of the shared practices and revealing her long-term com-mitment to the shared enterprise of role-playing. By storytelling, she is teaching others about the community's practices, engaging their imagination, and providing a context for the future expansion of the community's enterprise, by enticing others to engage in it. Others can see potential trajecto-ries and ways of being for themselves, which will in turn transform their identities, the very crux of what learning is all about, according to Wenger.

I want to turn now to talk about Wenger's notion that learning is also a process of combining modes of being. This is concerned with the idea that what we can learn from belonging to one com-munity, or through engaging in retreats, sabbaticals, or workshops, can be adapted and realised in another community, the new learning assimilated and applied to a different context. Wenger states "our identities must be able to absorb our new perspectives and make us part of who we are" (Wenger, 1998, p. 217) and this both transforms our identities and is at the heart of what learning is all about. I found this to be the case in the *Gathering of the Elves* community and will illuminate how learning occurs in this manner by drawing upon my interviews with Percirion. In asking him about how he role-played different emotions for his character, he revealed the following transcript of a recent post, to show his "bubbly happy self":

During the dead of night, a certain carriage rolls down the streets. The road is muddy, the weather is foul, but the occupant is as happy as ever. He sings a happy and simple tune to himself, for he has returned from war. The occupant leaves the carriage, his robes as orderly as always, his hair bun neat and precise; he knocks on the door to his own house, waiting with anticipation. As his wife opens the door, he smiles broadly, to see her shining, shocked face and wide eyes…He moves quickly in, and picks her up…or very nearly tries. He is physically weak, but manages to plant a kiss on her lips before falling head over heels.

After laughing with him in appreciation of his beautiful, descriptive language and in celebration of the humour of writing, I proceeded to ask him about what he knew about the person who was role-playing his wife. To my amazement, he revealed that HE also role-played the character of his wife!! In my previous research (Thomas, 2004), I had spent four years as a virtual ethnographer, studying children's behaviour and language in online chat contexts, and in all but two isolated incidents, the data revealed that children never switched gender (something adults have a tendency to do in online contexts), but in fact performed exaggerated behaviours to emphasise characteristics of their real gender. However for the purposes of role-playing, children are quite happy to swap gender roles, with Percirion being just one illuminative example for my purposes here. I asked Percirion how he was able to convincingly role-play a female character, and I also asked him how his language and role-playing changed to reflect his female character. The following excerpt is the conversation that ensued:

Percirion:	Whereas Wei is more 1000-words-per-minute, Xiao is more…quiet and low, I guess
Percirion:	When Wei gets angry he tends to go all pale and speak slowly and angrily
Percirion:	Xiao doesn't speak. period.
Percirion:	She attempts to conjure laser beams from her eyes
Anya:	so she is a docile quiet little woman?
Percirion:	docile?
Anya:	oh. laser beams. I guess not hehehe
Percirion:	lol, she tends to glare
Percirion:	But she isn't docile.
Anya:	oh ok
Percirion:	If need be she'll take down that old halberd and shove it through someone's throat
Percirion:	Mainly because Zhou Wei can't use it that well
Anya:	ok so…tell me more about how your "wife" behaves
Percirion:	aaaa hahahaha
Percirion:	Well
Percirion:	Quite thoughtful actually, she often speaks softly.
Percirion:	But she has a look about her that makes people know that something is wrong
Percirion:	Wei's been living with it so long he can almost smell it
Percirion:	And she only speaks in soft tones because, why bother speaking loudly? Wei can hear. He's the one that needs to hear it
Anya:	but did you model her from anything else, like what you have seen in movies, or from real people at all?
Percirion:	um.
Percirion:	Well I kind of based her around a friend from school
Anya:	what bits of your friend do you use in your character?
Percirion:	Quite reserved and happy, but completely willing to get into a scratch

Anya:	ahhh excellent
Percirion:	I learnt a lot about my friend.
Anya:	oh what did you learn about her?
Percirion:	She appears…strong quite a bit of the time
Percirion:	But once you get past that exterior, she's like a kitten

Percirion's study of his female friend to portray the character of the wife he role-plays is a good example of his use of imagination to transfer new learning into a new context, in order to transform his role-playing experience, making it more enriching, convincing and authentic. The role-playing community gave Percirion the space to learn what it was like to play a female character, and the opportunity to use and modify language for different purposes. The medium of the digital environment provided a safe place for this exploration, not limiting but opening up the scope of possibilities for Percirion's imagination. The culture of the community, being one of character development, theatre and performance, allowed, encouraged and applauded such explorations. The context of community here provides a unique opportunity to reconfigure and transform identities, so much so that all the usual markers of identity (age, gender, race, class) can be disrupted. In this context, identity is marked and mediated specifically through language.

Language, Power and Belonging

What is most striking about the community is the respect and support the children give to each other's writing. They regularly comment upon each other's role-playing, poetry and fan fiction writing, showing encouragement and expressing emotional responses to the beauty of the words of others. Several children commented to me that one of the most special things about their involvement in the community was the way in which they established friendships and felt a real sense of support for their writing. In addition to commenting upon each other's writing, there's also a culture of interacting and responding to writing through the very nature of the role-playing games. The role-playing requires each person to carefully read the contributions of others and use the cues provided by them to insert their own character's next actions meaningfully into the text. The sense of pleasure children gain from seeing their own character and words being reacted to by others is both instantly rewarding their efforts and highly motivating for them to continue.

As far as language is concerned, children are learning that to be literate is to have power. Literate behavior is one of the most valued forms of capital in the community. The ability to weave each other's words into a narrative and engage in stimulating, collaborative storytelling is considered the highest practice of the community. Literate behavior is also privileged and sets up its own form of class system within the community. The popular children are those who engage in the most articulate storytelling and who interact with the storytelling of others. Percirion told me that he loved to role-play with somebody who really knew the historical context of the characters, because "it can get so interesting…it just makes you glow." When I asked Percirion what his friends would say were his strengths, his immediate response was his ability to use language for varying contexts. He told me "as a matter of fact I am a top student at English, so I can easily adapt to a certain selection of language choices. I am good at strategy, politics, I am patient, and I can charm/persuade the pants off anyone if I put my mind/silver tongue to it." He then said that he and his friends have a saying for his character, which was "I am noble when I am good; I am cold and calculating when I am angry. Now, get out of my way before I lock you in a room and watch you slowly starve." Percirion is clearly engaged in the role-playing and feels a strong sense of belonging to the community due to his command of the English language—something he is very proud of and exercises at every opportunity. His role-playing texts are valued and adopted by others, and so his identity in the group is negotiated through the power of his language.

However, there is one girl in the community who is neither articulate nor able to always contribute meaningfully to the role-playing, often contributing posts that do not fit in with the established narrative storyline. The children found this frustrating at first and either ignored her or had the admin staff simply remove her posts from the board. By doing this, the children were taking away her right to participate, minimalising her ability to engage and therefore belong to the community, thus constructing her as a marginalized identity. This was forced upon the girl and clearly hurt her. This caused much dissension, as Elianna wanted to promote a culture of respect and tolerance for difference in the community. The situation was resolved eventually by having the girl private message her intended posts to one of the admin staff first to check and discuss with her before it was posted publicly. Through a series of discussions about her various posts, the girl learned the acceptable practices of the community and learned that to belong required her to work with the ideas of others, and to role-play meant staying true to the narrative lines that were built by the other characters. She is now permitted to contribute posts without prior checking, as she has learned the community expectations about the language choices she makes.

Leggy has been involved in role-playing for several years. He is one of the admin staff members for *Gathering of the Elves* and his particular area of responsibility is the poetry discussion board. He established some rules for his board that included a rule that poems had to be private messaged (PMed) to him first, so that he could check that the content was "G-rated" before they went public. However at a meeting of the admin staff, Leggy found himself the centre of a dispute and some heated discussion related to this strict regulation, as they felt he didn't trust the other community members to do the right thing. He told me, "people were getting really mad at me in a GotE meeting on palace [a kind of chat space] and I felt kind of cornered and that people didn't like me. And so I was thinking about it and I just decided, maybe people would like it if I left, so I started a poll on it, and I wrote a poem about it." The poem Leggy wrote expressed his confusion and dismay, and was a genuine reflection of his angst about the situation. I was so astounded to hear that a 13-year-old boy would solve a problem through writing a poem, that I want to include the poem here to show how Leggy negotiated himself out of conflict and into a position of power.

I don't know if I should go,
or if I should stay.
some want me here, others want me away.
If you want me to stay,
prove it to me,
or I shall go,
across the sea.

You are all so nice,
but sometimes mean,
I don't know what to do,
should I cry or should I sing?
I've come so far,

but can still turn back
for I have some flaws,
and things I lack.

(Leggy)

This poem caused a flurry of messages from other members who reassured him that he was a valued community member, as in this extract:

> I agree with Lia so much Leggy. I know that lately things have been really stressed, and I lot of it's my fault. I am sooo sorry that any of this ever happened, and I will do whatever I can to make it up to you. But you have done so much for all of us here, and you are such a big help to me, that if you left, it would leave us an empty hole that we couldn't fill. We love you to death, and none of us want you gone. Please don't leave us ☹☹. (Elianna)

Leggy, feeling valued once again, remained in the community but tempered his rules so that people had a little more freedom in posting their poetry, allowing them to feel like they were trusted to do the right thing in their writing. The new rule he posted was, "It needs to be clean poetry (no cussing, sexual themes, or things like that). If you're not sure about something being 'clean,' than pm me and ask me. No racism/hate comments or anything like that." Leggy successfully used language to resolve conflict, but in a creative way that would not be possible offline. He went from feeling excluded and attacked, to being included and in fact very popular (he was voted "August's hottest guy" in the "Girls Only" discussion board!), as a direct result of the negotiation of his role and place in the community by confronting the issue in poetry.

As Wenger notes, it is through these disruptions of the transparency of identities that negotiated identities are formed and reified within a community. This also resonates closely with Fairclough's notion that power is not an undisputed given or attribute of a person, but instead it is "won, exercised, sustained and lost in the course of social struggle" (Fairclough, 1989, p. 68). By doing something that the community was unhappy about (the perceived lack of trust by enforcing such stringent rules), Leggy had met a boundary, which was a lack of mutuality between him and the community. Leggy had a choice. He could leave the community. This in fact is much easier to do in online communities, as they have the distinct characteristic of being transient communities for the very reason that many people find it a disembodied experience and find it difficult to feel that sense of belonging to the community. But Leggy was unwilling to let go his membership of the community because he had invested so much of himself into the design, the organization and the life of the community. Instead, Leggy chose to stay, sharing his feelings, through the medium in which he felt he had a special strength—his poetry. This act, and his subsequent willingness to adapt the stringency of his procedures with poetry posting, served to dissolve the boundary and bring him back into the fold, so to speak, developing a sense of mutuality and belonging once again. Not only that, but it elevated his status in the community.

Conclusion

Wenger asserts that a community of practice in which a history of mutual engagement has evolved around a joint enterprise is an ideal context for the acquisition of knowledge. He states that when the condition of this mutual engagement is achieved, the community is "a privileged locus for the creation of knowledge" (Wenger, 1998, p. 214). The most important implication of this study is to understand the degree and nature of learning that occurred, and the intensity of interactions that occur in online communities such as the *Gathering of the Elves*. The nature of this learning challenges some previous beliefs about learning. Here, children are working at a complex level in order to communicate effectively and efficiently. But through their desires to negotiate the mediated environment of communication, children work together to solve problems, or they teach themselves through self-study, self-initiated research, and trial and error. Sometimes children do have an expert other to assist them, as articulated in Vygotskian notions of learning. But more often than not, the desire to get things done quickly, for the social purposes of both personal development and for the betterment of the community, inspires a passion and hunger in them to learn for themselves or in collaboration with other novices.

The key points to be drawn from this chapter include:

1. Children and young people are forming communities of practice through which develop their identities with respect to their roles in those communities
2. They are able to develop new social and literacy practices as they push the limits of what technology affords them, for purposes of pleasure and fun, and are highly motivated as they learn together and teach each other the rules of engagement in their communities
3. They invest a significant amount of time in their pursuits and in their relationships with others, to maintain a cohesive community
4. They are able to make sophisticated use of language resources to create and sustain believable fictional characters, whilst also sustaining a personal "real" identity in their out of character interactions, which are of more significance than their fictional characters
5. Storying, storytelling and literary criticism is a characteristic of role-playing communities, and these children are deeply immersed in all of the features and linguistic characteristics of the fantasy genre
6. Whilst children maintain their real gender in their "real" identity roles, they have no compunction about swapping gender when engaged in fictional contexts, and openly state that by role-playing the opposite gender they are at the same time learning about that gender in new ways, including social and linguistic nuances
7. Clearly, to be powerful and have status or social capital in this and other communities like it, one must be literate—good writing equals power inside the narrative, regardless of the character status being role-played

In this study, the level of skills children achieve in the pursuit of active and committed citizenship in virtual communities may exceed expectations of teachers in schools. The opportunities for freedom of expression, for the exercise of power, and for the opportunities to create meaningful relationships with others, offer children a place where they can be themselves, and the motivation to belong is the drive for learning. In my view, the *Gathering of the Elves* community offers these children fulfilment of needs that do not seem to be offered in schools. I would challenge educators to bridge this gaping difference to account for the children of this technological age. The challenge for parents, teachers, policy makers, librarians, software developers and so forth is that they all need to respond to the new characteristics displayed by children such as the *Gathering of the Elves* children, and do so quickly in order to ensure that children get the best support in developing these new literacies. It will be critical to offer professional development to teachers in the area of the cultures of cyberspace and the characteristics of cyberliteracies to enable children's growth and success in this sensorially complex, technological age, where computer-mediated communication is becoming increasingly common. As the knowledge from students, teachers, and children regarding new and changing literacies is developed, used and shared, teachers and policy makers will need to become curriculum builders, to make the necessary changes at the curriculum policy level. And when they do build new curricula, they too, like 13-year-old Elianna, may be able to create a community of learning which can become a privileged locus for the creation of knowledge.

Note

* This chapter was originally published as: Thomas, A. (2007). Youth participation: Learning and growth in the forum. *Youth Online: Identity and Literacy in the Digital Age.* (pp. 94–112). New York: Peter Lang.

References

Cox, E. (1995). *A truly civil society.* Sydney: Australian Broadcasting Corporation.

Falk, I. (2006). Essence of engagement: Social capital in workplace learning. In G. Castleton, R. Gerber & H. Pillay (Eds.), *Improving workplace learning: Emerging international perspectives* (pp. 21–34). Hauppauge, NY: Nova Science Publishers.

Fairclough, N. (1989). *Language and power.* London: Longman.

Holeton, R. (1998). *Composing cyberspace: Identity, community, and knowledge in the electronic age.* Boston, McGraw-Hill.

Jones, S. G. (Ed.) (1998). *Cybersociety 2.0: Revisiting computer-mediated communication and community.* Thousand Oaks, CA: Sage Publications.

Lesser, E., & Storck, J. (2001). Communities of practice in organizational performance. *IBM Systems Journal, 4*(4): 831–842.

Lipnack, J., & Stamps, J. (1997). *Virtual teams.* New York: John Wiley & Sons Inc.

Phillips, L., & Jørgensen, M. W. (2002). *Discourse analysis as theory and method.* London, Sage.

Smith, M. A., & Kollock, P. (Eds.) (1999). *Communities in cyberspace.* London: Routledge.

Stewart-Weeks, M. (1997). Voluntary associations: Social capital at work or post-modern romance? *Social capital: The individual civil society and the state. CIS policy forum 14.* Canberra, ACT: Centre for Independent Studies.

Mitchell, J. (2000). *Re-framing the future: An e-commerce operation.* Melbourne, VIC: ANTA.

Tapscott, D. (1999). *Creating value in the network economy.* Cambridge, MA: Harvard Business Review Book.

Thomas, A. (2004). Digital literacies of the cybergirl. *E-Learning. 1*(3): 358–382.

Thomas, A. (2007). *Youth online: Identity and literacy in the digital age.* New York: Peter Lang.

Tolkien, J.R.R. (1977). *The Silmarillion.* London, Allen and Unwin.

Turban, E., Lee, J., King, D., & Chung, M. H. (2000). *Electronic commerce: A managerial perspective.* Englewood Cliffs, NJ: Prentice Hall.

Turkle, S. (1995). *Life on the screen.* New York, Simon and Schuster.

Vygotsky, L. (1981). The genesis of higher mental functions. In J. Wertsch (Ed.), *The concept of activity on soviet psychology.* New York: M. E. Sharpe.

Wenger, E. (1998). *Communities of practice: Learning, meaning, and identity.* London: Cambridge University Press.

Wenger, E., & Snyder, W. (2000). Communities of practice: The organizational frontier. *Harvard Business Review, 78*(1): 139–145.

Young, S. (2000). Managing long-term impacts of short-term projects. *Australian vocational education and training association (AVETRA).* Canberra: AVETRA.

CHAPTER FIFTEEN

Which *South Park* Character Are You?

Popular Culture and Online Performance of Identity

BRONWYN WILLIAMS

Context

*B*ronwyn Williams' book Shimmering Literacies *examines "how the discourse and rhetorical forms of popular culture are significant in a culture of multiliteracies in shaping students' perceptions of reading and writing, and their conceptions of audience, authorship, text, and identity" (Williams, 2010, p. 3). The research informing the book involved reading and analyzing a wide range of online material, and interviewing and observing first-year university students. Online artifacts included material created by popular culture producers (e.g., television and movie studios, bands, computer game companies etc.), as well as student-produced texts like personal profiles on social networking sites, blogs, posts to fan forums, and so on. Williams interviewed 21 university students in the U.S. (approx. 2 hours per interview) about their online practices and engagement with popular culture. Of these, he selected 15 students to observe and interview further over the course of a number of sessions (roughly 8 hours in all per student). All students owned their own computers and reported spending time online each day. Williams describes the students as predominantly middle class. All but four of the initial pool were Caucasian, and five described themselves as belonging to affluent families. All students named below (e.g., Jenny, Natalie, Mitchell, Ashley, etc.) were study participants.*

Introduction

If I handed out sheets of paper with the heading "About Me" on them to a group of writing teachers and asked them to fill them out, I've little doubt that most would fill the page with expository passages about themselves, their backgrounds, accomplishments, family descriptions, and so on. Every *MySpace* page has a section titled "About Me" where the person creating the page is invited, similarly, to write expository, biographical descriptions. Yet the "About Me" sections on the *MySpace* pages of, say, university students are often among the least used, least detailed, and least informative parts of the page.

Here is Tony's:

"Hey! How are ya? Well a little about me. I'm a pretty laid back guy for the most part. I enjoy hanging out with my buds and kinda just relaxing. I just like to go out and have fun, but I know my limits. But feel free to talk."

Or Jenny's:

"Oh, you know me. Just a girl who likes the sun on her face and the smell of popcorn. Say 'hi' if you want. Maybe I'll answer. Maybe not."

Or Ashley's, which just has her name in glittering type.

The brevity of these "About Me" entries might lead a person unfamiliar with *MySpace* to believe that the pages reveal little about their creators. But the truth is that the pages are filled with information that the writer of the page has composed to construct a performance of identity. This information is drawn from multiple media and, very often, directly connected to popular culture.

In this chapter, I focus on *MySpace* and *Facebook* pages and the university students who created them. When I interviewed them, their answers to questions of intent, audience, and rhetorical choices vary, but what is common on these students' personal pages is their reliance on popular culture content and references they can appropriate from other sites to enable them to compose their identities and read the identities of others. They use popular culture icons, catchphrases, music, text, and film clips in postmodern, fragmented collages that present selves that seem simultaneously sentimental and ironic. The construction of these pages illustrates how popular culture practices that predate online technologies have been adopted and have flourished with new technologies that allow content to flow across media as well as to increase the ease of audience participation. The intertextual nature of popular culture texts creates opportunities for multiple readings of social networking webpages in ways that destabilize the identity students believe they have created. These multiple readings create ambivalence for students who realize that their practices in composing pages online may be in conflict with how they read other pages, and how their own pages are read.

Identity on the Page or Screen

Issues of identity have been important areas of discussion in both literacy and popular culture. Composing texts, whether in print or in multiple modes, requires deliberate decisions about how identity is going to be communicated, just as interpreting texts always includes making decisions about the identity of an author. Though the cultural contexts may vary, we are always negotiating identity when we read and write. Even when writers try not to reveal explicitly personal information, the audience then reads the text to a default identity according to the cultural context. For example, for scholarly writing that attempts to be detached and impersonal, the default identity remains the white male in the lab coat (or in the humanities and social sciences, perhaps it is the tweed jacket). In the choices we make about audience, how we choose and arrange words and images, what we choose to disclose about ourselves, we are making choices that both emerge from and shape identity.

Accepting that literacy is a social practice is to accept that identity is central to both how texts are created and how they are interpreted. What we perceive we are allowed to write and read, the resources we can employ in our reading and writing, the ways in which we present identities in texts are all shaped by the social and cultural contexts in which we live. As Barton and Hamilton (1998) maintain, literacy practices are influenced by social rules. Such rules

> [r]egulate the use and distribution of texts, prescribing who may produce and have access to them. They straddle the distinction between individual and social worlds, and literacy practices are more usefully understood as existing in the relationships between people, within groups and communities, rather than as a series of properties residing in individuals (p. 7).

Ethnographies of literacy practices (Heath, 1983; Street, 1995; Barton & Hamilton, 1998; Gregory & Williams, 2000; Pandey, 2006) have offered extensive evidence of the complex and powerful interrelationships of literacy and identity. Rather than reveal a single authentic "self," such research has emphasized that our performances of identity through literacy may be shifting and are always contingent on the cultural context. Context determines our ability to make meaning from language, as well as the material and cultural resources to create and interpret texts (Gee, 2004). Regardless of the genre or the technology, when a literacy event occurs an identity is performed and it is important to consider the possibilities and effects of such performances.

What Gee (1990) says about "Discourse" is also appropriate to questions of literacy in that reading and writing act as "a sort of 'identity kit' which comes with the appropriate costume and instructions on how to act, talk, and often write so as to take on a particular social role that others will recognize" (p. 142). Online writing is deeply connected with social roles and identities, even more so for secondary and university students who are in particularly important and often turbulent years of social and emotional development. Adolescents are struggling toward understanding their sense of "self," in both physical and psychological terms. Their performances of identity and their relationships with social groups are under constant negotiation and often significant alteration. It is not unusual to see adolescent identities shift remarkably over a single school term as social and personal circumstances change (de Pourbaix, 2001).

As adolescent identities shift, so do their perceptions of literacy practices. Where almost any form of reading and writing is praised in young children, by middle school and beyond, the cultural and institutional limitations on how literacy is defined become more pronounced. Literacy in school and the larger culture, very often, is restricted to the reading and writing that accomplishes work. Reading a textbook or a literary novel is acceptable; reading a romance or science fiction novel is not. Schools then reinforce larger dominant cultural attitudes about literacy that are based largely on issues of social class and cultural capital. Writing and reading that emphasize detachment and aesthetic or analytical appreciation are valued, and writing and reading that evoke emotions or are sentimental are not. Consequently, most people would see reading a textbook or writing a research paper as evidence of literacy but not writing Christmas cards or reading a comic book.

As the last example illustrates, literacy practices connected to popular culture—unless they are detached analytic critiques—are dismissed by school and the dominant culture as frivolous (Newkirk, 1997). Even as students described their online reading and writing about popular culture with much more enthusiasm and authority, when asked to define literacy, they did not include this pleasurable, emotional, out-of-school reading and writing for which they were highly motivated. Distinctions of race, gender, and—perhaps most of all—social class contribute to the gap in what is considered legitimate literacy practices. Reading and writing that evoke emotions or use images or video or take a more explicitly personal approach to a text are regarded as being "easy" and lacking the detachment and rigor of the work assigned in schools. Oftentimes, detachment and aesthetic appreciation of texts are perceived as demonstrating a higher social class status (Bourdieu, 1984). Mass popular culture is almost always regarded as the domain of those from a more common and less intellectual social class. When they are in school, many in our culture, including students, are encouraged to discount and apologize for the direct pleasure and emotion they find in popular culture.

Like all literacy practices, then, those connected with popular culture are formed and perceived through our cultural constructions of identity. Often, issues of race, social class, gender, and sexual orientation are explicit in popular culture. For example, the computer game industry and audience has been overwhelmingly male and this has been reflected both in the kinds of games that have been created, such as first-person shooters, as well as in the way young people approach and interact with the games. Though students such as Natalie, who is an avid player of a fantasy only role-playing game called *Furcadia*, illustrates how the gender balance of gaming culture is changing. People are drawn to online affinity spaces, then interact with others on fan forums and lists based on shared identity expectations.

Locker Decorations and T-Shirts

Issues of identity and popular culture certainly predate online technologies. Mass popular culture has led people to make statements or judgments about identity and taste based on the popular culture references of those they met. A person might ask new acquaintances about the movies they had seen or look through their record collections as a way of evaluating potential social relationships. Similarly, people appropriated popular culture images and references in their daily identity performances. Part of the allure of mass popular culture has always been the identification of audience members with celebrity as people performed identities through public appropriation of celebrity images. For example, students decorated school lockers with photos of celebrities or wore rock concert T-shirts to connect the attributes of the popular culture reference to their own identities. Consequently, the high school girl with the preppy pop star's photos pasted all over her locker and the boy walking down the hall wearing a heavy metal band T-shirt might give each other one glance but, on seeing the popular culture references they had appropriated, not bother with a second.

The performance of identity obviously is always a social phenomenon. Thus, popular culture has not only been an element of identity construction but has also been a central part of creating community in contemporary society. Clearly, mass popular culture has created common cultural references that are shared by millions of people who may have never met. Joshua Meyrowitz (1985) noted that the casual discussion of popular television programs has served the same social function as conversations about the weather in terms of providing material of which everyone could have both some knowledge and an opinion. Popular culture has also provided the basis for social activities (groups that get together to watch television programs such as *Sex and the City* or parties that took place when it was revealed "who shot J.R." on *Dallas*) or shared social interests.

In the general population, such casual interactions with popular culture have been widespread. More intense, inter-media and interactive uses of popular culture such as fan clubs or fan magazines existed before online technologies, though they were the province of a much smaller group of devoted "fans" back when that term and such behaviors had more derogatory connotations. Before the advent of interactive online technologies, writing fan fiction, attending a fan convention, or belonging to a fan club required a commitment of time, emotion, and resources beyond that of more casual members of the audience. Still, such devoted fans existed and did engage in such interactive activities of textual poaching (Jenkins, 1992) in regard to mass popular culture texts. The activities of fans were motivated both by the desire to appropriate control of the popular culture text as well as the opportunity to become part of a "collective identity, to forge an alliance with a community of others in defense of tastes which, as a result, cannot be read as totally aberrant or idiosyncratic" (23). As people have read and adopted popular culture texts to their social contexts, popular culture has long served functions of both identity construction and community building.

Finding community through shared popular culture interests is, again, a long-standing phenomenon for young people. People have identified communities through their statements and interests about popular culture. Liking particular movies or television programs or bands created spaces through which people could not only identify shared interests but also could perform identity through the popular culture texts. For example, young people feeling particularly alienated may be drawn to punk or goth bands and fashions. Other young people connected more to books than sport may be drawn to the *Harry Potter* books and movies as texts that celebrate school and learning. Popular culture communities are also created by exclusivity and rejection. A group of people may find common ground by deriding a particular band or program, particularly if it has become largely popular in the culture. The preferences of people for their own popular culture preferences over others may become intense—so that Rolling Stones fans disdained the Beatles or *Star Wars* and *Star Trek* fans argue for the superiority of their favorite science fiction franchise. Even university professors engage in such identity performances by professing to ignore all popular culture except public broadcasting.

The elements of inter-media and interactive popular culture that Jenkins (2006a) emphasizes as central to convergence culture existed before online technologies. Consequently, online technologies did not create the desire for such activities but rather provided opportunities and media that enabled more people to engage in such activities more easily. It is not difficult to see that fan webpages seem so like fan clubs or that online fan forums seem like larger watercooler conversations.

Online and new media technologies have not only expanded the abilities of people to participate in popular culture by making it easier and faster for everyone to engage in activities once the province of the most committed fans but also created the possibilities for performing different identities at the same time. One element of online activity that has fascinated people from the first days of electronic bulletin boards is the opportunity it offers for playing with identity. As it was so neatly encapsulated by Peter Steiner (1993) in his famous cartoon, where one dog at a computer says to another dog, "On the Internet, nobody knows you're a dog." When they are online, people can discard or transform many of the "semiotics of identity" that define their daily lives and portray themselves as somehow other than they are in their daily lives (Thomas, 2007). Online, people can alter identities and do so for a variety of reasons—safety, play, disguise, harassment, or hiding the fact they are fans. In participatory popular culture, some of the more popular activities, such as fan fiction, fan forums and lists, online game playing, and posting videos and comments on *YouTube* often involve people using pseudonyms or otherwise transforming their identities. For example, on fan forums, people sometimes use a title that pertains to the program or film or band about which they are writing, say "fanoffrodo" for *Lord of the Rings*, or just one that strikes their fancy, such as "gossipguerilla." There is often a profile link through which people can provide some information, such as age or nationality, but just as often the profile spaces are not filled out.

As with the famous internet dog, it can be difficult to determine the identity characteristics of people who post online or to verify whether the information people do provide is accurate. A student posting fan fiction might alter her age on the profile to look older and get different readings of her work. On multi-user role-playing sites, such as *SecondLife* or *World of Warcraft*, the larger point is to create avatars that play with identity. Yet when the point of the site is not to play with identity, such as a fan forum or fan fiction site, people often want to protect their full identities but at the same time be honest about their ideas and emotions. As Genevieve put it, "I did conceal some of the stuff because I didn't want people to look at it and judge me. . . . The type of stuff I put in there was really limited. I didn't reveal a whole lot about myself because I didn't want people—a certain type of person—to contact me, you know." For the readers of the posts or narratives, however, there is no way to determine who the person is except for discursive and rhetorical cues that may or may not be accurate for placing a person in terms of identity characteristics. People may try to create digital bodies, to write themselves into being using words and images and video, but such "digital bodies are fundamentally coarser, making it far easier to misinterpret what someone is expressing" (boyd, 2008, p.129). We might imagine that a writer of a post using aggressive language and unconventional grammar and spelling is male and has less formal education, but we could also be very wrong in our assumptions.

As *MySpace* and *Facebook* pages make clear, however, to say that people can play with identity online does not necessarily mean that their play is detached from their offline lives. As Angela Thomas (2007) argues, composing identities online through the semiotic resources is inextricable from our embodied reactions and emotions. Our desires and anxieties over what we compose online as well as our emotional responses are very much part of our embodied identities. Other research (Stern, 2008) has indicated that students can use posting online or composing personal pages as an outlet for expressing powerful emotions in a cathartic or therapeutic way. What writing and reading with participatory popular culture online do is connect such emotions not only with representations of self but also with intertextual representations of popular culture content. In this way, the individual's identity is mediated through the texts he or she composes by drawing on and appropriating a variety of other resources (see also Williams, 2010, Ch. 3). For example, the photos on a *Facebook* or *MySpace* page of the author with friends and family are read with the images of movie or music stars to create an identity through the juxtaposition of the images. If the images of a female student are accompanied by images of female pop stars or athletes, for example, the celebrity photos can be read as "an extension or projection of their bodies, a desiring or coveting of another's appearance" (Weber & Mitchell, 2008, p. 31). It is not as simple as drawing a line between online and offline identities. Indeed, for many young people, "there is no dichotomy of online and offline, or virtual and real—the digital is so much intertwined into their lives and psyche that the one is entirely enmeshed with the other" (Thomas 2007, p. 163). For students composing identities online, then, there is both the familiar and strange, the embodied and the detached, all of which can create tensions as they struggle to determine how their online texts will be received.

Social Networking Sites and Templates of Identities

It is well accepted in the rhetoric and composition community that both definitions of literacy and performances of identity are complex social phenomena situated in cultural contexts. Those working with online technologies have extended these ideas to the performance of identities on webpages that are instantly accessible to people across town or around the world. The emergence of *MySpace* and *Facebook* has created an explosion in the number of people posting personal webpages. The ease with which the templates of these social networking websites allow individuals to create personal sites means that such expressions of identity have suddenly become available to anyone, not just people who can write HTML code or even use point-and-click web writing software. Although the templates may be criticized for the limitations they place on composing texts (see also Williams, 2010, Ch. 5), there is no doubt that the ease and predictability of the templates have encouraged wider creation and consumption of such webpages with both *MySpace* and *Facebook* claiming users in the multiple millions.

The *MySpace* and *Facebook* pages of many high school and college students include the kinds of material that have regularly shown up on personal webpages in the past, such as photos of friends and family; they remind us how online texts draw from preceding genres such as locker doors or yearbooks or diaries. What is distinctive about the webpages on these social networking sites is how much more material and emphasis there is on popular culture. Most of them have a great deal of popular culture-related content, often comprising more than half the information presented on the page and often numbering between fifty and seventy-five distinct popular culture elements.

The templates that shape *MySpace* and *Facebook* pages raise a chicken-and-egg question about the influence of popular culture in the performance of students' identities online. The templates ask people to think of their identities in terms of popular culture references with the requests for lists of favorite movies, television programs, and books, with the capability to choose a song to play when the page opens, and with the capability to load images and video from other sources. We shouldn't be surprised; that's how people respond to the templates. Still, it is easy to see why these social networking sites set themselves up to emphasize popular culture content if we again think about how popular culture texts serve as the common cultural touchstones by which we first judge other people. If when we initially meet people we often ask about their tastes in movies or music or we scan their bookshelves, it is a natural move by *MySpace* and *Facebook* to replicate such information on their pages. Students such as Sarah talked about using the pages to gather just such information about people before meeting them in person:

> I think you can learn a lot. At least more than you could if I just met you, you know. . . . If you're going to meet someone, if you're going to go on a date, that gets annoying. What books do you like, what movies do you like? What's your favorite quote? That's not stuff that people say anymore, I don't know if they used to but we don't really talk like that. So it's good to already have that information and then if you are going to like meet someone the first time it does start conversations because you already know what type of music you like, I already know what type of movies you like and I can always bring that up and I've done that before. Been like, "Oh, I saw that you like this on *Facebook*, I love that movie."

The popularity of the sites indicates that the decision to construct the templates around popular culture contents resounds with users who are comfortable with this approach. I've yet to see a student's *MySpace* or *Facebook* page that does not have the popular culture lists filled in, though I'm sure they exist. Even when other forms of identification are asked, like political or religious affiliations on *Facebook*, they are not filled in as regularly and, perhaps more significantly, they offer users only a few predetermined choices on drop-down menus rather than the ability to create an individual list. Nor are there options available for other lists that might be used to construct identities, for example, "most important social issues," or "places I have lived" or "childhood illnesses."

In addition, on both social networking sites, lists of popular culture references are linked so that, for example, by clicking on the name of a band on *MySpace*, one can connect to the band's page or, on *Facebook*, to others who have also listed the band. Such linking encourages thinking about popular culture preferences in terms of communities of others who share the same tastes. The capability of online technologies to facilitate the affinity spaces around popular culture texts is a key element of convergence culture that influences the reading of personal pages, as I will illustrate later in the chapter.

What also makes the lists of references on social networking sites different than conversation one might strike up with a new acquaintance is the capability of online technologies to publish the information for a broader audience. This is another instance where media technologies and popular culture practices converge to create new concepts of performing identity. The popular culture content and references on social networking pages are available for others, casual acquaintances, or even sometimes strangers, who encounter it in contexts that perhaps lead to significantly different interpretations than the authors intended. Students creating webpages on social networking spaces do so with the expectation that others will not only visit the page but respond to them and the page's content. Just as they often will respond to the popular culture content they encounter, students expect friends to make judgments and comments about their choice of songs, images, or video or to respond to fan forum ideas or fan fiction stories. The question of how the presence of an audience beyond the local influences how students regard identities on these sites is an important one to consider in thinking about convergence culture, and one that can provoke students' anxieties as I will discuss later. Such performances of identity through popular culture content that reach beyond the local are changing the way students compose and read their identities on such pages.

Reading Friends and Strangers

Ashley's *MySpace* page is a fairly representative example. As is true with many pages, a song plays when her page is opened; her page's song is by pop musician Josh Groban. She has lists of favorite movies (*Pirates of the Caribbean, Star Wars, Madagascar, Dirty Dancing*, etc.), music (Josh Groban, Justin Timberlake, Nickelback, Nichole Norderman, Green Day, etc.), books (the *Harry Potter* series, *The DaVinci Code, the Bible*), and television (*Charmed, Veronica Mars*, etc.). Embedded in the lists are images of some of the films and television series she mentions, such as *Eragon, The Lord of the Rings, Pirates of the Caribbean,* and *Charmed*). The two largest images on the page are under the heading of people she wants to meet. There, you find a large photo of Orlando Bloom reclining on a couch, shirt unbuttoned to the waist, and Johnny Depp in *Pirates of the Caribbean.* In addition, Ashley has downloaded from another site a questionnaire about personal preferences that includes popular culture questions such as her favorite CD or favorite candy bar. The page also includes other images, such as an American flag, and a statement of support for U.S. soldiers; the page's background is an image of an angel with a rosary draped over its shoulders.

Other students' *MySpace* pages have other forms of popular culture content in addition to the kinds on Ashley's page. For example, Mitchell's page includes the results of online personality quizzes he has taken on sites such as *Quizilla.* These quizzes allow him to download the image and description of his results. He has, among others, the results of "What *South Park* Character Are You?" (Kyle), "What *Pirates of the Caribbean* Character Are You?" (Barbossa), and the kind of rock star he is most like (punk rocker). Jenny's *MySpace* page includes downloaded music videos, including the video of Fatboy Slim's "Weapon of Choice," and the video of "The Evolution of the Dance," which became hugely popular on *YouTube.*

I first asked students how they read the *MySpace* and *Facebook* pages of their friends and people they had only just met. Although the responses varied in terms of what students looked at first, they were surprisingly consistent in the way the students interpreted the authors' performances of identity. Shannon, for example, paid particular attention to the song on a person's *MySpace*:

> As for their song, I listen to music a lot so that tells me a lot about them. What kind of song they would like. Maybe more is that it tells me what kind of song they would put up on their page for me to see. Because if it's more of a rap song, then it's not so much for me. You can tell a lot about a person by the song.

Although Jenny also paid attention to the song, she mentioned other items that also helped her interpretation of the page:

> You can tell from their quotes if they have a perverted sense of humor, depending on what their quotes say. Or music-wise you can tell if you like the same genre. If someone has a lot of rap listed, I won't get along with them as well because I'm not the biggest rap person. Rap or country. Usually, I think by figuring out what a person listens to, you can figure out more about them. There are some things you can just tell in an instant. If they list a lot of Disney movies, it's going to be a little weird to talk to them.

Though the popular culture elements that drew students' attention varied, they all mentioned that it had an influence on how they read the page owner's identity. The only other element mentioned by a significant number of the students were personal photographs placed on the page. Popular culture influenced how people read identities on the pages, and also the judgments such readings led them to make about others. As Jenny and Shannon mention in their quotations, their judgments about someone they did not know well could be shaped by the popular culture content included on the page. Some of the students even mentioned the shock of looking at a friend's *MySpace* or *Facebook* page to find popular culture preferences that surprised them or seemed inconsistent with the person they thought they knew. Brianna said:

> I was looking the other day (at a friend's page) and they had Lil' Wayne on there and I was like "Wow, you wouldn't even have thought they liked Lil' Wayne." I was like, "I am so sorry but seriously like, I said look at her!" It was a girl too, she doesn't even look like she like even knows who Lil' Wayne is. It was like her number one favorite artist, she was obsessed with Lil' Wayne, I thought it was so funny.

Another student likened such revelations to "guilty secrets," and Shannon noted that "Some of the people I've known since long before *MySpace* have things on their pages that I can hardly believe and I think 'What is that?' or 'That doesn't make any sense' or 'I don't like that.' I try not to let it make me like them any less, but it makes you think twice about them anyway."

Again, the judgments people make about the popular culture preferences of others are nothing new. We have all been shocked at the revelation that a movie we loved is one a close friend loathed. Yet as I noted previously, in the past, those judgments were made most often in face-to-face interactions, one person at a time and usually only about one form of popular culture at a time. The performance of identity though popular culture forms on *MySpace* and *Facebook* pages, however, happens in a virtual space, to an audience that may or often may not be known to the writer, and offers multiple pieces of popular culture content that are read both quickly and in relation to each other.

James Gee (2004) has noted how interactive popular culture has allowed for the creation of "affinity spaces." These affinity spaces, which Gee argues can be virtual or physical such as websites or fan magazines, bring people together by a shared interest or activity. Affinity spaces allow individuals "to any degree they wish, small or large, affiliate with others to share knowledge and gain knowledge that is distributed and dispersed across many different people, places, Internet sites, and modalities" (p.

73). Interactive popular culture has allowed the creation of multiple affinity spaces for any single popular culture text or interest, such as the television program *Lost,* where those with an interest in the show have the opportunity to engage in fan forums, fan fictions, online games, and so on. These online affinity spaces can easily be accessed and so demand little commitment, though they also often allow levels of commitment that become habitual and defining for the individual. Popular culture content on social networking pages creates small affinity spaces demanding minimal commitment; an image or a song may result in a comment from a visitor to a page but usually little in sustained discussion. Though the image or list of favorite movies may be linked to further content that broadens the affinity space. Even so, the popular culture content on these pages creates opportunities for affinity spaces between the owner of the page and the user that are sustained by the popular culture content, not necessarily by age or gender or educational level (Jenkins, Clinton, Purushotma, Robison, & Weigel, 2006). What is different with these spaces in contrast to a fan forum for a television program is that the popular culture is not the motivation for visiting the page. Yet once visited, the popular culture content mediates the relationship between writer and reader. The identity of the page owner cannot be read without making connections to outside popular culture content.

The Anxiety of Real Audiences

The students' affection for using the images, songs, and templates of social networking pages to make quick judgments about others, including friends, stands in contrast to their awareness that the identities they were creating on *MySpace* or *Facebook* were incomplete and could result in incomplete or inaccurate readings of their identities. Tony, for example, realized that the incomplete representation of identity could be misread by others, particularly those who did know him face to face:

> I would say that my friends are the audience. But I know they're not the only ones who look at it. But on here I guess it's almost a surreal kind of thing. People who are looking at *MySpace* aren't real. It's almost like they don't exist as people, like they're not going to look at my profile page and think that is what they should think about me and think that is me. Which really they probably do. But my chances of knowing who these people are is slim to none so it doesn't really bother me how they view me as a person.

Students like Tony displayed an understanding of the slipperiness of representation that would make any postmodern theorist proud. Tony makes the distinction between the people who might read his page online and the people he would know face to face. In part, this understanding comes from the different perceptions of the audiences of the pages. It also, however, comes from the understanding that the audience in such situations is double, regardless of the website. Although Amy said that she hoped her audience was like her, she had to admit, "I really have no idea . . . I wonder how many people actually come to mine because there's no way to really tell." Students like Tony and Amy understand that while they may be constructing an identity for their friends, the nature of the online text is that it is extended to an audience that is beyond the knowledge and beyond the control of the writer of the page.

The practice of using popular culture images to create an identity or proclaim an affinity extends back as least as far as those decorated school locker interiors many of us remember from our youth. Unlike the locker, however, the webpage is not just seen by friends or even passing acquaintances but by anyone who can access the page. The removal of face-to-face interactions also means that, as I noted previously, identities can be falsified or altered, even on personal web pages. Students displayed an acute awareness that the identity they might be seeing performed on someone's page—particularly someone they didn't know face to face—might very well be constructed in ways the students would find misleading if they knew the person offline. Genevieve's skepticism was typical:

> I think that people put those [lists of popular culture references] down a lot to put forth an image so I don't trust them as much because you can control what's on there. If I knew that I wanted to be in a group with everybody who liked AC/DC, you know if I really liked this group of kids, then I'd put on my *MySpace* page music, AC/DC. So I don't really trust the music, movies, and books because I think a lot of people put down stuff they don't like just to put an image forward.

And Kevin said that the only way to be certain about identity was to limit his online friends to people he already knew: "Anybody can put anything up there and try to portray themselves as something they're not. You have to go onto the pages realizing that." But he said he tried to make his page an accurate portrayal of himself so that "if someone that I don't know well looks at it, it would create an interest in learning more about me, about the real me."

The affinity that those visiting the page feel for different popular culture content may be in conflict from one person to the next. Davies and Merchant (2007) note in their research on blogs that the tensions between known readers and unknown readers often create anxiety for writers and result in surprising and often disruptive responses from readers. Students who had not set their page viewing preferences to private, or limited to friends, quickly realized how they might be read in different and disturbing ways by others online. The realization that others were reading their pages struck some students as if the notes they were passing in school for an audience of friends had suddenly been posted outside the school. Several of the students talked about having had confrontations with their parents over content on their personal pages, particularly while they were in high school. Students with public settings also reported receiving unwelcome and often deeply disturbing messages from strangers, particularly on *MySpace*, at least until they changed their settings. These kinds of messages, particularly for the women, made the kind of detached position that Tony assumed toward his unknown audience much less available to female students. As Ashley said:

> There's kids the age of twelve on there (*MySpace*) and they try to act like they're teenagers. They try to act like they're in their twenties, the way they dress, the way they act, their profiles. And people wonder why these thirty- and forty-year-old psychos who are on there end up finding these girls because they [the girls] don't know better than to not say something.

Even students who had set their preferences to private realized that, while it might make them uncomfortable to think about, they could be read by friends of friends of friends, or people they might only meet through a social networking site, and who would be reading their identities only through their pages.

For some of the students, this raised questions and concerns about their intent in creating their pages and the reality of being read differently than that intent. Brianna pointed out that she had changed the background on her *MySpace* page, even though she had liked the image: "I had Mickey Mouse. I love Mickey Mouse and Mickey Mouse was my background. But I finally changed it because I thought people would think it was really childish." And Jenny said she began to think about the self she was composing as she looked at the music she was listing as her favorites:

> When I fill out my own I try to think, "This is what I do like, this is what I don't like." But when I take a step back from it, I think, "Does that really describe me or not?" It kind of makes you think, "Oh wow these musicians I'm listing have a lot of dark music. Is that really me? I just like the music."

Jenny's thoughtful reflection on how her page is representing a particular identity is indicative of the kind of care many students put into the choices of popular culture content they employ in composing their social networking pages. Though there may be many audiences that students are aware of, it is clear that the primary audience that frames their composing is that of their peers. They want to appear as attractive and "cool" in their online performances of identity for their friends and potential friends as they do in their face-to-face lives (boyd, 2008). Though they may dismiss the pages as frivolous or fun in their initial comments, during the course of an interview, it was not uncommon for students to report spending many hours *tweaking*—a verb that can mean either minor or substantial revisions—their pages and thinking about how these pages and their images, references, and songs will be read by friends, acquaintances, and strangers. Catherine said that when she began to list her popular culture preferences on her pages, it was "really hard for me to sit down and write about myself like that. I remember constructing my list of like favorite music or whatever and I'm sitting here for hours. I have like days of music in my, you know, music library . . . but sitting down actually writing that down was really hard for me to focus on." Angela Thomas (2007) calls this kind of attention and revision of identity online "a close editing of self" (p. 9), and it illustrates how the commonly held belief that social networking pages are composed without thought or even anxiety is about as believable as thinking that university students don't pay attention to which clothes to wear.

Jenny's comment also illustrates the tension a number of the students mentioned about how their pages might be open to multiple readings they did not intend. The source of the anxiety in her comment can be traced in part to issues of competing and conflicting contexts in the use of popular culture content. Although the templates and conventions of the sites guide interpretation, the intertextual connections created through popular culture content can be greatly varied. We often think of popular culture as a set of communal texts with which we are all familiar. While this commonality may have been more accurate in years past with few television networks to choose from, in today's convergence culture of multiple popular culture sources that flow across media and invite participation from audience members, the interpretation of any popular culture text is necessarily more situated and dependent on the specific context. The context of a social networking site personal page, and the juxtaposition of different popular culture content on such a page, creates multiple meanings of the kind that concerned Jenny.

The Multiple Readings of Popular Culture

As I mentioned previously, the popular culture content on individual pages varies widely. What is consistent across student pages, however, is that the popular culture content is almost always displayed without comment or explanation. The writer of the page offers little guidance about the way the various popular culture elements are to be interpreted or why they have been placed on the page. The meaning, then, must be arrived at through the reader's intertextual connections to the popular culture references and the juxtaposition of these popular culture elements on the page.

The question of context is crucial in how popular culture content is written and read on social networking pages. Take, for example, on the *MySpace* pages I described previously, a single image from Ashley's page and Mitchell's page. Ashley has, under the heading of "Who I'd Like To Meet," a photomontage of Johnny Depp in *Pirates of the Caribbean*. On Mitchell's page, he has an image of the character Kyle from the television program *South Park* as the result of an online quiz he took on "What *South Park* Character Are You?" The image has this caption: "You are clever, and often come up with intelligent and funny comebacks to other people's stupid remarks."

Each image exists on the page as one element within the template of the page. Obviously, putting the Depp photos under the heading of who Ashley would like to meet asks us to read them as an object of romantic fantasy, whether humorous or not. It also could indicate a preference for dark-haired men with beards. The image of Kyle and the caption ask us to consider that Mitchell thinks of himself as smart and funny or that he perhaps sees that conception of himself as ironic. It also indicates an interest in animated television programs. What is just as important in how we read the images on the page, however, are our connections to the popular culture content that extend beyond the page. Because these images are adopted from larger popular culture texts, how we respond to them will be influenced by our relationship to the original text, and the original text's position in the larger culture. Thus, highly contextual affinity spaces create contexts for interpretation that may provide one set of meaning for those within those spaces and another for those unfamiliar with the texts.

If we look at an image of a *South Park* figure without a knowledge of the television series, it is just a crudely constructed image of a young boy smiling. Our knowledge of *South Park*, however, can change our reading. If we see *South Park* as juvenile and offensive, our reading will be different than if we think of it as irreverent and creative satire. *South Park* has a reputation in the larger culture beyond that of a simple animated television series. It has been the focus of numerous public debates about offensive material on television and written about in mainstream media many times. At the same time, its popularity can be charted in the T-shirts, posters, and catchphrases from the show that float through the culture disconnected from specific episodes. Consequently, an image from *South Park* can be read as a reference to more than a television program; it becomes instead a synecdoche for a particular popular culture sensibility of subversive, transgressive humor and cultural critique.

The reading of a *South Park* image becomes even more complicated if we know the characters on the show. Kyle is smart and funny, so we might see Mitchell's posting of the image on the page as in some way a sincere reflection of the identity he is constructing. Had the character posted been Eric Cartman, the selfish and bigoted character from the program, we might see it as a more ironic statement. The fact that either character is the result of a "personality quiz" from a page that has countless parodies of such quizzes also would influence our reading. Such quizzes, on everything from favorite ice cream flavor and favorite movie monster to which television characters people resemble are hugely popular on *MySpace* and *Facebook*.

Similarly, Ashley's image of Johnny Depp is read not only as an image of an attractive young man. Our reading of the image will also depend on whether we have seen the movie from which it was taken and how we felt about the film, as well as our knowledge of other Depp films and even our knowledge of his public life as a celebrity. How differently might an image from Depp's film *Ed Wood*, about the cross-dressing cult film director, be read on the page? Even with the image on Ashley's page, do we assume that Ashley is aware of Depp's roles in other films when she includes it, or is it his image in only one film that appeals to her?

Convergence culture has allowed individuals to use popular culture content to compose identities on social networking sites with unprecedented ease. Students have taken advantage of this opportunity to use such content to create texts that they feel represent themselves in some specific way because they feel they can count on readers understanding the meaning of the popular culture references. They count on readers of their pages sharing affinity spaces and understanding which references should be read seriously or ironically. Yet because popular culture texts have meaning outside of a personal page, the way photos of family or friends do not, the intertextual layers of meaning in popular culture texts can undermine or at least be read far differently than the writer of the page intended. A few students noted an awareness of how intertextual connections of popular culture content opened up interpretations for readers. Genevieve said, "If you don't write something in the 'About Me' section, if you put up a bunch of pictures (of celebrities) instead, then it's like you're letting people draw conclusions for themselves." But more of them said they would assume their audience understood the meaning behind the content. This is but one way the changes in technology that allow media convergence have altered the relationships of audience members to each other. A member of the *South Park* audience, for example, now has ways to perform his or her identity to other members of the audience by using images from the show in ways that may or may not be dialogic but certainly influence interpretations of identity.

The use of popular culture content and references to compose an identity online inevitably raises complicated questions about the role of consumer culture in the process. Popular culture content is also consumer culture content. After all, regardless of their artistic merits, movies are made to put paying customers in the seats, television programs are meant to keep eyeballs occupied until the commercials come on, computer games are made to be bought or rented. And for all the discussion of the democratic and liberatory possibilities of the internet, it has also quickly become a consumer culture machine. From the viewpoint of the producers of popular culture, convergence culture offers the opportunity for greater marketing and greater profits. Students now in adolescence may have been on popular culture websites such as *Pokemon-* or *Harry Potter*-related sites—designed as part of the marketing apparatus for the films, books, and other materials—since they were young children (Mitchell & Reid-Walsh, 2002).

It is perhaps a truism that consumers of popular culture are also consumed by it, but certainly what happens when students use popular culture content to define and perform identities reflects this idea. As students use popular culture to compose identities, they place themselves in the service of the consumer demands of that culture. Every movie star, every CD or book cover, every list of favorite television programs, every song that starts playing when a *MySpace* page opens is not only an illustration of preferences but is also an advertisement for the further consumptions of the popular culture. Just like young people wearing T-shirts sporting corporate logos, personal pages on social networking sites turn individuals into billboards. As personal pages also function as advertisements, they reproduce and reinforce the ideology of material gain that accompanies consumer culture. The choices that students make in determining what images or songs to put on their pages are not only a result of aesthetic or personal preferences but are influenced by the ideology perpetuated by consumer culture. For example, a person putting an image of a *Star Wars* character on a page may be in part responding to narrative and character but has also no doubt been influenced by the marketing machine that has made *Star Wars* a ubiquitous brand. No one would deny that consumer culture is a relentless force in affecting the fashions and tastes of young people—or all people. While we should resist seeing the power of consumer culture as inescapable for young people, we also must realize that if identity is embedded in consumer culture in our daily lives, then it is also a present and substantial force in popular culture and online identity. In the same way that a student will dress or listen to music in part because marketers have succeeded in making it cool or desirable, the same consumer culture forces will influence which images, sound, and video students put on a personal page.

A further wrinkle in terms of consumer culture is the way in which audience members have become the content providers in participatory popular culture. On the one hand, individuals in the audience now have the opportunity to respond to programs, talk with other fans, and create new content with sampled material on personal pages. At the same time, however, by posting this material, the audience is providing the content that makes profit for the websites. If people didn't have personal pages on *Facebook* and *MySpace*, then those sites could not make money from the advertising they sell. Yet the people posting on personal pages or blogs or fan forums are not receiving compensation for their work, even as some of these sites become profitable enough to be purchased by other corporations. (The purchase of such sites has not been without controversy, as several students said they had closed their *MySpace* pages once the site was sold to Rupert Murdoch's News Corp. because they opposed his conservative political positions.) This is another way that the consumers of popular culture become the consumed in convergence culture.

When I raised the question of consumer culture with students, either as an influence on how they constructed their pages or in terms of the content they provided for sites, most of them brushed off the question. Either they hadn't thought about it or they did not believe that it was relevant to them. The only comments were along the lines of Greg's, who said, "I don't care if they make money off of it. I mean, that's capitalism. But it's not going to matter about what I do with my page." The lack of interest in questions of consumer culture is not surprising. Students are not encouraged either in school or at home to look critically at the mechanisms and ideology of consumer culture. What's more, in a culture such as the United States, where the mythology of individual agency is powerful, students resist the idea that their choices might be in any way subject to social forces. Even when they express skepticism or cynicism about advertising, for example, their comments are usually couched in terms of how it might manipulate others but that they would never fall prey to it themselves.

Bonding the Self with Social Groups

The question of authorial intention in creating social networking personal pages is, of course, a slippery one. Even for the students I spoke with, different elements on the page reflected different levels of interest. Tony had many images of college and professional sports logos and athletes on his page and talked at length about how central his interest in sports was to his life. Also on his page, however, was a favorite *South Park* character that he said he had included on a whim. "I have my favorite *South Park* character, even though I've probably only watched *South Park* about four times. But I saw a friend had one up on his page and I thought it was really funny." There was nothing on the page to indicate these differences, however, so a reader of the page might see the *South Park* reference as an important part of the representation of his identity.

It is important to understand that students often see these pages as created for friends, as online extensions of face-to-face social relationships. This is reflected in the personal photos, quotations, and jokes from friends posted on the pages. Indeed, one common reason given for creating a personal page is what the author's friends have done (boyd, 2008). The pages not only allow friends to post messages, either privately or on the public page, or share photos or other content, they allow users to form social groups. The groups cover interests including politics, sports, and local social organizations, or just playful ideas ("Because I Am Senior, That's Why!" or "Treehouse Lovers"). Popular culture, again, provides the focal point for many of these groups. Some are organized around a specific movie or show while others focus more on a genre of music or film. Each group then has a page where comments, images, videos, and so on can be posted. Some groups, particularly the sillier ones, tend to be fairly short-lived fads. But other groups, including some of the popular culture groups that have a broader focus, have longer life spans. How involved students were with groups varied. Some belonged to few or none while others belong to fifty or more.

The *Facebook* popular culture groups Pat belonged to included "Dane Cook is Awesome" and "I Understand Monty Python Jokes." He said, "I don't go to the groups all the time but every now and then, just for fun. And sometimes I find out something I didn't know or I'm reminded of something. But mostly I just see who is there." For other students, popular culture groups occasionally provided affinity spaces through which to gain information, though most students—if they talked about making use of the collective intelligence of online communities—talked of doing so through fan forums and lists. In general, however, the participation students reported in the popular culture groups on *MySpace* and *Facebook* was much more about belonging and community. Like Pat, students went to groups to see who else was there. Or, perhaps even more tellingly, a number of students said they rarely visited popular culture groups once they had joined them. It was the joining, the declaration of an affiliation to the group that would be a visible link on the personal page, that motivated most students' choices to join. Once again, the performance of identity through proclaiming group affiliations enters into how students read and write these personal pages. As boyd (2008) notes, "For better or worse, people judge others based on their associations: group identities form around and are reinforced by the collective tastes and attitudes of those who identify with the group. Online, this cue is quite helpful in enabling people to find their bearings" (p. 130). Angela said, "If I don't know the person I scan their groups. I can sometimes get more than a lot of other things about them through their groups. I can even get a sense of humor." Like all popular culture statements of affiliation, identity with the community is created both through inclusion and exclusion. By stating which groups a person has joined, and which a person has not, students add important elements to their pages. Does the person have a lot of groups that seem like fads, one-time groups that may soon fade such as "Paris Hilton for President"? Or are the groups more obscure, making statements of hipness and cool through their esoteric and limited appeal?

As group membership indicates, popular culture content is often an extension of social relationships. An image from a movie may reflect a shared interest in that film with a particular group of friends who may have watched the movie together. A catchphrase from a television series may reflect a social discourse specific to one group of friends who use that catchphrase as part of sharing a particular affinity space. Such a catchphrase is an extension of daily activities used to reinforce social bonds.

But a person with a social networking page is connected to multiple social groups whose interests, and relationships to the multiple popular culture texts on a page, overlap and conflict with each other. These overlapping affinity spaces mean that some readers of the page may be drawn to certain images or videos or songs and simultaneously puzzled or even disconcerted by others. This is why even close friends when encountering the multiple popular culture texts on a page can respond with surprise and consternation about the identity represented.

One quick example of how the slippage between daily social life and the content of social networking pages can lead to misreadings comes from Jenny's *Facebook* page. She has, among her quotations, one from the film *Forrest Gump*. When I first read the quotation, "Run, Forrest, Run!" I assumed she was a fan of the film and was drawn to the quotation because of the way, in the film, it represents the title character's quest for independence and dignity. I also assumed she enjoyed the film and that led me to assumptions about the kinds of movies she liked and what that indicated about her personality. When she talked about the quotation, however, she said, "I'm on the rugby team and my nickname is 'Forrest.' I am supposed to run, apparently, so they nicknamed me 'Forrest' and yell that at me when we play." Clearly, her teammates visiting her page would understand the reference and appreciate her attempt to reinforce her bonds with them. For others reading the page, however, the social context is lost and replaced with the context of the original popular culture text and its meaning in the larger culture. Such misreadings, several students said, also resulted in parents not understanding popular culture references or whether such references were meant ironically, and responding with concern or puzzlement.

The result of the multiple popular culture references or content on a page is more than the creation of multiple and overlapping affinity spaces where one person might like *Pirates of the Caribbean* while another likes *Charmed*. Obviously, these multiple images, videos, songs, and lists do not exist in isolation but are regarded in juxtaposition to each other. On Ashley's page, for example, we do not see Johnny Depp without also seeing images of Orlando Bloom, *Eragon*, *The Lord of the Rings*, *Pirates of the Caribbean*, *Charmed*, the American flag, and an angel with a rosary draped over its shoulders. This collage of images is also juxtaposed with lists of favorite songs and movies and a downloaded song. Some of the juxtapositions may seem complementary, such as the image of Bloom and an image from *The Lord of the Rings* films in which he acted. Other images, depending on our readings, may seem contradictory—Depp as a critic of U.S. foreign policy next to the U.S. flag—or puzzling—the angel as the background to all the images. For the writer of the page, these multiple images may seem like different aspects of identity or may only represent different motivations at different moments (see also Williams, 2010, Ch. 3). Either way, however, the juxtaposition of disparate popular culture elements shifts the meaning of each as it arranged with the next.

Culture and Identity on Personal Pages

Finally, a discussion of identity performance would be incomplete without a consideration of how these pages are composed and read in terms of larger identity constructions such as gender, sexual orientation, race, and social class. Popular culture preferences often reflect cultural identities. Say *country music* and the default audience is expected to be European American and rural; say *hip hop* and the default audience is expected to be more urban and African American. A list of romantic comedies would be more likely to indicate a woman's page and a list of crude sex comedies would indicate a man's. Clearly, there are exceptions to all of these statements—and the exceptions students highlight raise interesting questions—but the reality, supported by years of research too lengthy to list, is that popular culture is often a vehicle through which people both perform identities and make judgments about others in terms of these larger identity characteristics. If students use popular culture content and references to compose identities on their personal pages, then they are also making statements about how they position themselves in terms of social identities. When Sandy said about her *MySpace* pages that "Here's my music. See, I like anything but rap. (She reads a label on her page) 'Rap Stands for Retards Attempting Poetry' Yes, I found it clever." Although Sandy seemed slightly embarrassed at showing me the language on her page, her statement about rap also helps her perform her identity as a white student from a small rural community (for more on the complex influence of culture on performances of identity see Williams, 2010, Chs. 6 and 7).

Students' identities on their personal pages are, of course, first determined from the photos at the top of their pages. On most pages, the age, sex, and race of an individual are quickly apparent. What can be discerned from the photos is fairly limited, however, leaving the popular culture content to complete the representations of identity. More often than not, the representations reflect what would be considered fairly conventional identity constructions. For example, men's pages tend to have more action and horror movies, such as *300* or *Dawn of the Dead*. Women's pages had more comedies and romantic dramas such as *The Notebook* or *The Sisterhood of the Traveling Pants*. Of course, not all references are as revealing of identity. Still, in general, if you removed the name and personal photos from most personal pages on social networking sites, you could use the popular culture content and references to make a fairly accurate determination of at least the age, sex, race or ethnicity, social class, and nationality of the author.

When I asked students how they thought their pages represented their identities, most of them deflected the question by saying they did not think about such issues when composing their pages or, even more often, saying their pages represented only themselves, not any larger cultural identities. This is not surprising, particularly in the United States, where, again, the dominant mythology is that individual agency is unfettered by cultural or social forces of any kind. The students I talked with resisted the idea that their ways of representing themselves might be influenced by culture just as they resist such conversations in the classroom, and indeed just as the larger public resists such conversations. The exception to this position from students was when they felt they had put something on their page that they felt would defy the dominant cultural expectations. Sometimes such moves were meant to be rebellious. Natalie, who mixed goth images with fairies on her page, said, "I would never want people to think that I'm too girly-girl. I want to keep them guessing." Other students pointed out references or material they felt was inconsistent with their cultural identities to explain the incongruities. Greg, for example, had *Pride and Prejudice* listed under his favorite movies and pointed to it saying, "That's just on there because it's my girlfriend's favorite movie."

The students I talked with were more willing to consider cultural identities when reading the pages of others, however. Catherine said that she sometimes looks at pages with "lots of sports stuff or action movies all over it and I'm like 'God, what a guy page. Dial it back a notch, will you?.'" Or Genevieve noted that how pages are read could be dependent on gender: "You know, if I go and see a bunch of pictures of beautiful women and Britney Spears on some girl's page, I think that she has self-image problems. And then again maybe if a male would look at the same page, he would say she really idolizes beauty, you know she wants to be beautiful." As so often happens, the students were willing to see culture as an influence on their peers, even as they denied its possible effect on them. Given the judgments that students make about the pages they read, and given the ways that identity influences popular culture tastes and affinities, it is easy to see that students use identity characteristics to make decisions about the pages they visit and the ways they evaluate the authors of those pages.

Another intriguing issue of popular culture and identity that social networking sites raise is the ways in which different sites appeal to different groups of students. Among the university students I spoke to, there was a common narrative in which they discussed having had *MySpace* pages in high school but having migrated to *Facebook* once they entered university. Amy said, "*MySpace* is getting more and more ridiculous. So *Facebook* is more aimed toward like the college audience and people that are of college age at least." Francesca had a similar response: "I got it (a *MySpace* page) my sophomore year (of high school) but I don't get on it. It's just, I don't know, it's silly. It's more like stupid junk stuff all the time than anyone actually having a conversation with anyone." Over and over again, students described *Facebook* as more serious, more mature, or cleaner and easier to use. They also talked about preferring the more exclusive nature of *Facebook*, which at the time was limited to university and high school students, to the more open environment of *MySpace*. This is interesting in light of boyd's (2008) research that indicates *MySpace* memberships cut across economic, gender, and racial lines. What the student response may reinforce is boyd's (2007) speculation that *Facebook* has become identified with more affluent, college-bound students while *MySpace* is seen by these students as the province of a younger, more marginalized, and less affluent population. Not only are different populations drawn to the different sites, but boyd points out that while *MySpace* has flashy imagery more reminiscent of Las Vegas, *Facebook* cultivates a clean and modern look more akin to websites and publications that target affluent audiences. Of course, it is difficult to raise the possibility to students that their choices may be grounded in class status and aspirations because, again, they dislike thinking that their choices are influenced by culture or that the United States as a society has powerful class divisions. Such responses are not limited to students, as can be seen when boyd's blog entry on this subject, which was careful and nuanced as a piece of initial theorizing on the subject, was subjected to fierce and angry responses from readers that revealed how sensitive social class is as a subject.

Conclusion

Online media technologies have allowed students to construct new performances of identity and yet also reinforce existing social identities from their face-to-face relationships with all the excitement—and anxiety—that accompany such activities. Online media have also allowed, and encouraged, students to appropriate and reuse popular culture content and references as resources for composing and revising their identities on a daily basis. Students' use of popular culture to compose identities online is not a haphazard event but instead is a conscious process of self-inquiry and self-editing (Thomas, 2007; Stern, 2008) and as considered and reflected upon as what clothes to wear and which group to sit with at lunch.

The use of collected elements to create a collage of meaning has been interrogated in different settings as a move characteristic of authorship in a postmodern culture. The use of unexpected juxtapositions and associative meanings composed from appropriated texts has been addressed in such contexts as the creation of zines (Knobel & Lankshear, 2004), memes (Knobel & Lankshear, 2007), webpages (Alexander, 2006), and new video (Stephens, 1998). According to Stephens, new identities can be created not only through the linear exposition of print texts but also "through the deft juxtaposition of carefully selected aspects of surfaces" (p. 217). Indeed, the students I spoke with were comfortable with and confident about the creation of identities through the composition of fragmented, associative collages of popular culture texts. Immersion in popular culture, as discourse, as epistemology, as a text for creating identity is the everyday life of our students and ourselves. Added to the already pervasive nature of popular culture are the technological capabilities of online communication that have not only made easier this kind of appropriation of and composition with popular culture texts but have often made the cutting, pasting, and creating with such texts easier and faster than composing with print (Lewis, 2007). It would, indeed, be more remarkable if students bypassed popular culture as a means of composing personal pages than that it has become the foundation for such performances of identity.

Note

* This chapter was originally published as: Williams, B. (2010). Which *South Park* character are you? Popular culture and online performances of identity. *Shimmering Literacies: Popular Culture and Reading and Writing Online* (pp. 91–120). New York: Peter Lang.

References

Alexander, J. (2006). *Digital youth: Emerging literacies on the world wide web*. Cresskill, NJ: Hampton Press.

Barton, D., & Hamilton, M. (1998). *Local literacies: Reading and writing in one community*. London: Routledge.

Bourdieu, P. (1984). *Distinction: A social critique of the judgement of taste*. Trans. R. Nice. Cambridge, MA: Harvard University Press.

boyd, d. (2007). Viewing American class divisions through Facebook and MySpace. Apophenia blog essay. Retrieved January 26, 2009, from: http://www.danah.org/papers/essays/ClassDivisions.html

boyd, d. (2008). Why youth (heart) social network sites: The role of networked publics in teenage social life. In *Youth, identity, and digital media*. (pp. 119–142). Cambridge, MA: The MIT Press.

Davies, J., & Merchant, G. (2007). Looking from the inside out: Academic blogging as new literacy. In M. Knobel and C. Lankshear (Eds.), *A new literacies sampler* (pp. 167–198). New York: Peter Lang.

de Pourbaix, R. (2001). Emergent literacy practices in an electronic community. In D. Barton, M. Hamilton and R. Ivani (Eds.), *Situated literacies: Reading and writing in context* (pp. 125–147). London: Routledge.

Gee, J.P. (1990). *Social linguistics and literacies—Ideology in discourse.* London: Falmer.

Gee, J.P. (2004). *Situated language and learning: A critique of traditional schooling.* London: Routledge.

Gregory, E., & Williams, A. (2000). *City literacies: Learning to read across generations and cultures.* London: Routledge.

Heath, S.B. (1983). *Ways with words: Language, life, and work in communities and classrooms.* Cambridge: Cambridge University Press.

Jenkins, H. (1992). *Textual poachers: Television fans and participatory culture.* London: Routledge.

Jenkins, H. (2006a). *Convergence culture: Where old and new media collide.* New York: New York University Press.

Jenkins, H., Clinton, K., Purushotma, R., Robison, A., & Weigel, M. (2006). *Confronting the challenges of participatory culture: Media education for the 21st century.* Chicago: The John D. and Catherine T. MacArthur Foundation.

Knobel, M., & Lankshear, C. (2004). Cut, paste, publish: The production and consumption of zines. In D. Alvermann (Ed.), *Adolescents and literacies in a digital world* (pp. 19–39), New York: Peter Lang.

Knobel, M., & Lankshear, C. (2007). Online memes, affinities, and cultural production. In M. Knobel and C. Lankshear (Eds.), *A new literacies sampler* (pp. 199–228). London: Peter Lang.

Lewis, C. (2007). Sampling "the new" in new literacies. In M. Knobel and C. Lankshear (Eds.), *The new literacies sampler* (pp. 1–24). New York: Peter Lang.

Meyrowitz, J. (1985). *No sense of place.* New York: Oxford University Press.

Mitchell, C., & Reid-Walsh, J. (2002). *Researching children's popular culture: The cultural spaces of childhood.* London: Routledge.

Newkirk, T. (1997). *The performance of self in student writing.* Portsmouth, NH: Boynton/Cook Publishers: Heinemann.

Pandey, I. (2006). *Imagined nations, re-imagined roles: Literacy practices of South Asian immigrants.* University of Louisville, Louisville, KY.

Steiner, P. (1993). On the internet, nobody knows you're a dog. *New Yorker,* July 5, 1993, 61.

Stephens, M. (1998). *The rise of the image, the fall of the word.* Oxford: Oxford University Press.

Stern, S. (2008). Producing sites, exploring identities: Youth online authorship. In D. Buckingham (Ed.), *Youth, identity, and digital media* (pp. 95–117). Cambridge, MA: The MIT Press.

Street, B. V. (1995). *Social literacies: Critical approaches to literacy in development, ethnography, and education.* London: Longman.

Thomas, A. (2007). *Youth online: Identity and literacy in the digital age.* New York: Peter Lang.

Weber, S., & Mitchell, C. (2008). Imaging, keyboarding, and posting identities: Young people and new media technologies. In D. Buckingham (Ed.), *Youth, identity, and digital media,* (pp. 25–47). Cambridge, MA: The MIT Press.

Williams, B. (2010). *Shimmering literacies: Popular culture and reading and writing online.* New York: Peter Lang.

PART 5

Researcher Perspectives on New Literacies and Learning

CHAPTER SIXTEEN

Learning about Learning from a Video Game

JAMES PAUL GEE

This chapter develops the argument that computer and video games have a great deal to teach us about how to facilitate learning, even in domains outside games. Good computer and video games are complex, challenging, and long; they can take 50 or more hours to finish. If a game cannot be learned well, then it will fail to sell well, and the company that makes it is in danger of going broke. Shortening and dumbing games down is not an option, since most avid players don't want short or easy games. Thus, if only to sell well, good games have to incorporate good learning principles in virtue of which they get themselves well learned. Game designers build on each other's successes and, in a sort of Darwinian process, good games come to reflect better and better learning principles.

The learning principles that good games incorporate are by no means unknown to researchers in the learning sciences. In fact, current research on learning supports the sorts of learning principles that good games use, though these principles are often exemplified in games in particularly striking ways (for a survey and citations to the literature, see Gee, 2003). However, many of these principles are much better reflected in good games than they are in today's schools, where we also ask young people to learn complex and challenging things. With the current return in our schools to skill-and-drill and curricula driven by standardized tests, good learning principles have, more and more, been left on the cognitive scientist's laboratory bench and, I will argue, inside good computer and video games.

Game design involves modeling human interactions with and within complex virtual worlds, including learning processes as part and parcel of these interactions. This is, in fact, not unlike design research in educational psychology where researchers model new forms of interaction connected to learning in classrooms (complex worlds, indeed), study such interactions to better understand how and why they lead to deep learning, and then ultimately disseminate them across a great many classrooms (see, for example, the papers in Kelly, 2003).

There are many different types of computer and video games, such as shooters (e.g., *Deus Ex, Return to Castle Wolfenstein, Unreal II: The Awakening*), squad-based shooters (e.g., *Tom Clancy's Ghost Recon, Operation Flashpoint: Cold War Crisis*), adventure games (e.g., *The Longest Journey, Siberia*), simulations (e.g., *The Sims, SimCity 4, Black and White*), role-playing games (e.g., *Baldur's Gate II: Shadows of Amn, The Elder Scrolls III: Morrowind, Star Wars: Knights of the Old Republic*), real-time strategy games (e.g., *Age of Empires, Age of Mythology, Rise of Nations*), action/arcade games (e.g., *Sonic Adventure 2 Battle, Super Smash Brothers, Sly Cooper and Thievius Raccoonus*), and a good number of other types.

This paper discusses one real-time strategy game, namely *Rise of Nations*. Hereafter I will refer to real-time strategy games as "RTS games" and to *Rise of Nations* as "*RoN.*" RTS games are among the most complex and demanding of computer and video games. In such games, players play a civilization of their choosing, a civilization for which they must make a myriad of decisions. They send their citizens out to gather resources (e.g., food, wood, minerals, gold, etc.) and use these resources to build domestic and military buildings and engage in various forms of research. In these buildings, they can train soldiers and other sorts of people (e.g., leaders, priests, scientists, and/or professors), as well as build military and other sorts of apparatus. As they gather and build, they can advance to different ages, allowing their civilization to achieve higher levels of complexity and sophistication. All the while they must go to war against or engage in diplomacy with other civilizations.

All of this is done in real time. While the player builds up his civilization, other players (or the computer representing other players) are building up theirs as well. Players must decide when to attack or engage in diplomacy. Victory may come to the swift, that is, to those who attack early (a strategy called "rushing"), or to those who wait and patiently build up (a strategy called "turtling").

RoN is one of the best RTS games ever made (along with such excellent games as *Civilization III, StarCraft, WarCraft III: Reign of Chaos*, and *Age of Mythology*). *RoN* allows the player to play one of 18 civilizations (e.g., Aztecs, Bantu, British, Chinese, Egyptians, Mayan, Nubians, Russians, Spanish, etc.), each with different advantages and disadvantages. The player can play against one to seven opponents (other real people or the computer playing other civilizations). Players can move through eight ages from the Ancient Age to the Information Age through various intervening ages such as the Medieval Age, the Gunpowder Age, and the Enlightenment Age. Like all RTS games, *RoN* involves players learning well over a hundred different commands, each connected to decisions that need to be made, as they move through a myriad of different menus (there are 102 commands on the abridged list that comes printed on a small sheet enclosed with the game). Furthermore, players must operate at top speed if they are to keep up with skilled opponents who are building up as they are. *RoN* involves a great deal of micromanagement and decision making under time pressure.

This chapter is based on an analysis of my own learning and personal interactions with the game as a game player. Learning differs from individual to individual, so we need to base our discussions of learning around actual cases of actual people learning. This is not to say, however, that no generality exists here. How any one of us learns throws light, both by comparison and contrast, on how others learn. Learning is not infinitely variable, and there are patterns and principles to be discovered, patterns and principles that ultimately constitute a theory of learning. Indeed, what I am offering here is a case study meant to offer suggestions for a theory of how deep learning works (see, also, Barsalou, 1999a, b; diSessa, 2000; Glenberg, 1997; Glenberg & Robertson, 1999). In the end, I hope to convince you that today's young people often see deeper and better forms of learning going on in the games they play than in the schools they attend.

Though some of the information below is personal, I intend and hope readers will think about the comparisons and contrasts of my learning experience with *RoN* to the sorts of learning that go on in schools. Ironically, perhaps, a baby-boomer trying to learn a modern computer or video game is not, in some respects, unlike a child in school trying to learn science or math. Both parties are being asked to learn something new and, in some respects, alien to their taken-for-granted ways of thinking.

Preparation for Learning: Before *RoN*

By the time I started up *RoN* I had played lots of computer and video games. They had taught me new ways of learning and new things about myself as a learner (Gee, 2003). However, I had not had good experiences with RTS games. I felt overwhelmed by their many details and by the pressure of competing in real time. I had watched my twin brother play RTS games at a high level and was amazed by the number of details he had mastered and the speed with which he had acted and thought in the games. I had watched my seven-year-old play the wonderful *Age of Mythology* and was stunned that he and his friends could play such a complicated game so well. Far from giving me confidence these experiences just made me think that I was not suited for the micromanagement and on-the-spot decision-making RTS games demand. In regard to RTS games, I was an "at risk" learner, at risk for failing to be able to learn and enjoy these sorts of games.

Though timid about RTS games, when *WarCraft III* came out, I tried it, prodded by my brother who loved the game. I made some progress in the single-player campaign, but eventually found the game "too hard." We should pause a moment, though, at this phrase "too hard." *WarCraft III* is a superbly designed game. In fact, it is well designed to get itself learned. So when I say it was "too hard," what I really mean is that I failed to engage with it in a way that fully recruited its solid design and learning principles. Good games are never really "too hard." They fail, for some players, either because their designers did not use good learning principles or because players have, for one reason or another, failed to engage the good learning principles that are built into the games.

So something has to come even before good learning principles. What has to come before is *motivation for an extended engagement* with the game. Without a commitment to an extended engagement no deep learning of a complex domain can happen (diSessa, 2000). So what made me motivated to offer such extended engagement to *RoN* and not earlier to *WarCraft III*? Well, as good as *WarCraft III* is, *RoN* is yet better at allowing newcomers to learn it. But, more importantly, and ironically, perhaps, my "failure" at *WarCraft III* motivated me to try *RoN*. I had liked *WarCraft III*. It had made me feel that RTS games were important and worth playing. Though I had had limited success with the game, I had had some small success that made me feel that at another time and place, perhaps, I would do better. It had led me to read about RTS games and reflect on them. *WarCraft III*, it turned out— though I realized this fully only when I started *RoN*—had *prepared me for future learning* (Bransford & Schwartz, 1999) of RTS games. When I started *RoN*, I realized that I already knew something, somewhat more than I had thought. I felt I had a small foot up.

In a school setting, my experience with *WarCraft III* would simply have been seen as a failure as I received my low or failing grade. In reality, it was not a failure, but an important precursor for later learning. My experience with *WarCraft III* is what I will call, following the work of Stan Goto (2003), a "horizontal" learning experience. "Vertical" learning experiences are cases where a learner makes lots of incremental progress on a scale from low skills to high skills, as if moving up a ladder. "Horizontal" learning experiences are experiences where one does not make a lot of progress up the ladder of skills, but stays on the initial rungs awhile, exploring them and getting to know what some of the rungs are and what the ladder looks like. Horizontal experiences look like mucking around, but they are really ways of getting your feet wet, getting used to the water, and getting ready, eventually, to jump in and go swimming. They may, in one form or another, be essential to learning, or, at least, essential for learners who are "at risk."

So, is there a contradiction in saying that when I started *RoN* I was still an "at risk" learner, but that my experiences with *WarCraft III* were important preparation for future learning? No. All that my being "at risk" meant, in the end, was that if *RoN* had failed to reward my preparation for future learning (the future was here with *RoN*) or had been a bad learning experience—a real failure—then I may have given up on RTS games forever, assuming I was too "dumb" to learn them. This is all "at risk" needs to mean in schools, too, though there it often means giving "at risk" learners a special dumbed-down curriculum meant to catch them up on "basic skills," a curriculum that all too often is a bad learning experience for these students.

Computer and video games have a built in advantage in the creation of motivation for an extended engagement. Human beings feel that their bodies and minds extend, in a rather intimate way, to the area around them over which they have direct control, usually a fairly small area (Clark, 2003). Thus, as I type, I feel that my keyboard and mouse seem almost like extensions of my fingers, just as blind people often feel that their cane is an extension of their hand. The space closely around my body seems to be connected to it in such a way that I can feel that it is being "invaded" by others.

When humans can manipulate something at a distance, for example controlling with a keyboard a far-away robot seen on a screen, they get an uncanny feeling that their minds and bodies have been vastly extended (Clark, 2003; Goldberg, 2001). When people are playing a computer or video game they are manipulating a character (or many different things in a RTS game) at a distance in a very fine-grained way—in this case a virtual distance. They feel that their minds and bodies have been extended into this virtual world. This process appears to allow players to identify powerfully with the virtual character or characters they are playing in a game and to become strongly motivated to commit themselves to the virtual world the game is creating with their help.

When students are learning a content area in school—such as some area of science—this domain could be seen as a special world of its own, the world of doing science in a certain way and acting with certain values. Students could be encouraged to take on identities as scientists of a certain sort, to see and think about themselves and their taken-for-granted everyday world in new ways. In this case, school would be functioning more like a good game than traditional schooling, which stresses knowledge apart from action and identity.

RoN's Tutorials: Fish Tanks

Let's begin to explore what makes *RoN* a good learning engine. When a player starts *RoN*, the designers immediately have two problems. First, learners are all different and the designers don't know what each one already knows, nor what their favored style of learning will be. Second, learners don't necessarily themselves know how much they do or do not already know and what their best style of learning will be in a given situation. Schools tend to handle these problems by assessing the learner and then deciding for the learner how these problems ought to be dealt with. *RoN*, like many other good games, solves the problem by letting learners assess themselves and learn things about what they do and do not know and what style of learning suits them here and now. Learners then decide for themselves how they want to proceed. Of course, *RoN* is designed to assist learners in this task; they are not left solely to their own devices. By the time you have interacted with *RoN*'s tutorials and skill tests and played your first few real games, you know a good deal about yourself as a learner, in general, and a learner of RTS games, in particular. (In this chapter the games called "Quick Battles" in *RoN* are what I refer to as the "real" game; a game called "Conquer the World" is also part of *RoN*, but I do not discuss that game in this chapter. Conquer the World is composed of Quick Battles and other elements.)

When *RoN* starts, you see a screen with the following choices (the numbers on the right are dates, ranging from 60 AD to 1940):

Tutorial		
Learn to Play	Quick Start	
Boadicia	Beginning Player	60
Alfred the Great	Beginning Player	878
The 100 Years War	Experienced Real-Time Strategy Player	1337
Henry VIII	Experienced Real-Time Strategy Player	1513
Battle of Britain	Advanced Topics	1940

Right away the learner sees choices: jump right in (Quick Start), learn step-by-step (moving from beginning player to experienced player to advanced topics), start with the experienced or advanced topics (thereby testing one's own assumptions about one's previous knowledge), or skip the tutorials altogether. Choice is built in from the beginning. Notice, too, there is no "remedial" in this learning world. You begin where you begin and move to advanced when you move there. None of this is timed. There are no invidious judgments based on one's previous "failures."

When the learner places the mouse on each choice above, a box is displayed at the bottom of the screen detailing just what historical event each choice will deal with and what skills the learner will learn by making that choice. Table 16.1 (p. 310) shows each choice and what is displayed in the box when the learner places the mouse over that choice:

All is not as it at first seems here, though. What you see in the boxes are by no means all or even the majority of the skills you need to play *RoN* well. They are the "basic skills" you need to play the game, but "basic" in a special sense: they are the skills that allow you to actually start playing and learning from playing. I will point out below that the designers of *RoN* don't just take it for granted that players will be able to move from the basic skills in the tutorials to learning by playing. Once the player actually starts the "real" game, they ensure that this transition—from basic skill learning to learning by playing—will happen. But before I tell you how they do this (it's all about players being able to customize the game to their own desires and goals), let me finish my discussion of the tutorials.

If we look back at the terms "experienced real-time strategy player" and "advanced topics" in Table 16.1 we see something interesting. "Experienced" and "advanced" mean something quite different here than they do in places like schools. The skills taught in the tutorials, as we have said, are "basic" (in the sense defined). They are not the deeper skills required to play *RoN* or any other RTS game well, skills like time management, speed, micro-managing many details at once, and strategic thinking. So it may seem odd that terms like "experienced" and "advanced" are used. But "experienced" and

Table 16.1: Tutorial Screens

Learn to Play	Quick Start	
Quick Learn Learn-As-You-Play Introduction • One-on-one battle • Hints and suggestions as you play		
Boadicia	**Beginning Player**	60
Boadicia—Tutorial 2 Help a queen fight off the Romans to reclaim her nation • unit selection • movement • map scrolling • help text • basic combat		
Alfred the Great	**Beginning Player**	878
Alfred the Great—Tutorial 3 Turn back the raging Viking hoard • Constructing and using buildings • Training units • Minimap		
The 100 Years War	**Experienced Real-Time Strategy Player**	1337
The 100 Years War—Tutorial 4 • Library research • Food, timber, and metal gathering • Capturing cities • Repairing buildings • Unit combat advantages and disadvantages • Transporting units across water		
Henry VIII	**Experienced Real-Time Strategy Player**	1513
Henry VIII—Tutorial 5 Defend against Scottish raids • City construction • National borders • Knowledge and wealth gathering • Merchants and rare resources		
Battle of Britain	**Advanced Topics**	1940
Battle of Britain—Tutorial 6 Battle the Germans in Britain's finest hour • Diplomacy • Air combat • Generals • Oil • Enhancement buildings • Formations		

"advanced" here mean what players need to know to begin to take yet greater control over their own learning by discovery through playing. They don't mean "at the top of the vertical ladder of skills" (or "you get an A in this subject"). The player is experienced and advanced in the sense of being prepared for future learning "on site," not in the sense of necessarily being an expert.

Each tutorial places its basic skills in a scenario that is just a simplified version of the real game. This allows learners always to see how these basic skills fit into the game as a whole system and how different skills integrate with each other. In school, on the other hand, very often these days children are exposed to basic skills one-by-one, step-by-step. For example, in early reading instruction they are taught first awareness of the sounds that compose words, then the decoding of letters, then reading aloud to attain more fluent decoding, then comprehension skills (Coles, 2003). Then and only then do they get to play the real "game" of reading, namely reading for meaning and to carry out their own purposes. In schools, too often, skills are decontextualized from the system (the "game") and from each other. This never happens in *RoN* or any other good game.

As an example of what I am trying to get at here, consider the tutorial labeled "Alfred the Great" (see Table 16.1, p. 310). When you click on this tutorial, while the scenario is loading, you see the following in print, while listening to the same thing (my own remarks below are placed inside square brackets):

> Eight hundred years after Boadicia rebelled against the Romans [this event was dealt with in the preceding tutorial labeled "Boadicia"], Britain was savaged by repeated Viking attacks. Alfred King of Wessex has been paying tribute to stave off the raiders, but in 878 the Vikings prepare for conquest. After a defeat, Alfred retreats to rebuild his forces and drive the Vikings away.

Once you press "Start" to start the scenario, you see the Vikings attacking the British town of Ethandum and hear the following:

> Alfred suffers a stinging defeat when the Vikings attack in battle. The Norsemen loot the town and Alfred is driven back to his stronghold in Carlisle. Alfred must rebuild his forces and attempt to retake Ethandum.

Here we see that the scenario opens with a short context within which to understand and make sense of what one is going to do. After the Vikings' victory, the scene changes to the British town of Carlisle, the place to which Alfred has retreated. This is where we will play out our tutorial. We don't start from scratch, though. We start in the Classical Age, the second of *RoN*'s eight ages, not in the Ancient Age where real games start. We also start with a large city, granary, lumber mill, market, and fort, as well as several citizens and their farms. While the game always starts with a (small) city and some citizens, the rest of these things players would normally build for themselves. Furthermore, while players in the real game always start with a library where they can do lots of different types of research, including research that leads to new ages, this scenario has no library, because we are not going to use it.

The setting of the scenario has been designed to be a minimal game setting with no more and no less than we need to learn at this point, but with enough to see how things fit together as a system. I will call this a "fish tank tutorial," because a fish tank can be, when done right, a simplified environment that lets one appreciate an ecosystem (e.g., a river, a pond, or a reef in the ocean) by stripping away a good deal of complexity, but keeping enough to bring out some basic and important relationships.

As we stare at the town of Carlisle, we hear and see the following, which importantly gives us an overall purpose and goal within which to situate the actions we are going to carry out and the skills we are going to learn:

> The Vikings now control Ethandum. Before we can rally the nation, we must retake that city. Our first goal is to scout the Viking position and find a route for our attack. We need to keep watch on the Viking preparations and defenses. A Lookout [a type of building] is needed as close to the Vikings as possible. This is a good spot for the look out [the camera moves to a spot at the edge of the town, and we see a big red circle marking the spot], close enough to see what's happening, but not so close that they'll notice it and attack. Now we'll learn how to construct new buildings. The actions a selected citizen [the camera moves back to town, and we see a big red circle marking a citizen] can perform are found in the lower left panel [we see a red arrow pointing to the panel]. Click the Build Military Button [we see a small yellow circle marking the button in the panel] to access a menu of building choices, one of which is the Lookout.

While you would normally have to click on the citizen to get the panel for types of buildings you can build (e.g., domestic ones, military ones, public monuments, etc.), in this case it is done for you when the game highlights the citizen. All you have to do is click on the Build Military Building button, which has a small flashing yellow circle around it. When you click on it, you see another panel appear, a panel for building different sorts of military buildings. This time there is a flashing yellow circle around the button for building a Lookout. We also hear "Select the highlighted Build Lookout button." Once we do this, we hear "Select the location for your Lookout by clicking near the target marker. Your citizen will begin construction there" and see a big red flashing circle at the spot that had been indicated earlier. When we click this spot, we hear: "Good, now your citizen will move to that site and begin construction."

We are having our hands held as we move through the fish tank (it's what we can call a "supervised fish tank"). But notice some crucial features of this hand-holding. Information is given multimodally (Kress & van Leeuwen, 2001), that is, in print, orally, and visually (note, as well, that if you place your mouse cursor on any person, building, or environmental object on the screen, a box will appear that tells you what it is and what you can do with it). There is lots of redundancy. Information is always given "just in time" when it can be used, and we can see its meaning in terms of effects and actions. Unlike in school, we don't get lots of verbal information up front and then have to remember it all when we can actually use it much later.

We see clearly how each piece of information we are given and each skill we are learning (and doing) is inter-connected to everything else we are learning and doing. We see the game as a system, not just a set of discrete skills. For example, we see how selecting a citizen, selecting a spot, and building a building are an integrated skill set. We see also how they relate to our overall purpose in this case; that is, to observe the enemy without getting too close. This lets us see that this skill set is both a general one (used for building and placing all sorts of buildings) and a *strategy* in the specific case when we are building Lookouts. In fact, we learn that all skills and skill sets are always ultimately strategies when they are concretely instantiated in practice.

This fish tank tutorial is also, of course, an example of what Vygotsky (1978) called learning within the learner's "Zone of Proximal Development." The "teacher" (in this case, the very design of the game) helps learners (players) pull off more than they could on their own and yet still feel a sense of personal accomplishment. Furthermore, the "teacher" (the design) tells the learner how to interpret things (what they mean), but these interpretations (meanings) become part and parcel of the learner's own mind as he or she carries out actions that embody those interpretations, such as, for example, building a Lookout as an initial plan in battle.

RoN's Tutorials: Supervised sandboxes

All the tutorials below "Quick Start" in Table 16.1 (p. 310) function as fish tanks. So, then, what about the Quick Start tutorial? By its placement at the top of the list you are coaxed to take this choice first, though you need not (and if you don't like it, you can always quit, go back to the main menu, and make another choice). If you click on Quick Start what you get, in fact, is something a bit different from a fish tank. You get what I call a "sandbox tutorial." In the real world, a sandbox is a piece of the real world, but sealed off to be a protected and safe place where children can explore. You can throw anything you want in the sandbox for the kids to play with so long as it isn't dangerous (there may be spiders in there, but, presumably we don't let the family python in). It need not be as controlled and clean an environment as a fish tank.

So, too, the Quick Start tutorial is a space where the player is really playing the game, but is protected from quick defeat and is free to explore, try things, take risks, and make new discoveries. Nothing bad will happen. In other sorts of games, for example shooters, the first or first couple of levels of the game often function as sandbox tutorials (e.g., the excellent *System Shock 2*), though they are not labeled as tutorials, but as real levels of the actual game (in the first level of *System Shock 2*, though it looks as if you must escape a failing space ship rapidly and are in great danger, in actuality the level is not timed and the player cannot get hurt).

Quick Start begins by telling the player:

> This is a preformed scenario where you can play the game at your own pace. Try to capture the Barbarian capital or conquer 70% of the map. There'll be hints and reminders to help you as you play.

The Quick Start scenario is actually the "real" game set at an easy level of difficulty with copious comments and hints. There is an opponent (in the real game you can have multiple opponents), but the opponent builds up slowly and does not make the smartest choices. The player gets a real sense of being in the game, even a sense of urgency, but can't really lose or, at least, lose at all early before having put up a very good stand.

Let me just show you the beginning of the Quick Start tutorial, so that you get the flavor of what is going on. The material below deals with how I operated in the Quick Learn tutorial. Here, once again, I print my own remarks in square brackets:

> [Voice:] The leadership of your fledging tribe has fallen on your shoulders. The first task is to unify a new nation under your rule. You're free to build your nation at your own pace. Occasionally you may receive advice to help keep things moving, but otherwise it's all up to you.

> [If you wait, eventually you will read and hear hints about what to do. But there is "wait time" here to allow you to explore the screen and click on whatever you like. I clicked on the scout. When I did so I saw the box printed below and simultaneously heard the remarks listed below that:]

> Scout: Currently selected (hotkey)
> Scouts, Ancient Age [picture with hotkey]–fast, but unarmed; good for exploring the map and finding enemies
> - Can spot hidden enemy units, such as spies and commandos
> - Can also destroy enemy spies
> - Strong vs. spies; Weak vs. Archers, Gunpowder Infantry

[Voice:] This is your scout. Use him to discover rare resources or locate the enemy position. Scouts are very fast and can see farther than most units, but cannot attack. You can move your scout around the map manually or click the auto explore button to have him explore on his own.

[After a few moments, I saw the message printed below on the top left of the screen and simultaneously heard the words below that:]

[Top Left Corner:] Create citizens to gather more resources

[Voice:] Your first priority in the Ancient Age is to create citizens and gather resources. Click your capital city and click Create Citizen to add to your work force. Put as many of your people to work gathering food and timber as you can. If you're running low on resources, you can always build farms to gather food and fill up woodcutters' camps with citizens to gather timber.

[During another "wait time," I clicked on the library and then clicked on a red button that lets the player research military technologies. Once this research is finished, the player can build military buildings. After clicking on the red button, I hear the following]:

[Voice:] Now that you have studied the first red military technology, you can build a barracks and begin training troops to protect your nation.

[After a few moments, I hear the following:]

[Voice:] If you want to see more of the map, you can always zoom in and out by using the mousewheel or pressing Page Up and Page Down on the keyboard.

The Quick Start tutorial goes on in this way for a while. If the player explores and does things, the tutorial confirms these acts and explains them. If the player waits, the tutorial prints a hint about what to do on the top left of the screen and says the hint orally and explains what it means. There are also, from time to time, remarks about how the game works, for example, the remark above about how to see more of the map. The tutorial is a nice dance of the player's actions and designers' guidance and instructions.

Midway through the Quick Start scenario the following box pops up:

MID GAME

At this point you should be having fun exploring the game and following some of the prompts that appear in the top left of the screen. If you're not having fun, you may want to try one of the following options.
- I'm having fun I want to continue playing
- I need to know more basic information, take me back to the tutorial screen
- The game is too slow. Let me start a Quick Battle.

This text box is an excellent example of alerting players to the fact that they need to assess their own progress, desires, and learning styles. They need to be proactive, make decisions, think about what they are doing and learning, and take control of their own learning.

When I started *RoN*, I started by doing the Quick Start tutorial. I did this for a rather perverse reason. I was so sure I would fail that I wanted to reconfirm my own view that actually playing the game would be too tedious and complex for me. What happened was that I got excited, feeling, "Wow, I'm actually playing a RTS game and winning, to boot!" (Of course, this may remind you of the great scene in the movie *What About Bob?* where the ever-fearful Bob is lashed to the sail of a sail boat and yells to his friends, "Look, I'm sailing, I'm actually sailing!"). The Quick Start tutorial is a sandbox. The sandbox feels like the real world to a child, but is guaranteed not to destroy the child's trust and ego before the child is strong enough to face more significant challenges. But this tutorial is a specific type of particularly efficacious sandbox. It is a sandbox with a wise parent present to guide and confirm efficacious play in the sandbox, in this case proactive game designers. Let's call this a "supervised sandbox."

Once I had done the Quick Start tutorial, I was energized to learn more, but, of course, I could not remember all the details the tutorial had introduced—nor was I meant to. Now I could turn to the specific fish tank tutorials and make each of these details, through focused practice, a part of my embodied intelligence and not just the caprice of my risky verbal memory. But I also knew now how these details fit into the larger scheme of the whole game, remembering that even in the fish tank tutorials skills are also introduced in terms of how they relate to other skills and to a simplified game system. Of course, other learners might do the fish tank tutorials first and use the supervised sandbox of the Quick Start tutorial to assess their learning and readiness to jump into the "real" game.

There is one last important point to make about the Quick Start tutorial. What it does, in addition to what we have already surveyed, is introduce the *genre* of RTS games to players who may have not played such games before. "Genre" just means what *type* of thing a thing is, for example whether a novel is a mystery, romance, science fiction, etc., or a piece of writing is a story, report, essay, and so forth. RTS games are one type of computer/video game (there are many others, e.g., shooters, adventure games, role-playing games, etc.). They involve typical actions, rules, and strategies that are different from those involved in other types of games.

Schools often try to teach kids to read and write, rather than read or write specific types of things like stories, reports, field notes, essays, or expositions. But, just like games, these different types of reading and writing operate by different principles and are used to carry out different types of actions. Good learning always involves knowing early and well what *type* of thing we are being asked to learn and do (Christie, 1990; Cope & Kalantzis,1993; Martin, 1990). Learners need to see this type of thing in action, not to be given static rules, if they are really to understand. In fact, for most types of things— like types of games, writing, movies, and so forth—there are no clear and static rules that define different types. Each type (e.g., a RTS game or an essay) is composed of many different instances that are variations around a theme. The only way to learn is to see some instances and live with them concretely.

Sure, there are some things you need to learn that help you to play most games, regardless of their type (e.g., moving and clicking a mouse), but these are the tip of an iceberg compared to what you need to know about how different specific types of games work. Thinking a RTS game is a shooter will make you a particularly bad learner of the RTS game or, at the least, will make you disappointed with it and not like it. The same thing is true of writing—there are some basic all-purpose things to learn (e.g., where to put commas and periods), but they, too, are but the tip of an iceberg, and writing an essay thinking it is supposed to be a personal narrative won't work.

RoN: Unsupervised Sandboxes

We are now ready—as the player is—to leave *RoN*'s tutorials and start the "real" game. I said that the skills *RoN*'s fish tank tutorials taught were "basic skills" in the sense that they are the skills that will allow you to actually start playing and learning from playing the game. The designers of *RoN* have ensured that these skills, once you learn them, will function just this way by building certain devices into the game play itself. When you leave the tutorials and actually start playing, there is a pause key that will stop time. This allows you to explore what icons on the screen mean and think about what you want to do. When time is paused, your opponent(s) do not continue building, and so you do not have to worry about falling behind. Furthermore, you can set the game at one of two easy difficulty settings (easiest and easy) that greatly decreases the pressure of time. On these settings, opponents move slowly and not always in the smartest fashion. Finally, you can turn on (or off) hints that appear from time to time to remind you of what you have learned in the tutorials and teach you new things.

What all this means is that the player learns in the tutorial just enough to move on to learn more—and more subtle things—by actually playing the game, but playing it in a protected way so that deeper learning can occur through playing. The player can customize the game play to be, in fact, another sort of sandbox, in this case what we might call an unsupervised sandbox. The player is protected to explore and take risks, but, aside from the small hint notes that can be turned off and on, there is much less guidance and direction from *RoN*'s designers.

We see, then, that in *RoN* there is no clear division between the tutorials as a learning space and the player's first "real" games with difficulty set on easiest or easy and use of the pause key. These first real games are actually "hidden tutorials" which assist players in teaching themselves how to play *RoN*, not as a set of discrete skills, but as strategic thinking using an integrated system of skills. These unsupervised sandboxes make for a smooth transition between official tutorials and "really" playing the game (set on normal or a harder level).

Learning and Playing

But there is a yet deeper principle at work here than the smooth transition between tutorials and playing. In a good game like *RoN* there is never a real distinction between learning and playing. The tutorials are simplified versions of playing the game. The game itself has a number of difficulty levels and at each level players must refine their skills and learn new ones. Players can also play other players in a multiplayer form of *RoN* on the internet, getting into games with others whose skill levels are equivalent to their own. They can move up to play better and better players as their own skills progress and, in doing so, will constantly be learning new things. When learning stops, fun stops, and playing eventually stops. For humans, real learning is always associated with pleasure, is ultimately a form of play—a principle almost always dismissed by schools.

There is one crucial learning principle that all good games incorporate that recognizes that people draw deep pleasure from learning and that such learning keeps people playing. Good games allow players to operate within, but at the outer edge of their competence. At lots of moments, a good game feels highly challenging, but ultimately "doable." Perhaps the player fails a few times at a given task, but good games show how much progress the player has made on each try and the player sees that this progress is increasing each time he or she "fails." Eventually success comes. This feeling of being highly challenging, but ultimately doable, gives rise to a feeling I have called pleasurable frustration, one of the great joys of both deep learning and good gaming.

Good games, however, do not at all points operate at the outer and growing edge of the player's competence. This is because they also recognize another important learning principle, what I call the "principle of expertise," because it is the foundation of expertise in all significant domains (Bereiter & Scardamalia, 1993). When learners learn a new skill set/strategy, they need to practice it over and over in varied contexts in order to make it operate at an almost unconscious routinized level. Then they are really good at it. But they are also in danger of resting on their laurels and learning nothing new. At this point, a good game throws a problem at the player where the routinized skill set/strategy won't work. This forces the player to think consciously again about skills that have become unconscious, taken-for-granted, and routine. The player must integrate his or her old skills with new ones, forming a new and higher skill set/strategy.

Now, in turn, the game will let this new skill set/strategy get practiced until it is routine. The player has moved to a new level of expertise and will then eventually face a yet harder problem that will start the process all over again. Thus, good games cycle through times when they operate at the outer edge of (but within) the player's competence and times when they allow players to solidify their skills. The times where players are solidifying their skills to the point of routine and taken-for-granted application give rise to another form of pleasure, the pleasure of mastery. Games cycle through periods of pleasurable frustration and routine mastery, a cycle of storm and calm.

These cycles are actually clearer in games like shooters (e.g., *Return to Castle Wolfenstein, Deus Ex, Unreal 2*, etc.) than they are in RTS games like *RoN*. In a game like *RoN* they are partially under the players' own control through the ways in which players can customize the game to their own skill level and interest. Players can themselves choose periods of skill solidification and high challenge, though the game gives them plenty of feedback as to when things are getting too easy or too hard.

But how do players know when they are prepared to move beyond the unsupervised sandboxes they can create by playing the game on easy difficulty levels? How do they know when they are ready to move on to the more rigorous challenges of the normal difficulty level and harder levels, as well as multiplayer play? As it happens—as happened with me, in fact—the player can certainly tell the game is becoming too easy by how fast and thoroughly he or she gains victory over the opponent(s). However, I found that when I moved on to the normal level, it was, at first, too hard, harder than I had thought it would be, given my swift victories on lower difficulty levels. The problem, of course, was that I had not properly evaluated my skills. I did not realize that my skill sets/strategies were not fast and efficient enough to take on harder challenges.

RoN does two things to speak directly to this problem. First, it offers players a whole set of "Skill Tests." I list the skill tests in Table 16.2 (p. 318). Note that some tests are defined in terms of skills (e.g., mouse clicking) and others in terms of strategies (e.g., getting to the Classical Age fast). As we have said, in games, skills are always seen as strategies.

These skill tests allow players to assess how well their skills fit into an efficient strategy set—how well integrated with each other and with the game as a system they are. The skill tests are, as they often are not in school, developmental for the learner and not evaluative (judgments carried out by authority figures). Furthermore, they are tests of what skills mean as strategies, not decontextualized tests of skills outside contexts of application where they mean quite specific things.

The second thing *RoN* does to solve the problem of letting players know where the cutting edge of their competence is is to render the whole matter *social*. Sadly, I failed my very first skill test several times. But I knew just how to increase my learning curve so I could pass the test. Every player knows there are an immense number of internet sites and chat rooms from which loads of things can be learned and to which lot of questions can be directed.

One very effective thing—though there are a great many others—that players can do is download recordings of *RoN* games played by players at different levels of expertise. Players can watch these to learn new things at ever increasing levels of expertise. Players can also easily record their own games and review them. They can also pit the computer against itself—at whatever level of difficulty they choose—and watch how things are done. On line, there is a world-wide university of peers and experts available to any player all the time. *RoN* lists its own web site on its program file, a site with much information, chat rooms, and links to other sites. There are also published strategy guides and many game magazines that will discuss games like *RoN*, offering hints, guides, and other sorts of helpful information.

Table 16.2: *RoN* Skill Tests

Aging Madness—Age 2
How fast can you get to Classical Age? Find out if your resource management skill is good enough.

Aging Madness—Age 4
How fast can you get to Gunpowder Age? Find out if your resource management skill is good enough.

Aging Madness—Age 8
How fast can you get to the Information Age? Find out if your resource management skill is good enough.

Raiding Party
Take your bloodthirsty Mongol horde and pay a visit to some enemy towns in an exercise of micromanagement.

Hotkey Handling
Do you know your hotkeys? This is a test of hotkey knowledge.

Protect the Wonder
Protect your Wonder from jealous enemies in an exercise of defense.

Tactics
Defeat the enemy troops to take control of a valuable resource without losing more than half your army in this test of generalship.

Whack the General
How fast can you click your mouse? This is a test of clicking ability.

This social aspect of *RoN*, and games in general, makes *RoN* and other games the focus of what I have elsewhere called an "affinity group" (Gee, 2004; see also Gee, 2007, Ch. 8) An affinity group is a group of people who affiliate with others based primarily on shared activities, interests, and goals, not shared race, class, culture, ethnicity, or gender. The many sites and publications devoted to *RoN* create a social space in which people can, to any degree they wish, small or large, affiliate with others to share knowledge and gain knowledge that is distributed and dispersed across many different people, places, internet sites, and modalities (e.g., magazines, chat rooms, guides, recordings, etc.). Distributed and dispersed knowledge that is available "just in time" and "on demand" is, then, yet another learning principle built into a game like *RoN*. Too often in schools knowledge is not shared across the students, is not distributed so that different students, adults, and technologies offer different bits and pieces of it as needed, and is not garnered from dispersed sites outside the classroom (for a case where it was, see Brown, 1994). *RoN* has no such problems.

Conclusion

By way of summary, let me collect together here in a list some of the learning principles that are built into *RoN* and reflected in my interaction with the game. I believe that these principles would be efficacious in areas outside games, for example, in science instruction in schools, though I must leave that argument until later. However, it is clear that these principles resonate with what theorists in the learning sciences have said about learning in content areas in school.

1. Create motivation for an extended engagement
2. Create and honor preparation for future learning
3. Create and honor horizontal learning experiences, not just vertical ones
4. "At risk" doesn't need to mean any more than that you don't need another bad learning experience
5. Let learners themselves assess their previous knowledge and learning styles and make decisions for themselves (with help)
6. Build in choice from the beginning
7. Banish "remedial"—the word and the experience
8. "Basic skills" means what you need to learn in order to take more control over your own learning and learn by playing
9. "Experienced" doesn't need to mean "expert," it can mean being able to take more control over your own learning and being able to learn by playing
10. Teach basic skills in the context of simplified versions of the real game so that learners can see how these skills fit into the game as a system and how they integrate with each other
11. Teach skills as sets and make it clear how they are instantiated in practice as strategies for accomplishing specific goals or carrying out specific activities
12. Offer supervised (i.e., guided) fish tank tutorials (simplified versions of the real system)
13. Offer supervised (i.e., guided) sandbox tutorials (safe versions of the real system)
14. Give information via several different modes (e.g., print, orally, visually). Create redundancy
15. Give information "just in time" and "on demand"
16. Learning should be a collaborative dance between the teacher's (designer's) guidance and the learner's actions and interpretations
17. Let learners create their own unsupervised sandboxes (i.e., let them be able to customize what you are offering)
18. Teach learners the genre they are involved with early and well (supervised sandboxes are good for this)
19. Ensure that there is a smooth transition between tutorials and actually playing (customized unsupervised sandboxes are good for this)
20. There should be no big distinction between learning and playing at any level
21. Allow learners to discover the outer edge of their competence and to be able to operate just inside that edge
22. Allow learners to practice enough so that they routinize their skills and then challenge them with new problems that force them to re-think these taken-for-granted skills and integrate them with new ones
23. Offer learners developmental (not evaluative) skill tests that allow them to judge where the outer edge of their competence is and that let them make decisions about what new things they need to learn on their path to mastery

24. Ensure that learners at every level of expertise can readily use knowledge that is distributed and dispersed across a great many other people, places, sites, texts, tools, and technologies
25. Ensure that the learners become part of an affinity group composed of peers and masters near them and spread across the community and world

Young people exposed to these principles so powerfully in a game like *RoN* are engaged in a form of learning that, in my view, makes many schools look uninspired and out of touch with the realities of how human learning works at a deep level. Perhaps, too, this exposure causes in some of these young people a critique of schooling as it currently exists.

Note

* This chapter was originally published as: Gee, J. (2007). Learning about learning from a video game: *Rise of Nations*. In his *Good Video Games and Good Learning* (pp. 45–66). New York: Peter Lang.

References

Barsalou, L. W. (1999a). Language comprehension: Archival memory or preparation for situated action. *Discourse Processes, 28*: 61–80.

Barsalou, L. W. (1999b). Perceptual symbol systems. *Behavioral and Brain Sciences, 22*: 577–660.

Bereiter, C., & Scardamalia, M. (1993). *Surpassing ourselves: An inquiry into the nature and implications of expertise.* Chicago: Open Court.

Bransford, J. D., & Schwartz, D. L. (1999). Rethinking transfer: A simple proposal with multiple implications. *Review of Research in Education, 24*: 61–100.

Brown, A. L. (1994). The advancement of learning. *Educational Researcher, 23*: 4–12.

Christie, F., Ed. (1990). *Literacy for a changing world.* Melbourne: Australian Council for Educational Research.

Clark, A. (2003). *Natural-born cyborgs: Why minds and technologies are made to merge.* Oxford: Oxford University Press.

Coles, G. (2003). *Reading the naked truth: Literacy, legislation, and lies.* Portsmouth, NH: Heinemann.

Cope, B., & Kalantzis, M., Eds. (1993). *The powers of literacy: A genre approach to teaching writing.* Pittsburgh: University of Pittsburgh Press.

diSessa, A. A. (2000). *Changing minds: Computers, learning, and literacy.* Cambridge, MA: MIT Press.

Gee, J. P. (2003). *What video games have to teach us about learning and literacy.* New York: Palgrave/Macmillan.

Gee, J. P. (2004). *Situated language and learning: A critique of traditional schooling.* London: Routledge.

Gee, J. (2007). *Good video games and good learning.* New York: Peter Lang.

Glenberg, A. M. (1997). What is memory for? *Behavioral and Brain Sciences, 20*: 1–55.

Glenberg, A. M., & Robertson, D. A. (1999). Indexical understanding of instructions. *Discourse Processes, 28*: 1–26.

Goldberg, K., Ed. (2001). *The robot in the garden: Telerobotics and telepistemology in the age of the Internet.* Cambridge, MA: MIT Press.

Goto, S. (2003). Basic writing and policy reform: Why we keep talking past each other. *Journal of Basic Writing, 21*: 16–32.

Kelly, A. E., Ed. (2003). Theme issue: The role of design in educational research, *Educational Researcher, 32*: 3–37.

Kress, G., & van Leeuwen, T. (2001). *Multimodal discourse: The modes and media of contemporary communication.* London: Edward Arnold.

Martin, J. R. (1990). Literacy in science: Learning to handle text as technology. In F. Christie (Ed.), *Literacy for a changing world* (pp. 79–117). Melbourne: Australian Council for Educational Research.

Vygotsky, L. S. (1978*). Mind in society: The development of higher psychological processes.* Cambridge, MA: Harvard University Press.

CHAPTER SEVENTEEN

Situated Play

Instruction and Learning in Fighter Games

AARON HUNG

Context

*A*aron Chia Yuan Hung's book, The Work of Play, *takes an ethnomethodological approach to understanding what video game players actually do when they play. His study of a group of video game players—many of whom speak Mandarin or Cantonese as their first language—captures situated language use and learning. Hung shows how moment-by-moment interactions around and during game-play shape meaning over time and how understandings of games themselves change with experiences over time.*

Hung uses analytic and transcript conventions from conversation analysis in this chapter. The following key will help with reading his transcript excerpts (taken from Hung, 2011, p. 55).

[	*Overlapping talk, with bracket marking the point of overlap*
:	*Lengthened syllable, indicated by number of colons*
-	*Cut off utterance*
?	*Rising intonation*
=	*No interval between end of prior sentence and beginning of next*
( )	*Uncertainty over verbatim transcription*
(( ))	*Action or other non-linguistic feature*
(0.0)	*Number of seconds of silence*

Hung also provides direct and glossed translations of the game players' language, too. For example:

Li	you biancheng ling	*original*
	again turned into zero	*gloss*
	(My score turned into zero again.)	*translation*

==============

It is the case that all developments in learning theory, from Vygostsky to Lave, have established that individuals do not learn by themselves. They learn with others, and the social worlds they build make all the difference for what all will be known to have been known. "Learning," thus, is always a political process, and there cannot be any learning without some form of teaching.

—HERVÉ VARENNE (2007, P. 1561)

The popularity of videogames has gained educators' attention, in part, because videogames often contain complicated rules and narratives that need to be taught to its players. Their popularity over the years suggests that game designers have been successful in communicating these complex systems to large numbers of players with different learning styles and backgrounds. But what do players learn when they play a videogame? Some game researchers suggest that, through playing the game, players acquire the game designer's underlying epistemology (Shaffer, 2007) or ideology (Squire, 2006). Others, such as Bogost (2007), suggest that games serve as rhetorical devices that have a persuasive component in their composition.

The goal of this chapter is to unpack some of the questions about what and how players learn when they interact with a videogame, specifically with fighting games. Much of what players learn depends on their prior knowledge of the game, the genre conventions, and of videogames in general. For this study, I had asked players to select games they have not played before, in order to describe their "first time through" experience with the game. This builds on the ethnomethodological notion that people's first experience with a phenomenon is an interaction that cannot be fully recaptured in a post hoc recollection. Learning is messy. Learning tends not to be a linear progression that advances from Point A to Point B; instead, learning (as it unfolds in time) tends to be exploratory, filled with trial-and-error, ventures down blind alleys, and back-tracking, and the goal here is to capture and preserve this messiness in its qualitative richness.

This chapter focuses on learning in relation to a novice and three expert players. The novice, in this case, is a non-player who not only has to understand the Nintendo controller, but also the conventions of fighting games as well as how to play with this particular group of players.

Methodology

This investigation was influenced by Suchman's (2002) study of users and photocopiers and Goodwin's (2006) study of playground games in a middle school. As with these studies, the goal was to understand the participants' orientation to the activity through their social organization. Since their communicative work was the focus, I was interested in videogames that could be played as a group in the same physical space. While there are many game genres that afford this type of interaction, the participants all gravitated towards fighting games. The participants' conversations were recorded through a digital voice recorder, their off-screen interactions were captured with a video camera, and their onscreen interactions were captured with a videocassette recorder. The onscreen interaction and conversations were later spliced together using Final Cut Pro, thus having a final product that included both onscreen and conversation data. In addition to the recordings, I took field notes during my observations. In most cases, my role as a participant was limited to an observer. However, there were some occasions when they needed me to "fill out" the game, during which I joined in the play (see aso Hung, 2011, Ch. 7).

All the participants were Asian adolescents, ages between 14 and 18, some of whom had recently immigrated to the United States and were English language learners. I met an initial group during an earlier pilot study, and through snowball sampling, some of them recruited their friends from high school to be part of the study described here. Since this study required considerable time commitment, there were seven participants whom I was able to observe on a regular basis (over the course of a year)—six boys and two girls (although not all of them are mentioned here).

The sessions occurred after school, on weekends, or during their summer break. A few of the sessions lasted close to four hours, with the average being around two hours. Typically, the players mixed up their play within the session, occasionally breaking into smaller groups or trying out new facets of the game. Part of my attempt here is to preserve the essence of the session being described while highlighting key moments of their interactions. Whenever possible, I have preserved the chronology of the interactions as they occurred.

Fighting Games

Fighting games tend to involve a large cast of characters that players select to represent them. Each of these characters has unique abilities and weaknesses. Two of these fighting games used in this study are *Super Smash Brothers Melee* (SSBM) for the Nintendo GameCube, and *Super Smash Brothers Brawl* (SSBB), its follow-up on the Nintendo Wii system. Both are similar in their design. The *Super Smash Brothers* series involves characters from the larger Nintendo game universe, such as *Legend of Zelda*, *Super Mario Brothers*, *Donkey Kong*, *Pokémon*, and *Star Fox*. The characters in *Super Smash Brother* fighting games tend to be diluted versions of the characters they represent, usually reflecting only the main traits of the original character. For example, Link, the protagonist from the *Legend of Zelda* series, carries his characteristic bow and arrow in *Super Smash Brothers Melee* but is less sophisticated in his design and capabilities than he is in the *Legend of Zelda* games.

Super Smash Brothers starts players with a dozen or so selection of characters, and additional ones to unlock after the player has achieved certain goals in the game. These goals are usually unspecified, so players can only unlock them by continuously playing through and trying out different characters and stages. The players usually do not know who the unlockable characters are (unless they look it up online), and part of the excitement seems to be to guess who might be unlocked next. When the players have met the requirements of unlocking a character (e.g., playing in a particular setting a certain number of times), the game announces that a new challenger has appeared. In order to unlock the new character and make it a playable character, the player has to first beat the character in a one-to-one duel. This also serves as a way for the players to see what abilities the new characters have. The game also allows players to change initial settings, such as the duration of each fight and the ability to respawn (the ability to return to the game after your character is defeated). In this case, the players kept the fight duration at two minutes along with the ability to respawn. This means that the only way for the game to end is for the time to run out (as opposed to, when all the opponents are defeated).

For the sake of clarity, "player" refers to the human person playing the game and the "character" refers to the virtual character the player controls in the game. At the start of each game, the player selects a character, then the stage in which the fight is to occur. The game can accommodate up to four characters, at least one of which must be a player-controlled character. The other three characters can either be player-controlled or computer-controlled. More than one player can select the same character. However, once the game starts, the player cannot change characters until the end of the game.

Like the playable characters, all the stages in *Super Smash Brothers* fighting games are based on preexisting settings drawn from other Nintendo series. These stages fall into two general designs. One design features a relatively stable camera perspective that zooms in or pans out, depending on where the characters are spread out. For example, if the characters are spread apart from one another, the camera will pan out so that the players can see where their characters are; if they are close together, the camera zooms in on the characters' location. Another design has a moving camera that continuously forces the players to keep up with where the camera is panning. If the players fail to keep up, their characters will disappear off the stage and they will lose a life. In addition to the camera, each stage also contains its unique features, such as speeding cars, sinking platforms, and collapsing roofs, all of which force players to pay attention not only to their opponents but also to how the stage is transforming.

The Novice

The Order of the Design

Balancing out the players seemed to be an important part of fighting games. Presumably, having an odd number of players in the game means that two players will always be ganging up on another player, thus creating unfairness (see also Hung, 2011, Ch. 6). Although the game itself permitted up to four characters, most games were either two- or four-player games. Thus, when the expert players—Jason, Kevin, and Andrew—found themselves one short, they always had to seek a fourth player to balance them out. On some occasions, I filled in as the fourth, but on this particular occasion, it was Li.

Li, the novice, did not play videogames as much as the other participants. Not only did she have to learn the specifics of *Super Smash Brothers Melee*, but also about the genre, the controllers, and how to interact with the other players. In addition to being new at videogames, Li also spoke mostly Mandarin, while the other players in this session spoke mostly Cantonese. Mandarin and Cantonese are both dialects of Chinese, but sound quite different, and while it is possible to infer general meaning by identifying a few words, it is not easy to understand the other dialect without knowing it relatively fluently. Jason and Andrew seemed most fluent in Mandarin, and spent most of the time communicating with Li in Mandarin; Kevin spoke less frequently to Li, and his Mandarin was also the least fluent. Li spoke only Mandarin, although she seemed to know a few Cantonese words. This linguistic complication meant that there were many times that Jason, Andrew, and Kevin would talk about Li without addressing her directly.

For conversation transcription purposes, I use (C) to indicate when a speaker is using Cantonese, and (M) to indicate when a speaker is using Mandarin. Cantonese is transcribed using the *jyutping* romanization system, and Mandarin is transcribed using the *pinyin* romanization system. (For more on the conversation analysis transcription conventions used in this chapter, see Hung, 2011, pp. 54–55.) The numbers in brackets represent the amount of time that has transpired since the start of the recording. Figure 17.1 shows the chronological order of excerpts 5.1 to 5.14, which together represent a sequence of instructional work that ultimately ends in frustration and failure.

Let's start with excerpt 5.1, which occurs just as Li begins to learn about fighting games. This excerpt occurs right after a game of *Super Smash Brothers Melee* had ended. After the game displays the winners and losers, each of the players has to click a button on their controller to acknowledge that they are still there. After that, the game takes the players to a "Character Selection" screen, which

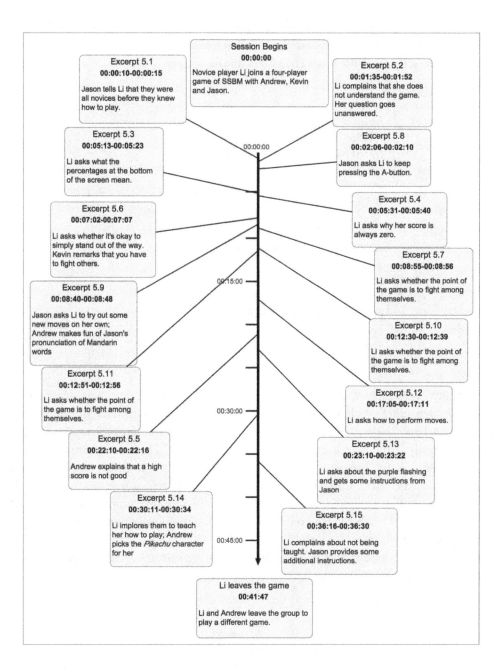

Session Begins
00:00:00
Novice player Li joins a four-player game of SSBM with Andrew, Kevin and Jason.

Excerpt 5.1
00:00:10-00:00:15
Jason tells Li that they were all novices before they knew how to play.

Excerpt 5.2
00:01:35-00:01:52
Li complains that she does not understand the game. Her question goes unanswered.

Excerpt 5.3
00:05:13-00:05:23
Li asks what the percentages at the bottom of the screen mean.

Excerpt 5.8
00:02:06-00:02:10
Jason asks Li to keep pressing the A-button.

Excerpt 5.4
00:05:31-00:05:40
Li asks why her score is always zero.

Excerpt 5.6
00:07:02-00:07:07
Li asks whether it's okay to simply stand out of the way. Kevin remarks that you have to fight others.

Excerpt 5.7
00:08:55-00:08:56
Li asks whether the point of the game is to fight among themselves.

Excerpt 5.9
00:08:40-00:08:48
Jason asks Li to try out some new moves on her own; Andrew makes fun of Jason's pronunciation of Mandarin words

Excerpt 5.10
00:12:30-00:12:39
Li asks whether the point of the game is to fight among themselves.

Excerpt 5.11
00:12:51-00:12:56
Li asks whether the point of the game is to fight among themselves.

Excerpt 5.12
00:17:05-00:17:11
Li asks how to perform moves.

Excerpt 5.5
00:22:10-00:22:16
Andrew explains that a high score is not good

Excerpt 5.13
00:23:10-00:23:22
Li asks about the purple flashing and gets some instructions from Jason

Excerpt 5.14
00:30:11-00:30:34
Li implores them to teach her how to play; Andrew picks the *Pikachu* character for her

Excerpt 5.15
00:36:16-00:36:30
Li complains about not being taught. Jason provides some additional instructions.

Li leaves the game
00:41:47
Li and Andrew leave the group to play a different game.

00:00:00
00:15:00
00:30:00
00:45:00

Figure 17.1: Sequencing of events in Li's instructional session (excerpts 5.1–5.15).

lets them pick a new character. Then, it takes them to a "Stage Selection" screen, which lets them pick a stage or lets the game randomly assign one for them. I refer to these as *transition screens*.

In this excerpt, we see three kinds of instructions going on. Jason had picked the Pikachu character for Li to use. However, Pikachu was also the character he used most frequently, and it became confusing for Li to see two of the same characters on the screen:

EXCERPT 5.1 (00:00:10–00:00:15)

1	Andrew(C)	*nei mhou tung keoi gaan jatjoeng*
		you don't with her pick same
		(Don't pick the same color character as
2		*ngaansik laa::::: diu:::*
		color final particle fuck
		she does, damn it.)
3	Jason(M)	=*women gang kaishi doubuhui*
		=we just begin also don't know
		=**(When we started playing, we didn't**
4		*da (yi da) jiu hui*
		play (once play) then know
		know how to play either. Once we started
		playing, we knew [how to play].)
5	Kevin(C)	=*gam gam gam*
		=press press press
		=**(Press it. Press it. Press it.)**

Andrew instructs Jason (lines 1–2) not to use the same color, so that Li can have an easier time differentiating her character from Jason's. Jason addresses Li in Mandarin (lines 3–4), telling her of their own experience when they started with the game, and making it sound as if learning to play would come relatively easily with enough practice. Finally, Kevin (line 5) instructs them to press through the transition screens in order to get the next game started. This excerpt demonstrates a typical interaction between the experts and the novice. Among the three experts, Jason tends to provide the most instruction. Andrew tends to provide instruction more indirectly, by commenting on how Li *should* be instructed; and Kevin tends to give no instruction and, instead, tries to move the action along so that the next game can start.

Li spends the next game trying to orient herself to the game, repeatedly asking "where am I?" but most of her questions are ignored:

EXCERPT 5.2 (00:01:35–00:01:52)

1	Li(M)	*wo zai nali a? (1.5) ( ) (2.0) (wo) fei*
		at where final particle (I) flew
		(Where am I? (1.5) ( ) (2.0) I flew
2		*zou (0.9) ta ma de kan bu mingbai*
		away that mother's see not understand
		away. (0.9) Damn it, I don't understand.
3		*(1.0) zhe ganma yong a?*
		this what use question marker
		what's going on. (1.0) What does this do?)
		(5.2)

4	Kevin(C)	*waa:: pukgaai:: aa! zeng! saat*
		wow damn exclamation great kill
		(Wow, damn it. Ah! Great, killed
5		*jatgo*
		one
		one (of you).)

The timescale of fighting games is such that there is no occasion to provide any detailed instruction when the game is in process without interrupting the play. In the two-minute duration of the game, the action is nonstop. While Li talks to herself throughout the game, this is one of many occasions when she asks a specific question (line 3). No one answers her and when Kevin speaks (lines 4–5), instead of answering her question, he comments about the ongoing game in general. In conversation analysis, questions are considered first-pair parts of adjacency pairs, which means that a second-pair part (a response to the question) is expected. Throughout this early episode, Li's many first-pair parts get ignored by the experts, which eventually leads to her voicing her frustration.

Li's questions in excerpt 5.2 also signal that her struggle is not simply about understanding the controls, but that she is having trouble identifying her character on the screen (line 1) and that she does not know what is happening on the screen (lines 2–3). Her words "*kan bu mingbai*" (I don't understand what's going on) suggest that it is not just a sensorimotor issue but also that she does not understand what she is *seeing*. In videogames, there is a visual aspect to affordance that depends on the game genre, and understanding a game requires that the player understand the visual meanings embedded in the game. As Li tries to learn the basic controls, she asks about the percentages that appear on the bottom of each screen (see Figure 17.2 below). The percentages for each character start at zero percent.

Figure 17.2: *Super Smash Brothers Melee* screenshot.

The more you are attacked, the higher the number climbs. The percentages can exceed 300 percent, and there is no clear indication of what the maximum percentage is. (Theoretically, the percentage indicator can go up to 999 percent if a player is able to execute a complicated combination move. This is, however, a rare occurrence.) As such, players do not always know exactly when their character is about to be killed, only that it is more likely to be killed when the percentages approach or exceed 300 percent. Furthermore, there isn't an indication of what the percentages refer to. The percentages do not seem to represent *damage, health, chance of survival,* or *chance of death,* nor are they used in the same way percentages are used in everyday life (i.e., to mark the fraction of something).

In Excerpt 5.3, Li asks what the percentages mean:

EXCERPT 5.3 (00:05:13–00:05:23)

1	Li(M)	*xiamian de fenshu shi*
		Below possessive score is
		(What's the meaning of the score below?)
2		*shenme yisi a?*
		what meaning final particle
3	Andrew(M)	*shi ni*
		is you—
		(You-)
4	Jason(M)	=*shi ni shi ni dale dale duoshao*
		=is you is you hit hit how much
		=**(It shows how much you've been hit.)**
5	Andrew(M)	*shi a*
		Yes final particle
		(Right.)
6	Li(M)	*a shisi? shi bei ren dale*
		Ah fourteen? Is by someone beaten
		(Fourteen? It shows how much someone's
7		*duoshao ma?*
		how much question marker
		beat me?)
8	Kevin(M)	=*dui*
		=Correct
		=**(Correct.)**

As this excerpt unfolds in the midst of a game, the other players do not give a precise answer to Li's query (lines 3–5). Even so, Li seems to have understood their explanation (lines 6–7) when she reiterates her understanding and receives an affirmation from Kevin. This is technically the correct response even though there appears to be possible confusion in her understanding. Her use of the word *"fenshu"* (score) suggests that she had interpreted the percentages to refer to a numerical score, as used in a test or a sports game. Seconds after, in excerpt 5.4, she asks for further clarification on the percentage system and seems to veer further away from its designated meaning:

EXCERPT 5.4 (00:05:31–00:05:40)

1	Li(M)	*weishenme wo yizhi dou shi*
		why I continue still is
		(Why (does my score) stay at zero?)

2		*ling a?*
		zero question marker
3	Andrew(M)	*yinwei* [*ni yizhi ni si*
		Because [you continue you die
		(Because you keep dying.)
4	Kevin(M)	[*yinwei ni si a*
		[because you die final particle
		[(Because you died.)
5	Li(M)	*a* (1.4) *najiu shi xiamian fenshu*
		ah then I below score
		(Ah. (1.4) So whoever has the higher score
6		*yuegao jiu shui ying luo?*
		higher then who wins final particle
		wins?)

Her continual use of the word "score" (*fenshu*) suggests that the conventional use of percentages to indicate the score is more salient than the game's intended meaning. Thus, even though, in excerpt 5.3, she seemed to understand what it meant and was able to articulate its literal meaning accurately, she found the need to clarify her understanding, as she seemed surprised that her "score" was not higher. She asks why her percentage remains at zero and the other players tell her it is because she keeps dying (lines 3–4). Their explanation is vague because it can be understood in at least two ways:

- *Explanation A*: high percentage is better, probably indicates your score; your percentage is zero because you just died and lost your score

- *Explanation B*: low percentage is better, probably indicates the amount of damage you sustained; when your character dies, your new character starts at zero damage

Explanation A seems relatively straightforward. In most games, scores count up while health counts down over the course of the game. If understood to mean score, then it makes sense for the score to drop if your character dies. It is possible to achieve higher than 100 percent on a test, so this also helps explain why it is possible to exceed 100 percent. This seems to be Li's preferred understanding as well (lines 5–6). Explanation B makes less sense because the percentages lack a reference point. It should be noted that the game manual itself refers to the percentage as indicator of *damage*, but even that defies understanding. How is it possible for a character's damage to exceed 100 percent and still survive?

The percentage/damage indicator is a good example of the *et cetera provision* as used in ethnomethodology. Garfinkel (2002) uses it to refer to the unarticulated "stuff" that is glossed over in communication to allow us to carry on with the task at hand. The indexicality of language means that our communication is always ambiguous and situated. The fact that we can communicate, not only in conversation, but across space and time means that we have to rely on the *et cetera provision* to "fill out" all that is left unspoken, unwritten, or unexplained. The damage indicator may be difficult to explain but that does not bother the other players. They do not need to know what the percentages refer to, nor do they care. All they need to know for them to continue with the game is that if a character has a high percentage, it is weak. Everything else is part of the *et cetera provision* and does not need to be further clarified.

The *et cetera provision* is what allows games to be games. It helps players accept and move beyond the arbitrariness of rules and embrace them within the context of the game. What is part of the *et cetera provision* varies from genre to genre. As a novice, Li did not understand what should be part of the provision and calls for clarification. Finally, a few games later, Li says:

EXCERPT 5.5 (00:22:10–00:22:16)

1	Li(M)	*yo::::! cong 130 ji bian*
		exclamation from 130 something change
		(Damn, I went from 130 something
2		*cheng ling!*
		to zero!
		to zero!)
		(0.4)
3	Andrew(M)	*duo bush hao ni zhidao*
		many isn't good you know
		(It's not good to have a higher (number),
4		*ma?*
		question marker
		you know?)

A few things are worth pointing out. First, Li did not seem to notice a connection between how often her character was killed and the percentage indicators. Her exclamation that her "score" went from 130 to 0 suggests that she thought it was good to have a high number, which led Andrew to correct her (lines 3–4). In other words, although she was not a good player (she had died multiple times), there was no contradiction in her experience of the game. This could suggest either that Li *believed* herself to be a good player, or that Li did not see any relationship between her playing and the "score." This is an example of Li using Garfinkel's notion of the *documentary method of interpretation* to look for an underlying order or pattern in the game design. Whatever Li was experiencing, she was selecting certain aspects of the game and ignoring others in order for her experience to be coherent. Second, although Li was "misinterpreting" the game, she still played relatively well, finishing in second place in two of five games. This raises the question of whether it is possible to play a game and misunderstand its rules and still be considered a competent player. (I myself have "misinterpreted" games before and the games have made sense, both before and after I discovered my misunderstanding. In some cases, it was more fun to misunderstand a game because it made the game more challenging.) For Li, it seems that, provided that she continued to perceive an underlying order, it did not matter whether that underlying order was congruent to the game designers' plan. Third, it is just as interesting that Andrew found the need to re-orient her to the "accurate" interpretation of the game—that it is not good to have a high percentage. This is an example of "accountability work" emerging in context, during which members of the activity are oriented such that they are all *mutually* accountable to one another. Thus, the players felt that it was not enough for Li to be playing with them, nor was it enough that she was doing rather well for herself, despite being a novice; it was important that she was oriented to the game in the same way that they were.

Orientation to the Game

Sharing an orientation means that the players have the same way of interacting with the game. In other words, players understand that "this is the way you play this type of game" and others who play with them should share the same orientation. In conversation, we continually adjust one another's orientation through what conversation analysis scholars refer to as *repair*. We also do it through opening and closing sequences, such as when we start a conversation with "Guess what happened to me?" as a way of indicating to the audience that we are about to tell a story.

What should we consider to be the "right" orientation to a fighting game? What does it mean to play a fighting game? For Li, the initial goal was not to fight, but to survive:

EXCERPT 5.6 (00:07:02–00:07:07)

1	Li(M)	*na jiu shi yizhi zhan zai*
		then just is continue stand at
		(So, if I keep standing up here,
2		*shangmian jiu mei shi luo?*
		up there just no issue question marker
		I won't have a problem?)
		(0.9)
3	Kevin(M)	*danshi ni yao ying renjia*
		but you have to win others
		(But you have to win against the others.)
4		*ma:::::*
		final particle

Li had found a spot on the stage that was safe to stand on. In lines 1 and 2, Li continues to probe whether this was the "point" of the game. Kevin instructs her that the point is not simply to survive, but to fight other players (lines 3–4). Li eventually seems to realize this point later on in the session:

EXCERPT 5.7 (00:08:55–00:08:56)

1	Li(M)	*zhe shi zijiren da zijiren*
		this is ourselves attack ourselves
		(So, here we are fighting against one another.)
2		*wo*
		final particle

Dourish (2001) points out that, "*users, not designers, create and communicate meaning*" (p. 170, emphasis in original). While the game's design structures constrain the possible meanings of a game, the eventual interpretation comes only through interaction that players have with the game. It is easy, especially for those familiar with a genre, to overlook how easy it is to assume the "point" of a given game. Fighting games usually do not have a context, so there is usually no explanation as to why these characters are fighting each other in the first place. Furthermore, Li's initial goal in the game—simply to stay at a safe location—seems perfectly reasonable. By staying out of the way, she managed to come out in second place a couple of times. However, even though she was ranking higher than a few of her fellow players, they did not consider her to be a proper part of the game unless she engaged in direct combat.

Li's gradual understanding of the game helps unravel the taken-for-granted elements we have toward game genres. The term "fighting game" (its Chinese name—*gedou youxi*—translates roughly to the same thing) is quite a vague concept, as it can be applied to nearly every other game genre that has a fighting component. Novices like Li are left to figure out on their own what makes a fighting game a fighting game. The phrase *zijiren* (line 1)—literally "self people" but usually translated to mean either "ourselves" or "one another"—implies a we-orientation to the players and shows her surprise that the "point" of this particular game is more antagonistic than she initially presumed. Her fellow players were not comrades in arms but opponents in combat. It should also be noted, however, that in *Super Smash Brothers Melee*, there are occasionally computer-controlled characters that make momentary appearances on the stage that typically last a few seconds. These are meant as an added challenge to the players, who have to fend off these other characters or seek a safe location. Thus, the players are not simply fighting among themselves but also navigating the stage. Furthermore, many of the stages in *Super Smash Brothers Melee* resembles another genre—called *platformers*—in which the goal is to move through the game as if it were an obstacle course, going from one location to the next and dodging any obstructions along the way. Although there might be brief encounters that require minor combat, direct combat is usually not a central part of the game. One of the earliest and most recognizable platformer games is *Super Mario Bros.*, whose main characters—Mario, Luigi, Bowser, and Princess Peach—are playable characters in *Super Smash Brothers Melee*. Thus, it is no surprise that Li should think of *Super Smash Brothers Melee* more as a platformer than a fighting game.

When Is Instruction?

Li's orientation to the game eventually led to problems. She continually complained that her fellow players were ganging up on her and bullying her. This is further aggravated by her perception that the others were not properly instructing her on how to play. It is usually quite hard for a player to teach another to play a fighting game without interrupting the play itself. This is perhaps one reason why most of the instruction occurred only during the transition screens, and even those moments were short, as Kevin tried to hurry to start the next game (excerpt 5.1, line 5).

So, what does instruction between players look like and when does it happen?

In classroom interaction, the structure of the lesson and its participants are socially organized such that an instruction act consists of an initiation-response-evaluation sequence (Mehan, 1979). In videogames, the relationship between an expert and novice player might be more akin to an apprenticeship. For example, Steinkuehler (2004) describes instruction between expert and player in an MMOG using Gee's (1996) discourse analysis, paying particular attention to the relationship between expert and novice and the way the novice is guided into the "Discourse" of the game.

Fighting games pose a particular problem because the relationships between the players are essentially antagonistic. It could be argued that by "bullying" and "ganging up" on Li, the others are teaching her something about the identity of the player in fighting games and it could be argued that Li eventually did learn this by excerpt 5.7. Prior literature on learning in videogames has noted the benefits of the learning-by-doing aspect of games, where players are put into direct interaction with the rules of the game. But this form of "situated learning" does not always work well and can be particularly frustrating for a novice who needs to learn the more basic features of a genre.

To be able to play well in a fighting game, the player needs to know what the characters' moves are and how to perform them. In excerpt 5.8, Jason offers some guidance:

EXCERPT 5.8 (00:02:06–00:02:10)

1   Jason(M)   *ni yizhi an A hen lihaide*
                      you continue press A very powerful
                      (Keep pressing the A-button. It's very powerful.)

((Li taps the A-button repeatedly))

2 Jason(M) dui! Yizhi yizhi an
correct! continue continue press
(That's right, keep pressing it.)

In *Super Smash Brothers Melee*, the A-button is one of the main attack buttons. However, pressing the A-button only unleashes one of many combination attack moves. Jason's instruction itself is vague in that he states that it is "powerful" but does not clarify what it is used for. Li obliges and begins to tap on the button and Jason moves on to interacting with the other players.

EXCERPT 5.9 (00:08:40–00:08:48)

1 Jason(M) *ni shishi sheng e zhashu*
you try "new" moves
(You should try some new moves

2 *ma . . . ziji shishi kan*
question marker self try see
yourself, try and see.)

3 Andrew(M) *sheng de* [*sheng de sheng de . . .*]
"new" ["new" "new"]
("New, new, new . . ."])

4 Jason(M) [*zhao::::::shu*]
[moves]
(["Moves."])

5 Andrew(M) *zhao::::::shu*
moves
(Moves.)

6 Li(M) =*zhaoshu*
=moves
=**(Moves.)**

7 Jason(M) =*shi zhaoshu*
=try moves
=**(Practice moves.)**

In excerpt 5.9, a game has ended and Li came out in second place. Jason asks Li to try some new moves on her own (lines 1–2). He mispronounces the word "new"—*xin* as *sheng*—and Andrew makes fun of it (line 3). Jason continues to struggle a bit with the pronunciation of "move"—*zhaoshu*—and Andrew and Li help him along. Jason's instruction to Li, however, is simply to try out new moves on her own. He did not try to show her what to press on the controllers, how many new moves there are, or what it even means to try out new moves.

Li eventually does figure out a new move, one that the other players have not seen:

EXCERPT 5.10 (00:12:30–00:12:39)

1 Li(M) *wo wo yizhi an zhu A ranhou*
I keep press down A then
(When I keep pressing the A-button,

2 *ta jiu you zisede nage*

		it then has purple that one
		a purple thing appears.
3		*dongxi shi shenme a?*
		thing is what question marker
		What is that?)
		(2.0)
4	Jason(C)	*waa gam ging ge?*
		wow so powerful question marker
		(Wow, that's so powerful?)
5	Li(M)	=*ni kan ni kan*
		=you see you see
		(Look, look.)
6	Andrew	( )
7	Jason(C)	=*Li go ziu gam ging*
		=Li that move so powerful
		=**(Li's move is so powerful.)**

In lines 1 to 3, Li asks about the "purple thing" that appears when she follows her given instructions and presses the A-button. However, she receives no feedback or response. Instead, while Li is talking to Jason in Mandarin, Jason addresses the others in Cantonese. After pausing to look at the move she describes, Jason remarks that Li has discovered a new, powerful move. Neither Jason nor the other players respond to her question about the new move. Seconds later, Andrew and Jason have this exchange:

EXCERPT 5.11 (00:12:51–00:12:56)

1	Andrew(C)	*waa pukgaai Li gam gangging*
		wow damn Li sodamn powerful
		(Wow, Li's gotten so powerful.)
2		*ge?*
		question marker
		(1.4)
3	Jason(C)	*hai wo goziu1 m zi matje*
		yeah that move not know what
		(Yeah, I don't know what the move is.)
4		*wo (jathaa) hoji congsei*
		final particle (suddenly) can crash dead
		(It can suddenly kill your character.)
5		*jandi ge wo*
		others final particles

Again speaking in Cantonese, Andrew and Jason do not address Li, even though they refer to her by name. They do recognize it as a powerful move, however, but they don't explain that to Li. When the game is in progress, Andrew, Jason, and Kevin are usually engaged in continuous taunts and challenges against one another, much akin to what some might call "smack talk" or "ritual insults." Li's questions are usually ignored or given vague responses. For example:

EXCERPT 5.12 (00:17:05–00:17:11)

1	Li(M)	*weishenme wo yi peng nimen*
		whyI once touch you
		(Why is it that, once my character touches
2		*jiu hui fei fei zou diao?*
		will fly flyaway
		yours, it will fly away?)
3	Jason(M)	*yinwei wome yon zhaoshu*
		because We use moves
		(Because we use attack moves.)
4	Li(M)	*na wo yao zenme yong*
		then I want how use
		(Then how do I use it?)
5		*a?*
		question marker
6	Andrew(M)	=*yong shou*
		=use hand
		=**(Use your hand.)**
7	Jason(M)	=*ziji shi shi kan*
		=self try try see
		(Try on your own and see.)

Li calls for an explanation about particular elements of the game (lines 1–2). When she says "fly away," she is referring to how one character can suddenly kill a character with one hit. These attacks occur only when the character's percentage indicators are high (i.e., above 100%). When it occurs, the character that is attacked sails into the air and disappears off over a horizon, then a new character appears, and the percentage indicators turn to zero. Jason's response (line 3) is somewhat vague because he does not explain what constitutes a move. The word "move" (*zhaoshu*) in this context refers specifically to an attack move or style. In fighting game jargon, it is called a *combo move*, and knowing how to perform these moves at the right time is a key aspect of fighting games. When Li asks them how to execute a move (lines 4–5), she gets a sarcastic response from Andrew (line 6) and a suggestion from Jason to, once again, try it out on her own (line 7).

As the game progresses, Li persists in asking about the "purple thing" as well as what it means to attack others. Jason and Andrew try to provide more detailed explanations, but are given only 12 seconds to teach something new before the new game begins:

EXCERPT 5.13 (00:23:10–00:23:22)

	((game ends))
1	Li(M)	*wo zise nage wo zise nage yonglai*
		I purple that I purple that use
		(That purple flashing thing, what is
2		*ganma ya?*
		do what question marker
3	Kevin(M)	*da [renjia]*
		attack [other]
		(Attacking others.)
4	Li(M)	[*zenme da?*]

		[how to attack]
		[(How do I attack?)]
5	Andrew(M)	=*da renjia*
		=attack others
		(Attacking others.)
6	Li(M)	[*( )*
7	Jason(M)	[*ni yao hen jin . . . duizhu renjia*
		[you have to very close facing others
		[(You have to be very close and facing
8		*an (ni zhidao) A a?*
		press (you know) A question marker
		them, then press, you know the A button?)
9	Li(M)	*dui a:::: an A ranhou ne?*
		right press A then question marker
		(Right, press the A-button. Then what?)
10	Jason(M)	*jiu hui yizhi an yizhi an*
		then will continue press continue press
		(Then, if you keep pressing the button
11		*duizhu renjia renjia jiu hui*
		facing others others then will
		while facing another, it will cause them to
12		*fei lai fei qu fei lai fei qu*
		fly here fly there fly here fly there
		fly all over the place.)
13	Li(M)	*o*
		Okay
		(Okay.)
		((game begins))

Excerpt 5.13 occurs during a transition between two games. Since she first discovered the purple flashing (about 11 minutes ago), Li had asked six times about its purpose and received no response. This time, she manages to get some instructions. She asks specifically what it is *used for* (lines 1–2), as opposed to what it means visually or what it does to her character. Kevin and Andrew both give her the kind of vague answers that she has received in the past. Jason offers more specific instructions and tells her that she has to be close to the opponent and facing them (line 7). This is useful to know because not all attacks need to be done up close, and most characters have a long-range attack. He again talks about pressing the A-button (line 8), and Li acknowledges that she knows about the A-button, and asks for the next part of the instruction (line 9). Jason simply tells her to keep pressing the button (line 11) and that it would cause people to "fly all over the place" (line 12).

It should be noted that each character has seven to nine moves associated with the A-button, and four moves associated with the B-button. (This is from consulting the manual and online guides. There are likely to be additional moves that game designers have concealed.) Pressing the A-button alone executes a close-range attack, but there are additional moves that can be performed if the A-button is combined with other moves, such as "A-button + up-direction," "B-button + down-direction," "jump + A-button," and so on. The expert players themselves do not seem to know all the possible combinations because they continue to discover them as they stumble across them over time. Interestingly, this group of players seemed to prefer this form of discovery instead of acquiring advanced knowledge about a character through online guides and other sources. From my interaction with the expert group, this discovery process is itself part of the "fun" because it allows individuals to develop their own expertise instead of depending on outsiders. This might explain why they seemed less interested in providing direct instruction to Li, leaving her to discover on her own. In other words, they are not teaching her to play this particular game, as much as they are teaching her to play this particular game *with them*.

Excerpt 5.14 is a slightly extended sequence. By this point, they have been playing for approximately 30 minutes, and Li implores them to teach her how to play. Andrew offers to change the character she was using to Pikachu, which Andrew and Kevin perceive to be slightly easier to use:

Excerpt 5.14 (00:30:11–00:30:34)

		((game ends))
1	Li(M)	*jiao wo zhenme wan la*::::::: !
		teach me how to play exclamation
		(Teach me how to play!)
2	Andrew	[( )
3	Li(M)	[*hao jian a nimen laoshi*
		[very mean exclamation you always
		[(You're all so mean to always kill me.)
4		*sha wo*=
		kill me=
5	Kevin(C)	=*gam (nego) gam laa wai*=
		=press (this)press exclamation=
		=(Hey, press that button.)=
6	Andrew(M)	=*ni bie yong zhege la*
		=you don't use this exclamation
		(=Don't use this character, use Pikachu.)
7		*yong* Pikachu
		use Pikachu
8	Jason(M)	( ) Andrew *eryi a*:::
		( ) Andrew only final particle
		(( ) Andrew only.)
		((players at the character selection screen))
9	Kevin(C)	*aa jung lego sin lego ging*
		ah use this first this powerful
		(Ah, I'm using this character, it's cool.)
10	Andrew(M)	*ai?*
		ah?
		(Ah?)
11	Kevin(C)	*gam laa diu nei loumou*
		press exclamation fuck your mother
		(Press the button, motherfucker.)
12		*hai aa?*
		vagina final particle
		(2.5)
13	Andrew(C)	*peikaajau*
		Pikachu
		(Pikachu.)
		((Andrew chooses Pikachu for Li))

14 Kevin(C)   *peikaajau [gam jungji waan4:::*
                   Pikachu [so easy play
                   (Pikachu is so easy to use.)

15 Andrew(M)   [*ni an xia ranhou*
                   [you press down then
                   [(Press the down-button, then

16   *an B jiu hao le*
                   press B just fine final particle
                   press the B-button, and you'll be fine.)

17 Li(M)   *a*
                   okay
                   (Okay.)

   ((new game starts))

18 Andrew(M)   *tiaolai tiaoqu*
                   jump around
                   (Jump around.)

19 Andrew(C)   *aai pukgaai gaanzo lego coeng*
                   oh damn chose this stage
                   (Oh damn it, it chose this stage.)

Li's complaints in lines 1 and 3 indicate her frustration that she has not been properly taught the game and that the others are treating her unfairly. Andrew suggests that she use a new character, Pikachu, instead (lines 6–7), and proceeds to instruct her how to execute one move (lines 15–16). He then tells her that that move alone should allow her to play, and that all she has to do it "jump around" the game (line 17). Throughout this exchange, Kevin is eager to move on to the next game. *Super Smash Brothers Melee* requires that players click a button before they can move out of some of the transition screens. Kevin hurries them out of the victory screen (line 5) and character selection screen (lines 11–12). Soon after the game started, Andrew switched back to Cantonese (line 19), complaining that the game, which was set to randomly select the stage designs, had picked one that was unfavorable to him. Throughout this (and earlier) instruction, Andrew and Jason had reduced the instruction to vague procedures such as "fly all over the place," "jump around," "keep pressing" and so on. These are, to some extent, accurate instructions but are not particularly helpful ones as they don't convey when or why you would perform any of these actions. In the next excerpt, Li claims that they have yet to teach her how to play:

EXCERPT 5.15 (00:36:16–00:36:30)

((players at the character selection screen))

1 Li(M)   *nimen you bu jiao wo*
                   you again not teach me
                   (You never teach me.)

2 Kevin   *( )*

3 Andrew(M)   *jiaole ni a*
                   taught you exclamation
                   (I taught you already.)
                   (0.3)

4 Li(M)   *na jiu meici yizhi an*
                   Then every time   keep press

		(You always just tell me to keep pressing)
5		*a:::::*
		exclamation
6	Andrew(M)	*ni yao tiao ma::::::::::::::::::*
		you have to jump final particle
		(You have to jump,
7		[*tiao dao renjia xiamian*
		[jump to others below
		jump underneath others.)
8	Jason(M)	[*ni an (zhege)* Li *an zhege*
		[you press (this) Li press this one
		[(Press (this), Li, press this one to attack
9		*da zhege an tui ren chuqu*
		attacks this one press push people away
		Press this one to push people away.
10		*haiyao an xia an xia*
		also press down press down
		And also press down to—)
	((new game begins))	
11	Andrew(M)	[*ni keyi dian ren*
		[you can electrocute people
		[(You can electrocute people.)
12	Li(M)	[*ba ren tui xiaqu*
		[*preposition* people push down
		(Does it push people off the edge?)
13		*ma?*
		question marker

Here, Li still expresses that they did not teach her how to play (line 1). Andrew says that he did (line 3), and Li tells him that all he did was tell her to keep pressing buttons (line 4). Jason, who is more familiar with the Pikachu character, steps in (lines 8–10) with more detailed instruction. He points to the controller to show her what to press. In the meantime, the next game has started and instruction promptly ends.

This series of instructional sequences has a number of possible implications. First, we might characterize Jason, Andrew, and Kevin as poor instructors because they don't seem to teach Li anything. Their instructions are vague, and they often do not respond directly to her questions. However, their vague instructions might partly be due to the difficulty in providing instruction while a game is in progress. Videogames, particularly action-packed ones, command considerable attention. Jason, Andrew, and Kevin do talk a lot during the game, but it is usually to comment on the game in progress. To provide instruction would require them to break out of that frame. It is hard for Li to know whether the instruction she receives during the transition screens is helpful until she tries it out for herself when the game is in progress.

Second, although the experts are not always clear, they do give her some idea of how to use the controller. However, participating in a fighting game is a lot more than just knowing the controls. While the game is in progress, the experts engage in constant conversation: they taunt and challenge one another; create alliances only to break them a few seconds later; feint and counter feint; argue about who's the better player, which character is stronger, which move is most powerful, which stage is most tedious; and so on. Li is left out of this interaction. Although none of what they said would have made her a better player—most of it being their opinions of the game—this talk is a significant part of what it means to play in that context, with these particular players.

Finally, these excerpts—particularly excerpt 5.15—bring us back to the questions: what does instruction between players look like and when does it happen? Li did not consider Andrew's explanations adequate, and he insists that instruction took place. The question "When is instruction?" alludes to Varenne's (2007) question "When is education?"; specifically, what should we study if we want to study education? Varenne builds on Garfinkel's notion of social order and argues that instruction reflects the work needed to maintain the order. Instructional work occurs during the most mundane activities, every day, whenever one person speaks out about a perceived disturbance to the constitution of the order (e.g., when we explain to someone how something *should* be done). Li's circumstances are reversed in that she senses an underlying order—a way of playing the game—that she does not understand. She continually asks what the others are laughing at or arguing about through the games, but these questions are ignored. Li struggles to understand not simply the "how-to" part of the game, but the broader ethos surrounding it.

The excerpts so far (5.1–5.15) occurred within a roughly 40-minute segment, during which the experts tried to teach Li how to play. Li eventually left the game to play on a separate game with Andrew, leaving Jason and Kevin to play *Super Smash Brothers Melee*. For the remainder of the session, Jason repeatedly implored Li to return, but Li stayed away. Andrew returned to the game after a while, but the three experts did not play at the same time. Li's departure created a fracture in the player configuration for this game. Between the three of them, there was an instability in which one player was often being attacked by the two others. Jason also felt that it was more fun to have more people in the game. After almost two hours, Li is persuaded to return to the game, but only under the conditions that they teach her properly how to play.

Educating the Novice

The following excerpt unfolds in around four minutes and shows a more earnest attempt by the experts to instruct Li. These have been broken down into smaller segments for easier discussion. It is worth comparing this extended sequence with earlier attempts at instruction and to see why Li considered this second round of instruction more useful.

The instruction begins when Li rejoins the experts after having abandoned them for two hours. The experts break out of their two-player game to accommodate four players (e.g., moving chairs, creating more space, plugging in additional controllers to the console). However, they hold off on starting the game to provide time to instruct Li:

EXCERPT 5.16a (02:36:33–02:37:18)

    ((game ends))
    ((Jason and Andrew reorganize the room to accommodate more players))
1   Li(M)   *qu jiao wo wan la::::::*
                      go teach me play exclamation
                      (Come and teach me how to play!)
2   Jason(M)   *ni zuo zhe*
                      you sit here
                      (Sit here.)
                      (1.0)

3	Andrew(C)	[*gaau keoi waan* (0.9)
		[teach her play
		[(Teach her how to play.)
4	Jason(C)	[( ) *nei mhoji waan zyu* ((to Kevin))
		[( ) you cannot play yet
		[(( ) You can't play yet.)]
5	Andrew(C)	*nei waa bingo gaau keoi waan*
		You say who teach her play
		(Who should teach her how to play?)
		(1.0)
6		[*bei jan waan lo*
		[let people play final particle
		["Let me play."
7	Jason(C)	[(*neidei*) *haigam saat* Li. .
		[(you all) keep killing Li
		[(You all) keep attacking Li.)
8	Andrew(C)	*nei m bei ngo gaau*
		you don't let me teach
		(You don't let me teach.)
9	Jason(C)	*gaau keoi laa maa*
		teach her final particles
		(Time to teach her.)
10	Andrew(C)	=*hai lo*
		=right final particle
		=(That's right.)
		((Jason moves them through the last game results screen))
11	Kevin(C)	*diu::::::::::::::*
		fuck
		(Fuck.)
		((Li laughs))

First, the players reconfigure their group to include Li as a novice. Jason explicitly asks her to sit next to him (line 2) to facilitate instruction, suggesting that playing games are about interaction in actual spaces, and that it is likely easier for the expert to teach the novice how to use the controller by sitting close together and watching what buttons she presses. In lines 3 to 11, Andrew, Jason, and Kevin struggle to control the situation. As Kevin reaches for the controller, Jason bars him from playing (line 4). Andrew agrees with teaching Li (line 3) even though he wants to be involved (lines 5–6). Jason says that both of them just keep ganging up on her (line 7) without teaching her properly, apparently recalling the earlier failed attempt at instruction. Kevin, who in the past was eager to get the game moving, voices his frustration (line 11). This negotiation occurs in Cantonese, which means Li is not part of this exchange. Jason and Andrew's position suggests that they understand the need to find time to teach Li specific instructions, and that doing so while the game is happening might not be the most effective way to teach.

EXCERPT 5.16b

((Jason moves to the character selection screen))

| 12 | Andrew(C) | (*hou lo*) *gaan jan laa* |
| | | (fine) choose person final particle |

(Fine, choose the character.)
((Li begins picking her character))
13 Jason(M)   *ni::: shi:::*
                   you are
                   (You are—)
                    (1.0)
14 Li(M)   *wo xiang nage [jiu—*
                   I think that one [then
                   (I think, that one then—)
15 Jason(M)   [P2 *a?* (0.9)
                    [P2 final particle
                   [(Player 2?
16   *(ni shi P2) shibushi?*
                   (you are P2) aren't you?
                   Are you player 2?)
17 Kevin(C)   *gam laa*
                   press final particle
                   (Press it.)
18 Li   ( )
19 Jason (M)   *ni an zhege shi::::: (0.9) ni qu*
                   you press this one is you go
                   (Press this one.
20   *zheyangzi*[( )
                   like this
                   Go like this.)
21 Li(M)   [*xian le ma?*
                   [choose already
                   [(Choose now?)
                    (0.6)
22 Kevin(C)   *wulei laa::::::::::: wulei ciu ging*
                   fox final particle fox super great
                   (Choose Fox. Fox is really awesome.)
                    (0.7)
23 Jason(M)   *na guolai* ( )
                   bring over here ( )
                   (Bring (the cursor) over here ( ).)
24 Li(M)   *o*
                   okay
                   (Okay.)
25 Andrew(M)   [*yong zhege . . . ranhou xuan*
                   [use this one then choose
                   (Use this (button) to select your character.)
                   ((Li selects the character Mewtwo))
26 Li(M)   *wo haishi yao zhege*
                   I still want   this one
                   (I still want to use this character.)
27 Kevin(C)   *ciumungmung*
                   Mewtwo
                   (Mewtwo.)
28 Jason(M)   =*zhege buhao yong* (0.7)

=this one not good use
=(**This one is not easy to use**

29
      hennan yong
very difficult use
Very difficult to use.)

When instruction starts, Jason switches back to Mandarin. First, he tries to understand which player represents Li (lines 15–16). In prior situations, Li had little say in choosing the character. She is usually rushed along to the next game as the other players—usually Kevin—moved the game forward. Kevin tries to do this again (line 17) but is ignored. Instead, Jason shows her how to navigate the character selection screen with her controller (lines 19–20) and Li tries to follow along (line 21). In lines 23 to 25, Jason tries to teach another unusual feature in *Super Smash Brothers Melee*, in which players select their characters by moving a token across the screen (Li gets confused by this later, see excerpt 5.17). Li expresses wanting to use a kangaroo-like character called "Mewtwo" (line 26), but Jason cautions her against it, saying that it would be hard for her to use (lines 28–29).

After teaching Li how to select the Pikachu character, Jason starts a new game with only the two of them as players:

EXCERPT 5.17 (02:37:56–02:38:05)

1 Jason(M)   *you ji zhao la zheyang*
          there are few moves final particle like this
          (**There are a few moves, like this.**)
   ((new game starts))
2 Jason(M)   *ni kan a ni guolai*
          you see final particle you come over
          (**Look at this, come over here**
3   *ni buyao dong*
          you don't move.
          and don't move.)
4 Li(M)   *buyao dong*
          don't move
          (**Don't move.**)
5 Jason(M)   *ni an xia ranhou an* B
          you press down then press B
          (**Press the down-button, then the B-button.**)
6 Li(M)   (*ranhou ne?*)
          (then question marker)
          ((**Then what?**))
7 Jason(M)   *xia* B
          down B
          (**The down-button, then B-button.**)
   ((Li's Pikachu character creates thunderbolts))
8 Kevin(C)   (*si ziu laa*)
          (try move final particle)
          (**Let me try some moves.**)
9 Jason(M)   (*kanbukandao?*)
          (do you see?)
          ((**Do you see?**))

10	Li(M)	=*en he*
		=uh huh
		=(Uh huh.)
11	Jason(M)	*ranhou:::a an A zai an*
		then ah press A then press
		(Then, press A, and then press)
		(2.5)
12	Li(M)	*zhe—ta zai ganma?*
		this it at doing what
		(What is it doing?)
13	Jason(M)	*tiao a*
		jump final particle
		([Make it] jump.)
14	Andrew	( )
15	Jason(M)	*tiao a*
		jump final particle
		([Make it] jump.)
		(1.5)
16	Jason(M)	*wo jiao ni yi zhao a*
		I teach you one move final particle
		(I'll show you [another] move.)
17	Li(M)	*ranhou ne?*
		then question marker
		(Then what?)
18	Jason(M)	zheyangzi tiaoqilai an zhege
		like this jump up press this one
		(Like this, jump up, then press this.)
19	Li(M)	*dengyixia man yidia*n
		wait a moment slow a little
		(Wait a moment, slow down.)

Unlike earlier attempts at instruction, this time Li has more control over the timing of the lesson. After Jason teaches a move, he watches Li perform it, and lets her signal for him to continue (lines 6, 10, 17, and 19). He also switches between letting her perform the moves herself (lines 5, 7, 11) and demonstrating it himself (line 18). The instructions are also broken down into smaller steps, which take roughly the form: (1) expert describes the button combinations; (2) expert watches as the novice tries the move; and (3) expert repeats instructions or starts the next set of instructions. Most game tutorials seem to follow a similar format when providing onscreen instructions, giving players opportunity to fail and correct their moves. Many of the instructions (e.g., line 5, 7) represent indexical expressions that are difficult to understand. For example, "press down"—in both English and Chinese—can mean both "press the down-directional button" or "press down the button." This is made clear when Jason shows Li the controller and points to what action he wants her to perform.

Excerpt 5.18 involves two simultaneous conversations. Up until now, Jason and Li have been passing the same controller back and forth, leaving the second controller unused. Kevin and Andrew have been sitting back and watching them interact. Eventually, Andrew picks up the unused controller and begins trying out some moves of his own. Kevin joins in, and takes the controller from him.

EXCERPT 5.18 (02:38:27–02:38:45)

1	Li(M)	*dengyixia ni an ni an*
		wait a moment you press you press
		(Wait, show me for a second what
2		*yixia wo kan*
		a moment I see
		[buttons] you press.)
		((Andrew picks up the unused controller))
3	Andrew(C)	*ngo ( ) ngo taihaa nego jau matje ziu*
		I ( ) I see this has what moves
		(Let me see what moves this character has.)
4	Kevin(C)	*gaau gaau nei jat ziu*
		teach teach you a move
		(Let me teach you a move.)
5	Jason(M)	( )
6	Kevin(C)	*gwolai aa ngo gaau nei jat ziu*
		come here ah I teach you one move
		(Come over here. I'll teach you one move.)
7	Li(M)	=*zenme yong a?*
		=how use question marker
		(How do I use it?)
8	Kevin(C)	=*ngo gaau nei jat ziu*
		=I teach you one move
		=**(I'll teach you a move.)**
9	Jason(M)	*tiaoqilai an zhege*
		jump up press this one
		(Jump up, and then press this [button].)
10	Li(M)	*ni yao (dong) zhege de ma*
		you have to (move) this question marker
		(Do you have to move this?)
11	Jason(M)	=*tiaoqilai an shang zai an B*
		=jump up press up then press B
		=**(Jump up, press the up-button, then the B-button.)**

Both Andrew and Kevin are allowed to participate in the game provided that they do not interrupt the instruction. Kevin, who had been denied a role earlier, frames his participation in terms of teaching Andrew some new moves (lines 4, 6, 8).

EXCERPT 5.19a (02:39:03–02:39:26)

1	Jason(M)	*zhegea? ( ) an xia*
		this one final particle ( ) press down
		(This one? ( ) press down.)
2	Li(M)	*ganma ya?*
		do what question marker
		(What are you doing?)
3	Jason(C)	Andrew *bei ngo bei ngo* Andrew
		Andrew let me let me Andrew

		(Andrew, let me, let me, Andrew,
4		*bei ngo bei ngo si ziu bei ngo*
		let me let me try move let me
		let me show her a few moves.
5		*si di je bei heoi tai*
		try some things let her see
		Let me show her a few things.)
6	Jason(M)	*an xia*
		press down
		(Press the down-button.)
		((Pikachu zaps the other character with thunderbolt. Li laughs.))
7	Jason(M)	*haiyou haiyou haiyou zheyang*
		also also also like this
		(Also, also also, like this, push it,
8		*tui guoqu zuo you* [*dou keyi*
		push over left right [also can
		either left or right.)
9	Kevin(C)	[*ne ziu*
		[this move
		[(This move.
10		*lo zungjau* (0.4) *si sihaa*
		final particle also try try
		There's this move, too. Try this move,
11		*ne ziu lo nei ziu*
		this move final particle this move
		this move.)
12		*lo*
		final particle

In excerpt 5.19a, instead of showing only the button combinations, Jason shows Li what effect certain moves have on opponents. He asks Andrew to stop playing (lines 3–5) and then demonstrates the effect of thunderbolts. In the meantime, Andrew and Kevin pass the controllers back and forth, taking turns to show what additional moves they can perform.

EXCERPT 5.19b

13	Jason(M)	*haiyou*
		also
		(Also)
14	Li(M)	=*shibushi keyi diansi ta ma?*
		=is it can electrocute him final particle
		=(Can it electrocute him?)
15	Jason(M)	*haiyou haiyou*
		also also
		(Also, also)
16	Jason(C)	Andrew *mhou gaau*
		Andrew don't play
		(Andrew, quit playing.)
		(0.7)
17	Kevin	( )

18	Jason(C)	=(*ganzyu* [*zoi*—)
		=(then [again—)
		=((After that, then—))
19	Andrew(C)	[*haa* B *lo*
		[down B final particle
		[(Then, the down-button and B-button.)
20	Jason(C)	*mhai hai lo ganzyu zoi*
		no yes final particle then again
		(No, [I mean] yes, then you press this.)
21		[*gam nego lo* Andrew
		[press this final particle Andrew
22	Kevin	[( )
23	Jason(C)	*nei zoi gam nego hoji*
		you again press this can
		(When you press this, you can fling
24		*fing dou jandei*
		fling others
		others away.)

As the instruction continues, Jason tries to maintain control over the game and stop Andrew from interfering (line 16). Jason seems to lose track of his instruction, as he switches back to Cantonese (line 19), after which Andrew joins in and discusses with Jason what combination of moves to use in this given situation (lines 19–21). Specifically, Jason suggests that there are moves that can cause characters to fly off into the horizon and be killed (lines 23–24).

At this point, the instruction has transitioned to a new phase, in which Jason is not just showing Li the buttons to press, but also how to use them against other characters. In excerpt 5.20 below, Jason tries to explain the percentage indicator to Li (which had confused her earlier, see excerpts 5.3–5.5):

EXCERPT 5.20 (02:39:28–02:39:52)

1	Andrew(C)	din *kyun mou matje jung*
		electric power not much use
		(Thunderbolt isn't very useful.
2		*jausi jaujung jausi moujung*
		sometimes useful sometimes useless
		Sometimes it is, sometimes it isn't.)
3	Kevin(C)	(*nei aamaa waa?*)
		(your mother say)
		(Says who?)
		(0.7)
4	Andrew(C)	din *kyun jausi jausi*
		electric power sometimes sometimes
		(Thunderbolt sometimes, sometimes
5		[*daa dak ( )*
		[hit
		[can hit ( ).)
6	Kevin(C)	[( )
7	Jason(C)	[*nei jiu heoi do* percent *lo:::*

		[you need him many percent final particle
		[(**You need [your opponent] to be at high percentage.**)
8	Kevin(C)	[*ngo seizo mei aa::: wai!*
		[I died yet final particle hey
		[(**Is my character dead yet? Hey!**
9		[*wai!* (0.8) *diu::::::*
		[hey fuck
		[**Hey! Fuck!**)
10	Jason(C)	[*aa zik haang*
		[ah straight go
		[(**Ah, go straight.**)
		(1.4)
11	Li(M)	*shi* [*ganma ya?*
		is [do what question marker
		(**What does it do?**)
12	Kevin(C)	[*sei sei bei heoi tai sei* [*bei heoi tai*
		[die die give her see die [give her see
		[([**I'll] show her how she can kill.**)
13	Li(M)	[*ni ni*
		[you you
		[(**You, you**)
14	Jason(M)	=( ) *ni you ni you xie zhao*
		=( ) you have you have some moves
		=(( ) **For some of your moves,**
15		*zhaoshu ni shi—*
		moves you try
		you should try—)
		((Andrew goes to the TV and points to the percentage indicators on the screen))
16	Jason(M)	*ni zheli* [percent
		you here [percent
		(**The percentages here**)
17	Kevin(C)	[*sei bei heoi tai*
		[die give her see
		[(**Show her how to die, okay?**)
18		*haa?*
		question marker
19	Jason(M)	=percent *yueduo de hua ni zhe—*
		=percent more you here
		(**The higher the percentage here—**)
	((to Kevin))	
20	Jason(C)	*aai aa mhou gaau zyu sin laa*
		hey don't play yet exclamation
		(**Hey, don't play yet.**)
		(0.8)
21	Jason(M)	*ni zheli* percent *yueduo de hua*
		you here percent more
		(**The higher the percentage indicator here,**
22		*ni an shang zhexi* ( ) *jiu keyi*
		you press up these then can
		when you press the up-button, you can

23   *da ( ) renjia fei zou*
                         hit others fly away
                         attack others and send them flying.)

This excerpt shows the multilayered conversations that can occur simultaneously during a game session. It also shows how difficult it is for experts, who have the jargon needed to understand a game between themselves, to switch to a different vocabulary in order not to confuse the novice. As Jason teaches Li how to use thunderbolts, Andrew begins commenting about whether it is an effective attack (lines 1–2, 4–5). Jason jumps back and forth between his conversation with Andrew and instructing Li, while Li almost gets sidelined during this exchange, barely getting a word in. Jason tells Andrew that thunderbolts are useful if the opponent's percentage indicator is high, and then explains this to Li (lines 16, 19, 21–23). Jason uses the slightly clumsier wording that Li uses to describe characters dying (as "sending them flying"). Kevin tries to play around with the character, and frames his actions to make himself seem helpful. He takes control of the second, unused character and says that he will "show her how to die" (lines 12, 17) by raising its percentage indicator, presumably to get it high enough that it will die when attacked. However, Jason finds this distracting and stops him (lines 20-21).

EXCERPT 5.21 (02:40:07–02:40:18)

1   Li(M)   *na ni gangcai an nide—*
                         then you just now press your
                         (Then, just now, you were pressing—)

2   Jason(M)   *=zhege shi zhuazhu ren lai da*
                         =this one is grab onto someone come hit
                         =(This [button] lets you grab onto someone and attack.)

3   Li(M)   *zhuazhu ren lai da?*
                         grab onto people come hit
                         (Grab onto people and attack?)

4   Jason(M)   *a danshi yao hen jin*
                         ah but needs very close
                         (Ah, but you have to be very close.)

5   Li(M)   *o*
                         okay
                         (Okay.)

6   Jason(M)   *=suoyi ni. . zou jin deshihou*
                         =so you move close when
                         (So, when you move close,

7   *keneng hui gei ren da*
                         maybe will let others hit
                         you might be attacked by others.)

          ((Li laughs))
          Li(M)   *[zheyang mingbai la*
                         [like this understand   final particle
                         [(In that case, I understand.)

9   Jason(C)   *[aa ngodei hoici ( ) hoibo hoibo*
                         [ah we begin play ball play ball
                         [(Ah, we can start now, let's go, let's go.)

By the end of excerpt 5.21, Jason finishes his instruction with Li and moves onto the real game. This instruction activity has been more successful than the previous attempts because the activity was more one of collaboration between Jason and Li, instead of it being unidirectional (from expert to novice). Since action occurred both on the controller and the screen, instruction had to be given in relation to both these spaces. More importantly, Li had to be instructed on how to connect the events on the screen with the moves she can perform on the controller. Excerpt 5.21 above is also an example of the importance of using backchanneling to provide feedback to the speaker. In lines 3, 5, and 8, Li provides different forms of backchanneling to signal whether she has understood a remark made by Jason, and this helps facilitate the instructional process. Interestingly, when Jason calls for the actual game to begin (line 9), he switches into Cantonese, excluding Li in the process. This suggests that he considers actual-play to be what he does with Andrew and Kevin, while what he does with Li is more instructional and not-really-play (for more on this see Hung, 2011, Ch. 7).

Discussion

This chapter addressed what instruction looks like in situated play; that is, what players do and say when they try to instruct another player in how to play the game. Their interaction has been presented with all its messy complexity and has shown that learning in videogames is not always smooth.

It is also worth pointing out again that what the experts are teaching is not so much "how to play *Super Smash Brothers Melee*," but "how *we* play *Super Smash Brothers Melee*." Embedded within their instructions are signs of their own orientations to the game, such as which characters are easier or better to use, which moves are powerful, what stages benefit certain characters, and so on. The experts are continuously learning about the game themselves, and their individual orientations are made visible through their discussions, or what Varenne (2007) calls "deliberations," about the game's design as an observable "fact."

Game researchers often talk about "situated learning" or "just-in-time" learning in videogames (Gee, 2003, 2004, 2007; Squire, 2008), specifically as it relates to the ways in which games teach people how to play. Situated learning builds on Lave and Wenger's (1991) theory of learning, which describes learning as an "integral part of a generative social practice in a lived-in world" (p. 35). Central to this theory is the notion of *legitimate peripheral participation*, which is embedded in power relations within the "community of practice." Lave and Wenger point out that this theory is more of an analytical viewpoint on learning, not a pedagogical strategy (p. 40), and should be seen as a way of describing how learning takes place. "Just-in time" learning refers to learning that occurs when an individual is given information needed to accomplish a task at hand (Collins & Halverson, 2009). This is often used in comparison to learning in schools, where students learn skills and knowledge for situations they need in the future. Oftentimes, this means that learning will be decontextualized and reduced to memorization or rote learning. Just-in-time builds on new capitalist vocabulary and alludes to an ideal organization in operations management aimed at reducing inventory costs. Suppliers provide materials *just in time* for a manufacturer to put together the end products, thus lowering the need to carry unused materials in inventory. While the notion of just-in-time makes sense, it does not fully address what it means for learning to happen "in time." To say that good instruction is provided just in time is a tautological statement. To give an instruction "just in time" tells us nothing about whether the *right* instruction was given in time. Hand a non-gamer a controller and you are likely to see that even the most well-designed game tutorials can be difficult to follow. Both game designers and expert gamers have to assume a basic level of understanding of how games work; when novices, like Li, enter at a level that is below this expected level of competency, misunderstanding and frustration can happen on all sides.

Instruction is a mutually constituted event between an instructional source (a game tutorial or an expert player) and the learner. We can compare the two phases of instruction that Li went through: one that resulted in frustration (excerpts 5.1–5.15) and one that resulted in enough understanding to allow for meaningful participation (excerpts 5.16–5.21). Much of what occurred in the early phase resembled situated or just-in-time learning, but this had failed. Clearly, providing an instruction "in time" alone is not enough for it to be a successful instruction. The experts thought that they were teaching Li, but Li did not feel they were. In the later phase, Li seemed to have learned better because Jason broke the instructions into smaller steps and addressed some of Li's questions. Li's case has shown the importance of the instructional act to be co-constructed between the expert and novice. The expert needs to know what instruction the novice needs, and the novice needs to give feedback to the expert in order to communicate whether the instruction was heard correctly and whether they can move onto the next skill. These backchannels played a significant role in helping Jason break the instructions down. In the earlier segments (excerpts 5.1–5.15), even though instruion was given, it was not understood properly, and learning did not take place. In other words, the act of giving someone an instruction to follow does not mean that learning happens, regardless of whether it is given "in time" or not.

Note

* This chapter was originally published as: Hung, A.C.Y. (2011). *The Work of Play: Meaning Making in Video Games* (pp. 89–130). New York: Peter Lang.

References

Bogost, I. (2007). *Persuasive games*. Cambridge, MA: The MIT Press.

Collins, A., & Halverson, R. (2009). *Rethinking education in the age of technology: The digital revolution and schooling in America*. New York: Teachers College Press.

Dourish, P. (2001). *Where the action is: The foundations of embodied interaction*. Cambridge, MA: MIT Press.

Garfinkel, H. (2002). *Ethnomethodology's program: Working out Durkheim's aphorism*. Lanham, MD: Rowman & Littlefield Publishers.

Gee, J. P. (1996). *Social linguistics and literacies* (2nd ed.). London: Taylor and Francis Group.

Gee, J. P. (2003). *What video games have to teach us about learning and literacy*. New York: Palgrave Macmillan.

Gee, J. P. (2004). *Situated language and learning: A critique of traditional schooling*. New York: Routledge.

Gee, J. P. (2007). Pleasure, learning, video games, and life: The projective stance. In C. Lankshear & M. Knobel (Eds.), *A new literacies sampler* (pp. 95–113). New York: Peter Lang.

Goodwin, M. H. (2006). *The hidden life of girls: Games of stance, status, and exclusion*. Malden, MA: Blackwell.

Hung, A.C.Y. (2011). *The work of play: Meaning making in video games*. New York: Peter Lang.

Lave, J., & Wenger, E. (1991). *Situated learning: Legitimate peripheral participation*. Cambridge: Cambridge University Press.

Mehan, H. (1979). *Learning lessons: Social organization in the classroom*. Cambridge, MA: Harvard University Press.

Shaffer, D. W. (2007). *How computer games help children learn*. New York: Palgrave Macmillan.

Squire, K. (2006). From content to context: Videogames as designed experience. *Educational Researcher, 35*(8): 19–29.

Squire, K. (2008). Open-ended video games: A model for developing learning for the interactive age. In K. Salen (Ed.), *The ecology of games* (pp. 167–198). Cambridge, MA: MIT Press.

Steinkuehler, C. (2004). Learning in massively multiplayer online games. In Y. B. Kafai, W. A. Sandoval, N. Enyedy, A. S. Nixon, & F. Herrera (Eds.), Proceedings of the Sixth International Conference of the Learning Sciences (pp. 521–528). Mahwah, NJ: Erlbaum.

Suchman, L. A. (2002). *Human-machine reconfigurations: Plans and situated actions* (2nd ed.). Cambridge: Cambridge University Press.

Varenne, H. (2007). Difficult collective deliberations: Anthropological notes toward a theory of education. *Teachers College Record, 109*(7): 1559–1588.

CHAPTER EIGHTEEN

Kongregating Online

Developing Design Literacies in Play-Based Affinity Space

SEAN DUNCAN

Gee's (2004) affinity space notion has been quite productive in recent years, providing "new literacies" (Lankshear & Knobel, 2006) and New Literacy Studies (e.g., New London Group, 1996) scholarship with an interesting and important new domain of inquiry. Understanding learning and literacy in the 21st century entails moving beyond solely understanding the formal instructional contexts that educators impose upon learners, to further developing an "ecological perspective" (Jenkins, Purushotma, Clinton, Weigel, & Robison, 2006) that values informal engagement with popular media. The affinity space represents an attempt to meld several strands of "new literacy" research into the principled investigation of overtly fan-oriented spaces, casting a light upon "everyday" learning and literacy practices, in part as a means to address jarring inadequacies of standard space, "traditional schooling" (Gee, 2004) environments.

It is clear that these *spaces*—and this chapter will emphasize that term, relying upon an interpretation that values Gee's spatial metaphor—are locales that can at once facilitate and constrain participation. They exist both because of a shared affinity for a common topic (e.g., a television series, musical group, book series, videogame) and for the affinities that are developed between members within the space. They are both persistent, staying put long enough for valuable practices to evolve within them, as well as *ad hoc*, featuring a constantly shifting membership that thwarts any attempt to think of them simply as "communities." These contrasts are both appealing and vexing. In this chapter, I will explore Gee's notion further through the investigation of a specific gaming-related affinity space, striving to further develop Gee's (2004) nascent conception of the affinity space through an analysis of participation within a single, small case.

Affinity space research has been applied to a variety of domains, addressing online spaces as varied as adolescent anime fan fiction communities (Black, 2008) to the multifarious play and instructional spaces around games such as *The Sims* (Gee & Hayes, 2010) to studies of celebrity-centric affinity spaces around web television series such as *The Guild* (Ellcessor & Duncan, 2011). In this chapter, I will attempt to outline another way forward, better spelling out an affinity space that overtly attempts to bridge media consumption and production, and showing how game design can be fostered within a predominantly game play-oriented affinity space. In addition to this, I will attempt to uncover new paths of inquiry and concerns for the future study of affinity spaces: What methodological approaches are most useful for understanding both the predominant and small-scale exchanges that occur within affinity spaces? How might a look at an informal game design competition "push back" on Gee's conception of the affinity space? What are the *boundaries* of affinity spaces, and how do engaged fans suggest new directions we might take in studying them?

One of the challenges in moving affinity space research forward to date has been primarily methodological. Many studies of affinity spaces have relied heavily upon Gee's (2006) big-D Discourse theory, unpacking the detailed meaning-making exchanges that occur within the textual content of many affinity spaces. While these studies have often revealed fascinating and compelling moments of verbal exchange between participants within affinity spaces, very little work has sought to characterize the overall character of an affinity space's textual content. In other words, the approach has been generally qualitative and *idiographic*—attempting to discern the details of one specific affinity space's inner workings. In this chapter, I propose that idiographic methods may be bolstered through the judicious application of *nomothetic* approaches—though the present chapter deals with an analysis of a *single* affinity space, the research methodologies explored here are designed to attempt to find regularities across multiple affinity space cases, and may help address the preponderance of specific practices within several affinity spaces' data corpi.

A key inspiration for the present study was Steinkuehler and Duncan's (2008) work, which applied a content analysis (à la Mayring, 2000) scheme to the understanding of informal scientific reasoning within an online gaming affinity space. Uncovering the predominance of discursive, informal scientific, and tacit epistemological activities across posts within a sample of online text drawn from the *World of Warcraft* affinity space, Steinkuehler and Duncan were able to effectively characterize not only the learning and literacy practices within a given affinity space, but also the commonality of them. In addition to better avoiding the appearance of "cherry-picking data," I argue that the incorporation of content analysis methodologies may help to uncover "new literacy" practices occurring within affinity spaces that might otherwise be difficult to ascertain using solely Discourse analysis methods.

Additionally, understanding the participatory cultures (Jenkins, 2006) that inhabit affinity spaces may mean characterizing the designed elements of the spaces and the ways that the space's stakeholders shape them (such as the influence of *World of Warcraft*'s designers as seen in Duncan, 2012, or the creators of *The Guild*, as seen in Ellcessor & Duncan, 2011). How are affinity spaces actively constructed by the managers of the space to foster certain kinds of "new literacies"? Gee (2004) presents affinity spaces as open realms of possibility, but few studies have to date addressed the designed constraints that can shape activity within them—especially the economic investments that may give us pause in the advocacy for the educational use of affinity spaces around commercial games.

While Gee presents affinity spaces as enabling a variety of productive activities within them, it is also the case that the gaming world has changed significantly since 2004, when Gee initially developed these concepts. Current games such as *Little Big Planet* and *Minecraft* involve a high degree of user-created content, often shared with others within the gaming space. In 2011, gamers have increasingly desired to go beyond "simple" gameplay, becoming game *designers* who can employ available tools to make their own game artifacts. This move, driving gaming consumers toward becoming producers of games or game content, has been studied elsewhere through analyses of game "modding" (Steinkuehler & Johnson, 2009), the creation of new game scenarios (Squire & Giovanetto, 2008), and the leverage of game design practices toward learning outcomes (see Hayes & Games, 2008, for an overview of game design tools).

These concerns, then, leave us considering an investigation of a gaming affinity space that can address a meaningful combination of factors: What might learning look like within an affinity space in which we can further investigate "gamers as designers" (Duncan, 2010a), one in which the designed constraints of the space may help to shape the activities within it, and one where idiographic and nomothetic research methodologies may be meaningfully employed in tandem? In this chapter, I outline a multi-methodological investigation of a case that may just fit this bill: A careful look at the "design talk" (Schön, 1983, 1988) present within an online "casual" gaming space, *Kongregate* (http://kongregate.com).

Kongregate as an Affinity Space

Kongregate provides an interesting example of shift in "casual" gaming affinity spaces that began to take hold in the mid-2000s. Serving as a "YouTube of Flash games" since 2006, *Kongregate* has provided an interesting model for gaming sites, providing an easy-to-use Web 2.0 interface, a wide variety of games for players to engage with, and a dedicated, ongoing community that designs, critiques, and plays the many game artifacts available on the site. It is most overtly a game *play* site, but one in which gamers quickly realize they can critique each others' games, they can make a little money by sharing their own games, and they can (potentially) develop collaborations with other budding game designers.

Most applicable to the concerns in this volume is the recent attempt (in November, 2008) by *Kongregate* developers to begin to formally foster some form of game design skills within their existing user base of Flash game players. Developers for *Kongregate* created a set of tutorials and an associated gaming contest—dubbed *Kongregate Labs*—that provides us with an interesting opportunity to analyze the scaffolding of game design literacies within a pre-existing affinity space centered around gaming. Investigating the online forums on *Kongregate* dedicated to *Kongregate Labs*, I address the following questions: What kinds of design practices are fostered in this community? How can we understand the ways that the affinity space of the online forum have both supported and constrained the employment of specific forms of design talk (Schön, 1983, 1988)? And, how might this case highlight the relationship of skills development to interest-driven learning within affinity spaces?

Toward this end, I will employ a linked content/Discourse analysis approach (à la Duncan, 2010b). That is, in this chapter, I will first describe a content analysis (Mayring, 2000) coding scheme developed and applied to investigate the discursive practices and design talk evinced by participants in the *Kongregate Labs* affinity space, as well subsequent Discourse analyses (Gee, 2006) designed to further unpack the ways that this "design talk" was employed by participants within this space. First, however, I describe in greater detail the design of *Kongregate*, the design-oriented affinity space of *Kongregate Labs*, as well as the structure of the online forum data that will serve as the basis for the present study.

Kongregate *Labs*

Kongregate is relatively young (launched in October 2006), but has grown significantly in recent years. When the data were originally culled for this study (February 2009), *Kongregate* had 2,454,879 users and 21,231 games—in a little over two years, the number of games had doubled (currently over 42,000), and *Kongregate* has been acquired by the United States' largest games retailer, GameStop. *Kongregate* serves up games primarily created in the Adobe Flash development environment, with other design platforms now represented (e.g., Unity). Any user can play, rate, and comment upon games within the site, and players are encouraged to present their own games within it as well. The site features games from a wide variety of common game genres, including shooters, puzzle games, real-time strategy games, tower defense games, and even Flash-based virtual worlds (e.g., *Runescape*). While not alone among primarily Flash-based, often "casual" gaming affinity spaces (other sites, such as Newgrounds.com have been historically dominant within this space), *Kongregate* has contained a persistently unique mix of professional game designers, independent game developers, and novices desiring to learn how to become game designers.

If we think of the site itself as representing a loose affinity space for the play, sharing, and critique of primarily Flash-based, casual games, it includes several elements presumably intended to foster engagement within its component communities, many of which are evocative of massively multiplayer online games and share structural similarities with other online gaming networks (such as Steam, Xbox Live, and Playstation Network). These include player "leveling" through the accrual of "points" associated with game-specific badges (analogous to Xbox Live "achievements"), as well as customizable social-networking information with individual profile pages, customizable avatar images, and private messaging functions. It seems to have been a central concern for *Kongregate's* developers to make the site more than simply another Flash game portal, and to begin to foster practices that both evoke community-building tools present in other spaces while also guiding players into design. Through the use of these social networking and community tools familiar within global gaming culture, *Kongregate* is actively involved in both attempting to drive new "casual" game players to the site, but also to begin to blur the lines between "simple" game play, game critique, and game design more broadly.

One of the most interesting developments within the *Kongregate* affinity space was the advent of *Kongregate Labs*, a set of tutorials and contests sponsored by *Kongregate* developers and a corporate partner (Toyota, producer of the Scion which was branded as sponsor of the contest) to provide opportunities for its player users to start the process of learning game design skills in Adobe Flash. Beginning with a set of tutorials on how to create a simple "shooter" style Flash game ("Shootorials," see Figure 18.1, below), the apparent goal of *Kongregate Labs* was to scaffold the instruction of game design through the use of Flash Actionscript code, and to also provide incentives for participation with the tutorials through a meager monetary prize ($250 for the game awarded the first prize in an associated game design contest).

Kongregate Labs

Learn to create your first game

Making games is easy! Well, okay, maybe it's actually kind of hard, but starting out is easy at least! Especially when you have Kongregate's shootorials (shooting tutorials) to guide you through the process.

Check out the link below to play through the game you can learn to build yourself.

Play 'Shoot!' now »

If you'd like to discuss the shootorials with other Kongregate members, join the Kongregate Labs discussion on our forums.

Figure 18.1: The introduction to the first "shootorial" on the Kongregate Labs web site, explicitly linking the "Shootorials" to both the Flash game-design tutorial ("Play 'Shoot' now") and Kongregate Labs' online discussion forum (at the bottom of the window).

As part of *Kongregate Labs*, the site's developers provided standard sets of Actionscript code for a variety of standard gaming functionalities, from the basic behavior of a "shooter" (ship movement, firing at enemies, etc.) to specific game tropes such as the "miniboss" (a challenging single opponent of intermediate difficulty within the course of a game level). By giving participants these potentially useful tools, and a contest with monetary rewards as incentive to learn how to use them, both the acquisition of common game design practices and the learning of Actionscript programming skills appear to have been among the goals of the site developers. And, given that there was already a pre-existing community of participants within the online discussion forums, chat, and social networking aspects of *Kongregate*, I suggest that this particular community provides researchers with a unique opportunity to see how *gamers* can be scaffolded into *designers* through interaction within an affinity space that features the use of shared reference materials, instructional materials, design tools, and financial incentives. Like many of the other cases presented within this volume, the representatives of *Kongregate* are largely absent, and participants were left to discuss game design among themselves, with only the tutorials and provided resources as tools. Unlike recent other research into affinity spaces and design (e.g., Duncan's, 2012, analysis of *World of Warcraft* player/designer interactions) every participant was a potential designer, and many appeared to participate in the affinity space to learn aspects of game design or Actionscript programming.

Additionally, I should identify that, though much of the affinity space research in gaming contexts focuses solely upon online discussion forums, it is arguable that *Kongregate*'s affinity space includes a "Web 2.0" model (O'Reilly, 2005). This approach, popularized by sites like *YouTube* and *Flickr*, has been employed by *Kongregate* toward the creation of games, the critique of games, and the scaffolding of game development skills. The locus of this affinity space can be most clearly seen within the online forums within *Kongregate* and *Kongregate Labs* in particular, but extends out into *Kongregate*'s broader affinity space. I focus on *Kongregate Labs'* online forums initially, in order to assess how specific discursive and design practices (through the use of Donald Schön's design domains, types, and rules; Schön, 1983, 1988) are developed within them; and yet, as I will argue in later sections, a more "full" account of this case's gaming affinity space will necessitate moving beyond the online forum as the sole locus of productive interactions. By applying the content and Discourse analyses to forum text from *Kongregate Labs*, I aim to capture how game design (involving both narrative and ludic elements; Duncan, 2010a) can be supported within one part of the informal learning environment positioned within *Kongregate*'s pre-existing affinity space, while acknowledging that this is only the beginning of a full analysis of this space.

Data Corpus and Collection

I chose to focus on a subset of the online discussion forums present within *Kongregate*'s larger affinity space. Containing online forums for technical support, programming, collaborations, and specific promoted games (e.g., "Kongai," a site-specific online collectible card game), the *Kongregate* forums featured breakout discussions on a number of topics. By selecting the *Kongregate Labs* online discussion forums for analysis, I have therefore limited the larger affinity space to a smaller, focused subcommunity of participants who have been drawn to the *Kongregate Labs* forums presumably in order to learn how to make games and/or to develop successful games to win the *Kongregate Labs* contest.

It should be noted, though, that the *Kongregate Labs* forums were segregated from the rest of the talk on the *Kongregate* forums by the design of the site's online discussion forum structure. Within their own demarcated discussion forum, *Kongregate Labs* threads were easily discernible from threads on other topics. The choice to assess the *Kongregate Labs* forum provided a clear match to Steinkuehler and Duncan's (2008) analysis of a *World of Warcraft* class forum, at least at the level of forum structure, with implications for random sampling of the discussion posts. Though some discussions relevant to the *Kongregate Labs* contest and the activities of game design and Flash programming can be found in other sections of the *Kongregate* forums ("Collaborations" and "Programming," respectively), it was decided to limit the present analysis to the *Kongregate Labs* forums in order to adhere to the site's designed demarcation of content.

In the next section, I describe the data corpus as well as the methods chosen for sampling this corpus to analyze for an initial pass with a content analysis coding scheme.

Data Sampling

The *Kongregate Labs* forum featured numerous threaded discussions, with a clear delineation between this space and the other discussion spaces on the *Kongregate* site. In July 2009, I culled the entirety of the *Kongregate Labs* forum text at that time, a total of 472 threads containing 3,758 posts. While the contest was completed on November 28, 2008, the forums remained active at the time of the data cull (and at the time of this chapter's writing), perhaps pending another installment of the tutorials and another contest.

With only 3,758 posts, the data corpus was found to be only moderately active compared to other affinity spaces, and even other sub-forums within *Kongregate*—the mean number of posts per thread was small, at nearly 8 posts per thread (population mean = 7.96). With a median thread length of 4.5, we can see that the distribution of thread lengths is quite positively skewed (see Figure 18.2, below), indicating that the vast majority of threads were clustered at the lower end of the size spectrum, with a few longer thread outliers pulling the mean higher. Seventy-seven percent of the threads within the *Kongregate Labs* forums were between 1 and 9 posts long, with a steep drop-off after that point (to 15% for threads 10–19 posts long, 4% for threads 20–29 posts long, and so on).

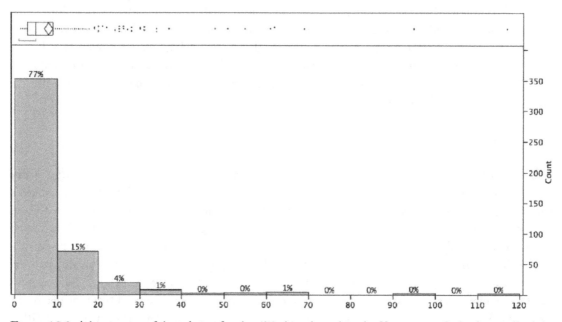

Figure 18.2: A histogram of thread size for the 472 threads within the Kongragate Labs forum. Each bar represents intervals of 10 posts.

Using the precedent of Steinkuehler and Duncan (2008), random sampling of posts from complete threads in the *Kongregate Labs* forums was based on a confidence interval (margin of error) of 9%, with a 95% confidence level for estimates made upon this sample. This yielded a necessary minimum sample size of 115 posts (calculations were conducted with the Raosoft sample size calculator; Raosoft, 2009), and threads were randomly sampled from this data corpus until the necessary minimum number of posts had been reached. A total of 16 threads were randomly sampled, containing 130 total posts in the sample. The data sampling was slightly higher than the minimum needed to ensure representativeness of the sample, as entire threads were sampled in order to maintain the context of the discussions within each thread for intelligibility purposes (and to capture potential back-and-forth interactions in the subsequent Discourse analyses to be conducted from this sample). This follows the method adopted by Steinkuehler and Duncan (2008), in order to facilitate the intelligible analysis of these online exchanges, but may have implications for representativeness—if threads were sampled randomly, but not individual posts, posts that dealt with a specific thread topic (say, reflections on good gaming practice) might be over-represented in the sample.

In the next section, I describe the application of the content analysis coding scheme to this data sample in order to uncover design thinking practices within this affinity space, applying the framework based upon Schön's constructs of domains, types, and rules.

Content Analysis: Characterizing Design Talk in an Affinity Space

As the activity within the *Kongregate Labs* forums was conceived as a necessarily *design*-oriented activity, a content analysis (Mayring, 2000) coding scheme needed to be developed to capture the forms of design discussions that participants employed within the affinity space. As part of a larger study of design practices in online affinity spaces (described in Duncan, 2009; 2010a), the coding scheme was developed *a priori* to the analysis of the forum, based, in part, upon a consideration of the forms of design talk uncovered by Donald Schön (1983; 1988) in several early studies of design thinking. Schön's work aimed to develop an abstracted set of classifications of design thinking embodied in the ways designers discussed their work. By extension, I hypothesized that several design-oriented gaming affinity spaces would feature many similar forms of design talk, and that the nature of artifacts being produced within these affinity spaces may affect the forms of talk in each. For the purposes of this chapter, I focus only on the *Kongregate Labs* case, and the forms of design talk uncovered within the *Kongregate Labs* affinity space.

Schön's emphasis was on design talk in both professional design mentorship and the analysis of protocols of design tasks. This was appealing for the present study in that several of the component factors—certainly design "types" and "rules" (Schön, 1988)—were abstracted categorizations of design practice which are not closely tied to the specific context of design that they were gleaned from. That is, while the category of "design reference" (one of Schön's types) evolved from his reading of architectural practice (e.g., using Frank Gehry's Experience Music Project museum as a case of "bad design" to justify deviations from that design), Schön's structure allows for a "design reference" to be applicable in a very different design field (say, a game designer arguing that Valve's *Portal* provides a good reference for conceiving level structure in a new first-person "shooter" game).

Thus, for the present study, Schön's types and rules served as the initial basis for a coding scheme, which, as I discuss in detail in the next section, was developed then tested on a sample of forum posts for applicability. As per content analysis and verbal analysis (Chi, 1997) techniques, revisions to this coding scheme were necessary, factoring in more than the initial *a priori* framework from Schön's work.

A Coding Scheme

In this section, I discuss the generation of a coding scheme that was initially developed using affinity space text in an analysis of design practices within three gaming affinity spaces (Duncan, 2010a), before I move into the case-specific analysis of *Kongregate*'s affinity space in subsequent sections. The discussion here will refer to the genesis of a coding scheme that was originally intended to capture discursive, design, and content talk within three design-related gaming affinity spaces (around the games *The Legend of Zelda*, *World of Warcraft*, and *Kongregate*, the focus of the present chapter). The discussion in this section will first begin by describing the concerns that drove the creation of this general coding scheme before later addressing how this scheme was applied to the analysis of *Kongregate*.

As the general coding scheme was developed, it became clear that Schön's categories were interestingly capturing elements of design talk, but not *how* the talk was being conducted. That is, design talk was conflated with discursive practices for Schön, and given the emphases of Steinkuehler and Duncan (2008), it seemed appropriate to assess discursive practices separately from the forms of scientific, mathematical, or design talk present within the affinity space text. As part of the larger study's concerns (Duncan, 2010a), a general coding scheme was developed that was hypothesized to help capture the design practices as well as other elements of the affinity space talk.

First, discursive practices needed to be better captured, including a means for capturing the co-construction of knowledge, argumentation, and development of ideas within the forums. Secondly, elements of "design talk" which were prevalent but not necessarily classified within the types/rules framework needed to be accounted for. As a consequence, the coding scheme was iterated and revised to capture more elements of the "talk" present within each of the three affinity spaces (see Duncan, 2010a), as well as adding a means of assessing narrative/ludic content as a "manipulation check" to assess if the structuring framework of narrative play, ludic play, and game design were accurately capturing the activities within them. The final set of codes was clustered into three major areas: *Discursive practice*, *design practice*, and *narrative/ludic content* codes.

As the present research is in some ways an extension of the nomothetic inclination and content analysis methodologies employed by Steinkuehler and Duncan (2008), the coding scheme for informal design practices employed the same *discursive practice* codes used in their work. These codes captured social knowledge construction, participants' building on each others' ideas, the use of counter-arguments, uses of data/evidence, alternative explanations of data/evidence, and referencing of outside resources in informal scientific reasoning discussions around *World of Warcraft*. I argue that Steinkuehler and Duncan's discursive practices codes effectively captured the co-construction of knowledge and argumentation practices prevalent in many online discussions, not just those found in informal scientific reasoning contexts. By utilizing this part of their coding scheme, I have sought to test its applicability to constructive, design-oriented discussions online while also consciously blurring the line between online science reasoning practices and online design practices; while featuring very different goals, I hypothesize that both "science" and "design" employ many of the same common argumentation and discursive practices in these informal settings.

Second, the set of codes to capture *design practices* was a distillation of Schön's design types, and design rules (1988), with the addition of a subset of Schön's (1983) design domains included. Starting with the four design types specified in Schön (1988)—functional types, design references, *gestalts*, and experiential types—plus the identification of explicit design rules, I have added three codes from Schön's (1983) description of design domains (use, structure/technology, and a combined code of character/form based on two design domains). In other words, in order to address inadequacies in the initial versions of the coding scheme, design domains were brought in to capture forms of design talk discussed within these three cases' forum text. I have included Schön's emphasis upon intermediate representations that are brought into the design discussions, the statement of explicit design rules that arise out of these types, as well as three codes which are "closer to" the contexts of design. In this fashion, the coding scheme is an attempt to address, in a context-free manner, several levels of design talk.

Finally, a set of simple *narrative/ludic* content codes were added to the coding scheme. As part of the larger project (including *Kongregate*, as well as the aforementioned two other affinity spaces), it served as a means of conducting a loose form of "manipulation check" for each case—not a manipulation per se, of course, but a means of "checking" that the forum's content matched the affinity space's hypothesized content (see Duncan, 2010a for a more detailed discussion of expected practices in each space). By selecting each of these three cases, I implicitly posited that each case's talk was of a primarily narrative, primarily ludic, or combined narrative/ludic nature. Therefore, these assumed topics of discussion should be also borne out in an analysis of each forum's actual talk. These codes are very simple, addressing if the design discussion at each post was about issues of narrative around the game, game series, or platform under discussion; about ludic elements of the game, game series, or platform under discussion; or if it was uncodable/ambiguous. The content codes are not mutually exclusive—the present study of *Kongregate Labs* was selected because of its emphasis upon scaffolding game design (presumably involving both narrative and ludic elements), and thus I hypothesized that both narrative and ludic discussions would be found. The final coding scheme, along with descriptions of each code, can be seen in Table 18.1 (p. 362).

In order to determine a rough measure of the reliability of this coding scheme, inter-coder agreement was calculated between two experienced coders on a subset of the data corpus for multiple cases. Both coded the same subset, which comprised approximately 9.5% of the cross-case data corpus (48 posts from the *Kongregate Labs* data, but also including data from *World of Warcraft* and *The Legend of Zelda* gaming affinity spaces). The two coders reached 93.5% inter-coder agreement using the above coding scheme.

For the content analysis, it was necessary to identify the ways that each of the coding scheme elements mapped onto specific issues faced within the *Kongregate Labs* affinity space. To explicate exactly how these general codes were interpreted with the *Kongregate Labs* forum data, I include (in Table 18.2, p. 362) a set of examples drawn from the data sample that illustrate how each code was interpreted for this case of game design. In the *Kongregate Labs* case, each of the content codes was found to be applicable to at least one post in the data sample, including an array of content ranging in topic from asking for help for pressing *programming issues* (coded D8, structure/technology), to discussions of designing games for other game *genres* (coded D9, character/form), to statements of good *design practice* (coded D15, design rules).

Following the lead of Steinkuehler and Duncan (2008), the unit of analysis in this *Kongregate Labs* analysis was determined to be at the level of individual post. Multiple codes could be applied to each post, with the exception of the uncodable/ambiguous codes (D67 and C67), which were mutually exclusive with other sets of codes (D67 was only coded when D7–D15 were not, and C67 was only coded when C1–C66 were not). Each of the codes was applied within this data set, perhaps attesting to the potential variety of forms of design talk that could be employed in an affinity space with an emphasis upon game design. In the next section, I evaluate the coding saturation for this data sample, attempt to tease out exactly which of these codes were most applied in the *Kongregate Labs* case, as well as interpreting why they were.

Table 18.1

Discursive Practices		
Code	*Title*	*Description*
D1	**Social Knowledge Construction**	Designers construct knowledge in collaborative groups (AAAS.D.12.6 & 1.A.12.2; Chinn & Malhotra, 2002).
D2	**Build on Others' Ideas**	Participate in design discussions by restating or summarizing accurately what others have said, iterating designs. (AAAS)
D3	**Use of Counter-Arguments**	Suggest alternative claims or proposals, criticize arguments in which data, explanations, or conclusions are represented as the only ones worth consideration with no mention of other possibilities, suggest alternative trade-offs in decisions and designs, criticize designs in which major trade-offs are not acknowledged (AAAS.12.E).
D4	**Uses Data/Evidence**	Use data or evidence in making arguments and claims (AAAS).
D5	**Alternative Explanations of Data/Evidence**	No matter how well one theory fits observations, a new theory might fit them just as well or better, or might fit a wider range of observations. (AAAS.1.A.12.3, AAAS.12.A.8.3).
D6	**References Outside Resources**	References outside resources in making arguments and claims (e.g., other threads, online articles, databases).
Design Practices		
D7	**Use**	Designers address uses of designs; specifications for use. (Schön, 1983)
D8	**Structure/Technology**	Designers reference structures, technologies, and processes used in designing and implementation. (Schön, 1983)
D9	**Character/Form**	Designers reference form of design or components, the character of a design, markings of organization of spatial relationships, and genre. (Schön, 1983)
D10	**Cost**	Designers need to consider the cost of the design and construction of a design, both in terms of financial capital and human resources. (Schön, 1983)
D11	**Function**	Designers refer to the function of designs, either functional elements of designs or the function of a design. (Schön, 1988)
D12	**Design References**	Designers reference other designs, as exemplary "leading ideas" or as examples of designs to avoid. (Schön, 1988)
D13	**Gestalt**	Designers refer to "coherent wholes," or the ways that subcomponents of a design fit together into larger systems and relationships. (Schön, 1988)
D14	**Experience**	Designers refer to the experiential significance, emotive power, or universality of designs. (Schön, 1988)
D15	**Rules**	Designers state explicit design rules, maxims, or heuristics codifying good design practice. (Schön, 1988)
D66	**Social Banter**	
D67	**Uncodable/Ambiguous**	
Narrative/Ludic Content		
C1	**Narrative Play**	Is the content of the post about a narrative aspect of a game?
C2	**Ludic Play**	Is the content of the post about a ludic aspect of a game?
C66	**Not Relevant to Narrative/Ludic**	The content of the post does not discuss narrative or ludic elements of a game.
C67	**Uncodable/Ambiguous**	

The coding scheme for the current study, including discursive practice, design practice, and narrative/ludic content codes. Individual codes reference sources from which they were drawn, when applicable: American Association for the Advancement of Science standards (American Association for the Advancement of Science, 1993), Chinn and Malhotra (2002), and Schön's (1983, 1988) framework for understanding design.

Table 18.2

	Discursive Practices	
Code	*Title*	*Examples*
D1	Social Knowledge Construction	"I'm not sure what your saying, but if you mean that a first time develaoper has no chance at winning, I agree. It's a shame, but how could they make it otherwise?" (thread K24, post 2).
D2	Build on Others' Ideas	"What do you think the next shootorial should be, if you think there should be one?" (thread K22, post 12).
D3	Use of Counter-Arguments	"[T]ry making more onPress functions containing a single trace statement. This is to see if maybe something else is catching your mouse clicks... maybe you have something on top of the button?" (thread K292, post 8).
D4	Uses Data/Evidence	"Here are my errors i copied the code exactly from the tutorial any suggestions?" (thread K373, post 4).
D5	Alternative Explanations of Data/Evidence	"The problem is that the Flash compiler expects all the .as files to be in the same directory as the .fla, and doesn't check any subdirectories unless you tell it to" (thread K446, post 2).
D6	References Outside Resources	"Since you bumped this, I will mention that I wrote a TD tutorial [links to external website]" (thread K22, post 25).
	Design Practices	
D7	Use	"When I get to step 11, and try to test the ship velocity movie, it says that my ship should move back and fourth across the screen... This is not happening for me, and several other people in the chat room are having the same problem" (thread K373, post 1).
D8	Structure/Technology	"I haven't changed the GameOver function()... so what could the problem be?" (thread K258, post 2).
D9	Character/Form	"Did they confirm whether it will be platformer or what genre?" (thread K22, post 3).
D10	Cost	"If you are on favor to stop working on Kongai or even work less, say it" (thread K22, post 29).
D11	Function	"I learned to weight the introduction of new recurring enemies (or powerups, obstacles, whatever) HEAVILY towards the beginning of the game" (thread K154, post 9).
D12	Design References	"I plan on having extremely high scores a-la giga wing 2" (thread K258, post 1).
D13	Gestalt	"Because it's boring, and if you do it wrong, the entire game sucks" (thread K22, post 16).
D14	Experience	"Even if only a handful of people really like your game it;s totally worth it" (thread K154, post 2).
D15	Rules	"People who aren't impressed by the first four levels aren't going to play the next ninety-six. Give players a reason to invest their time, or they won't" (thread K154, post 9).
D66	Social Banter	"Your friggin awesome... And so are your games!" (thread K123, post 4).
D67	Uncodable/Ambiguous	"Nope." (thread K120, post 3).
	Narrative/Ludic Content	
C1	Narrative Play	"I can program to do almost everything I want to, but I can't come up with a good story..." (thread K22, post 20).
C2	Ludic Play	"Yeah everything works perfectly except for the health going down when the Boss gets shot" (thread K16, post 3).
C66	Not Relevant to Narrative/Ludic	"nothing is stopping them from making another account, but kongregate does validate their revenue reports" (thread K34, post 7).
C67	Uncodable/Ambiguous	"The tutorials would be a big help for beginners. Especially with code concepts. I think its a great idea!" (thread K22, post 26).

Examples of selected talk from the Kongregate Labs affinity space coded for each discursive, design, and content code.

Coding Saturation

In the coding saturation graph for this case (Figure 18.3, below), as with the other cases, the degree of coding for "social knowledge construction" (D1) was quite high—93.8% of the posts within this sample—with a large degree of "builds on others' ideas" talk as well (D2, 60.8% of the data sample coded). However, D3–D6 were relatively lightly coded, with none crossing 14%. A key question arises: What are participants talking about, if not using counter-arguments, evidence, alternative explanations of evidence, or referencing outside resources to a significant degree?

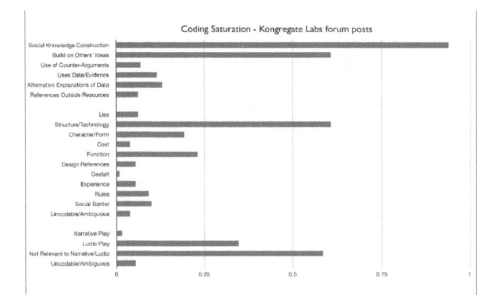

Figure 18.3: Coding saturation for the Kongregate Labs content analysis (n = 130 posts).

Looking at the content codes, it immediately becomes clear that, while there were a variety of design codes applied to the data from this case, one hypothesized "manipulation check" vis-à-vis expected discussion content was not confirmed. Focusing first on the content codes, the code with the largest degree of application to the posts in this data sample was "Not Relevant to Narrative/Ludic" (C66) at 58.5%. Though ludic play (C2) followed with 34.6% of the data sample coded, narrative play was virtually *nonexistent* in the sample, coded in only 1.5% of the posts. This result was unexpected, though perhaps the expectation of there being any degree of narrative play in this case was naïve—as these were players learning to become game designers, much of the discussions within the forums centered on issues that, I suspect, necessarily *preceded* the higher order design practices indicative of combined narrative/ludic game design.

Talk in the C66 category featured a variety of content, such as determining fixes for persistent bugs in Actionscript code and interpreting instructions to the game design tutorials, which were technical discussions that did not explicitly engage with narrative or ludic elements of games. This result indicates that while it was reasonable to assume that *Kongregate Labs* featured a community working towards game design, the nature of the player base (and their unfamiliarity with Actionscript programming) likely skewed the forum activity toward it serving as a *debugging resource* more than a space for explicit discussion of design during the course of the contest. Unsurprisingly, it seems that learning the proximal skill of "creating code" precedes the higher-order engagement with gaming and game design that many of the participants desired to do within this affinity space, and novice designers perhaps focused on developing programming skills before considerations of user experience, "good design," and so on.

This interpretation appears to jibe with the results found in the Schön-inspired design codes, which featured a preponderance of structure/technology (D8) talk, coded on 60.8% of the data sample. If participants were using the online discussion forum primarily as a means of addressing specific issues with the construction and structuring of their contest entries, this would be coded quite highly. And, if the level of this talk was at Actionscript code issues (not addressing narrative or ludic elements of games), it is conceivable that posts would be coded both structure/technology and not be relevant to narrative/ludic distinction. Yet, there was some discussion of game functions (D11, at 23.1%) and character/form (D9, at 19.2%), which reflected participants' discussions related to functional elements of games and, often, the pre-existing game genres that they attempted to emulate or modify through their game designs.

Notable as well were the low degrees of coding on use (D7, coded on 6.2% of the posts) and experience (D14, coded on 5.4% of posts). Participants within this affinity space thus seemed especially inclined towards the construction of their gaming artifacts, without much concern (or interest) in how they would be used. That is, concerns over the use of a game were, I suggest, limited due to the lack of game design expertise among the participants within the affinity space and, perhaps, overshadowed by the difficulties in learning how to use Adobe Flash by many of the novices engaged with the tutorials. These results bolster the interpretation that posters were more concerned with developing solutions to programming problems, and less with viewing their games as either potentially usable or conveying an experience to another player (concerns indicative of a more advanced game design sensibility).

Therefore, we're left with a potentially interesting emergent finding, indicating that within this affinity space, there may have been multiple channels of participation, and a variety of forms of design talk may have been "drowned out" by the dominance of technical support chatter. We need to consider that the affinity space for *Kongregate Labs* featured, in general, participants with distinctly separate goals than those initially anticipated in this space, pointing us to consider that there were a multiplicity of purposes that drew participants into engaging with one another in the *Kongregate Labs* forums. I conjecture that a variety of design goals not captured with the content analysis coding scheme—expressive, competitive, and educational—might have influenced the forms of talk within the *Kongregate Labs* forum. With a dominant trend of structure/technology talk and talk not relevant to narrative/ludic distinctions present within these data, this indicates that we need to delve into factors uncaptured by the application of this particular coding scheme.

Another emergent finding within the content analysis of the *Kongregate Labs* forums was the potential differences between uses of design talk at different time periods during the design process. As the forum existed both during and after the *Kongregate Labs* contest had completed, I suggest that the forms of technical support captured by the application of this coding scheme may have ceased to be quite so pressing after the contest's deadline had passed (November 28, 2008). In other words, with the forum remaining open for participants to continue to discuss the "Shootorials," each others' games, and the next steps for the *Kongregate Labs*-using community, how can we characterize what participants were engaging in during this period? With some distance from the immediate needs of creating games to compete versus one another for the social and fiscal rewards of the contest, do participants within the affinity space take up different topics for discussion? How can we interpret the role of "skills training" vis-à-vis design within a game-based affinity space?

In order to better address these findings, I have selected an exchange from the sample of online discussion forum data from January, 2009, several months after the conclusion of the *Kongregate Labs* contest. Investigating a short exchange between participants seeking to negotiate potential next game design tutorials, and game genres that these tutorials addressed, I perform a Discourse analysis on the text to better discern the means by which players move from players to designers and, in some cases, to becoming instructors of good game design practice. That is, an attention to the ways that participants subsequently "step back" from the contest itself to take on new topics can reveal factors influencing the enacting of design practices within this affinity space.

Discourse Analysis: Unpacking Meaning-Making in an Affinity Space

In this section, I apply Discourse analysis to a small set of posts from a thread from within the sample of *Kongregate Labs* forum text entitled "Jumptorials: Learn To Make A Platformer." Started on January 23, 2009, nearly two months after the conclusion of the *Kongregate Labs* "Shootorial" contest, the thread began with a simple, yet very telling question by poster "Flav02K"[1]:

> Would anyone else also like to see Kongregate Labs make a new set of tutorials that show you how to make a simple Mario-style platformer?
>
> If yes, please post in this topic—the more replies the more Kongregate staff will notice it and make it a reality :D

Immediately, the context of this thread was framed as being about the next set of tutorials, opening the discussion to another popular game genre (the "Mario-style platformer," harkening to *Super Mario Bros.* and its many two-dimensional sequels). But, most interestingly, we see a different use of the forums emerge here than simply technical support; Flav02K claims "the more replies the more Kongregate staff will notice it and make it a reality," implying that the forums are (for this poster at least) useful as a means of *advocating* for future instructional content ("a new set of tutorials"). In other words, the affinity space two months after the end of the *Kongregate Labs* contest *could* become a tool for discussing and promoting desirable future game design instruction tools, if only enough people would reply to Flav02K's post.

As the thread progressed, more game genres became entertained by the participants in the community—"tower defense games," such as *Gemcraft* or *Desktop Tower Defense*—while some participants decried the desire to create platformers, or the likelihood that good platformer games would even be achievable by novice participants within this affinity space. Concerns raised included the difficulty of the mathematics needed to make a good tower defense game, and the story-building expertise needed to come up with a "good story" (see code example for C1, in Table 18.2) to justify making a game in this genre. After a number of responses within the next two weeks, the thread activity died out; there was a subsequent period of over one month in which no further arguments were forwarded and no further posts were contributed to this particular thread.

On March 13, 2009, the thread was "bumped" (revived with a new post) by a poster referred to here as "Oscar." Though it is unknown how advanced within the community Oscar was at the time of his post, as of the time of this chapter's writing, Oscar's *Kongregate* level was 35 (quite high, reflecting many dozens of games played within the space), and he self-reported on his *Kongregate* profile page that he was a 25-year-old male. Oscar's post will be the focus of this analysis, and is replicated in its entirety below:

> I could see a platformer being a nice tutorial. A TD game wouldn't be as good though. Not only is the TD lag an issue for new coders, but the logic for shooting may also be a bit advanced for a newbie tutorial. A big part of shootorial is that a simple space shooter really is a nice start for coding knowledge. A platformer gets into a little bit more complex logic with the collision detection and movement physics and isn't as good a starting project because of level design being such a large portion. It might be a good tutorial to complete after shootorial though because level design can be a massive part of producing games. A tower defense would make a really good 3rd tutorial because it could get even more advanced with things like predictive shooting, pathing AI, and game balance.
>
> With a trio of tutorials like that, a player who could complete and retain the information in them would be set for pretty much all parts of the design outside of music and graphics that many people hire out when they make games anyway.

Here, we see Oscar taking the relatively unfocused discussion into a new direction, arguing for a framework that would support *both* the utility of furthering the *Kongregate Labs* tutorials through the use of, first, games in the platformer genre (e.g., *Super Mario Bros., Metroid, Viewtiful Joe,* or *Shadow Complex*) and then moving into the tower defense genre (referred to by Oscar as "TD"; e.g., *Desktop Tower Defense, Protector,* and *GemCraft,* the latter two of which were very popular Flash games hosted on *Kongregate*). Oscar's post was heavily coded with the content analysis coding scheme, with codes for social knowledge construction (D1), builds on others' ideas (D2), use of counter-arguments (D3), structure/technology (D8), character/form (D9), function (D11), experience (D14), and ludic play (C2) applied. Oscar did not make explicit, declarative statements for particular forms of design *practice,* thus design rules (D15) was not applied, though there is a set of implicit beliefs expressed here about good game design that I will unpack through the rest of this analysis.

Following Gee's (2006) Discourse analytic method, we can break Oscar's post into stanza form first based on the natural paragraph breaks in his post, then roughly by clauses within each sentence. The following structure emerges:

Stanza 1
1—I could see a platformer being a nice tutorial.
2—A TD game wouldn't be as good though.
3—Not only is the TD lag an issue for new coders,
4—but the logic for shooting may also be a bit advanced for a newbie tutorial.

Stanza 2
1—A big part of shootorial is that a simple space shooter really is a nice start for coding knowledge.
2—A platformer gets into a little bit more complex logic
3—with the collision detection and movement physics
4—and isn't as good a starting project
5—because of level design being such a large portion.
6—It might be a good tutorial to complete after shootorial though
7—because level design can be a massive part of producing games.
8—A tower defense would make a really good 3rd tutorial
9—because it could get even more advanced with things
10—like predictive shooting, pathing AI, and game balance.

Stanza 3
1—With a trio of tutorials like that,
2—a player who could complete and retain the information in them
3—would be set for pretty much all parts of the design
4—outside of music and graphics that many people hire out when they make games anyway.

In Stanza 1, Oscar began by expressing (in line 1) a personal preference, addressing the ostensible topic of the thread before quickly moving into an evaluative statement (line 2) about tower defense (TD) games, justified by the next two lines (3 and 4), discussing issues of "lag" and "logic for shooting." These were brought up as a form of justification to argue against the tower defense genre as "a bit" too advanced for a "newbie tutorial," and reflected a reframing of the discussion from what the next tutorial should be to a discussion of the tutorials in general.

Right off the bat, we can see a number of assumptions encapsulated within Oscar's post: That there are technical hurdles that players would need to achieve to successfully write tower defense games, and that the goal of the next tutorial may still be to create a "newbie tutorial," even after the completion of the "Shootorials" and connected contests. That is, Oscar has framed his post in a useful manner to support the argument he was about to make in the subsequent paragraphs—the goal should not necessarily be to argue for a particular game *genre* but to argue for an *experience* that could address new skills in a manageable manner, while also addressing the state of game design literacies that participants developed through the first set of tutorials. Unlike other posters in the thread, Oscar's emphasis quickly became one of developing a *scaffolding* for game design instruction; one that may indicate that certain desired game genres and formats may not be wholly applicable at the level of programming and design proficiency that participants in *Kongregate Labs* had developed at this point.

In the next stanza, Oscar developed his argument further. Starting with a declarative statement about the previous tutorial, "a simple space shooter really is a nice start for coding knowledge," Oscar moved from framing the post as about instruction to declaring which elements of game design have been addressed by the existing instructional materials on *Kongregate*. This jibes with the results of the content analysis and perhaps speaks to the coding scheme's effectiveness to some degree—if Oscar's assessment was correct, then we should not have been surprised to see such a high degree of discussion about ActionScript programming in the sample of *Kongregate Labs* forum data. While not explicitly stated as such, the "Shootorials" may have been viewed by *Kongregate Labs*'s developer as a useful way to develop programming competencies and familiarity with Adobe Flash more so than as a tool to foster interaction design and other "higher order" game design literacies.

Oscar continued, stating that platformers feature "complex logic" (stanza 2, line 3) as well as "collision detection and movement physics" (stanza 2, line 4), evaluating the platformer genre as not "as good [as] a starting project" (stanza 2, line 5). Immediately, we can see that elements that cross between game design and programming become evident; "collision detection" and "movement physics" are technical terms that describe desired states within the game, but do not necessarily imply a specific coding solution, and also flagged Oscar's pre-existing knowledge (and, presumably, higher-order issues in game design) with such terminology. Oscar argued that, therefore, the platformer "isn't as good a starting project" (stanza 2, line 4), evaluating, based on this argument, that the platformer should not be the first tutorial presented to novice game designers.

However, at this point, we need to assess this statement for another curious feature of Oscar's post: Why would Oscar argue about a "starting project" when the first tutorial (the "Shootorials") had already been completed? The discussion in the thread to that point had featured a number of game genres and opinions on their merits, but all participants appear to have understood that the first tutorials had been completed two months before and the ostensible discussion topic was on *next* steps for the *Kongregate Labs* tutorials. This further reflects Oscar's desire to "step back" from the tutorials in general and his intent to evaluate the overall process of game design instruction as promoted by *Kongregate Labs*. Therefore, the stakes are higher for Oscar than just contributing to a discussion about "what to do next"; Oscar's post reflects a (perhaps unconscious) desire to declare to other participants that the game design instruction tools on *Kongregate* were inadequate, potentially questioning the efficacy of the "Shootorials" to foster useful, foundational game design skills. Oscar was, in part, taking control of *Kongregate*'s initial forays into game design instruction away from the site's developers and reminding the "everyday" affinity space participant that it is also within their control.

In the next utterance (stanza 2, line 5), Oscar justified why platformers were not useful as first steps in game design (focusing on "level design," or the construction of interactive spaces in a game-world which players inhabit and work through during the course of a game). Arguing for a placement of level design after foundational skills have been developed ("a good tutorial to complete after shootorial," stanza 2, line 6), Oscar continued by acknowledging level design's importance in making good games ("level design can be a massive part of producing games," stanza 2, line 7). Here, we can see him stating an explicit ordering of stages for game design: first, programming skills are fostered through design of "Shootorials," then level design can be fostered (along with collision detection and movement physics) through the implementation of platformer tutorials.

Oscar advocated using tower defense games as a "really good 3rd tutorial" (stanza 2, line 8), because of its "advanced" (stanza 2, line 9) elements, such as "predictive shooting, pathing AI [artificial intelligence], and game balance" (stanza 2, line 10). For Oscar, then, a "trio of tutorials" (stanza 3, line 1) would help move a "player" (stanza 3, line 2) into a position where he or she "could . . . retain the information within them" (stanza 3, line 2) and "would be set for pretty much all parts of the design" (stanza 3, line 3). Line 2's reference to "player" then line 3's reference to "design" made explicit that Oscar was talking about moving from *play* based literacies into *design* based literacies. The "trio of tutorials" laid out in Oscar's post present one such possible means of scaffolding these skills, while also building upon pre-existing familiarities with games and game genres. To wit, Oscar differentiated these game design skills from other elements of the game development process ("music and graphics," in stanza 3, line 4), appealing to conceptions of game design as it is currently construed in professional game design and development contexts ("many people hire out when they make games anyway"; stanza 3, line 4). With this, Oscar ended his post by implicitly advocating for a desired end state that mirrors the game design professions that he assumes many of the *Kongregate Labs* players would like to enter, or, perhaps, one he viewed as the logical end state of learning how to design games.

We can see that Oscar's proposal here follows an interesting path—first, he presented a clear reassessment of the entire project of tutorials (gauging the specific design practices afforded by each game genre), then he forwarded an argument for structuring a series of tutorials to develop game design skills. And, finally, Oscar cast the goal of this to "retain the information" of game design, while also tacitly adopting roles in the game design process that match professional practice. While the predominant trends for the data sample as a whole were toward providing technical support for novice ActionScript learners, we can see that after some time and distance were taken away from the contest, some players began to evaluate the experience and develop critical stances toward the designers' intentions for the *Kongregate Labs* affinity space as a whole. A significant part of the impact of the *Kongregate Labs* contest may have been as a touchstone to drive discussions within the affinity space that could push the affinity space members toward making their own instructional materials.

I suggest that assessing the context of learning may be an important stage in game design development; the emergent findings of this case present a form of Schön's (1983) *reflection-on-action* not adequately captured by the present content analysis coding scheme. By engaging with others on the online discussion forum after the activity in the process of arguing for new configurations of instructional materials, Oscar embodied a reflective stance after the *Kongregate Labs* contest experience through proposing ways to *redesign* it for future participants and alternative game genres. Oscar used the interactional tools presented by *Kongregate Labs* (in this case, the online discussion forum and the framework of game design tutorials) to advocate for the modification of the instructional context, but also, implicitly, the *ownership* of the affinity space.

Additionally, this highlights an important yet often overlooked factor in the design of tools to support these kinds of affinity spaces. *Kongregate* had no real incentive to keep the forums open for several months after the game design contest had ended and could have shut down these forums or personally engaged with these proposals in the space (like employees of Activision Blizzard have with *World of Warcraft*; Duncan, 2012). By remaining relatively absent yet maintaining the forum, the developers of the site have implicitly provided the "room" for these kinds of discussions to occur, and, I suspect, view them as potential community-building environments for *Kongregate* as a whole.

While it is beyond the scope of this chapter to fully evaluate the quality of Oscar's proposed tripartite game design "curriculum," it is worth noting that his attempts to forward an instructional model for game design are not alone in the *Kongregate Labs* context, and spill out of the confines of the online forum. As the *Kongregate Labs* affinity space was left to the participants for the most part, it should not be a surprise that participants took the spirit of the forum discussions, the "Shootorials," and the dominant forms of gameplay found on *Kongregate* at large, then moved these discussions into sites that they could shape more directly (beyond the designed constraints of *Kongregate* and its forums). In the next section, I present examples of other posts from within the "Jumptorials" thread and elsewhere from the data sample which highlight additional ways in which participants within the *Kongregate Labs* affinity space extended beyond the *Kongregate Labs* forum, and attempted to make sense of not just the specific contest and tutorials, but of good game design practice itself.

Rethinking the Boundaries of the Affinity Space

Finally, as we consider the ways that affinity spaces evolve over time, and how the goals of participants may clash with the designed elements of a particular affinity space, we need to consider how affinity spaces are not necessarily confined to a single online "space" (website, blog, online forum). Though Gee (2004) and much subsequent affinity space work has largely construed each affinity space as synonymous with a single online discussion forum, the *Kongregate* analysis indicates that the agency of an individual participant may drive valuable learning and literacy practices out of the initial affinity space, and into satellite spaces controlled by the individual participant. This syncs with Steinkuehler and Duncan's (2008) findings, in which some of the most active participants in the *World of Warcraft* affinity space linked to user-created, intricate mathematical spreadsheets to support their claims. Instead of simply supporting the activities of the *Kongregate Labs* affinity space, I argue that participants within it desired to push future game design instruction out of the traditional affinity space, and onto sites in which they had more control of the content.

This can be seen through further analysis of the same "Jumptorial" thread as discussed in the previous section. Oscar's post was not the only one which further addressed game design and game design instruction after the close of the contest. The very next post in the "Jumptorial" thread was a very brief contribution by a poster referred to here as "JonBulova":

> Since you bumped this, I will mention that I wrote a TD tutorial (well kinda, more a "here's what I learnt" than "do this") and therefore a platformer would be my preference for a Kong sponsored one!

This is a referral to Oscar's "bumping" of the previous post (posting to the thread after a long period in which the thread had dropped in the forum) and his discussion of the instruction of tower defense game design. In his post, JonBulova presented a simple yet evocative post which shows that individuals within the evolving *Kongregate Labs* affinity space were increasingly interested in teaching game design to one another within the forums themselves. JonBulova, according to his *Kongregate* profile page, was a 26-year-old male who had achieved a *Kongregate* level of 25 at the time of this chapter's writing (not quite as high level as Oscar, but still involving hours of gameplay on the site).

The underlined "TD Tutorial" referred to in JonBulova's post was actually a hyperlink to a lengthy and detailed tutorial on designing tower defense games in Adobe Flash, presumably hosted on JonBulova's personal website. The tutorial site included a three-part instructional sequence, including snippets of ActionScript code, sample features for a reader to include within his or her own tower defense game, and downloadable examples of the ActionScript code employed within embeddable Flash objects. While certainly not common to see a participant take the conversation away from the forum to their own tutorials—JonBulova's one was one of the few posts coded D6 (referencing outside resources)—it represents a step forward for the affinity space to move beyond the *Kongregate Labs* forum discussion of the *Kongregate* tutorials. In essence, some members of the community had begun to take seriously the ostensible goal of the *Kongregate Labs* project in general, and had begun to craft instructional materials that could support game design instruction, even when *Kongregate* had not yet made clear what their future intentions were in this regard.

Furthermore, note the informal manner in which JonBulova described his tower defense tutorial site—"more a 'here's what I learnt' than 'do this'"—indicating his intent that it serve as an instructional tool, but less a constraining, prescriptive tool than one which might illustrate the idiosyncratic manner with which JonBulova's made tower defense games. This interpretation is also supported by a look at the legal disclaimer on JonBulova's site, which stated:

> Appendix: Legal stuff
> The code and image assets provided in this series are copyright to me, except where acknowledged otherwise, and are provided for the sake of instruction only. You are granted a non-exclusive license to use them for personal use only. You should not upload any game incorporating them to a publicly available location without explicit permission from me.
> *Besides, they are not worth stealing! Make your own, make them better and wow the world with your artistic abilities.*

The italicized text above (emphasis mine) shows that JonBulova's self-deprecation with regard to his tutorial site belies a desire to foster personal expression in others within the community ("wow the world with your artistic abilities"). That is, we begin to see an ethic evolving within this expanding affinity space to take the *Kongregate Labs* tutorials and use them to help others build new game designs, new game genres, instructional tools, and promote personal expression through games (if, of course, one doesn't use JonBulova's code verbatim, as specified in his "Legal stuff").

It's tantalizing to consider how these sites may crop up *around* an existing affinity space, and challenging for researchers to understand how they may or may not represent extensions of the original affinity space. Additionally, while the attempts to reshape the learning experience provided in this case appear off-site several months after the end of the contest, there is some evidence that a small number of participants also engaged with "lessons learned" *immediately* after contest games were submitted, as a part of the *Kongregate Labs* forum. On November 30, 2008, a thread was started with the title, "What have you learned?" featuring individual responses ranging from the snarky ("There are bigger prizes out there.") to the rather eloquent, such as this post from a participant I have pseudonymized as "Ascension":

> I learned to think ahead. For example, I didn't put music/sound buttons in my game until after I'd coded in all of the enemies and levels. Then when I added in mute buttons, I had to go into every enemy and bullet class and add in the same "if sound is on" code in several dozen places. All too often I had to go change fifteen classes that could have been changed in just one, and next time it will be just one.
>
> I learned to weight the introduction of new recurring enemies (or powerups, obstacles, whatever) HEAVILY towards the beginning of the game. If it's a good recurring enemy, it should be introduced early so as to maximize usage. Introducing it late is a waste. But most of all I learned the importance of first impressions. People who aren't impressed by the first four levels aren't going to play the next ninety-six. Give players a reason to invest their time, or they won't.

Featuring both explanations of personal experiences ("I had to go into every enemy and bullet class…") as well as a number of proclamations of good design practice ("Give players a reason to invest their time…"; coded D15, design rules), Ascension's post speaks to the potential of game design-oriented affinity spaces to draw out conclusions and good practices as an open channel for ever-shifting communities of participants to make sense of an instructional experience.

This implies a number of conclusions regarding affinity spaces and their role in the evolution of these design discussions. Perhaps, then, the original affinity space may not constrain discussion of design activities in any significant way, at least after the contest ended. As the set of "Shootorials" provided by the site produced a number of games of varying success, it is unclear how successfully ActionScript programming was conveyed through the tools present on the site, and while reflections were afforded by the online forums within the affinity space, perhaps further instruction required a bridging of the discussion to personally controlled instructional materials (JonBulova's tutorials).

Ascension's post above also implies that there is not necessarily a purely temporal component to the *Kongregate Labs* experience that led to later serious consideration of the game design experience's greater significance and movement of instructional materials off the *Kongregate* site. Rather, I argue that the *competitive framing* of the *Kongregate Labs* tutorials and contest may have had something to do with the reticence of participants to engage in sophisticated design talk/instruction until after the contest's conclusion. By using social status (winning games were featured on the front page of *Kongregate*) as well as monetary rewards ($250 for top game) as "carrots" to motivate the learning of game design, *Kongregate* may also have forestalled a design community from evolving around the game design tutorials until after the contest had ended. The constraints of competition and monetary reward present within this particular affinity space may have, in a fashion, pushed the higher-end design discussions of the site.

After all, if one is competing against others within the affinity space, engaging in design practices "out in the open" with other contestants could be seen as dangerous to one's own chances at winning the prizes offered through the contest. Proposals and descriptions of games were not found in the forum data sample, potentially because (1) novice player/designers had not yet reached the level of technical proficiency where they were comfortable sharing tentative designs; and (2) the competitive ethic of the space led participants to believe that there was a chance their good ideas might be appropriated by others. Designed *constraints* thus play a role within the activities found within online gaming affinity spaces—the *Kongregate Labs* case may provide insights into how design talk is curtailed when the entire community contains potential designers competing against all of the others.

Final Thoughts

Though this study is overtly regarding the affinity space concept, and represents an attempt to more precisely analyze the forms of learning and literacy that occur within them, there are also implications for the broader use of game design as an implement for fostering learning. While many in games and learning research put an emphasis upon using engagement with games as a tool to drive a much-needed educational emphasis in, say, computational thinking (e.g., National Research Council, 2010), the example of *Kongregate's* "in the wild" affinity space may cause us to better specify the directionality of this relationship (an engagement with gaming vs. the learning of skills) for both researchers and participants. The goals of participation in the space as defined by the participant and by the researcher are quite different—rather than becoming engaged with games with the goal of learning technical (programming) skills, the participants within the *Kongregate Labs* affinity space *used programming instrumentally*, developing needed technical skills to aid them during the duration of the contest, only delving into the "meatier" issues of game genre, game design best practices, and game design instruction once the contest was over. That is, while the goal of the educator may be to use games to foster these kinds of skills, evidence from this affinity space research indicates that participants in affinity spaces may use programming to build a broader sense of engagement with games and gaming culture, only picking up the technical skills along the way.

The affinity space participant and education scholar's perspectives are, of course, not incommensurate ways of viewing the relationship of gaming culture and skill development within an online affinity space. Rather, this disparity reinforces Gee's (2004) argument that affinity spaces can be valuable contexts for learning because, in part, they address real-world interests and have real-world consequences. In the case of *Kongregate Labs*, the meager consequence of a contest and $250 (not to mention the social or cultural capital that might be gained within the community of *Kongregate* users) was an incentive to spur on the instruction of game design, while also constraining when certain activities would be ascendant within the space. While educational literatures still focus inordinately upon decontextualized *content* (say, developing programming skills or computational literacies more broadly), a deeper look at game design affinity spaces highlights that, in the real world, the acquisition of these is motivated by a concern to engage with media and the cultures around them. Gamers become designers not because they're desiring to learn programming for its own merits, but because participation within gaming cultures and game design affinity spaces is benefitted by being able to *situate* learning practices in the development of one's own games.

In sum, this study spells out three chief conclusions regarding Gee's (2004) affinity space notion. First, the study of online gaming affinity spaces can be undertaken in both a nomothetic and an idiographic manner—a characterization of the forms of "talk" within an affinity space is better understood through a principled look at the meaning-making within the space, and vice versa. The nomothetic approaches allow us to better characterize the prevalence of discursive, design, and content discussions within the *Kongregate Labs* affinity space, while the idiographic give us a better sense of how meaning was made within them. Specifically, in this case, the content analyses illuminated that the dominant design-and-content-coded data regarded learning programming skills, while the

Discourse analyses provided a means of assessing how conversations within this affinity space moved beyond the initial programming-oriented discussions. Additionally, as argued in Duncan (2010b), using a content analysis to better justify the selection of data for a Discourse analysis helps to avoid the perception of "cherry picking" data—the representativeness of a selection of data should be taken into account when characterizing the discursive exchanges within an affinity space.

Second, it seems that there are designed constraints that influence the shape and timing of valuable practices that occur in affinity spaces; the *Kongregate* developers' desire to impose a contest within the *Kongregate Labs* experience drove the learning of specific programming literacies during its duration, and the designers' absence at its conclusion may have driven participants' subsequent reflections (and movement off of the *Kongregate* site). For the dedicated participants involved in the *Kongregate Labs* affinity space, there were few avenues by which one could significantly build off of the existing "Shootorials," and little useful in an online forum to provide detailed extensions of tutorials into other game genres. With the lack of further *Kongregate Labs* tutorials (at the time of this chapter's writing), the absence of *Kongregate*'s involvement may have, I suspect, driven participants to take the design of instructional materials into their own hands. While certainly speculative at this stage, I suggest that the project of "games and learning" research in affinity spaces needs to better address the ways that the goals of participants in these spaces might contrast with the goals of researchers investigating these media.

With regards to this last point, future research in the learning and literacy potential of online affinity spaces needs to further address this disparity. If the goals of participants within these spaces are to, ultimately, participate more meaningfully with the broader culture of gaming and game design, is it problematic that the goal(s) of education researchers tend to focus on the skills developed in service of engagement within these cultures? How might we better address the big-L literacies (Lankshear & Knobel, 2006) that drive the play within these spaces, when they may not be as valued in educational literatures as the small-l literacies of programming and developing technical skills? Do we, as affinity space researchers, face ethical quandaries in attempting to appropriate the "in the wild" participation within the spaces for goals that the participants might not share?

That is, what motivates participants to delve into *Kongregate Labs* or other similar spaces needs to be better addressed. As affinity space research matures beyond simply highlighting the learning potential of these spaces toward better understanding how meaning is made within them, they may continue to serve as critical spaces to drive educational innovation (à la Gee's, 2004, goals). Yet, I suggest that we may need to build more nuanced understandings of the forms of *affinity* that are at the core of affinity spaces. Research on gaming and game design affinity spaces is currently inadequate in several regards (this study included), and it may be beneficial to address the many ways players wish to, say, become game designers not necessarily as a career goal, not for the proximal goal of developing a "skill," but perhaps because of their desire to be involved with *games for games' sake*. If affinity space research is to continue to blossom, I suggest that the goals of the educational researcher must be further reconciled with the goals of participants within affinity spaces, taking into account practices that participants undertake within them, the constraints that guide how participants shape and reshape them, and, ultimately, the goals that drive participants to devote themselves to such engagements.

Notes

* This chapter was originally published as: Duncan, S. (2012). Kongregating online: Developing design literacies in play-based affinity space. In E. Hayes and S. Duncan (Eds.), *Learning in Video Game Affinity Spaces* (pp. 51–83). New York: Peter Lang.

1. I have pseudonymized this poster name, along with all other poster names found within this chapter.

References

American Association for the Advancement of Science (1993). *Benchmarks for science literacy.* New York: Oxford University Press.

Black, R. (2008). *Adolescents and online fan fiction.* New York: Peter Lang.

Chi, M. (1997). Quantifying qualitative analyses of verbal data: A practical guide. *Journal of the Learning Sciences, 6*: 271–315.

Chinn, C. A., & Malhotra, B. (2002). Epistemologically authentic inquiry in schools: A theoretical framework for evaluating inquiry tasks. *Science Education, 86*(2):175–218.

Duncan, S. (2009). *Gamers as designers: Online communities as informal spaces for learning and literacy.* Unpublished doctoral dissertation, University of Wisconsin-Madison.

Duncan, S. C. (2010a). Gamers as designers: A framework for investigating design in gaming affinity spaces. *E-Learning and Digital Media, 7*(1): 21–34.

Duncan, S. (2010b). A dual-level approach for investigating design in online affinity spaces. In K. Gomez, L. Lyons & J. Radinsky (Eds.), *Learning in the Disciplines: Proceedings of the 9th International Conference of the Learning Sciences (ICLS 2010)–Volume 2, Short Papers, Symposia, and Selected Abstracts* (pp. 346–347).Chicago, IL: International Society of the Learning Sciences.

Duncan, S. C. (2012). *World of Warcraft* and "the World of Science": Ludic play in an online affinity space. In T. Wright, D. Embrick, & A. Lukacs (Eds.), *Social exclusion, power, and video game play: New research in digital media and technology* (pp. 177–198). New York: Lexington Press.

Ellcessor, E., & Duncan, S. C. (2011). Forming *The Guild*: Star power and rethinking projective identity in affinity spaces. *International Journal of Game-Based Learning, 1*(2): 82–95.

Gee, J. P. (2004). *Situated language and learning: A critique of traditional schooling.* London: Routledge.

Gee, J. P. (2006). *An introduction to Discourse analysis: Theory and method, 2*nd. ed. New York: Routledge.

Gee, J. P., & Hayes, E. R. (2010). *Women and gaming: The Sims and 21st century learning.* New York: Palgrave Macmillan.

Hayes, E., & Games, I. A. (2008). Making computer games and design thinking: A review of current software and strategies. *Games and Culture, 3*(3–4): 309–332.

Jenkins, H., Purushotma, R., Clinton, K., Weigel, M., & Robison, A. (2006). *Confronting the challenges of participatory culture: Media education for the 21st century.* Chicago: Macarthur Foundation.

Jenkins. H. (2006). *Convergence culture: Where old and new media collide.* New York: NYU Press.

Lankshear, C., & Knobel, M. (2006). *New literacies: Everyday practices and classroom learning.* 2nd edition. New York: Open University Press.

Mayring, P. (2000). Qualitative content analysis. *Forum: Qualitative Social Research, 1*(2). Retrieved November 24, 2012, from: http://www.qualitative-research.net/index.php/fqs/article/view/1089 2385

National Research Council. (2010). *Report of a workshop on the scope and nature of computational thinking.* Washington, DC: National Academies Press. Retrieved October 20, 2010, from: http://www.nap.edu/catalog.php?record_id =12840

New London Group. (1996). A pedagogy of multiliteracies: Designing social futures. *Harvard Educational Review, 66*(1): 60–92

O'Reilly, T. (2005). What is Web 2.0: Design patterns and business models for the next generation of software. *O'Reilly Media*, retrieved November 24, 2010, from: http://oreilly.com/web2/archive/what-is-web-20.html

Raosoft, Inc. (2009). *Sample size calculator, Raosoft Inc.* Retrieved November 24, 2012, from: http://www.raosoft.com/samplesize.html

Schön, D. A. (1983). *The reflective practitioner.* New York: Basic Books.

Schön, D. A. (1988). Designing: Rules, types, and worlds. *Design Studies, 9*(3): 181–190.

Squire, K., & Giovanetto, L. (2008). The higher education of gaming, *E-Learning,* 5(1): 2–28.

Steinkuehler, C., & Johnson, B. Z. (2009). Computational literacy in online games: The social life of a mod. *International Journal of Gaming and Computer Mediated Simulations, 1*(1): 53–65.

Steinkuehler, C. A., & Duncan, S. C. (2008). Scientific habits of mind in virtual worlds. *Journal of Science Education and Technology 17*(6): 530–543.

Name Index

Subject Index